The Lancaster House Conference and the Independence of Zimbabwe, 1979

DOCUMENTS ON BRITISH POLICY OVERSEAS
Series III, Volume XIV

DOCUMENTS ON BRITISH POLICY OVERSEAS

Series Editors: Patrick Salmon and Richard Smith

SERIES I (1945–1950)
Volume I   The Conference at Potsdam, July–August 1945
Volume II   Conferences and Conversations 1945: London, Washington and Moscow
Volume III   Britain and America: Negotiation of the United States loan, August–December 1945
Volume IV   Britain and America: Atomic Energy, Bases and Food, December 1945–July 1946
Volume V   Germany and Western Europe, August–December 1945
Volume VI   Eastern Europe, August 1945–April 1946
Volume VII   The United Nations: Iran, Cold War and World Organisation, January 1946–January 1947
Volume VIII   Britain and China, 1945–1950
Volume IX   The Nordic Countries: From War to Cold War, 1944–1951
Volume X   The Brussels and North Atlantic Treaties, 1947–1949
Volume XI   European Recovery and the Search for Western Security, 1946–1948

SERIES II (1950–1955)
Volume I   The Schuman Plan, the Council of Europe and Western European Integration, May 1950–December 1952
Volume II   The London Conferences, January–June 1950
Volume III   German Rearmament, September–December 1950
Volume IV   Korea, June 1950–April 1951

SERIES III (1960–)
Volume I   Britain and the Soviet Union, 1968–1972
Volume II   The Conference on Security and Co-operation in Europe, 1972–1975
Volume III   Détente in Europe, 1972–1976
Volume IV   The Year of Europe: America, Europe and the Energy Crisis 1972–1974
Volume V   The Southern Flank in Crisis, 1973–1976
Volume VI   Berlin in the Cold War, 1948–1990
Volume VII   German Unification, 1989–1990
Volume VIII   The Invasion of Afghanistan and UK-Soviet Relations, 1979–1982
Volume IX   The Challenge of Apartheid: UK-South Africa Relations, 1985–1986
Volume X   The Polish Crisis and Relations with Eastern Europe, 1979–1982
Volume XI   The Unwinding of Apartheid: UK-South African Relations, 1986–1989
Volume XII   Britain and the Revolutions in Eastern Europe, 1989
Volume XIII   Britain and China, 1967-72

The Lancaster House
Conference and the Independence
of Zimbabwe, 1979

DOCUMENTS ON BRITISH POLICY OVERSEAS
Series III, Volume XIV

Edited by
Patrick Salmon, Richard Smith and Paul Bali

FOREIGN, COMMONWEALTH AND DEVELOPMENT OFFICE

First published 2025
by the Foreign, Commonwealth and Development Office
King Charles Street, London, SW1A 2AH

© 2025 Crown Copyright

Cover illustration: The Zimbabwe Independence State Banquet:
Robert Mugabe, Lord Soames, Lord Carrington

Picture credit: Soames MSS: Churchill Archives Centre, Cambridge

ISBN 978-1-905181-19-3 (hardback)
ISBN 978-1-905181-20-9 (paperback)
ISBN 978-1-905181-21-6 (pdf)

CONTENTS

Preface		ix
Abbreviations for printed sources		xxv
Abbreviated designations		xxv
List of persons		xxvii
Document summaries		xxxiii
I	Before the Conference April – September 1979	1
II	Agreement on the Constitution September – October 1979	133
III	The Pre-Independence Arrangements October – November 1979	220
IV	Negotiations of the Cease-Fire and the Return to Legality November – December 1979	288
Index		355

PREFACE

Rhodesia's Unilateral Declaration of Independence (UDI) in 1965 had confronted successive British governments with an intractable political issue. In the face of world opinion and the wave of decolonisation across Africa, the white minority government led by Ian Smith had maintained a position of stubborn defiance. The United Kingdom, nominally responsible for Rhodesia (or Southern Rhodesia, as it was still officially termed) as a British colony, had ruled out the use of force, relying instead on economic sanctions which proved easy to evade. Repeated attempts to reach a negotiated solution had failed. Britain's position was one of responsibility without power. Since the early 1970s, however, Rhodesia's position had become more precarious. The independence of the former Portuguese colonies of Angola and Mozambique had left Rhodesia isolated, supported only by apartheid South Africa. Two liberation movements—the Zimbabwe African People's Union (ZAPU), led by Joshua Nkomo, and the Zimbabwe African National Union (ZANU), led by Robert Mugabe—were waging an increasingly effective guerrilla war. In the short term, the Rhodesian armed forces, led by Lieutenant-General Peter Walls, were more than a match for the guerrilla armies and frequently launched punishing assaults against their bases in neighbouring Zambia and Mozambique. But the war debilitated the white population as young men were conscripted, many to be killed or injured, and the guerrillas controlled much of the countryside. Only the cities of Salisbury, the capital, and Bulawayo remained largely untouched by the conflict. Thousands emigrated from the country every year, leaving the position of the white minority increasingly untenable and Rhodesia's economy on the verge of collapse. Many Rhodesians, as well as their South African allies, were coming to realise that the war was unwinnable.

Yet a negotiated settlement seemed as far away as ever. Attempts to reach a direct agreement with the Rhodesians had foundered on Ian Smith's intransigence and duplicity. International efforts had also failed. The Geneva Conference, held in 1976 as the first attempt to bring the contending parties together—the Salisbury government and the newly formed Popular Front of ZAPU and ZANU, along with the internal parties led by Bishop Abel Muzorewa and the Reverend Ndabaningi Sithole—ended in deadlock and acrimony. Dr David Owen, appointed Foreign Secretary by Labour Prime Minister James Callaghan in 1977, drew the conclusion that it was unrealistic to try to weld such antagonistic forces together and expect them to agree on a constitution.[1] Agreement on a constitution must come first: then the various parties could contend for power through free elections. Over the next two years, Dr Owen made Rhodesia a priority, continuing the collaboration with the United States that had begun with Dr Henry Kissinger as President Gerald Ford's Secretary of State, under the new Presidency of Jimmy Carter and

---

1 David Owen, *Time to Declare* (London: Michael Joseph, 1991), Chs. 13, 16, 18); interview with Lord Owen, 13 May 2005, in Sue Onslow and Michael Kandiah (eds.), *Lancaster House 1979, Part II: The Witnesses* (London: FCO Historians, 2019), pp. 15-59.

in close partnership with Secretary of State Cyrus Vance. Elements of a settlement began to fall into place: Field Marshal Lord Carver was appointed British Resident Commissioner; the UN agreed to provide a peacekeeping force; a constitution was drafted and a constitutional conference was scheduled to open at Lancaster House in November 1978.

But the forces working against a settlement proved far stronger. In August 1977 President Carter clumsily undermined the Anglo-American initiative by declaring that the future army of Zimbabwe would be 'based primarily' on the Patriotic Front's armed forces (ZANLA, and ZIPRA, the armed wings, respectively, of ZANU and ZAPU), thus alienating white Rhodesians. Within the Patriotic Front, Mugabe was convinced that ZANLA was winning the war; while Nkomo, more inclined to do a deal, was discredited by the downing of a Rhodesian Viscount airliner by ZIPRA in September 1978. Above all, Ian Smith once again wrong-footed his opponents by concluding an 'internal agreement' with Bishop Muzorewa and other black leaders in March 1978. Reluctantly, Dr Owen concluded that there was simply no basis for agreement and that the plan for a conference at Lancaster House must be shelved. By the beginning of 1979, with a minority Labour government unwilling to take decisive action and a British general election looming, there was little prospect of progress.

The presence of black ministers in the government of 'Rhodesia-Zimbabwe' and the prospect of nominally free elections in April 1979 gave the Smith regime a veneer of legitimacy which carried little weight with international opinion but did reassure the influential section of the British Conservative party that sympathised with 'our kith and kin' in Rhodesia. Their power had been shown in the annual vote on the renewal of sanctions in November 1978. When their leader, Margaret Thatcher, and her frontbench colleagues decided to abstain, they were confronted with the largest Conservative backbench revolt since the Second World War.[2] Mrs Thatcher's personal sympathies lay with the internal settlement; she recognised, nevertheless, the need to avoid making any public statement in its favour—although at times she came close to doing so. The pressure to recognise the Muzorewa government became stronger when it won the April 1979 elections. As Leader of the Opposition, Mrs Thatcher sent Lord Boyd, a former Colonial Secretary, to monitor the elections. By the time he reported, on 18 May 1979, the general election of 3 May had returned Mrs Thatcher to power with a large majority and a radical domestic agenda.

At the Foreign and Commonwealth Office (FCO) it was clear that the advent of a Conservative government presented both a risk and an opportunity. The risk was that, prompted by strong grassroots support and the Prime Minister's own instincts, the new government would accept the outcome of the Rhodesian elections and recognise Bishop Muzorewa. This was reinforced by Lord Boyd's conclusion (already known in Whitehall) that the elections had taken place in conditions that were, by African standards, free and well conducted—although the black electorate had had no opportunity to vote for either of the Patriotic Front parties. It was also clear that, with a large Conservative majority, Parliament would not vote to renew sanctions in November, leaving the United Kingdom isolated and no closer to a solution

---

2 Charles Moore, *Margaret Thatcher: The Authorised Biography*, Vol. I, *Not For Turning* (London: Allen Lane, 2013), p. 373.

acceptable to world opinion. The opportunity was that, knowing her personality, Mrs Thatcher might be attracted by a bold new answer to the Rhodesian impasse.[3]

Before the Conference, April – September 1979

As was customary, FCO officials had the task of presenting foreign policy options to a new government, of whatever party. Those dealing with Rhodesia included Sir Antony Duff, the Deputy Under-Secretary responsible for Africa, and Robin Renwick, who had been appointed head of a demoralised Rhodesia Department in November 1978. Sir Antony, a former submariner, had experienced the dispiriting Geneva Conference in 1976 and was determined that its mistakes should not be repeated. In March 1979, Mr Renwick, 'one of the most thrusting and dynamic operators at his level in the Foreign Office',[4] had been sent on a tour of southern Africa, where he met Rhodesian leaders before going on to Mozambique. Here he met Robert Mugabe, confident that ZANLA could achieve military victory, and the young British official responsible for liaison with the ZANU leadership who told him: 'They will not take you seriously until they get to Lancaster House. They know it is there that the independence constitutions for the other British colonies were decided.'[5] The answer, evolved under pressure, on the one hand, to avoid premature recognition of the Muzorewa government and, on the other, to reach a settlement before the debate on sanctions in November (Nos. 1, 3, 6-7), was to offer incoming Ministers a bold new plan. The United Kingdom should resume its full responsibility as a colonial power and should do so alone. In order to bring Southern Rhodesia to independence—the resumption of its old name was deliberate—Britain would convene a constitutional conference and see it through to the end. The warring parties would be forced to confront each other and to make hard choices. If they did not agree, the conference would simply proceed without them and they would have no say in its outcome. Britain would show favour to neither side. Once a constitution was agreed, a British Governor-General would return to Salisbury to supervise free elections with the support, if necessary, of British soldiers. The outcome of those elections would be entirely a matter for the people of Zimbabwe, black and white. Until then, it would be entirely a British-run show; and it would be choreographed at Lancaster House.

The first challenge faced by Duff and Renwick was to persuade the new Foreign Secretary, Lord Carrington, to accept a novel approach fraught with dangers on all sides. Lord Carrington was persuaded, although not without some initial reservations. With his military background, charm, good humour and—when necessary—ruthlessness, he would prove crucial to the ultimate success of the Lancaster House Conference. Without his appointment as Foreign Secretary, Renwick wrote, 'there

---

[3] For the origins and course of the Lancaster House Conference, as well as the transition to independence, see the internal report completed by Robin Renwick in July 19980, now published as Patrick Salmon (ed.), *The Rhodesia Settlement, 1979-1980: An In-house Study* (London: FCDO Historians, 2021), available at https://issuu.com/fcohistorians.

[4] British Diplomatic Oral History Programme (BDOHP) interview with Sir Roderic Lyne, 2006, https://oa.churchillarchives.libnova.com/view/1653. George Walden, then Private Secretary to Dr Owen and later to Lord Carrington, later claimed credit for the appointment of both Robin Renwick and Charles Powell to Rhodesia Department: George Walden, *Lucky George: Memoirs of an Anti-Politician* (London: Allen Lane, 1999). p. 198.

[5] Robin Renwick, *Unconventional Diplomacy in Southern Africa* (Basingstoke and London: Macmillan, 1997), p. 11.

would have been no Rhodesia settlement'.⁶ Lord Carrington was also key to the next part of the plan, persuading Mrs Thatcher: he was one of the few senior colleagues for whom the Prime Minister had respect and to whose advice she would listen. It took some time, nevertheless, before she was fully brought on board, and there were some bumps along the way. Her dislike of conventional thinking was revealed by her indignant marginal comments and underlinings on the briefing document on Rhodesia provided by the Cabinet Secretary, Sir John Hunt, on the day she assumed office (No. 2). She bridled at the advice that a 'cautious' approach was required: 'I agree we need *care* but a little courage is necessary too.' Left to herself, courage would have taken her in the direction of recognising Bishop Muzorewa; and she came close to doing so in a notorious speech in Canberra on 1 July.⁷ At one point Sir Antony Duff felt the need to collect 'those of the Prime Minister's opinions which we believe to be unfounded or which are likely to be presented in such a way as to produce the worst possible reaction amongst her African interlocutors' in order to 'counter her misapprehensions' (No. 19).

However, once converted to a plan that was both bold and British-led, the Prime Minister proved unshakeable. She liked the element of risk and the opportunity to wrong-foot her critics—never more so than at the Commonwealth Heads of Government Meeting (CHOGM) held at Lusaka from 1 to 7 August. Overcoming her fears for both her safety and that of The Queen, she famously danced with President Kenneth Kaunda and announced, confounding expectations, that the United Kingdom would resume its colonial responsibilities and convene a constitutional conference aimed at bringing Rhodesia to legal independence. After the Lancaster House Conference opened in September, she remained publicly distant from its proceedings, impervious to the appeals of white Rhodesians or their right-wing Conservative sympathisers (No. 68) and invoked only occasionally to speak to visiting dignitaries such as South African foreign minister Pik Botha, or to mollify or cajole heads of state such as President Julius Nyerere of Tanzania and President Kaunda when important matters were at stake.

Many more elements needed to fall into place before the Conference could open. Perhaps the least difficult task, though challenging enough, was to persuade the United States that they would no longer play the role of equal partner as they had done in the Owen-Vance years; but the Americans would still need to be kept on side and Congressional opinion placated (Nos 8, 10-12, 24, 28, 34, 44-45). International opinion, as represented by the United Nations, must be persuaded that this time Britain meant business (Nos. 30, 37, 47, 49, 55). The Commonwealth, led by Secretary-General Sir Shridath (Sonny) Ramphal, was generally suspicious of British motives (No. 19).⁸ Some members, such as President Nyerere's Tanzania,

---

6 *Ibid.*, p. 16. For Lord Carrington's recollections of the Conference see *Reflect on Things Past: The Memoirs of Lord Carrington* (London: Collins, 1988), Ch.13, and his contributions to a witness seminar held on 5 July 2005: Sue Onslow and Michael Kandiah (eds.), *Lancaster House 1979, Part I: The Witness Seminar* (London: FCO Historians, 2019), available at https://issuu.com/fcohistorians.

7 Available on the website of the Margaret Thatcher Foundation, https://www.margaretthatcher.org/document/103888.

8 Interviews with Sir Shridath ('Sonny') Ramphal and Patsy Robertson, 16 March 2006, in Onslow and Kandiah (eds.), *Lancaster House 1979, Part II: The Witnesses*, pp. 209-30, and with Sir S. Ramphal alone, 10 May 2006, ibid., pp. 231-44.

were strong supporters of the Patriotic Front; others, notably Nigeria, were openly hostile to the United Kingdom and could do serious damage to British economic interests (No. 57); while the volatile President of Zambia, Kenneth Kaunda, laboured under the burden of hosting ZAPU and seeing parts of his country being blown to pieces by Rhodesian forces (No. 65). Tanzania and Zambia were members of another grouping, the Front-Line States (FLS) dedicated to the defeat of white minority rule in Southern Africa, which also included Botswana, Lesotho and the two former Portuguese colonies of Angola and Mozambique. In June, Lord Harlech was sent on a mission to gauge the opinion of these states and to convince them that Britain meant business (Nos. 13-18, 22-23, 28). The Marxist President of Angola, Samora Machel, was later to prove remarkably helpful; but this could not have been predicted at the outset. Then there was South Africa, tiring of having to support the Rhodesians but determined not to have another radical black regime on its northern doorstep (Nos. 33, 52). In the United Kingdom, meanwhile, any suggestion of concessions to the Patriotic Front would be denounced as a sell-out by a vocal minority of the Conservative party, who could be relied on to make their feelings known at the party's annual conference in September (No. 68).

And all this assumed that the three elements of the Salisbury government – led by Ian Smith, Bishop Muzorewa and the Rev Ndabaningi Sithole—could somehow be persuaded to sit down in the same room as their enemies in the Patriotic Front led by Nkomo and Mugabe—and vice-versa—and stay there long enough to reach agreement before the deadline imposed by the vote on sanctions in November. Sir Antony Duff paid an early visit to Salisbury; he was followed later by another senior FCO official, Derek Day, in order to maintain contact with the Rhodesian authorities (Nos. 22, 26),[9] and the Prime Minister herself brought her influence to bear on Bishop Muzorewa (No. 29). As the plans for the Conference developed, the attitudes of ZANU (Nos. 36, 50) and ZAPU (Nos. 46, 51, 54) also became clearer.

The agreement reached at the Commonwealth meeting in Lusaka marked a breakthrough (No. 38). As the Prime Minister informed the Cabinet on 10 August, 'all Commonwealth Governments had accepted the primacy of Britain's role' and the plan for a constitutional conference could now go ahead (No. 39). On the same day invitations were issued to Bishop Muzorewa's government and the leaders of the Patriotic Front alone (No. 40). They were to send delegations of no more than twelve persons each, for whom the Government would cover first-class fares and expenses; any additional members would have to come at their own expense. From the outset, therefore, it was made clear that the British Government was in absolute control. But the risks remained enormous and the prospects doubtful. Lord Carrington later confessed that, 'having got the Lancaster House Conference on the agenda with everyone agreeing to it, I did not think for a moment that it would be a success'.[10] His pessimism is confirmed by a revealing conversation with Mrs Thatcher a few days later. While she wished to do everything possible to make the Conference a success, he regarded 'such agreement as virtually inconceivable' and 'more as a means of enabling the British Government to get off the Rhodesia hook' (No. 49). As he informed the Prime Minister at the end of August, it was highly unlikely that the

---

9 BDOHP interview with Sir Derek Day, 1996, https://oa.churchillarchives.libnova.com/view/1507.
10 Onslow and Kandiah (eds.), *Lancaster House 1979, Part I: The Witness Seminar*, p. 79.

Patriotic Front would 'accept reasonable constitutional proposals and agree to participate in new elections': it was therefore essential to ensure that if the Conference broke down, the responsibility lay with them, not the British Government (No. 56). A steering brief by Rhodesia Department on 6 September outlined the Government's negotiating strategy (No. 61). Reversing the approach adopted at Geneva, it set out a sequence of stages, each more difficult than the last. First, and most straightforward, would be agreement on a constitution; then would come procedures for the transfer of power; finally there would be the arrangements for a cease-fire between the warring parties. Each would be based on firm proposals by the British side, on which there would have to be full agreement by all parties before embarking on the next stage. The three stages were therefore interlinked: there could be no progress unless all the delegations agreed to go on to the next stage. If any party failed to agree, the conference would simply proceed without them.

Stage I: Agreement on the Constitution, September – October 1979
Lancaster House was an ideal location for a conference. Begun in 1825 as a residence for the Duke of York and completed in 1836 in an ornate Louis XIV style, it enjoyed a central London location which could be easily sealed off from outside intrusion. The building combined grand, gilded state rooms, where plenary sessions were held, with smaller rooms and spaces where informal meetings and social encounters could take place (and much of the most important business was conducted). Organisations like the FLS were welcome to send observers to London but they would not be admitted to the Conference: they would be kept informed of progress 'through the usual diplomatic channels' (No. 40). Even the Commonwealth was excluded, while the information that reached the media was tightly controlled by a press office headed by Nicholas Fenn, with press briefings, on and off the record, being held away from Lancaster House.[11] The full resources of the FCO were deployed. Officials, some very junior, were seconded to the conference from across the organisation, often at short notice, to ensure that the proceedings ran smoothly. Ministers other than Lord Carrington also played a major part. Sir Ian Gilmour, the Lord Privy Seal, represented the FCO in the House of Commons and chaired meetings in the Foreign Secretary's absence; Richard Luce, Parliamentary Under-Secretary of State, undertook three visits to Africa before and during the conference (Nos. 123, 135, 170). No opportunity was lost to gain insight into the thinking of the delegates, whether in casual conversation at Heathrow Airport (No. 63) or over lunch with Robert and Sally Mugabe (No. 155). Every morning, Ministers and officials met at the FCO to discuss the latest information before the day's proceedings began at Lancaster House.[12]

The arrangements were carefully planned. The aim was to introduce a sense of theatre: to make the delegates realise that Britain was in control and expected them to reach a result.[13] In the Conference chamber, the seating was arranged so that the

---

11 BDOHP interview with Sir Nicholas Fenn, 2010, https://oa.churchillarchives.libnova.com/view/1523.
12 Interview with Lord Luce, 26 January 2006, in Onslow and Kandiah (eds.), *Lancaster House 1979, Part II: The Witnesses*, pp. 120-138 (p. 128).
13 Interview with Lord Renwick, 30 January 2006, in Onslow and Kandiah (eds.), *Lancaster House 1979, Part II: The Witnesses*, pp. 139-151 (p. 141).

contending parties faced each other, with Lord Carrington and his advisers at one end of the room and the Conference Secretariat, headed by John Willson, at the other.[14] An early attempt by the Patriotic Front to change the seating was instantly rebuffed (No. 66). One of the main tasks of the Secretariat was to produce a full record of the plenary sessions, working until two or three in the morning to get the minutes into pigeonholes by eight o'clock that day. Yet, as Nigel Sheinwald, a young diplomat drafted in to join the Secretariat, quickly realised, the real negotiations took place out of sight; the minutes were there mainly to be argued over.[15] The unofficial aspects were equally important. The members of the two delegations—all of them Rhodesians far from home—were obliged to socialise during the breaks between conference sessions, sometimes producing surprising encounters such as the occasion when Josaiah Tongogara, ZANU's military leader, asked after the health of Ian Smith's mother, who had been kind to him as a child. Ministers and members of the House of Lords attended dinners and arranged other informal gatherings for the leading participants (Nos. 70, 87, 155). Less eminent delegates had to endure the vagaries of London life, like the two members of the ZAPU delegation who were subjected to a racist attack in the East End (No. 100).

By the time Lord Carrington delivered his opening statement to the Conference on 10 September (No. 67), the delegates were already familiar with the British Government's outline proposals for an independence constitution. Confounding expectations, they were extremely brief. Instead of the 'thick mass of documentation' with which delegates were familiar from the Owen-Vance era, Carrington tabled a very short note. 'It was a few bullet points on the page,' recalled Roderic Lyne, a junior member of Rhodesia Department. 'And they were all apple-pie and motherhood. So of course there wasn't a great deal for people to disagree with.' The aim 'was get them over the first hurdle into agreement, get the process going, get people talking to each other before he tackled the more difficult issues. So he deliberately left the most difficult issues at the back; they weren't even on the table.'[16] Even so, the negotiations on the constitution proved arduous. While Bishop Muzorewa's delegation objected to holding new elections and discussing anything other than the constitutional arrangements, key elements of the British proposals—that 20 per cent of the parliamentary seats should be reserved for the white electorate, and that there should be a constitutional rather than an executive Presidency—were unacceptable to the Patriotic Front as well as to many African governments.

It was evident, however, that 'neither delegation was able to maintain more than a semblance of unity'.[17] Each therefore had to be dealt with separately, its internal divisions identified and, if possible, exploited. In the first phase of the conference, efforts were focused primarily on the Salisbury government. The most important initial task was to isolate Ian Smith and neutralise his 'hypnotic influence' over his fellow delegates (Nos. 74, 77).[18] This occupied much of the first month of the Conference, with the British seeking to sway those members of the delegation who held a more

---

14 BDOHP interview with John Willson, 2005, https://oa.churchillarchives.libnova.com/view/1795.
15 BDOHP interview with Sir Nigel Sheinwald, 2016-17, https://oa.churchillarchives.libnova.com/view/1757.
16 Interview with Sir R. Lyne (note 4 above).
17 Salmon (ed.), *The Rhodesia Settlement*, p. 30.
18 *Ibid.*, p. 31.

realistic view of Rhodesia's prospects for survival, notably David Smith, the Deputy Prime Minister and Minister of Finance, and General Walls, the head of the armed forces, as well as Bishop Muzorewa himself. On 6 October Muzorewa announced his acceptance of the British proposals and of new elections (No. 97). Ian Smith immediately left for Salisbury, where he attempted to rally opposition to the agreement; but his influence over the delegation had been broken.

The focus now turned to the Patriotic Front. In addition to the formal bilateral meetings at Lancaster House, the task of liaising with Joshua Nkomo and Robert Mugabe fell primarily to Robin Renwick and Charles Powell, a close friend who had recently joined Rhodesia Department. They met the two leaders almost daily in their London hotels, and there were elements of farce as they witnessed furniture threaten to collapse under Nkomo's weight, or Mugabe wrapped in a mackintosh watching children's television.[19] Sometimes the meetings were very informal. After one evening session at which no notes were taken, Sir Ian Gilmour apologised to Lord Carrington for 'the rather hazy nature of what follows' and concluded his account of the constitutional discussions: 'While Nkomo was in the loo, Mugabe picked up my book on Conservatism and asked for a copy. This is unlikely to have decisive influence on his views.'[20]

It had been clear from the outset that, while Nkomo might be persuaded to reach a deal, Mugabe would hold out for much longer, confident in his ability to achieve a military victory sooner or later. Their negotiating styles were also very different:

> I remember Nkomo thumping the coffee table in Carrington's office time and again. He and Mugabe would come in glowering to complain, to threaten to walk out. Nkomo would do a lot of talking and shouting and ranting. He was a big powerful man and he'd bring his fists crashing down on the coffee table; we were always waiting for the day when the coffee table would break, but it never did.
>
> Mugabe would sit there saying very little, but he was an extremely clever, very astute man. Then he would come in at a certain point with a rapier thrust. He would make some killer point, a point that was really difficult to answer. Nkomo and Mugabe didn't like each other; they were rivals for power. They were very suspicious of each other, but they were also a pretty clever double act and tough to negotiate with; a very wearing process.[21]

Whether one could be separated from the other, and the desirability of doing so, remained an open question and one that would recur throughout the Conference. Yet through patient negotiation and judicious diplomatic pressure (from, among others, President Machel and Sir Sonny Ramphal), the Patriotic Front gradually relented. It was at this point that the inbuilt momentum of the Conference started to pick up speed. For Lord Carrington announced on 15 October that, in view of their failure to accept the constitution, discussions on the next phase would simply

---

19 Interviews with Lord Renwick (note 11 above) and with Lord Powell of Bayswater, 1 February 2006, in Onslow and Kandiah (eds.), *Lancaster House 1979, Part II: The Witnesses*, pp. 152-65.
20 Minute of 14 September 1979, TNA, FCO 73/725.
21 Interview with Sir R. Lyne (note 4 above).

proceed without the Patriotic Front. By this time, they had been persuaded to agree to a constitutional Presidency and white seats in Parliament but still held out on many other issues, notably the question of land reform (Nos. 87, 91-92). Within three days of Carrington's ultimatum, they had fallen into line (No. 122) and he was able to announce the successful conclusion of the first phase of the Conference (No. 125).

Stage II: The Pre-Independence Arrangements, October – November 1979
The British Government had already begun to make preparations for the next stage of the Conference. On 28 September Lord Carrington set out for the Prime Minister the main conditions that would need to be fulfilled in order to bring Rhodesia to legal independence (No. 89). The most important question was whether it should take place under direct British control or with the Muzorewa government still in place. The Foreign Secretary advised that only British control—requiring a British Governor, with full legal authority to direct Rhodesian civil servants and armed forces, and a British military force to be in place in order to supervise the elections within at most two months—would carry conviction with the international community. Lord Carrington outlined the British plan in plenary session on 19 October, having already secured Bishop Muzorewa's agreement to the holding of new elections (No. 125). Having been elected Prime Minister only a few months earlier, the Bishop understandably insisted on remaining in office until they took place: Britain was therefore faced with the challenging task of persuading him to relinquish power. But it was equally vital that the Patriotic Front should agree not only to elections under British supervision but also to a cease-fire. Going ahead with the consent of the Salisbury government alone would mean that the elections would have to be held under wartime conditions and in the face of international disapproval—leaving Britain diplomatically isolated and the Governor and the small British force dangerously exposed. The scene was set for a second and even more difficult round of negotiations.

The United Kingdom's detailed proposals for implementing the independence constitution were tabled in plenary session on 22 October (No. 130). Two days later, Mr Renwick submitted a series of papers discussing tactics for the next stage of the Conference, the measures required to allow sanctions to be maintained beyond the 15 November deadline and the implications of going ahead with Muzorewa alone (No. 131). An Enabling Bill to promulgate the constitution and allow the continuation of sanctions would have to become law by 15 November. It would also have to make provision for the appointment of a Governor by Order in Council. If Bishop Muzorewa and General Walls announced that they would accept the Governor's authority and the dissolution of the Salisbury Parliament, the UK would be able to inform the UN Security Council that legality was in the process of being restored, even if the Patriotic Front refused to accept the pre-independence arrangements. Britain would still face hostile reactions in Africa and from the wider international community but might be able to rely on a measure of support from the United States and France. Much diplomatic activity was therefore devoted to explaining the British proposals, particularly to the Americans (Nos. 127-128, 133-134, 150, 158, 161-162) and the Front-Line States (Nos. 126, 135).

By this time, too, the appointment of a British Governor was under active consideration. In a minute of 5 October Mr Renwick canvassed the names of several potential candidates (No. 96), but he was already convinced that only one of these was of sufficient stature to undertake such a critical mission. Christopher Soames, under whom he had served in Paris, 'was, arguably, the most effective Ambassador we had sent there since the war'.[22] He was now Lord President of the Council and Leader of the House of Lords. Only Lord Soames could 'make up in force of personality what he lacked in real power'; his wife Mary, Winston Churchill's daughter, would also prove a valuable asset. In the course of November, Ministers and officials sought first to secure his agreement to the appointment and then to reassure him about the considerable risks that he would face (Nos. 143, 165, 187). As early as 7 November, two British diplomats arrived discreetly in Salisbury to prepare Government House for the Governor's arrival.

On 27 October, after protracted negotiations in London and Salisbury, Bishop Muzorewa accepted the broad principles of the interim arrangements; acceptance of the detailed proposals followed on 5 November (No. 150). The task now was to secure acceptance by the Patriotic Front and to ensure the passing of the Enabling Act by 15 November. Lord Carrington told the Cabinet on 2 November that definitive proposals would be tabled that day, requiring a reply from the Patriotic Front by the 5th (No. 144). If they agreed, the Conference would move on to consider cease-fire arrangements. The parliamentary timetable, approved by the Cabinet Defence and Oversea Policy Committee (OD) on 5 November (Nos. 145-146), was tight and designed to exert maximum pressure on the Patriotic Front. If it went according to plan, a Second Reading debate on 8 November would allow the Enabling Bill to receive Royal Assent on 14 November and come into force the following day. Unsurprisingly, however, the Patriotic Front did not accept the British proposals, having tabled alternative proposals, including a lengthy transitional period under United Nations auspices, that seemed designed to drag out the negotiations indefinitely (No. 134). It was therefore necessary not only to find ways of bringing pressure to bear on the Patriotic Front, but also to consider what options were available if they simply chose to walk out of the Conference.

Of the external actors able to influence the Patriotic Front, President Kaunda of Zambia was among the most important, but also least predictable. He remained loyal to Joshua Nkomo and ZAPU, enduring repeated Rhodesian attacks on his country for doing so, while his personal representative in London, Mark Chona, was an even stronger supporter who 'seemed on occasions to be defending positions already abandoned by Nkomo'.[23] Mr Luce had explained Britain's objectives to President Kaunda during his tour of the Front-Line States (No. 135). Now Mrs Thatcher's influence was brought to bear in a personal message (No. 138), and both the Foreign Secretary and the Prime Minister had lengthy meetings with the President when he visited London between 8 and 11 November (Nos. 154, 157, 159). These ranged between the amicable and the 'singularly unproductive' (No. 159). Other means of pressure were therefore sought, with appeals to Nigeria and other Commonwealth governments (Nos. 139, 149, 166-167, 170).

---

22 Renwick, *Unconventional Diplomacy*, p. 57.
23 *Ibid.*, p. 49

Knowing that Mr Nkomo was more inclined to strike a deal than Mr Mugabe, thoughts also turned to exploiting the divisions between the two Patriotic Front leaders, possibly to doing a deal with Nkomo alone and excluding Mugabe (No. 147). How seriously this option was pursued, and who might have been in favour of it, remains an open question.[24] Another option might be to go ahead with Bishop Muzorewa alone, hoping that the international community would acknowledge that Britain had done its utmost to bring about an agreement and that only the Patriotic Front had prevented it from materialising. Mr Mugabe certainly remained convinced that the British were 'strongly in favour of Muzorewa and [were] working to ensure that he is head of the next Government' (No. 155). Some junior FCO officials shared that suspicion.[25] By 11 November, however, Mr Nkomo 'appeared to realise that matters could not be delayed', and his remaining objections had to do more with form than substance (No. 163). President Kaunda, too, 'was sure that Nkomo wanted a settlement', though 'he was much less sure about Mugabe' (No. 164). Eventually Mr Mugabe calculated that he had procrastinated enough. On the day the Enabling Bill passed into law, the Patriotic Front relented and agreed to the proposals for the interim period, 'subject to a successful outcome of the negotiations on a cease-fire' (No. 171).

Stage III: Negotiations on the Cease-Fire and the Return to Legality, November – December 1979

From the outset, the British had known that the final stage of negotiations would be the most difficult. Even though both sides were now committed to free elections, a civil war would have to be wound down and brought to an end before they could take place. Both sides had much to fear: the Rhodesians that the rebel armies stationed in Zambia and Mozambique would infiltrate the country before the elections took place and establish their grip over areas they did not yet control; the Patriotic Front that if their forces agreed to assemble at designated points and laid down their arms, they would be at the mercy of the Rhodesian military. The British had their own anxieties: how a British Governor could assert his authority over a resentful white community and a black population whose loyalties were difficult to predict, and how the cease-fire was to be supervised. They would have to win the confidence of General Walls and his colleagues in the Rhodesian high command, without whom no cease-fire could be enforced. Departing from its previous position, the Government decided to send a British military force, supported by forces from Commonwealth countries that did not back the Patriotic Front (Australia, New Zealand, Fiji and Kenya); but their combined strength would still be small in comparison with the responsibilities they would take on and the risks they would face. The British knew, too, that in the previous two stages the Patriotic Front had reached agreement only when pushed to the brink. To make them accept the independence settlement in its entirety, brinkmanship would have to be redoubled.

On 16 November Lord Carrington put forward the UK's outline proposals for a cease-fire. The initial reactions of General Walls and other members of the

---

24 Differing views are expressed by Lord Luce in Onslow and Kandiah (eds.), *Lancaster House 1979, Part II: The Witnesses*, p. 126, Lord Renwick, ibid, p. 144, and Lord Powell, ibid, p. 153.

25 BDOHP interviews with Sir Stephen Gomersall, 2023. https://oa.churchillarchives.libnova.com/view/1547, and Sir Kieran Prendergast, 2012, https://oa.churchillarchives.libnova.com/view/1693.

Salisbury delegation were promising, and even General Tongogara admitted that there were positive aspects, including the idea of a cease-fire commission on which both sides were represented (No. 176). At this point, the Conference was nearly derailed by massive Rhodesian incursions into Zambia (authorised without General Walls's knowledge) aimed at stemming the infiltration of ZIPRA forces into the country and inflicting severe damage on Zambia's infrastructure. Holding Britain to blame, Zambian demonstrators seriously threatened the safety of the British High Commissioner, Sir Leonard Allinson, and his staff. Again, Mrs Thatcher did her utmost to defuse the situation in a long telephone conversation with President Kaunda (No. 177).

The crisis soon passed, and the UK's full cease-fire proposals were presented on 22 November with instructions that they should be sent quickly to Dar es Salaam, where Nkomo and Mugabe were meeting leaders of the Front-Line States—and where President Machel brought pressure on them to reach agreement (No. 179). However, the two leaders were not yet in any mood to agree. On 26 November they failed to attend the plenary session at which the Salisbury delegation accepted Britain's proposals (No. 184). Bilateral meetings with the Patriotic Front proved unproductive and acrimonious (Nos. 188, 190). In a heated meeting on 30 November Lord Carrington reacted strongly against their latest paper ('It was not an answer, but an interpretative statement') and gave them an ultimatum: 'Lord Carrington said that we had been discussing the ceasefire arrangements for over two weeks and had gone out of our way to allay the PF's fears. We had to have an answer' (No. 193). Behind the PF's truculence, however, the British side detected a widening rift between the two leaders: 'It was by this stage clear that there was considerable pressure within ZAPU to agree to a settlement on this basis.'[26] Even if the Patriotic Front accepted the British proposals, it remained vital for the UK to retain the initiative. This meant pushing to enact the independence constitution, appointing the Governor and getting him to Salisbury as quickly as possible, if necessary before the conclusion of the Conference.

Yet the Conference was in danger of unravelling on both sides. On 3 December Lord Carrington informed the OD Committee that it 'was now close to break-down' (No. 194). The problem did not lie only with the Patriotic Front, since 'the Salisbury delegation who had accepted the British proposals were reaching the end of their patience'. Meeting the Salisbury delegation later that day he was told that 'that the British Government had lost the concept of time and were trying to get the Patriotic Front in at almost any price' (No. 195). To retain Rhodesian cooperation, the British pushed ahead on 3 December with the legislative arrangements for the appointment of a Governor (No. 196), while behind the scenes British officials were talking privately to Nkomo, and Sir Sonny Ramphal was talking to both leaders. He told Mrs Thatcher on 3 December that 'Mr Nkomo recognised that 'the bus was on the move' and that he intended to be on it. Of the other members of the Patriotic Front, Mr Ramphal said that Mr Tongogara wanted a settlement and that Mr Mugabe probably did too although he was still 'in a dialectic'. He was confident, however, that 'the Patriotic Front would come up to the mark, probably on the following day' (No. 197). Sir Sonny's confidence proved well founded. In plenary session on 5 December the

---

26 Salmon (ed.), *The Rhodesia Settlement*, p. 103.

Patriotic Front stated that 'They now felt that our proposals provided the basis for an agreement and for moving on quickly to settle the details of implementation' (No. 198). Lord Carrington was able to inform the Cabinet of their agreement on 6 December (No. 199). Maintaining the momentum, the appointment of Lord Soames as Governor was announced on 7 December, with the date of his arrival in Salisbury still to be decided (No. 202).

It remained necessary to placate the South Africans and secure American support for the final stage of negotiations. The South Africans were increasingly alarmed by the draining away of Bishop Muzorewa's electoral support and the prospect that 'another hostile, Marxist regime will come to power on their borders' (Nos. 172, 173). Following the advice of Colonel Laurens van der Post, who had acted as an intermediary throughout the Conference, Mrs Thatcher and Lord Carrington sent private messages of reassurance to both Pik Botha and Prime Minister P.W. Botha (No. 201). With the Americans (and with a visit to Washington by Prime Minister and Foreign Secretary impending), it was a matter of explaining that the Patriotic Front were filibustering, hoping to infiltrate as many of their forces as they could. A clear American statement of support, together with an early decision to lift sanctions, would 'exert real pressure on the Patriotic Front finally to agree to the settlement' (No. 203). Similar requests for support were sent to Commonwealth and other friendly countries, along with a personal message from the Prime Minister to President Machel (Nos. 204-205).

The despatch of Lord Soames to Salisbury was announced on 10 December (No. 206); he arrived there in the early afternoon of the 12th, bringing the Rhodesian state of rebellion formally to an end and leading to the lifting of sanctions by the United Kingdom. In order to give the Patriotic Front a further push, Lord Carrington had made a final presentation of Britain's cease-fire proposals to the Conference on 11 December. The Salisbury delegation accepted these proposals on 13 December, subject to two provisions, reflecting concern that the Patriotic Front would not concentrate all its forces in the assembly points and might continue to infiltrate further forces into the country (No. 208); and indeed the Patriotic Front was still wrangling about assembly points in further animated meetings on 13 and 14 December (Nos. 207, 210). The final plenary session of the Conference was held on 15 December. While Nkomo was relatively helpful, Mugabe was still clearly holding out for a break (No. 212). Despite very strong pressure from General Tongogara and President Machel (No. 214) he broke off negotiations and was preparing to leave for New York to address the United Nations. Only a further strong message from Machel, delivered by his personal representative in London Fernando Honwana, stating that if he rejected the agreement he could no longer count on Mozambican support, made Mugabe change his mind.

With sanctions now being lifted by countries such as New Zealand and Germany, it was urgently necessary, as Mrs Thatcher was advised before her visit to Washington on 17-18 December, for the United States to do the same. If not, the Patriotic Front might be encouraged to continue to hold out for better terms (No. 209). Following her personal appeal (No. 211), President Carter decided that American sanctions would be lifted with effect from midnight on 16 December. At 6 p.m. on 17 December Nkomo and Mugabe initialled the agreement, having finally been brought round by the offer of one further assembly point, bringing the total to sixteen (No. 215). The real reason, as the FCO explained to Lord Soames in Salisbury, was that Mr Mugabe '[had] been under very strong pressure to accept from (*a*) Tongogara, who has been pressing for a settlement throughout (*b*) Machel, who is fed up with the war' (No. 214). Even at this late stage there was further delay caused by the reaction of Rhodesian military commanders to a provocative press conference held by the Patriotic Front. However, the final agreement was signed at Lancaster House at noon on 21 December (No. 218). Both the Cabinet and the Prime Minister herself congratulated Lord Carrington and Sir Ian Gilmour on their 'outstanding achievement in the face of so many obstacles' (Nos. 217, 219).

The Transition to Independence, December 1979 – April 1980

When Lord Soames arrived at Government House in Salisbury on 12 December, the Union Flag was raised and he was greeted, in a symbolic moment, by Sir Humphrey Gibbs, the last Governor of Southern Rhodesia before UDI. Lord Soames's team included his deputy, Sir Antony Duff, Major-General John Acland, who would command the monitoring force, and Sir John Boynton, the election commissioner, as well as Robin Renwick, Nicholas Fenn and a number of junior FCO staff. An advance party of British officials had been in the country since 22 November: it included Robin Byatt from the FCO and Brigadier Adam Gurdon, who was largely responsible for devising the system of assembly points. Lord Soames was due to make a broadcast on the first evening. 'This broadcast was to be fairly important; many Rhodesians told me afterwards they had been much influenced by it,' Robin Byatt recalled:

> We got to work on the text and got a very good text, but he wanted a suitable peroration, something with a real kick in it, we all struggled away and suggested this and suggested that, he was dissatisfied with all of them, nothing would do, 'Oh', he said, 'I'll ask Mary, she'll get it right' (Mary being his wife). He stumped off, Mary was in the bath, and from the bath she came up – she wasn't Winston Churchill's daughter for nothing – she came up with two sentences which just fitted the bill absolutely right.[27]

Lord Soames's arrival had helped to accelerate the negotiations in London but was still a moment of great risk. It marked the formal resumption of British rule, but effective authority required the cooperation of the Rhodesian authorities: most of all the military, who were still conducting active operations against the guerrillas and doubted the capacity of the Commonwealth monitoring force to impose any kind of order in the war-torn countryside. There was still no cease-fire and ZANU and ZAPU remained banned; a large body of South African troops was known to remain in the country, but the full extent of South African involvement remained to be discovered. The offer of an additional assembly point helped to bring the Patriotic Front closer to agreement and on 21 December, the day of the Lancaster House Agreement, Lord Soames lifted the bans on ZANU and ZAPU and granted a general

---

27 BDOHP interview with Sir Robin Byatt, 2016, https://oa.churchillarchives.libnova.com/view/1425

amnesty. The monitoring force arrived immediately afterwards, its men and equipment airlifted by the US Air Force and the RAF. They were then deployed to the most remote and dangerous parts of the country to await the unpredictable response of the guerrilla fighters.

Dangerous incidents followed: a helicopter crash that killed three members of the RAF but turned out to have been accidental; and the death of General Tongogara on 26 December in a car crash in Mozambique that may or may not have been accidental but ended his close working relationship with General Walls. The cease-fire was announced on 29 December. It now remained to be seen whether the guerrillas would come in from the bush. They began to trickle in slowly at first, then arrived in very large numbers. The process was nearly complete by 6 January 1980, with over 20,000 men having come in from the bush; a further 2-3,000 men came in over the next nine days. Apart from isolated incidents, the cease-fire largely held, though it remained difficult to hold the disgruntled Rhodesian military in check. With the end of hostilities, the two Patriotic Front leaders returned to the country and began their electoral campaigns. There was talk of a Muzorewa/Nkomo deal to exclude Mugabe from power; some suspected that this had been the British intention all along.[28] Nkomo himself hoped for a joint campaign with Mugabe but this came to nothing: ZANU was confident of its support from the Shona tribe, representing 80 per cent of the population. Lord Soames resisted pressure to exclude Mugabe from the elections on grounds of intimidation: he would take action against any breaches of the cease-fire, but he could not justify taking action against one party alone.

The situation remained volatile: intimidation was widespread; assassinations were attempted and carried out by all sides (the most serious attempt, on 10 February, came close to killing Mugabe). The election was held between 27 February and 4 March. Twenty seats had been reserved for the white voters. As many, but not all, had expected, the black vote exactly reflected the country's tribal balance, with Nkomo winning the entire Ndebele vote and gaining all 20 seats in Matabeleland, while Mugabe won 57 seats in Mashonaland, giving him an absolute majority of the 80 African seats. The election supervisors, led by Sir John Boynton, concluded that, while intimidation might have distorted the voting in some areas, the overall result was a fair reflection of the wishes of the people. The scale of Mugabe's victory nevertheless came as a shock to the white population, as well as to the South Africans. Back in London, most people had expected Mugabe to win the largest number of seats; few had expected a landslide. In a sweepstake held at the FCO, only one person correctly predicted the actual result: Paul Lever, Lord Carrington's Assistant Private Secretary, who knew nothing at all about Rhodesia. Lord Soames invited Mugabe to form a government; he did so, constructing a broadly-based coalition that included Nkomo. The independence of Zimbabwe was proclaimed at midnight on 17 April in the presence of the Prince of Wales. Lord Soames and his staff left Salisbury on the following day.

---

28 BDOHP interview with Edward Chaplin, 2021, https://oa.churchillarchives.libnova.com/view/1449.

Acknowledgements

In accordance with the Parliamentary announcement cited in the Preface to the first volume of *Documents on British Policy Overseas*, the editors have had the customary freedom of selection and arrangement of documents, including full access to all classes of documentation. Original versions of all the documents printed in this volume are available at The National Archives, Kew. In one instance it has been necessary for reasons of national security to excise passages from a selected document (No. 60). These omissions are indicated with square brackets and appropriate footnote references.

The editors wish to thank Sir Philip Barton, Permanent Under-Secretary of State, Adrian Blundell, Chief Information Officer, and Stewart MacLeod, Head of Knowledge and Information Services for their support. For assistance in providing documents they are grateful to colleagues in the Archives Management Team at Hanslope Park, and to staff at The National Archives. They have benefited greatly from the advice and information provided by Chris Collins, Professor Sue Onslow, Lord Powell of Bayswater and Lord Renwick of Clifton. They are grateful to their colleagues in the Historians team, including Sue Fleming, Nevil Hagon and Tom Goodwin, for editorial support, and to Linda Lundin for typesetting the volume.

PATRICK SALMON
RICHARD SMITH
PAUL BALI

January 2025

ABBREVIATIONS FOR PRINTED SOURCES

Parl. Debs.,   *Parliamentary Debates (Hansard), Fifth Series, House*
5th ser., H. of C.   *of Commons, Official Report* (London, 1909f.)

ABBREVIATED DESIGNATIONS

AAP	Anglo American Proposals
APC	All Party Conference
BBC	British Broadcasting Corporation
BP	British Petroleum
CHGM/ CHOGM	Commonwealth Heads of Government Meeting
CTB	Comprehensive Test Ban Treaty
EEC	European Economic Community
ECGD	Export Credits Guarantee Department
FCO	Foreign and Commonwealth Office
FLS	Front Line States
FMG	Federal Military Government
FRELIMO	Liberation Front of Mozambique
GMT	Greenwich Mean Time
HE	His Excellency
HM	Her Majesty's
HMG	Her Majesty's Government
IFT	Immediate Following Telegram
MIFT	My Immediate Following Telegram
MIPT	My Immediate Preceding Telegram
MP	Member of Parliament
NATO	North Atlantic Treaty Organisation

NCO	Non-Commissioned Officer
OD	Cabinet Defence and Oversea Committee
PF	Patriotic Front
SAG	South African Government
SWAPO	South West Africa People's Organisation
TEL	Telegram
TELNO	Telegram Number
TUR	Telegram Under Reference
UANC	United African Council
UDI	Unilateral Declaration of Independence
UK	United Kingdom
UKDEL	United Kingdom Delegation
UKMIS	United Kingdom Mission
UN	United Nations
UNGA	United Nations General Assembly
US	United States
USSR	Union of Soviet Socialist Republics
VS	Verbatim Series
Z	Zulu (Greenwich Mean Time)
ZANLA	Zimbabwe African National Liberation Army
ZANU	Zimbabwe African National Union
ZANU-PF	Zimbabwe African National Union-Patriotic Front
ZAPU	Zimbabwe African People's Union
ZIPRA	Zimbabwe People's Revolutionary Army

LIST OF PERSONS

Adefope, General Henry Edmund Olufemi, Nigerian Minister of Foreign affairs, 1978-30 September 1979
Alexander, Michael O'Donel Bjarne, Private Secretary (Overseas Affairs) to the Prime Minister, 1979-81
Allinson, Sir (Walter) Leonard, British High Commissioner, Lusaka, 1978-80
Allum, Peter Kevin, Rhodesian Police Commissioner
Anderson (Andersen), (Jonas) Christian, Rhodesian Minister of Justice, 1 June 1979-12 December 1979

Bafanah, Zephaniah, Rhodesian Minister of Water Development, 1 June 1979-12 December 1979
Banda, Hastings Kamuzu, President of Malawi, 1964-94
Barlow, Peter John, Special Assistant (Planning), Rhodesia Department, FCO
Barltrop, Roger Arnold Rowlandson, Head of Commonwealth Coordination Department, FCO, 1978-81
Baron, Leo, Legal Adviser to the Patriotic Front delegation at the Lancaster House Conference
Binaisa, Godfrey Lukongwa, President of Uganda, 1979-80
Blaker, Peter Allan Renshaw, Minister of State, FCO, 5 May 1979-1981
Bonde, Stephen Robin, Rhodesia Department, FCO, 1978-79
Botha, Pieter Willem, Prime Minister of South Africa, 1978-84
Botha, (Roelof Frederik) Pik, South African Foreign Minister, 1977-94
Boyd, Alan Tindal Lennox-, (first Viscount Boyd of Merton), British Conservative Peer; Secretary of State for the Colonies, 1954-59
Brewster, Kingman, US Ambassador, London, 1977-81
Brown, Mervyn, British High Commissioner, Lagos, 29 January 1979-1983
Bulle, Ernest Leonard, Rhodesian Minister of Commerce and Industry, 1 June 1979-12 December 1979
Burgess, Anthony Reginald Frank, Rhodesia Department, FCO, 1979-80
Byatt, Ronald Archer Campbell, Assistant Under-Secretary of State for Africa, August 1979-1980

Carter, James 'Jimmy' Earl, President of the United States, 1977-81
Carrington, Lord (Peter Alexander Rupert), Secretary of State for Foreign and Commonwealth Affairs, 4 May 1979-1982
Cartledge, Bryan, Private Secretary (Overseas Affairs) to the Prime Minister, 1977-79
Chambati, Ariston, ZAPU Secretary for Research; Joint secretary for the Patriotic Front Delegation at Lancaster House
Chikerema, James Robert Dambaza, Leader of the Zimbabwe Democratic Party
Chinamano, Josiah Mushore, Vice-President, ZAPU
Chona, Mark, Special Adviser for Political Affairs to President Kaunda, 1968-80

Crabbie, Christopher Donald, First Secretary, British Embassy, Washington, 1979-83
Cronje, Rowan, Rhodesian Deputy Minister for Lands, Natural Resources and Rural Development, 1 June 1979-12 December 1979

Day, Derek Malcolm, Assistant Under-Secretary of State, FCO
Doble, John Frederick, First Secretary (Chancery) and Consul, British Embassy, Maputo, 1978-81
Dos Santos, José Eduardo, President of Angola, from 21 September 1979-2017
Duff, Sir Antony, Deputy Permanent Under-Secretary of State, FCO; Deputy Governor of Rhodesia, 12 December 1979-18 April 1980

Fenn, Nicholas Maxted, Lancaster House Conference Spokesman; Head of News Department, FCO, 1979-82
Fifoot, Paul Ronald Ninnes, Legal Counsellor, FCO
Fourie, (Bernardus) Brand Gerhardus, Director-General, South African Department of Foreign Affairs, 1966-83
Fraser, (John) Malcolm, Prime Minister of Australia, 1975-83

Gaylard, Jack, Secretary to the Rhodesian Cabinet, 1970- 20 June 1979
Gibbs, Sir Humphrey Vicary, Governor of Rhodesia, 1959-69
Gilmour, Sir Ian Hedworth John Little, Lord Privy Seal, from 5 May 1979-1981
Gomersall, Stephen John, Private Secretary to the Lord Privy Seal
Graham, Sir John Alexander Noble, Deputy Under-Secretary of State, FCO, 1977-79; HM Ambassador, Tehran, January 1979-80

Hall, Michael, Conference and Visits Section, Protocol and Conference Department, FCO
Harlech, Lord (William David Ormsby Gore), British Conservative Peer; HMG Special Envoy to Africa, from 26 May 1979
Hawkins, Air Vice Marshal Harold, Rhodesian Diplomatic Representative in South Africa
Haydon, Walter Robert, HM Ambassador, Dublin, 1976-80
Helms, Jesse Alexander, US Senator for North Carolina, 1973-2003
Henderson, Sir (John) Nicholas, HM Ambassador, Washington, 12 July 1979-1982
Hunt, Sir John, Secretary to the Cabinet, 1973-79
Hurd, Douglas Richard, Minister of State, FCO, 5 May 1979-1983

James, Cynlais Morgan (known as Kenneth), Minister, British Embassy, Paris, 1976-80
Johnson, John Rodney, Head of West African Department, FCO, 1978-80

Kamba, Professor Walter, Legal Adviser to the Patriotic Front delegation at the Lancaster House Conference

List of persons

Kamusikiri, Dr James, Private Secretary to Bishop Muzorewa
Kissinger, Dr Henry, US Secretary of State, 1973-77
Khama, Sir Seretse Goitsebeng Maphiri, President of Botswana, 1966-80
Kaunda, Kenneth David, President of Zambia, 1964-91

Lake, (William) Anthony Kirsopp, Director of Policy Planning, US State Department, 1977-81
Layden, Anthony Michael, Rhodesia Department, FCO, 1977-82
Leahy, John, HM Ambassador, Pretoria/Cape Town, 26 July 1979-1982
Lever, Paul, Assistant Private Secretary to the Secretary of State for Foreign and Commonwealth Affairs
Lewen, John Henry, HM Ambassador, Maputo, 1975-29 September 1979
Luce, Richard Napier, Parliamentary Under-Secretary of State, FCO, 5 May 1979-1981
Lyne, Roderic Michael John, Assistant Private Secretary to the Secretary of State for Foreign and Commonwealth Affairs, 1979-81

McHenry, Donald Franchot, US Ambassador to the UN, 23 September 1979-1981
Machel, Samora Moisés, President of Mozambique, 1975-86
MacLehose, Sir (Crawford) Murray, Governor of Hong Kong, 1971-82
Msika, Joseph, ZAPU Party official; and Patriotic Front delegate at Lancaster House Conference
Manley, Michael Norman, Prime Minister of Jamaica, 1972-80
Manning, Keith Quentin Frederick, Private Secretary to Mr Luce, 1979-81
Mansfield, Philip Robert Aked, Minister and UK Deputy Permanent Representative to the UN, UKMIS New York, 1979-81
Mkapa, Benjamin William, Tanzania Minister of Foreign Affairs, 1977-80
Mlambo, Eshmael Ephial Mtshmayeli, ZAPU delegate at the Lancaster House Conference
Moi, Daniel Toroitich arap, President of Kenya, 1978-2002
Moon, Sir Peter James Scott, British High Commissioner, Dar es Salaam, 1978-82
Moore, Sir Philip Brian Cecil, Private Secretary to HM The Queen, 1977-86
Moose, Richard Menifee, Assistant Secretary of State for African Affairs, US State Department, 1977-81
Mugabe Robert Gabriel, Leader of ZANU and then ZANU-PF; First Prime Minister of Zimbabwe, from 18 April 1980
Mugabe, (Sarah Francesca) Sally, First wife of Robert Mugabe; ZANU-PF Deputy Secretary for the Women's League, 1978-80
Mubako (Mubaku), Dr Simbi, Legal Adviser to the Patriotic Front delegation at the Lancaster House Conference
Mukome, David, Rhodesian Foreign Minister, 1 June 1979-11 December 1979
Mundawarara, Dr Silas, Deputy Prime Minister of Rhodesia, 1 June 1979 to 11 December 1979

Muzorewa, Bishop Abel Tendekayi, Leader of the UANC; Prime Minister of Rhodesia, 1 June 1979-11 December 1979
Ndiweni, Chief Kayisa, Leader of the United National Federal Party; Minister for Works in Bishop Muzorewa's Government
Neto, Antonio Agostinho da Silva, President of Angola, 1975-10 September 1979
Nkomo, Joshua Mqabuko Nyongolo, Leader of ZAPU
Nyemba, Leonard, Rhodesian Minister of Roads and Traffic, 15 August 1979-12 December 1979
Nyerere, Julius Kambarage, President of Tanzania, 1964-85

Obasanjo, Chief Olusegun, President of Nigeria, 1976-1 October 1979

Palliser, Sir (Arthur) Michael, Permanent Under-Secretary, FCO, 1975-82
Papadopoulos, Achilles Symeon, HM Ambassador to Maputo, 30 September 1979-1980
Parsons, Sir Anthony, UK Permanent Representative to the UN, New York, and UK Representative on the UN Security Council, from July 1979-1982
Pattison, Michael, Private Secretary to the Prime Minister
Powell, Charles David, Special Counsellor for Rhodesian Negotiations, FCO, 1979-80
Preston, Sir Peter, Permanent Secretary, Overseas Administration, FCO, 1976-82
Pym, Francis Leslie, Secretary of State for Defence, 4 May 1979-1981

Ramphal, Sir Shridath 'Sonny' Surendranath, Commonwealth Secretary-General, 1975-90
Reid, (Harold) Martin, Minister, British Embassy, Pretoria/Cape Town, 1979-82
Renwick, Robin William, Head of Rhodesia Department, FCO, 1978-80
Richardson, Michael John, Private Secretary to the Lord Privy Seal, FCO, 1979

Salim, Salim Ahmed, Permanent Representative of Tanzania at the UN, 1970-80
Seitz, Raymond George Hardenbergh, First Secretary (Political), US Embassy, London, 1975-79
Shagari, Alhaji Shehu Usman Aliyu, President of Nigeria, 1 October 1979-1983
Sibanda, Siwanda Kennedy Mbuso, Member of the Patriotic Front Legal Team at the Lancaster Hose Conference
Silundika, (Tarcisius Malan) George, ZAPU Party official and member of the Patriotic Front delegation at the Lancaster House Conference
Sinclair, Sir Ian (McTaggart), The Legal Adviser, FCO, 1976-84
Sithole, Reverend Ndabaningi, Leader of the Zimbabwe African National Union-Ndonga Party and member of Bishop Muzorewa's Government
Smedley, Sir Harold, British High Commissioner, Wellington, 1976-80

Smith, David Colville, Deputy Prime Minister of Rhodesia, 1976-1 June 1979; Minister of Finance, 1976-12 December 1979

Smith, George, Secretary to the Rhodesian Cabinet, 21 June 1979-11 December 1979

Smith, Ian Douglas, Prime Minister of Rhodesia, 1964 to 1 June 1979, Leader of the Rhodesian Front

Soames, Lord ((Arthur) Christopher John), Lord President of the Council and Leader of the House of Lords, from 5 May 1979-1981; Governor of Rhodesia from 11 December 1979-18 April 1980

Solarz, Stephen Joshua, Member of the US House Foreign Affairs Committee and Chair of the Subcommittee on Africa

Spencer, Rosemary Jane, Assistant Head, Rhodesia Department, FCO, 1977-80

Squire, Clifford William, Counsellor and Head of Chancery, British Embassy, Washington, 1976-79

Sule, Alhaji Maitama, Special Representative of the President of Nigeria, from 1 October 1979

Tebbit, Sir Donald Claude, British High Commissioner, Canberra, 1976-80

Tekere, Edgar Zivanai, Secretary-General, ZANU

Thatcher, Margaret Hilda, British Prime Minister, from 4 May 1979-1990

Thomson, Sir John Adam, British Commissioner, New Delhi, 1977-82

Tomlinson, Stephen Eric, Foreign Secretary's Private Office

Tongogara, General Josiah Magama, Commander of ZANLA until his death on 26 December 1979

Tungamirai, Josiah, ZANLA Officer and Patriotic Front delegate at the Lancaster House Conference

Vance, Cyrus Robert, US Secretary of State, 1977-80

Van Der Byl, Pieter Kenyon Fleming-Voltelyn, Rhodesian Minister of Foreign Affairs, 1974-1 June 1979

Van Der Post, Colonel Laurens, Writer and explorer; unofficial adviser to Margaret Thatcher on Southern Africa

Vest, George Southall, Assistant Secretary of State for European Affairs, US State Department, 1977-81

Walden, George Gordon Harvey, Principal Private Secretary to the Secretary of State for Foreign and Commonwealth Affairs, 1978-81

Waldheim, Dr Kurt Josef, UN Secretary-General, 1972-1981

Wall, (John) Stephen, Assistant Private Secretary to the Secretary of State for Foreign and Commonwealth Affairs, 1977-79

Walls, Lieutenant General (George) Peter, Head of the Rhodesian Armed Forces and Head of Rhodesian Joint Operations Command

Walston, Lord (Henry David Leonard George), Labour Peer; Parliamentary Under-Secretary of State, Foreign Office, 1964-67

Whitmore, **Clive Anthony**, Principal Private Secretary to the Prime Minister, 1979-82
Willson, **John Michael**, Lancaster House Conference Secretary
Windsor, **Elizabeth Alexandra Mary**, HM Queen Elizabeth II, 1952-2022

Young, **Andrew Jackson Jr.**, US Ambassador to the UN, 1977-16 August 1979
Zvobgo, **Eddison Jonasi Mudadirwa**, ZANU Party spokesman

DOCUMENT SUMMARIES

	NAME	DATE	MAIN SUBJECT	PAGE
		1979		
1	Mr Barlow FCO	18 Apr	Minute to Sir A. Duff enclosing an options paper on Rhodesia for an incoming Conservative Government.	1
2	Sir J. Hunt Cabinet Office	4 May	Minute to Mrs Thatcher updating on elections in Rhodesia; and how HMG could respond to the new Rhodesian Government.	9
3	Sir A. Duff FCO	4 May	Minute to Mr Walden advocating the need to consult with Muzorewa and HMG allies e.g. the Americans.	11
4	Sir A. Parsons FCO	9 May	Minute to Mr Walden stating that whatever course of action HMG takes on Rhodesia, the US needs to be involved.	12
5	To Sir L. Allinson Lusaka Tel. No. 150	10 May	Informal steer on HMG's expected next steps on Rhodesia; and instructions to report any statements made on Rhodesia by host governments.	13
6	Cabinet Defence and Oversea Committee OD(79)3	11 May	Memorandum by Lord Carrington on bringing Rhodesia back to legality and how best to achieve this.	14
7	Cabinet Defence and Oversea Committee OD(79)1st	14 May	Discussion of No. 6, including how Mrs Thatcher should update Parliament during the debate on the Queen's speech.	20
8	Mr Day FCO	18 May	Minute to Mr Walden outlining the US position on Rhodesia, ahead of Lord Carrington meeting Mr Vance.	22
9	Sir A. Duff FCO	19 Apr	Minute to Lord Carrington recording the main points of his meeting with Bishop Muzorewa and next steps required.	23
10	Note of a Meeting	4 May	Record of a discussion between Lord Carrington and Mr Vance at the FCO.	25

11	Sir A. Duff FCO	23 May	Minute to Lord Carrington on the need to reassure the US that HMG is not ruling out Patriotic Front involvement in the future of Rhodesia.	29
12	Mr Cartledge 10 Downing Street	24 May	Note of Mrs Thatcher's discussion with Mr Vance on Rhodesia.	29
13	Mr Renwick FCO	24 May	Minute to Mr Walden detailing plans for a political emissary to travel to the Front-Line states for consultations on Rhodesia.	31
14	To Sir L. Allinson Lusaka Tel. No. 194	25 May	Instructions to posts in the Front-Line States to approach host governments to advise them of Lord Harlech's appointment as political emissary.	32
15	Mr Wall FCO	25 May	Letter to Mr Cartledge informing him of Lord Harlech's itinerary for his visit to Africa; and the need, post-visit, to avoid early discussions or statements by HMG.	33
16	Mr Cartledge 10 Downing Street	29 May	Response to No. 15. Mrs Thatcher is content with Lord Harlech's itinerary, except that he should not meet the leaders of the Patriotic Front.	34
17	Mr Cartledge 10 Downing Street	1 June	Letter to Mr Wall. Mrs Thatcher agrees to Lord Harlech meeting the Patriotic Front, only if others are present.	35
18	Mr Cartledge 10 Downing Street	6 June	Letter to Mr Wall recording the main points arising during the meeting between Mrs Thatcher and Lord Harlech, ahead of his mission to Southern Africa.	36
19	Sir A. Duff FCO	19 June	Minute to Rhodesia Department after the Mrs Thatcher's meeting with Sir S. Ramphal. Briefing for Lusaka requires careful handling for maximum Commonwealth support on Rhodesia.	37
20	Mr Renwick FCO	20 June	Minute to Sir A. Duff proposing future options on Rhodesia, including action in the event of no improvement on the internal settlement.	38
21	Mr Day FCO	21 June	Minute to Sir A. Duff attaching a paper recording his views on prospects for a settlement in Rhodesia, following his visit to Salisbury.	39

Document summaries

22	Mr Barlow FCO	25 June	Minute to Mr Wall attaching Lord Harlech's report of his mission to Southern Africa.	43
23	Mr Cartledge 10 Downing Street	26 June	Note of a meeting held between Mrs Thatcher, Lord Carrington and Lord Harlech to discuss the outcome of Lord Harlech's first mission to Southern Africa.	47
24	Mr Renwick FCO	26 June	Minute to Sir A. Duff enclosing a note with points to make for his meeting with US officials.	49
25	Cabinet Defence and Oversea Committee OD(79)11	2 July	Memorandum by Lord Carrington on how HMG can bring Rhodesia to legal independence by the Autumn with the widest possible international acceptance.	51
26	Mr Day Mirimba (Salisbury) Tel. No. 350	3 July	Lord Harlech update on a meeting with Bishop Muzorewa and the Rhodesian Deputy and Foreign Ministers.	55
27	Sir A. Duff FCO	4 July	Minute to Mr Renwick suggesting further guidance for posts to rebut media reporting HMG is bargaining with Bishop Muzorewa to recognise his Government.	56
28	Mr Cartledge 10 Downing Street	4 July	Letter to Mr Wall summarising the main points made during a meeting between Mrs Thatcher and Senator Jesse Helms.	58
29	Mr Cartledge 10 Downing Street	13 July	Letter to Mr Wall enclosing his note of the discussion between the Mrs Thatcher and Bishop Muzorewa.	59
30	Sir I. Sinclair FCO	18 July	Minute to Sir A. Duff on how HMG should handle the UN aspects to Rhodesia.	65
31	Cabinet Defence and Oversea Committee OD(79)21	19 July	Memorandum by Lord Carrington outlining proposals and strategy for a Rhodesian independence constitution.	68
32	Cabinet Defence and Oversea Committee OD(79)5th	23 July	Discussion of No. 31 and a memorandum by Lord Carrington on potential dangers to British political & commercial interests in Africa.	74

33	Mr Reid Pretoria	26 July	Letter to Mr Renwick detailing South African policy towards Rhodesia.	76
34	Mr Crabbie Washington	27 July	Letter to Mr Lyne about Dick Moose's appearance before the US House Foreign Affairs Sub-Committee; and implications for US policy on Rhodesia.	78
35	Mr Luce FCO	3 Aug	Minute to Lord Carrington covering all the main developments and contingencies on Rhodesia, post Constitutional Conference.	79
36	Sir P. Moon Dar es Salaam Tel. No. 660	8 Aug	Readout of a meeting with Mr Chimbandi, ZANU, to discuss Rhodesia, post CHOGM.	82
37	Mr Cartledge 10 Downing Street	9 Aug	Letter to Mr Wall covering Mrs Thatcher's meeting with Sir A. Parsons to discuss Rhodesia handling in the UN Security Council.	83
38	Lord Carrington FCO C(79)33	9 Aug	Memorandum to the Cabinet updating on Rhodesia strategy and policy following CHOGM.	84
39	Cabinet Conclusions CC(79)13th	10 Aug	Discussion of No. 38. The Cabinet endorsed agreement reached at CHOGM and approved next steps set out in the memorandum.	92
40	To Mr Lewen Maputo Tel. No. 139	10 Aug	Instructions to deliver written invitations to Bishop Muzorewa, Mr Mugabe and Mr Nkomo to attend a Constitutional Conference in September.	94
41	To Mr Lewen Maputo Tel. No. 140	10 Aug	Text of written invitation to attend the Constitutional Conference.	95
42	To Sir N. Henderson Washington Tel. No. 1010	10 Aug	Update on a meeting between Lord Carrington and Mr Brewster, following CHOGM, to discuss Rhodesia.	96
43	Sir L. Allinson Lusaka Tel. No. 894	9 Aug	Reports Mr Chinamano's views of the ZAPU conditions that need to be met before Rhodesia can achieve independence.	97
44	Mr Wall FCO	13 Aug	Minute to Ms Spencer about No. 42. Lord Carrington hoping for US support, especially if the Constitutional Conference breaks down.	98

Document summaries

45	To Sir N. Henderson Washington Tel. No. 1016	14 Aug	Text of a message from Mrs Thatcher to President Carter updating him on the Constitutional Conference.	98
46	To Sir L. Allinson Lusaka Tel. No. 710	14 Aug	Reports Mr Nkomo's reaction to receiving the text of the Conference invitation and outline independence Constitution.	99
47	To Sir A. Parsons UKMIS New York Tel. No. 412	14 Aug	Instructions to transmit a message from Lord Carrington to Dr Waldheim updating him on CHOGM and the Constitutional Conference.	100
48	Bryan Cartledge 10 Downing Street	15 Aug	Note of a conversation held by Mrs Thatcher and Lord Carrington regarding proposed changes to the Rhodesian Constitution.	100
49	Mr Renwick FCO	16 Aug	Minute to Mr Walden providing detailed advice on the legal and political implications of handling Rhodesian independence in the UN Security Council.	101
50	Mr Doble Maputo	20 Aug	Letter to Mr Bonde reporting conversations with Mr Tekere, on how Zimbabwe would be governed by ZANU.	104
51	Sir L. Allinson Lusaka Tel. No. 922	21 Aug	Reports media coverage of a press conference held by Mr Nkomo to announce the Patriotic Front's participation in the Constitutional Conference.	106
52	Sir A. Duff FCO	23 Aug	Minute to Mr Hurd reporting his visit to South Africa and difficult discussions with the South African Government on Rhodesia policy.	106
53	Mr Doble Maputo Tel. No. 224	24 Aug	Requests guidance on points to make to Mr Tekere, beyond standard lines on Rhodesia, before he leaves for London and the Conference.	108
54	Sir A. Duff FCO	24 Aug	Minute to Mr Renwick reporting a conversation he had with Sir S. Ramphal, who requests points to make to Nkomo ahead of meeting him.	109
55	Mr Renwick FCO	29 Aug	Letter to Mr Mansfield outlining the courses of action HMG could take at the UN Security Council for revoking sanctions on Rhodesia.	109

56	To Mrs Thatcher PM/79/74	undated	Minute from Lord Carrington on the approach HMG should take at the Constitutional Conference.	112
57	Mr Brown Lagos Tel. No. 673	30 Aug	Reports a meeting with President Obasanjo to discuss the upcoming Constitutional Conference.	115
58	Mr Doble Maputo	31 Aug	Letter to Miss Spencer expanding upon No. 50.	118
59	Mr Alexander 10 Downing Street	3 Sep	Letter to Mr Walden confirming that Mrs Thatcher endorses No. 56, apart from HMG assuming full responsibility for overseeing an election if agreement reached.	120
60	Mr Renwick FCO	4 Sep	Minute to Sir A. Duff enclosing a note on the attitudes the parties are likely to adopt at the Constitutional Conference.	121
61	Rhodesia Department FCO	6 Sep	Steering brief for the Constitutional Conference.	125
62	Mr Lyne FCO	6 Sep	Letter to Mr Alexander responding to No. 59. Lord Carrington agrees HMG should oversee an election, although a referendum may be required if Patriotic Front withdraw from negotiations.	129
63	Mr Hall FCO	6 Sep	Reports conversation with ZANU delegates arriving at Heathrow Airport, ahead of the Constitutional Conference.	129
64	Mr Lyne FCO	7 Sep	Letter to Mr Alexander on the role Mrs Thatcher should play in relation to the Constitutional Conference.	130
65	Sir A. Duff FCO	10 Sep	Minute to Rhodesia Department reporting his lunch with Mr Chona to discuss the Conference.	131
66	Mr Renwick FCO	10 Sep	Minute to Mr Walden on ZANU demands about changing the seating arrangements at the Conference.	133
67	Mr Renwick FCO	10 Sep	Opening statement as the chair of the Constitutional Conference.	133
68	Mrs Thatcher 10 Downing Street	11 Sep	Letter to Nicholas Winterton MP, responding to a constituent query on HMG policy towards Rhodesia.	139

Document summaries

69	Mr Lyne FCO	12 Sep	Letter to Mr Alexander providing handling guidance for Mrs Thatcher ahead of her meeting with President Nyerere.	140
70	Mr Manning FCO	13 Sep	Minute to Mr Renwick reporting Mr Luce's dinner with Mr Chona, Mr Rowlands and Lord Duncan-Sandys to discuss the Conference.	142
71	Mr Squire UKMIS New York	13 Sep	Letter to Mr Renwick responding to No. 55.	143
72	Mr Alexander 10 Downing Street	15 Sep	Record of Mrs Thatcher's discussion with President Nyerere over a working dinner at No. 10.	147
73	Mr Walden FCO	17 Sep	Letter to Sir Philip Moore providing HM The Queen with an update on the Constitutional Conference.	150
74	Mr Lyne FCO	17 Sep	Minute to Mr Renwick on discussion between Lord Carrington and Bishop Muzorewa's delegation regarding the implications of their not accepting a new constitution.	151
75	Sir A. Duff FCO	18 Sep	Minute to Lord Carrington on HMG alternative objectives at the conference if a total settlement is not achieved.	152
76	Mr Alexander 10 Downing Street	18 Sep	Letter to Mr Walden reporting Mrs Thatcher's meeting with Col. van der Post.	154
77	Mr Walden FCO	18 Sep	Minute to Mr Renwick reporting the meeting held between Lord Carrington and Mr David Smith.	155
78	Mr Barltrop FCO	19 Sep	Minute to Mr Johnson recording his lunch with Mr Oba, the Nigerian High Commissioner to Zambia.	156
79	Rhodesia Department FCO	19 Sep	Minute recording a meeting between the UK and Patriotic Front delegations held on 18 Sept.	157
80	Rhodesia Department FCO	20 Sep	Minute recording a meeting between the UK and Salisbury delegations held on 19 Sept.	159
81	To Sir L. Allinson Lusaka Tel. No. 777	20 Sep	Updates on the meetings held with the Salisbury and Patriotic Front delegations respectively on 19 Sept.	161

82	Mr Renwick FCO	21 Sep	Minute to Mr Walden with press lines for State Department use in clarifying US position on lifting sanctions by 1 October.	162
83	To Sir L. Allinson Lusaka Tel. No. 781	22 Sep	Updates on further meetings held with the Salisbury and the Patriotic Front delegations. Salisbury agrees UK proposals for constitutional change.	163
84	Sir A. Parsons UKMIS New York Tel. No. 1098	24 Sep	Record of Lord Carrington's meeting with Dr Waldheim on Rhodesia.	164
85	To Sir L. Allinson Lusaka Tel. No. 787	25 Sep	Reports meetings held with the Salisbury and the Patriotic Front delegations. Patriotic Front not accepting UK proposals on the constitution.	165
86	Mr Walden FCO	27 Sep	Letter to Mr Alexander, responding to No. 76, providing text of a message Col. van der Post can pass to the South African Government.	165
87	Mr Manning FCO	27 Sep	Minute to Mr Renwick in which Mr Luce suggests more entertainment and social functions could be organised for delegates.	166
88	To Sir L. Allinson Lusaka Tel. No. 796	28 Sep	Update on the latest meetings held with the delegations. Intention is to table in plenary a full version of the constitution for UK Parliamentary approval.	166
89	To Mrs Thatcher 10 Downing Street PM/79/83	28 Sep	Minute from Lord Carrington setting out proposals for Rhodesian pre-independence arrangements.	167
90	Mr Day FCO	1 Oct	Minute to Sir A. Duff on efforts to bring Rhodesia to legality with wide international agreement and planning for next steps.	174
91	To Sir L. Allinson Lusaka Tel. No. 799	2 Oct	Instructions to give host governments the text of the full proposals for the Independence Constitution.	176
92	Rhodesia Department FCO	2 Oct	Record of a meeting held with the Patriotic Front delegation to discuss provisions in the Declaration of Rights.	179

93	To Sir L. Allinson Lusaka Tel. No. 801	2 Oct	Update to Front Line States regarding No. 92; advised HMG constitutional proposals expected to be tabled the next day.	181
94	Mr Lyne FCO	3 Oct	Letter to Mr Alexander on the full HMG proposals for the Independence Constitution to be tabled at the Conference.	182
95	Mr Manning FCO	4 Oct	Minute to Mr Gomersall. Mr Luce suggests closer working with ZAPU at the Conference, given differences of approach with ZANU.	185
96	Mr Renwick FCO	5 Oct	Minute to Sir A. Duff providing a list of potential candidates for consideration as British Governor of Rhodesia.	185
97	To Sir L. Allinson Lusaka Tel. No. 820	6 Oct	Instructions to advise host governments; Patriotic Front needs to react positively to HMG constitutional proposals, following concessions from Salisbury delegation.	186
98	Sir A. Duff FCO	2 Oct	Minute to Mr Walden forwarding a message from Mr Vance who is concerned about Rhodesian military action in Mozambique.	187
99	Mr Renwick FCO	8 Oct	Minute to Sir A. Duff on measures that could be taken to enact the Independence Constitution and lift sanctions if the Patriotic Front do not agree HMG terms.	188
100	Mr Burgess FCO	8 Oct	Minute to Ms Spencer reporting a racist attack on members of the ZAPU delegation in East London.	189
101	Sir A. Duff FCO	8 Oct	Minute to Lord Carrington outlining ways forward if the Patriotic Front walk out of the Conference.	190
102	To Sir L. Allinson Lusaka Tel. No. 829	9 Oct	Update on Patriotic Front position regarding the Independence Constitution. Sticking points remain and 11 Oct is the deadline for them to accept.	191
103	To Sir L. Allinson Lusaka Tel. No. 831	11 Oct	Update of No. 102. Patriotic Front reserved its position on a number of major issues. Conference adjourned by the Chair.	192
104	Mr Lyne FCO	11 Oct	Letter to Mr Alexander updating Mrs Thatcher on the need to adjourn the Conference, given Patriotic Front intransigence.	193

105	Mr Alexander 10 Downing Street	11 Oct	Handwritten note to Mrs Thatcher about the South African Government 'containing' Mr Ian Smith.	194
106	To Mr Leahy Pretoria Tel. No. 380	12 Oct	Message received from the South African Government critical of Patriotic Front intransigence, urging HMG to lift sanctions.	195
107	To Mr Leahy Pretoria Tel. No. 381	12 Oct	Lines to take in response to No. 106. Lifting of sanctions will not resolve the problem.	196
108	To Sir L. Allinson Lusaka Tel. No. 833	12 Oct	Instructions to deliver a message to President Kaunda (No. 109) and to clarify HMG's position as Mr Chona appears to be mis-representing the Conference discussions to him.	197
109	To Sir L. Allinson Lusaka Tel. No. 834	12 Oct	Text of a message from Mrs Thatcher responding to President Kaunda.	198
110	Mr Lyne FCO	12 Oct	Letter to Mr Alexander enclosing a paper on potential developments in Rhodesia, post Constitutional Conference.	200
111	Mr Alexander 10 Downing Street	12 Oct	Handwritten note to Mrs Thatcher about messages received from Bishop Muzorewa and the South African Government about Mr Ian Smith.	202
112	To Sir N. Henderson Washington Tel. No. 1406	14 Oct	Text of a message received from Mr Vance offering US support for the Constitutional proposals, as well as his views on the transitional arrangements.	203
113	Mr Renwick FCO	14 Oct	Minute to Sir A. Duff in response to No. 112. Need to inform US of HMG views on the transitional arrangements, given divergence of thoughts.	204
114	To Sir N. Henderson Washington Tel. No. 1411	14 Oct	Instructions to pass Lord Carrington's response to Mr Vance, setting out HMG views on the interim period, and updates the latest position of the Conference.	204
115	Rhodesia Department FCO	15 Oct	Record of a meeting held between Lord Carrington and the leaders of the Patriotic Front, discussing mainly the question of land transfer.	206

Document summaries

116	To Sir L. Allinson Lusaka Tel. No. 838	15 Oct	Instructions for posts in Front Line States and Lagos to lobby host governments to encourage the Patriotic Front to accept the Independence Constitution.	208
117	Mr Walden FCO	15 Oct	Minute to Mr Renwick recording a call on Lord Carrington by Mr Brewster.	209
118	To Sir L. Allinson Lusaka Tel. No. 844	17 Oct	Reports latest meeting with the Salisbury delegation. Door remains open for Patriotic Front to re-join the discussions.	211
119	Mr Lyne FCO	17 Oct	Letter to Mr Alexander enclosing a paper outlining HMG's proposals for the pre-independence period in Rhodesia.	211
120	Mr Alexander 10 Downing Street	17 Oct	Letter to Mr Walden recording the discussion between Mrs Thatcher and Mr Pik Botha.	213
121	Sir A. Parsons UKMIS New York Tel. No. 1284	18 Oct	Readout of Mr Hurd's calls at the UN on Dr Waldheim and Mr Salim.	216
122	Rhodesia Department FCO	18 Oct	Record of a meeting between Lord Carrington and the Patriotic Front, who agree to accept the Independence Constitution.	216
123	Mr Tomlinson FCO	18 Oct	Letter to Mr Pattison seeking Mrs Thatcher's approval for Mr Luce to be sent as an envoy to the Front-Line States.	217
124	Mr Renwick FCO	18 Oct	Minute to Sir A. Duff, ahead of his meeting with Mr Lake, detailing arrangements for the interim period in Rhodesia.	218
125	To Sir L. Allinson Lusaka Tel. No. 853	19 Oct	Reports resumption of the conference with Lord Carrington setting out the interim arrangements, notably holding elections.	220
126	Mr Renwick FCO	19 Oct	Message to Mr Manning with points to make for Mr Luce when he visits the Front Line States.	221
127	To Sir N. Henderson Washington Tel. No. 1467	20 Oct	Readout of a meeting held with US officials to discuss the Conference and interim arrangements for Rhodesia.	222

128	To Sir N. Henderson Washington Tel. No. 1468	20 Oct	Regarding No. 127, US officials advised HMG might have to proceed with Bishop Muzorewa alone, thereby granting Rhodesia independence on this basis.	225
129	Rhodesia Department FCO	21 Oct	Record of a meeting held between Sir I. Gilmour and Bishop Muzorewa to discuss a UK Governor replacing his Government.	226
130	To Sir L. Allinson Lusaka Tel. No. 858	22 Oct	Instructions to pass to host governments HMG proposals for implementing the Independence Constitution, as well as points to raise on the election process.	227
131	Mr Renwick FCO	24 Oct	Minute to Sir J. Graham enclosing papers on future tactics at the Conference, sanctions legislation and proceeding to independence with Bishop Muzorewa alone.	229
132	To Sir N. Henderson Washington Tel. No. 1510	25 Oct	US Embassy advised of proposals for the interim period in the hope the US will support them.	236
133	Mr Renwick FCO	25 Oct	Minute to Mr Walden seeking Lord Carrington's approval to ask the Americans to instruct their African posts to support HMG proposals.	237
134	To Sir L. Allinson Lusaka Tel. No. 876	26 Oct	Reports Patriotic Front calls for UN supervision of elections in Rhodesia. Posts should inform host governments the UK will take responsibility.	238
135	Mr Luce FCO	26 Oct	Minute to Lord Carrington regarding his visit to the Front Line States and Nigeria.	239
136	To Sir L. Allinson Lusaka Tel. No. 880	27 Oct	Update to posts on the Conference; issues remain between the delegations as to who will monitor the elections.	241
137	To Sir N. Henderson Washington Tel. No. 1527	29 Oct	Message from Lord Carrington to Mr Vance seeking support with the Front Line States.	242
138	To Sir L. Allinson Lusaka Tel. No. 888	30 Oct	Text of a message from Mrs Thatcher to President Kaunda, responding to his concerns about the transitional period.	243

Document summaries

139	To Sir D. Tebbit Canberra Tel. No. 526	30 Oct	Text of a message from Mrs Thatcher to Mr Fraser, setting out HMG proposals for the pre-independence period.	245
140	Mr Lyne FCO	30 Oct	Minute to Mr Renwick recording a meeting between Lord Carrington and Mr Nkomo.	247
141	Sir H. Smedley Wellington Tel. No. 362	31 Oct	Seeks clarification as to whether message sent from Mrs Thatcher to Mr Muldoon was specific to him.	249
142	To Sir H. Smedley Wellington Tel. No. 257	31 Oct	Response to No. 141. Mrs Thatcher has sent messages to other Commonwealth leaders looking for support on the interim arrangements.	249
143	Mr Day FCO	31 Oct	Minute to Mr Walden recording his meeting with Lord Soames, ahead of his appointment as Governor of Rhodesia.	249
144	Cabinet Conclusions CC(79)19th	1 Nov	Lord Carrington sets out HMG's plans for the transitional period, which are endorsed by the Cabinet.	251
145	Cabinet Defence and Oversea Committee OD(79)38	2 Nov	Memorandum by Lord Carrington on prospects for the Conference, steps required to lift sanctions and the legislative process for Rhodesian independence.	252
146	Cabinet Defence and Oversea Committee OD(79)12th	5 Nov	Consideration of No. 145. Committee endorsed approach outlined and agreed no viable alternative to HMG proposals for the pre-independence period.	256
147	Mr Renwick FCO	5 Nov	Minute to Mr Day about Sir I. Gilmour raising with Mr Nkomo the prospect of a settlement without Mr Mugabe.	258
148	Mr Whitmore 10 Downing Street	Nov 5	Record of Mrs Thatcher's meeting with the Leader of the Opposition to discuss the Parliamentary Enabling Bill on Rhodesia.	259
149	Mr Brown Lagos Tel. No. 937	6 Nov	Reports the views of the Nigerian Government on developments at the Conference.	261
150	To Sir N. Henderson Washington Tel. No. 1584	6 Nov	Instructions for posts to update host Governments on the Conference; decisions on the pre-independence period need to be agreed within days.	263

| 151 | Mr Lyne
FCO | 6 Nov | Letter to Mr Alexander suggesting Mrs Thatcher sends a personal message to selected recipients stating UK has done all it can to reach a fair settlement. | 264 |
| --- | --- | --- | --- | --- |
| 152 | Sir A. Parsons
UKMIS
New York
Tel. No. 1483 | 7 Nov | Reports meeting with chair of the UN Fourth Committee who agrees to adjourn a debate on Rhodesia. | 265 |
| 153 | Mr Gomersall
FCO | 8 Nov | Minute to Mr Walden recording a meeting between Sir I. Gilmour and Mr Nkomo, who still has concerns about HMG interim arrangements. | 266 |
| 154 | Rhodesia
Department
FCO | 8 Nov | Record of Lord Carrington's discussion with President Kaunda in London. | 267 |
| 155 | Lord Walston
House of Lords | 8 Nov | Memorandum to Lord Carrington about his lunch with Mr Mugabe. | 268 |
| 156 | Mr Day
FCO | 8 Nov | Minute to Sir M. Palliser about the extent of South African military involvement in Rhodesia and implications for the UK. | 270 |
| 157 | Mr Alexander
10 Downing Street | 8 Nov | Letter to Mr Walden about Mrs Thatcher's meeting with President Kaunda, where she stresses the need for the Patriotic Front to accept the interim proposals. | 271 |
| 158 | To Sir N. Henderson
Washington
Tel. No. 1614 | 8 Nov | Reports Sir M. Palliser's meeting with Mr Brewster to discuss Rhodesia, including US views on the lifting of sanctions. | 273 |
| 159 | Mr Lyne
FCO | 9 Nov | Minute to Mr Renwick about a message for President Kaunda, urging him to persuade Mr Nkomo to accept an agreement. | 273 |
| 160 | Mr Lyne
FCO | 9 Nov | Letter to Mr Alexander with points for Mrs Thatcher to make to President Kaunda to encourage Patriotic Front acceptance of an agreement. | 274 |
| 161 | Sir N. Henderson
Washington
Tel. No. 3664 | 9 Nov | Reports meeting with Mr Vance to discuss Conference latest; and how US might assist breaking the impasse. | 275 |
| 162 | Sir N. Henderson
Washington
Tel. No. 3665 | 10 Nov | Reports discussion with Mr Vance on lifting of sanctions in the UN Security Council and by the US. | 278 |

163	Mr Powell FCO	10 Nov	Minute to Mr Walden recording his meeting with Mr Nkomo on the proposed interim arrangements.	279
164	Mr Walden FCO	11 Nov	Minute to Mr Renwick reporting Lord Carrington's latest meeting with President Kaunda.	281
165	Mr Day FCO	13 Nov	Minute to Ms Spencer about his discussion with Lord Soames on the pre-independence arrangements.	281
166	Mr Alexander 10 Downing Street	13 Nov	Letter to Mr Lyne reporting the meeting held between Mrs Thatcher and Mr Sule.	282
167	Mrs Thatcher 10 Downing Street	14 Nov	Letter to President Shagari of Nigeria about the transitional arrangements.	283
168	Mr Lyne FCO	14 Nov	Minute to Mr Renwick about Lord Carrington's discussion with Bishop Muzorewa on when he will depart for Salisbury.	284
169	Mr Leahy Pretoria Tel. No. 852	14 Nov	Reports South African pessimism on the state of negotiations at the Conference.	285
170	Mr Luce FCO	14 Nov	Minute to Lord Carrington recording his meeting with Mr Sule.	285
171	To Sir L. Allinson Lusaka Tel. No. 947	15 Nov	Patriotic Front accepts proposals for the interim period. Instructions to lobby host governments for support in completing the settlement.	286
172	Mr Leahy Pretoria Tel. No. 856	15 Nov	Reports pessimism from Mr Pik Botha on progress at the Conference and Bishop Muzorewa's chances of re-election.	288
173	Mr Leahy Pretoria Tel. No. 860	15 Nov	Discusses possible South African courses of action if Bishop Muzorewa loses the election in Rhodesia.	290
174	To Mr Leahy Pretoria Tel. No. 479	16 Nov	Text of a message from Lord Carrington to Mr Pik Botha, offering reassurance on Rhodesia.	291

175	To Sir L. Allinson Lusaka Tel. No. 958	17 Nov	Conciliatory message from Mrs Thatcher to President Kaunda, emphasising the need to reach a settlement as a means of ending the civil war.	292
176	To Sir L. Allinson Lusaka Tel. No. 960	20 Nov	Updates relevant posts on meetings held with the Salisbury and Patriotic Front delegations discussing ceasefire proposals.	293
177	Note of Conversation	20 Nov	Transcript of a call between Mrs Thatcher and President Kaunda on Rhodesian incursions into Zambia and prospects for a ceasefire.	294
178	Mr Renwick FCO	22 Nov	Minute to Mr Walden enclosing a message from Mr Vance to Lord Carrington.	297
179	To Sir A. Parsons UKMIS New York Tel. No. 860	23 Nov	Text of a statement by Mrs Thatcher stressing the need to agree UK ceasefire proposals at the Conference.	298
180	To Mr Brown Lagos Tel. No. 886	23 Nov	Readout of Lord Carrington's meeting with Mr Sule.	299
181	Mr Renwick FCO	24 Nov	Minute to Mr Walden on the courses of action left open at this point in the Conference.	300
182	Note of Conversation	24 Nov	Telephone conversation between Mrs Thatcher and Lord Carrington discussing the non-cooperation of the Patriotic Front over ceasefire arrangements.	302
183	Mr Manning FCO	25 Nov	Minute to Mr Walden recording Mr Luce's views on No. 181.	305
184	To Sir L. Allinson Lusaka Tel. No. 983	26 Nov	Update on a meeting held with Patriotic Front who offer no substantive response on the ceasefire proposals.	306
185	Mr Renwick FCO	26 Nov	Minute to Mr Walden addressing tactics and objectives for Lord Carrington's meeting with the Patriotic Front leaders.	307

Document summaries

186	NOTE OF CONVERSATION	27 Nov	Record of a conversation between Lord Carrington and Pik Botha.	309
187	MR LYNE FCO	28 Nov	Minute to Ms Spencer regarding queries Lord Soames has about his impending Governorship.	312
188	MR WALDEN FCO	29 Nov	Minute to Mr Renwick on Lord Carrington's meeting with the Patriotic Front leaders on accepting the ceasefire proposals.	313
189	MR RENWICK FCO	29 Nov	Minute to Mr Walden on processes required to implement the ceasefire if the Patriotic Front accept, as well as the necessary legislative steps.	314
190	TO MR HAYDON Dublin Tel. No. 259	29 Nov	Update for Lord Carrington on a meeting held between officials and Mr Nkomo at which he tried to extract concessions.	315
191	MR DAY FCO	30 Nov	Minute responding to No. 189. Has reservations on a return to legality and lifting sanctions whilst ceasefire discussions are ongoing.	316
192	MR SINCLAIR FCO	30 Nov	Minute to Mr Walden in response to No. 189. Is concerned about the proposal to send an acting Governor to Rhodesia ahead of a ceasefire agreement.	317
193	MR WALDEN FCO	30 Nov	Minute to Mr Renwick about a difficult meeting between Lord Carrington and the Patriotic Front leaders over accepting the ceasefire proposals.	318
194	CABINET DEFENCE AND OVERSEA COMMITTEE OD(79)5TH	30 Nov	Discussion of necessary legislative steps for Rhodesian independence, given likely Conference breakdown over Patriotic Front not accepting ceasefire proposals.	320
195	MR LYNE FCO	3 Dec	Minute to Mr Renwick recording Lord Carrington's meeting with the Salisbury Delegation, about delays in sending a Governor.	321
196	TO SIR L. ALLINSON Lusaka Tel. No. 1034	3 Dec	Mr Nkomo willing to accept ceasefire proposals, Mugabe not. Order to send a Governor to Rhodesia to be made today.	322

197	Mr Alexander 10 Downing Street	3 Dec	Letter to Mr Lyne recording a call on Mrs Thatcher by Sir S. Ramphal to discuss the present situation at the Conference.	323
198	To Sir L. Allinson Lusaka Tel. No. 1012	4 Dec	Reports that the Patriotic Front has accepted the ceasefire proposals. HMG now looking to implement agreements quickly.	325
199	Cabinet Conclusions CC(79) 24th	5 Dec	Cabinet endorse next steps, including sending a Governor to Rhodesia, despite a risk the ceasefire may break down.	326
200	Mr Alexander 10 Downing Street	6 Dec	Record of a meeting held between Mrs Thatcher and General Walls to discuss implementation of the ceasefire.	327
201	Mr Lyne FCO	6 Dec	Letter to Mr Alexander suggesting Mrs Thatcher send a message of appreciation to Mr P.W. Botha for his help and restraint.	330
202	To Sir P. Moon Dar es Salaam Tel. No. 411	6 Dec	Update to relevant posts on Lord Soames's appointment.	331
203	Mr Renwick FCO	7 Dec	Minute to Mr Walden about lines to take when Lord Carrington meets Mr Vance.	331
204	To Sir D. Tebbit Canberra Tel. No. 609	9 Dec	Instructions to advise host governments to support a final push to reach agreement and lift sanctions.	334
205	To Mr Papadopoulos Maputo Tel. No. 173	10 Dec	Text of a message from Mrs Thatcher to President Machel urging him to persuade the Patriotic Front to accept the ceasefire proposals	336
206	To Sir J. Thomson New Delhi Tel. No. 833	10 Dec	Instructions to relevant posts to pass to host Governments a message from Mrs Thatcher.	338
207	Mr Gomersall FCO	10 Dec	Minute to Mr Renwick recording a meeting between Sir I. Gilmour and the Patriotic Front to discuss the Conference and implementation of the ceasefire.	339
208	To Sir L Allinson Lusaka Tel. No. 1034	13 Dec	The Salisbury delegation accept the full ceasefire proposals. Conference documents are ready for signature by all parties.	340

Document summaries

209	RHODESIA DEPARTMENT FCO	13 Dec	Briefing for Mrs Thatcher ahead of her visit to Washington.	341
210	NOTE OF A MEETING	13 Dec	Record of a meeting held between Lord Carrington and leaders of the Patriotic Front to see if they will sign the Conference agreement.	343
211	MRS THATCHER 10 Downing Street	14 Dec	Letter to President Carter urging the US to lift sanctions against Rhodesia.	345
212	TO SIR L ALLINSON Lusaka Tel. No. 1039	15 Dec	Update to relevant posts on Patriotic Front intransigence on the location of the assembly places for its forces.	346
213	TO SIR L ALLINSON Lusaka Tel. No. 1040	15 Dec	Full text of the statement made by Lord Carrington at the final plenary session of the Conference.	348
214	TO LORD SOAMES Salisbury Tel. No. 527	15 Dec	The Patriotic Front appears to accept the agreement; now need them to initial the Conference documents.	349
215	TO SIR L ALLINSON Lusaka Tel. No. 1051	17 Dec	Patriotic Front leaders have now initialled the Conference documents. Focus on implementing the ceasefire and assembly of forces.	350
216	MR PATTISON 10 Downing Street	17 Dec	Letter to Mr Walden enclosing a record of the meeting between Mrs Thatcher, Lord Carrington and Dr Waldheim at the UN.	351
217	CABINET CONCLUSIONS CC(79) 26TH	19 Dec	Lord Carrington reports the conclusion of the Conference with all parties signing final documents tomorrow.	353
218	TO LORD SOAMES Salisbury Tel. No. 594	20 Dec	Reports that the final Conference documents were signed by all parties.	354
219	MRS THATCHER 10 Downing Street	21 Dec	Personal minute to Lord Carrington congratulating him and the FCO on securing a successful outcome at the Conference.	354

CHAPTER I

Before the Conference
April – September 1979

No. 1

Minute from Mr Barlow to Sir A. Duff, 18 April 1979
Confidential (FCO 36/2480)

Rhodesia: Papers for Incoming Government
1. I attach (without the annexes referred to in the text and listed at the end), a draft substantive paper on the options for Rhodesia which a Conservative administration might wish to consider. It incorporates amendments by Mr Renwick but has not previously been seen by Mr Steel.[1]

P.J. BARLOW

ENCLOSURE IN No. 1

Rhodesia
The Problem
1. Since the illegal declaration of Independence in 1965, successive British governments have maintained sanctions against Rhodesia and have refused to recognise the Rhodesian authorities as a lawful government. There are mandatory resolutions of the UN Security Council which require HMG and all other signatories of the UN Charter to impose economic sanctions against Rhodesia. Other resolutions call on us not to recognise the government which has emerged following the April election, but do so in terms which can be argued not to be binding.

2. Important changes have, however, taken place inside Rhodesia since and in consequence of the 'Salisbury Agreement' of 3 March 1978. A Parliament has now been elected on the basis of universal adult suffrage, although in circumstances which are unlikely to satisfy international opinion generally as to the significance of the result (a detailed assessment of the election is at Annex I). The country is under majority rule in the sense that the future Prime Minister, a majority of the Executive Council and a majority of the parliament will be black. But the constitution is drafted in terms which guarantee the whites representation greatly out of proportion with their numbers in both Government and Parliament and which effectively remove a large measure of control over the public services, the security forces and the judiciary

---

[1] Mr Henry Steel was a Legal Counsellor. This draft was submitted by Sir A. Duff to the new Foreign Secretary, Lord Carrington, on 4 May 1979, with no changes apart from the inclusion of the five annexes: see No.3.

from the executive for the next 10 years. These provisions and others (see Annex II) have been criticised as contradicting claims that Rhodesia has now achieved genuine majority rule.

3. Bishop Muzorewa has won a clear parliamentary majority in the election and can be expected to head the new government which will be formed about the end of May once the complex procedures laid down in the new constitution have been completed. He will call on HMG to declare Rhodesia legally independent, and to bring about international recognition for his government and the removal of sanctions. The leaders of the Patriotic Front, with the virtually unanimous support of the rest of Africa, will on the other hand demand that Britain maintains sanctions and continues to withhold recognition from the administration in Salisbury.

4. Meanwhile the war in and around Rhodesia continues with increasing intensity (for an up-to-date assessment, see Annex III). Victory is not in sight for either side. Neighbouring countries have become increasingly affected by the conflict and there is a risk of increased Soviet and other Communist involvement on the side of the Patriotic Front (for whom they are already providing arms, equipment and training). The attitudes of the parties themselves appear to be hardening, though neither side is politically united. The security situation, which has deteriorated steadily over the last three years, is crucial to the survival of Bishop Muzorewa's government. He can only hope to reverse the present slow, but apparently inexorable trend in favour of the Patriotic Front, if he succeeds in attracting African support away from it (and in particular from ZANU (Mugabe)) and in retaining in Rhodesia the present white population who provide the professional and conscript backbone of the armed forces. There can be no guarantee that recognition by Britain would put the new administration in a position to win the war, though it might help to prolong it. It may need increasing South African support even to maintain the status quo, thus further undermining Muzorewa's international credibility. If there is no improvement in the security situation, there is likely to be a further exodus of whites (14,000 left last year). The next six months will be the testing period for the new government's ability to survive.

5. The so-called 'Front Line States'—Zambia, Tanzania, Botswana, Mozambique and Angola—are likely to remain committed to the cause of the Patriotic Front and none of them (with the possible exception of Botswana) is likely to want to extend any degree of recognition or co-operation to the new Government (apart from the reluctant economic co-operation which survives between Zambia and Rhodesia). Although both have guerrilla camps on their territory, Angola and Tanzania are not really in the front line. Although both Zambia and Mozambique have reasons of self-interest to want a settlement, and they are increasingly exasperated with the military incompetence and the political disunity of the Patriotic Front, they do not regard themselves as able to accept one which excludes the Patriotic Front. There is no prospect of an early change in this attitude. In addition to the material support which they will go on giving to the Patriotic Front, the front line states are in a position to ensure that any resolution on Rhodesia in the Security Council which does not have their backing will not get the votes necessary for adoption.

6. The South African Government are concerned to avoid the emergence in Rhodesia of a government dominated by the Patriotic Front. They will support a Muzorewa-led government so long as they believe it has any prospects of survival.

They are already providing massive financial and covert military support. But they will continue to be wary of committing combat troops and in general of linking their fate too closely with that of the Rhodesian administration if the security situation continues to deteriorate. They feared that Mr Smith's decision to remain in politics would damage the credibility of Bishop Muzorewa's government, but have taken no positive action to persuade him to stand down.

HMG's Objectives

7. The aim of successive British Governments has been to grant legal independence to Rhodesia on terms which would be internationally acceptable, enable sanctions to be lifted, and end the war. This aim may not now be attainable in full. All attempts since 1974 to promote an all-party settlement in Rhodesia leading to an agreed constitution and election under international supervision have failed. The new situation inside the country, however, may offer the Government opportunities at any rate to approximate to its objective by different routes. The Government will be under strong pressure to make some gesture of support to the new administration in Salisbury and will want to consider how to respond to it.

8. Papers are, therefore, attached which discuss four broad alternative approaches:

Option A is to go straight for legalisation of the present government in Rhodesia and the lifting of sanctions. The international repercussions of doing this would be very serious. The Government might find itself without the support of the US administration or of other members of the Nine[2], and the Commonwealth could break up.

Option B has the same objective as Option A, but does not involve the immediate legalisation of the Rhodesian government. It assumes however the Government may choose not to seek (or might fail to secure) Parliamentary approval in November for the renewal of Section 2 of the Southern Rhodesia Act 1965. This would result in the disappearance of much of the sanctions enforcement machinery. This would afford strong encouragement to the Salisbury parties and could put the Government in a similar position to that which could arise in the United States. But it would put the Government in breach of its treaty obligations under the UN Charter.

Option C would legalise the 'internal' settlement in Rhodesia, but only after a negotiation between HMG and the Salisbury government designed to secure improvements in the present constitution and the way in which it is operated.

Option D is to make a further attempt to bring about a settlement between the Salisbury government and the Patriotic Front in the hope that even if (as is probable) it did not achieve its ostensible aim, it might succeed in detaching support from the Patriot Front and, if they continued to adopt an intransigent attitude, put HMG in a better position to exercise one of the other options already discussed.

9. These approaches are, it will be seen, not mutually exclusive. Nor do they claim to exhaust all the possibilities. Further work can be done on them as Ministers wish. Our consideration of them so far suggests, however, that a major concern for the Government is likely to be the degree of international support which it can expect for whatever course of action it now decides to adopt in relation to Rhodesia, and that this should be taken into account in determining not only the nature but the timing of the Government's next moves.

2 The Group of Nine was an alliance of European states that met to discuss matters of mutual pan-European interest.

The Next Steps

10. For, example, the United States administration has at present a commitment to a solution through UN supervised elections following a ceasefire. It will be reluctant to abandon this commitment even if the Congress succeeds (as it may do) in obliging it to lift US sanctions on Rhodesia. The Nine have so far adopted a reserved attitude to the election in Rhodesia. The French recognise our special legal relationship with Rhodesia, but would be reluctant to back us in taking action which might jeopardise their relations with some francophone African countries. The Dutch and the Danes will be reluctant in principle to recognise the Bishop's governments, and so too may the Germans. An early decision to recognise the new Government and/or lift sanctions would also be certain, as has been said, to consolidate a hostile Commonwealth reaction.

11. On the other hand, the Bishop has shown that he undoubtedly enjoys a considerable measure of popular support in Rhodesia. He may be able to build on this and on a more sympathetic attitude from Britain and the United States to attract Shona support away from ZANU (Mugabe); (there does not seem much prospect of a Shona-led government attracting support away from Nkomo in Matabeleland). If he can do this—but without relying too obviously on South African backing—he could conceivably succeed also in undermining the Front Line's support for the Patriotic Front. The process could start with Botswana, which is particularly weary of the war. Even Nigerian attitudes might change, given their impatience with Patriotic Front strategy, and this in turn could have a powerful influence elsewhere in Africa. This process would take time, but it might eventually create conditions where HMG could recognise the Bishop's government with less adverse effects than at present seem likely to flow from Option A if it were exercised now.

12. At the same time the Government might wish to demonstrate very soon an overtly sympathetic attitude to the Bishop's government, while it may also be necessary to persuade him in turn that it is in his own interests to follow a conciliatory approach to the outside world during the early months of his administration. If the Government decides that it would be imprudent to go directly for Option A, it will be desirable to reassure the Bishop that this is not because we are unsympathetic to him but because we believe it would be less helpful to him in the long run than a more gradual approach to the problem. This points to the need for early action to establish a permanent link with him. This could be done without formal recognition—though this too would require careful presentation to minimise hostile reactions elsewhere in Africa.

13. The international dimensions which the Rhodesia problem has acquired are, in short, such that almost any conceivable approach to it by HMG must, to have a prospect of success, be based on some degree of consultation with other governments. This is true even of the least spectacular of the options (D)—indeed there might be scope for some direct US involvement in this, even if the US administration were not prepared initially to share the Government's expectation of what the ultimate outcome might be. Before deciding on the content of this first approach to the Bishop's government, the Government may therefore wish to discuss its appreciation of the problem with the Americans at least. The need for consultation with the rest of the Nine is less pressing. But some account will have to be taken at an early

stage of the views of the other African governments concerned; and the Government will wish to decide also whether and how to make contact with the external parties.

OPTION A
Action
1. The Government would invite Parliament to declare, by Act of Parliament, that Rhodesia is no longer part of Her Majesty's dominions, and that the Government and Parliament of the United Kingdom no longer have responsibility or jurisdiction for any and in respect of it. The Southern Rhodesia Act 1965 would be repealed (this in itself would remove the sanctions provided for by order under Section 2 of that Act). Consequential action would be necessary *inter alia* to dismantle the rest of the sanctions machinery. The Act could, but need not, say that independence was being granted on the basis of the present constitution. If it did not, the Government could take other steps to recognise the Rhodesian government and put its legality in British law beyond doubt.

Consequences
2. The Government would be in a position to argue that the legislation of the Salisbury government had removed the basis for the existing mandatory resolutions of the Security Council on sanctions. It would not get the endorsement of the Security Council for this interpretation of international law. It would be argued strongly that a threat to the peace still existed in Rhodesia and that in any case the act of legalisation was contrary to Security Council resolutions requiring us not to recognise the 'illegal regime'. On the latter point the Government could argue in reply that the regime being legalised was not that which was referred to in the mandatory resolutions, and that it did not accept that Parliament could be fettered in any way in the exercise of its responsibilities in relation to Rhodesia. It could if necessary veto any moves in the Security Council designed to prevent it acting in the way suggested or to declare the proposed action illegal. Some other countries might follow our lead in lifting sanctions (others would simply cease to apply them), though they might not extend formal recognition to the new Rhodesian government and would probably not want to back us openly on the Security Council or elsewhere.

Advantages
3. This course would be legally defensible. It would make a clean break with the past and enable the Government to conduct its relations with Rhodesia on the same basis as it would with any other independent state.

Disadvantages
4. It will be strongly argued that the April elections held under censorship and martial law and without the participation of the external partners cannot be regarded as a fair test of the wishes of the people of Rhodesia as a whole. The present US administration would have great difficulty in supporting recognition of the post-April regime even if (as is possible) it were obliged by Congress to lift sanctions. There will be question-marks also about the attitude of the Nine. We could expect very strong reactions in Africa and throughout the Commonwealth, not confined to the more radical members. Nigeria and Zambia amongst others would be likely to break off diplomatic relations with HMG; and quite possibly also to take action against their economic interests. British communities and interests

in other African countries would be at risk (see Annex IV for a breakdown of trade relations with, investment in and size of British communities in key African countries). A number of countries would be likely to leave the Commonwealth or seek to expel Britain from it. If the action were taken before 1 August, there would be grave implications for CHOGM, which is due to begin in Lusaka on that date in the presence of HM The Queen. There would be a high risk of increased Soviet/Cuban involvement in the war. We would quickly be confronted by requests from Salisbury for arms supplies. Unless action of this kind were very carefully prepared, we could find ourselves in a very exposed position in support of the Rhodesian regime, in the company of South Africa and in opposition to virtually all African and Commonwealth opinion.

OPTION B
Action
1. The Government would fail to get, or choose not to seek, parliamentary approval for the continuance of those sanctions which need annual Parliamentary renewal i.e. those which depend on Section 2 of the Southern Rhodesia Act 1965. But it would not (or at least not immediately) divest itself of sovereignty over Rhodesia or formally recognise the new government.

Consequences
2. If this happened, sanctions would not immediately disappear and there would be awkward administrative consequences which would have to be dealt with by new legislation (see Annex V for a detailed analysis). But sanctions would become more difficult to enforce and the moral effect on the administration in Salisbury would be considerable. It would be open to the Government to anticipate this effect by announcing in advance that it did not propose to seek renewal of Section 2 of the 1965 Act in November. It could continue to delay formal recognition of the new Rhodesian government until it had demonstrated whether or not it was likely to survive. But it could establish working relations with it. It could (if it wished) continue to prevent the supply of British arms to Rhodesia.

Advantages
3. There would be some hope of containing reactions at a lower level than in the event of outright legalisation of the new government. The Government could say that it had no option but to defer to the wishes of Parliament in the matter.

Disadvantages
4. The main disadvantages of proceeding in this way is that failure to renew Section 2 without legalising the Rhodesian Government would put the Government in breach of its treaty obligations under Article 25 of the UN Charter. Such a course would attract severe criticism in the Commonwealth and elsewhere. The consequences would still be serious but might turn out to be less dramatic than in the case of Option A.

OPTION C
Action
1. The Government would announce that the April elections in Rhodesia and the installation of a black majority government there were significant steps forward.

Nevertheless, it acknowledged the strength of the international criticism of the new constitution, and of certain features of the administration (e.g. censorship, summary execution under martial law, etc.). It therefore proposed to enter into negotiations with the Salisbury administration to see whether adjustments could be made which would justify HMG in according recognition.

2. On this basis the Government could seek to persuade the Bishop and his colleagues to agree, for example, to:

(*a*) reduce the proportion and/or duration of special white representation in Government and Parliament;

(*b*) suspend or modify censorship and martial law, e.g. by halting summary executions;

(*c*) take more positive steps to improve the social and economic position of Africans;

(*d*) arrange for Mr Smith to make an honourable but definitive exit from politics; and

(*e*) offer realistic terms for the return of ZAPU and ZANU (Mugabe) to political life.

3. Depending on its success in this effort, the Government could then decide whether to proceed to recognise the Bishop's government on this basis, or to seek to undermine international criticism further by offering (in agreement with the Bishop) to organise itself a test of acceptability of the new constitution as amended, and subject to the conclusion of a ceasefire with the Patriotic Front. 'Bankable' guarantees would be offered about the conduct of the administration and security forces during the ceasefire (e.g. Britain might offer to introduce senior officers to supervise the police). If (as is probable) the Patriotic Front refused a ceasefire, it could be argued that they had excluded themselves from a reasonable test of acceptability. If they accepted, HMG would face a difficult task in conducting the test of acceptability. But any attempt to carry out the task would be predicated on a ceasefire.

Consequences

4. The consequential action would be as for Option A.

Advantages

5. There would be some hope of lessening international criticism of the eventual decision to recognise and of securing a degree of support from the US Government and the rest of the Nine. The time needed to lay the groundwork for and conduct such a negotiation might also give the Government a breathing space in which to deal with action at the United Nations and get through CHOGM without serious damage to the Commonwealth or to our economic interests in Africa.

Disadvantages

6. Even an 'improved' internal settlement would be unlikely to attract either the participation of the Patriotic Front or the support of the Front Line Presidents, and legalisation would still be likely to provoke hostile reactions in the Commonwealth and at the United Nations.

7. The internal parties—particularly by the Rhodesian Front—might resist changes. But HMG would have strong negotiating counters to offer in return—legalisation and the lifting of sanctions, positive economic co-operation and aid, and more hope for (if not the certainty of) wider international recognition.

OPTION D
Action
1. The Government would announce publicly that, whatever criticisms might be levelled against the new constitution in Rhodesia, there had been obvious political progress in the emergence of a Parliament and Government with a black majority. But the war was still going on, and the need to bring it to an end was greater than ever. The change in circumstances in Rhodesia called for a fresh attempt to be made to achieve a settlement which would include all parties. The Government's intention would be to send a senior political representative as soon as possible to help to inform it fully of the attitudes of the Rhodesian parties and of the other states concerned and to advise whether a basis for such a settlement now existed or could be created. Until then it was reserving its position on the question of recognition and the lifting of sanctions.

2. At the same time contact would be made with the Bishop. It would be put to him that the Government was disposed to favour his government and to confer legality on it, but that they could not themselves ensure that this would end the war or bring him international recognition. To have any hope of doing this and of securing a degree of US, Commonwealth, etc. support, it would be necessary for HMG to demonstrate first that it had made an effort to negotiate a comprehensive settlement. There would clearly be no hope of this if the Government moved immediately to recognition of the new regime in Rhodesia. But if the Bishop would co-operate sincerely in an effort to mount a negotiation involving all the parties, there would be every chance that this would increase sympathy for him in the Commonwealth and elsewhere, and that at the same time the Patriotic Front would lose sympathy, as they had done in the past, by the intransigence of their attitudes. If the Patriotic Front were seen to be wholly unreasonable in their demands, the way would then be open for an agreement between the Bishop and HMG. As a first gesture to him, we were therefore proposing in the course of the consultations foreshadowed in the Government's statement to establish in Salisbury a senior official who would nominally be visiting Rhodesia from London and would not be accredited as High Commissioner, but would in fact be the channel of communication between the new government and HMG.

3. The Bishop would have to be warned that he should not seek to exploit the presence of this official to press demands for reciprocity, recognition or the lifting of sanctions. He should understand that this would be counterproductive. But we would be prepared if all went well to go on to relax sanctions immediately in such limited ways as were open to the Government without legislation (e.g. in relation to exchange controls and the operation of the 'stop-list'[3]). In the meantime he should be patient.

Advantages
4. The Government could hope to keep its options open for a time while the Bishop demonstrated his prospects for survival. There would be a high probability of the Patriotic Front striking attitudes which would alienate the US administration and put the impossibility of successful all-party negotiation beyond all doubt. If the Bishop (and the South Africans) behaved in a statesmanlike manner, there would

---

3 Following UDI, the UK imposed sanctions on Rhodesia. This included depriving members of the Rhodesian Government of the right to travel to and enter the UK.

be opportunities for diplomatic action in Africa aimed at eroding support for the Patriotic Front and encouraging acceptance of the internal settlement.

Disadvantages

5. The Government would encounter intense suspicion from the start that its actions were really designed to further recognition of the Salisbury government. It would find difficulty in persuading Bishop Muzorewa to display the flexibility and discretion necessary to help us create a favourable climate for him, especially if he is much under the influence of Mr Smith. Mr Smith has a well-earned reputation as a tough negotiator. It would be essential to persuade him (if possible with the help of the South Africans) of the desirability of a moderate approach.

Annexes[4]

I Assessment of the Election
II Criticisms of the Constitution
III The Security Situation
IV British Interests in Africa
V Consequences of Failure to renew Section 2 of the Southern Rhodesian Act 1965

4 Not printed.

No. 2

Minute from Sir J. Hunt (Cabinet Secretary) to Mrs Thatcher, 4 May 1979[1]
Confidential (PREM 19/106)

Rhodesia

1. The Rhodesian elections which ended on 21 April pose the urgent question of how we should react to them and to the new Rhodesian Government which will be formed at the end of May under Bishop Muzorewa. Indeed much international attention will focus on the first indication which the new British Government gives of its intentions and this will need to be carefully considered.[2] You will of course wish to obtain the early advice of the Foreign and Commonwealth Secretary and to discuss the matter with him and other senior colleagues: but here are my preliminary views.

2. There is now a new situation in Rhodesia. The main question is how best to take advantage of it in order to bring Rhodesia as rapidly as possible to independence without leaving behind a situation which would only be exploited by anti-Western elements.

3. The elections. You will wish to consider reports from Lord Boyd and other non-official observers.[3] Most comment so far indicates that the elections were well

1 This document contains a number of Mrs Thatcher's typically trenchant underlinings and marginal comments. The more important ones are indicated by underlining and footnotes at the appropriate points.
2 Mrs Margaret Thatcher had taken office as Prime Minister on 4 May 1979, following the Conservative victory in the general election of the previous day.
3 Lord Boyd led a team of Conservative Party observers to report on the elections held in Rhodesia in April 1979.

conducted. A number of criticisms have been made (under pressure to vote, plural voting, under-age voting, under-estimates of the total number of voters and so on). But the fact remains that a very large number of Africans did turn out happily to vote, and the Patriotic Front, despite their previous threats, were unable to stop them doing so.

4. The problem, however, is that the election, and the establishment of a black government, are not of themselves going to bring the war to an end, nor to bring international recognition of the new government. On the contrary, the initial reaction of the African governments most immediately concerned is violently negative, and the rest of Africa and the Third World are likely to follow this lead.[4] Whatever we may say, our own friends and allies will not be easily persuaded to take a strong line against this tide. And of course the Security Council resolution on 30th April (on which we, the Americans and French abstained but did not veto) condemned the elections as null and void and called for continued non-recognition and sanctions.

5. A lot of this reaction is of course emotional and the result of fixed attitudes, but it will not go quickly away and we cannot afford to disregard it without having regard to our other interests. There is moreover some substance in the contention[5] that the election was held under conditions of martial law and with ZANU and ZAPU banned. It is also fair comment that the constitution, which was approved by a referendum of Whites only, contains a number of clauses which leave room for serious doubt as to whether real power will be exercised by representatives of the black majority.

6. I think you will need therefore to handle the matter in a way which will be acceptable to those parts of the Conservative Party who would like to see early recognition and a lifting of sanctions, but which will at the same time avoid:

(i) very severe reactions in Black Africa[6] (where we have increasingly large economic interests)—and from other Commonwealth governments; condemnation at the United Nations and a call for mandatory sanctions;

(ii) the blame being laid at our door for disruption[7] of plans for The Queen's State Visit to Lusaka and for the Commonwealth Heads of Government Meeting immediately thereafter (1st-8th August);

(iii) danger of increased Soviet exploitation of black African nationalist frustration and of Zambia's acceptance of Cuban and Soviet aid[8] and influence (despite Kaunda's reluctance and Zambia's recent heavy dependence on the southern route through Rhodesia and South Africa for its copper exports);

(iv) the end of hopes for a negotiated independence for Namibia on the lines supported by the Five Powers (United States, United Kingdom, Germany, France and Canada) and by the United Nations[9] (because SWAPO and the Front Line States would not co-operate and South Africa might feel free to proceed with an alternative internal settlement).

Precipitate action could risk all these without achieving the main objective.[10] But that is an argument for playing the hand carefully rather than inaction.

4 'Not if we give them a firm lead in the opposite direction.'
5 '?No. Tell me another country in Africa which has one person/one vote for 4 different political parties.'
6 'They will react for a time but Zambia will still use the railway through Rhodesia.'
7 'They will do the disruption.'
8 'How much do we give to Zambia?'
9 'who have gone back on their agreements.'
10 'Agreed, but let there be no doubt what we intend to do. The only question is how and when.'

7. A further important point is the close involvement of the Americans in a joint United Kingdom-United States Rhodesian policy hitherto. Once a new Rhodesian government is installed President Carter is required by the 'Case/Javits' amendment to decide whether it was chosen by free elections.[11] The United States Administration will be anxious for early consultations on the line the British Government intends to pursue. Present indications are that they will acknowledge the progress made and the possibility of building on it but will not at this stage wish to recognise the new government. They will, however, face strong Congressional pressures to lift sanctions.

8. My own view is that we should seek to build on the undoubted advance which the Rhodesian elections represent. But the line between missing this opportunity on the one hand and causing great damage to our wider interests on the other (without necessarily gaining our aim of a stable democratic future for Rhodesia) is very narrow. It <u>will need great care to find</u> and tread it successfully. The first steps, after you have discussed the matter with the Foreign and Commonwealth Secretary and other senior colleagues, may be to make early contact with the new Rhodesian Government (and with the South Africans); to consult with the Americans and other allies: and to consider how best to play the cards we have in order to achieve adequate international support for the new regime and real progress towards ending the war. At home this would mean a cautious welcome to recent developments; an impression of being willing to seize the opportunity now present: but an avoidance of commitments until these consultations (particularly with the Americans) have taken place.[12]

JOHN HUNT

11 The Case/Javits amendment, approved on 26 July 1978, required President Carter to lift sanctions against Rhodesia if he determined the Salisbury elections were free and fair; and that all of the population and political groups had been allowed to participate.
12 'I agree we need care but a little courage is necessary too.'

No. 3

Minute from Sir A. Duff to Mr Walden, 4 May 1979
Confidential (FCO 36/2480)

Rhodesia

I attach a paper (with supporting annexes) in which Mr Renwick discusses possible future policy options on Rhodesia and their implications.[1] It has, of course, been necessary to produce these papers in advance of Lord Boyd's report.

2. Bishop Muzorewa is expected to take office as Prime Minister at the end of the month. There is no external requirement on the British government to take action in the immediate future of a kind which would commit us irrevocably on the issues involved—though we may well have to fight off moves in the Security Council to try to foreclose our freedom of action. But I think there is much to be said for regaining as soon as possible a process of consultation with Muzorewa and his future government colleagues; with our allies and partners—in the first instance, the Americans; and before long with the other African Governments principally concerned.

1 No. 1.

3. When the Secretary of State has had time to consider these papers, he may wish to discuss the options with officials and to give directions for further work or for action to be put in hand. Depending on the course to be taken, there are certain immediate practical questions, such as:

(*a*) *a possible mission to Salisbury and elsewhere headed by a senior political figure;*

(b) the establishment of a link with Bishop Muzorewa; and

(c) the form and timing of consultations on Rhodesia with the Americans, and subsequently with our other partners and allies.

ANTONY DUFF

No. 4

Minute from Sir A. Parsons to Mr Walden, 9 May 1979
Confidential (FCO 36/2480)

Rhodesia

I have studied the paper submitted by Rhodesia Department.[1] My particular interest is in the UN and United States aspects.

2. Whatever option or series of options is finally chosen, it seems to me of crucial importance that we should persuade the US to associate themselves fully with our course of action. We cannot expect much active help from our EEC partners or from e.g. the old Commonwealth. None of them is sufficiently involved to put their own interests at serious risk. Some of the more cynical will be quite content to see us in the role of Uriah the Hittite.[2]

3. The United States is a different matter. The active involvement of the US in Southern African problems, initiated by Dr Kissinger in his last days, was a turning point. President Carter followed this up both as a matter of principle and with his own black vote in mind—Andy Young and all that. The US is now internationally recognised as an active participant in attempts to reach a Rhodesian settlement. Both in the UN and, I imagine, in terms of the repercussions on our interests in Africa and elsewhere, proceeding in harness with the US should provide us with a substantial cushion. It is interesting that the US has in recent years attracted comparatively little flak over its breaching sanctions through the import of Rhodesian chrome (the Byrd amendment[3]). It has been fashionable in the UN for many years to carp at the US, but that is a different matter to a head on confrontation with the western super power. If the US were fully associated with us in any of the options described in the Department's paper there is no doubt in my mind that the UN repercussions against us would be significantly diminished.

1 No. 1.
2 According to the Hebrew Bible, Uriah was an elite soldier in the army of King David of Israel. David impregnated Uriah's wife whilst he was serving in David's army abroad. David recalled him, in an effort to hide his misdeeds, hoping he would visit his wife so that the pregnancy could be passed off as by him. However, Uriah, as a disciplined soldier, refused to visit his wife and was subsequently killed in battle.
3 In 1971, Senator Harry F. Byrd Jr. tabled an amendment allowing for Rhodesian chrome and nickel to be imported into the US, in violation of UN sanctions. Passed by Congress, imports began from January 1972.

4. The above is another argument for urgent action to solve the problem. By the end of this year, President Carter will be heavily bogged down in the Presidential Election campaign. This may either produce pressures to adopt certain attitudes for electoral reasons (bearing in mind the importance of the black vote in President Carter's last victory) or, more likely, stymie decision making.

A. D. PARSONS

No. 5

Lord Carrington to Sir L. Allinson (Lusaka), 10 May 1979, 1.25 p.m.[1]
Tel. No. 150 Secret, Immediate (FCO 36/2480)

Following personal for Head of Mission from Duff: Rhodesia

1. It will be a little while before you receive formal guidance on the new Government's policy on Rhodesia, and have Ministerial statements, etc. to pass to the Government to which you are accredited. In the meantime, you may like to have an informal steer on certain points.

2. Some press commentators (and no doubt governments) have drawn the conclusion from statements made during the election campaign that a Conservative government would move rapidly to recognise Rhodesia and lift sanctions. This had led to obvious concern about the consequences for our relations with the rest of black Africa of a sudden shift in our Rhodesia policy. To counter this in contacts with local officials, you may wish to draw attention to Lord Carrington's statement in an ITN interview on 6 May (Retract 23807, not all) that the Government intend to consult their 'friends and allies, the Commonwealth, the Americans and so on' about Rhodesia. You could also refer to Mr Pym's statement of 15 April that it would not be possible or right to make a snap judgement on the result of the Rhodesian election: that the issue would require full consideration: and that it might be appropriate to have detailed discussions with our European and American allies and the Commonwealth.

3. For your own information at this stage, we are in touch with Muzorewa and others in the Rhodesian administration. The Prime Minister and Lord Carrington will next week receive the report of the Conservative delegation led by Lord Boyd which observed the Rhodesian elections. Rhodesia is one of the subjects likely to be discussed at the Informal Meeting of Foreign Ministers of the Nine on 12/13 May. It will also be discussed during Mr Vance's visit to London on 21/22 May. It is likely that thereafter there will be further moves to extend the area and scope of consultations. But the first public pronouncement of policy on Rhodesia will be made during the debate on the Queen's Speech next week. You should be guided by this.

4. It follows from this timetable that Ministers will have an opportunity to give all aspects of the Rhodesian question thorough consideration. Though we should spare them a flood of telegrams warning against policies favoured by large sections of their

---

[1] And Immediate to Dar es Salaam, Gaborone, Nairobi, Lilongwe, Maputo, Lagos, Khartoum, Cape Town, Mirimba, Salisbury; Priority Accra, Freetown, Kinshasa, Luanda, Cairo, Rabat, Mogadishu.

party, you and other recipients of this letter should report immediately any relevant statement by the Governments to which you are accredited. We should also like to know quickly of any evidence that the new administration in Rhodesia is seeking to develop contacts with African governments, and whether these Governments are disposed to take a more favourable view towards the Rhodesian regime in the light of the high turnout achieved during the recent elections there.

5. Before long we may have to ask you to comment more formally on the likely consequences of the various courses which might be pursued. In replying you will wish to pay attention to the tone of your drafting and to bear in mind for example that Ministers are likely to have little patience with the attitude displayed by the African Group in New York. But they will want to have your assessment of the practical consequences for British interest of any moves towards recognition or the lifting of sanctions. (Such assessments will of course carry more weight in the care and objectivity with which they are prepared to manifest).

(For High Commissioner Lagos only)

6. The above was drafted as a response to your personal letter of 17 April, for which many thanks.[2] The point is well taken that a sudden change in our Rhodesia policy could have particularly drastic consequences for Britain's extensive interests, and for British people, in Nigeria. Your telno 1372 was opportune, and has been put before the Prime Minister and Lord Carrington.

2 Not printed.

No. 6

Memorandum by Lord Carrington for the Cabinet Defence and Oversea Policy Committee, 11 May 1979
OD(79)3 Confidential (CAB 148/183)

Rhodesia

The Objective

1. Our objective is clear—to bring Rhodesia back to legality and to do our utmost to ensure that Rhodesia gains widespread international recognition. The question at issue is how best to achieve this.

The Rhodesian Elections

2. Lord Boyd's report is expected to be made available to the Government on 16 May. The question of publication will then fall to be considered. Lord Boyd is thought likely to conclude that the election in Rhodesia was fairly conducted and that it was as free as was possible in the circumstances.

3. Once the new government in Rhodesia is formed, it will be open to the Government at any time to introduce the legislation necessary to repeal the Southern Rhodesia Act 1965, recognise Rhodesia's legal independence and lift sanctions. To do so at once would be widely popular in the Party and in the country. I do not however recommend it for two reasons:

(*a*) we can be more helpful to Rhodesia by playing our hand rather differently;

(*b*) to recognise immediately would risk considerable damage to our interests, both economic and political throughout the world.

I think we should work to return Rhodesia to legality in such a way and in such a timescale that the country is launched into independence with the best start that may be attainable, while at the same time limiting damage to our own interests.

4. So far as 3(*a*) is concerned, immediate recognition would not bring the war to an end, nor achieve international acceptance. On the contrary, few if any of our allies and partners would follow suit; and it would be likely to harden attitudes throughout Africa, the Commonwealth and the Third World rather than giving them a lead. We need urgent consultation with friendly countries to help us form a judgement on this. The American attitude will be of particular importance. The President is required by the 'Case/Javits' amendment to determine, once the new government is installed in Rhodesia, whether it was 'chosen by free elections in which all political and population groups have been allowed to participate freely'. Our first step will be to talk to the Americans. I shall be discussing Rhodesia with Mr Vance on 21-22 May.

5. We shall do better for the Rhodesian government if we can persuade other governments to accept that a real change has taken place on which a secure, stable and democratic country can be built. The Rhodesian government can help in this process by conducting themselves in such a way as to attract international approval and to undermine the support given to the Patriotic Front. We should encourage them in this.

6. As regards paragraph 3(*b*), if we proceed to immediate recognition some African countries, led by Nigeria (our biggest market outside Europe and the USA) would take action against our economic interests and break off diplomatic relations. British communities and interests in other African countries would be at risk. (See Annex A for a summary of likely international repercussions.) A number of African countries and possibly some others might leave the Commonwealth or seek to expel Britain from it. If the action were taken before 1 August, the Commonwealth Heads of Government Meeting (CHOGM) which is due to begin in Lusaka on that date in the presence of HM The Queen would probably collapse.

Sanctions

7. In view of the change of circumstances inside Rhodesia, one cannot envisage asking Parliament in November to renew Section 2 of the 1965 Act. Section 2 will then lapse automatically and so will the sanctions which depend on it; others will not, and we shall have to take executive and legislative action to remove the remaining anomalies. But the removal of our domestic sanctions legislation would put us in breach of our obligations under mandatory Security Council resolutions if we had not by then secured a return to legality. To announce forthwith that we intended to allow Section 2 of the Act to lapse would lay us open to much the same consequences as an announcement that we were going to recognise the Rhodesian Government. Our objective should be to ensure that sanctions are lifted, not only by us but by other members of the international community.

The Next Steps

8. Our first objective must be to establish a relationship with the Rhodesian Government which will enable us to initiate the process I suggest at the end of paragraph 3. We should then seek to obtain the support of influential members of the

international community; and begin the process of trying to turn the minds of the African leaders most directly concerned into more constructive channels.

9. In the first place, we ought to establish a regular means of communication with Bishop Muzorewa and his colleagues. I have already made arrangements for a senior official to visit Salisbury to discuss *inter alia* how we can arrange this. Secondly, we should launch consultations with Mr Vance on 21 May. Thirdly, I believe we should take early steps to appoint a senior figure whose terms of reference would be to advise the Government on the steps to be taken to bring Rhodesia to a state of legality and to international recognition, and who would be prepared to devote his full attention to this task. In carrying out this task he would aim to be in constant touch not only with the new government in Rhodesia but with other Rhodesian leaders and with other influential leaders in Commonwealth Africa and elsewhere, and to provide the Government with authoritative advice. I envisage that this adviser might be either a Cabinet Minister, a senior and respected political figure, or a distinguished former official with good political experience.

10. Finally, we should put a senior official into Salisbury to act as a channel of communication with Bishop Muzorewa and to keep us closely informed of developments. We should do this in such a manner as to forestall objections that we were already recognising the new government (by presenting the official's presence as being part of a consultative mission—as indeed would be the case).

The Debate on the Queen's Speech

11. If my colleagues endorse this approach, we should be able to take a positive line in the debate on the Queen's speech in the Commons next week. This could be, in outline, that we fully appreciate what has been achieved in Rhodesia and welcome the progress which has been made there. Fundamental changes have taken place, leading to the emergence of an African majority in government and parliament. We are already in touch with Bishop Muzorewa [a senior official is in Salisbury for this purpose this week]. We are awaiting (or—assuming we have already received it—are studying) Lord Boyd's report and hope to make its conclusions public in due course. We wish to build on what has taken place in Rhodesia to achieve our basic objective—a return to legality—and to do our utmost to give her the best possible chance of securing wide international recognition. But this involves consultation with our allies and the Commonwealth Governments concerned. We are giving high priority to making contact with Bishop Muzorewa and with them at a level which recognises the importance of the changes in Rhodesia, and which will help HMG to discharge the special responsibility for the territory which the UN Security Council has so often reaffirmed.

12. I invite my colleagues to endorse the action outlined in paragraphs 9 and 10 above and the line suggested for the debate next week in paragraph 11.

ANNEX A

Rhodesia: Recognition: The International Repercussions

1. This paper examines briefly the possible consequences of an early decision by HMG to recognise a government in Rhodesia and/or lift sanctions against Rhodesia.

The severity of the international reaction would depend to some extent on whether or not we were acting in company with the United States and France. But the brunt would probably fall on Britain in any case in view of our status as the colonial power in Rhodesia.

2. There is a strong likelihood that Nigeria, conscious of its status as the richest and most populous state in black Africa, would play a leading role on organising the African response to moves of this kind by HMG. The Federal Military Government issued a statement on the Rhodesian elections of 2 May, threatening reprisals against any government which recognised the outcome.

Political Retaliation

3. There would be moves by African members, led by Nigeria, Tanzania and Zambia, to try to expel us from the Commonwealth, and threats of withdrawal from the Commonwealth by these and some other African and Asian members.

4. There would be expulsions of British Heads of Missions, and quite possibly a total breach of diplomatic relations by many African and possible some other Third World countries. There would be a strong probability of demonstrations and attacks on official British buildings. In some places the local authorities would be unwilling or unable to contain such demonstrations.

5. There would also be some risk to United Kingdom citizens and their families. There are substantial British communities in Zambia (at least 26,000) and Nigeria (15,000) who would be particularly at risk. It might be necessary to consider evacuating communities which were particularly endangered especially in Zambia.

6. There would be serious conflict at the Commonwealth Heads of Government meeting in Lusaka. It would almost certainly be necessary to advise the Queen not to attend. If she had not already been so advised by the Zambian Government. There might be a boycott of the meeting by several African, Asian and Caribbean governments.

7. Britain's standing at the UN would be affected. Even, if, by recognising the Rhodesian government before lifting sanctions, we had satisfied ourselves that we were acting legally and in accordance with the terms of mandatory UN resolutions, we should find that this interpretation of international law was challenged. There would be repeated moves in the Security Council to condemn our actions or declare them illegal. This would result in an intensification of existing pressure on our Permanent Member status.

8. *Per contra*[1] the Soviet Union and its allies would receive a substantial diplomatic boost of which they would make the most for propaganda purposes throughout Africa. They would seize this as a pretext for offering increased military support to the Front Line States—and it would probably be acceptable. A big step would be taken towards the consolidation of Soviet influence in Southern Africa.

Economic Retaliation

9. The incidence and severity of this would vary greatly. But there would certainly be moves by African countries, and possibly some other Third World states, to enforce a trade boycott against us and/or confiscate British assets. Action could include nationalisation of remaining British shareholding in major companies,

---

1 On the other hand, on the contrary.

discrimination against British imports, or denial of key raw materials (see the attached table for a breakdown of British economic interests in Africa). Whatever the precise outcome, important commercial interests would be at risk. The economic consequences could be particularly serious in Nigeria where visible exports worth £1144.4 m net, invisible receipts worth £108.8 m, and direct investment with a bulk value of £508 m would be at stake. By Comparison, British exports to Rhodesia in 1965 at 1978 prices totalled £123.4 m. The book value of British assets in Rhodesia is estimated at £113.6 m (1974)).

The Longer Term

10. There will be a risk of increased Soviet and other Communist involvement in the war in Rhodesia on the side of the Patriotic Front. This might take the form of:

(*a*) increased quantities of arms and equipment already being supplied;

(*b*) provision of different kinds of weapons, e.g. air defence systems for host countries, possibly requiring Soviet or surrogate technicians to operate them;

(*c*) direct involvement of Soviet or surrogate personnel, perhaps initially as 'advisers' or as technicians operating the equipment at (*a*).

11. The risks of destabilisation would be high in Zambia and Botswana, whose own defence forces are inexperienced, outnumbered by the guerrillas, and humiliated by Rhodesian incursions which they are incapable of resisting effectively.

TABLE

British Interests in Africa

1. United Kingdom economic interests in Africa (1978 figures)

£ million

	South Africa	Total Other Africa	of which Nigeria
Visible exports	669.3	3464.4	1133.4
Net invisible receipts	426	708	108.8 (1977)
Direct investment* (book value)	1347	1296.1	508.1* (1977)
(market value)	4500		
Portfolio investment	650		
ECGD commitment[1]	763	2653	753.0
Gross banking claims	1250	2586	NA
UK aid debt	Nil	195.5	39.6

Key supplies	Uranium (from Namibia)	Coffee
	Platinum	Cocoa
	Chromium	Bauxite
	Vanadium	Copper
	Manganese	Cobalt
	Gold	Manganese
	Diamonds	Phosphate rock
	Antimony	Tin

* excludes oil, banking and insurance

(1) Part of the ECGD commitment, representing ECGD guarantees of bank lending, duplicates amounts in the gross banking claim figures.

2. British communities in Black Africa: There are substantial British communities, as well as very important economic interests, in Zambia (26,000), Nigeria (15,000) and Kenya (11,000). These are based on registrations by patrial UK citizens; the total British community is probably a good deal larger in each case.

ANNEX B

The Six Principles

1. The principle and intention of majority rule, already enshrined in the 1961 constitution, would have to be maintained and guaranteed.
2. There would have to be guarantees against retrogressive amendment of the constitution.
3. There would have to be immediate improvement in the political status of the African population.
4. There would have to be progress towards ending racial discrimination.
5. The British Government would need to be satisfied that any basis for independence was acceptable to the people of Rhodesia as a whole.
6. It would be necessary to ensure that, regardless of race, there was no oppression of majority by minority or of minority by majority.

No. 7

Extract from the minutes of a meeting of the Cabinet Defence and Oversea Policy Committee, 14 May 1979[1]
OD(79)1st Meeting, Secret (CAB 148/183)

1. Rhodesia[2]

The Committee had before them a memorandum by the Foreign and Commonwealth Secretary (OD(79) 3) on future policy towards Rhodesia.[3]

The Foreign and Commonwealth Secretary said that the purpose of his paper was to discuss how to carry out the Manifesto commitment in regard to Rhodesia. This was to the effect that if the six Principles were satisfied, it would be the duty of the Conservative Government to bring Rhodesia back to a state of legality, to lift sanctions and to seek to secure international recognition for the Salisbury regime. Expectation in the Party and also generally in the country was that the Government would move to early recognition, especially if, as seemed likely, Lord Boyd reported that the elections had been fairly conducted. On the other hand, if we moved too quickly, this would have adverse consequences for our international interests. Time was therefore needed for consultation. He had had an opportunity on 13 May to explain the Government's position to his Community colleagues who had shown understanding but had expressed concern at the possible effect on Namibia of any early move on Rhodesia. He was due to see the United States Secretary of State, Mr Vance, on 21 May. A senior official of the Foreign and Commonwealth Office, Sir Antony Duff, was due to leave that day for Rhodesia in order to make contact with Bishop Muzorewa. The aim would be to discover from the Bishop how he intended to proceed. Depending on his talks with Mr Vance and Sir Antony Duff's report, he was in favour of sending a high level emissary out to discuss both with Bishop Muzorewa and with others how to handle the question of recognition. We should need to urge the Bishop to make his Government appear more African than it looked like being at present, and try to negotiate an amendment to the Constitution to reduce the built-in safeguards for the Whites, which were an obvious target for criticism. No immediate decision was required about recognition and Bishop Muzorewa was not due to take over the Government until the beginning of June. It would be desirable to avoid any action which would disrupt the Commonwealth Heads of Government Meeting in early August. On the other hand, we would have to complete the process before the Sanctions Order was due to come up for renewal in November.

In discussion it was argued that we might have to move faster than suggested. In particular, the Prime Minister would need to say something positive in the

---

[1] Present were: The Rt Hon Margaret Thatcher MP, Prime Minister; The Rt Hon William Whitelaw MP, Secretary of State for the Home Department; The Rt Hon Lord Hailsham, Lord Chancellor; The Rt Hon Lord Carrington, Secretary of State for Foreign and Commonwealth Affairs; The Rt Hon Lord Soames, Lord President of the Council; The Rt Hon Sir Ian Gilmour MP, Lord Privy Seal; The Rt Hon John Nott MP, Secretary of State for Trade. Secretariat: Sir John Hunt; Sir Clive Rose; Mr C.A. Whitmore.
[2] This section is marked Confidential.
[3] No. 6.

House of Commons on 15 May.[4] She could refer to consultations which were going on and would wish to say that she had been in touch with Lord Boyd. She might also make the point that both sides of the House were agreed on the Six Principles and that the need now was to confirm whether they were satisfied. The Australian Government had already expressed some anxiety about the effect on the Commonwealth of the Government moving too fast. But there was a case for giving an early lead which, after initial objections, might in due course, be generally accepted. The main difficulties would be with Tanzania, Zambia and Nigeria. On the other hand Kenya, Malawi, Botswana and Mozambique were unlikely to cause serious trouble. As regards the legal position, it was suggested that in order to avoid difficulties in the Security Council, where progress might be blocked by a Soviet veto, we should consider taking steps to return Rhodesia to legality by declaring that the rebellion was terminated, which would remove the basis for the original United Nations action.

The Prime Minister, summing up the discussion, said that in her speech in the House she would follow generally the line in paragraph 11 of the Foreign and Commonwealth Secretary's memorandum. She would welcome the developments which had led to the elections in Rhodesia, report that a senior Foreign and Commonwealth Office official had been sent out to establish initial contact with Bishop Muzorewa on behalf of the Government, refer to the forthcoming consultations between the Foreign and Commonwealth Secretary and Mr Vance and undertake to arrange for publication of Lord Boyd's report. As regards the latter, she would see Lord Boyd before speaking in the house with a view to being able to tell the House in general terms of his conclusions. The Foreign and Commonwealth Secretary should arrange for a passage to be drafted covering these points. Consultations should proceed on the basis proposed by the Foreign and Commonwealth Secretary, but we should not assume that we had much time before we would need to reach and announce a firm decision on recognition.

The Committee—

Took note, with approval, of the Prime Minister's summing up of their discussion, and invited the Foreign and Commonwealth Secretary to take action accordingly.[5]

---

[4] The first public pronouncement was made in guarded terms in the Queen's Speech on 15 May. Every effort would be made to end the conflict and bring about a lasting settlement based on democratic wishes, and there would be international consultation. The Prime Minister said in the debate: 'I assure the House that we intend to proceed with vigour to resolve the issue.' (Parl. Debs., 5th ser., H. of C., vol. 967, col. 87).

[5] The other two items discussed at this meeting were (2) Strategic Arms Limitation Talks and (3) European Economic Community Matters.

No. 8

Minute from Mr Day to Mr Walden, 18 May 1979
Confidential (FCO 36/2539)

The Secretary of State's Meeting with Mr Vance: Rhodesia

1. The brief for the discussions with Mr Vance covers the principal ground. The following additional thoughts are offered subject to Sir A. Duff's views on his return.[1]

2. The US Administration is under intense pressure from the Senate to lift sanctions. This pressure should shift American policy closer to our own. We have indications that the President's determination on the Case-Javits amendment is likely to be positive in tone. He is likely to recognise that the Rhodesian elections were well-conducted, that the turnout was impressive and that they represent a basis on which to build. He will probably resist the proposition that sanctions should be lifted and recognition accorded forthwith. This would put the Americans out in front of us. It would cause damage to their interest in Africa and (they believe) increase the opportunities for Soviet penetration in black Africa.

3. In seeking to square the circle, the Americans will be looking for 'something more' to be done before moving towards the lifting of sanctions and, eventually, recognition. It will not be much use urging Bishop Muzorewa at this stage to agree to new UN-supervised elections. The Patriotic Front have in any case never accepted that these should take place without their occupying a dominant position in advance.

4. There are other possibilities. Sir A. Duff can advise if any of them look feasible.

5. The offer to conduct a 'test of acceptability' and/or some negotiation on the constitution is mentioned in paragraph 10 of the brief. We should not rule out the possibility of some final attempt at a negotiation between the internal and external parties. Rather than simply allowing ourselves to be pilloried at the Commonwealth Conference, we might encourage the idea that a Commonwealth 'Contact Group' should try to promote a negotiation between Bishop Muzorewa and the Patriotic Front (Mr Smith could not of course be involved). The Australians seem to be thinking along these lines. The Malawi High Commissioner at today's Commonwealth meeting urged his colleagues to produce constructive ideas rather than destructive criticism.

6. In short, in order to render the ultimate granting of independence to Rhodesia more acceptable—and thereby limit the damage to our own interests—we may need to make some positive proposal. The Patriotic Front are likely to be intransigent—but it will be no bad thing to expose their intransigence. It would of course be essential to carry Bishop Muzorewa with us. It will be the task of the 'political emissary' to advise on this.

7. At the moment the Americans find themselves in the awkward position of having to take decisions (the President's determination) on a time-scale more compressed than ours. We want to achieve a realignment of US policy on our own —but not at the expense of ourselves moving at this stage out in front of the Americans: we are much more vulnerable to African retaliation than they are. We need to carry them with us; but we cannot solve their problems for them.

D.M. Day

1 Sir A. Duff had flown to Salisbury on 17 May.

No. 9

Minute from Sir A. Duff to Lord Carrington, 19 May 1979
Confidential (FCO 36/2561)

Secretary of State,

1. My telegram No. 230[1] from Salisbury gave you an account of my conversation with the Bishop.[2] I do not think I need trouble you with the full record. The main point is that he was very pleased (as were many others in Salisbury) at the swift action to get in touch with him and the clear demonstration of our intention to work with him rather than against him. I think we must follow this up soon, by sending an official to Salisbury by the end of this month. I believe that we have the opportunity to gain and retain the Bishop's confidence. This will be important when, in the general interest, we wish to advise him to do things he does not much want to do like making moves towards the Patriotic Front, or modifying the Constitution. Even before then there will be a need, I suspect, for someone to push the Government in Salisbury to make presentational initiatives such as accelerated Africanisation in the public service and a new attractive presentation of the amnesty for guerrillas.

2. I deliberately did not press on the Bishop, nor indeed on anyone else, the thought that quite painful concessions may well be necessary in the interests of undermining the Patriotic Front and attracting African support. I think Muzorewa and his supporters, and most Rhodesia officials, would find the thought unacceptable at present and I judged it better to concentrate on establishing a basis of goodwill and sympathy. In any case, until we have talked to Mr Vance I was not altogether sure how we ourselves would wish to handle this issue. But we shall have to begin to educate the Rhodesians in it soon after the government is formed, and in the light of African reactions to the Muzorewa overtures; the continuation of the war; the rate at which guerrillas do or do not lay down their arms and so on.

3. On the other hand, I do not think that I gave any hostages to fortune. I was careful throughout to speak of bringing Rhodesia to legal independence, building on what has been achieved already, moving forward together, working together to give an independent Rhodesia the best possible start in life, and so on, without I hope implying that at the end of the day we would necessarily recognise the present government as it stands. At the same time I made it quite clear to everyone to whom I talked that we had to watch our own backs, as well as working for Rhodesia, and that a damage limitation exercise was very much part of our thinking.

4. Most people I spoke to understood our reasons for favouring a fairly cautious approach to recognition or the lifting of sanctions. But I met everywhere of course the argument that it would be better to grasp the nettle now, and endure a short sharp reaction which would dissipate quite quickly; rather than dragging out the process and encountering greater difficulty at a later date. There is also the perfectly tenable thesis that lifting sanctions now would set the economy in motion and enable the government to find money for job training, minor development schemes and so on, calculated to persuade young people to stay in Rhodesia rather than crossing the

1 Not printed.
2 Sir A. Duff had flown to Salisbury on 17 May.

border to join the guerrillas; and the more arguable thesis that recognition by Britain and others would so impress those guerrillas who are sitting on the fence that they would immediately come flowing back.

5. Various people in Salisbury assured me that Muzorewa had recently become more decisive. I do not myself believe that he is going to be a strong Prime Minister, and we may of course see a fragile and increasingly disunited government failing to run the country properly let alone creating the sort of new image which is basic to acceptance by the outside world. However, I would judge that there will probably be enough sensible white support and guidance to enable the government to hold together and to make a reasonable showing.

6. I am not sure how attached the Bishop is to the idea of working only discreetly and privately, at the present stage, to attract international support. It is in his nature, and I think it is also a fair point that certain countries (e.g. Ivory Coast, Senegal, Kenya) will not thank us if we put them too obviously *au pied du mur*.[3] On the other hand, we have perhaps a domestic need to be seen to be active. Moreover some countries (e.g. Nigeria) will probably respond better to the top-level treatment than to a quiet approach—though even in these cases there may be advantage in a more private contact first. I do think however that it is important to get on with it, at any rate so far as the African countries are concerned.

7. I see little hope at present of arranging Ian Smith's departure from the government.

8. Against this background, I think the immediate needs are as follows:

(*a*) To define and agree with the United States the general direction in which we are trying to go. I take this to be: 'To bring Rhodesia to legal independence by building on the new Rhodesia Government and Constitution, while seeking such changes as may be necessary to attract the support of other African countries, and seeking an end to the war either by negotiation or by undermining the support given to the Patriotic Front.'

(*b*) To get in touch quickly and discreetly with as many of the moderate African governments as we think worthwhile.

(*c*) To decide whether to let Nigeria stew for a bit; or to tackle her now and, if so, how.

(*d*) To consider similarly the question of tackling the front line states.

(*e*) To decide, in the light of our contacts with the front line states, how and when to talk to Mugabe and Nkomo.

(*f*) To decide whether to talk privately to the South Africans.

(*g*) To consult the Europeans, and seek to persuade them of the validity of our defined policy.

(*h*) To begin now to talk to some of the non-African Commonwealth, as preparation for the CHGM.

9. I think it is only after the initial contacts with the African states and especially Nigeria and the front line states, that we shall be able to form a view as to the best way forward.

10. We need to discuss with the Americans the extent to which they should involve

---

3 Have one's back to the wall.

themselves in all this, and take the lead in some of it: e.g. Nigeria. As a sweeping generalisation it may be preferable at this stage to think of a division of labour between the US and ourselves, rather than making our approaches hand-in-hand.

ANTONY DUFF

No. 10

Record of a discussion between Lord Carrington and Mr Vance at the FCO, 21 May 1979, 10.10 a.m.
Confidential (FCO 36/2539)

Present:
All the time:
The Rt. Hon. Lord Carrington
Sir Ian Gilmour MP
Mr Peter Jay[1]
Sir M. Palliser
Sir A. Duff
Mr G. Walden

The Hon. Cyrus Vance
Mr Kingman Brewster
Mr George Vest
Mr Dick Moose
Mr Tony Lake
Mr Peter Tarnoff[2]
Mr Ed Streator (US Embassy)

For some of the time:
Mr Peter Blaker MP
Mr Douglas Hurd MP
Mr Richard Luce MP
Sir A. Parsons
Mr D.M. Day
Mr M.R. Melhuish[3]
Mr P. Yarnold[4]
Mr P. Lever
Mr J.S. Wall

Mr Jim Dobbins (US Embassy)
Mr Ray Seitz (US Embassy)
Miss April Glasbury (US Embassy)

Rhodesia

29. *Lord Carrington* opened the afternoon session by explaining the new Government's attitude to the Rhodesia question. For some years successive Governments had asked the Rhodesians to satisfy the six principles, which they had been reluctant to do. There had been a breakthrough as a result of the Kissinger initiative, and up to March this year all the principles had been satisfied except for the test of acceptability. Both Conservatives and Labour had said that a return to legality would result from the satisfaction of the six principles.

30. The Conservatives had sent six observers to the elections and the Boyd Report, a copy of which had been sent to the Americans, concluded (as had a separate report

---

1 British Ambassador to the United States, 1977-79.
2 Mr Peter Tarnoff, Special Assistant to the Secretary of State and Executive Secretary.
3 Mr Michael Ramsay Milhuish, Head of North America Department.
4 Mr Patrick Yarnold, Assistant Head of North America Department.

by Mr Drinkwater)[5] that the election had been free and fair. Both Lord Boyd and Mr Drinkwater considered that the election result implied acceptance of the constitution, thus fulfilling the sixth principle.

31. The new Government felt it was required to honour the undertakings given in the Conservative manifesto. Of course there were problems of presentation to the Commonwealth Heads of Government, the EEC, the United States and the Third World in general. But the Conservatives had said that if they were satisfied that the principles had been carried out they would have a duty to return Rhodesia to legality and seek to secure international recognition.

32. The Government was not committed to a time scale but there were intense political pressures. The general public broadly felt that the internal settlement had been shabbily treated and there was a great deal of pressure in the Conservative Party and Parliament for progress. In November the Sanctions Order would fall due for renewal, and there was no prospect of getting this through either house.

33. Invited by Lord Carrington to report on his visit to Rhodesia, *Sir A. Duff* said that his chief purpose was to make early contact with Bishop Muzorewa and demonstrate that Britain desired constant future contact. The Bishop had greatly welcomed the visit, particularly the speed with which it had taken place.

34. The general mood in Salisbury was still fairly confident, as a result of the success of the election and its organisation. A new African government was slowly and deliberately being installed. The next step was the election of the President: if unopposed this would happen on 22 May, otherwise in a week's time. Then Bishop Muzorewa would be appointed Prime Minister and would soon form a Government, though there might be some delay.

35. Mr Smith would certainly be a part of the Government: there was talk that he would be a Minister without a portfolio, but no confirmation. It was not known who the other four white Ministers would be, but the rumour was that they would be the more moderate ones.

36. *Sir A. Duff* said he was disappointed by the lack of views among professional white administrators in Rhodesia on how the new government could make itself more acceptable in Africa. Bishop Muzorewa was more alive to this need, but he had not pressed him. The Bishop had written 'reconciliatory' letters to President Kaunda, Nyerere, Machel and Seretse Khama, saying that there was no need for the war to continue since an African government had been elected, and that there was no further need for large numbers of Rhodesians to remain outside Rhodesia's borders, since the amnesty applied to all. In addition the UANC emissaries were now visiting moderate countries, and would continue on to Europe and the USA, to drum up support.

37. Sir A. Duff said he had pressed Bishop Muzorewa on the need for maximum international acceptance and also had spoken a little about the Patriotic Front and the need for some political move. The Bishop clearly had not given this much thought. He brushed Mr Nkomo aside as impossible, but said there had been some contact between the UANC and Mr Mugabe's people and that he had been told by visitors that Mr Mugabe wanted fresh contacts. He was coming round to the view that his letter should also go to Mr Nkomo and Mr Mugabe.

---

5 Mr John Drinkwater QC.

38. *Lord Carrington* stressed that the need was to appear to be moving forward. Britain would send a senior official to Salisbury, who would not be accredited there but would be there virtually all the time. This could make it possible to exert some pressure on Bishop Muzorewa.

39. The Government also thought it necessary to talk to the Front Line States and Nigeria, and thought it best to send someone, not a Minister but a suitably high-level emissary, to talk to them. It would be for consideration whether he should also talk to Mr Nkomo and Mr Mugabe. The emissary would put it to the Africans that the election had changed the situation and would seek their views. Something might come from this which would produce progress. He hoped that Britain and the USA could keep in step.

40. Mr Vance said that the Americans recognised the new reality created by the elections. The President had not yet made a decision on the determination required by the Case-Javits Amendment, nor what the ultimate US position would be. But time was running out. Mr Carter was committed to a determination not later than two weeks after the installation of the new government in Salisbury. In a sense, the Administration was required to put the cart before the horse, since the burning question was the lifting of sanctions. The Case-Javits Amendment put forward two conditions: that free and fair elections should be held and that there should be a readiness to take part in All Party Conference under international auspices.

41. The Americans wished to know British thinking on how the situation should be addressed since they would like to keep in line. There were two main dangers in lifting sanctions:

(i) The US would be seen by many countries including most black Africans and non-aligned, as aligning themselves with South Africa against black Africa.

(ii) It would increase the leverage of the Russians and Cubans in Africa.

He wondered if there was a solution on the lines of a conditional determination. Would it be possible to say that sanctions would be lifted once certain events had taken place? No decision had yet been taken but the conditions might be:

(a) some revision of the constitution;

(b) an attempt to move the Salisbury Government towards some form of All Party Conference (but without a blocking veto for the Patriotic Front);

(c) an election after such a conference under some form of international supervision, ratifying the modified constitution (but again PF refusal to take part would not block the process).

42. Mr Moose said that in thinking about constitutional changes the US did not envisage mere efforts to produce changes emotionally satisfying to the Front Line States and Nigeria. But the Front Line had practical problems and any solution must address those problems. They needed an offer so acceptable that they could justifiably criticise the PF if the latter turned it down.

43. Mr Vance briefly outlined the Congressional position. It was clear that a majority in the Senate would vote now to lift sanctions, although the majority would not be as large as last week's vote had seemed to indicate. In the House the situation was more doubtful. The Africa Sub-committee under Rep. Solarz argued powerfully against lifting sanctions at present. Whatever happened the Administration faced a very divisive political battle, with the black community feeling particularly strongly.

44. *Lord Carrington* expressed doubts about the attractions for Salisbury of a conditional determination by President Carter. Bishop Muzorewa needed to avoid amending the constitution in order to keep the whites in Rhodesia, while a revival of the APC suggestion would be derided. *Sir A. Duff* added that the difficulty was the need to announce the conditions by the second week of June, but he agreed with Mr Moose that the Front Line States needed something. Perhaps the President could make a conditional determination *without spelling out the conditions*. As it was, Bishop Muzorewa, the Front Line States and the PF would reject the proposed conditions out of hand.

45. *Mr Lake* commented that the whites could be kept in Rhodesia by strengthening some parts of the constitution to increase the guarantee of economic and social rights for whites, while reducing their political strength. After some further exchanges *Lord Carrington* and *Mr Vance* agreed that Mr Luce, Sir A. Duff and American officials should continue discussing Rhodesia in a separate session, returning later to report.

46. When they returned *Mr Lake* reported that the meeting had agreed that it might be best for the British representative to speak alone to the Front Line States but that in the case of Nigeria a US representative should brief them while the British representative was still on his way. This was on the assumption that the Nigerians would wish to avoid getting out in front of the Front Line States as they had done previously. At the same time Britain and the US could make quiet approaches through diplomatic channels to other African States. Mr Lake continued that officials had agreed that in the President's determination the US should work towards:

(*a*) acknowledging that the elections were a significant advance;

(*b*) establishing a position which would be credible with the Front Line States.

Mr Carter could say that the Case-Javits criteria had not been fully met, but that the Administration would keep the question under close review and report back to Congress after six months, not specifying precise conditions. He could further reiterate the view that the best solution would be a second internationally supervised election with a number of other unspecified conditions. There might perhaps be a reference to the Administration's wish to see some attempt at an accommodation with the outside parties, to assessing Salisbury's ability to bring peace to areas where fighting was now going on (although this had its dangers) and also to the new government's commitment to democratic principles, such as ending discrimination, opening up top jobs to Africans etc. The disadvantage for the Administration of not being precise about conditions was that they needed a clear policy in order to make it acceptable to Congress.

47. After *Mr Vance* had said that he needed time to think about these new ideas, it was agreed that Rhodesia would be discussed at a further session on Wednesday 23 May, together with other Southern African questions.

No. 11

Minute from Sir A. Duff to Lord Carrington, 23 May 1979
Unclassified (FCO 36/2539)

I have discovered what is fussing the Americans is the thought that we are ruling out, from the beginning, any possibility that there might be something to be done even at this stage with the Patriotic Front. I am not certain whether they genuinely believe this, or whether (which is perhaps more probable) they are acutely conscious of the need to convert certain strands of opinion in Washington. However that may be I have told them that we are at this stage ruling out nothing. In theory there is at one extreme the possibility (however remote) of re-opening some sort of negotiation between the Rhodesian parties; or at least of contriving a political accommodation between some of them. At the other extreme is the possibility of making minimum changes within Rhodesia sufficient to save the faces of the Front Line Presidents so that they can abandon the Patriotic Front. In between these two extremes there are a number of other possibilities. We cannot begin to focus on them until the first report comes in from your emissary.

If you can make some reassuring noises on this aspect it would be helpful.

A. DUFF

No. 12

Extract from a note of Mrs Thatcher's discussion with Mr Vance, at 10 Downing Street, 23 May 1979, 10 a.m.
Confidential (FCO 36/2539)

Present:
The Prime Minister
The Foreign and Commonwealth Secretary
The Lord Privy Seal
Mr B. G. Cartledge

Mr Cyrus Vance
H.E. The US Ambassador

Rhodesia

The Foreign and Commonwealth Secretary explained the respective roles of the three emissaries whom the Government were sending to Southern Africa in the near future—Mr Luce for discussions on Namibia, a political emissary to have discussions with the Front Line Presidents and others and a senior FCO official to maintain contact with Bishop Muzorewa in Salisbury. Lord Carrington explained that it might be necessary for the political emissary to have discussions with Mr Mugabe and Mr Nkomo as well as with some of the Front Line Presidents and that he might pay subsequent visits to Salisbury and South Africa. The emissary would be leaving on this mission as soon as possible. *The Prime Minister* commented that if these discussions did not succeed in moderating African positions, some alternative approach would have to be devised in advance of the meeting of Commonwealth Heads of Government in Lusaka: her concern was that African attitudes might freeze if the momentum were not sustained. It was essential to secure the maximum possible recognition for a Rhodesian regime since that country held the key to the whole Southern African region. The Prime Minister thought that Mozambique would welcome a settlement but acknowledged that President Nyerere would be difficult. *Lord Carrington* commented that President Kaunda would almost certainly be difficult as well.

Mr Vance told the Prime Minister that the United States Ambassador in Dar es Salaam[1] had called on President Nyerere on 22 May. President Nyerere had expressed the view that it would be possible for some kind of negotiation to be arranged; but he remained very fearful of recognition of the Muzorewa regime. President Nyerere had not excluded the possibility of playing a helpful role in negotiations and had mentioned the need for some revision of the new Rhodesian constitution. President Nyerere had acknowledged that Bishop Muzorewa did have a Government. The American Ambassador's impression had been that there was now slightly more flexibility in the Tanzanian approach. *Lord Carrington* said that the deputation of Commonwealth High Commissioners who had called on him earlier in the morning had dismissed the Rhodesian elections as irrelevant and had criticised the constitution. He had taken the line that the elections had in fact transformed the situation. His own view, however, was that there was some force in the criticisms which had been made of the constitution, which did entrench white control in a number of important areas. Lord Carrington went on to say that if the provisions of the constitution posed a real problem, the Commonwealth African leaders should go to see Bishop Muzorewa themselves and take the matter up with him to make the necessary changes. *The Prime Minister* asked whether Bishop Muzorewa was talking to Mugabe. *Lord Carrington* said that he was; they were both from the Shona tribe.

Mr Vance said that he had been disturbed by the report in that morning's *Daily Telegraph* to the effect that the United States were opposed to the UK official presence in Salisbury which Lord Carrington had mentioned. It was fully appreciated in the State Department that this did not amount to recognition and he would take an opportunity later in the day to make it clear that the *Daily Telegraph* report was wholly incorrect.

---

1 Mr James William Spain.

No. 13

Minute from Mr Renwick to Mr Walden, 24 May 1979[1]
Confidential (FCO 36/2480)

Consultations on Rhodesia

Timing and Scope

1. The President of Zimbabwe-Rhodesia will probably be elected on 28 May. The new government is expected to be formed by 1 June. Mr Day will be travelling to Salisbury towards the end of next week. Against this background, it would seem right to plan for the Government senior political emissary to embark on the first stage of the mission in their course of the following week (i.e. by 8 or 9 June).

2. The Government's public commitment is to send a *political emissary* to have discussions with the Commonwealth and other African governments most directly concerned. I *recommend* that in his first visit the emissary should go to Zambia, Tanzania, Botswana, Mozambique and—probably—Nigeria. Angola is the least influential of the front-line states and consultation with President Neto is unlikely to add anything useful to what the emissary will hear from the other Presidents. The talks in Mozambique may not be very profitable in view of President Machel's strong commitment to the Patriotic Front and radical attitude; but it would be unwise to leave the Mozambique government out of the first round of consultations. The consultation with President Kaunda will be of particular importance. In view of Nigeria's status in the old OAU and the Commonwealth and important as a trading partner, I recommend (subject to confirmation by the High Commissioner in Lagos, whom we are consulting) that the emissary should also go to Lagos.

3. Allowing for a full day in each capital, travelling time and rest, and using a chartered aircraft after the first stop in Africa (in view of the poor connection by scheduled flights in the region) a mission to Lusaka, Dar es Salaam, Maputo, Gaborone and Lagos, could be completed in about 10-12 days. The starting point could be either Lusaka or Dar es Salaam.

4. I recommend that in the course of the visits to Lusaka and Maputo arrangements should be made for the emissary to meet Mr Nkomo and Mr Mugabe if they are available at the time. There will be strong criticism if he does not do so. If there is any difficulty about arranging meetings with the Patriotic Front leaders we should make clear our intention to hold consultations with them in due course.

Consultation with Other Governments

5. There would be presentational advantage in arranging a first round of consultations with the *South African government* in a more discreet way, in the first instance at senior official level, rather than by the political emissary.

6. We have submitted separately instructions to posts in Commonwealth and OAU countries to make an early high-level approach to the government to which they are accredited to give them an account, with reference to Ministerial statements, of the Government general approach to Rhodesia. They will be drawing attention in particular to the importance which the Government attaches to consultation before it

[1] Also sent to Mr Day.

decides on its next moves. There will be a strong case for subsequent approaches at a political level in selective countries in the following categories:

(*a*) *Major non-African Commonwealth countries*. The Secretary of State will wish to consider whether he will be able to hold consultations with some of the Asian Commonwealth countries in the course of his Far Eastern visit at the end of June. There would seem to us to be considerable advantage to this. The Australians are already well covered (e.g. Mr Peacock's[2] visit).

(*b*) *Moderate African countries* with influence in the OAU e.g. Sudan, Liberia, Ghana, and possibly the Ivory Coast and Senegal. It will be important to make contact with these countries before the OAU Foreign Ministers' Meeting in Monrovia on 5 July. Depending on his other commitments, Mr Luce might be able to undertake some of these consultations.

7. We shall need to keep in close touch with the *Americans*. There will be a strong case for the political emissary to go to Washington and also to consult with the new *Canadian* government, after his first visit to Africa.

8. So far as the *Nine* are concerned, the best opportunity for consultation with the French will be afforded by the Prime Minister's visit to Paris on 5 June. The meeting of the Political Committee on 5-6 June will provide a further opportunity for consultation with the Nine generally, as will the subsequent political cooperation meeting at Ministerial level on 18 June.

9. I *submit* a draft letter to No. 10, setting out arrangements we have in mind for the political emissary.[3] We shall meanwhile be making provisional plans for an itinerary on the lines set out in paragraph 2 above.

R.W. R<small>ENWICK</small>

2 Mr Andrew Sharp Peacock, Australian Minister for Foreign Affairs, 1975-80.
3 See No. 15.

No. 14

Lord Carrington to Sir L. Allinson (Lusaka), 25 May 1979, 1.41 p.m.[1]
Tel. No. 194 Confidential, Flash (FCO 36/2480)

Rhodesia: Political Consultation

1. You should now approach the government to which you are accredited at the highest appropriate level and speak on the lines of paragraphs 2-4 below.

2. As I announced on 22 May, the Government intend to arrange for a high level emissary to travel to Africa in the very near future to talk to the Commonwealth and other African governments most directly concerned with the problem of the future of Rhodesia. The Government have asked Lord Harlech who, as you will remember, is a former Minister of State at the FCO and British Ambassador in Washington and was

1 And Flash to Dar es Salaam, Gaborone, Maputo, Lagos; Info Flash Luanda; Info Immediate Deskby 251400Z Washington, UKMIS New York, Cape Town, Mirimba, Salisbury.

Deputy Chairman of the Pearce Commission[2], to act as their personal representative to carry out this task. I hope that the President/Head of the FMG will be prepared to receive Lord Harlech in the course of his mission. The High Commission/Embassy will be in touch as soon as possible about the details of his itinerary. The plan is that, in the first instance, he should visit Dar es Salaam, Gaborone, Lusaka Maputo and Lagos (though not necessarily in that order).

3. As the government have emphasised in all their public statements on Rhodesia since taking office they attach special importance to the closest possible consultation with the country's most directly concerned before they decide on the next steps they will take on this question. Their overall objective is to bring Rhodesia back to legality in conditions of wide international recognition which will give the country the prospect of a more peaceful future. They have taken no decision yet as to how this is to be done, and no possible way of achieving this aim will be excluded from the scope of these consultations.

4. I therefore expect Lord Harlech's talks with his interlocuters in Africa to be frank and wide-ranging. He will be reporting to the Prime Minister on his return from his mission and we shall be giving full weight to what he has to tell us about the views of the Frontline States and Nigeria in further consideration of this problem.

5. For your own information, it is envisaged that there will be further consultations on Rhodesia with Commonwealth governments in Africa before the Commonwealth Heads of Government Meeting in Lusaka. We shall be in touch shortly about consultations with the South Africans and African governments.

6. Please inform Luanda by immediate telegram if you are unable to carry out these instruction before departure of Head of State/Government for Luanda so that action can be taken by Mr Byatt if possible.

7. We do not (not) propose to announce Lord Harlech's appointment until early next week.

2 This was a UK Commission set up in 1971, by the then Foreign Secretary, Sir Alec Douglas-Home, to test acceptability of a proposed constitutional settlement in Rhodesia. The chairman was the retired British judge, Lord (Edward) Pearce.

No. 15

Letter from Mr Wall to Mr Cartledge (No. 10), 25 May 1979
Confidential (FCO 36/2563)

Dear Bryan,

Rhodesia

As you know, Lord Harlech has agreed to be the Government's emissary on Rhodesia.

Lord Carrington envisages (subject to confirmation by our posts in the countries concerned) that the emissary's first round of talks should include consultations with Presidents Kaunda, Nyerere, Machel and Sir Seretse Khama and General Obasanjo. Lord Carrington considers that the emissary should offer to meet the co-leaders of the Patriotic Front in Lusaka and Maputo, as we should not appear to be excluding them from our consultations. Lord Carrington does not believe it is necessary for the emissary to see President Neto of Angola. On the other hand, Nigeria's political and economic importance justifies the inclusion of Lagos in the itinerary. We are at present planning on the assumption that the itinerary can be carried out between, say, 11 and 22 June.

I enclose a copy of the telegram which we have sent to front line posts telling them about Lord Harlech.[1] It is not now certain that the front line Presidents will meet over this weekend but Lord Carrington thought it important to let them know straight away what we had in mind, partly in the hope that we might pre-empt unhelpful public statements.

We would hope to delay an announcement about Lord Harlech until approaches have been made to the governments concerned. We have told Lord Harlech that we would hope to make the announcement next week and I enclose a copy of the text we have in mind.[2] In public comment, Lord Carrington suggests that we should avoid creating the expectation that the emissary's mission will be followed by early discussion or statements by the Government. He believes that it will be best to take the line that the Government will be considering the next steps in the light of what the emissary has to say about his consultations and of Mr Day's reports on his mission to Salisbury. It is clear that further extensive consultation with other Commonwealth and African governments will be desirable before the OAU meetings in Monrovia in July and the Commonwealth Heads of Government meeting in Lusaka. It will probably be necessary for the emissary to return to Africa, and to report further to the Prime Minister before the Commonwealth Conference.

I am copying this letter to the Private Secretaries of other members of OD and to Martin Vile (Cabinet Office).

Yours ever,
STEPHEN

1 No. 14.
2 Not printed.

No. 16

Letter from Mr Cartledge (No. 10) to Mr Wall, 29 May 1979
Confidential (FCO 36/2563)

Dear Stephen,

Rhodesia

Thank you for your letter of 25 May about Lord Harlech's mission to Southern Africa.

The Prime Minister has seen your letter and, with one important exception, is content with the arrangements envisaged for Lord Harlech's consultations. The Prime Minister agrees that Lord Harlech should have talks with President Kaunda, President Nyerere, President Machel, Sir Seretse Khama and General Obasanjo. The Prime Minister does not, however, consider that Lord Harlech should meet the co-leaders of the Patriotic Front. The Prime Minister has commented that she has never done business with terrorists until they become Prime Ministers.

The arrangements foreshadowed in your letter for the announcement of Lord Harlech's mission and for handling publicity have, of course, now being overtaken by the leak of his appointment which occurred over the weekend.

I am sending copies of this letter to the Private Secretaries to other members of OD and to Martin Vile (Cabinet Office).

Yours ever,
BRYAN CARTLEDGE

No. 17

Letter from Mr Cartledge (No. 10) to Mr Wall, 1 June 1979
Confidential (FCO 36/2563)

Dear Stephen,

Rhodesia

I wrote to you on 29 May to convey the Prime Minister's views on Lord Harlech's forthcoming consultations in Southern Africa.[1]

The Prime Minister and the Foreign and Commonwealth Secretary had a further discussion about Lord Harlech's mission this morning. Lord Carrington explained that Lord Harlech's tour of Southern Africa would have two objectives: to find out whether there was any flexibility in the position of the Front Line Presidents, and also to minimise, so far as possible, the damage which might result to British interests from their current attitude towards the Government's Rhodesia policy. If Lord Harlech did not make contact with the Leaders of the Patriotic Front, the Front Line Presidents would be unlikely be regard his mission as a genuine attempt to achieve settlement, and would probably dismiss it as bogus. Lord Carrington said that he entirely shared the Prime Minister's opinion of Joshua Nkomo and Robert Mugabe, but believed that it would be right for Lord Harlech to see them. The Prime Minister suggested that Lord Harlech might meet President Kaunda and Nkomo together. It was agreed that if this were not, in the event, practicable, Lord Harlech should see Nkomo and Mugabe only in the presence of additional UK witnesses such as our High Commissioner in Lusaka and our Ambassador in Maputo. Lord Carrington pointed out that if, in the event, Nkomo were to refuse to see Lord Harlech, this would do no harm to the Government's public case.

I am sending copies of this letter to the Private Secretaries to the other members of OD and to Martin Vile (Cabinet Office).

Yours ever,
BRYAN CARTLEDGE

1 No. 16.

No. 18

Letter from Mr Cartledge (No. 10) to Mr Wall, 6 June 1979
Confidential (FCO 36/2563)

Dear Stephen,

Lord Harlech's Mission to Southern Africa

The Foreign and Commonwealth Secretary brought Lord Harlech to call on the Prime Minister this morning, to discuss his mission to Southern Africa as the emissary of the Government.[1] The following is a summary of the main points which arose during a short discussion.

The Prime Minister told Lord Harlech that President Giscard[2], judging from her talk with him on the previous day, was disposed to be helpful over Rhodesia. There was clearly the beginnings of a more realistic appraisal in Africa of the Rhodesian situation and we should do our best to build on this. Lord Harlech told the Prime Minister that his recent talk with the American envoy, Mr Loewenstein[3], who had just returned from unofficial talks with presidents Nyerere and Kaunda, showed that there was some sign of movement in the thinking of the Front Line Presidents and that some of them might be keen to get off the hook. If they could be persuaded to give a lead, many other African Heads of Government would be only too ready to follow.

The Prime Minister expressed some concern that if Bishop Muzorewa could not be persuaded to move quickly, Mr Sithole might abandon the internal settlement which would make it much more difficult for the British Government to defend. She recalled that President Kaunda had told her that his whole attitude towards Rhodesia would change if Mr Smith were to retire from the scene; looking at it from Mr Smith's point of view, however, she could well understand that he would wish to hang on until recognition was certain. The Prime Minister went on to say that she thought it was essential to make a thorough assessment of the relationship between the guerrillas and their supporters and how these could be changed to the disadvantage of the former. We should look for any leverage which the UK could bring to bear on the Front Line Presidents to induce them to deny money or territory to the Patriotic Front forces. Lord Carrington said that one future possibility might be a fresh test of acceptability of an amended constitution: if this were to be internationally supervised, or at least internationally recognised, the ground would be cut from under the feet of Nkomo and Mugabe, who would be reluctant to take part in an election themselves since their relatively meagre popular support would thereby be exposed. Lord Carrington told the Prime Minister that the Soviet Union were evidently trying to persuade the Front Line Presidents to form a Rhodesian Government in exile but Lord Harlech thought that the Russians could be encouraged not to make trouble, on the grounds that this would endanger the ratification of the SALT 2 Treaty. Lord Carrington said that if the United States were to lift sanctions within the next few weeks, the UK would be in a very difficult position at Lusaka.

---

1 Lord Harlech left for Southern Africa on 11 June and returned on 22 June.
2 M. Valéry Giscard d'Estaing, President of France, 1974-81.
3 Mr Allard Loewenstein.

The Prime Minister agreed that Lord Harlech would have to see Nkomo and Mugabe, since they were essential factors in bringing about a ceasefire, distasteful though she found the prospect. (The Prime Minister asked whether Mugabe was still receiving aid from the Chinese: I should be grateful for advice on this.)

There was some discussion on what would happen to Nkomo and Mugabe, and to their guerrilla forces, if the new Government in Salisbury were to win recognition: how would Presidents Kaunda and Machel get rid of them? Lord Harlech said that it might prove necessary to send a minimal Commonwealth force to give President Kaunda some assistance in clearing the guerrillas out of Zambia.

The Prime Minister said that it was essential to make President Kaunda do something about the ground-to-air missiles in guerrilla hands in advance of the CHGM in Lusaka. If the missiles could once be taken away from the guerrillas, it might prove possible to ensure that they did not receive any more. The Queen's visit to Zambia, and the Conference in Lusaka, were strong cards which should be used to put pressure on President Kaunda.

Yours ever,
BRYAN CARTLEDGE

No. 19

Minute from Sir A. Duff to Rhodesia Department, 19 June 1979
Confidential (FCO 36/2529)

I attended yesterday evening a meeting between the Prime Minister and Mr Ramphal. The Prime Minister said a good deal about her attitude towards the Rhodesia problem, and the need she foresees to make her attitude absolutely clear to her fellow Heads of Government. A study of the record will show you the sort of things that, at present, she has it in mind to say.[1] You will conclude that we shall need a very careful brief and speaking note if we are to persuade her that the discussion on Rhodesia in Lusaka does indeed provide an opportunity to carry the Commonwealth along with her, rather than confronting them with all the facts which they find so unpalatable.

2. In this general connection, I believe it might be useful if we were to collect, from this conversation and from others, those of the Prime Minister's opinions which we believe to be unfounded or which are likely to be presented in such a way as to produce the worst possible reaction amongst her African interlocutors. Once we have such a collection, I would hope that it would be possible to counter her misapprehensions either in the brief for Lusaka, or in a separate letter to Mr Cartledge. Obviously this needs very careful handling, but I think it has to be done.

J. MOYSE[2]
FOR (ANTONY DUFF)

---

1 Not printed.
2 Ms Jacqueline Arlette Moyse, Personal Assistant to Sir A. Duff.

No. 20

Minute from Mr Renwick to Sir A. Duff, 20 June 1979
Confidential (FCO 36/2480)

Rhodesia

1. The Secretary of State has asked for some preliminary consideration to be given to future options, including our course of action if it is not in fact possible to achieve significant changes or improvements in the internal settlement. You may wish to have some thoughts to focus discussion when Lord Harlech returns.

2. It is clear from Lord Harlech's consultations that it would be extremely difficult to justify the granting of legal independence even to our friends in Africa—and elsewhere—unless we are able to satisfy ourselves about the Constitution and its acceptability.

3. Our preliminary thinking in the Department is that, subject to Lord Harlech's views, the best way ahead may be for us to try to agree with Bishop Muzorewa:

(*a*) some *limited amendments to the Constitution*, relating in particular to the number of white seats and the blocking minority and to modification of the public service commissions in such a manner as to permit progressive Africanisation; and

(*b*) a *test of acceptability* of the amended Constitution.

4. In our discussions with Bishop Muzorewa we should make it clear that it is our responsibility to satisfy ourselves about the constitutional basis on which legal independence is granted. Bishop Muzorewa is not therefore in a position to present us with a *fait accompli* in relation to the Constitution. For the Constitution to be legal, it has to be agreed by us.

5. This line of approach would go some way to meet the requirement stated by all of Lord Harlech's interlocutors, including Presidents Banda and Seretse Khama, that the final basis for a solution must flow from HMG and not from the internal settlement; and that there must be some impartial test of the acceptability of what has been achieved. We should impress on Bishop Muzorewa that if we granted independence simply on the basis of the *status quo* it is unlikely that even the Americans, French and Germans would follow us. There would be no prospect of achieving a de-escalation of the war.

6. If it is not possible to secure the Bishop's agreement to amendments to the Constitution which would improve his chances and ours of winning wider acceptance, it would still be open to us to insist on a test of *acceptability of the existing Constitution*. If the Bishop refused such a test, we should be satisfied in withholding the granting of legal independence. Sanctions would, however, be allowed to lapse in November. This would leave us in the awkward position in the United Nations—we should be in formal breach of our obligations—but this is a situation in which the Americans have found themselves before and are likely to again.

7. If this approach is presented—as it is intended to be—as designed to help the Bishop, it should not come to that. It should be in the Bishop's interest to agree to limited amendments of the Constitution. We could then present the constitutional arrangements as flowing from us. It should be possible to create

a degree of political momentum which would help to ensure that the test was positive. Lord Cledwyn Hughes[1] might perhaps be involved in it.

8. Among the *white community*, the business and farming leaders will be prepared to contemplate modest constitutional changes. The difficulty, as always, will lie with the Rhodesia Front. It should, however, be possible to achieve agreement if we can enlist the support of Bishop Muzorewa and Mr David Smith. It will be important to impress upon them that, while they may take lifting of sanctions virtually for granted, it is worth making a further effort for the major prize of legal independence and the degree of international acceptance that will ensue.

9. We should make it clear that *we are not looking for changes on a scale which would be likely to upset the confidence of the white community.* We should make it equally clear that the departure of Mr Smith and Mr Van der Byl is a *sine qua non*[2].

10. This approach should be accompanied by *moves to demonstrate that the Patriotic Front are the obstacle to a wider agreement.* If the Font Line Presidents continue to insist, as they no doubt will, that they must be included, we should challenge them to demonstrate whether they could deliver the Patriotic Front for a reasonable constitutional settlement (we would not allow them to block an agreement between us and Muzorewa); or for a genuinely fair test of opinion. If the Front Line Presidents were in a position to commit the Patriotic Front to participate in new elections under some form of neutral supervision, we should be bound to consider this: it would offer the prospect of an end to the war. But it is most unlikely that they would be able to do so. The Patriotic Front will continue to insist, as Mugabe did to Lord Harlech, on control in advance of elections. This intransigence should be exposed.

11. I shall be submitting separately on Lord Harlech's ideas about a statement.

R.W. RENWICK

[1] British Labour politician; and Special Envoy to Rhodesia under the previous Labour Government, from November 1978 to April 1979.
[2] An essential condition.

No. 21

Minute from Mr Day to Sir A. Duff, 21 June 1979
Confidential (FCO 36/2562)

Prospects for a Settlement

1. I attach a paper recording my views on various aspects of the Rhodesia problem in the light of my discussions in Salisbury. The broad conclusions are that:
   (*a*) Smith will not easily be removed;
   (*b*) Constitutional change, and a further test of acceptability under outside supervision, are not excluded;
   (*c*) The Muzorewa Government will not, without some pressure or incentive, move at the speed required if wider international acceptance is to be achieved.

2. Against this background, HMG will need to initiate positive action if progress is to be made. Helpful initiatives will not be volunteered from within Rhodesia and seem unlikely to be forthcoming from the Patriotic Front.

3. The steps that we might now contemplate are:

(*a*) A final attempt to bring all Rhodesian Political Leaders to negotiate an agreed process for the return to legality;

(*b*) A recasting by HMG of the present Constitution to diminish the blocking power of the minority white community and to provide a Constitutional framework for a return to legality that would be endorsed by Parliament and acceptable to responsible opinion within Rhodesia and outside;

(*c*) Provision for a test of acceptability of the revised Constitution.

4. If any party or group declined to be associated with such steps they would have to understand that they would have no veto on further progress. I believe that the Muzorewa Government could be brought to accept proposals on these lines.

D.M. DAY

ENCLOSURE IN NO. 21

Prospects for a Settlement

1. The attitude of the various elements within Rhodesia to proposals for a settlement cannot be stated with certainty. The following is an assessment based on my discussions during the past three weeks.

The Political Future of Ian Smith

2. Smith still attracts the support of a fair number of the white population. They concede he has made many mistakes. They blame him for the uncertainty and the suffering of the present. But in a strange way they still trust him to see them through. He himself feeds on this attitude. We shall not see a concerted effort by the whites to induce him to withdraw. He believes that his continued presence in Government; at least for the time being, is essential to ensure continued 'responsibility'. He can't bring himself to go until he is confident that the internal agreement and the resulting government is going to survive more or less intact, with sanctions off and Rhodesia given constitutional sovereignty and independence. Bishop Muzorewa shows no disposition to force a show-down with Smith. He needs the whites in the Security Forces and the administration to keep his government safe and efficient. He may believe that he has to accept Smith as the price for white support. To a degree he is right. What the Bishop does not however recognise is that Smith needs him more than *vice-versa.* The internal settlement could survive Smith's departure (and would be strengthened thereby). It could not survive the defection of the Bishop and the UANC.

Conclusion

Smith will not go quietly. The whites must be brought to realise that he is now a threat to stability, not its guarantor. The Bishop must be encouraged to use the leverage he has to get Smith to stand down.

The Constitution

3. The Constitution is a compromise hammered out by the three black parties and the one white party to the 3 March agreement. Smith probably secured more in-built white protection than he expected—or needed. There should be scope for amendments which will not provoke a white exodus or undermine the morale of

the Security Forces. The Bishop shows no sign at present of taking any initiative in this direction and will certainly not be prompted to do so by his white advisers. He will have to be encouraged either by HMG or by some of his black associates. He will probably also have to be advised which aspects of the Constitution should be amended to make it:

(*a*) more acceptable to international opinion;

(*b*) still acceptable to the whites; and

(*c*) a document which HMG could commend to Parliament as fulfilling all of the Six Principles.

Conclusion

The Constitution is not regarded as inviolate. The Bishop will have to be led into amending it. Moderate changes will not drive the whites out.

Test of Acceptability

4. There will be a reluctance to embark upon a further general election or test of acceptability. The recent election was costly in money and manpower. It involved an enormous security effort. A further test in similar conditions would impose a heavy burden. If, however, this was the price to pay for an ultimate solution to the Rhodesian problem, it would be accepted. The test would therefore need to be on a basis which would produce an outcome which would, in any circumstances, be acceptable to HMG. This means that any constitutional arrangements put to the test, or the constitutional arrangements under which such a test were held, would have to be in accordance with the Six Principles. A straight contest, could it be arranged, between the existing Constitution (as amended) and a PF Constitution (should it be prepared) could present problems. The latter would be unlikely to accord with the Six Principles. If it were nevertheless accepted by the majority of the people of Rhodesia, HMG would have to decide which of the Six principles had precedence.

Conclusion

A further test of acceptability would be accepted inside Rhodesia if it were clearly seen to be the final step before a legal transfer of power.

Further Negotiation

5. The Bishop has said that he will talk further with the FLS and the PF. He will not however, agree to talk himself out of power. He regards himself as the elected leader of the people of Rhodesia. He will only negotiate from that position of strength. Whereas he could almost certainly be brought to discuss amendments to the Constitution (para 3 above), he will not agree to start again from scratch. He will argue that it is for the external leaders to put their parties and policies before the Rhodesian electorate and accept the verdict of the ballot box, which he is prepared to do. He takes this view in the almost certain knowledge that the external leaders will *not* be prepared to proceed on that basis and that his position is not therefore seriously at risk.

Conclusion

The Bishop would agree to further talks with the PF but sees no prospect of these arriving at any mutually acceptable solution.

Internationally Supervised Elections

6. If there were to be a further test of acceptability, with or without PF participation,

it could not be held under the sole auspices of the present Rhodesian Government. Within Rhodesia, the preference would probably be for the test to be conducted by HMG on terms agreed with the present Government. This is because they would regard HMG as (*a*) fair and (*b*) disposed to achieve a positive result. They would not necessarily reject further outside involvement, subject to the following reservations:

(*a*) *The United States*

The Carter Administration is suspect, following the Presidential Determination. Nevertheless the significance of US support and recognition is recognised. The Bishop, having studied and lived in the US, attaches importance to his relationship with Washington. US involvement in a test would be accepted;

(*b*) *The Commonwealth*

The Commonwealth is regarded as generally sympathetic to the PF. Its involvement in a test would not be welcomed. There would be strong resistance to the participation of any of the Front Line Commonwealth countries or Nigeria, who would not be regarded as impartial. We need not, however, exclude the inclusion of less committed states such as Australia, India, Kenya and Sierra Leone.

(*c*) *The OAU*

OAU participation would be less acceptable than that of the Commonwealth. The Government would only be brought to accept this if they were confident that OAU endorsement of the outcome was assured. They would not be prepared to countenance a situation in which HMG found the outcome acceptable, and the OAU rejected it. (But neither would HMG.)

(*d*) *The United Nations*

The reputation of the United Nations is low, with both black and white. They would prefer to avoid UN participation in any further test, though would go along with it, if essential. There would however, be reluctance to any suggestion that the UN should itself conduct the test. The prime responsibility would have to be that of HMG, with such outside support as they considered desirable and the internal Government regard as tolerable.

Conclusion

The preference would be for any further test to be conducted by HMG, with minimal outside involvement.

The Credibility of the Muzorewa Government

7. The Bishop has yet to convince opinion outside Rhodesia and some within the country that he is in firm command of a genuine majority government. Neither he, nor a number of his Ministers, seem to recognise that some early tangible evidence is required to demonstrate the reality of the transfer of power. The Bishop's inclination, encouraged by his white advisers, will be to move cautiously and by compromise. He and his Ministerial colleagues do not have the fervour or ideological zest of other African nationalist leaders. Their style and approach is more European than contemporary African. This renders them suspect. We will not be able to change the Bishop's nature. We shall, however, have to continue to impress upon him the need for demonstrable change and to encourage him to adopt bolder actions and policies. We will have to work direct upon the Bishop and upon those most closely associated with him, such as the Deputy Prime Minister.

Conclusion

The Bishop will not of his volition, move at the speed that we would wish in order to enhance the credibility of his Government in the Third World. We will have to urge him on.¹

---

1 In a minute of 25 June, Sir A. Duff asked: '(*a*) how do we bring the whites to realise that Ian Smith should go, and that the Constitution must be amended' and '(*b*) how to bring the Bishop and his colleagues not only to accept the need for demonstrable change, but to do something about it?' In a minute of 26 June Mr Day responded that many white Rhodesians accepted that Ian Smith's continued participation in the government was a major obstacle to a settlement but few were prepared to call publicly for his departure. The only way to force the issue would be to make it clear that his departure would finally open the way to recognition and the lifting of sanctions. Until then, all that was possible was to keep up discreet pressure in this direction. He also believed that white Rhodesians would accept further amendments to the Constitution provided they did not undermine the overall stability of the government and the changes led irrevocably to recognition and the removal of sanctions. Mr Day thought point (*b*) was more difficult, and all they could do was continue to press the Bishop and his colleagues on the need for demonstrable change and persuade them that reasonable changes would not frighten the majority of the whites out of Rhodesia. The areas to concentrate on were political detainees, prohibited immigrants, censorship, and Africanisation. Two other areas on which progress would help would be redistribution of the land and improvement in educational facilities and prospects for black Rhodesians.

No. 22

Minute from Mr Barlow to Mr Wall, 25 June 1979
Covering Confidential (FCO 36/2563)

Rhodesia—Lord Harlech's Report

1. I attach copies of Lord Harlech's report on his mission to Africa from 11 to 22 June.

P. J. BARLOW
RHODESIA DEPT.

ENCLOSURE IN NO. 22

Rhodesia: Moving Towards a Settlement

1. The purpose of the mission to Africa which I undertook from 11 to 22 June was to begin a process of consultation with African and other governments in order to promote the Government's stated objective for Rhodesia—a return to legality in conditions of the widest possible international recognition, and a de-escalation of the war.

2. In the course of this first round of visits, my task was to consult the 'Front Line' Presidents (i.e. those of Tanzania, Zambia, Botswana, Mozambique and Angola), the Nigerian government and President Banda of Malawi in an attempt to establish:

(*a*) to what extent they were prepared to accept that fundamental political change has taken place in Rhodesia, and

(*b*) what prospect there was of their supporting or at least acquiescing in a settlement of the Rhodesian question which is based on that political change or on some further development of it.

I also met leaders of the external Rhodesian nationalist parties (ZAPU and ZANU) in order to hear their own views on recent developments in Rhodesia and to gauge the prospects for their joining in some wider agreement which would take those developments as its starting point. A summary of my telegraphic reports on these meetings is annexed.[1]

3. In explaining the government's objectives and my mission to those I met, I generally sought to make the following points:

(*a*) Successive British governments, including the present government, have been committed to bringing Rhodesia to legal independence on the basis of the six principles.

(*b*) Political change has taken place in Rhodesia on lines which in the Government's view can be argued to satisfy to a very large extent those principles. It is not alone in welcoming this change (I cited the views of President Carter and President Moi as instances of this). But it is also aware that the change has been criticised as not going far enough.

(*c*) The government has genuinely not made up its mind about the next steps to be taken towards achieving its objectives and wishes to consult other governments before deciding. There is thus no question of merely 'playing for time', until, say, after the Commonwealth Heads of Government Meeting.

(*d*) The British and American governments take a similar view of what has happened in Rhodesia and we agree with them that Bishop Muzorewa's government should not be recognised or sanctions lifted at this time.

4. My aim then was to try to initiate as soon as possible a discussion of the ways by which the Government might move towards its objective. At no point did I suggest that the Government was itself trying to establish further conditions which Rhodesia would have to satisfy before independence could be granted. My concern was rather to try to draw out from those I met a statement of what might have to be done, even as a mere matter of form, to carry them with us in pursuing the Government's objective.

5. It was obvious that not one of the governments whose leaders I met would give us even tacit support if we granted Rhodesia independence on the basis of the *status quo*. There was a unanimous view that, whatever the content of an eventual settlement, in form it must be seen to be British and not merely the legalisation after the event of a solution which Britain, the colonial power, has played no part in working out. Going on from there, however, the course of my discussions showed that there were two broad areas of concern to almost everyone I met:

(*a*) the present constitution and power structure of Zimbabwe Rhodesia, and

(*b*) the need for some further step which would either bring about a wider agreement among the parties or settle in some other satisfactory way their conflicting claims to have the support of the people.

The Constitution

6. Under this heading I am including everything which relates to the *status quo* in Rhodesia. There are several features of this about which almost everyone I met expressed serious misgivings once we had embarked on a discussion of the options which seemed to be open to HMG.

---

[1] Not printed.

7. In the first place, it is clear to me that there can be little hope of gaining wider acceptance of a Rhodesian government which includes *Mr Ian Smith*. He is universally distrusted and regarded as a symbol of white domination. It is true that some regard his personal position as less important than what they see as the disproportionate powers given to the whites as a group under the new constitution (which I discuss later). Others (like President Nyerere) would be prepared in theory to see him play a role if he were elected as part of what they would regard as a genuine democratic process. But so long as he remains in office on present terms even the most moderate African states will maintain a reserved attitude to Bishop Muzorewa, and the Patriotic Front will have a major propaganda advantage. It seems essential to the Government's objective that he should first leave government, and, if possible, political life as a whole, for good.

8. Everyone I spoke to also expressed concern about certain features of the *constitution* itself. I do not believe we should encounter serious opposition in the Commonwealth to the idea of a least temporary special representation for the whites in Parliament or even in Government. There are many precedents for this in other constitutions which we have granted at independence. What does encounter strong resistance is the power given to the whites at present to block constitutional changes on their own.

9. There is also much concern about the need to affirm government control over the armed forces and the police, and about the powers of the white-dominated commissions controlling senior appointments in the armed forces, police, judiciary and civil service. The Government's hand would in my view be strengthened if we could secure some modification of these provisions of the constitution. Alternatively, or in addition, the Rhodesians might modify or balance their effect by some extra-constitutional commitment to an effective policy of Africanisation.

Acceptability

10. It was repeatedly put to me that the new constitution had never been submitted to a test of its acceptability to the black electorate and that the election could not be interpreted as such a test. If we ourselves, or some other impartial authority, were to carry out such a test of the constitution, preferably amended in the respects which have attracted most criticism and presented as a British proposal, this would carry much weight. Such a test would in present conditions probably have to take the form of a properly conducted referendum or election on the basis of an electoral roll if it were to carry conviction. A commission of enquiry would probably not be enough, despite the precedent of the Pearce Commission which is regarded as having been impartial. However if it had reached an opposite conclusion I expect it would have had a very different reputation.

11. This question is, however, almost inextricably linked with that of a possible wider agreement between Bishop Muzorewa and the external parties. As President Nyerere pointed out to me, we have not found tests of acceptability a necessary preliminary to independence in the case of other colonies where a constitution has been drafted at a conference of all the parties concerned and with their general approval. There is probably not the slightest chance that a meeting of all the Rhodesian parties now would produce agreement on an independence constitution—though if it did, that would clearly eliminate the need for a separate test

of acceptability and we could go straight for an election on the basis of the new constitution as the preliminary to independence. But to convene such a conference might be a necessary step towards proposing a constitution acceptable to us and the Salisbury parties, while at the same time exposing the intransigence of the Patriotic Front. A subsequent test of acceptability might be desirable in that case in order to weaken Front Line support for the Patriotic Front still further and to demonstrate that Bishop Muzorewa was adopting a reasonable attitude. But it must be at least doubtful whether a test of acceptability would carry conviction unless we had gone through the preliminary of a conference (or at any rate an attempt to convene a conference). African governments are great believers in precedent. A positive test of acceptability would in any case still have to be followed by new elections in which either all parties took part, or those who did not could be seen to have excluded themselves on unreasonable grounds.

12. My consultations during this round suggested that any idea of establishing a Commonwealth or African 'contact group' to explore the possibility of agreement between the two sides would arouse little enthusiasm. It would suggest a parallel with Namibia which most would find unacceptable, and would be criticised as an attempt to evade our duty as the colonial power. I have also found it difficult to imagine a composition for such a 'contact group' which would be acceptable to all parties and at the same time even remotely sensible.

13. Nor did I find much interest in the concept of a temporary return to legal dependent status as a preliminary to legal independence (I prefer 'return to legal dependent status' to 'return to legality' because Rhodesia would also, in a sense, 'return to legality' if we granted legal independence). We should not dismiss this idea ourselves if it seems at a later stage to offer a way of lifting sanctions without more extensive damage to our interests. But we cannot expect it to seem more relevant to others until we have advanced much closer towards a means of achieving our overall objective. If we do decide to adopt this device, it will clearly have to be on fairly stringent conditions. We could not for example, afford to contemplate a situation in which a legally recognised dependent government in Rhodesia was carrying out attacks on Mozambican and Zambian territory for which we would be held responsible.

Conclusion

14. In the broadest terms my conclusion is that we need not despair of an internationally acceptable solution which would take as its *de facto* starting point the present settlement in Rhodesia. But:

(*a*) Such a solution would have to be recognisably British, not Rhodesian, in its terms;

(*b*) It would have to include some amendment of the *status quo,* including the departure of Mr Smith and elimination of the white veto in parliament; and

(*c*) There would have to be some means of neutralising the claims of the Patriotic Front through an attempted negotiation, a test of acceptability, a new election or some combination of two or three of these devices.

15. At an early stage I think it would be useful if I could discuss my findings so far with the Americans and also explore the present areas of difficulty with Bishop Muzorewa and, possible, the South Africans. But before doing so, I would need

to know at least in broad outline how we now intended to proceed. It could also be that at some time in the future I should have further consultations with at least some of the Front Line Presidents, but much will depend on how things go at the Commonwealth Heads of Government Meeting in August.

HARLECH

No. 23

Note for the Record by Mr Cartledge (No. 10), 26 June 1979
Confidential (PREM 19/107)

Rhodesia

The Foreign and Commonwealth Secretary, Lord Harlech and Sir Antony Duff called on the Prime Minister on 26 June at 10.30 in order to discuss the outcome of Lord Harlech's first mission in Southern Africa and its implications for the Government's next moves. *Lord Harlech* agreed with the Prime Minister's conclusion, from his reporting telegrams, that no change of heart would take place among the Front Line Presidents unless there was some amendment to the present constitution of Zimbabwe-Rhodesia. He said that even President Banda and Sir Seretse Khama were unable to stomach the idea of a constitution which had been cobbled together by Mr Smith and his assistants and owed nothing to UK sponsorship. The Africans seemed to attach great importance to British input into any constitutional arrangement: even the Nigerians admitted that the UK's record on independence was good. It was, therefore, important to give the constitution a measure of UK sponsorship. *The Prime Minister* commented that the constitutional arrangements which had been offered to Rhodesia in 1963 and then on 'Tiger' and 'Fearless' were in fact less favourable than the present constitution.

The Foreign and Commonwealth Secretary said that there were certain constraints of timing on the Government's future steps. There was a House of Lords debate on 10 July. Bishop Muzorewa would be going to Washington on 7 July and to London, where he would see the Prime Minister, on 11 or 12 July. Lord Carrington said that he proposed that Lord Harlech should go to Salisbury on 2 July, have exploratory discussions with Bishop Muzorewa and then report to a meeting of OD on 5 July.

Lord Carrington went on to say that it was clear that if the UK were to recognise Zimbabwe-Rhodesia straight away, without securing any amendments to the constitution, nobody in black Africa would support us. If, on the other hand, the UK were to make arbitrary changes in the constitution, the Government would have considerable political difficulties at home. It was therefore essential to convince Bishop Muzorewa that he must himself introduce constitutional changes. Sir Antony Duff was working out the minimum degree of change which would be necessary to win African support without upsetting the Rhodesian whites. Lord Harlech's consultations had shown that some of the Front Line Presidents accepted that there had to be a degree of constitutional entrenchment for the whites. If the Bishop could be persuaded to move beyond purely cosmetic changes towards a position which other Africans might be disposed to accept, the British Government could then make a public proposal to the effect that the constitution would be amended in certain respects, which would be specified, and that they therefore wished to invite the Patriotic Front Leaders and Bishop Muzorewa to attend a constitutional conference in London. One of two things would then happen. Either the Patriotic Front would refuse the invitation, in which case they would be publicly wrong-footed: or they would attend the conference with the result that it would break down and they would be seen to be responsible for this. In either event, the British Government could then recognise Zimbabwe-Rhodesia on the basis of the amended constitution.

The Prime Minister said that it would be important to ensure that the amended constitution had aspects in common with the 'standard' UK-sponsored constitutions which had been given to Tanzania, Kenya, Uganda and other countries; a degree of similarity would be needed for use in argument with the Front Line Presidents. *Sir Antony Duff* agreed and said that the amended constitution had to be sufficiently similar to the existing one but at the same time sufficiently different to be defensible outside Rhodesia. At present, the FCO judgement was that the first factor was the more important of the two. As an example of the kind of change which might be made, Sir Antony Duff said that the white representatives in Parliament could be reduced from 28 to 20 and the arrangements for Commissioners could be altered. *Lord Carrington* agreed that the power of the Commissions to impose a veto was a major problem with the present constitution.

The Prime Minister enquired about the timescale which was envisaged for this procedure. *Lord Carrington* said that he thought that the Prime Minister might float the Government's ideas at the CHGM in Lusaka. *The Prime Minister* indicated that she thought that progress would have to be faster than this, since Bishop Muzorewa's party might otherwise fall to pieces before the Government had taken action. *Lord Carrington* said that Sir Antony Duff would be giving further thought to the question of timing and proposals would be put to the Prime Minister in due course.

The Prime Minister said that, in answer to questions in the House, she would say that Lord Harlech's purpose during his forthcoming visit to Salisbury would be to engage in friendly consultations with Bishop Muzorewa in order to find a basis for a way forward.

In a short discussion of the activities of Mr Tiny Rowland and Lonrho[1], *Lord Carrington* commented that Mr Rowlands was evidently trying to cobble together an opposition faction in the African National Congress which could eventually topple Bishop Muzorewa and bring Nkomo back to Salisbury.

In further discussion, it was agreed that the suggestion that junior FCO Ministers might begin to disclose some of the Government's thinking to backbenchers in the corridors of the House should not be pursued. Enough would be happening during the next few weeks to convey the feeling of movement and Lord Carrington would say in the debate on 10 July that the Government would have certain proposals to make in due course. It was agreed that a meeting of OD should be arranged for 5 July.

---

1 Mr Rowland was chief executive, later Chairman, of the London and Rhodesian Mining and Land Company (Lonrho), 1962-93.

Lord Carrington told the Prime Minister that in Mr Andy Young's view the US House of Representatives would not support the lifting of sanctions. If they did, President Carter would veto. But, in Mr Young's view, the President would not impose his veto if the Zimbabwe-Rhodesia constitution had been modified in the meantime. Mr Young had indicated that the British Government should not read too much into President Carter's Determination on the sanctions issue; his main concern had been to establish the best basis for himself on which to argue with Congress. Mr Young thought that President Carter was basically in favour of Bishop Muzorewa. It was agreed that when the Prime Minister saw President Carter bilaterally in Tokyo she should inform him about Lord Harlech's mission and consultations with Bishop Muzorewa but that she should not, at this stage, apprise him of the Government's plans for further moves. She would impress on him the need for Bishop Muzorewa to be made aware, when he visited Washington, of the importance of being seen to govern in Salisbury and to make his government a going concern. The Prime Minister would tell President Carter that Lord Harlech's talks had revealed a measure of flexibility among the Front Line Presidents; and that they had shown that there was some possibility of finding a formula in which they could acquiesce—there was a chink of light, she would say, for a possible solution. The Prime Minister would also stress to President Carter that the Front Line Presidents would not necessarily object to a special constitutional position for the whites in Zimbabwe-Rhodesia.

Uganda

In a short discussion of current developments in Uganda, *the Prime Minister* agreed that the British Government should take no action on the question of recognition of President Binaisa's regime for the time being but should await developments. She did not dissent from Lord Carrington's suggestion that ex-President Lule[2] should be allowed to come to the UK when President Nyerere agreed to release him from detention.

2 Mr Yusuf Kironde Lule, President of Uganda, 13 April 1979-20 June 1979.

No. 24

Minute from Mr Renwick to Sir A. Duff, 26 June 1979
Confidential (FCO 36/2539)

Rhodesia: Discussions with US Officials

1. Mr Moose and Mr Lake from the State Department will call on Lord Harlech at 10:30 am tomorrow. They will be accompanied by Mr Seitz from the US Embassy and by Mr Davidow, who, though nominally based in the US Embassy in Pretoria, will be the US representative in Salisbury.

2. After the discussions with Lord Harlech, the talks will be continued about 11.15 a.m. in your office. Lunch has been arranged at Kettners at 12:45.

3. I attach a short note which might serve as a basis for the discussions.

R.W. RENWICK

Enclosure in No. 24

Rhodesia: Points to Make to US Officials 27-28 June

1. We welcome Mr Vance's statement of 12 June. The concept of 'encouraging further progress' is the way we intend to proceed.

2. Lord Harlech's talks in Africa suggested that there is a widespread mood of weariness with the war. We believe that we have convinced African leaders that we are not just playing for time. Bishop Muzorewa's claims were not dismissed out of hand. There was a disposition to acknowledge that some progress had been made. But to gain acceptance in Africa it seems clear that:

(*a*) A solution will have to stem from us, as the legal authority, and not purely from the internal settlement;

(*b*) It will have to include some improvements on the *status quo*, including the departure of Smith and the removal of the white veto in parliament, and

(*c*) It will have to involve a final attempt to resolve the conflicting political claims of Muzorewa and the Patriotic Front.

3. Lord Harlech will be putting these points to the Bishop next week before he leaves Salisbury for Washington. We will report his response to the Americans. We hope that they will strongly support the action we will be taking with the Bishop; and will make clear to him that, if he wishes to win international acceptance, he must work with us to achieve this. There is a danger that the Bishop will believe that he can get sanctions lifted without further changes. It should be made clear to him that his real need is for international acceptance. Otherwise there will simply be an intensification of the war.

4. In the meantime we shall be making clear to the Front Line States and Nigeria and to other African governments that we have taken note of their views, that we are reflecting on them, that the next step will be for Lord Harlech to visit Salisbury, and that we will be continuing our consultations with them. It would be helpful if the US government would now support our position with the Front Line Presidents and other African governments by making clear, in their contacts with them, before the OAU meetings in July, that we are engaged in genuine consultations, that we want to proceed in cooperation with our friends in Africa, and that the possibility of an attempt to achieve a wider agreement is not excluded. We hope that they will put it to OAU governments that it will be unhelpful to the prospects for a settlement to accord exclusive recognition to the Patriotic Front and that there is a need to recognise that Muzorewa represents a very large section of Rhodesian opinion.

5. The Americans are likely to insist on the need to make a genuine effort to bring in the Patriotic Front. On this we might say that we recognise that it is important that an opportunity should be offered to the Patriotic Front to come in. Lord Harlech's conversations with them did not give us much encouragement to believe that either wing of the Patriotic Front is at present ready to discuss a settlement except on terms which are neither compatible with political reality in Rhodesia nor defensible to British—or, we suppose, American—opinion. It is as desirable as ever to get, if we can, a settlement which will end the war. But we cannot negotiate on the basis of a Patriotic Front takeover.

No. 25

Memorandum by Lord Carrington for the Cabinet Defence and Oversea Policy Committee, 2 July 1979[1]
OD(79)11, Secret (CAB 148/183)

Rhodesia

1. Our objective is to bring Rhodesia to legal independence by the Autumn with the widest possible international acceptance.

2. Lord Harlech's consultations showed that a solution stemming purely from the Internal Settlement would not attract the support even of Presidents Banda and Seretse Khama (I am arranging for his report to be circulated to the Committee). If we proceed simply to legalise the *status quo,* we are unlikely to be able to carry other Western countries—including the French, Germans and Americans—with us. This would be liable to lead to an intensification of the war, with increased Soviet and Cuban involvement.

3. Opposition to Bishop Muzorewa's Government focusses chiefly on defects in the Constitution. There is a general demand that HMG should make their own proposals for a solution, and that the eventual independence constitution should be seen to stem from us.

4. As the constitutionally responsible authority, we cannot in any event disclaim responsibility for the constitutional arrangements under which Rhodesia is brought to legal independence.

5. We could hope to arrive at a settlement which would command a wider measure of international acceptance (though not that of the more radical African states) by:

(*a*) persuading Bishop Muzorewa's government to accept changes to the Constitution;

(*b*) attempting to reach agreement on these changes and, in the likely event of Patriotic Front intransigence, demonstrating that it was the Patriotic Front who were the obstacles to a wider settlement.

6. Our aim would be a public announcement of policy after the Commonwealth conference in August. We would seek to agree this in advance with Muzorewa, through confidential consultation, or at least to persuade him not to dissent from it. Our announcement would be on the following lines:

(*a*) the changes that had taken place in Rhodesia marked a major advance, but we recognised that there were controversial aspects to the Constitution;

(*b*) our objective was to reach a settlement which would be consistent with the Six Principles, and which could provide for the participation of all Rhodesians;

(*c*) we had now consulted widely in the Commonwealth and Africa and were able to make our own firm proposals for a new settlement;

(*d*) as the responsible authority, we believed that the independence constitution for Rhodesia should be on the following lines. There would follow a broad outline of the main elements, which would be based on the present constitution, but would envisage a reduction in the number of white seats and of their power to block con-

---

1 The text of this memorandum had been sent in tel. No 468 of 29 June 1979 to Sir M. MacLehose (Hong Kong) and other posts. (FCO 36/2480).

stitutional amendments without some African support, and provide for changes in the defence and public service commissions to allow for Africanisation. The kind of changes we would have in mind are set out at Annex A;

(e) we are convening a conference in the first week of September to seek agreement on a constitution on these lines;

(f) when agreement has been reached we would go on to discuss how to assure ourselves that these proposals were acceptable to the people of Rhodesia as a whole, and how the first elections under the independence constitution should be conducted;

(g) after the conference, it would be for the British Parliament to approve the independence constitution and to grant independence on that basis;

(h) we would call for an immediate cease-fire.

7. The Patriotic Front might not come to such a conference, except on conditions which we would be able to describe as unreasonable. Alternatively, if they did come, it is likely that the conference would break up on Patriotic Front intransigence. We would then plan to go ahead with our constitutional proposals on the basis of acceptance by the internal parties.

8. If this is accepted as a basis for our policy and for progress towards granting legal independence to Rhodesia, a programme of preliminary steps has to be worked out:

(a) a public statement, for which Lord Harlech's consultations have shown a need, to create confidence in our intentions. In my speech in the House of Lords' debate on Rhodesia on 10 July, I would propose to say that our consultations were continuing, and that when we had completed them we would be making firm proposals to achieve our objective of bringing Rhodesia to legal independence with wide international acceptance. Although we shall come under some political pressure at home, I hope that this statement and other elements in my programme will carry us through to the organisation of African Unity Summit Meeting from 16-19 July and the Commonwealth Heads of Government Meeting (CHGM) from 1-8 August;

(b) further discussions with Bishop Muzorewa to begin to secure his acquiescence in the eventual policy statement;

(c) at the CHGM to tell the Heads of Government something of what is in our minds—the purpose being to secure their acquiescence in our general approach, while not exposing our policy in such detail that they would have a chance to try to impose conditions or constraints.

A time-table is attached at Annex B.

9. To secure international acceptance of the implementation of our constitutional proposals, we should be prepared to demonstrate the acceptability to the people of Rhodesia of what had been agreed, if possible in a manner designed to secure bi-partisan support in Britain. We should also ensure that Mr Smith honours his promise to leave the government. We should then grant legal independence to Rhodesia, lift sanctions and call upon other countries to follow suit.

10. There will be repercussions in Africa and in the Commonwealth. There have already been strong reactions in Nigeria and elsewhere. But this course of action will give us the best basis to contain these; and a firm basis also on which to deal with other Commonwealth governments at Lusaka.

ANNEX A

Controversial Features of the Rhodesian Constitution

1. Changes should be made to the Rhodesian constitution in the following main areas:

(*a*) the extent of white representation in Parliament and the power of the white representative to block legislation acting on their own; and

(*b*) the membership and terms of reference of the defence and public service commissions, which at present inhibit even gradual Africanisation.

Our objective would be to achieve changes which would not go so far as to undermine the confidence of the white community, but which would go far enough to render the independence constitution defensible to international and democratic opinion and more comparable to those we have agreed in granting independence to certain other African countries.

White Representation in Parliament

2. Special representation of white and other minorities in Parliament—at least for a limited period after independence—is acceptable in principle to much African opinion: and there are precedents elsewhere in the Commonwealth. Thus in *Tanganyika* out of the 71 seats in the existing National Assembly which was continued in office at independence 10 were reserved for Europeans on a 'reserved roll'. Thereafter, there was provision for up to five additional nominated members. In *Kenya* there was no express reservation of seats for racial minorities, but 12 out 117 seats in the Lower House were specially elected by the Constituency members sitting as an electoral college. This was designed to achieve, and did achieve, the election of Europeans. There was no comparable provision in *Nigeria*, which had no permanent non-indigenous population of any size: minority interests (essentially tribal and regional) were supposed to be protected by the Federal Structure of the Constitution.

3. Under the present Rhodesia constitution, the whites have the power, acting on their own, to block a wide range of constitutional and a very wide variety of bills, not restricted to those involving constitutional amendment, require a positive vote of 78 member before they can become law.

This situation is without parallel elsewhere.

4. Criticism of it could be met in several ways, alone or in combination, e.g.:

(*a*) the majority required to pass the bills in question could be altered so that the Europeans no longer had a blocking power by themselves;

(*b*) the number of white seats could be reduced. (But to curtail the blocking power this would need to be accompanied by a reduction in the required majority, as at (*a*), or by an increase in the black seats, as at (*c*);

(*c*) the number of black seats could be increased to give them the required majority; or

(*d*) the range of bills required to be passed by the required majority could be restricted.

5. We suggest that we might aim for 15 white seats in a Lower House of 100, with 75 votes to be required for major constitutional measures.

Powers over the Public Services and Defence Forces

6. Under the present arrangements there are independence commissions and

similar boards controlling appointments to, and removals from the Public Service, the Police Force, and Defence Forces and the Judiciary. These provisions are not objectionable in themselves, but the qualifications for membership of the commissions and boards are such that almost all members in each case will for many years be Europeans. This, coupled with the terms of reference of the Commissions, will inhibit even gradual Africanisation of the senior ranks of the Defence and Public Services and of the Judiciary. There is a need for simple amendments to attenuate the European dominance of the various commissions, to open up the way for progressive Africanisation and to give the Prime Minister a greater voice in the selection and retention of his senior officials and service commanders.

Other Matters

7. Changes in other areas are less essential. In addition, however, the present constitution makes a coalition government obligatory for the life of the first Parliament and entitles every group with more than five MPs to automatic representation in the Cabinet. The Prime Minister has to accept the parties' nominees for Cabinet seats: *He has no power to dismiss a Minister*. Bishop Muzorewa is already finding these requirements irksome and in practice almost unworkable. There may well be a need for changes in the constitutional requirements in this area, without prejudice to the political desirability of a coalition government on more normal terms.

8. There are other areas of the constitution where improvements though not essential, may be desirable—e.g. to make it easier to acquire land (with adequate compensation for existing owners) for settlement by Africans.

ANNEX B

Timetable

10 July	Lord Carrington's Speech in the House of Lords
13 July	The Prime Minister and Lord Carrington hold discussions with Bishop Muzorewa in London
1-8 August	Commonwealth Conference in Lusaka
15 August	Policy statement by HMG. We announce our intention to hold a constitutional conference, with a statement of the principles on which the Independence Constitution will be based
3-7 September	Constitutional Conference at Lancaster House. We table more specific proposals, the general lines of which should be agreed in advance with Muzorewa
October	There is a demonstration within Rhodesia (by an election, a referendum or other test) of the acceptability of the Independence Constitution
5-15 November	Rhodesia Independence Bill passed by Parliament.

No. 26

Mr Day (Mirimba Salisbury) to Lord Carrington, 3 July 1979, 6.15. p.m.[1]
Tel No. 350 Confidential, Immediate (FCO 36/2563)

From Lord Harlech: Rhodesia

1. I had a meeting lasting one and a half hours on 3 July with Bishop Muzorewa, Mundawarara (Deputy Prime Minister), Mukome (Foreign Minister), Gaylard and George Smith were also present.

2. My main impressions from the discussion were that Muzorewa:

(*a*) Has made a totally different assessment from us of the likely African reactions to a decision by HMG to grant independence and lift sanctions on the basis of the status quo:

(*b*) Deeply resents the unfairness, as he sees it, of others in Africa and elsewhere passing unfavourable judgement on a settlement which the parties in Rhodesia have worked out themselves: and

(*c*) In spite of his disappointment at HMG's not having legalised his government or lifted sanctions, is at the same time highly appreciative of the Government's general attitude towards him and of their willingness, which I emphasised, to work with him and not against him for a solution.

3. In my introductory remarks I sought to bring out the Government's determination to seize the opportunity which they saw at present to work quickly for a solution to our respective problems. There was no question of allowing any extremist party or government to stand in the way of a settlement which was by objective standards fair and reasonable and had a prospect of wide international support. At the same time, my consultations and Mr Luce's so far had shown that, despite the widespread appreciation of what had already been achieved in Rhodesia, there was criticism of some shortcomings in the present constitution and a wish for a final solution which derived its authority from Britain. Not even the most moderate African states we had consulted so far would follow our example if we simply recognised on the basis of the status quo. Nor would we get backing from our friends and allies in the United States or the EEC. This was the problem to which we now had urgently to address ourselves.

4. Muzorewa countered this vigorously, claiming that the teams he had sent round Africa immediately after the Rhodesian elections had reported to him that practically all the countries consulted had given the impression that they were simply waiting for a British lead to recognise his government. It was blatantly unfair for anyone else now to expect him to show signs of greater flexibility before they would make a move towards him. The parties to the present constitution were thoroughly representative and had had a respectable election, which was more than could be said for most of their critics. Gaylard argued at this point that whatever they did they would never get the agreement of the Front Line States to any solution which took the present set-up as its starting-point. What they needed was an end to sanctions so as to improve their prospects of winning the war. Mundawarara and Mukome spoke in support (the former with impressive fluency for a beginner in government). HMG

[1] And Information Immediate Washington; Information Priority Lusaka, Dar es Salaam, Gaborone, Maputo, Lagos, Luanda, UKMIS New York and Pretoria.

were now shifting their ground and seeking to establish fresh conditions for recognition in addition to the Six Principles. If they complied, how were they to know we would not shift our ground again?

5. I denied there was any intention of adding to the Six Principles, and in further argument I hinted very broadly to Muzorewa that, regardless of the rights and wrongs of his present stand, he might find it tactically advantageous to show himself willing to offer improvements on the status quo in order to expose the intransigence of the Patriotic Front and cut the ground from under their feet. He refused to rise to the bait and did not respond directly to my suggestion that for similar reasons he should continue to express willingness to talk to the Patriotic Front.

Conclusion

6. In spite of the Bishop's apparent stonewalling, I formed the clear impression that he was talking to a large extent for the effect on his colleagues. When you see him in London, you may perhaps find that he is susceptible to argument on the basis that constitutional changes are needed to produce a solution which will be acceptable to the British Parliament and perhaps to the international community (although he purported to believe either that they were a lost cause or would simply follow our lead). I am due to have another meeting with him tomorrow afternoon. I hope to arrange for this to be in private: in that case I shall try to probe his attitude further than was possible today. I urged him to listen carefully to Vance.

7. See MIFT[2] for a report of subsequent meetings with Ndiweni, David Smith and Ian Smith.

2 Not printed.

No. 27

Minute from Sir A. Duff to Mr Renwick, 4 July 1979
Confidential (FCO 36/2480)

Rhodesia Random Thoughts from the Bathroom

I am tempted to think that we need a further guidance to posts along the following lines:

'The press and the BBC are both tending to take the line (e.g. Michael Vestey[1] from Salisbury this morning) that we are engaged in working out a bargain with Bishop Muzorewa along the lines that we will "recognise" his government, in return for changes to the constitution and an all-party conference. This is far from the truth. We are not (not) at this stage making proposals to anyone. We are still consulting. We look forward to further discussion at CHGM. You should do everything possible to dispel the impression that

(*a*) what we are doing is seeking a way of 'recognising' Muzorewa

(*b*) we have made any proposals to anyone.

1 BBC Foreign Correspondent who spent a year reporting in Southern Africa.

In particular, you should avoid the use of the word 'recognition' which is imprecise and misleading in that it implies attachment to the present situation in Rhodesia. You should continue to emphasise that we are searching for the way to bring Rhodesia to legal independency with the widest possible international acceptance.'

2. None of the above is new, and it might be thought that it might be irritating to posts to receive this message again. But I do feel strongly that for the rest of this month we have to move quickly, on each occasion when the press are wrong footing us, to try to restore the situation. It is also I think relevant that short guidances can be used (as in the above case) as part of the attempt to influence Ministerial statements and the choice of Ministerial language at home.

3. I wonder whether we ought not at this point to make a definite assault on a selection of the African High Commissioners. Some of them are, I fear, assiduous reporters to capitals of what the British press is saying. In their capitals this, unfortunately, is likely to make as much if not more impression than what is being said by our local High Commissioners. Should we for example ask Lord Harlech to see some of the Africans on Friday?

4. It would of course be particularly important to work out in advance the press line we need for Muzorewa's visit to London next week. Having got agreement on how to present the visit, it will be important (as well as very difficult) to persuade Ministers and others to stick to it. We need some discussion with News Department and with the No. 10 Press Office, before the Bishop ever gets here, to try to ensure that the visit does not simply result in such few cards as we have being exposed prematurely.

5. As part of the process of trying to persuade the Prime Minister that there really is a hand that she could usefully play at Lusaka, which will avoid too confrontational an atmosphere and at the same time carry us forward to the policy declaration we want to make in August, this gambit should be carefully spelled out in the Secretary of State's brief for the Ministerial discussion tomorrow.

6. From the oral account I have received from Sir J. Hunt about the Prime Minister's discussion with Mr Fraser on Rhodesia, it seems that the Australians are hankering for the presentation to the CHGM of a precise proposal for 'the way forward' and for seeking if not a vote at least a consensus of approval for it. This is not at all the way we would want to handle the CHGM and we shall have to find a way of limiting the damage the Australians could do.

ANTONY DUFF

No. 28

Letter from Mr Cartledge (No. 10) to Mr Wall, 4 July 1979
Confidential (FCO 36/2506)

Dear Stephen,

Call on the Prime Minister by Senator Jesse Helms at 10 Downing Street on 4 July 1979

Senator Jesse Helms (Republican, North Carolina), following a written request by him for a private and confidential discussion with the Prime Minister about Rhodesia, called at No. 10 at 10.30 this morning by prior arrangement. He was accompanied by Mr Carbaugh[1] and another personal assistant. The following is a summary of the main points which arose during half an hour's discussion.

The Prime Minister began the conversation by telling Senator Helms that she thought it desirable that their meeting should be given no publicity. In particular, she hoped that he would not consider it necessary to inform the other Conservative Members of Parliament whom he was meeting later in the day that he had called on her. In answer to questions, No.10 would if necessary confirm that he had made a brief call on the Prime Minister, in return for the Prime Minister's own meeting with him in Washington during her visit as Leader of the Opposition. Senator Helms accepted this, but with evident reluctance.

Rhodesia

Senator Helms told the Prime Minister that when President Carter had announced his 'unfortunate' Determination concerning sanctions against Rhodesia, he had suggested to the President that he should take an early opportunity of meeting Bishop Muzorewa. President Carter had telephoned him on the following day to ask him to invite the Bishop to visit the United States as his (the Senator's) guest. This was the genesis of Bishop Muzorewa's forthcoming visit to Washington on 7 July. President Carter, Mr Vance and Dr Brzezinski[2] were taking the line that the US could not unilaterally move ahead of the UK on the Rhodesia issue. The Senator greatly feared, however, that any inordinate delay in recognising the Muzorewa Government would cause it to fall apart. The Prime Minister's own statements had been helpful but what was now needed was a clear statement by the US and British Governments together that sanctions would be lifted. This might enable Bishop Muzorewa to survive. The present mood on the Hill was generally supportive of lifting sanctions although some highly placed members of the Administration were in favour of holding back, thereby playing, in the Senator's view, into the hands of the terrorists. The best way of defeating the terrorists would be to revive the Rhodesian economy by lifting sanctions.

Mr Carbaugh said that President Carter was now seeking a way out of the impasse. The Prime Minister should make it clear that the British Government intended to lift sanctions after Bishop Muzorewa's forthcoming visits to Washington and London. If she did not make this move before the Commonwealth meeting in Lusaka, the pressures there would be hard to resist. It would be much

1 Mr John Carbaugh, foreign policy advisor to Senator Helms.
2 Mr Zbigniew Brzezinski, National Security Advisor to President Carter, 1977-81.

better to present the Lusaka meeting with a *fait accompli*. Mr Carbaugh said that it would be wrong to anticipate that in these circumstances the Commonwealth would fall apart. It would be useful if Bishop Muzorewa could have some firm indication of support and of an end to sanctions from the Prime Minister before he went to see President Carter.

The Prime Minister told Senator Helms that most African countries now accepted that there was a new situation in Rhodesia, following the elections in April. The next step was to determine whether the existing constitutional arrangements were, in accordance with the Fifth Principle, acceptable to the people of Rhodesia as a whole. The Prime Minister said that she did not share Senator Helms' approach to the Lusaka meeting. She thought it essential that the UK should attend that meeting in the position of being able to point to continuing consultations with all the parties concerned. The impact of any premature move on the forthcoming meeting of the Organisation of African Unity also had to be borne in mind. The Prime Minister said that she disagreed with Mr Carbaugh on the desirability of presenting the Commonwealth Heads of Government Meeting with a *fait accompli*: it was essential to persuade some countries to go along with the UK—a wide degree of international acceptance would be essential to the future of Bishop Muzorewa's Government, which would be gravely handicapped by an unnecessary measure of African hostility towards it. For all these reasons, the Prime Minister said, she did not think it wise to make any further move before the Lusaka meeting.

As you know, the Prime Minister wishes knowledge of her meeting with Senator Helms to be confined to the smallest possible circle. The above account, therefore, is for the personal information of the Foreign and Commonwealth Secretary only. Lord Carrington may wish to authorise you to convey the gist of it to the one or two senior officials who were directly concerned in preparing the brief for Senator Helms' call.

Yours ever,
BRYAN CARTLEDGE

No. 29

Letter from Mr Cartledge (No. 10) to Mr Wall, 13 July 1979
Confidential (PREM 19/108)

Dear Stephen,
Bishop Muzorewa's Call on the Prime Minister on 13 July, 1979
Bishop Muzorewa, accompanied by his Minister for External Affairs, Mr Mukome, called on the Prime Minister at No.10 this afternoon at 1445. The Foreign and Commonwealth Secretary and Sir Antony Duff were present at the meeting. I enclose a copy of my note of the discussion, which lasted for just over three-quarters-of-an-hour.

I should be grateful if you would ensure that the record, parts of which are particularly sensitive, is given a very restricted distribution indeed.

I am sending a copy of this letter, and enclosure, to Martin Vile (Cabinet Office).

Yours ever,
BRYAN CARTLEDGE

ENCLOSURE IN NO. 29

Note of the Prime Minister's Discussion with Bishop Abel Muzorewa, Prime Minister of Zimbabwe-Rhodesia, at 10 Downing Street on 13 July 1979

Present:

The Prime Minister	Bishop Muzorewa
Foreign and Commonwealth Secretary	Mr Mukome
Sir Antony Duff	(Minister for External Affairs)
Mr B.G. Cartledge	

When the Prime Minister had welcomed Bishop Muzorewa, and the Bishop had in turn congratulated the Prime Minister on her election victory, the *Prime Minister* said that although she did not wish to cover the same ground as Lord Carrington during the Bishop's morning session of talks with him, she thought it would be useful to summarise the British Government's position once more.

The Prime Minister told Bishop Muzorewa that everybody in the United Kingdom recognised that he and his colleagues had come a tremendously long way. She never failed to tell everybody she met that Rhodesia had held elections on the basis of one person, one vote, in which there had been a 65 per cent turn out and which had resulted in the election of a black Prime Minister, with a black President, a black majority in Parliament and a black majority in the Cabinet. Zimbabwe-Rhodesia had covered the greater part of its journey towards independence. The British Government wished to take as many people as they possibly could with them in winning acceptance for the new situation in the country; this was the purpose of the consultations which had been carried on in recent weeks. From these consultations, two points had come across very strongly. The first was that the constitution of Zimbabwe-Rhodesia would have to be comparable to the constitutions which the UK had given to other African countries at their independence. Secondly, the constitutional arrangements would have to be seen to have originated with, and to have been approved by, the UK.

The Prime Minister went on to say that the constitutional changes which the UK thought necessary would not be such as to undermine the confidence of the white population in Rhodesia. Bishop Muzorewa was very wise to insist on retaining this confidence, in the interests of his country's future economic success. The changes would, moreover, be quite small in relation to the distance which Rhodesia had already travelled. The Prime Minister pointed out to Bishop Muzorewa that the kind of changes the UK had in mind would in fact increase his own powers as Prime Minister. It was astonishing that he, as Prime Minister, should have to submit new appointments to the independent commissions. There were also too many white Members of Parliament, who were able to operate a blocking mechanism. The Prime Minister repeated that changes to these aspects of the constitution would, nevertheless, be minor in relation to what Rhodesia has already achieved. Rhodesia had already covered 90 per cent of the distance: the UK wanted her to travel the remaining 10 per cent of the way, so that the British Government could say that the constitution was legal and comparable to those which had been granted in the past.

The Prime Minister said that the British Government was determined that if they regarded revised constitutional arrangements as being right, they would not be blocked or dictated to by anybody at the conference. Having come so far, it would be foolish if Rhodesia were to fail to take the final step. The Prime Minister repeated that the British Government had no wish to undermine the confidence of the whites. They were speaking to Bishop Muzorewa as friends and they wanted to see rapid progress over the last phase. Sir Antony Duff was already engaged in a detailed comparison of the constitution of Zimbabwe-Rhodesia with the constitutions of other former British colonies in Africa. Many of these constitutions had allowed for the special representation of minorities: there could be no objection of principle to this and minorities had to be protected. The Prime Minister emphasised that the British Government were not seeking immediate or instant changes. They were concerned to work towards the ending of sanctions, as rapidly as possible; but, at the forthcoming conference in Lusaka, they would not propose to set out the constitutional changes which they had in mind in detail. This was purely a matter between Bishop Muzorewa and the UK. At Lusaka, she and Lord Carrington would simply say that they would be making proposals for a constitutional basis on which Zimbabwe-Rhodesia could be brought to legal independence. Thereafter, if the proposals were acceptable to the Bishop, the British Government would invite him and the representatives of the Patriotic Front to a conference. If the Patriotic Front refused to attend, this would not give them a power to veto over progress to independence. There would then have to be a test of acceptability but it should be possible to complete the whole process by the end of October.

Lord Carrington said that he had only one point to add, namely that unless the kind of changes which the Prime Minister had outlined took place, no country of any importance would recognise Zimbabwe-Rhodesia, even if the UK had done so. The *Prime Minister* agreed and pointed out that Lord Harlech's consultations had shown that even President Banda and President Seretse Khama had made it clear that changes to the constitution were essential. The British Government must be able to argue, with other African governments, that they had themselves accepted comparable constitutions when they had achieved independence and that they consequently had no right to object to the constitution of Zimbabwe-Rhodesia.

Lord Carrington said that it was important to be able to wrong-foot the bullies: if this were done, there would be a much better chance of putting an end to the war in Rhodesia. In a brief reference to Mr Ian Smith, the *Prime Minister* said that he would presumably leave the Government as soon as he was certain that independence and the lifting of sanctions were in prospect.

Bishop Muzorewa told the Prime Minister how much he appreciated the new and positive attitude of the British Government towards his country. The visits to Salisbury of Sir Antony Duff, Mr Day and Lord Harlech had made a very great difference to the situation and he and his colleagues in Salisbury now knew that the British Government were trying to help. The Bishop said that the Prime Minister clearly understood some of his concerns. But he still believed, on the basis of the reports which he had received from his representatives, that many in Africa would follow a clear lead from the UK. If the British Government were to decide to lift sanctions or to recognise his regime, they would find that they had support even if no changes had taken place in the existing constitution. Sanctions, after all, had not been imposed because of defects in a constitution; they had been imposed as a result of rebellion against the British Crown. But now the people of Zimbabwe-Rhodesia were sovereign and had spoken up for government by the people. Zimbabwe-Rhodesia nevertheless remained Britain's responsibility and it was therefore up to Britain to give a lead. Inevitably, there would be some shouting and name-calling: but, the Bishop said, many would follow the UK.

The *Prime Minister* replied that she wished that this were true. But it did not accord with the British Government's own information. Telegram after telegram which she had read showed that there was still some way for Rhodesia to go. The Prime Minister emphasised that it would strengthen the Bishop's own hand if he were to get rid of the commissions and if he were to increase the number of black Members of Parliament—it might be easier to add to the black membership rather than reducing the white membership.

Bishop Muzorewa said that a key problem was the fact that in the present situation all the members of the white community were sensitive and frightened. The situation following the achievement of black majority rule was in any case a delicate one: but in Zimbabwe-Rhodesia it was greatly aggravated by the war. The whites were wondering in what way Bishop Muzorewa was any different from other African leaders. He could only show them how different he was through his own actions. Any move towards constitutional change would frighten the whites. The *Prime Minister* replied that the British Government was only asking that Rhodesia should have a constitution similar to that which had been given to other African states on independence. She asked the Bishop whether it would be helpful for Lord Carrington to visit Salisbury immediately after the Lusaka conference. This might strengthen the confidence of the white population. *Lord Carrington* said that it might be better if somebody other than he were to go; such a visit could, in any case, have an unsettling rather than a reassuring effect on the whites.

The *Prime Minister* said that the opponents of the internal settlement argued that power had not really been transferred to the Africans. She assured them that it had. The critics then pointed to the blocking mechanism and the commissions. If these aspects of the constitution were changed, the critic's argument would crumble. The British Government would also be able to say that the constitution was comparable to others. It would be possible, in those circumstances, for the UK to bring the United States along with her; The American attitude had already changed significantly, as a result of the British Government's efforts.

Lord Carrington said that the United States would probably come along with the

UK. But the US would certainly not support the UK if recognition were to be given on the basis of the constitution as it stood.

Bishop Muzorewa said that Zimbabwe-Rhodesia's problem was that they had already done so much and would have hoped for some reward for what they had already achieved. For example, sanctions could be lifted now, in return for what had already been done, and legality restored in return for the further changes which the British Government wanted. This procedure would create greater confidence in the white community. If they were given some reward now, the whites would face the second stage of change with greater confidence. The *Prime Minister* said that this approach would create political problems in her own Party. The timescale of the process which the British Government had in mind would in fact be very short: once constitutional changes had been made, the UK would move very fast. *Lord Carrington* pointed out that a further difficulty in the course suggested by the Bishop would be that it would undermine the procedural approach which the Government had in mind: If sanctions had already been lifted, nobody would take the British Government's further efforts at all seriously. The *Prime Minister* asked Lord Carrington whether it would be possible for him to go to Salisbury any earlier, before Lusaka. *Lord Carrington* pointed out that this would be interpreted, at Lusaka, as collusion between London and Salisbury; the British would be accused of ganging up with the Rhodesians.

Sir Antony Duff, referring to the comparative constitutional study on which he was working, said that the independence constitutions of both Tanzania and Zambia had provided for special minority representation. *Bishop Muzorewa* agreed and commented that the Tanzanian constitution, in particular, had been extremely generous to minorities.

The *Prime Minister* repeated that it would be necessary to work very fast. Bishop Muzorewa would not have long to wait. The UK would send somebody to visit Salisbury, with specific proposals, very soon after the end of the Lusaka conference on 8 August. *Lord Carrington* said that Lord Harlech's and Mr Day's talks with members of the white community in Zimbabwe-Rhodesia showed that many whites, for example David Smith, admitted that there was a need for some change.

Mr Mukome said that the unfortunate factor in the situation was that his country was engaged in a war. Any leak concerning the possibility of constitutional change would gravely undermine the confidence of the white members of the security forces, since they would have no means of knowing how extensive the changes were likely to be. Their suspicions would be aroused. The whites argued that the British Government had set out six principles which must be fulfilled. These had all now been carried out and they would have expected the British Government to acknowledge this. Instead, they were told that there were still weaknesses in the constitution and that they could not reap the benefit of what they had done until changes had been made. They were always being asked for more. It was true that some of the changes which the British Government wanted to see concerned aspects of the constitution which the Africans themselves had tried to get rid of. But their retention was the price which the Africans had to pay for being able to keep the terrorists down, which could not be done without the help of the whites. The *Prime Minister* said that it would have to be made very clear to the white community that the changes for which the British Government were asking represented the end of the process. She told Bishop Muzorewa that she would have to take the whole of her party with her if sanctions were to be lifted. *Lord Carrington* added that unless there was some move on the constitution, a number of Conservatives would vote against the removal of sanctions.

The *Prime Minister* said that the way forward which she had indicated should be acceptable to the Bishop and his people and it would also enable the British Government to bring the Americans, and others, along with them. She and her colleagues had no interest in those who wanted the bullets to win in Rhodesia. *Bishop Muzorewa* told the Prime Minister that at the end of his meeting with President Carter, the President had said that the US Government would follow whatever lead the British Government gave.[1] *Lord Carrington* pointed out that what the President had in mind in saying this was precisely the kind of procedure which he and the Prime Minister had been outlining.

Bishop Muzorewa asked about the timetable which the Prime Minister had in mind. The *Prime Minister* said that the UK's proposals for changes in the constitution could be put forward by the middle of August and a constitutional conference convened in September. The whole process could be completed by the end of October. When the British Government made its proposals, Bishop Muzorewa could make it clear that he and his people would accept the new constitution if the UK were to grant Zimbabwe-Rhodesia legal independence. *Lord Carrington* pointed out that if Nkomo and Mugabe did, in fact, agree to attend the constitutional conference, the next steps would have to be arranged rather differently; but they were very unlikely to come. The *Prime Minister* said that if they did attend, and accepted the proposals, there would be no argument against an immediate return to legality.

Mr Mukome said that he feared that the Patriotic Front leaders might be advised by the Front Line Presidents to accept invitations to the constitutional conference in order to buy more time.

If this happened, the confidence of the whites would be undermined and Zimbabwe-Rhodesia would lose a great many of her most skilled people. He could foresee a situation in which the Patriotic Front might attend a conference and drag it out while the war continued. Sanctions would remain in force at the same time, while the Patriotic Front were supplied with more new weapons. The timescale of what the UK was proposing was much too long.

Bishop Muzorewa said that another problem lay in the Prime Minister's reference to a further test of acceptability. The British Government should not under-estimate what the people of Zimbabwe-Rhodesia had been through during the last election, turning out to vote at the risk of their lives. *Lord Carrington* said that this stage was still some way off. *Sir Antony Duff* told Bishop Muzorewa that he was permanently concerned by all the things which might go wrong along the road to a settlement. It was impossible to perceive exactly how matters would turn out: but both the British Government and the Bishop were certain of their objectives and the only sensible approach was to move forward step by step, tackling problems as and when they arose. He was now more optimistic about the prospects for a settlement than he had been for a very long time.

---

1 Bishop Muzorewa had visited Washington on 11-12 July.

Before the Conference

The *Prime Minister* said that the British Government certainly possessed the resolve to carry matters to a conclusion. *Lord Carrington* added that they were also working to a timetable.

After a short discussion of what should be said to the press, it was agreed that both sides would adhere strictly to the three paragraphs of the attached note, omitting the second paragraph of the original draft press line.

Concluding the discussion, the *Prime Minister* repeated that the British Government had the resolve to help Zimbabwe-Rhodesia towards legal independence within a limited time.

The meeting ended at 1535.

No. 30

Minute from Sir I. Sinclair to Sir A. Duff, 18 July 1979
Confidential (FCO 36/2549)

Rhodesia: UN Aspects

1. I think it might be helpful if I were to comment on Sir A. Parsons' minute of 11 July[1] which opens up the question of how we should handle the UN aspects of the Rhodesia problem in the coming months.

2. By way of introduction, it might be as well to note that, ever since we first agreed to mandatory Security Council resolutions on Rhodesia in 1965 and 1966, we have been conscious of the need to preserve some possibility of arguing that these resolutions automatically lapsed on the happening of certain events. This is why careful consideration was given to the wording of original Chapter VII determination. I recall an exchange of correspondence between myself and Sir Francis Vallat[2] as early as 1966 which bore upon this very point.

3. In considering how we should handle the UN aspects of the Rhodesia problem in the coming months, we have to bear in mind that there are at least five possible sets of political circumstances in which we may have to confront the UN problem, and that our handling of the UN aspects will almost certainly depend upon which set of political circumstances we are faced with at the time. Broadly speaking, however, I can envisage the following five different sets of circumstances:

(*a*) as a result of discussions and negotiations with the régime in Salisbury and the external parties over the next few months, the internal régime agrees to make radical constitutional changes (accompanied perhaps by a test of acceptability) sufficient to make the resulting settlement acceptable to the external parties, the Front Line States, and international opinion generally;

(*b*) as a result of discussions and negotiations with the internal régime and the external parties over the next few months, the internal régime agrees to make constitutional changes sufficient to satisfy moderate African opinion, but insufficient to satisfy the external parties, the Front Line States and the more radical Africans (in

---

1 Not printed.
2 The Foreign Office Legal Adviser, 1960-68.

this eventuality it is extremely unlikely that the moderate Africans, even if sympathetic, would publicly endorse the settlement);

(c) as a result of discussions and negotiations over the next few months, the internal régime agrees to make only presentational changes to the constitution insufficient to satisfy even moderate African opinion, far less the external parties, the Front Line States and the radical Africans;

(d) we are unable to make any progress with the internal régime over the next few months, but nonetheless it is decided, for political reasons, to enact legislation effectively giving independence to Rhodesia (on the basis of its present constitution—though there would, of course, be no need to say this and best not to);

(e) we are unable to make much progress with the internal régime over the next few months, but have not, by November, entirely given up hope of bringing about some constitutional change; it is nevertheless decided not to seek renewal of Section 2 of the Southern Rhodesia Act 1965, and the situation we are confronted with in the UN is limited to our breach of mandatory Security Council resolutions.

4. On case (a), which is no doubt very unlikely, it may be possible to envisage some positive action by the Security Council, whether in the form of a resolution or (and this may be more likely) in the form of a consensus, acknowledging in more or less direct terms that the rebellion in Rhodesia has been brought to an end and that therefore the basis for mandatory sanctions resolutions has lapsed.

5. In any of the other four sets of circumstances, it is quite clear that the basis for positive Security Council action will simply not exist, in the sense that (leaving aside possible vetoes by others) it would be impossible to obtain nine positive votes for any satisfactory Security Council resolution, far less the unanimity necessary for a satisfactory consensus.

6. Assuming that the most likely case is (b) or (c), or possibly something between the two, we are then confronted with the necessity to argue along the lines of paragraph 3 of Sir A. Parsons' minute. It is almost certain that the legal arguments which we would advance in these circumstances would be strongly challenged. There might well be at least nine votes for a resolution which would affirm the continued validity of previous mandatory sanctions resolutions; and it is clear that we should have to veto such a resolution. Nevertheless, the opponents of the settlement may well recognise that it would be damaging to their case to promote a resolution of this kind which would inevitably attract our veto, and may therefore try more subtle tactics posited on the assumption of the continued validity of existing mandatory sanctions resolutions and simply calling upon all States to continue to respect them. This would no doubt also, in the events contemplated, attract our veto, but in politically more damaging circumstances.

7. Case (d) is much more difficult. If we grant independence to Rhodesia in circumstances where we have failed to secure any changes in the constitution (despite our announced policy of seeking such changes), I doubt very much whether we can maintain with any semblance of plausibility that the rebellion has been brought to an end (the terminology on which we have to base the argument outlined in paragraph 3 of Sir A. Parsons' minute)—even though, by the grant of independence, the concept of 'rebellion' has no further meaning. To use this argument, in this particular set of circumstances, would be so unconvincing that we would be

unlikely to get even friendly Governments to pay lip service to it. If this is right, it would be damaging for us generally to rely on it. We may therefore need to try to develop a bolder line of argument for use in this eventuality. The argument might be that developments in Rhodesia over the past year, including the installation of a majority Government following upon nation-wide elections, had brought about such a fundamental change of circumstances that the issue of whether the régime currently exercising power in Salisbury was a legal or illegal régime was no longer relevant, so that the Chapter VII determination on the basis of which sanctions had been imposed, had ceased to be operative. I have no illusions about the viability of an argument on these lines. Traditionally, reference to a 'fundamental change of circumstances' argument has been the last resort of States wishing to release themselves from inconvenient treaty or other international obligations. I would like to think a bit more about how we could most respectfully run an argument of this kind in the circumstances contemplated. It is far from being satisfactory, but it may be marginally preferable to the alternative of our seeking to assert that the grant of independence to Rhodesia (without any constitutional change) had brought the rebellion to an end.

8. In case (*e*), the legal argument outlined in paragraph 3 of Sir A. Parsons' minute would *not* be available to us and we would presumably be reduced to running the purely political argument that we could not persuade Parliament to renew the legal basis for imposing sanctions under UK law (but, on this, see paragraph 10 below).

9. In all this, we have to bear in mind the relationship between the legislative action we will have to take in Parliament and possible developments in the Security Council. As soon as we go to Parliament with a Bill, we are likely to be hauled before the Security Council in an attempt to wrest the initiative from us (at least in every possible case except (*a*)). This seems to point to the desirability of rapid Parliamentary action. If there is going to be a 'bang' in any event as soon as we lay draft legislation before Parliament, the sooner it is enacted (together with any consequential subordinate legislation) the better. Otherwise, there is a danger that the outcry in New York and in Africa will have an impact upon Parliamentary consideration of the proposed legislation.

10. One further difficult problem arises in connection with case (*e*). It is *not* going to be at all easy to convince international opinion that the British Government are unable to secure from Parliament the renewal of Section 2 of the Southern Rhodesia Act 1965. This difficulty will be compounded if simultaneously we take *positive* action to revoke subordinate legislation which gives effect to mandatory sanctions and resolutions under other enactments (e.g. Exchange Control Act 1947 and Import, Export Customs Powers (Defence) Act 1939). There is the additional consideration that some of our critics will almost certainly be aware that we could, even if Section 2 of the Southern Rhodesia Act 1965 were not enacted, make provision for the application of sanctions in our domestic law by virtue of Orders in Council made under the United Nations Act 1946, which require to be laid before Parliament after being made but which otherwise require no Parliamentary approval.

11. These are inevitably by way of being preliminary comments on Sir A. Parsons' minute of 11 July. I need hardly say that I entirely agree with Sir A.

Parsons in his judgement that we must bear constantly in mind, and indeed make an integral part of our Rhodesia policy, the problem of how we are going to handle the inevitably explosive situation which (except in the most unlikely circumstances) we will be confronted with in New York.

IAN SINCLAIR

No. 31

Memorandum by Lord Carrington for the Cabinet Defence and Oversea Policy Committee, 19 July 1979
OD(79)21, Secret (CAB 148/183)

1. Following the meeting of the Committee on 5 July, I stated in my speech in the House of Lords on 10 July[1] the Government's intention to make firm proposals, once our consultations are completed, to bring Rhodesia to legal independence with wide international acceptance.

2. In their talks with him on 11 and 12 July President Carter and Mr Vance impressed on Bishop Muzorewa the need to work with us. They made clear that in their view constitutional changes would be essential to win international acceptance; and that the Bishop should make a genuine attempt to negotiate with [the] Patriotic Front. They added that they could see no prospect of a normalisation of relations with Rhodesia's neighbours so long as Mr Smith remained in the Government. In private conversation with Mr Vance, Bishop Muzorewa indicated that he was prepared to consider reducing the blocking power of the 28 white MPs, but emphasised his concern to preserve white confidence.

3. In discussion with Bishop Muzorewa in London on 13 July, the Prime Minister and I sought in the first place to leave him in no doubt about the Government's appreciation of the magnitude of his and his colleagues' achievement. Thereafter, we concentrated on the need for some measure of constitutional change which, without undermining white confidence, would make the present Constitution more comparable with those which we had granted to other African countries at independence. We also put it to him that in proceeding towards legal independence it would be essential to offer the external parties an opportunity to participate, though we should not allow them to block a settlement on terms we believed to be right and defensible internationally. It was our impression that the Bishop and his African colleagues are prepared to consider constitutional change, though for obvious reasons they are reluctant to say so at present. In this they would have the support of important elements in the European population who will be attracted by the major prize of legal independence. There will be resistance from the Rhodesia Front: Mr Ian Smith has declared himself against any change in the Constitution.

4. Our objective should be to publish, by mid-August, a statement of our outline proposals for an independence Constitution. Such a statement should meet the following criteria:

---

1 Parl. Debs., 5th ser., H. of C., vol. 401, cols. 757-763.

(*a*) It should clearly indicate an eventual independence constitution which would be comparable with the terms on which independence was granted to other Commonwealth countries, especially in Africa;

(*b*) It should enable Bishop Muzorewa to make clear to white opinion in Rhodesia that he can discuss our proposals without compromising essential minority interests. We should be ready to make a separate statement at the time the proposals are published, emphasising the importance we attach to enabling the white community to play a full part in the future of the country;

(*c*) It should be in such terms that we could claim to the African Presidents and others that a refusal by the Patriotic Front to attend a constitutional conference on this basis would be unreasonable and a proof of bad faith on their part.

5. It will be desirable to confine our initial presentation to the outline of the independence Constitution. If we exposed the full extent to which we were prepared to incorporate the substance of the existing Constitution into our own proposals, we should give the Patriotic Front and their supporters in Africa a chance to claim that we were clearly aiming for a solution based on the internal settlement. We can expect the Patriotic Front to reject any proposals we make at the Conference. But we should not make it easy for them to claim that it is not worth their while attending the Conference at all. This would defeat our objective of demonstrating that it is their intransigence which is the main obstacle to a wider agreement.

6. I attach at Annex A a draft for such a statement of our outline proposals for a Constitution. This is largely compatible with the existing Rhodesian Constitution; but the side-lined passages indicate the points on which changes will have to be made. I believe that it should be possible to secure Bishop Muzorewa's acquiescence in such changes, without serious damage to white confidence. The limited changes we have in mind are set out in Annex B which has been revised in the light of the Committee's discussion on 5 July.

7. The proposals would be issued simultaneously with an invitation to the Bishop's government and the external parties to attend a Constitutional Conference in London in early September. The terms of the invitation should make clear that:

(*a*) Our objective is agreement on an independence Constitution to be granted by Britain;

(*b*) Our proposals outline the sort of Constitution which we are prepared to enact and which we believe should commend itself to the parties and to international opinion as a basis for legal independence (though if alternative arrangements were agreed by all the parties, we should be prepared to accept a solution on that basis).

8. Immediately after the CHGM, we should begin to discuss, in detail, with the Bishop and his officials, the changes set out in Annex B, so as to be in a position to table fully worked out proposals at the Constitutional Conference. It would be my intention, in the light of our discussions with the Rhodesians, to circulate to my colleagues for approval in August the detailed proposals we would table at the conference.

9. Our aim at the CHGM in Lusaka should be to secure the acquiescence of the Heads of Government in our general approach, while not exposing our policy in such detail that they will have a chance to try to impose conditions or constraints. We can expect attempts by President Nyerere and others to involve us in negotiating

specific proposals with the Commonwealth at Lusaka which we should then persuade Muzorewa to accept. He may also try to initiate a discussion of the arrangements for the transition to independence, which he will wish to load in favour of the Patriotic Front. We should not permit the discussion in Lusaka to develop in this way. There will be a general desire at the Conference to avoid a confrontation; and, on the basis of the approach I have outlined above, it should be possible to do so.

10. I recommend that the Prime Minister should deal with the problem at Lusaka by including in her statement on Southern Africa a passage on Rhodesia on the lines suggested at Annex C. The announcement that there will be a Constitutional Conference should cut much of the ground from under the radicals. It may be best to hold this back until after the discussion had gone round the table. The Prime Minister will wish to decide this in the light of the circumstances in Lusaka.

ANNEX A

Rhodesia: Outline of Proposals for an Independence Constitution

1. Zimbabwe will be an independent sovereign republic in which all citizens will enjoy equal rights under the law.

2. The Head of State will be a President elected by Parliament.

3. The Head of Government will be the Prime Minister, who will be a member of the House of Assembly having the support of a majority in that House. Power to appoint and dismiss Ministers will be vested in the Prime Minister.

4. Parliament will consist of a Senate, and a House of Assembly. The Senate will be indirectly elected, and a majority of its members will be Africans. It will have power to delay but not block bills passed by the House of Assembly. The House of Assembly will be directly elected by universal adult suffrage (but see para 5).

5. For a specified minimum period after independence the House of Assembly will contain a minority of seats reserved for representatives to be elected by the European community. The proportion of these seats to the total number of seats in the House will be a matter for discussion between the British Government and the Rhodesian parties.

6. Parliament will have power to amend the constitution, which will prescribe procedures to be followed for effecting such amendments on lines similar to those contained in other independence constitutions granted by Britain.

7. The constitution will protect the independence of the judiciary.

8. Under the law, public servants will carry out the instructions of Ministers. Power to appoint, dismiss and discipline members of the public service will be vested in an independent Public Service Commission. The Constitution will protect the pension rights of public servants.

9. The Commanders of the Police Force and the Defence Forces will act in accordance with general policy directives given by the Prime Minister or other responsible Minister. The Police Commissioner and each Defence Force Commander will be responsible for the administration and operational control of their forces. There will be independent Service Commissions for the respective forces which will have prescribed powers in the disciplinary and establishment fields.

10. The Public Service Commission, and other Service Commissions, will be appointed on a basis, and with terms of reference, which will take due account of the need to preserve a high standard of efficiency and which also recognise the legitimate claim of the majority of the population to increasing representation in all forms of public office. The power to make certain senior appointments in the Public Service and other services will be vested in the Prime Minister, acting after consultation with the appropriate Commission.

11. There will be a fully justiciable Declaration of Rights and an independent official to assist in its enforcement.

ANNEX B

The Rhodesian Constitution

1. The areas of the Rhodesian Constitution which have been most widely criticised are:

(*a*) The extent of white representation in Parliament and the power of the white representatives to block legislation action on their own; and

(*b*) The membership and terms of reference of the defence and public service commissions, which at present inhibit even gradual Africanisation.

Our objective will be to achieve changes which would not undermine the confidence of the white community, but would render the Independence Constitution defensible to international and democratic opinion and more comparable to those we have agreed in granting independence to certain other African countries.

White Representation in Parliament

2. Special representation of white and other minorities in Parliament—at least for a limited period after independence—is acceptable in principle to much African opinion; and there are precedents elsewhere in the Commonwealth. Thus in *Tanganyika* out of the 71 seats in the then existing National Assembly which was continued in office at independence, 10 were reserved for Europeans and 11 for Asians. This arrangement lasted for the remainder of the life of that National Assembly and was then replaced by provision for up to 10 additional nominated members who included Europeans and Asians. Similar arrangements were made for *Zambia* where, for the remainder of the life of the existing National Assembly which was continued in office at independence, 10 out of 75 members had been elected by Europeans on a 'reserved roll'. Thereafter, there was provision for up to 5 additional nominated members. In *Kenya* there was no express reservation of seats for racial minorities, but 12 out of 117 seats in the Lower House were specially elected, the constituency members sitting as an electoral college. This was designed to achieve, and did achieve, the election of Europeans. (There was no comparable provision in *Nigeria*, which had no permanent non-indigenous population of any size; minority interests—essentially tribal and regional—were supposed to be protected by the federal structure of the Constitution).

3. Under the present Rhodesian Constitution, the whites have the power, acting on their own, to block a wide range of constitutional and other bills. They have 28 seats out of 100 in the Lower House and a very wide variety of bills, not restricted

to those involving constitutional amendment, require a positive vote of 78 members before they can become law. *This situation is without parallel elsewhere.*

4. Criticism of it could be met in several ways, alone or in combination, e.g.:

(*a*) The majority required to pass the bills in question could be reduced so that the Europeans no longer had a blocking power by themselves;

(*b*) The number of white seats could be reduced. (But to curtail the blocking power this would need to be accompanied by a reduction in the required majority, as at (*a*), or by an increase in the black seats, as at (*c*));

(*c*) The number of black seats could be increased to give them the required majority; or

(*d*) The range of bills required to be passed by the required majority could be restricted.

5. *We suggest that we might aim for*:

(*a*) 20 white seats in a lower house of 100, with 70 or at most 75 votes to be required for major measures (i.e. those dealing with specially entrenched sections of the Constitution); or

(*b*) 28 seats in a house of 120, with 80 or 85 votes required for major constitutional measures.

Powers over the Public Services and Defence Forces

6. Under the present arrangement there are independent Commissions and similar Boards controlling appointments to, and removals from, the public service, the police force, and defence forces and the judiciary. The qualifications for membership of the Commissions and Boards are such that Europeans will have a controlling voice in them for many years. This, coupled with the terms of reference of the Commissions, will inhibit even gradual Africanisation of the senior ranks of the defence and public services and of the judiciary in the foreseeable future. We know that Bishop Muzorewa wished to appoint an African to succeed the Cabinet Secretary, but was unable to do so in the face of opposition from the Public Service Commission. Nor was he able to appoint an African as Deputy Secretary. There is a need for simple amendments to attenuate the European dominance of the various Commissions, to open up the way for progressive Africanisation and to give the Prime Minister power over the selection and retention of his senior officials and service commanders (subject to consultation with the appropriate Service Commission).

Other Matters

7. Changes in other areas are less essential. But the present Constitution makes a coalition government obligatory for the life of the first Parliament and entitles every group with more than five MPs to automatic representation in the Cabinet. The Prime Minister has to accept the parties' nominees for the Cabinet seats: he has no power to dismiss a Minister. Bishop Muzorewa is already finding these requirements irksome. There may be a need for changes in the constitutional requirements in this area, without prejudice to the political desirability of a coalition government on more normal terms.

8. There are other areas of the Constitution where improvements, though not essential, may be desirable—e.g. to make it easier to acquire land (with adequate compensation for existing owners) for settlement by Africans.

ANNEX C

Commonwealth Heads of Government Meeting:
Statement by the Prime Minister on Southern Africa: Rhodesia

1. The problem of Rhodesia has hung over the Commonwealth for many years. A disastrous course was taken when, in 1965, the then Rhodesian government made the illegal declaration of independence. This was followed by years in which the efforts of successive British governments to achieve a settlement based on the wishes of the majority of the people of Rhodesia were frustrated, and in which the political rights of the majority were denied, leading in the end to a war which has brought great hardship and suffering both inside Rhodesia and in neighbouring countries—none more so than here in Zambia.

2. What began as a struggle between the white minority and the black majority has more recently taken on a very different dimension. There is now an African President, an African Prime Minister, and an African majority in Parliament. There have been elections in which for the first time the African majority have been able to elect the leaders of the government. There are those who seem to believe that the world should simply go on treating Bishop Muzorewa as if he were Mr Smith. But that is not the view of the British Government.

3. It is my Government's view that we must try to exploit the opportunity which has been created, by the changes which have taken place inside Rhodesia, to see if we can now find the solution which has eluded us for so long, and in doing so seek a way to bring an end to the war. We owe the people of Rhodesia the best effort we can make, all of us, to help all of them, if we can, to resolve their political differences peacefully rather than by force. I simply do not believe that there is anything now dividing the people of Rhodesia which is worth the use of the bomb and the gun to kill and maim men, women and children by the thousand, or can justify the misery of the hundreds of thousands in refugee camps, to put it right. In the changes which have now taken place, we surely have a basis from which to try to develop a solution which will command general international acceptance. The consultation we have had so far have helped my Government in seeking to identify what that solution should be, and I should like to thank all those Heads of Government here today who have contributed to them.

4. Important aspects of the Constitution under which Bishop Muzorewa has come to power have been criticised. [These clauses are indeed not ones that we would have included in a constitution granted by Britain.] But the principle that there should be some guaranteed representation of minority views during a certain minimum period following the transfer of power is not new; and the importance of enabling the European minority to continue to play a part in the life of the new country is widely recognised.

5. There is also natural concern that the search for a solution should involve the present external parties, so that their supporters outside the country may return home in peace and play their full part in political life. We all attach importance to that. It takes both sides to make an agreement and therefore we expect both sides to show that they are prepared to seek a negotiated solution.

6. Finally, I have been impressed by the general conviction that any solution of

the Rhodesia problem must derive its authority from Britain as the responsible colonial power. The international community has lost few opportunities to remind us that it is Britain's constitutional responsibility to bring Rhodesia to legal independence on a basis of justice and democracy fully comparable with the arrangements we have made in granting independence to other countries. We accept that responsibility and have every intention of discharging it honourably.

7. Mr Chairman, as I mentioned earlier, the consultations we have had with our Commonwealth partners over the last two months, and indeed with many other governments, have been most helpful. We have looked forward to this meeting as an important stage in that process of consultation before we put together our policy and initiate what we all profoundly hope will be the final approach to a solution. I look forward very much to hearing the further views of my colleagues round this table; but you will have gathered that we think we can begin to see the form that an attempt at a solution ought to take.

[For later use: As I indicated earlier, we intend to put forward proposals to bring Rhodesia to legal independence. These will take account of the consultations carried out by Lord Harlech; of the discussions we have had with other Commonwealth governments; and of the discussions at this Conference. The intention of my Government is to summon a constitutional conference at Lancaster House in September to discuss an independence constitution on a basis comparable to that on which we have granted independence to other countries. The present Rhodesian administration and the external parties will be invited to participate. The next steps will depend on the progress made at that Conference.]

No. 32

Extract from the minutes of a meeting of the Cabinet Defence and Oversea Policy Committee, 23 July 1979[1]
OD(79) 5th Meeting, Secret (CAB 148/183)

1. *Rhodesia*[2]

Previous Reference: OD(79) 3rd Meeting

The Committee had before them a memorandum by the Foreign and Commonwealth Secretary (OD(79) 21)[3] on policy to carry forward the Government's strategy of bringing Rhodesia to early legal independence with the widest possible international acceptance; and a memorandum by the Foreign and

---

1 Present were: The Rt Hon Margaret Thatcher MP, Prime Minister; The Rt Hon William Whitelaw MP, Secretary of State for the Home Department; The Rt Hon Lord Hailsham, Lord Chancellor; The Rt Hon Lord Carrington, Secretary of State for Foreign and Commonwealth Affairs and Minister of Overseas Development; The Rt Hon Sir Geoffrey Howe QC MP, Chancellor of the Exchequer; The Rt Hon Francis Pym MP, Secretary of State for Defence; The Rt Hon Lord Soames, Lord President of the Council; The Rt Hon Sir Ian Gilmour MP, Lord Privy Seal; The Rt Hon John Nott MP, Secretary of State for Trade. The following were also present: Sir Antony Duff, Foreign and Commonwealth Office (Item 1). Secretariat: Sir John Hunt; Mr R.L. Wade-Gery; Mr R M Hastie-Smith; Air Commodore J.D. Duxbury.
2 This section was classified Confidential.
3 No. 31.

Commonwealth Secretary (OD(79) 19)[4] on possible dangers to British political and commercial interests.

The Foreign and Commonwealth Secretary said that the course proposed in his policy paper (OD(79) 21) seemed to be the best available in the circumstances. A difficult time lay ahead, in the Parliamentary debate on 25 July, at the Lusaka Conference and thereafter. But so far the situation had evolved less unfavourably than might have been expected, despite some unhelpful public comment from among the Governments own supporters. Following his visit to Washington and London Bishop Muzorewa seemed to have taken in the case for changes in the Rhodesian constitution. At Lusaka it could be best to avoid revealing our intentions beyond announcing, at a fairly late state, our plan for a constitutional conference. When issuing invitations to that conference, we should announce our outline plans for an independence constitution. Details would then be explained to the Bishop, with a view to securing at least his tacit agreement when we tabled them at the constitutional conference, which would meet in London on 4 September. The Patriotic Front would probably attend but soon walk out having rejected our proposals. We should then negotiate these with the Bishop's Government and then defend them internationally as being comparable to the terms on which others of our former territories had been brought to independence. Finally, we should need to persuade the Bishop to arrange a Test of Acceptability with our help, probably in the form of a referendum, on the basis that at its successful conclusion we should grant full legal independence. This strategy offered our best chance of carrying with us the United States Government, our European partners and moderate opinion in Africa and elsewhere. We could not expect support from Nigeria, Tanzania, Zambia or Mozambique; and some damage to our interests was therefore likely, particularly in Nigeria. But if moderate opinion supported us we could hope to avoid the full range of political and economic damage described in OD(79) 19.

In discussion there was general agreement that the proposed strategy offered a reasonable prospect of carrying with us moderate opinion in the United States and elsewhere. Speed was essential. But the timing would be very tight, particularly between Lusaka and the constitutional conference; and if all else failed we might still need to fall back on granting independence on the basis of whatever minimum political changes the Rhodesian Government would accept. We could not expect help from the Commonwealth Secretary General, Mr Ramphal, whose views were clearly one-sided. But others, such as the Australian Government were now showing more understanding. We had a good case on solidarity grounds for insisting on full political support from our European allies, although we could not altogether hope to avoid their profiting economically at our expense in Nigeria and elsewhere. It would be important to do all we could to avoid economic damage to our interests from spreading beyond the minimum, and to involve others with us in any aid operation which might in due course be needed to restore the Rhodesian economy.

In that context it was noted that the economic benefit for Rhodesia of sanctions being lifted would be very great if others followed our example, but not if we acted almost alone; and that in the worst case, if our strategy failed, we might have to cope

---

4 Not printed.

by ourselves with a major rescue operation which would not necessarily be limited to financial measures.

The Prime Minister, summing up the discussion, said that the Committee endorsed the strategy proposed. We should aim for constitutional changes affecting particularly the blocking power of the whites and the status of the Public Commissions. In Parliament on 25 July the Government should make no bones about being unable to disclose their negotiating hand. At Lusaka and afterwards, our tactics would need to be kept flexible enough to deal with the situation as it developed. At the same time great care would be needed to avoid undermining the internal position of Bishop Muzorewa.

The Committee—

Took note, with approval, of the Prime Minister's summing up of their discussion.[5]

---

[5] The other two items discussed at this meeting were (2) Arms for the Royal Ulster Constabulary and (3) Future Light Torpedo.

No. 33

Letter from Mr Reid (Pretoria) to Mr Renwick, 26 July 1979
Confidential (FCO 36/2512)

Dear Robin,

South African Policy Towards Rhodesia

1. I thought it might be helpful to you to have a brief account of South African policy towards Rhodesia.

2. In my teleletter of 11 May,[1] I reported Van Heerden[2] as saying that the South African Government wished Muzorewa well. They hoped that he would be successful in running his new Government and that, when this began to be seen, a trend would develop in black Africa towards recognition. The South Africans knew only too well that if they recognise the Muzorewa Government too soon they would frighten off the very countries who they hoped would recognise.

3. I was able to confirm that this remained the basic position of the South African Government in the talk which I had yesterday with Ray Killen, the Deputy Secretary for Central and Southern Africa in the Department of Foreign Affairs. But he had quite a lot to add.

4. Killen's first point was that South Africa attached little importance to recognition as such since in itself it would give Muzorewa no material benefit. What mattered was the lifting of sanctions: that would put life back into the country's economy, demonstrate to the people of the country that Muzorewa's Government was doing them some good, and thus help to end the war. (The Canadian Counsellor recently gave me the enclosed extract of a telegram from Ottawa which shows that the South African Ambassador had made much the same point to the Canadian

---

[1] Not printed.
[2] Mr Neil Peter van Heerden, a senior official in the South African Department of Foreign Affairs.

government.¹ Why the South Africans should have taken the formal step of putting this in writing to the Canadians is unclear. The American ambassador tells me that the South Africans have not made the same approach to the Americans nor have they, as far as I know, to us. Perhaps the South African Ambassador in Ottawa was acting on his own initiative on the basis of whatever is the South African equivalent of a guidance telegram.)

5. When I asked Killen for his assessment of the present situation, he said that the South African Government's view was that the sort of constitutional and other changes which we seem to want Muzorewa to make would upset the delicate balance and might result in an exodus of whites which, if it extended to the armed forces, would be disastrous to Muzorewa's prospects. I explained our position on the basis of Lord Carrington's speech on 10 July. Killen took this in and after some further discussion said that he at least understood what we were seeking to achieve, and why (the implication being that in that respect he was in a minority here).

6. Killen said that the South Africans had not recently expressed any public views of Zimbabwe/Rhodesia but he referred to the (important but cautious) passage in Mr P.W. Botha's BBC TV interview (Cape Town tel. 310) and to Mr Pik Botha's equally cautious answer to a written PQ on recognition (Cape Town tel. 296).¹ He might also have mentioned an earlier comment by Mr P.W. Botha that the principles repeatedly put forward by the international community for an acceptance settlement had been satisfied and that he lamented that the West was not prepared to recognise this (Cape Town tel. 204 of 20 April).1 Dr Koornhof[3] has said much more recently that Rhodesia is in mind as a member of the constellation of Southern African States: that is, as we understand it, still the position, but little has recently been said in public here on the constellation of states.

7. For obvious reasons I did not ask Killen about South African assistance to Zimbabwe/Rhodesia. But our assessment is that it remains South African policy to give all necessary support to Muzorewa including military supplies and technical assistance as well as some key military personnel. None of this is, however, acknowledged and great care is taken to conceal South African military personnel. (Lieutenant General Dutton[4] told me the other day that his son who is a helicopter pilot and had been serving in Rhodesia. He said jokingly that it was a relief during the elections when his son's presence as a Puma pilot transporting the observers could be openly acknowledged.)

Yours ever,
MARTIN

---

3 Dr Pieter Koornhof, South Africa Minister of Cooperation and Development, 1978-84.
4 Lieutenant General Jack Raymond Dutton, South African Chief of Staff Operations, 1976-81.

No. 34

Letter from Mr Crabbie (Washington) to Mr Lyne, 27 July 1979
Restricted (FCO 36/2507)

Dear Roderic,

Rhodesia

1. Dick Moose today appeared before the House Foreign Affairs Sub-Committee. He was fulfilling an obligation made by President Carter on 7 June to keep Congress informed of the situation in Rhodesia. Moose's presentation and the questions asked of him were straightforward, although there was one point of particular interest.

2. Chairman Solarz asked whether the United States would automatically follow suit if HMG were to lift sanctions against Rhodesia later this year, even if no satisfactory progress towards genuine majority rule had been achieved. Solarz asserted that it would be wrong for US policy to be decided in London rather than Washington. (He was obviously pursuing the line of thought mentioned in UKMIS Geneva tel. no 352 to FCO).[1] Moose replied to the effect that the US supported HMG's attempts to bring about an internationally acceptable settlement in Rhodesia and that our perceptions of the problems involved were essentially the same: he added however that the Administration's attitude was in the final analysis based on what happened in Salisbury and that it was events on the ground in Rhodesia itself that would ultimately decide the US policy.

3. The implication of Moose's reply is, I think, that for political reasons the US Administration cannot appear in Congress simply to be following in British footsteps, although there is a growing impression on the Hill, as there has for some time been in the Administration, that it will be prudent for the United States to emphasize HMG's primary responsibility for solving the Rhodesian problem. *Time* magazine's Africa correspondent commented to me the other day that 'if windows have to be broken in Africa, it is better that they should be British rather than American'.

4. I should perhaps add that Moose was also asked whether he agreed with the distinction drawn by the Prime Minister between recognition and the lifting of sanctions. He replied that the two actions were essentially the same since they would produce virtually identical African reactions.

Yours ever,
C.D. CRABBIE

---

1 Not printed.

No. 35

Minute from Mr Luce to Lord Carrington, 3 August 1979
Confidential (FCO 36/2480)

Rhodesia

1. Since we are now reaching the second stage in our Rhodesian policy which involves planning a Constitutional Conference, I am submitting a few points for you to consider. I think that it is essential for us to think through the whole process to legal independence so that we can anticipate all the main developments and work out contingency and fallback plans. The Office have produced excellent proposals for handling the Conference but I would like to anticipate various stages after that.

2. *Objective*: Our aim must remain to withdraw from our Rhodesian responsibilities as soon as possible (and certainly within a year) on the most honourable and credible basis that we can achieve, and with support from at the very least the United States and the main EEC partners. We shall do temporary damage to our interests in the process but in the long term we should gain by having disposed of a problem which has debilitated us, has given us responsibility without power and has damaged our post-imperial relationship with the rest of the world.

3. *Constitutional Conference*: This has already been planned in great detail and I have only two points:

(i) *Sithole and Chikerema*: I think it is essential to find a formula to enable them to participate. It is better to involve them than to alienate them.

(ii) *No agreement with Muzorewa*: Although it is more likely that Muzorewa will go along with our proposals or a variation, we should anticipate the possibility of a total rejection of our proposals. If so, do we proceed to legal independence on the basis of the 'status quo'? Since we are fully committed to constitutional change we would lose all credibility in the outside world if we were to do this. Moreover, a considerable number in our Party would oppose such a move, along with the Labour Party. We need to assess the implications.

4. *Reassurances to Muzorewa and Whites*: It will be singularly important that we should anticipate Muzorewa's main anxiety by finding an early opportunity (mid-August?) to try and establish the confidence of the whites in our moves. I know that you have this in hand but we have to make it clear to them that the prize for accepting further changes is recognition and an end to sanctions. A visit by Lord Harlech or Lord Boyd might help in this process. It needs to be carefully presented so that we make it clear we won't come back for more concessions later. We may need to consider making some counter-balancing gesture towards the Patriotic Front to avoid giving them an excuse to back out of the discussions.

5. *Confidence-building measures*: We must be ready, at the appropriate stage, to offer other measures which will act as an incentive to all the parties to agree to our proposals. To this end the concept of an international aid effort should be revived. We must work out urgently details of the scale of Western economic assistance which HMG would be prepared to co-ordinate and which would be applicable not just to Rhodesia after legal independence, but to the neighbouring states as well. In addition we must clarify our views on other relief measures including the underpinning

of the white civil servants' pension arrangements and debt rescheduling. Sir Roy Welensky[1] told me that at least £1½ billion would be required for all these purposes, though I think this may be difficult to obtain.

6. *Referendum and Elections*
(i) *Referendum*: If the Patriotic Front walk out, then it is essential to hold a proper referendum on the constitution. We know from the April experience that an election is not regarded by the outside world as a clearcut test of acceptability on the constitution. We should of course anticipate what action to take if there is a 'No' vote.
(ii) *Election*: The argument for this is less strong but, if a new constitution is to be devised and, if we are to give an opening to the Patriotic Front to participate, then a fresh election prior to independence will give greater weight to the newly independent government. It might enhance the prospect of wider international recognition. If, however, the internal parties strongly object to this, I do not think it is worth making a stand on it.

If we decide on both processes then is there any reason why they could not be carried out simultaneously? We should also examine whether it would be possible to carry out these measures by 15 November.

7. *Diplomatic offensive*: We should be ready with plans for a major diplomatic offensive, presumably immediately after the Constitutional Conference, in order to gain the confidence and support of our main Western allies and the more moderate and friendly Commonwealth and African governments. We should consider how to set about this. I am assuming moreover that we carry the United States with us at each stage.

8. *Legal independence and sanctions*
(i) I entirely agree that, by the Party Conference in early October, we have got to be able to indicate a clear process towards legal independence and the removal of sanctions. We do seem, however, to have formed a view that the first move must be to lift sanctions. I take it that this is because we must do something concrete to satisfy our Party by mid-November. I see the purpose of this. But I believe that this proposal has a major flaw in another context. Since our main objective is to present as credible and honourable a plan as possible to the international community, then lifting sanctions before legal independence weakens it. Since sanctions at the UN are linked to the question of the legality of Rhodesia, we will make our task more difficult if we remove sanctions first.
(ii) We should therefore consider other ways of moving forward which will have the support of our Party, and, if possible, of Parliament as a whole. For example we should consider the introduction of an Act to allow us to renew sanctions for a defined period (2 or 3 months only) whilst we proceed to legal independence on completion of the referendum and election. Or we could renew the Order for a year giving an undertaking that we will move to independence much earlier. This would only be plausible if there was a clear and agreed timetable.
(iii) Alternatively we could look seriously at the proposition of moving to a legally dependent status by mid-November, purely for the transition period. This would enable us to lift sanctions at the same time, on the basis of legality. All this is on the assumption that it is not possible to complete a referendum and elections by mid-November.

---

1 Prime Minister of the Federation of Rhodesia and Nyasaland, 1956-1963.

9. *The transition*
(i) Even if the Patriotic Front agree to the constitution, the prospect for a breakdown over the transitional arrangement is almost inevitable.
(ii) At one stage I felt that there was a very strong case for Britain 'holding the ring' for a defined period. This could only be done on condition that all parties to the dispute accepted the arrangement and a ceasefire were to be agreed. The prospects for this are very remote but we should not rule it out. We cannot in my view take on this task without the agreement of the Patriotic Front. Otherwise we would be drawn into the conflict with all the inevitable consequences.
(iii) We should, however, be ready for this and work out in more detail other possible transitional arrangements. The proposal, for example, of a 'legally dependent status' should be taken seriously. I agree also that we should be ready to supervise the referendum and elections, perhaps in conjunction with the United States?
(iv) One of the biggest obstacles on the transition will be the objections of the Patriotic Front over the composition of the security forces. We cannot make major changes without undermining the internal parties and the whites. But we could draw up proposals with Muzorewa which would involve a concrete offer to absorb a proportion of guerillas in the forces. There are precedents for this, including the culmination of the Southern Sudan rebellion.

10. *Onus on Patriotic Front*: At every stage in the process to independence we must be seeking to put the onus on the Patriotic Front for any failure to agree and to make progress.

11. *Post independence*
(i) We must not lose sight of the implications of our moves to final legal independence or our longer term relations with Rhodesia and in Southern Africa. Even if we have somehow managed to lead Rhodesia to independence on a reasonably honourable and credible basis, we are nevertheless still bound to have to face up to the prospects of a continuation of the war and a running threat to the stability of Zimbabwe.
(ii) In these circumstances Britain and the Western allies should not shirk from the possibilities of providing economic assistance and perhaps even military equipment (but certainly not troops). If it is a reasonably credible settlement then it will be in our interests to assist this experiment in a multiracial society.
(iii) It is important that we should be ready to move on to the diplomatic offensive with self-confidence. Moreover, we should study seriously with our Western allies the possibility of linking Soviet and Satellite policies in regard to the Patriotic Front with our general relations (grain supplies, credit facilities, Western oil technology, SALT II). To this end Peter Blaker and I have asked the office to produce a paper on the subject of 'linkage'.
(iv) In addition we should be reviewing our relations with those African states who follow policies inimical to ours on Rhodesia. There is a case for making it plain to these countries, principally Tanzania and Zambia, that we cannot contemplate the continued provision of substantial aid and other assistance until we obtain co-operation on Rhodesia. I hope the office will produce their ideas on this.

RICHARD LUCE

No. 36

Sir P. Moon (Dar es Salaam) to Lord Carrington, 8 August 1979, 6 a.m.[1]
Tel. No. 660 Priority, Confidential (FCO 36/2409)

ZANU Comments Following Lusaka

1. Uncharacteristically the local ZANU Office contacted us yesterday and John Chimbandi, their Chief Representative for East Africa called on our Senior First Secretary[2] in Chancery today.

2. Although as yet unbriefed by those attending Lusaka he made the following points:

(i) ZANU was surprised at the change in the British attitude moving from, as they saw it, almost automatic recognition of Muzorewa to the Lusaka agreement.

(ii) Even more surprising however was the change by African Heads of State from the OAU resolution at Monrovia to Lusaka. Chimbandi attributed this to an excessive preoccupation over Uganda at Monrovia by Heads of Delegations which otherwise could have been expected to have amended the Resolution on Zimbabwe which had been mainly drafted by ZANU here in Dar es Salaam.

(iii) ZANU would have no objection to a negotiated settlement.

(iv) There could be no question this time of a cease fire before a settlement. They retained painful memories of the last time they had stopped fighting during negotiations and were confident of ample historical precedence for only ceasing hostilities when full agreement has been reached.

(v) The present constitution, even if there are parts of it which in theory they could accept, will have to be scrapped and a new one drawn up as not even Muzorewa was involved in the drafting of it and they could not be expected to live under a white man's (Smith's) constitution.

3. Speaking personally Chimbandi saw no difficulty in an election being held in Zimbabwe provided:

(*a*) The present government's security forces were contained and supervised by external forces;

(*b*) Supervision was not by Britain.

Chimbandi said it would then be for the government emerging from this election to decide on the composition of security and law enforcement forces. He also foresaw no difficulty about keeping ZANU forces outside Zimbabwe during the election period as this would create fewer problems and the loss of their votes would be of minimal importance.

4. When asked what he envisage would become of the present standing army Chimbandi said that the rank and file black soldiers who, in his words, had been driven by poverty into joining the army would be forgiven, re-educated and retained but what he described as the hard core senior blacks, NCOs etc, who have been deliberately fighting for the retention of a hostile regime would have to go. He thought that some whites would need to be retained for their expertise.

---

1 And for Information Priority to Lusaka, Maputo, Mirimba Salisbury, Pretoria; Information Routine to Luanda, UKMIS New York, Washington, Gaborone.
2 Mr Peter Robert Mossom Hinchcliffe.

5. Edgar Tekere, ZANU's Secretary General and Head of the Delegation at Lusaka is expected in Dar tomorrow on his way back to Maputo, and after briefing from him Chimbandi has promised to get in touch.

6. We do not know to what extent Chimbandi reflects ZANU policy but given his position he is obviously an important figure and we would expect him to be in close touch with the ZANU leadership. It will be interesting to see if he modifies his views after his meeting with Tekere.

No. 37

Letter from Mr Cartledge (No. 10) to Mr Wall, 9 August 1979
Confidential (FCO 36/2549)

Dear Stephen,

Rhodesia and the Security Council

Sir Anthony Parsons called on the Prime Minister this morning for a short discussion before leaving to take up his new appointment as UK Permanent Representative to the United Nations.

The Prime Minister said that she was concerned about the possibility that unhelpful statements on Rhodesia might emerge from the forthcoming conference of the Non-Aligned in Havana next month. She said that everything possible should be done to ensure that the Commonwealth participants in the Non-Aligned conference stuck to their commitment to the Rhodesia section of the Lusaka Communique. In particular, the Prime Minister would like the maximum advantage to be taken of such leverage as our aid programmes towards those Commonwealth countries may give us in keeping them in line. As you know, the Prime Minister has already asked that the new £10 million grant aid to Zambia for agricultural development should be kept up our sleeve for the time being: she would like the same tactic to be adopted so far as any other impending aid agreements with Non-Aligned Commonwealth members are concerned.

Sir Anthony Parsons told the Prime Minister of his views on how the issue of sanctions against Rhodesia should be handled in the Security Council if a constitutional conference were to produce proposals acceptable to all the parties, except the Patriotic Front, and to 'reasonable Governments' in general. Sir Anthony Parsons said that his recommendations would be that the UK should address a letter to the Secretary General of the UN, or to the President of the Security Council, stressing the UK's status as the power responsible for ending the state of rebellion in Rhodesia and setting out the steps by which the UK had brought or proposed to bring Rhodesia to legal independence. Depending on the stage reached at the time of sending the letter (and in particular on whether elections had been held or were still in the stage of preparation), it would set out the grounds for the UK's view that the rebellion in Rhodesia was at an end: and would go on to state that, in this situation, the UN resolutions on mandatory sanctions against Rhodesia had fallen away. The letter would not call for any reply. The onus would then be on the UK's adversaries in the UN

Council (Soviet Union, Czechoslovakia and possibly China) to launch a counter-attack against the UK's statement of the position.

Sir Anthony Parsons said that when the counter-attack had been launched, it would be open to the UK to veto a resolution reaffirming sanctions. Much the better course, however, would be to bring about a situation in which such a resolution failed to attract a requisite number of votes in the Council. The UK could, if the proposed constitutional arrangements were reasonable and defensible, count on the abstentions of the five Western members of the Council. Two more would be needed: these should be available from among Kuwait, Bolivia (to whom a new offer of UK aid was in the pipeline) Gabon, Jamaica, Bangladesh or Zambia itself. Sir Anthony Parsons said that, on this basis, there should be a fair chance of ensuring that the Security Council was unable to demonstrate its capacity to reaffirm the resolution on sanctions.

On the question of the form of a Rhodesia settlement, Sir Anthony Parsons expressed the view that transitional periods should be kept to an absolute minimum (e.g. 24 hours if practicable). The Prime Minister agreed and said, with reference to the FCO paper on the preparation of new elections in Rhodesia which she had read on her way back from Lusaka, that the period of 3 months envisaged in the paper for the preparation of elections was much too long and that some means would have to be found of completing all the preparations within one month.

I am sending a copy of this letter to Martin Vile (Cabinet Office).

Yours ever,
BRYAN CARTLEDGE

No. 38

Memorandum by Lord Carrington for the Cabinet, 9 August 1979
C(79)33, Confidential (CAB 129/207)

Rhodesia

1. I attach at Annex A the speech which the Prime Minister made in the debate on Southern Africa at Lusaka, and at Annex B the passage on Rhodesia in the communique to which we managed to secure agreement.

2. The agreement closely follows the line of our policy as set out by the Prime Minister in the House of Commons and in her speech to Heads of Government last week. Its main features are:

(*a*) Recognition by the Commonwealth that there is a new dimension in Rhodesia. President Nyerere drew particular attention to this in his own statement to the meeting. The change of attitude which the Prime Minister and I found in Lusaka is significant.

(*b*) Total absence of condemnation of Bishop Muzorewa or of endorsement of the Patriotic Front—in complete contrast to the Resolution adopted at the Organisation of African Unity Summit only ten days before.

(*c*) Commonwealth affirmation that it is Britain's constitutional responsibility to grant legal independence to Rhodesia on the basis of majority rule with appropriate safeguards for minorities, and Commonwealth agreement to work to that end and to help bring about a cessation of hostilities and an end to sanctions.

(*d*) Agreement that it is for Britain to arrange supervision of fresh elections in Rhodesia. There would be Commonwealth observers, which is in our interest. There would be no international supervision.

3. The Prime Minister made clear in the House of Commons on 25 July[1] that we intended to put forward firm proposals designed to bring Rhodesia to legal independence on a basis comparable to that on which we granted independence to other former British territories. This implied that we would seek changes in the constitution of the internal settlement which contains two features not found in any independence constitutions granted by Britain; the blocking power of the whites (the Cyprus constitution of 1960 did give the minority community (i.e. the Turks) power to block certain constitutional amendments. But the constitution itself was not granted by Britain, and the population ratio was 70:30 (as against 97:3 in Rhodesia)), and the power given to the four Commissions controlling appointments to the Police, Armed Forces, Public Services and the Judiciary. It is these aspects of the constitution to which the Lusaka communique refers.

4. Our colleagues in the Defence and Oversea Policy Committee agreed before Lusaka that we should aim to discuss the form of a revised constitution at a constitutional conference in the classic decolonisation pattern. We would have preferred not to mention this in the Lusaka communique but changes in the constitution so clearly implied a constitutional conference that the Prime Minister and I agreed to the formula used, which protects the full authority of Cabinet. The communique also draws attention to the obvious fact that a government formed under an independence constitution would have to be chosen through new elections. Such elections are anyway essential to a settlement if it is to gain international acceptance and bring the war to an end.

5. I believe that we must now move quickly to take advantage of the agreement reached at Lusaka. We have been in close touch with Bishop Muzorewa throughout and he already knows, from his talks with the Prime Minister in London, what we have in mind. I therefore propose that I should issue invitations next week to the parties to the conflict to attend a constitutional conference at Lancaster House beginning on 4 September. At the same time, I shall give to the parties, and publish a statement of our outline proposals for an outline constitution (draft at Annex C). The draft is designed to indicate an eventual independence constitution which:

(*a*) would be comparable to the terms on which independence was granted to other Commonwealth countries in Africa;
(*b*) would offer enough protection to the whites to encourage them to stay; and
(*c*) would be in such terms that we could claim to the African Presidents and others that a refusal by the Patriotic Front to attend the constitutional conference or to work within the traditional framework of an independence constitution would be unreasonable and a proof of bad faith on their part.

6. I would intend to make a separate statement at the time the proposals were

---

1 Parl. Debs., 5th ser., H. of C., vol. 971, cols. 620-630.

published, emphasising the importance we attach to enabling the white community to play a full part in the future of the country and holding out a firm promise of legal independence and the lifting of sanctions once the proposals are implemented.

7. I believe we should confine our initial presentation to the bare outline of the independence constitution. If we expose the full extent to which we were prepared to incorporate the substance of the existing constitution into our own proposals, we should give the Patriotic Front and their supporters in Africa a chance to claim that we were clearly aiming for a solution based on the internal settlement. It is very likely that, once they get to a conference, the Patriotic Front will reject our proposals. But we should not make it easy for them to claim that it is not worth their while attending the conference at all. This would only make it more difficult for us to demonstrate that it is their intransigence which is the main obstacle to a wider agreement.

8. The constitution we would put forward at the conference would be largely compatible with the existing Rhodesian constitution (a great deal of which is comparable to provisions contained in constitutions we have granted). But certain changes are essential if we are to carry world opinion (including United States and European Allies) with us. These are described in Annex D.

9. I invite my colleagues to agree that I should:

(*a*) issue next week invitations to a constitutional conference to begin on 4 September;

(*b*) table for discussion at the Conference constitutional proposals along the lines described in Annex C;

(*c*) begin now the varied preparatory work and consultations with the parties to the conference, with the Commonwealth and with our other friends and allies, which are necessary if we are to obtain the best possible psychological conditions in which to begin a conference.

Annex A

Statement by the Prime Minister during the Opening Debate on Southern Africa, 3 August

I imagine that it is on the question of Rhodesia that my colleagues will wish me to speak; and I therefore propose to confine my own intervention to that subject.

The problem with Rhodesia has hung over the Commonwealth for many years. The present trouble began in 1965 when the then Rhodesian Government made the illegal declaration of independence. This was followed by years in which the efforts of successive British Governments to achieve a settlement based on the wishes of a majority of people of Rhodesia were frustrated, years in which the political rights of the majority were denied. Then came the war which has brought great hardship and suffering both inside Rhodesia and in neighbouring countries.

What began as a struggle between the white minority and the black majority has more recently taken on a very different dimension. There is now an African President, an African Prime Minister and an African majority in parliament.

There have been elections in which for the first time the African majority have been able to elect the leaders of the Government. There are those who seem to believe that the world should simply go on treating Bishop Muzorewa as if he were Mr Smith. But the change that has taken place in Rhodesia cannot be dismissed as of no consequence.

It is the British Government's view that we must use the opportunity created by the changes which have taken place in Rhodesia to see if we can now find the solution which has eluded us for so long and to bring an end to the war.

We owe it to the people of Rhodesia to do all we can, all of us to help all of them, to resolve their political differences peacefully rather than by force.

I simply do not believe there is anything now dividing the people of Rhodesia which is worth the use of the bomb and the gun to kill and maim men, women and children by the thousand, or which can justify the misery of the hundreds of thousands in refugee camps. In the changes that have now taken place we surely have the basis from which to try to develop a solution which will command general international acceptance.

As you know, on the British Government's behalf, Lord Harlech saw the Heads of Government of seven African states and also Mr Mugabe and representatives of Mr Nkomo.

Richard Luce saw the governments of a further five African countries. We have also been in touch with all our other Commonwealth friends as well as with our European Community partners and the United States. The consultations we have had so far have been of great value to the Government in helping to identify what the solution should be.

I should like to take this opportunity to thank personally all those Heads of Government here today who have helped us in this way.

From our consultations certain common factors emerge clearly. The strongest is the view that the constitution under which Bishop Muzorewa has come to power is defective in certain important respects.

I refer of course to the provisions which make it possible for the white minority to block, in the Parliament, constitutional changes that would be unwelcome to them.

This is a valid criticism—such a blocking mechanism has not appeared in any other independence constitution agreed to by the British Parliament.

The principle that there should be some guaranteed representation for minority communities during a certain minimum period following the transfer of power on independence is not new—and I think we all recognise the importance to Rhodesia of encouraging the European minority to remain and continue to play a useful part in the life of the community. But that is a very different matter from enabling them to block.

The other main criticism of the Constitution relating to the composition and powers of the various service commissions is also valid. It is clearly wrong that the Government should not have adequate control over certain senior appointments.

Those consulted also considered it essential that the search for a solution should involve the present external parties, so that their supporters outside the country might return home in peace and play their full part in political life.

Lastly, in considering the consultations we have had so far, I have been impressed by the general conviction that any solution of the Rhodesia problem must derive its authority from Britain as the responsible colonial power.

The International Community has lost few opportunities to remind us that it is

Britain's constitutional responsibility to bring Rhodesia to legal independence on a basis of justice and democracy full comparable with the arrangements we have made for the independence of other countries.

We accept that responsibility and have every intention of discharging it honourably.

Mr Chairman, as I mentioned earlier, the consultations we have had with our Commonwealth partners over the last two months, and indeed with many other governments, have been most helpful. We have looked forward to this meeting as an important stage in that process of consultation before we decide our policy and initiate what we all profoundly hope will be the final approach to a solution.

I look forward very much to hearing any further views of colleagues here: but you will have gathered that we think we can begin to see the form that an attempt at a solution ought to take.

Let me therefore, before this debate continues, make certain points about the British position quite clear.

(i) The British Government are wholly committed to genuine black majority rule in Rhodesia:

(ii) We accept that it is our constitutional responsibility to grant legal independence on that basis and that only Britain can do it:

(iii) We accept that our objective must be to establish that independence on the basis of a constitution comparable with the constitutions we have agreed with other countries:

(iv) We are deeply conscious of the urgent need to bring peace to the people of Rhodesia and her neighbours: we will therefore present our proposals as quickly as possible to all the parties, and at the same time call on them to cease hostilities and move forward with us to a settlement.

Our aim is, as I stated it during our opening session, to bring Rhodesia to legal independence on a basis which the Commonwealth and the International Community as a whole will find acceptable.

I believe that we now have a chance to achieve this, and we must take it.

Annex B

Commonwealth Heads of Government Meeting
Communiqué— Rhodesia

1. Heads of Government had a frank discussion on the current problems of Southern Africa and their implications for the Commonwealth and the wider international community. While recognising that certain developments since their Meeting in London have added new dimensions, they remained concerned by the potential dangers inherent in the existing situation. They therefore stressed the urgent need for finding satisfactory solutions to the remaining problems of this region.

2. In relation to the situation in Rhodesia, Heads of Government therefore:

(*a*) confirmed that they were wholly committed to genuine black majority rule for the people of Zimbabwe;

(*b*) recognised, in this context, that the internal settlement constitution is defec-

tive in certain important respects;
(*c*) fully accepted that it is the constitutional responsibility of the British Government to grant legal independence to Zimbabwe on the basis of majority rule;
(*d*) recognised that the search for a lasting settlement must involve all parties to the conflict;
(*e*) were deeply conscious of the urgent need to achieve such a settlement and bring peace to the people of Zimbabwe and their neighbours;
(*f*) accepted that independence on the basis of majority rule requires the adoption of a democratic constitution including appropriate safeguards for minorities;
(*g*) acknowledged that the government formed under such an independence constitution must be chosen through free and fair elections properly supervised under British Government authority and with Commonwealth observers;
(*h*) welcomed the British Government's indication that an appropriate procedure for advancing towards these objectives would be for them to call a constitutional conference to which all the parties would be invited; and
(*i*) consequently, accepted that it must be a major objective to bring about a cessation of hostilities and an end to sanctions as part of the process of implementation of a lasting settlement.

ANNEX C

Rhodesia: Outline of Proposals for an Independence Constitution

1. Zimbabwe will be an independent sovereign state in which all citizens will enjoy equal rights under the law.

2. There will be a 'constitutional' Head of State.

3. The Head of Government will be the Prime Minister, who will be a member of the House of Assembly having the support of a majority in that House. Power to appoint and dismiss Ministers will be exercised in accordance with the advice of the Prime Minister.

4. Parliament will consist of a Senate and a House of Assembly. The Senate will be indirectly elected, and a majority of its members will be Africans. It will have power to delay but not block bills passed by the House of Assembly. The House of Assembly will be directly elected by universal adult suffrage.

5. For a specified minimum period after independence the House of Assembly will contain a minority of seats reserved for representatives to be elected by the European Community. The proportion of these seats to the total number of seats in the House will be a matter for discussion between the British Government and the Rhodesian Parties.

6. Parliament will have power to amend the constitution, which will prescribe procedures to be followed for effecting such amendments on lines similar to those contained in other independence constitutions granted by Britain.

7. The constitution will protect the independence of the judiciary.

8. Under the law, public servants will carry out the instructions of Ministers. Power to appoint, dismiss and discipline members of the public service will be

vested in an independent Public Service Commission. The Constitution will protect the pension rights of public servants.

9. The Commanders of the Police Force and the Defence Forces will act in accordance with general policy directives given by the Prime Minister or other responsible Minister. The Police Commissioner and each Defence Force Commander will be responsible for the administration and operational control of their forces. There will be independent Service Commissions for the respective forces which will have prescribed powers in the disciplinary and establishment fields.

10. The Public Service Commission, and the other Service Commissions, will be appointed on a basis, and with terms of reference, which will take due account of the need to preserve a high standard of efficiency and which also recognise the legitimate claims of the majority of the population to increasing representation in all forms of public office. The power to make certain senior appointments in the Public Service and other services will be vested in the Prime Minister, acting after consultation with the appropriate Commission.

11. There will be a fully justiciable Declaration of Rights and an independent official to assist in its enforcement.

Annex D

The Rhodesian Constitution

1. The areas of the Rhodesian Constitution which have been most widely criticised are:

(*a*) the extent of white representation in Parliament and the power of the white representatives to block legislation acting on their own; and

(*b*) the membership and terms of reference of the defence and public service commissions, which at present inhibit even gradual Africanisation.

Our objective will be to achieve changes which would not undermine the confidence of the white community, but would render the Independence Constitution defensible to international and democratic opinion and more comparable to those we have agreed in granting independence to certain other African countries.

White Representation in Parliament

2. Special representation of white and other minorities in Parliament—at least for a limited period after independence—is acceptable in principle to much African opinion; and there are precedents elsewhere in the Commonwealth. Thus in *Tanganyika* out of the 71 seats in the then existing National Assembly which has continued in office at independence, 10 were reserved for Europeans and 11 for Asians. This arrangement lasted for the remainder of the life of that National Assembly and was then replaced by provision for up to 10 additional nominated members who included Europeans and Asians. Similar arrangements were made for *Zambia* where, for the remainder of the life of the existing National Assembly which was continued in office at independence, 10 out of 75 members had been elected by Europeans on a 'reserved roll'. Thereafter, there was provision for up to 5 additional nominated members. In *Kenya* there was no express reservation of seats for racial minorities, but 12 out of 117 seats in the Lower House were specially elected by the

constituency members sitting as an electoral college. This was designed to achieve, and did achieve, the election of Europeans. (There was no comparable provision in *Nigeria*, which had no permanent non-indigenous population of any size; minority interests—essentially tribal and regional—were supposed to be protected by the federal structure of the Constitution).

3. Under the present Rhodesian Constitution, the whites have the power, acting on their own, to block a wide range of constitutional and other bills. They have 28 seats out of 100 in the Lower House and a very wide variety of bills, not restricted to those involving constitutional amendment, require a positive vote of 78 members before they can become law. *This situation is without parallel elsewhere.*

4. Criticism of it could be met in several ways, alone or in combination, e.g.:
(*a*) the majority required to pass the bills in question could be reduced so that the Europeans no longer had a blocking power by themselves;
(*b*) the number of white seats could be reduced. (But to curtail the blocking power this would need to be accompanied by a reduction in the required majority, as at (*a*), or by an increase in the black seats, as at (*c*));
(*c*) the number of black seats could be increased to give them the required majority; or
(*d*) the range of bills required to be passed by the required majority could be restricted.

5. *We suggest that we might aim for:*
(*a*) 20 white seats in a lower house of 100, with 70 or at most 75 votes to be required for major measures (i.e. those dealing with specially entrenched sections of the Constitution); or
(*b*) 28 seats in a house of 120, with 80 or 85 votes required for major constitutional measures.

Powers over the Public Services and Defence Forces

6. Under the present arrangements there are independent Commissions and similar Boards controlling appointments to, and removals from, the public service, the police force, and defence forces and the judiciary. The qualifications for membership of the Commissions and Boards are such that Europeans will have a controlling voice in them for many years. This, coupled with the terms of reference of the Commissions, will inhibit even gradual Africanisation of the senior ranks of the defence and public services and of the judiciary in the foreseeable future. We know that Bishop Muzorewa wished to appoint an African to succeed the Cabinet Secretary, but was unable to do so in the face of opposition from the Public Service Commission. Nor was he able to appoint an African as Deputy Secretary. There is a need for simple amendments to attenuate the European dominance of the various Commissions, to open up the way for progressive Africanisation and to give the Prime Minister power over the selection and retention of his senior officials and service commanders (subject to consultation with the appropriate Service Commission).

Other Matters

7. Changes in other areas are less essential. But the present Constitution makes a coalition government obligatory for the life of the first Parliament and entitles every group with more than five MPs to automatic representation in the Cabinet. The Prime

Minister has to accept the parties' nominees for the Cabinet seats; he has no power to dismiss a Minister. Bishop Muzorewa is already finding these requirements irksome. There may be a need for changes in the constitutional requirements in this area, without prejudice to the political desirability of a coalition government on more normal terms.

8. There are other areas of the Constitution where improvements, though not essential, may be desirable—e.g. to make it easier to acquire land (with adequate compensation for existing owners) for settlement by Africans.

No. 39

Extract from the conclusions of a meeting of the Cabinet, 10 August 1979[1]
CC(79) 13th Conclusions, Secret (CAB 128/66)

Rhodesia
1. The Cabinet considered a memorandum by the Secretary of State for Foreign and Commonwealth Affairs (C(79)33)[2] on the next steps towards a Rhodesia settlement, in the light of developments at the Commonwealth Heads of Government Meeting in Lusaka.

The Foreign and Commonwealth Secretary said that on arrival the atmosphere in Lusaka had been unfriendly and unpromising. But an early talk with President Nyerere of Tanzania revealed that the Front Line Presidents had agreed among themselves to leave the initiative to us. It emerged later that because of their domestic difficulties Presidents Nyerere, Machel (Mozambique) and Khama (Botswana) were all anxious to see a settlement. The same was probably also true of President Kaunda of Zambia, whose economic problems were even worse; but he was inhibited by the presence in Zambia of powerful Patriotic Front forces under Nkomo. The Prime Minister's speech at the opening session had been well received and had laid the basis for later progress. President Nyerere, President Moi of Kenya and the Commonwealth Secretary General had played helpful roles; and over the weekend agreement on a satisfactory communique passage had been reached in a caucus comprising President Kaunda, President Nyerere, Mr Fraser of Australia, Mr Manley of Jamaica, General Adefope of Nigeria, the Prime Minister, the Secretary General and himself. Despite difficulties caused by its premature

---

1 The following were present: The Rt Hon Margaret Thatcher MP, Prime Minister; The Rt Hon William Whitelaw MP, Secretary of State for the Home Department; The Rt Hon Lord Carrington, Secretary of State for Foreign and Commonwealth Affairs; The Rt Hon Sir Geoffrey Howe QC MP, Chancellor of the Exchequer; The Rt Hon Sir Keith Joseph MP, Secretary of State for Industry; The Rt Hon Francis Pym MP, Secretary of State for Defence; The Rt Hon Lord Soames, Lord President of the Council; The Rt Hon Sir Ian Gilmour MP, Lord Privy Seal; The Rt Hon Michael Heseltine MP, Secretary of State for the Environment; The Rt Hon George Younger MP, Secretary of State for Scotland; The Rt Hon Nicholas Edwards MP, Secretary of State for Wales; The Rt Hon John Nott MP, Secretary of State for Trade; The Rt Hon David Howell MP, Secretary of State for Energy; The Rt Hon John Biffen MP, Chief Secretary, Treasury; The Rt Hon Angus Maude MP, Paymaster General. The following were also present: The Rt Hon Norman Fowler MP, Minister of Transport; The Rt Hon Michael Jopling MP, Parliamentary Secretary, Treasury. Secretariat: Sir John Hunt; Mr R.L. Wade-Gery; Mr R.M. Hastie-Smith.
2 No. 38.

disclosure by Mr Fraser, this text had in the end been accepted by all the Heads of Delegations. It provided, if the Cabinet now agreed, for Britain to summon a Constitutional Conference. We would invite two delegations of equal size; one would be led by Bishop Muzorewa and would include other 'internal' representatives, while the other would represent both the Nkomo and Mugabe wings of the Patriotic Front. With the invitations we should circulate only an outline of our proposals for an independence constitution which would be comparable to those granted to other territories. Emissaries would be sent to both parties in preparation for the Conference; and Bishop Muzorewa should be told the details of the constitution we had in mind, which would in many respects simply incorporate existing arrangements. Care would be taken to reassure white opinion in Rhodesia. The Bishop could be expected to attend the Conference; and the Patriotic Front would probably also do so, under pressure from the Front Line Presidents. At the Conference, agreement with the Patriotic Front might well not be reached, but if so they would appear in a bad light and we could hope to carry moderate international opinion with us over the independence arrangements we would then reach with Bishop Muzorewa. If agreement were reached with all the parties at the Conference there would be even greater difficulties to be overcome as regards the transitional arrangements, including the elections to which it had been necessary to agree in the Lusaka document at the natural corollary of a new constitution; but these would be under British supervision and would be a price worth paying in order to end the war. The date of the Constitutional Conference might have to be 11 September, to avoid a clash with the Non-Aligned Conference in Havana.

The Prime Minister said that in the Lusaka document all Commonwealth Governments had accepted the primacy of Britain's role. It had also committed them to regarding a cessation of hostilities and an end to sanctions as major objectives. There had been no reference at Lusaka to the recognition by the Organisation of African Unity Summit of the Patriotic Front as the sole representative of the people of Rhodesia; and Presidents Kaunda and Nyerere had said privately that they would accept whatever government the proposed elections produced.

In discussion there was general agreement that the course followed by the Prime Minister and Foreign and Commonwealth Secretary at Lusaka had been highly successful; and that the action now proposed offered the best hope of further progress. A number of questions were raised, particularly about the handling of difficulties which might arise in the period during and after the Constitutional Conference. But it was accepted that our policy could only be followed on a step-by-step basis, and that the Government should avoid hypothetical public discussion about their intentions in the event of failure to achieve their present objectives. It was important to play for success and to be seen to be doing so.

The Prime Minister, summing up the discussion, said that the Cabinet endorsed the agreement which had been reached in Lusaka and which was set out in Annex B of C(79)33. They also approved the proposals for the next steps set out in that paper. She would arrange for the Press to be informed that the Cabinet had endorsed the Lusaka document; that invitations to a Constitutional Conference would be issued shortly; and that a further statement would be made in the course of next week. The strictest confidentiality should be observed over the details of the Cabinet's discussion.

The Cabinet—
Took note with approval of the Prime Minister's summing up of their discussion.

No. 40

Lord Carrington to Mr Lewen (Maputo), 10 August 1979, 4 p.m.[1]
Tel. No. 139 Confidential, Immediate (FCO 36/2435)

Rhodesia: Constitutional Conference

1. (For Mirimba and Maputo and Lusaka). My first immediately following telegram[2] contains the text of a written invitation to be delivered to Bishop Muzorewa, Mugabe and Nkomo as close as possible to 1000Z on 14 August, together with a copy of the outline proposals for an independence constitution the text of which is in my second immediately following telegram,[3] and of the accompanying statement in my third immediately following telegram[2] which is to be released in London later on 14 August.

2. (Front Line, Lagos, Washington, Pretoria and Commonwealth Posts). You should (not before 1000Z on 14 August) hand over copies of these texts also to the Government to which you are accredited and explain the action being taken vis-à-vis the parties. (Addis Ababa and Monrovia). You should take similar action respectively with the OAU Secretariat and with the President as current Chairman of the OAU.

3. Paragraphs 4 to 9 below set out points to be made orally.

4. You should make clear that our invitation is addressed only to Bishop Muzorewa and to the co-leaders of the Patriotic Front. We expect delegations of 12 from Salisbury and 12 from the Patriotic Front. We will pay all expenses (including first class fares) from these numbers. Others may come to London at expense of parties, but will not be admitted to the conference itself.

5. Who the leaders choose to bring with them is their business. (For Mirimba Salisbury: Please discuss with the Bishop whom he will choose. We want to ensure that he brings a delegation which will be seen to be broadly representative of the African spectrum, and will have adequate white representation. The latter point is particularly important because the white members are going to have to carry the white community with them. Our current feeling is that the presence of Mr Ian Smith in the delegation is unlikely to enhance the prospects of a successful conference).

6. We are prepared for the conference to last as long as progress is being made. There are no deadlines.

7. We cannot agree that the notice given for the conference is insufficient for the preparation (indeed we should have hoped to start earlier but for the fact that

---

1 Also sent to Mirimba, Salisbury and Lusaka Deskby on 11 August 0730Z; Repeated for Information Immediate Deskby on 11 August 0730Z to Gaborone, Dar es Salaam, Luanda, Washington, UKMIS New York, Pretoria, Addis Ababa, Monrovia, Canberra, Ottawa, Wellington, Deskby on 11 August 0830Z Lagos; Priority to Abidjan, Dakar, Kinshasa, Khartoum, Tokyo, EEC Posts and other Commonwealth Posts; Saving to Suva, Port Moresby, Honiara, Nuku'alofa and Tarawa.
2 Not printed.
3 No. 41.

the non-aligned summit opens in Havana on 4 September). Both sides have had ample time to consider their positions. We are prepared to meet delegates from either side in London, or to send officials to meet them, for bilateral preliminary work in advance of the conference itself.

8. The purpose of the conference is as stated. The form of a constitutional settlement is the first question to be resolved. We shall then seek agreement on measures for its implementation. We believe that if the parties can agree on a basis for independence, they can agree also on the steps to be taken towards it, including arrangements for a ceasefire, free and fair elections and so on (this was the order of discussion for which Mugabe, for example, expressed a strong preference in conversation with Lord Harlech on 18 June).[4] If agreement can be reached on an Independence Constitution, we will be ready, as the constitutionally responsible authority, to play a full part in making arrangements for all the parties to participate in a fair test of opinion on that basis, but we cannot accept a series of preconditions as to how we should carry out that responsibility.

9. On the question of observers—the Front Line, etc., will be welcome to send representatives to London, if they wish, to keep in touch with us and the parties. But we do not envisage that they will be admitted to the conference. We will in any case be keeping them informed of progress through the usual diplomatic channels.

10. (If necessary, with any parties left out of the Rhodesian Delegation). We will see that the legitimate interests of minority parties are not over-looked at the conference. But in the interests of rapid progress towards a settlement we think it best if the negotiations are confined to the principal parties involved in the war.

4 Not printed (but see No. 22).

No. 41

Lord Carrington to Mr Lewen (Maputo), 10 August 1979, 6 p.m.[1]
Tel. No. 140 Confidential, Immediate (FCO 36/2435)

MIPT: Rhodesia[2]

1. The British Government announced in July that they intended in due course to put forward firm proposals of their own for bringing Rhodesia to legal independence. They agreed with other Commonwealth Governments in Lusaka that an appropriate procedure would be to call a Constitutional Conference to which the Parties would be invited.

2. The British Government now formally invite Bishop Muzorewa/the Patriotic Front to appoint a delegation of up to 12 members to attend a Constitutional Conference to be held at Lancaster House, London, from 10 September 1979, under the chairmanship of the Secretary of State for Foreign and Commonwealth Affairs,

1 Also sent to Mirimba, Salisbury and Lusaka Deskby 11 August 0730Z; Repeated for Information Immediate Deskby 11 August at 7.30. a.m. to Gaborone, Dar es Salaam, Luanda, Washington, UKMIS New York, Pretoria, Addis Ababa, Monrovia, Canberra, Ottawa, Wellington, Deskby 11 August 0830Z Lagos; Priority to Abidjan, Dakar, Kinshasa, Khartoum, Tokyo, EEC Posts and other Commonwealth Posts; Saving to Suva, Port Moresby, Honiara, Nuku'alofa and Tarawa.
2 No. 40.

Lord Carrington. The purpose of the conference will be to discuss and reach agreement on the terms of an independence constitution. An outline of proposals for an independence constitution is attached.³

3. The British Government are of the opinion that the military questions associated with a transition to legal independence should be for discussion once the terms of an independence constitution have been agreed. They believe, nevertheless, and strongly urge on the parties, that the prospects for a successful conference will be greatly enhanced if both sides will observe a ceasefire.

4. The constitutional proposals attached represent in outline the kind of constitution which the British Government believe should be acceptable to the Rhodesian people, and on the basis of which the British Government would be prepared to grant independence. The British Government would also be ready to consider granting independence on the basis of alternative proposals, put forward by any of the parties, on which the parties themselves are able to reach agreement. During the period between now and 10 September, the British Government are ready to take part in consultations at official level with the parties to whatever extent the Parties themselves think useful in order to prepare for the conference and to clarify their respective positions.

5. The British Government believe that the need for a political settlement and an end to the war in Rhodesia is more urgent today than it has ever been. In addressing this invitation to the parties they therefore also appeal to them, in the interests of the people of Rhodesia, to approach these negotiations, as they will themselves, in a constructive and forward-looking spirit and to lay the foundations for a free, independent and democratic society in which all Rhodesians, whatever their race or political beliefs, will be able to live in security and at peace with each other and their neighbours.

3 Not printed.

No. 42

Lord Carrington to Sir N. Henderson (Washington), 10 August 1979, 7.02 p.m.
Tel. No. 1010 Confidential, Priority (FCO 36/2539)

Rhodesia: Call by US Ambassador
1. Kingman Brewster called on me at his request this afternoon to hear about Lusaka. He said the US Government was very pleased with the outcome and would support our efforts. I told him in confidence about the proposed date for the Constitutional Conference (on which you will be receiving separate instructions). I said it might be useful if Moose and Lake came over here after they got back to Washington. Brewster said it would be useful to have 'someone in the bushes' during the conference and thought he might suggest to Vance that Seitz be sent back for the purpose.

2. I told Brewster that if the constitutional conference broke down due to Patriotic Front intransigence we would look to the Americans for support. Brewster said that

it was a contingency which would need to be looked at and we should together plan how to handle it.

No. 43

Sir L. Allinson (Lusaka) to Lord Carrington, 11 August 1979, 7.55 a.m.[1]
Tel. No. 894 Priority, Confidential (FCO 36/2410)

ZAPU views of the Commonwealth Agreement

1. Unlike ZANU, the ZAPU wing of the Patriotic Front have to a large extent avoided public comment on the Commonwealth Agreement on Rhodesia. They are no/no doubt awaiting a lead from Nkomo who is on his travels again.

2. However, ZAPU Vice-President Chinamano told the Egyptian Counsellor yesterday (9 August) that ZAPU were likely to insist on three points:

(*a*) Agreement on the constitution must be reached before there could be a ceasefire;

(*b*) The elections should not be supervised by Britain (we pointed out to the Egyptian that the Commonwealth communique did not/not say this). Commonwealth supervision would be acceptable;

(*c*) In relation to all party talks ZAPU would talk to their enemies (e.g. Smith) but would not/not sit down with traitors (e.g. Muzorewa).

3. Chinamano also said that a formula for elections should be agreed before any ceasefire and should include the return of all refugees so that they could participate, the drawing up of electoral rolls and the delimitation of constituencies. ZAPU were aghast at suggestions that all this could be accomplished by November.

4. I realise that there is nothing basically very new in the foregoing. But it may be useful in the absence of a more substantive ZAPU reaction and of interest that ZAPU are apparently in a large measure of agreement with ZANU. Clearly ZAPU are not/not confident of their ability to win an early election and if there is agreement on the constitution in the first half of September, may try to play for time in order to build up their support with the internal electorate. On the other hand, if other problems can be satisfactorily resolved, (a very big 'if' of course) the Front Line States and Zambia in particular may turn out to be in more of a hurry.

---

1 And Information Priority to Dar es Salaam, Maputo, Gaborone, Luanda, Information Routine to Lagos, Nairobi, Addis Ababa, Washington, UKMIS New York.

No. 44

Minute from Mr Wall (No. 10) to Ms Spencer, 13 August 1979
Confidential (FCO 36/2539)

Rhodesia: Meeting with the Ambassador

I have recorded in a telegram the main points which emerged out of Kingman Brewster's call on the Secretary of State of 10 August.[1]

In addition, you may wish to know that the Secretary of State asked Mr Brewster if there was anything the Americans could do to soften up the South Africans. Mr Brewster thought that the Americans had little credit but wondered if the Germans might help. You may wish to consider this suggestion.

Lord Carrington expressed the hope that the Americans would come with us if our strategy worked and stick with us if the conference broke down due to Patriotic Front intransigence. Mr Brewster described this as 'the most difficult contingency' (see also the reporting telegram attached).[2]

J.S. WALL

1 See No. 42.
2 Not printed.

No. 45

Lord Carrington to Sir N. Henderson, 14 August 1979, 9.55 a.m.
Tel. No. 1016 Immediate, Confidential (FCO 36/2539)

Your tel. No. 6 to Lusaka: Rhodesia[1]

1. Following message from the Prime Minister to President Carter was sent over the hotline last night
Begins:
Dear Mr President,

Thank you so much for your kind message about Rhodesia which I received in Lusaka. I am very glad that you think the work we did there was valuable. We were encouraged by the attitudes we encountered amongst our Commonwealth colleagues, and by the outcome which we believe does represent a constructive step forward.

We are now going ahead, on the basis of the agreement reached in Lusaka, to invite the leaders of the Salisbury administration and the Patriotic Front to come to a Constitutional Conference, to open at Lancaster House in London on 10 September, we shall be making an announcement at 12.30 London time tomorrow 14 August. I am arranging for full details to be sent to our Embassy in Washington so that they can brief the State Department.

Thank you for your support. There are difficult negotiations ahead, but we shall work hard for success. If we are to achieve it, we shall indeed need the close and detailed consultation with your Government that you suggest.

1 Not printed.

Warm personal regards,
Yours sincerely,
Margaret Thatcher.
Ends

No. 46

Lord Carrington to Sir L. Allinson (Lusaka), 14 August 1979, 7.15 p.m.[1]
Tel. No. 710 Immediate, Confidential (FCO 36/2410)

Your telno 895 and Bucharest telno 187[2] (not to all):
Rhodesia: Constitutional Conference

1. Byatt (AUS) saw Nkomo at Heathrow this afternoon to deliver the text of the invitation and outline of the Independence Constitution (tels. Nos. 140[3] and 141[4] to Mirimba Salisbury).

2. Nkomo, who was in jovial and bantering mood, read both texts with great care several times but asked few questions. He remarked of the outline constitution that 'we have seen this language many times before' and objected to the provision for commissions for the police and armed forces for which he said there was no British Colonial precedent: 'If you insist on including that the whole thing will founder.'

3. When told that a similar invitation was being delivered to Muzorewa he asked 'formally' to know in what capacity the Bishop was being invited. If he raises this on return to Lusaka you should say that Muzorewa is being invited as a matter of political reality (the same goes for the Patriotic Front): He is Head of the Administration in Salisbury. If there is a disposition to pursue the point you should as necessary make clear that we have little patience with quibbles of this sort.

4. Nkomo's first reaction to the date for the conference was that it was 'impossible'. When Byatt explained that the date had been chosen to avoid any clash with the Havana Non-Aligned Conference he did not explain his difficulties with 10 September or pursue the point beyond asking whether the opening would be at official level. He was told that it would be at Head of Delegation level.

5. Nkomo said that he would have to consider whether he could attend, and consult his people, and that he would be in touch with you on his return to Lusaka.

6. He is staying overnight in London. He was evasive about his future movements but said that he expected to be in Lusaka in three to four days' time.

---

1 And for Information Immediate to Mirimba Salisbury, Gaborone, Dar es Salaam, Luanda, Maputo; Information Priority to Washington, UKMIS New York, Pretoria, Lagos, Addis Ababa; Information Saving to Bucharest.
2 Both not printed.
3 No. 41.
4 Not printed.

No. 47

**Lord Carrington to Sir A. Parsons (UKMIS New York),
14 August 1979, 4.20 p.m.**
Tel. No. 412 Immediate, Confidential (FCO 36/2549)

Rhodesia: Constitutional Conference

1. If you have not already done so, please draw the attention of Dr Waldheim or his staff to the Commonwealth Agreement on Rhodesia and to the texts in FCO telegrams Nos. 140-142 to Mirimba Salisbury.[1] You should also transmit the following personal message to Dr Waldheim from the Secretary of State.

Begins:

Dear Mr Waldheim,

Although I expect the Zambian Government will be sending you the full text of the communique issued by the Commonwealth Heads of Government in Lusaka, I wanted to let you know personally that a very helpful agreement on Rhodesia was reached. I believe that we now have a new basis for helping Rhodesia to attain legal independence with wide international recognition. We are inviting the parties to a constitutional conference to open in London on 10 September. My people in New York will be able to brief you in detail. This is the first stage in what is bound to be a difficult process. Complex negotiations lie ahead.

I am grateful for the helpful attitude you have always shown over this problem and I am sure that I can count on your continued support as we seek a settlement in accordance with the terms of the Commonwealth Agreement.

Yours sincerely
Peter Carrington
Ends.

1 Tel. No. 140 is No. 41. Tel. Nos. 141 and 142 are not printed.

No 48

Note for the Record by Mr Cartledge (No. 10), 15 August 1979
Unclassified (PREM 19/110)

Points arising from a conversation between the Prime Minister and the Foreign & Commonwealth Secretary on Tuesday, the 14th of August 1979

Rhodesia

Lord Carrington told the Prime Minister that the FCO were considering ways in which the wording of the 1979 Rhodesian Constitution could be changed, for presentational reasons vis-à-vis the Africans, without affecting the substance. The Prime Minister argued strongly against meddling with the wording of the Constitution for purely presentational reasons. She thought that changes should be confined to those substantive amendments which were necessary to remedy the Constitution's defects and that the wording of the rest of the Constitution should be left alone. After some discussion, Lord Carrington accepted this.

It was agreed that Mr Peter Blaker would accompany Sir Antony Duff to Salisbury at the end of August; and that Lord Harlech should visit the Frontline Presidents and the Patriotic Front at the same time. Lord Carrington suggested, and the Prime Minister agreed, that Lord Harlech should also visit the United States and brief Senator Kennedy[1] among others.

(It was clear from the discussion that the Prime Minister and Lord Carrington are approaching the forthcoming Constitutional Conference in rather different ways. The Prime Minister wishes to do everything possible to enable the Conference to succeed and to bring about agreement on the Constitution: Lord Carrington regards such agreement as virtually inconceivable and therefore tends to regard the conference more as a means of enabling the British Government to get off the Rhodesia hook.)

1 Mr Edward Kennedy, Senator for Massachusetts, 1962-2009.

No. 49

Minute from Mr Renwick to Mr Walden, 16 August 1979[1]
Confidential (FCO 36/2549)

Rhodesia and the Security Council

1. Mr Cartledge's letter of 9 August to Mr Wall reports Sir A. Parsons' conversations with the Prime Minister about handling of the Rhodesia problem in the Security Council.[2] The Secretary of State may wish to have some further comments on this and on the legal position. The following is based on minutes by and discussions with Sir I. Sinclair and Sir A. Parsons.

2. If it is possible to achieve agreement at a Conference which includes provision for elections with the participation of the Patriotic Front and is therefore acceptable to the Front Line States we should be well-placed, in consultation with Security Council members, to negotiate a method of providing for the termination of sanctions. We could proceed by a letter to the Secretary General or the President of the Council recording that a satisfactory settlement has been achieved and that existing mandatory resolutions should therefore lapse. We might agree informally with other Security Council members that this would not be contested; or there might have to be a resolution affirming the above to be the case. The Soviet Union would not veto whatever the Front Line States accepted. But we might have to cope with attempts to defer a formal decision of the Council until a newly elected Government had been installed in Salisbury.

3. It is more likely, however, that the Conference will not lead to agreement. If Bishop Muzorewa accepts constitutional changes and it is subsequently demonstrated

1 Also sent to Mr Byatt.
2 No. 37.

that these are acceptable to the people of Rhodesia then, as Sir A. Parsons indicates, we should have to consider addressing a letter to the Secretary General (or President of the Council) stressing our responsibility to bring Rhodesia to legal independence; that the conditions for this have now been achieved; that the sanctions resolutions had been predicated on the existence of a rebellion against the United Kingdom's authority and in consequence were no longer operative.

4. This will provoke a strong reaction designed to assert that the mandatory resolutions remain in force. Other members of the Security Council will probably put forward a new resolution affirming this to be the case. We would try to secure enough abstentions to prevent the resolution securing nine affirmative votes. Failing that, we would veto it. Particularly if we have to veto, our opponents will argue strongly that UN mandatory resolutions cannot be deprived of their force as a result of a 'unilateral' interpretation by us, whether or not we are the administering power. This argument will get extensive support. It would be part of our argument that since the state of rebellion had come to an end, the basis for the 'threat to the peace' and hence for the Chapter VII resolutions no longer existed; and that the language of the resolutions and the reservations we have expressed on them support our interpretation. But it will be argued on the other side that in reality a 'threat to the peace' manifestly does exist, with a continuance of the fighting in Rhodesia and on its borders. It is the latter interpretation which is likely to be accepted by most members of the Security Council, by Third World countries and—more important—by many other Western countries. We could find ourselves in a very isolated position at the UN, with attempts being made to question our right to continue as a Permanent Member.

5. The attitude to be adopted by the other Western members of the Security Council on this point will therefore be of particular importance to us. Sir I. Sinclair's discussions with a senior Legal Adviser in the State Department indicate that the Americans may themselves have divided views, with some inclined to uphold the view that UN sanctions can be ended only by positive action by the Security Council. But the State Department Legal Advisers, although considering that there are arguments on the other side, are disposed to favour the view that it is within our competence as the constitutionally responsible authority to determine when the state of rebellion has come to an end and that, when it has, the mandatory resolutions can be regarded as having lapsed. Clearly, however, the strength of the support we get from the US government will depend on the *political* context. If we have clearly made a genuine effort to reach a negotiated settlement, which clearly has been frustrated by the Patriotic Front, and the Rhodesian electorate have shown that they approve the new Constitution, the Americans can be expected to be helpful. I am sure that it is desirable, as Sir I. Sinclair suggests, that he or the Second Legal Adviser should hold further discussions with the State Department Legal Advisers in September with a view to ensuring that their views are brought as closely as possible in line with ours on the legal interpretation.

6. The Legal Advisers have had less satisfactory exchanges with the French. The Legal Adviser in the Quai d'Orsay has taken the view that mandatory resolutions of the Security Council can be terminated only by positive decisions of the Council, or, failing that, at least in a context in which no member of the Council demurs from a statement by us that the rebellion has been brought to an end and that the resolutions

have, accordingly, lapsed. We should make a further effort with the French. We are explaining the position to HM Embassy in Paris and asking them to impress upon the French at a political level the importance we attach to our interpretation, as the basis for the handling at the UN of the sanctions aspect of a settlement. There may well be a case for the Secretary of State in due course to raise this with the French Foreign Minister.

7. We shall at an appropriate moment also need to take steps to explain our legal interpretation to the other Western members of the Security Council (Portugal and Norway). It would be unwise to do so prematurely. We must continue to operate on the basis that what we are aiming for is comprehensive agreement. But we should be ready if the Conference breaks down to explain our interpretations in detail. I am not, however, optimistic in those circumstances of obtaining their support for it—though it *may* be possible to persuade them to abstain on resolutions seeking to reaffirm sanctions.

8. We will also give thought, nearer the time, to Sir A. Parsons' proposals about lobbying those other members of the Security Council who might possibly help us to muster enough abstentions to avoid a veto (Gabon, Bolivia and possibly Kuwait). But we should not base our planning on the assumption that it will be possible to get the votes we need. If the African countries are united in insisting on the continuance of sanctions, it is unlikely that other Third World countries will be prepared to abstain.

9. It will be seen from the above that our chances of sustaining our position in the Security Council without a risk of virtual isolation on our legal interpretation depend critically on the political context in which we go to the Council. This under-lines—if that were necessary—the need, if we are to proceed with the internal parties alone, to do so in conditions in which that failure to achieve a wider agreement is seen clearly to lie with the Patriotic Front; and the approval of the Rhodesian electorate for what is agreed has been clearly demonstrated. The American attitude, in this as in other respects, will be crucial. It will be all the more important to have their support if—as is quite likely—we are unable to get support from other western members of the Security Council for our legal interpretation.

R.W. RENWICK

No. 50

Letter from Mr Doble (Maputo) to Mr Bonde, 20 August 1979
Confidential (FCO 36/2409)

Dear Bonde,

ZANU

1. Tekere, ZANU Secretary General, has twice recently dropped in at my house in the evenings, the last time staying for four hours. However, he never comes alone. I find him, like most of the ZANU leadership, an intelligent, pleasant person. But I regret that I have been unable to get much useful information out of him during these visits. Once he gets his hands on a large whiskey, Tekere tends to preach at length (perhaps due to his church up-bringing) and is notably skilful and devious at evading questions.

2. He said no more about 'pre-conditions'; and I expect ZANU to come to a conference. But their concern over military matters remains fundamental. Not only do they believe that only with their forces in charge can there be a real transfer of power; but they genuinely fear the results of returning to take part in elections, controlled by existing forces, a fear made more acute by the slaughter of 'auxiliaries'. But I feel that they might not insist on the complete dismantlement of the existing forces and substitution of their own; I tried to persuade him that this was quite unrealistic, which he did not deny. Tekere said he could imagine the external political leaders returning to take a share in government in the context of a settlement: but, he asked, what is to be done with the armies existing in the country? I surmised that we could only aim at some kind of merger of units into a new force under acceptable leadership, on which both the internal and external parties were represented. While not actually agreeing, he at least did not revert to the dismantlement theme, and expressed respect for the proposals which Lord Carver had made to deal with this problem.[1]

3. On the future of Zimbabwe, he said that there would be one or at the most two multi-party elections, before Zimbabwe became one-party (ZANU) state. They would not exterminate opponents; but one-party states were the African system; the people would rally to ZANU. Yet he maintained that this would be no monolithic or dictatorial system: Zimbabweans were very volatile and argumentative: even now during a war, he said, ZANU is remarkable for the intensive debates and questioning of policies that go on in its ranks. This he thought was valuable in order to achieve progress.

4. I constantly try to estimate whether prolonged contact with FRELIMO, during a liberation war, would result in ZANU trying to establish a FRELIMO-type system, or whether to an extent they have become inoculated against it. I regret that during long discussion of life in Mozambique, Tekere expressed little except admiration for FRELIMO. He thought their system was a true democracy; the people really had a say in the choice of candidates for the Peoples' Assemblies

---

[1] In August 1977, Lord Carver, former Chief of the UK Defence Staff, was appointed Resident Commissioner designate for Rhodesia with responsibility for ending the dispute over independence. He resigned after 14 months of deadlock.

and of 'peoples' judges'. I tried to disabuse him, without much apparent success. He did, however, say that FRELIMO's interference in people's private lives went too far: he deplored that one of the main reasons for the sacking of the last minister of agriculture had been that the Central Committee disapproved of his private life (a girl-friend expecting a baby whom he would not marry: and then, when he decided to marry her, they held her to be unsuitable). Tekere evidently quite enjoys his trips to the UK; but he waxed really eloquent about the delights of North Korea.

5. He objects to private ownership of land: on 'day one' of independence all land would become the property of the people. He admits that there must be safeguards to keep white farmers in production: but they will have to operate in accordance with the directives and priorities of 'the people's government'. He sympathised with FRELIMO over the church: some clergy were enemies of the people and would have to go; the churches tended to propagate colonialist attitudes; but he said many clergy in Zimbabwe, including his own father, supported ZANU. He defended Mozambique's nationalisation of schools, doctors, lawyers and housing, without saying whether he thought Zimbabwe should follow exactly the same path. Any private system implied privilege; and ZANU was completely against any section of the community having a privileged position. Whites were welcome to stay, but as Zimbabweans, sharing the facilities and hardships of all other Zimbabweans. I tried to explain to him that if they followed the Mozambican pattern, as in Mozambique, there would be a massive white exodus, impoverishing a country which could be not only rich itself, but a granary for its neighbours. Such arguments seem to cut little ice; I get the impression that ZANU want power and want to create a new society; if this means ruining the economy and starting afresh, anyway in the intellectual luxury of an irresponsible exile, it does not worry them.

6. I am conscious that I am relatively new to ZANU (and Africa). Keith Evetts[2] knows them much better. On his return, with his help, I will try to send a fuller assessment of the sort of Zimbabwe which ZANU would try and create.

Yours ever,
JOHN DOBLE

2 First Secretary, British Embassy Maputo, 1977-80.

No. 51

Sir L. Allinson (Lusaka) to Lord Carrington, 21 August 1979, 8 a.m.[1]
Tel. No. 922 Immediate, Restricted (FCO 36/2410)

My telno 919: Rhodesia Constitutional Conference[2]

1. The Zambian press today (21 August) reports a press conference given in Lusaka at which Nkomo announced the PF's acceptance of their invitation to the Constitutional Conference.

2. Nkomo is, in fact, quoted as denying that the conference's first task would be to draw up a constitution. He said that the PF regarded the meeting as a 'get-together between those involved in armed conflict and Britain ... as such any talks ... will have to be on how to end the conflict and not ... about a constitution'.

3. Nkomo claimed that Britain no/no longer had sole authority over Rhodesia. The PF had, through the armed struggle, brought 'Smith to his knees. We now share the same powers and responsibilities as the British Government in that country as we have liberated big chunks of land'. Nkomo is also quoted as rejecting a ceasefire during the talks ('the war goes on until that which we have been fighting for is achieved'), as rejecting British supervision of elections and demanding the disbandment of the Rhodesian security forces during the transitional period.

4. Comment:

This seems to have been one of Nkomo's more blustering performances and was no/no doubt primarily for the consumption of his own followers. Nkomo explained that the jointly agreed PF statement would be issued in Dar es Salaam and we should presumably regard this as representing the Front's definitive response to their invitation.

1 And Information Immediate to Dar es Salaam, Maputo, Mirimba Salisbury; Information Priority to Gaborone, Pretoria, Luanda, Washington, UKMIS New York, Lagos, Addis Ababa.
2 Not printed.

No. 52

Minute from Sir A. Duff to Mr Hurd, 23 August 1979
Confidential (FCO 36/2513)

Rhodesia

My visit to South Africa (20-22 August) was chiefly directed towards trying to get the South African Government to understand that our policy on Rhodesia was designed to result in the sort of settlement they would wish to see, whereas the policy they had hoped for (immediate lifting of sanctions and the granting of independence) would have been disastrous. I doubt if I succeeded in convincing them of this proposition, but I may have helped to persuade them not to try to turn Muzorewa against us. A subsidiary objective, designed to support the main objective, was to indicate if possible to the South Africans that it was not the British Government's intention to allow the Patriotic Front to have a veto over the proceedings at the Constitutional

Conference, or indeed over a settlement in general; But to do so without risking a South African public statement that we simply intended to promote Muzorewa and undermine the Patriotic Front.

2. I had two meetings on 22 August with Brand Fourie, the Secretary of the Department of Foreign Affairs. In the course of these I gave a very full account of the objectives of our policy and the process all thinking by which we had arrived at it. I made strongly the point that, while attempting to get wide international acceptance for an independent Rhodesia, it remained one of our objectives to establish a situation in Rhodesia in which moderate, democratic forces would be able to assert themselves. We were not in business to undermine the present set-up but to build on and develop it. We recognise that our policy carried with it the risk of losing the Whites and weakening Muzorewa's own position. We believed however that the prize was worth the risk, and that we could avoid them. I defined the prize as an independent Rhodesia, accepted internationally, able to restore itself economically and defend itself militarily, in which a moderate democratic government held power and the Whites were content to stay and play their part in the development of their country.

3. In the course of these discussions, Fourie referred to the chief South African anxieties as being, first that the Rhodesian Security Forces should not be destroyed; and second that we should not unduly drag out the process of reaching a settlement. Delay would mean a decrease in African support for Muzorewa and increased opportunities for the Patriotic Front. I took occasion to say that a successful Constitutional Conference was by no means assured. We would not necessarily come out of it with all the parties in full agreement. We might well lose some of them on the way. If so, we would have to go on with what was left. Our objective was to give Rhodesia the best possible start in life while at the same time limiting, to the extent that might be possible, the damage to our own interests.

4. On 22 August, Mr Leahy and I called on the Prime Minister, P.W. Botha. Pik Botha and Fourie were also present. I opened the discussion with a short and rather compressed account of our policy, acknowledging that the judgement we had made about the best way forward was different from the judgement the South African Government had made for themselves. P.W. Botha heard me out and then reposted with a series of his, by now standard and largely unjustified statements about the Conservative reversal of policy, the British disinterest in the stability and economic development of Southern Africa, our intention to connive with Mugabe in the destruction of the Rhodesian Security Forces and so on. He could not understand British policy and was deeply disappointed. When I attempted to dispute some of his more outrageous statements he threatened in effect to throw me out. I think this was probably done only for effect. At any rate, we went on to have a total of forty-five minutes of somewhat more constructive talk in the course of which he said that although he disagreed with it, he understood British policy and supposed that I wanted to ask for South African cooperation. So far as he was concerned, provided we did not tamper with the Rhodesian Security Forces, provided we did not sell out the Whites, and provided we did not create instability by undermining the present government, he was prepared to co-operate 'on minor matters'. I asked him what he meant by 'minor matters'. He said that he would say to Muzorewa: 'If you consider it in your interests to go along with the British plan, you should do so.'

5. I told him that it was not our intention to create instability, nor to produce an exodus of Whites, nor to undermine their confidence in the Security Forces. I could not however undertake (in answer to his question) that we would have everything settled by the end of the year, although we meant to get on as quickly as we could.

6. It was left to Pik Botha, in almost his only intervention in this discussion, to pose the inevitable question—if Muzorewa agrees to certain amendments to the constitution, but Mugabe and Nkomo do not, what will the British government then do? I said that although I could not tell when or whether such a conjunction might arise, it was an obvious possibility. At that moment the British Government would have to decide how their objective (which I had earlier defined) would be best served. There was one obvious course of action at that moment and I thought the British government might well decide to take it. In my view, the British Government were not interested in the idea of 'an agreement at any price'. Pik Botha commented to P.W. Botha: 'I think we are getting somewhere.'

7. I do not think I need to trouble you with the full records of these discussions, but they are of course available if you should want them.

ANTONY DUFF

No. 53

Mr Doble (Maputo) to Lord Carrington, 24 August 1979, 7.18 a.m.[1]
Tel. No. 224 Immediate, Confidential (FCO 36/2409)

My Tel No 221[2] *Not Copied: Rhodesia*

1. I saw ZANU Secretary General, Tekere last night at a party and said that it might be difficult to reserve all the rooms that ZANU wanted. He said that it was most important that we should do so: He explained 'We are coming in force with a strong delegation. We think Mrs Thatcher means business and we mean business: we intend to exhaust ourselves in negotiation.' He understood that they would have to pay for extra rooms themselves. They are unlikely to be able to give exact numbers on their delegation list before Mugabe returns early next week from Rumania.

2. He accepted with alacrity a suggestion that he should come to my house for a talk before he left for London. I should be grateful for any points which I should make, beyond existing guidance, and any aspects of a settlement which I should try to explore with him. On his last visit to me there was some indication that he realised that their demand for internal forces to be replaced by the Patriotic Forces was unrealistic, and he seemed keen to discuss what might be done with the latter.

---

1 And Information Immediate to Lusaka, Dar es Salaam, Gaborone, Salisbury, Luanda, Pretoria, Washington.
2 Not printed.

No. 54

Minute from Sir A. Duff to Mr Renwick, 24 August 1979
Restricted (FCO 36/2410)

Mr Ramphal, with whom I had a talk this morning, telephoned me this afternoon that he had just heard that Joshua Nkomo would be passing through London on Sunday and was hoping for a talk with him, Ramphal. Ramphal would arrange to see him, and would let us know afterwards what transpired. If there were anything particular we would like him to say to Nkomo we could let him know.

2. I said that the main point to make to Nkomo was that this conference was a real opportunity, and very likely the last opportunity, to reach an agreed settlement; and it was also probably the last opportunity Nkomo had to obtain a political future for himself in Zimbabwe. He should therefore come to London prepared to negotiate properly and sensibly.

ANTONY DUFF

No. 55

Letter from Mr Renwick to Mr Mansfield (UKMIS New York), 29 August 1979
Secret and Personal (FCO 36/2549)

Dear Philip,

Action at the United Nations over Rhodesia

1. The Secretary of State has asked us to consider the situation which could arise over Rhodesia in the Security Council. What follows takes account of the preliminary views of Ian Sinclair and Tony Parsons. We should be grateful for your comments, and those of Bill Squire and Kenneth James.

2. In its simplest form, the question at issue is whether or not the UK has the right, as the constitutionally responsible authority, unilaterally to determine that, with the end of the Rhodesian rebellion, the basis of the Chapter VII determination and of the consequent mandatory sanctions against Rhodesia has lapsed. The extent of the support which we receive from our friends and allies at the UN in various contingencies will be affected by whether they can acquiesce in our interpretation of the basis required for the revocation of sanctions.

3. It will of course be our objective to try to achieve an agreement at the Constitutional Conference which provides for elections with the participation of the Patriotic Front and is therefore acceptable to the African Group at the UN. If we achieve this, our aim would be to negotiate the termination of sanctions, in consultation with the Security Council members on an appropriate procedure, as soon as the agreement came into force (possibly in the form of a 'return to legality'). One procedure might be to record in a letter to the Secretary General or the President of the Council that a satisfactory settlement had been achieved, and that existing mandatory resolutions should therefore lapse. We might agree beforehand with other Security Council members that this would not be contested. Alternatively, there might have

to be an affirmative resolution. We assume that the USSR would not veto whatever the Front Line States accepted. There might, however, be attempts to defer a formal Security Council decision until after a newly elected government had been installed in Salisbury (thereby allowing the Patriotic Front, if they lost the elections, to claim they had not been fairly conducted and that sanctions should continue). This renders it all the more important that we should seek to get sanctions lifted as soon as an agreement comes into force.

4. Although the Patriotic Front feel themselves to be under some pressure following the Lusaka agreement, we have no reason at present to believe that they will negotiate seriously at the Conference. Nor is there as yet any certainty that the Salisbury delegation will be prepared to accept revised constitutional arrangements, and a demonstration of their acceptability. We must, however, give thought to the course of action we should adopt if Muzorewa has accepted what we regard as a reasonable settlement, and it has been demonstrated that this is acceptable to the people of Rhodesia, while the settlement has not been accepted by the external parties. Our tactics might then be to address a letter to the Secretary General or President of the Council, stressing the UK's constitutional responsibility to bring Rhodesia to legal independence. The letter would say that the conditions for this had now been achieved; and that the sanctions resolution had been predicated on the existence of a rebellion against UK's authority, and in consequence was no longer operative.

5. In this situation, other Council members would assert that the mandatory resolutions were still in force. We imagine that the African Group might put forward a new resolution, affirming this to be the case. We would try to secure enough abstentions to prevent the resolution attracting nine affirmative votes. Failing that, we would have to veto it. Particularly if we had to veto, our opponents would have an opening to argue that UN mandatory resolutions cannot be deprived of their force as a result of a 'unilateral' interpretation by the UK whether or not we are the Administrative Power. It is this argument which would presumably be accepted by most other members of the Security Council.

6. We would argue that, as the state of rebellion had come to an end, the basis of the 'threat to peace', and hence for the Chapter VII resolution, no longer existed. We would claim that the language of the various Security Council resolutions and of the UK's reservations on them supported our interpretation. But the contrary argument —that in reality there is a manifest 'threat to the peace' with a continuance of the fighting in Rhodesia and neighbouring countries—would probably be accepted, not only by Third World countries and a majority in the Security Council, but by some western countries.

7. It is at this point that the attitude of the other Western members of the Security Council would be of particular importance to us. On 20 July Ian Sinclair had an informal discussion with Steve Schwebel (Deputy Legal Adviser in the State Department) on the handling of Rhodesia at the UN. It emerged from their talk that the UN Division of the State Department supports the view that UN sanctions can be ended only by positive action by the Security Council, but that the State Department Legal Advisers are disposed to agree with us that the UK had the competence to determine when the state of rebellion has come to an end and the basis for mandatory sanctions has lapsed.

8. As you know, the Legal Adviser at the Quai d'Orsay asked David Anderson[1] recently about our interpretation. It emerged that de Lacharrière[2] takes a different view. He supports the argument—somewhat curiously, for a French official—that mandatory resolutions of the Security Council can be terminated only by positive decisions of the Council, or, failing that, at least in a context in which no member of the Council demurs from a statement by us that the rebellion has been brought to an end.

9. Clearly our chances of sustaining our position in the Security Council will depend crucially on the political context in which we go to the Council. If we are seen to have made a genuine effort to reach a negotiated settlement and that agreement has been frustrated by the Patriotic Front, and if the Rhodesian electorate have shown that they approved the new constitution, we would expect the Americans to be helpful (this was borne out by Tony Duff's discussions yesterday with Moose and Lake).

10. The Legal Advisers are now working on the memorandum setting out our interpretation of the legal position which, at an appropriate moment, they will want to put as a basis for discussion to the State Department Legal Advisers. Our tactics with the Americans thereafter will have to be decided in the light of the State Department's reactions to the memorandum.

11. We shall also need to make an effort with the French, and would welcome Kenneth James's advice on this. The Secretary of State is likely to mention in general terms to M. Francois Poncet[3] on 3 September the importance which we attach to the co-operation with the French in the Security Council over Rhodesia, as over other Southern African issues. In subsequent contacts with the French, we might aim to build our arguments not so much on a narrow legal interpretation of the steps required to terminate sanctions, as on France's acceptance of the UK's constitutional responsibility for Rhodesia; and on general French doctrinal reservations about the United Nations and its competence. We shall have a technical hurdle to overcome with the French, in that their application of sanctions against Rhodesia derives directly from Security Council resolutions, rather than from specific domestic legislation enacted in France. We should of course argue, on the basis of our interpretation, that the Security Council resolutions were no longer in force and in that event we should have to leave the French in no doubt of the importance the Government would attach to their not being seen to be adopting a position undercutting our constitutional responsibility to bring Rhodesia to legal independence and our legal interpretation at the Security Council i.e. we shall at least need their *acquiescence* in this.

12. Discussion at this stage with other governments about the situation which would arise from a failure to reach an agreed settlement would obviously be liable to misinterpretation. In due course, however, we shall need to consider action with other members of the Security Council who might possibly help us to muster enough abstentions to avoid a veto (though we do not rate very highly our chances of securing abstentions from any Third World governments if we are opposed by the African Group). We are keeping in touch generally with the Portuguese and Norwegians over

---

1 Mr David Heywood Anderson, Legal Adviser, UKMIS New York.
2 M. Guy Ladreit de Lacharrière, Legal Adviser to the French Foreign Ministry.
3 M. Jean Francois-Poncet, French Minister of Foreign Affairs, 1978-81.

Rhodesia and would try to enlist their support. We should obviously have to consider approaching Gabon, Bolivia and Kuwait at a later stage.

Yours ever,
R.W. RENWICK

No. 56

Minute from Lord Carrington to Mrs Thatcher (undated)[1]
PM/79/74 Confidential (FCO 36/2435)

Rhodesia: Constitutional Conference

1. In its discussion on 10 August the Cabinet endorsed the approach set out in my Memorandum of 9 August (C(79)33).[2]

2. Formal invitations to a Constitutional Conference at Lancaster House on 10 September were issued to Bishop Muzorewa and to the Patriotic Front on 14 August.[3] At the same time we put forward the outline of our proposals for the Rhodesian Independence Constitution (Annex A).[4]

3. Bishop Muzorewa accepted our invitation 'without preconditions'. We made it clear that the composition of the Salisbury delegation was a matter for him to decide. The Bishop would have preferred to come without Mr Ian Smith, but Mr Smith insisted on attending. His presence offers the advantage that whatever is agreed should be acceptable to the white community—though this is more than offset by the propaganda advantage his involvement will give to the Patriotic Front. Sithole and Ndiweni have also been included. Chikerema has been excluded. The initial Rhodesian reactions in our private consultations with them about constitutional change show that there is some tough bargaining ahead.

4. The Patriotic Front, after some initial prevarication, also agreed to attend. It would have put them in an impossible position vis-à-vis the Commonwealth African Presidents if they had refused to do so. They issued a statement rejecting our constitutional proposals, the idea of special representation for the white minority and our responsibility to ensure that new elections are fairly conducted. In other statements they have insisted on control over the administration and that the army should be based on the 'liberation forces.'

5. This approach is incompatible with the Lusaka agreement. There has been a good response so far from the Commonwealth African governments to our outline constitutional proposals and to the speed with which we have acted to give effect to the Lusaka agreement. The Patriotic Front will be nervous of coming under further pressure from the Commonwealth African Presidents.

6. Our task at the Constitutional Conference must be to demonstrate clearly that we are making a determined effort to achieve a fair settlement. The chances that

---

1 'At the end of August', according to Robin Renwick's internal history of the Conference: Patrick Salmon (ed.), *The Rhodesia Settlement, 1979-1980: An In-House Study* (Documents from the British Archives, No. 4) (London: FCDO Historians, 2021), p. 72.
2 No. 38
3 See Nos. 40 and 41.
4 Not printed.

the Patriotic Front will be prepared to accept reasonable constitutional proposals and agree to participate in new elections are slight (though Nkomo is under some pressure from his own supporters to negotiate; Mugabe, who believes that he is gradually winning the guerrilla war, can be expected to stick to his extreme demands). It is more probable that we shall be able to wring sufficient concessions from Bishop Muzorewa to achieve constitutional arrangement comparable to those on which we had granted independence to other Commonwealth African countries and which we would be prepared to put into effect subject to their being demonstrated to be acceptable to the people of Rhodesia.

7. We must not however so proceed as to give rise to accusation that this was our objective from the outset. We should seek to ensure that, if there is a break-down at the Conference, the responsibility for this is clearly seen to rest with the Patriotic Front and their intransigence on the basic issues—their demands in relation to the Constitution and the arrangements for elections. We should proceed in such a way as to put maximum strain on Commonwealth African governments' support for the Patriotic Front; and on the relations between Nkomo and Mugabe.

8. There is widespread support for the line we have so far adopted that we must proceed step by step and that the first task should be to secure agreement on the constitutional proposals we have put forward. We have successfully resisted demands to display more detailed proposals in advance of the Conference, thereby giving the Patriotic Front—or the Front Line States—a chance to evade the main issues, and to seek to pre-negotiate the Constitution.

9. We should persist with this approach. We have made it clear that there are large sections of the existing Constitution which are acceptable so far as we are concerned and which we would regard as being comparable to provisions in other independence constitutions. But it would be prejudicial to the chances of agreement and give the Patriotic Front a major propaganda advantage if, from the outset, we put on the table the full text of the existing Rhodesian Constitution, with amendments to it. The Rhodesians will themselves put their constitution on the table.

10. We should allow the Conference to open with our existing proposals (Annex A) and seek to oblige parties to declare their position in relation to them. The Salisbury parties are likely to do so in much more constructive terms than the Patriotic Front. We should then be prepared, if we are asked to put forward proposals to give effect to those principles, to table a fuller outline Constitution on the lines of the draft at Annex B attached.[4] This draft is based on the existing Rhodesian Constitution which may be regarded as common form and to focus attention on the main questions at issue. The tabling of this draft will be seen as a further serious attempt to promote agreement at the Conference. The draft is fully compatible with the existing Rhodesian Constitution, subject only to those areas on which we have already indicated we will insist on amendment. It will be easier for the Commonwealth Africans Presidents and others to support this approach in the initial stages of the Conference than for them to support an amended version of the full text of the existing Constitution. Mr Vance has assured us that it will have his full support.

11. We should not however allow the Patriotic Front to engage in a protracted filibuster or to evade the main issues. In order to focus attention on these and to make

clear our view on what would be acceptable on the central issues we should at the appropriate moment be prepared to make a statement on the question of white representation and the blocking mechanism and the public service commissions on the lines set out at Annex C.[4] The proposal that 20% of the parliamentary seats should be reserved to the white electorate will be criticised in Africa, but is indispensable to retain the confidence of the white community. These proposals are likely to be rejected by the Patriotic Front (if they have not already broken off the negotiations on other issues).

12. We shall also be pressed at the beginning of the Conference to make clear how we would proceed to give effect to the commitment in the Lusaka agreement to hold new elections if agreement could be reached. The way in which we should deal with this problem is set out at Annex D.[4] We should take the line that the purpose of the Conference is to reach agreement on the destination—the future independence Constitution. Once this has been achieved discussion should then take place of the means of implementing that agreement.

13. In order to emphasise at each stage that we are genuinely seeking agreement and to maximise the chance of weakening Commonwealth African support for the Patriotic Front, we should be prepared if the Conference appears to be reaching deadlock to urge the Commonwealth African Presidents to intervene with the Patriotic Front to persuade them to moderate their attitude. You will have an opportunity to do this with President Nyerere on 14 September.[5] It may be necessary to arrange an adjournment of the Conference for this purpose. We should in any event seek to avoid bringing matters to a point at which we proceed with Muzorewa alone until the civilian government has been established in Lagos on 1 October.[6]

14. We should in the meantime proceed with our bilateral negotiations with the Salisbury parties to establish the kind of Constitution we could in the end accept. We must continue to make clear, as we have done from the outset to Bishop Muzorewa, that in order to be able to proceed with the internal parties alone, we must be able to demonstrate the acceptability to the people of Rhodesia as a whole of what has been agreed. This means that there will need to be a referendum or new elections on the basis of the independence Constitution and that this test of acceptability must be supervised or at least observed by HMG.

15. I believe that this approach is the best way to build on the success achieved at Lusaka and in particular the recognition that it is our responsibility to make the proposals for legal independence. By this approach we should be able to carry the United States government with us and to retain as long as possible the support of the Commonwealth African Presidents (though it remains to be seen if they will be prepared to put effective pressure on the Patriotic Front). If, as is to be expected, the Patriotic Front reject these proposals, we shall then be best placed to proceed with the internal parties with a chance of securing a measure of international support at any rate from our principle friends and allies.

16. We should not however suppose that, if we are left to negotiate with the Salisbury parties alone, all will be plain sailing. Their instinct at that stage will be to

---

5 See No. 72.
6 On 1 October 1979, Mr Shehu Shagari was sworn in as President of Nigeria, returning the country to civilian rule after 13 years of military rule.

hold out for a settlement that will look as nearly as possible identical with their present arrangements. They will not easily comprehend the need to make changes for the sake of gaining international respectability. Specifically, they will wish to proceed by way of minimum amendment to their own constitution—rather than accepting a similar document enacted by the British Parliament, and they will refuse any form of test of acceptability. We shall have to persuade them that to obtain their legal independence, the lifting of sanctions, and recognition by a respectable number of governments, they must accept as a minimum that:

(*a*) whatever procedures they may go through in their own (illegal) Parliament, their independence constitution must be enacted as a whole by the British Parliament (though many of the provisions will be based on the existing Constitution);

(*b*) there must be some form of test of acceptability.

The prize will be within their reach; but they will have to be persuaded to grasp it.

CARRINGTON

No. 57

Mr Brown (Lagos) to Lord Carrington, 30 August 1979, 3 p.m.[1]
Tel. No. 673 Immediate, Confidential (FCO 36/2509)

Your tel. No. 600 (to Lagos only)[2]
Rhodesia/Nigeria

1. General Obasanjo received me for forty-five minutes this afternoon. I began by thanking him for his message of condolence to the Queen on Lord Mountbatten's death[3] and congratulating him and his government for their recent successful diplomatic efforts on Chad and for their remarkable achievement in successfully concluding their programme of elections, which will lead to civilian rule.

2. I then handed over the two messages from the Prime Minister. After he had read them I said I would like to speak mainly about Rhodesia since this had been the main cause of our difficult relations in recent months. Nigerian suspicions of HMG's intentions regarding the Muzorewa regime and sanctions were perhaps understandable in the early stages. However, we had engaged seriously in consultations with our Commonwealth partners and had taken particular note of Nigerian views as expressed by the Chief of Staff to Lord Harlech. The Prime Minister's statements just before and during the Lusaka conference took Nigerian views fully into account and has subsequently been endorsed by the whole Commonwealth Lusaka agreement. We had shown our commitment to the Lusaka agreement by the speed with which we had proceeded to organise a constitutional conference for next month. Thus we had not only announced a policy which met African

---

1 And Priority to Dar es Salaam, Gaborone, Maputo, Luanda, Mirimba Salisbury, Pretoria, UKMIS New York, Washington.
2 Not printed.
3 On 27 August 1979, Lord Mountbatten, a senior member of the UK Royal family, was assassinated by members of the Provisional Irish Republican Army, who detonated a bomb on his boat in the Republic of Ireland.

and Nigerian wishes but were energetically pursuing it. It does seem to me that Rhodesia was no longer a bone of contention between us and we should be able to resume our close and friendly relations in an atmosphere of confidence and trust. I hoped that General Obasanjo agreed.

3. Obasanjo said that his attitude to the Lusaka agreement was 'I shall believe it when I see it'. He had to confess that he was sceptical about the chances of an agreement on Rhodesia having seen so many previous efforts run into the sand. If the forthcoming conference were successful 'it would be to the eternal glory of Britain and the courage and statesmanship of Mrs. Thatcher'. But he could not be optimistic.

4. I said I hoped that his scepticism would not preclude full Nigerian support for efforts at the conference. We certainly did not under-estimate the difficulties but we believed that there was a better chance of success now than for a long time. However, we could not succeed without the active support of all our friends because the divergent views of the Rhodesian parties would mean that great pressure would have to be brought to bear to bring them to agree to a settlement on the lines agreed at Lusaka. Obasanjo replied 'we shall certainly support it', while continuing to express reservations. Since the present British Government in its early days seemed to be ready to recognise Muzorewa, it was understandable that the Patriotic Front had reservations about Britain as an impartial arbiter. They were suspicious that the conference was just a device to make Muzorewa more respectable so that in due course his government could be endorsed. If this were so, Nigeria would certainly not support the Conference. However, if the aim was to produce a genuine independence constitution and elections which were seen by the world to be free and fair, then he would support the conference and would be ready to recognise whoever was the victor of the elections, whether it was Muzorewa or even Smith. 'So on this basis we will support it.'

5. I said that an immediate occasion for such support was coming up very soon, i.e. the Non-Aligned Conference in Havana. We were concerned that the Havana Conference would adopt an extreme resolution which would make our task in London even more difficult and we hoped it would be possible for Nigeria to give support to a resolution giving some endorsement to the Lusaka agreement. Obasanjo, without giving a positive reply, said that he did not think that the Havana Conference would adopt a resolution which would prejudice the success of the London Conference. (I am afraid I did not ask him whether he himself would be going).

6. I said it was important that we should be agreed on the way ahead on solving the Rhodesia problem itself. But I was also concerned to repair the damage which the recent disagreement had caused to our bilateral relations. The Nigerian press was still in general hostile to us and it had not reflected the fact that the Lusaka agreement had been a great success and had resolved Anglo-Nigerian differences over Rhodesia. I hoped it would be possible for his Government to make the statement expressing its endorsement of the Lusaka agreement and its full support for the forthcoming London conference. Obasanjo said he would prefer to wait and see how the conference went. Referring to the failure of previous attempts at a settlement, including the Anglo-American proposals which Nigeria had firmly supported, he said they had been bitten several times and were therefore very shy.

7. Picking up this last phrase I said that British commercial interests had been bitten very hard by the embargo on the receipt of tenders from British firms for major government contracts. This had been imposed specifically in the context of Rhodesia 'pending clarification of the British government's policy'. This policy had been clarified to the entire satisfaction of the Commonwealth and we hoped therefore of Nigeria. There was no justification whatever for its continuation and I hoped that he could assure me that it would be lifted forthwith. Obasanjo's first reaction was to say, 'let's wait and see what happens at the London conference'. I protested vigorously that this was most unfair. We could not guarantee success at the London conference: all we could promise was to do our best to achieve a settlement on the basis agreed by the Commonwealth. The conditions for lifting the embargo had been amply fulfilled and its continuation in present circumstances would only be regarded as an unfriendly act. He took this very well with a smile and said that he would consider it. As I knew these decisions were collective ones I agreed but asked him to put the question before the SMC[4] at the first opportunity.

9. I then referred to the passage in Mrs Thatcher's message in which she said she would be asking me to talk to him about BP. He said brusquely, 'Forget about it. I don't want to talk about BP'. The tone was such that I judged that I might jeopardise the gains from the meeting so far if I pursued the question.

10. Obasanjo in conclusion said that he shared my hope that Britain's relations could revert to their former friendliness, and he would be replying to Mrs Thatcher's message in due course. But as to the method of conducting these relations, he wanted to warn us against using people outside the Government as channels of communication: He was sure I knew to what he was referring. (I assumed from this that he was aware of BP's various efforts to establish contact with senior figures in the FMG and/or Shagari through various non-official people: but he might also have been referring to our own use of unofficial sources as well as official channels to get through to himself in order to fix my appointment.)

11. Finally, picking up an earlier comment of his about the irresponsibility of the Nigerian press, I said I had been concerned about criticism of Mrs Thatcher's message to the President-elect and suggestions that this involved interference in internal affairs. I said in these circumstances I hoped it would not be misunderstood if I asked to pay my respects to the President-elect at some time in the near future: I thought it would be particularly useful to keep him briefed on the progress of the Rhodesia Conference. Obasanjo said he saw no objection whatsoever but thought the second half of September would be the right time and advised me to seek an appointment through the Ministry of External Affairs.

Comment

12. This was a tough interview which confirmed Obasanjo's rather grudging acceptance of Lusaka. I therefore fear that Nigerian support at the London Conference will not be whole-hearted under the present military government, and from this point of view we must hope that the moment to apply full pressure on the Patriotic Front will come after the civilian government has taken over here.

13. As regards the embargo on contracts I think I succeeded in shifting him from

4 Supreme Military Council.

his position of 'wait and see'. If he does bring the matter up at the SMG as he indicated he would, then the support of Danjuma[5] and Yar'Adua[6] should ensure the lifting of the embargo.

14. I shall comment separately on BP (not to all).

---

5 Lieutenant-General Theophilus Yakubu Danjuma, Nigerian Chief of Army Staff, 1975 - 30 Sept 1979.
6 Major General Shehu Musa Yar'Adua, Nigerian Chief of Staff, Supreme Headquarters, 1976- 30 September 1979.

No. 58

Letter from Mr Doble (Maputo) to Ms Spencer, 31 August 1979
Confidential (FCO 36/2409)

Dear Rosemary,

ZANU

1. In my letter of 20 August[1], I undertook to write again, with the benefit of Keith Evetts' views, on the sort of Zimbabwe which ZANU would be likely to create. It does not seem worthwhile to attempt any detailed assessment, at such a busy and fast-moving time just before the Constitutional Conference.

2. One cannot estimate with any confidence, what a ZANU-ruled Zimbabwe would look like. For one cannot be sure how far their public remarks reflect private views, how far policies expounded in exile would be carried out in practise and how far they would be induced to modify their policies by those at present in the country and by those returning from education, work or refuge abroad.

3. They stressed that they are a revolutionary party, pledged to take full power from the existing white rulers and to create a socialist, non-racial Zimbabwe. Most of those whom we meet here are influenced to an extent by Marxist ideas on politics, property, agriculture, religion, and international affairs. But probably most of them aim at a system of their own, subservient to no outside power or ideology, but drawing on the best, as they see it, in both East and West. Their mainly Christian up-bringing and British education gives them anyway a certain superficial attachment to some of our ideals. They aim at democracy and elections: but they expect democracy to consist soon of a one-party state working in traditional African style by consensus and grass-roots consultation, rather than a contest between different parties. They claim to encourage diversity of opinions and debate within their party; but the splits and detentions in Mozambique in the last few years give the impression of diversity within very narrow limits, if at all. They have political commissars and set much store by political indoctrination of refugees and of the inhabitants of 'liberated zones'.

4. They claim to be non-racial. But from their foundation they have kept the Central Committee all black, as a matter of policy, and have attracted few, if any, whites as members of the party. They say that they want those whites to stay in Zimbabwe who will cooperate with them, but have so far done little or nothing publicly to persuade them to do so or to reassure them; however, Tekere admits that

---

1 No. 50.

a massive publicity programme to this effect will be necessary after the war. In one breath they say that all who are prepared to stay are Zimbabweans regardless of colour, in the next they say that they must undo the results of the 1890 conquest and in particular take back the land stolen from them.

5. The land, they say, is a special issue. Private ownership of land by black or white is 'out'. They concede that efforts should be made to get white farmers to remain; but although they are not specific, one gets the impression that most farms will sooner or later be taken over, especially for black resettlement. 'Zimbabwe News' continues to talk of 'liberating settler farms'.

6. I referred to their views on religion in my letter of 6 August to Bonde[2]. The similarity of ZANU's and FRELIMO's approach to religion is notable. A FRELIMO gala show for the Prime Minister of Jamaica and ZANU's show to mark their 16th anniversary both contained satirical theatrical sketches on the history of their countries, which served to strengthen my opinions as set out in the letter to Bonde. In both, the arch-villain was the Church. ZANU showed a missionary (the only white in the show) as the master-mind of the military and commercial exploitation of the country: Cecil Rhodes[3] (acted by a black) was portrayed as a mere tool of the Church. Of course missionaries helped Rhodes in his negotiations with the natives. But ZANU, even privately, are reluctant to admit the benefits brought by Christianity, to which the attitude of those we meet here seems to vary between hostility and indifference.

7. At their anniversary show on 12 August Zvobgo and Muzenda[4] made speeches, which were of course very much for the benefit of the party faithful. They emphasized the unity of ZANU, its aim of a 'socialist' society, the world-wide struggle of 'socialism' and the help of 'progressive forces'. There would be no compromise: freedom would only be achieved by armed struggle. Muzorewa, as a traitor, received even more brick-bats than Smith. Muzenda said that all means of production and distribution should be owned by the people. Their concept of unity, he said, left no place for minorities or special groups; but those whites who loyally supported the new government need have no fear. However, afterwards Zvobgo was repeating privately to diplomats his certainty that war criminals would be hung, as at Nuremberg; if in reality, as some said, Mugabe disapproved of Zvobgo's 'death-list' threats last year, it seems rather unlikely that Zvobgo would still be taking this line.

8. ZANU do not seem to attach much importance to the destruction caused by prolonged war. They claim to prefer to have to rebuild their country totally, rather than to accept any continued white political, military or economic power. Muzenda in his speech claimed that the whites were ruining the economy by taking money out of the country, a clear effort to divert attention from the destruction caused by the war itself.

9. It is said that ZANU's policies would be considerably altered by opinions of the many educated Zimbabweans at home and those who would return from abroad. It is pointed out that these are largely western-educated. I doubt if too much faith should be placed on western education. Radical, and even Marxist, views are widespread in our educational system, especially in interpreting the history of colonialism, so that

2 Not printed.
3 19th Century British imperialist in Southern Africa and Prime Minister of Cape Colony, 1890-96.
4 Mr Simon Vengai Muzenda, Member Central Committee ZANU.

western education in no way means that Zimbabweans will necessarily adopt and implement the principles of liberal western democracy on their return home.

10. ZANU's experience of deprivation of political rights, fruitless peaceful opposition, revolt, prolonged imprisonment and a war of increasing savagery, in which the only military help comes from 'socialist' countries, is in my view the main influence upon their political views and plans for Zimbabwe. There remains an amazing amount of goodwill towards the UK. But, as Hove[5] said to me earlier this year, the experience of the armed struggle was rapidly changing their ideas on the sort of country which they wished to create. Nationalism remains their dominant motive: they would thus be likely, after the war, to resist Soviet influence or manipulation. Economic realities would somewhat temper their idealism. But their main foreign policy aim would be the overthrow of the present South African regime. Nor should we, in our view, be under any illusions about the type of society which they would seek to create in Zimbabwe; this would be more akin to (but not the same as) Mozambique, than to Kenya, Tanzania or Zambia. But we should not consequently, in our view, seek to exclude them at the conference: for only if ZANU can be brought into a settlement can peace and reconstruction follow.

Yours ever,
J. F. DOBLE

5 Mr Dunn Mabika Hove, ZANLA Military Intelligence Officer.

No. 59

Letter from Mr Alexander (No. 10) to Mr Walden, 3 September 1979
Confidential (FCO 36/2436)

Dear George,

Rhodesia: Constitutional Conference

The Prime Minister has seen the Foreign and Commonwealth Secretary's undated minute to her about the Constitutional Conference due to open next week.[1] She is in general content with the line set out in Lord Carrington's minute.

The Prime Minister has, however, noted that Annex D, paragraph 3, provides for an election to take place 'under impartial supervision' and only adds subsequently (paragraph 4) that HMG is 'prepared to assume' its responsibility to see that this requirement, *inter alia*, is met. In the Prime Minister's view, HMG is *charged* with responsibility for the election, and the election should be held under British supervision.

The Prime Minister has also noted that Annex D makes no provision for a referendum, should that be thought preferable to an election.

Yours ever,
MICHAEL ALEXANDER

1 No. 56.

No. 60

Minute from Mr Renwick to Sir A. Duff, 4 September 1979[1]
Confidential covering Secret (FCO 36/2436)

Rhodesia: Attitude of the Parties and of the 'Front Line' States

1. No. 10 have asked for a note on the attitudes the parties are likely to adopt at the outset of the Rhodesia conference. I enclose a note on these and on the attitudes of the 'Front Line' states with a draft covering letter to No. 10.[2]

R.W. RENWICK

Enclosure in No. 60
Secret

Rhodesia: Constitutional Conference
Attitude of the Parties

The Patriotic Front
A. *ZANU (Mugabe)*

1. The indications [. .][3] are that ZANU, as expected, will not be coming to the Conference with any intention of negotiating seriously for an agreement. Mr Mugabe, influenced by the experience of FRELIMO in Mozambique, knows that to win a guerrilla war it is not necessary to defeat the Rhodesian security forces in the field (which is beyond his capacity); it is sufficient to go on fighting until the other side has had enough. He now has 11,000 men fighting inside Rhodesia with some 15,000 in reserve. It is more difficult for the Rhodesians to hit targets in Mozambique than Zambia and Mugabe's army (ZANLA) are more adept in the use of genuine guerrilla tactics, avoiding large concentrations. He has the support of the Mozambique government and also, though less unequivocally, of Nyerere. If the military pressure exerted by ZANLA can be sustained and increased, a point could come at which the white exodus would become a flood and victory would be attainable. But he is conscious that he could at that stage find himself in a military confrontation with Nkomo; and of the risk of South African intervention.

2. Mugabe is likely to adopt an intransigent attitude at the Conference. This is in his nature; he has never shown himself ready to compromise. His political strength lies partly in that fact that, alone among the nationalist leaders, he has never been caught negotiating with Mr Smith. He was able to exploit to Nkomo's disadvantage the latter's last attempt to negotiate with Mr Smith in August 1978. Mugabe believes, probably rightly, that he could win an election against Nkomo (being a Shona he has a wider tribal base) and that the longer the war goes on the stronger his position will become. Mugabe will be adamant in his insistence that the Patriotic Front should

---

1 Also sent to Mr Walden.
2 Sir A. Duff minuted on 4 September: 'Some of the judgments in the note are a bit stark—but I think the paper will serve its purpose.' Lord Carrington saw the note and approved its issue on 6 September.
3 A phrase is here omitted.

exert effective control over the administration *before* new elections are held and that the future army must be 'based on the liberation forces'. He will also seek to argue that there should be no separate white representation at all and no amnesty. He will not want any constraints on the kind we have normally written into independence constitutions. Much is sometimes made of Mugabe's Catholic education, which has certainly influenced his cast of thought. But he is a committed Marxist, though not of the pro-Soviet type. ZANLA receive no direct military support from the Soviet Union (though they do have access to older Soviet equipment supplied to them by the Mozambicans, Ethiopians and others). Mugabe dislikes and distrusts the Soviet government because of their support for Nkomo. He is intellectually in a much higher category than either Nkomo or Muzorewa. He is at present in more effective control of ZANU than in the past, though it is a collective leadership, within which he depends on Tekere (Secretary-General) and the military commander, Tongogara. Most of his senior colleagues are much less flexible. Mugabe is contemptuous of Nkomo whom he regards as an opportunist; but he will be concerned to maintain the semblance at least of Patriotic Front unity throughout the Conference and to drag Nkomo with him in a refusal to participate in new elections held under our authority. Mugabe would be in serious difficulty, both politically and militarily, if Nkomo agreed to participate while ZANU tried to continue fighting.

B. *ZAPU (Nkomo)*

1. The indications [. . .]³ are that Nkomo will be under considerable pressure from the Zambians and elements within his own party to negotiate seriously at the Conference. But he will be concerned not to appear to be being out-flanked by Mugabe or to be exposed to accusations of splitting the Patriotic Front. It is difficult to predict how he will re-act to these contradictory pressures. He may at the outset adopt a blustering and intransigent approach. But whereas Mugabe tends to take the same line in public and in private, Nkomo can be expected to give a number of private indications that he may be prepared to participate in new elections. The leading 'moderate' members of his party (Chinamano and Chambati) will be urging him to do so, provided they are satisfied that the pre-independence arrangements would give ZAPU a fair chance.

2. Nkomo at present has only about 2,800 men inside Rhodesia, but over 20,000 in Zambia. His troops are better equipped (by the Soviet Union) than those of Mugabe; but various plans for a conventional offensive have come to nothing in the face of Rhodesian air attacks.

3. Nkomo's strength lies in the fact that as the traditional nationalist leader he enjoys considerably more support in the OAU than Mugabe. He also has direct Soviet support. A settlement involving Nkomo (but excluding Mugabe) would get widespread support elsewhere in Africa. Nkomo dislikes and affects to despise the doctrinaire and physically unimpressive Mugabe but, in recent years, has been steadily out-manoeuvred by him. Nkomo launched a serious attempt in December 1975 to negotiate an orderly transition to majority rule with Mr Smith and it was only after the breakdown of that attempt in March 1976 that he took up the 'armed struggle', from which he had been isolated in any case during his ten years in detention (1964-74). His forces (ZIPRA) are more vulnerable to Rhodesian attack than those of Mugabe, because some of the units are formed on 'conventional' lines and it is

easier for the Rhodesians to attack bases in Zambia (where they have better intelligence). ZIPRA's strategy, in the event of a collapse inside Rhodesia, would be to use their conventional units to put themselves in a position to dictate terms to ZANU.

4. There has been an erosion of Nkomo's support inside Rhodesia, as Muzorewa and Mugabe have established themselves as the Shona leaders. But Nkomo still enjoys general support among the Ndebele (20% of the population) and there could be a rapid revival in his political fortunes if he returned to Rhodesia as the 'peace-maker'. He also has among his lieutenants some of the ablest and—in the past—most moderate of the older nationalist leaders. Despite President Kaunda's strong personal support for Nkomo there is a good deal of discontent in both Zambia and Botswana at the ill-disciplined activities of Nkomo's forces. He will not therefore want to put himself in a position where a failure of the Conference is attributed to him, to an extent which could affect Kaunda's continuing support. He will oppose the idea that up to 20% of the Parliament should be elected by whites on a separate roll. But he is likely to attach most importance to the pre-independence arrangements (that elections should not be influenced by the present administration, Muzorewa should not be permitted to campaign as 'Prime Minister' and there must be a UN or Commonwealth force).

The Salisbury Delegation
A. *Bishop Muzorewa*

1. When the Prime Minister saw Bishop Muzorewa on 13 July she made clear to him that the independence Constitution would have to be comparable to the constitution which we had given other African countries at independence.; the Constitution would have to be seen to have originated with and to be approved by the United Kingdom; and there would have to be a demonstration of the acceptability by the people of Rhodesia of what had been agreed. On this basis we would not permit any other party to exercise a veto over a settlement. Muzorewa is therefore in no doubt about the basis on which we will be prepared to grant legal independence.

2. As he demonstrated in the April elections, Muzorewa has extensive political support in the Shona population (though virtually none in Matabeleland). He has a well-organised party machine, some able lieutenants and is not regarded as an opportunist like Sithole or Chikerema. He has a genuine commitment to a solution in which the white community would be able to play a full part.

3. Muzorewa and the other UANC Ministers would, for their part, have no difficulty accepting the kind of constitutional changes we regard as indispensable. But they are concerned that if they lose the support of the defence commanders, they would no longer be able to hold off the Patriotic Front. There are signs that Muzorewa's inability since the April elections to bring about changes affecting the lives of the African population generally may be losing him some support. He is also concerned about the attitude of Sithole, Chikerema (leading a break-away faction of his own party) and Ndiweni. He realises that we have been doing what we can to bolster his authority, both in public statements and in leaving in his hands the composition of the Salisbury delegation.

4. Muzorewa is not a decisive leader. He will be looking to us to fight his battles for him both vis-à-vis the Patriotic Front and the Rhodesia Front. He will not be

able to impose his own views on the Rhodesia Front Ministers. But he will realise that it is essential to his own prospects of political survival to be seen to be making progress towards a settlement and the lifting of sanctions. He will at the outset make a strong defence of the existing Constitution, but is well aware that we will not be prepared to grant independence on that basis. We shall be impressing on him the need at every stage in the Conference for him to be seen to be adopting a reasonable attitude in the face of Patriotic Front intransigence. He will be worried about any combination involving Nkomo, which could threaten his political position. He will also show resistance to the idea of a new election, but has said publicly that he would be prepared to accept this if it would help to win international recognition and bring an end to the war. He would be well-placed to win such an election if he is able to show that he has succeeded in negotiating the arrangements for legal independence and the lifting of sanctions.

B. *The White Community*

1. *Mr Ian Smith* will come to the Conference with the intention of winning the political argument with the Patriotic Front, but also with the object of emerging with little or no change to the present Constitution. The defence commanders did not support his inclusion in the Salisbury delegation and his presence will render it more difficult for Muzorewa to present himself a real leader of his delegation.

2. Mr Smith has brought off the extraordinary feat of defying most of the rest of the international community for fifteen years, but has only been prepared to concede majority rule at a stage at which the security situation was already almost out of control. His deferment of the elections which were due to be held in December 1978 caused serious problems for Muzorewa. It was only under strong pressure from the South Africans that he went ahead with them in April 1979. He promised the South African Prime Minister and stated publicly that he would withdraw from politics before the April elections, and subsequently gave equally firm undertakings not to participate in the government thereafter. His present stated intention is to withdraw from politics once legal independence has been achieved and sanctions are lifted. His endorsement of a settlement would, however, be an important element in the maintenance of the confidence of the white community. His withdrawal from the Government could also be a useful element in presenting a settlement to moderate international opinion.

3. Mr Smith will hope that as the November date for the renewal of Section 2 of the Southern Rhodesia Act approached the Government will be under pressure to accept only minor changes to the Constitution (and no demonstration of its acceptability). It will be essential to disabuse him of any illusion on this score. Mr David Smith, who will be accompanying him, is likely to be prepared to accept reasonable constitutional change. But it will be difficult to get him to stand up to Ian Smith on any issue of consequence.

4. General Walls has told Muzorewa that it is extremely important that this opportunity to find a resolution should be seized. He does not appear himself to see serious difficulty about our proposals for constitutional change. He believes that the Rhodesian forces can contain the security situation, though Mugabe's guerrillas are exerting increasing pressure. The business and farmers' leaders are also anxious for a settlement.

5. The white officials in the Salisbury delegation will negotiate to preserve as much as possible of the existing constitution, in particular the numerous provisions which give them effective control over the administration, judiciary and the defence forces. It will be possible to reassure them that we have very much in mind the need to preserve standard of efficiency in the civil service, within which senior appointment must, however, be under ultimate governmental control. They will negotiate with considerable intransigence, but will be doing so against the background of a political and military situation which could deteriorate rapidly if no settlement is in sight; and the fact that the real pressure on the white community is exerted by the war.

C. *Other Parties*

1. *Sithole* will support the kind of constitutional changes we have in mind, though there is a danger that he will try to play a maverick role at the Conference. We have told him that it would be extremely unwise of him to put forward proposals (as he intended to do) for a transitional administration until agreement has been reached on the outline independence Constitution. He has been flirting, through his connections with Mr Rowland on Lonrho, with some kind of alliance with Nkomo, involving also Chikerema and, possibly, Ndiweni. Nkomo would only be interested in such an alliance on his own terms. Sithole detests Mugabe, who supplanted him as leader of ZANU.

2. *Chief Ndiweni* will try to use the Conference to put forward ideas for a Constitution giving greater representation to Matabeleland; and will be hoping to see an agreement involving Nkomo (as the real Ndebele leader).

[Note:
It will be apparent from the above that if the Salisbury delegation find themselves in an awkward position because of the intransigence of the Rhodesia Front, this is likely to put considerable strain on the cohesion of the various elements of the governing coalition.]

No. 61

Steering Brief by Rhodesia Department, 6 September 1979
Secret (FCO 36/2436)

Rhodesia: Constitutional Conference

Steering Brief
Objectives
1. Our objectives *at this stage* of the negotiations will be:
(*a*) to demonstrate that we are engaged in a serious attempt to achieve an agreement on terms which should be acceptable to both sides;
(*b*) to retain as long as possible the support of the Commonwealth African Presidents, thereby putting maximum strain on their support for the Patriotic Front if, as is probable, the latter adopt an obstructive attitude;
(*c*) to leave ourselves free, if the attempt to achieve a wider agreement is unsuccessful, to proceed with the internal parties, provided that:

(i) they will accept the constitutional changes we have made clear we regard as indispensable; and

(ii) arrangements will be made to show that the outcome is acceptable to the people of Rhodesia.

Tactics

2. We should aim by the end of the first week of the Conference to have put forward our fuller constitutional proposals (Annex B),[1] thereby leaving ourselves in the best position to urge President Nyerere when he comes to London on 14 September to support a settlement on these lines.

3. The Conference must not be allowed to develop into a replay of the unstructured and profitless 'all-party discussions' in Geneva.[2] We should at each stage seek to retain the initiative by putting forward *our* proposals (Annex B in the first week; and a statement on the key issues in the second week). We should be prepared to deal firmly with procedural quibbles by the Patriotic Front. We should not place any emphasis on confidentiality in the early stages of the Conference; we alone would be likely to observe any such constraints. Our aim in this stage will be to demonstrate publicly the reasonableness of our proposals (for example, we should publish Annex B) and the intransigence of the Patriotic Front.

4. The Patriotic Front may well put forward their own proposals. We cannot decide our response to these until we have seen them. Their general tactic, however, will be to try to discuss first the military and other transitional arrangements. We should make clear—on the lines of Annex D—that this is a *Constitutional* Conference. If agreement can be reached on the main provisions of the Constitution, this can be contingent on agreement on the pre-independence arrangements—the key element in which is acceptance by both sides that elections should be held under our authority. Military questions will fall to be discussed last. Our tactics throughout the early stages should be to concentrate on bringing the discussion back to the Lusaka agreement and to our outline constitutional proposals. We should encourage *both* wings of the Patriotic Front to express their views on the various questions at issue. Other members of Bishop Muzorewa's delegation will wish to speak and should be permitted to do so.

5. In the early stages it will be important not to rush the process. We must not expose ourselves to charges of having deliberately precipitated a crisis at the Conference. We should avoid bringing matters to a point at which it is clear that we intend to proceed with the internal parties alone, at least until after the civilian government is established in Nigeria on 1 October. This may point to an adjournment of the Conference—on the basis of our proposals on the key issues—at the end of the second week, allowing time for a final effort to persuade the Commonwealth African Presidents that a fair settlement is on offer if the Patriotic Front are prepared to participate.

6. It will be essential at each stage to retain the confidence of Bishop Muzorewa. He should start from the position of defending the present arrangements in Rhodesia

---

1 Annexes not printed.
2 The Geneva Conference took place from 28 October to 14 December 1976. It was mediated by the then Labour UK Government, but proved to be unsuccessful in its attempt to agree a new constitution for Rhodesia, as well as trying to end the fighting between the Rhodesian security forces and guerrilla forces led by Mugabe and Nkomo.

and the April elections, but must be persuaded to adopt a reasonable and constructive attitude towards our proposals, in contrast to the intransigence likely to be displayed by the Patriotic Front. He can be assured that whatever ideas we put forward at the Conference will be fully compatible with what we have throughout made clear to him are our pre-requisites for a settlement (as explained to him by the Prime Minister on 13 July); and that the Patriotic Front will not be allowed to exercise a veto. We should not, however, put ourselves in the position of pre-negotiating with the Rhodesians the action we consider it necessary to take at the Conference. There is a demand on both sides to make clear what *our* requirements are. We should remain in close political contact with the Salisbury delegation throughout, but should not enter into detailed negotiations with the Rhodesians in the early stages of the Conference (such negotiations would be likely to become public knowledge). The time for further detailed discussions with Rhodesian officials will come after the first stage of the Conference: it will be much easier to bring them to successful conclusion against the background of a firm statement (on the lines of Annex C) of what we will be prepared to enact on the key issues. The chances of winning international support for the eventual outcome depend on our proceeding this way.

7. After the adjournment, the Conference would in due course be resumed on the basis of the proposals we had put forward. The Patriotic Front would still have a chance to participate on that basis; but the probability is that they will reject them. We should then complete negotiations on the Constitution with the internal parties and, in parallel, arrange a demonstration of their acceptability.

The main issues

8. There is with one proviso nothing in our general *constitutional proposals* (Annexes B and C) to which Commonwealth African governments can reasonably object. The provisions for constitutional amendment are comparable to those in other Commonwealth countries. Public service commissions are unexceptionable provided they are under ultimate governmental control. If it is argued that there should be an executive President, we can say that we could agree to this, provided the parties did so. If questions are raised about the Senate, we can point to the very limited extent of its powers. There will, however be resistance to the idea that, for the first five or at most ten years, 20% of the members of the Assembly should be whites elected separately by the white electorate. This is a higher percentage than has been conceded in any other independence Constitution; and it will be argued that the white representatives should be chosen by the electorate as a whole. This is not, however, a point on which there can be any real give in our position. We must take the firm line that, in the circumstances prevailing in Rhodesia, this is not unreasonable as a transitional provision; and that the essential point is that the white members must not be able, acting by themselves, to block constitutional amendment or a wide range of legislation.

9. The way in which we should seek to enlist Commonwealth support for a reasonable settlement on this point is related to the question of *the pre-independence arrangements*. Presidents Nyerere and Kaunda—unlike the Patriotic Front—accept that elections should be held under our authority. We shall need to assure them that, if the Patriotic Front are prepared to participate, we will supervise the electoral process to the full extent necessary to ensure that the Rhodesian administration would

not be in a position to deprive them of any chance of success. This would apply to freedom to campaign and free access to the press, radio etc. The Commonwealth Presidents may argue that Bishop Muzorewa should not be able to campaign as 'Prime Minister'. We should reply that all parties would have to campaign as parties, with equal chances of success. They will argue that the policing of the elections by the Rhodesian police would not be acceptable unless they were brought under our control. We should have to be prepared to make provision for this. In short, if there is *an agreement involving both sides and a ceasefire* we should be prepared to say that we will contemplate a return to legality before independence—and the lifting of sanctions at that stage.

10. The Commonwealth Presidents are likely to say that there will be a need for some additional neutral force to support the police and watch over the maintenance of a cease-fire. As a final demonstration that we are prepared to give the Patriotic Front a fair chance to participate and, above all, to put maximum strain on Commonwealth support for them if they are not, we should at the appropriate moment be prepared to indicate to Nyerere and Kaunda that—if this is the final element required for a peaceful settlement and they are prepared to support our constitutional proposals—we do not exclude the idea of a Commonwealth force. But we should not put ourselves into a position of having to sell a Commonwealth force to Muzorewa unless there is firm evidence that the Commonwealth Presidents are prepared to 'deliver' the Patriotic Front. It will be for the Commonwealth African Presidents to decide whether they are prepared to oblige the Patriotic Front to participate in elections which they would have a fair (but no more than that) chance of winning.

11. We should have regard throughout to the possibility that Nkomo may be more seriously interested in a settlement than Mugabe. We should bear in mind, however, that the chances of split in the ranks of the Patriotic Front will be correspondingly less if we appear to be trying to engineer it. We are making arrangements to remain in touch with Nkomo throughout the Conference.

Conclusion

12. In the aftermath of the Lusaka agreement we are in a position in which we should be able to demonstrate that we are ready to give the Patriotic Front a fair chance to participate, if they are prepared to put their electoral popularity to a fair test. If not, we shall be well placed to proceed with Muzorewa, subject to the acceptance of constitutional change and demonstration of acceptability (whether by a referendum or an election). There will be resistance to this from the internal parties; but Bishop Muzorewa has said publicly that he does not rule this out if it is the key to legal independence and the lifting of sanctions. Such a demonstration is essential to our ability to carry the US government and some others with us, as well as to demonstrating beyond doubt that all six principles have been fulfilled. Although there will be tough bargaining ahead, key members of the Salisbury administration (e.g. General Walls) are conscious that a failure to seize this opportunity to reach a settlement would have serious consequences, both political and military.

No. 62

Letter from Mr Lyne to Mr Alexander (No. 10), 6 September 1979
Confidential (FCO 36/2436)

Dear Michael,

Rhodesia: Constitutional Conference

The Foreign and Commonwealth Secretary has seen the Prime Minister's comments, set out in your letter of 3 September, on his minute about the Conference.[1]

Lord Carrington agrees that there can be no question of any authority other than the British Government supervising the election. I enclose an amended version of Annex D[2] which makes this unequivocally clear.

You will see that this version still makes no reference to the possibility of a referendum as an alternative to an election. This is because the paper takes an all-party agreement on the independence constitution as a starting-point. In this context there is no need to canvas the idea of a referendum since an election would be inevitable. The question of a referendum would, we think, only become actual in the event of the Patriotic Front withdrawing from the negotiation. In that case a properly supervised or observed referendum, rather than an election, might, as suggested in paragraph 14 of Lord Carrington's minute, be an alternative test of the acceptability of an agreement with Bishop Muzorewa.

Yours ever,
RODERIC LYNE

1 Nos. 59 and 56 respectively.
2 Not printed.

No. 63

Minute from Mr Hall to Mr Powell, 6 September 1979
Confidential (FCO 36/2409)

I met-in further members of the ZANU Delegation last night at Heathrow, principally Mr E. Tekere and Robson Manyika[1]. Flights were delayed and consequently I had a long opportunity to chat to members of the ZANU Greeting Party.

2. The following points emerged which may be of interest:

(*a*) One member of ZANU somewhat scornfully described Mr Nkomo as 'that big shareholder in Tiny Rowland's Company';

(*b*) Zvobgo, who was part of the receiving party, kept referring to the Salisbury Delegation as 'the criminals or the traitors'—one does have to bear in mind however the emotional nature of this man;

(*c*) I noticed that although there was a large turn out for Tekere (which is an African greeting custom anyway), he was greeted far less effusively than Ushewokunze[2] and Zvobgo last Monday night;

1 ZANU Secretary of Manpower Planning and Labour.
2 Mr Herbert Sylvester Masiyiwa Ushewokunze, member of ZANU Central Committee, external wing; and member of ZANU Executive and Secretary for Health.

(d) Mr Shava[3] the London Representative made a number of interesting revelations about the organisation of ZANU in the UK. Apparently, they call the UK 'the British district' and he claims they have 1500 Zimbabwean members in the country all of whom are card-indexed and can be 'mobilised' to give administrative and other assistance to the Party on occasions like this. Most of these members are, according to Shava, students studying in the UK and presumably they could also be 'mobilised' to take part in demonstrations etc.

M.M. HALL

3 Mr Frederick Musiiwa Makamure Shava.

No. 64

Letter from Mr Lyne to Mr Alexander (No. 10), 7 September 1979
Confidential (FCO 36/2436)

Dear Michael,

Rhodesia: Constitutional Conference

You asked for Lord Carrington's advice on the Prime Minister's role in relation to the Constitutional Conference.

We understand that the Prime Minister will attend, for a short time, the reception for delegates at 18.00 on 10 September. Lord Carrington very much welcomes this. It will demonstrate her close interest in the Conference and give the participants the opportunity to meet her.

Apart from this, Lord Carrington thinks that it would be best for the Prime Minister to hold herself in reserve during the first week. Both sides are likely to appeal to her and to seek bilateral meetings. To agree to such meetings would risk running the Conference in effect at two levels. In Lord Carrington's view, it would be a mistake to agree to any bilateral meetings until it has become clear what the crucial points to be resolved are.

The Prime Minister's meeting with President Nyerere on the evening of 14 September will, however, be of particular importance as an opportunity to explain to him the proposals we shall probably by then have tabled and to persuade him to use his influence with the Patriotic Front leaders to negotiate seriously with them. We shall be submitting full briefing for this meeting in the light of progress at the Conference.

At a later stage, probably during the second week, there may well be a strong case for the Prime Minister to see the delegations separately (or possibly to give separate lunches for them). It might indeed be that a critical stage was reached during that week at which it would be advisable for the Prime Minister to intervene directly in order to emphasise that the British Government were, at the highest level, making every effort to reach an agreed solution.

Lord Carrington will not be able to make recommendations on these points until he has tested the temperature of the Conference next week. He would aim to let the

Prime Minister have his further thoughts and firm recommendations about bilateral meetings and lunches towards the end of the week.

Yours ever,
RODERIC LYNE

No. 65

Minute from Sir A. Duff to Rhodesia Department, 10 September 1979
Confidential (FCO 36/2523)

1. I gave Mark Chona lunch yesterday. He said that his instructions from President Kaunda were to give all the help he could to the British in the conduct of the conference. We should keep in close touch, and let the observers know at once about any problems that arose and in regard to which they should be exerting pressure on the Patriotic Front. I outlined our concept for the conference. Chona said it was quite right to deal with the constitution first.

2. Chona said that one area of difficulty for the Front Line States was not knowing exactly what was on offer. In regard to Namibia it had been clear enough. There was the UN plan and the Front Line Presidents had been able to tell Nujoma[1] categorically that he should accept it. But in regard to Rhodesia there was no complete plan. He accepted that there could not be, at this stage, but went on to rub in the message we have already had from Kaunda: viz. that the British should make it clear from the beginning that they had plans for supervising the elections and for maintaining security which they were prepared to put into effect. He was not asking what these plans were, nor was it necessary for us to reveal them. But it was, he asserted, essential that the Patriotic Front should know from the beginning that we should genuinely accept this commitment.

3. I said that we of course accepted it, and were planning on that basis. It was however difficult to have any cut and dried plans because we did not know what the circumstances would be in which we should be giving effect to our plans. There was a whole range of possibilities. Until we had gained some experience of the attitudes of the parties during the conference, and had reached agreement on a constitution, it would not be possible to be at all precise.

4. Chona said he expected that. In this connection, however, he regarded the Secretary of State's opening speech as an important point of reference. During the discussions, whenever the parties tried to get on to the difficult questions of the interim administration or the military question, the Secretary of State should be able to recall that in his opening remarks he had made it clear that we would be ready with proposals at the appropriate time; that that was still the position, but meanwhile 'let us get back to the constitution'.

5. In the course of further discussion I gave Chona to understand that, when it became necessary to do so, Mrs Thatcher and Lord Carrington would be prepared to lay down the law in regard to the constitutional or other arrangements that the British

---

1 Mr Samuel Shafiishuna Daniel Nujoma, President of SWAPO, 1960-2007; and first President of Namibia, 1990-2005.

Government were prepared to put into effect. He welcomed this. I asked about the attitude of the Patriotic Front. Chona said he could not give me a categoric answer in regard to Mugabe, but Nkomo was prepared to work for a settlement in which 'the ballot would replace the bullet'. He thought that Nkomo would certainly attempt to make common cause with Mugabe's opponents: i.e. Sithole and Chikerema, and presumably Ndiweni also. At the same time however he would be trying to preserve a common front with Mugabe.

6. I took occasion to tell Chona why I had visited Pretoria; and that the outcome had in effect been an undertaking by the South Africans not to interfere with our attempt to reach agreement. He said that that was all that was needed from the South Africans at the present time.

7. I explained to Chona why we could not allow the observers into Lancaster House. He said he accepted that for the first reason I had given: viz. the need to treat the conference in every respect as a normal decolonising constitutional conference.

8. He was marginally less elliptical, convoluted and slippery than usual.

ANTONY DUFF

CHAPTER II

Agreement on the Constitution
September – October 1979

No. 66

Minute from Mr Renwick to Mr Walden, 10 September 1979
Confidential (FCO 36/2436)

Rhodesia Conference: Opening Session

1. At the meeting with the delegations this morning, ZANU said that they might not be prepared to take up their seats at the Conference unless they were placed in a position facing the British delegation (they are at present to one side of the Chairman, with Bishop Muzorewa's delegation to the other and the Secretariat facing the Chair).

2. I have told Mr Powell in the meeting at Lancaster House that he is to give no indication that we would be prepared to agree to this. It is at this stage virtually impossible to change the seating arrangements. If we did so, this would be regarded by Bishop Muzorewa's delegation—to say nothing of press and public opinion in this country—as capitulation to an absurd demand.

3. Having consulted Sir A. Duff, I *recommend* that we should not agree to the ZANU request and that the Secretary of State should if necessary be prepared to start the Conference without them (and without ZAPU as well if they support ZANU).

4. The Secretary of State will wish to mention this at the meeting with the Commonwealth and Front Line observers. If ZANU choose to start off the Conference with a boycott on so ludicrous an issue, they are likely to get a very unfavourable public and international response.

R.W. Renwick

No. 67

Opening Statement by Lord Carrington, 10 September 1979
(FCO 36/2463)

Chairman: Gentlemen, now that we have got the preliminaries over, I am glad to welcome you to this Conference and to open its proceedings.

When the British Government issued invitations to this Conference on 14 August, after extensive consultations, we naturally hoped for and expected a positive response. Our consultations had revealed a strong desire that the United Kingdom should take the initiative in making a further attempt to achieve a final settlement of the problem of Rhodesia, in fulfilment of its constitutional responsibilities. There was also a widespread feeling that continuation or intensification of the war was not in the best interests of any of the parties to the dispute, nor of the people of Rhodesia as a whole. Nevertheless, it is not a simple matter for those who have been involved in a bitter and tragic military confrontation to sit round a conference table together. The British Government felt strongly that it had the responsibility to bring that about.

When inviting you here we appealed to you, in the interests of the people of Rhodesia, to approach these negotiations in a positive spirit and to seek to build up areas of agreement. We hope thereby to lay the foundations for a free, independent and democratic society in which all the people of Rhodesia, irrespective of their race or political beliefs, would be able to live in security and at peace with each other and with their neighbours. The act of coming together is important. It is now up to us to build on that.

Since 1965, and indeed long before, many meetings have been held to try to resolve this problem. I am under no illusions, nor are any of my colleagues with me under any illusion, about the magnitude of the task before us. The problem is one which has defeated the efforts of successive British Governments, all of whom sought to achieve the objective of a peaceful settlement in conditions which would guarantee to the people of Rhodesia the full enjoyment of their rights. But I have no intention of going back over the history of those attempts; and I hope that you also will be prepared to look to the future rather than to the past.

I would like to hope that there is a difference between this meeting and those which have preceded it. This is a constitutional conference, the purpose of which is to decide the proper basis for the granting of legal independence to the people of Rhodesia. Many conferences like this have been held in this very building. A great many former dependent territories of the United Kingdom have successfully made the transition to independent statehood on the basis of constitutions agreed here. It is our intention to approach this Conference on the basis of the same principles and with no less strong a determination to succeed than in the case of those other conferences, which resulted in the granting of independence by this country to our former dependent territories. I believe that we can take some pride in the part we have played at conferences held at Lancaster House in the process of decolonisation. As Commonwealth leaders agreed at Lusaka, Britain has had no lack of experience as a decolonising power.

The agreement reached at Lusaka has made it possible for the British Government to convene this Conference with the very real hope that it will lead to an internationally acceptable settlement. I would like to pay tribute to the Commonwealth Heads of Government and the Commonwealth Secretary-General, all of whom worked so hard at Lusaka to establish an agreed position. In summary, the Commonwealth Heads of Government at Lusaka confirmed that they were wholly committed to genuine majority rule for the people of Rhodesia, and accepted that this requires the adoption of a democratic constitution including appropriate safeguards for minorities. They reiterated that it is the responsibility of the British Government to grant legal independence for Rhodesia. They agreed that the government formed under the independence constitution must be chosen through free and fair elections, properly supervised under British Government authority, and with Commonwealth observers. They welcomed the British Government's intention to convene this Conference, and recognised that the search for a settlement must involve all parties to the conflict. We should do well, I think, to bear in mind throughout our discussions the framework thus set out in the Lusaka communique. Not only does it incorporate the views of the British Government, but it sets out the approach which the Commonwealth will support and which will gain international acceptance.

Against this background I approach the search for a fair constitutional settlement in Rhodesia with the conviction that it is illusory to think that any settlement can fully satisfy the requirements of either side. An agreement can only be reached if there is a willingness to compromise.

The British Government has put to you the outline of the kind of constitution on the basis of which we would be prepared to grant independence. We wish to discuss these proposals with you at this Conference, and will be prepared to elaborate them in the light of our discussions. If we can reach agreement at this Conference, there will be an end to the war. That is an outcome which I believe will be greeted with immense relief by the people of Rhodesia and throughout Africa. Rhodesia will proceed to legal independence with a government formed by whichever party and whichever leader can show that they command the confidence of the people. I must confess that I find it difficult to see how any party or group or leader can hope to benefit from what would follow failure to reach agreement along the general lines we have put before you, and those who would suffer most would be the people of Rhodesia, towards whom our real responsibility lies.

A quarter of the population of Rhodesia has been born since 1965. Their lives have been overshadowed, not merely by a tragic and unnecessary political dispute, but by armed conflict. Many of them have died as innocent victims of the war. Or they have lost their parents, or their brothers or their sisters. Or they have lost their homes. Many of them, black and white, face the prospect of themselves having to fight, on one side or the other, or of being deprived indefinitely of peaceful residence in the land of their birth—a quarter of a million people are now in refugee camps in other countries. If we, who are assembled in this room, cannot agree on a way to end the fighting and provide for you to settle your differences by political means, this is what will happen.

This generation now at risk had no part in the initial causes of conflict. It was not born when the problem of Rhodesia came to a crisis in 1965. But now there is acceptance by all the parties of a society free from racial discrimination, of universal suffrage and majority rule. We can make this objective a reality if—and only if—we are prepared to look at the problems on the basis of principles on which both sides should be able to agree. I believe that the people assembled in this room have it in their power to end the war and to enable the people of Rhodesia to decide their future by peaceful means. We—you and I—bear the heavy responsibility, and I do not believe that the people of Rhodesia will readily forgive any party which deprives them of this opportunity to settle their future by peaceful means. This is a thought which should be in all our minds throughout the whole of this Conference.

It is, I must say, a matter of great regret and disappointment to me and my colleagues that hostilities are continuing during this Conference. Progress towards agreement on political issues—which I hope we are all determined to achieve—will by definition mean progress towards removing the causes of the war. It must be our objective to proceed as soon as possible to a stage at which there can be agreement on a ceasefire. We shall fall short of what we set out to achieve for the people of Rhodesia if we do not give them a chance to make a fresh start, its cause and its consequences put firmly in the past.

Gentlemen, Britain has at times, and variously, been described on the one side as choosing to stand with arms folded on the touchline; and on the other as not being serious in its determination to decolonise. Let me assure you today, if anyone is in any doubt, that we could not be more serious in our intention to achieve a satisfactory basis for granting of legal independence for the people of Rhodesia, and in this attempt to bring about an end to the war.

Since we were elected the government of this country at the beginning of May we have engaged in extensive consultation on the best way of achieving these objectives. Lord Harlech visited Africa early in the life of this Government to consult with the parties to the dispute and with the Commonwealth and other African governments most closely concerned. He found a general conviction that a solution to the problem of bringing Rhodesia to legal independence must stem from Britain as the constitutionally responsible authority, and that we must put forward proposals to achieve that objective. He also found that there was criticism of the present constitutional arrangements, in particular of the blocking power given to the white minority over a wide range of legislation, and of the character of the Public Service and other Commissions.

In the period of consultations, we made it clear that we would attach particular importance to the Commonwealth Heads of Government meeting at Lusaka. At Lusaka the British Prime Minister said that the British Government were wholly committed to genuine majority rule in Rhodesia. The principle of majority rule has been accepted by all the delegates of this Conference. The Prime Minister, at Lusaka, also recognised the importance of encouraging the European minority to remain as an integral part of the community. The Prime Minister emphasised that Britain fully accepted its constitutional responsibility to bring Rhodesia to legal independence on a basis of justice and democracy, comparable with the arrangements we have made for the independence of other countries.

The British Government took action immediately to give effect to the Lusaka declaration by convening this Conference and by putting forward constitutional proposals in accordance with the principles which we agreed at Lusaka and which have formed the basis for other independence constitutions in Africa and elsewhere.

The constitution is the fundamental problem to which we must address ourselves. I am of course well aware that there are other aspects of a settlement which must in due course be resolved. But it is essential to the prospects of success that we should first seek agreement on our destination—which is the independence constitution. If that can be achieved it will be necessary to decide the arrangements to give effect to that agreement. The British Government has stated clearly that it will be prepared to accept its full share of the responsibility for the practical implementation of those arrangements. The central element will be free and fair elections, properly supervised under British Government authority.

The British Government's outline proposals for an independence constitution have been before you for four weeks. I did not suggest that this Conference should be held on the basis of prior acceptance of this document. Instead, I would like to take the document as the starting point for our discussions. The British Government have been asked to put forward proposals and we have done so. Unless there is a focus for our discussion it will be impossible to make progress.

There are certain general points which I would make in introducing them.

First, as the constitutional authority for Southern Rhodesia, the United Kingdom intends to take direct responsibility for the independence constitution. What you have before you are the British Government's proposals, taking account of the points made to us in our consultations. They are intended to give effect to the principles which have been accepted by successive British Governments as the proper basis for independence, and you will recollect them very clearly. They are that the principle of majority rule must be maintained and guaranteed. That there must be guarantees against retrogressive amendments to the constitution; that there should be immediate improvement in the political status of the African population; that racial discrimination is unacceptable; that we must ensure that, regardless of race, there is no oppression of majority by minority or of minority by majority; and that what is agreed must be shown to be acceptable to the people of Rhodesia.

Second, our proposals are comparable to the basis on which the United Kingdom has granted independence to other former dependent territories, in particular those in Africa. We have no doubt, therefore, that a solution on this basis will be accepted by the international community, as giving effect to the principles we have accepted in granting independence to other former dependent territories. In the case of Rhodesia, as in all other cases, a constitution must take account of special circumstances. But the broad lines of independence constitutions are clear enough; and in the precedents there are points which can help us towards a solution, for example on the representation of minorities.

Third, we have made it unequivocally clear that our constitutional proposals represent in outline the kind of constitution on the basis of which the British Government would be prepared to grant legal independence.

If agreement could be reached on alternative proposals which meet the British Government's criteria, we would be ready to grant independence on that basis. But we believe that the best hope of success lies in negotiation on the lines we have proposed, in accordance with the Commonwealth declaration.

If it is possible to get agreement on the general framework for the independence constitution, the British Government will be prepared to put forward more detailed proposals to give effect to that agreement. We shall therefore have further suggestions to put before the Conference. But, before we advance to that stage, we must establish what measure of agreement exists on the outline proposals, and where the major difficulties, if any, will lie. As the first step, therefore, I shall hope to hear *your* views on the outline proposals.

Before inviting you, in our next session—because I think it would be appropriate to leave it to the next session—to state your positions on the constitutional framework for independence, I would like very briefly to speak about the arrangements to give effect to an agreement on the constitution.

In other countries approaching independence, the United Kingdom's role has invariably been to establish just conditions for independence, and not to encourage the aspirations of this or that party. Our role in Rhodesia will be the same as in other dependent territories. The international community is well aware of this and of our constitutional responsibility. In many countries we have handed over power to people who had previously been confirmed opponents of the policy of the United Kingdom, if they have been elected by the people of their countries. In the position which we agreed with other Commonwealth Governments at Lusaka, we stated that there must be free and fair elections, properly supervised under British Government authority and with Commonwealth observers. This has been accepted by all Commonwealth Governments; and, as I have already said, the British Government will be ready to carry out its responsibilities in this regard.

I turn now briefly to the way in which we might proceed at this Conference. The Conference is being held under my Chairmanship. I attach the highest priority to bringing it to a successful conclusion, and I assure you I intend to play the fullest part in the proceedings. At times when I am prevented from being here, I would propose to ask that Lord Privy Seal, Sir Ian Gilmour, to take the Chair.

We have made no attempt to fix the duration of the Conference. I hope that we can move forward rapidly. I trust that we can show real progress towards agreement on the constitution. We for our part are prepared to continue for as long as it is necessary, provided of course that progress is being made. In the opening plenary sessions I would ask you to set out fully your views on constitutional questions and on the outline proposals before the Conference, as I have done. Depending on the progress made, it might then be appropriate to consider aspects of the constitution in more detail, perhaps on the basis of further proposals tabled by the British Government. We may also wish to consider meeting in less formal groups at different levels. We shall have between us to decide on that as we proceed.

The Conference Secretariat, headed by the Conference Secretary, Mr Willson, is at the service of all delegates. Any questions on administrative arrangements should be referred to Mr Willson and the Conference Officers assisting him.

The Secretariat will prepare summary records of discussions in the formal conference sessions, that is to say, records which give a resume of the main points made by each speaker. They will circulate these records within 24 hours. If you wish to make corrections of substance to your own interventions I would be grateful if you would do so within two days. These will also be circulated. The summary records will not be made available to the press.

There will—and I dare say you have already seen it—be world-wide interest in the progress of the Conference. A great many journalists have been accredited to it. I shall be making public my own statement this afternoon; you may wish to do the same with your opening speeches. The press will not be admitted to Lancaster House, but there is a fully equipped press centre just across the road. This is at the disposal of all delegations. Mr Fenn will act as my spokesman as Chairman of the Conference. He will also release to the press any joint statements on which we may from time to time agree, and I invite each delegations, if they would be so good, to nominate a member of their staff as Press Secretary, to be in touch with Mr Fenn about these matters. They will of course be welcome to use the facilities at the press centre.

If there are other papers which you wish to have circulated to all participants, the Secretariat will be ready to have them reproduced and distributed as Conference documents.

May I say this in conclusion. This conference has been convened in response to the statement agreed by the Commonwealth Heads of Government at Lusaka. We have put forward proposals designed to bring Rhodesia to legal independence. Your acceptance of our invitation has given hope to the people of Rhodesia and the neighbouring countries. It is within the power of the parties represented here to bring an end to the war.

I have deliberately avoided talking of a 'last chance' of a settlement. Last chances have come and gone before. But I would put it differently. Since Geneva, the conflict has reached new levels. The cost of continuing it is very high. Since 1976 the number of men under arms on both sides has more than doubled. The war has spread into neighbouring states. The toll in casualties inside Rhodesia and in the neighbouring countries has continued to rise. Neither side has infinite resources. The price of failure at this Conference would be further prolonged bloodshed and further destruction on the life of whole communities. The responsibility for preventing this lies upon all those present here, and the eyes of the international community will be upon us all to see that we live up to that responsibility. The British Government is determined for its part to do everything in its power to bring this Conference to a successful conclusion. It is in that spirit that I ask all of you to address the task before us.

Now, gentlemen, having said that, I think that the best thing that we can do is to adjourn until 10:30 tomorrow morning when I hope we shall hear the considered views on what I have said from the two sides; of course there is no limit on the number of those who can speak. Perhaps we might then adjourn now, and I hope very much to see as many of you as can come this evening, when we are having a small party downstairs.

Thank you very much.

No. 68

Letter from Mrs Thatcher to Mr Winterton MP,[1] 11 September 1979
(PREM 19/111)

Dear Nicholas,

Thank you for your letter of 15th August with which you enclosed a copy of a letter dated 9th August which you had received from your constituent Mr J.G. Stanley.[2]

If Rhodesia is to have a secure future as, we all wish, it is essential that there should be a settlement capable of winning wide international recognition. The agreement we reached at the Commonwealth meeting in Lusaka represents a helpful step forward. We have established a new basis for progress towards a peaceful solution for Rhodesia, and it is significant that we have the unanimous acceptance of the

---

1 Member of Parliament for Macclesfield, 1971-2010.
2 Not printed.

Commonwealth—including three of the Front Line States—that it must be a major objective to bring about a cessation of hostilities and an end to sanctions as part of the process of achieving a lasting settlement.

I do not accept that this agreement amounts to an 'about face' on the part of the Government. The Conservative Party manifesto made it clear that, if elected, we would consider it our duty to make every effort to achieve international recognition for Rhodesia, while in my speech in the House on 25th July I made it clear that some constitutional change would be required. I also said that our proposals would be put to all the parties. New elections would follow naturally from agreement at the Constitutional Conference.

I believe that we now have a prospect of ending the present hostilities with the tragic loss of life they involve. The way ahead will not be easy but I am encouraged that those concerned have accepted our invitation to the Constitutional Conference which opened in London yesterday.

Yours ever,
MARGARET

No. 69

Letter from Mr Lyne to Mr Alexander (No. 10), 12 September 1979
Confidential (PREM 19/112)

Dear Michael,

Rhodesia: Constitutional Conference

This letter follows Lord Carrington's minute PM/79/74 in which he set out our approach to the Constitutional Conference.[1]

Lord Carrington made clear in his opening speech that we regard it as essential in the Conference to seek a measure of agreement first on the general outline of the independence Constitution, before going on to tackle the pre-independence arrangements. In his opening statement, Bishop Muzorewa made a strong defence of the existing constitutional arrangements, but implied that he was prepared to discuss our outline proposals. The Patriotic Front, as expected, sought to evade discussion of the main elements of the constitution and to insist on prior agreement on the pre-independence arrangements.

We have now managed to get over the initial procedural hurdle and have moved to item one on our agenda: 'The Independence Constitution'. In an attempt to focus discussion on this item we have tabled our fuller constitutional proposals (Annex B to Lord Carrington's minute). The Prime Minister's meeting with Nyerere will therefore come at a most important stage. We have to continue to urge the Commonwealth African Presidents to persuade the Patriotic Front to negotiate seriously on the Constitution. This is a necessary preliminary to being able to demonstrate to them and to a wider audience that, if the Patriotic Front will not co-operate, the responsibility for failure to reach agreement will lie with them.

1 No. 56.

Agreement on the Constitution

It will be important to enlist Nyerere's support for our constitutional proposals. In doing so it will be necessary to make clear to him that we regard it as indispensable to an agreement that, for a limited period, there should be a reasonable proportion of white representatives in the House of Assembly elected by the white community. The proportion should not exceed 20% and must fall short of the minority required to block constitutional amendment or a wide range of legislation. This is the point of principle at issue for us.

In order to enlist Nyerere's support—if we can obtain it—for constitutional proposals on these lines it will be important to convince him that we are prepared to deal satisfactorily with the pre-independence arrangements. In discussion with him, and in our subsequent contacts with the other African presidents, we must make it clear that we are prepared to accept the implications of the call in the Lusaka communique for 'free and fair elections properly supervised under the authority of the British Government'. It will then be up to the Presidents to ascertain whether the Patriotic Front are prepared to put their political standing to the test in elections in which they would have a fair—but no more than that—chance of winning.

The brief which I enclose with this minute[2] is designed to achieve that objective. The Prime Minister could start from the position that we wish to enlist Nyerere's help in ensuring that the Patriotic Front continue (if they have so started) to begin (if they have not) to engage in serious discussion of our fuller constitutional proposals. If President Nyerere attempts to defend the Patriotic Front's initial attempt to stall on the independence Constitution until the 'transfer of power' had been discussed, it will be necessary to tell him that—so far as the British Government is concerned—the question of to whom power is to be transferred must be settled by the people of Rhodesia in free elections, supervised under our authority. We should obviously do so in terms designed to reassure him that we recognise that there are real issues to be settled in this connection, when the time comes to deal with them.

Exactly how far it would be prudent to go in discussing the pre-independence arrangements with Nyerere is a matter for careful consideration. I am enclosing, in addition to the brief for the meeting, background papers[2] which illustrate the kind of military and administrative arrangements for the transition which might need to be discussed in the unlikely event of an agreement on an independence constitution and of an expression of willingness by the Patriotic Front to take part in elections *without* a dominant position in advance. As these papers show, such a situation would pose many difficult problems, of which the difficulty of making military arrangements in these circumstances would be the worst, and quite possibly insuperable. But, as preparation for a talk with Nyerere, the Prime Minister may wish to have these problems in mind because he will expect us to have thought about them, and may himself mention them. He may, for example, ask whether we are prepared to contemplate a return to legality—which could involve the appointment of a British Commissioner—and the introduction of a Commonwealth, or some other neutral, force in the period before elections are held.

We have not yet discussed any such ideas with Bishop Muzorewa. There is a risk that what is said to Nyerere in this connection will be relayed to Muzorewa and

2 Not printed.

misunderstood by him. In talking to Nyerere this consideration should be balanced against the need to convince him of our readiness to accept the implications of the Lusaka agreement, and to make the Patriotic Front in due course a fair offer on the electoral process. The Prime Minister will probably not wish to go further than is suggested in paragraphs 12 and 13 of the notes for the meeting. On one point we must stand absolutely firm with Nyerere—that in our Conference there can be no discussion *with the parties* of the pre-independence arrangements until agreement has been reached on the independence constitution and on the principle of free and fair elections, properly supervised under our authority.

These papers are intended to provide a basis for the Foreign and Commonwealth Secretary's meeting with the Prime Minister at 5.30 pm tomorrow, to discuss the handling of the working dinner with President Nyerere. As I explained to you, the papers have been written in the light of Lord Carrington's comments on a previous draft, but have not yet been seen by him in their present form.

Yours ever,
RODERIC LYNE

No. 70

Minute from Mr Manning to Mr Renwick, 13 September 1979
Confidential (FCO 36/2523)

Rhodesia: Zambian High Commissioner's Dinner
12 September

1. Mr Luce went to dinner with the Zambian High Commissioner[1] on 12 September. The other guests were Mark Chona, Tiny Rowlands and Duncan Sandys.[2] The main points that emerged are set out below.

2. Duncan Sandys spoke to Mr Luce of his experience of previous constitutional conferences. He strongly recommended bilateral contacts during adjournments as a means of making progress and emphasised the value of private contacts, e.g. at weekends, with delegation members. He also offered his assistance should this be considered useful.

3. Tiny Rowlands told Mr Luce that Lonrho were paying for 120 participants at the conference. Mr Luce had the impression that Mark Chona was being financed by Lonrho. He also said that on 8 September Ndiweni, Sithole, Chikerema and Nkomo held a meeting to co-ordinate tactics for the conference. He said that this group had agreed to work together with a view to putting Nkomo at the head of a new government in Salisbury and to by-pass the Bishop. Mark Chona confirmed this account and added that he believed that the Bishop intended to get the constitution agreed at the conference and then return to Salisbury saying that he had done all that was required and now expected recognition.

4. Mark Chona told Mr Luce that he did not expect the Patriotic Front to cause any difficulty over the constitution. They might put up different views about white

1 Ms Lombe Phyllis Chibesakunda.
2 (Edwin) Duncan Sandys, Baron Duncan-Sandys, Secretary of State for the Colonies, 1962-64.

representation but there would be no major obstacles to agreement nor did he believe that the Patriotic Front would make difficulties over transitional arrangements provided that these did not include the Bishop as Prime Minister. His prescription for a successful transition was the assumption of colonial responsibilities by Britain, the creation of a balanced interim administration including all the parties and the appointment of a Resident Commissioner. Zambia would support arrangements on these lines and he believed the Patriotic Front would also do so.

5. Mark Chona complained that Britain had not published detailed proposals for the constitution at an earlier stage and suggested that detailed proposals for the transition period should be put forward at once. He made it clear that he wanted very close contact with the Government during the conference and the Zambian High Commissioner was at pains to tell Mr Luce that Chona had been given carte blanche by President Kaunda for the handling of the conference.

6. Mark Chona and Tiny Rowlands went out of their way to emphasise their opinion that the Bishop was now very isolated and had little support either with Rhodesia or with within the Salisbury delegation.

7. Mr Chona said that he thought the Patriotic Front would want a 5/6 day adjournment for the funeral of President Neto which many of their leading members would want to attend.

8. Mr Luce thinks that it would be valuable for him to maintain close contact with Mark Chona and would be grateful for advice on how and when further meetings could most advantageously be arranged.

K.Q.F. MANNING

No. 71

Letter from Mr Squire (UKMIS New York) to Mr Renwick, 13 September 1979
Secret and Personal (FCO 36/2549)

[No salutation]

Action at the United Nations over Rhodesia

1. Please refer to your letter of 29 August to Philip Mansfield.[1] You asked for our views on US reactions to a situation where 'Muzorewa has accepted what we regard as a reasonable settlement, and it has been demonstrated that this is acceptable to the people of Rhodesia, while the settlement has not been accepted by the external parties' (paragraph 4 of your letter). We do not address here the issues of international law and UN tactics, since we believe other factors will be decisive for US policy.

2. This situation will present the US Administration with a decision they have so far been able to avoid—making a public choice between their relations with Black Africa and embracing a less than perfect Rhodesian settlement. In my judgement the Administration have moved a long way towards eventually making the latter choice. We cannot take the support of the Administration for granted as each tactical

1 No. 55.

problem comes up, but we are reasonably confident that the Administration will:

(i) follow the British lead over sanctions, whether or not the British decision to lift them results from a comprehensive settlement acceptable to all the parties;

(ii) recognise in due course the Government which HMG grants legal independence.

3. The rationale for and the qualifications to the above propositions follow, based on our assessment of the US domestic political factors and the view taken here (both by the Administration and the Congress) of the British Government and its role in the Rhodesian question.

Domestic Political Factors

4. Over the past two years the Administration and the Congress have noted the electoral unpopularity of a too 'liberal' approach on Third World issues (this was one factor which contributed to the defeat in the mid-term elections last November of Senator Dick Clarke, ex-Chairman of the Africa Subcommittee of the Senate Foreign Relations Committee), particularly where this is perceived (rightly or wrongly) as being linked with a too soft approach to the USSR. Over Rhodesia Dick Moose and his associates have learnt the danger to public support of their policies if they appear to lean towards the Patriotic Front. The Congressional debates over the past year have rammed the point home, helped by Mugabe's frankness and Nkomo's ineptness in public statements and appearances in the US news media.

5. Our Congressional contacts on both sides of the issue concur in believing that the Administration's successful stand against the precipitate lifting of sanctions earlier this year marked the high water mark of the liberal approach; but this was essentially a successful rear-guard action by the Administration and its Congressional supporters, which only bought time, in the face of Congress's basic attitude of growing sympathy towards 'internal settlers' and hostility towards the Patriotic Front.

President Carter's Domestic Position

6. In so far as Rhodesia is a matter of public controversy here, and although it is not a major issue, it can only hurt the President domestically. If he accepts a settlement controversial in Africa he will be criticised by the black caucus in Congress and black intellectuals generally who claim the black vote gave him his victory in 1976. There is already a good deal of disenchantment with Carter within the black constituency; and the Andy Young affair[2] has given the black voice added assertiveness in foreign affairs. If instead he seeks to maintain sanctions and ostracises the Government to which HMG have granted independence, it is regarded as certain that the Congress will reverse the Administration's policy over sanctions, thus administering a public rebuff and fuelling the criticism of his ineptness. It will also increase domestic criticisms of his dealings with the USSR (see paragraph 9 below). Our Congressional sources therefore believe that the Carter White House want Rhodesia out of the way as soon as possible.

7. In addition President Carter's personal views should not be overlooked. You will recall that at the early stages of Anglo/American planning on Rhodesia (July 1977) President Carter told the then-Foreign Secretary privately that he would not

---

2 On 26 July 1979, Young had an unauthorised meeting with a Palestine Liberation Organisation observer and, once this was disclosed, misled the President about the nature of the meeting. This led to his resignation on 16 August 1979 as US Ambassador to the UN.

condemn a fair settlement (I paraphrase) just because Smith was involved. I am sure this will hold for any settlement based on the 1979 Commonwealth Communique.

The National Interest

8. The formal position of the US Government worked out between the Executive and the Legislature at the time of the Congressional moves to lift sanctions unilaterally earlier this summer is that sanctions will be lifted by November 15 unless the President determines 'it would not be in the national interest to do so'. The arguments around which Congressional views finally coalesced were:

(i) Rhodesia was a British responsibility; the US should not move before HMG;

(ii) Black African states opposed the Muzorewa Government, the US would incur their hostility and economic penalties if they recognised him or lifted sanctions (Nigeria is the second largest supplier of oil to the US);

(iii) the US would be associated with minority racist regimes in Southern Africa;

(iv) Russian influence in the area would increase if the US moved towards Muzorewa.

9. Of these arguments the most important currently (apart from paragraph 8 (i) which fails by definition) is the Russian factor. Instead of being a reason for holding back, it is now seen as a reason why the US should stop leaning towards the Patriotic Front and instead develop normal relations with whatever Government emerges from a recognizable democratic process in Rhodesia. The recent publicity given to the presence of a Soviet combat brigade in Cuba has intensified the feeling on the Hill that the voters expect the US 'to stand up to the Russians' and their proxies. The more the USSR takes the part of the Patriotic Front and oppose a settlement the stronger will be this feeling.

Role of HMG

10. The importance of the role of HMG will be apparent from the foregoing. A good deal of Congressional opinion was always uneasy over the degree of US involvement in what is seen primarily as a British responsibility. From all we hear, the prevailing opinion both in the Administration and among those concerned with the issue in Congress is that HMG are acting in good faith, though there may be lingering doubts in some quarters in Congress that we are looking for a respectable way of legitimizing the internal settlement. If the Constitutional Conference fails to result in general agreement, there will nevertheless be a strong presumption here that whatever positive action HMG take will deserve the moral and political support of the United States.

11. Despite the importance of domestic considerations, the issues to be addressed at the Constitutional Conference are also important because they will provide the evidence for accepting British good faith and for supporting the outcome as progress towards a democratic political process. In the past both the Administration and its supporters have criticised the Muzorewa government because:

(i) the constitution was defective;

(ii) the environment in which the elections were held was defective (no real freedom for the external parties to participate, security arrangements under the control of a biased authority etc.)

(iii) Consequently no presumption that the shape of the constitution or the results were acceptable to the people as a whole.

From the favourable way the Lusaka communique was received here, it is clear that HMG's subsequent constitutional proposals are seen as fair and reasonable.

12. I mentioned some qualifications to the judgement in paragraph 3 above. Dick Moose told us last week that it was possible the Congress would adjourn around its target date of November 15 until late January without action on a Presidential decision to maintain sanctions. (This was predicated on a hypothetical situation in which HMG had not yet acted.) We think it unlikely that

(*a*) the Congress will be able to adjourn so early

(*b*) that the opponents of sanctions would be out-manoeuvred so easily (see Washington telegram No 2629).[3]

Gerry Helman (Deputy Assistant Secretary, International Organisations Bureau) made the point to Martin Morland[4] and me earlier this week that when our experts discuss the UN dimension, there will be important issue of UN principle at stake which should not be overlooked. We can expect this view to be firmly pressed by McHenry and others. But if the analysis in this letter is near the mark the political imperatives of making progress over Rhodesia will prevail.

Recognition of an Independent Zimbabwe

13. The logic of this analysis is that the US will normalise relations when Britain, as the country with constitutional responsibility, does so. But it is open to the Administration to defer recognition if it seemed expedient. Congress could exert pressure but (unlike sanctions) would have no legal power to force the Administration's hand.

14. The main part of this letter assumes an active British role throughout the process up to and including a credible test of what is 'acceptable' to the people of Rhodesia. A Commonwealth role in this process would be a bonus, and the more African colouration the better. The less credible the constitution or subsequent test of opinion, the more difficult it will be to achieve full Administration backing particularly in such fora as the UN. But this will be obvious to you.

15. We have reported separately what Senator Helms' office have told us in private, namely that President Carter has given the Prime Minister an oral assurance that the US will follow us in lifting sanctions whether or not our decision results from a comprehensive settlement agreed by all parties. Without knowing the context it is difficult to interpret what such an assurance would mean in practice. But it certainly fits in with the domestic political scene as we see it. I need hardly add that as the winter goes on and Carter's prospects become increasingly uncertain, predictions about US reactions on this and some other subjects will become more and more difficult.

Yours ever,
C.W. SQUIRE

---

3 Not printed.
4 Head of Chancery, British Embassy Washington.

No. 72

Minute by Mr Alexander (No. 10), 15 September 1979
Confidential (PREM 19/112)

Record of the Prime Minister's Discussion with President Nyerere over a Working Dinner at 10 Downing Street on 14 September 1979 at 20.30

Present:

Prime Minister	President Nyerere
Foreign and Commonwealth Secretary	Mr Benjamin Mkapa (Minister for Foreign Affairs)
Lord Harlech	H.E. Mr Amon Nsekela (Tanzanian High Commissioner in London)
Sir Antony Duff	
Sir Peter Preston	Captain Joseph Butiku (Private Secretary)[1]
H.E. Sir Peter Moon	
Mr M.O'D.B. Alexander	

Constitutional Conference

President Nyerere said that so far as he could judge the Constitutional Conference had so far gone well. A good atmosphere had been established and this was important. It would be important not to push the participants too hard. He was confident that progress could be made. It was unlikely that the Conference would break down on the question of the constitution. In particular it would be surprising if the Patriotic Front were to try to break on this issue. *The Foreign and Commonwealth Secretary* asked whether the Patriotic Front might not find the concept of reserved seats for the white population unacceptable. *President Nyerere* said he did not see a major difficulty here. The Patriotic Front wanted a settlement and knew that, while they might be tempted to ignore Bishop Muzorewa, they could not ignore Mr Smith. President Nyerere commented that the original Tanzanian constitution had not accorded the President all the powers he needed: this had not prevented him from changing the constitution subsequently. (The implication that the Patriotic Front could change the constitution if and when they came to power was clear.)

Interim Arrangements

President Nyerere said that in his judgement the Conference would have to take up the question of the interim arrangements at an early stage. If he were leading the Patriotic Front delegation he would be saying that the constitution could be discussed by the lawyers while the main Conference got down to discussing the transitional period. He asked what Lord Carrington had in mind. *The Foreign and Commonwealth Secretary* said that he was conscious that the negotiations in Geneva had broken down on the question of transitional arrangements and that it would be important to try to keep the arrangements as simple as possible. *The Prime Minister*

---

1 Private Secretary to President Nyerere.

said that there would have to be a ceasefire and the armed forces in the field would have to return to their barracks. It has been agreed in Lusaka that the bullet was going to be exchanged for the ballot and that HMG should concentrate on the arrangements for the election. It would be the responsibility of the military commanders to get their soldiers into barracks before the election campaign began. It would be the responsibility of the victor in the election to weld the existing armies into a single national force.

President Nyerere rejected this approach. If HMG wanted a peaceful Zimbabwe the problem of the three armies had to be solved now. If the participants in the Conference wanted a free and fair election the armies would have to be merged before that election. This was a condition for a peaceful transition. If they were not prepared to accept the merging of the armies as it could only be because they were not prepared to accept the results of the election. The men who controlled the armies were at present in London and there was no need to postpone tackling the issue. If HMG allow the discussion to be postponed it would mean that they were only trying to get out of the situation and that they were prepared to condemn the country to civil war. If HMG and the Zimbabweans agreed to proceed to independence with three armies in the field, he would not seek to interfere. But, equally, he would not back the settlement. He would not support any arrangement that guaranteed a civil war and he had no interest in postponing the civil war. He would rather that it took place now.

Sir Antony Duff said that it would be impossible to achieve agreement now on the creation of a single Army. It might be possible to move to discussion of a merger once agreement had been reached on the constitution and other aspects of the interim arrangements but the negotiation was certain to be difficult and prolonged. A lengthy pause between agreement on the constitution and the holding of an election would be extremely dangerous. Analysing President Nyerere's fears about the implication of the continued existence of three armies after an election, Sir Antony Duff pointed out that the newly elected government would be basing the national force either on the forces at present based in Salisbury or on those at present opposing them. In the first case, the loyalty of the present defence force was assured. The Patriotic Front would have to decide to allow their forces to be merged and presumably, an election having being held and they having lost, they would be deprived of the support of the Front Line States. It would be impossible for them to continue the struggle. In the second case, the national force would be based on the Patriotic Front's own soldiers. Some of the forces of Bishop Muzorewa's administration would adhere and many would leave the country. Again, it would be impossible for them to continue fighting. *President Nyerere* asked about the South African reaction to the defeat of Bishop Muzorewa's administration in an election. Would they not back the Bishop Muzorewa and Mr Smith in continuing the struggle? *The Prime Minister* said that the South African reaction would be irrelevant because many of the whites would, in any case, leave Zimbabwe. *Sir Antony Duff* said that the risk of continuing civil war after the election, described by President Nyerere, existed but was not a large one. *President Nyerere* said that he was not prepared to accept it.

The Prime Minister asked whether it was realistic to suppose that in the aftermath of an election the losers would be able to continue the struggle. The pressure of world opinion would be intense. She asked President Nyerere whether he would continue to support the Patriotic Front, supposing they lost the election, against a democratic constitution and an elected government negotiated in accordance with the Lusaka agreement.

President Nyerere said that if he was not put in a position to tell the Patriotic Front to disband their forces before the election he would not be able to do so after an election. *Sir Antony Duff* asked whether, in the event that an effort was made to secure the merger of the armies before an election and failed, President Nyerere would be prepared to back whatever other agreements might be reached at the Constitutional Conference. *President Nyerere* said that if a serious effort to create a single Army were made and failed the question then would be whether HMG were prepared to put in a military force or to organise a Commonwealth force. If they were not prepared to do this, the Conference was a waste of time. *The Prime Minister* asked if President Nyerere thought it would be helpful to introduce a fourth army into Zimbabwe where it would simply become bogged down in guerilla warfare. *President Nyerere* did not respond. *The Prime Minister* asked what proportion of the Patriotic Front forces would be prepared to go on fighting once a constitution had been agreed and the arrangements for an election were in train. *Mr Mkapa* said that if no agreement on a merger had been reached, he would expect the Patriotic Front's commanders to ensure that their men remained in the field. So long as the various armies were in being a genuine election campaign would be impossible.

President Nyerere said that if his government were satisfied that HMG were implementing the Lusaka agreement in full, they would not back the Patriotic Front in rejecting it. They would if necessary ask forcefully why the Patriotic Front wish to keep their army in being. That they were already telling SWAPO that they could not use their troops in Angola and Namibia to reject the results of an election in Namibia. They were telling ZANU and ZAPU the same. But who was telling Smith? If HMG were not prepared to pursue the issue, they were, he repeated, wasting their time at the Constitutional Conference. One had only to think of what Mr Sithole would have done earlier this year if he had had an army behind him. If a civil war broke out following agreement on a constitution, the United Kingdom would not be involved but Tanzania would. *The Foreign and Commonwealth Secretary* said that President Nyerere's approach to the problem represented by the three armies was logical but, in his judgement, impracticable. He considered that HMG's approach was the right one and that the presidents fears were misplaced.

The Prime Minister asked whether, if General Walls were prepared to say before an election that he would accept the government resulting from that election whatever its complexion, the military commanders of ZANLA and ZIPRA would be prepared to do the same. *President Nyerere*, while not replying directly to the Prime Minister's question, said that it would be important to make an effort to secure commitments of the kind she had outlined. But once the commitments had been obtained, HMG would then have to ask why the commanders would not proceed forthwith to the creation of a single army. His test of the genuineness of any agreement would be the merger of the armies. *The Prime Minister* said that an undertaking from the military commanders would nonetheless be a very substantial step forward.

President Nyerere began the concluding part of the discussion by saying that he was sure that the Patriotic Front wanted a settlement. Long discussions with them in

Lusaka and Havana had convinced him that they had come to London to do business. It would be essential now to maintain the momentum of the discussions and not to allow any of the participants to absent themselves from London.

The Foreign and Commonwealth Secretary urged that President Nyerere should see the Patriotic Front while he was in London and press them to participate constructively in next week's discussion of the constitution. *President Nyerere*, having noted the importance of not allowing Bishop Muzorewa to get away with nothing more than agreement on the constitution, said that while he would tell the Patriotic Front of the Foreign and Commonwealth Secretary's concern, he was not prepared to exert any pressure on them. *The Prime Minister* ended the discussion by saying that if things did not go well at the Conference she might well wish to get in touch again with the Presidents of the Front Line States.

The talk ended at 2230.

M.O'D.B. ALEXANDER

No. 73

Letter from Mr Walden to Sir P. Moore (Buckingham Palace), 17 September 1979
Confidential (FCO 36/2437)

Dear Sir Philip,

Rhodesia: Constitutional Conference

You asked for a note on the Conference, which opened on 10 September. Agreement on an order of work was the first problem. The Patriotic Front sought to insist that the pre-independence arrangements should be discussed first. The Salisbury delegation, on the other hand, were (and remain) reluctant to indicate that they are prepared to discuss anything but the independence constitution. The Government's position is that both should be discussed, but that the outline of an independence constitution must be agreed in the first place. On 12 September the Patriotic Front conceded that the Conference should proceed to discuss the independence constitution first, on the understanding that agreement by the Patriotic Front on the constitution would be dependent on agreement on the arrangements for implementing it.

We then tabled a paper containing Constitutional proposals and asked both delegations for comments on it. After the delegations had considered these proposals the Patriotic Front on 14 September tabled their own summary of a constitution and Bishop Muzorewa's delegation gave notice that they proposed to table the present Zimbabwe/Rhodesia constitution. Discussion began on 17 September on the basis that points would be taken in the same order as in the British document.

It is encouraging that the Conference is now fully under way and that the procedural difficulties which have so far arisen have been dealt with. But the real difficulties are still ahead. As expected, the Salisbury delegation's opening position is that their present constitution already meets our requirements and should be on the basis on which we grant independence. Mr Ian Smith, and some others, called on Lord Carrington on 14 September to discuss safeguards for the white minority. Lord

Carrington told him that the whites' present power to block constitutional amendment must go; but that the provisions on white seats and the basic provisions of the declaration of rights, might be unamendable for a specified period. Lord Carrington impressed on him that the prospects for Rhodesia would be bleak if the Conference were seen to break down because the Salisbury delegation were unable to accept the constitutional change proposed by the British Government.

The Patriotic Front will continue to try to insist on pre-independence arrangements favourable to them before elections are held. The Government's position is that such questions as the composition of the future army must be decided by the elected government, in the light of the wishes of the people of Rhodesia.

Yours ever,
GEORGE

No. 74

Minute from Mr Lyne to Mr Renwick, 17 September 1979
Secret (FCO 36/2437)

Rhodesia Constitutional Conference: Bishop Muzorewa's Delegation

Following the afternoon session today, Lord Carrington, Sir Ian Gilmour and Sir Antony Duff had a discussion for half an hour with Bishop Muzorewa, Dr Mundawarara, Mr Bulle and Mr Kamusikiri.

Lord Carrington warned Bishop Muzorewa of the damage which would be caused if the Patriotic Front agreed to a new constitution while the Salisbury delegation failed to do so. He had put this frankly to Mr Ian Smith on 14 September and had stressed that it would be impossible to lift sanctions in November or gain acceptance even from moderate countries if constitutional amendments were not made. Lord Carrington said that it was essential that Bishop Muzorewa should either get Mr Smith to accept this, or should isolate him.

Bishop Muzorewa said that he had already spoken on these lines to Mr Smith. However, Mr Smith had asserted that he had received contrary information from two Ministers, one of whom was in the Cabinet. Lord Carrington said that this could not be true, though back-bench MPs might have spoken in this vein. Dr Mundawarara said that Mr Smith had had many meetings since coming to London (he mentioned Mr Amery, Lord Salisbury, Mr Bell and Mr Hastings[1]) and that as a result his attitude to constitutional change had stiffened. Lord Carrington emphasised that the delegation should believe what they were told by the Government, not by back-benchers.

Bishop Muzorewa thought he could get some of the whites 'on side'; but Mr Anderson would not be separated from Mr Ian Smith. There were like identical twins. Bishop Muzorewa said that Mr Smith had heard on the grapevine that the British Government would settle for 24 white seats. Lord Carrington said our proposal

---

1 Mr Julian Amery, MP for Brighton Pavilion, 1969-92; Robert Gascoyne-Cecil, 7th Marquess of Salisbury, MP for South Dorset, 1979-87; Mr Ronald Bell, MP for Beaconsfield, 1974-82; Mr Stephen Hastings, MP for Mid-Bedfordshire, 1960-83.

for 20 seats was not negotiable. Mr Smith's grapevine was faulty. He was receiving bad advice.

Mr Kamusikiri said that Mr Smith insisted on obtaining certain guarantees in return for movement in his own position. Sir A. Duff said that we could not give assurances to Mr Smith in confidence. Lord Carrington said that the guarantees were implicit in the Lusaka agreement, which made it clear that neither side would have a veto; that was why it was so important that the Salisbury delegation should not refuse to accept the constitution. Dr Mundawarara said that Mr David Smith was prepared to vote on his own if he was satisfied with the terms of the settlement, according to the dictates of his conscience.

It was agreed that Sir A. Duff would talk further to Mr D. Smith, and that it might be advisable for the Secretary of State to have a word with him in due course. It was also agreed that further approaches might be made to Mr Cronje.

Dr Mundawarara said the Salisbury delegation would be explaining to the press that they had not taken a leading part in the Conference session today because they had put their queries forward on 14 September ahead of the Patriotic Front, and were therefore awaiting the British Government's replies to them today.

Bishop Muzorewa said that he would need more time to deal with the problems within his delegation before arranging a full bilateral session with the British side. Lord Carrington said that he was at Bishop Muzorewa's disposal. It was agreed that the group might meet again on the morning of 18 September. Lord Carrington mentioned the possibility of bringing the Prime Minister in if Mr Smith become too difficult. He repeated that the key question was that the Salisbury delegation should not reject a constitution to which the Patriotic Front had agreed. Bishop Muzorewa said that he might have to get his delegation to agree to disagree. Dr Mundawarara said that they would not reject the constitution, but that he was worried about the timing; the Patriotic Front might steal a march on them by agreeing to it first.

R.M.J. LYNE

No. 75

Minute from Sir A. Duff to Lord Carrington, 17 September 1979[1]
Secret (FCO 36/2437)

Rhodesia Conference: Tactical Objective

1. We have to continue to work for a total settlement, and to be seen to be so working. It is unlikely that we will succeed. If we cannot succeed, there remain in essence two alternative objectives:

(*a*) to reach a point where the Patriotic Front walk out so that we can continue with the Bishop alone;

(*b*) to reach a point where the Front split—ZANU walking out and ZAPU continuing to negotiate.

---

1 Also sent to Mr Luce and Sir I. Gilmour.

2. We have concentrated on (*a*) so far. To know if (*b*) is likely we need, and do not yet have, a clear picture of views within the Patriotic Front. Intelligence and other information prior to their arrival in London suggested that ZAPU might want to negotiate more seriously than ZANU. So far they seem to be working together at the conference. We have little indication yet of Nkomo's own views in this area, except for his apparently tearful insistence on an Executive Presidency (for himself).

3. If we could achieve objective (*b*) it would have the following principal advantages:

(i) it would be likely seriously to diminish Front Line support for continuing the war;

(ii) if it removed ZAPU and Zambia from the war it would greatly reduce Rhodesia's security problems (and Zambia's);

(iii) it would greatly ease our task in securing international support for any agreement reached at the conference.

4. It would have the following main disadvantages:

(i) an agreement including Nkomo (allied, possibly, to Chikerema, Ndiweni and Sithole) could lead to realignment of the internal African political scene to the Bishop's disadvantage;

(ii) white Rhodesian attitude might be divided: most of those in the conference delegation seem to want ZAPU in, and getting ZAPU and Zambia out of the war would be a major fillip; but at grass-root level there is deep personal antipathy to Nkomo because of the shooting down of the Viscount aircraft last year.[2]

Conclusions

5. We should seek to keep the Patriotic Front in play at the conference long enough to see whether signs of division appear (perhaps because of intransigence by Mugabe over the Constitution). We should not in any circumstances be seen to have encouraged or engineered the split, since that would lose the Front Line and cause us major problems with Muzorewa; but we should be poised to take advantage of one if it occurs.[3]

ANTONY DUFF

---

2 Air Rhodesia Flight 825 was a scheduled passenger flight from Victoria Falls to Salisbury that was shot down by a ZIPRA missile on 3 September 1978. Of the 56 people on board, 38 died in the crash. Ten of the survivors were subsequently shot dead by ZIPRA forces who arrived at the crash scene.

3 Mr Luce minuted on 17 September: 'I remain of the view that it is infinitely preferable to achieve objective b and I therefore agree with Sir A. Duff's conclusion. No opportunity should be lost to achieve this objective.' The minute was seen and noted by Mr Gilmour, and seen by Lord Carrington (minutes of 17 and 18 September).

No. 76

Letter from Mr Alexander (No. 10) to Mr Walden, 18 September 1979
Secret and Personal (FCO 36/2513)

Dear George,

Laurens van der Post

As you know, Colonel van der Post saw the Prime Minister and the Foreign and Commonwealth Secretary yesterday morning.

As a result of that discussion, Colonel van der Post undertook to use his influence with the South African Government to try to get them to intervene with Mr Smith to take a more reasonable line at the Constitutional Conference. Colonel van der Post rang his contact, the Minister of Co-operation and Development, yesterday evening. Mr Koornhof rang back this morning to say that he had seen the South African Prime Minister and the Foreign Minister late yesterday evening and that instructions had been issued to the South African Ambassador in London to see Mr Ian Smith today and to urge him to play a more constructive role in the Conference. Colonel van der Post said that it would perhaps be optimistic to expect the effects of the South African interventions to be apparent at once. However, I undertook to ring him back this evening to tell him whether there were any signs of flexibility on Mr Smith's part.

By way of background, Colonel van der Post told me that he had said to Mr Koornhof that the South African Government would never have a better opportunity to secure a peaceful settlement in Rhodesia. They had an honourable and just Government in the United Kingdom with which to deal and to fail to back that Government's efforts to make a success of the Constitutional Conference would be suicidal folly on their part. This was an opportunity which the South African Government had to take. Colonel van der Post added that he thought the South African military were saying the same thing to Mr P.W. Botha. He added, finally, that he thought the South African Ambassador in London, Dawie de Villiers, was a significant figure whose influence, both as a result of his rugby playing prowess and of his membership of the Broederbond[1], should not be under-estimated.

It may be worth recording in this letter one point which struck the Prime Minister forcibly in what Colonel van der Post said yesterday morning. He claimed to have learned from one Harold Mockford, who is a regular visitor to Mozambique as a recruiter of labour for South Africa, that Presidents Machel and Nyerere both have instructions from the Soviet Government to delay progress in Zimbabwe for another year. This was primarily because the ZANU and ZAPU guerrillas needed more time to learn how to use the equipment with which they were now being supplied by the Soviet and East German Governments; and partly because the Soviet Government wished to delay the crunch in Zimbabwe until after the Olympic Games. According to Mr Mockford, Nyerere was willing to go along with the Soviet wishes, while President Machel was more resistant.

MICHAEL ALEXANDER

---

1 An exclusively Afrikaner Calvinist male secret society in South Africa dedicated to the advancement of the Afrikaner people.

No. 77

Minute from Mr Walden to Mr Renwick, 18 September 1979
Confidential (FCO 36/2437)

Meeting between the Secretary of State and Mr David Smith

Mr David Smith called on the Secretary of State at 2 p.m. today at Lord Carrington's request. Apart from myself, no-one else was present.

Mr Smith said that everyone knew that Ian Smith was a has-been. But he did not regret his part in including him in the delegation. The fact was that he could still swing white opinion in Rhodesia. He had been greatly affected by his reception in London (fan mail etc.). He was alone in the Salisbury Delegation in holding out against the British proposals. Even Chief Ndiweni had now, to Ian Smith's surprise, come out against him on the grounds that the Chief could not go back to his people without agreement.

However, there had been the first 'chink of light' in Ian Smith's position at a delegation meeting this morning. Ian Smith had said that, even if they knew that they would have to give in in the end, the Salisbury Delegation should be seen to have gone down fighting. This had been the first indication that his intransigence was tactical.

David Smith himself said that he had now finally made up his mind on his own position: he trusted the British Foreign Office under a Conservative Minister and was prepared to negotiate on the three points on the Constitution, provided that recognition and the lifting of sanctions would be granted at the end of the process. Ian Smith was placing great hopes on the Americans lifting sanctions, especially following his recent meeting with Senator Helms' two representatives[1]. He, David Smith, knew better however. White opinion in Rhodesia wanted a settlement.

David Smith expressed confidence in our joint ability to wear Ian Smith down. But it would be important to give him a chance to 'empty his stomach' in a prolonged session with Lord Carrington, perhaps with Bishop Muzorewa and others present. Ian Smith kept repeating that, whatever assurances Lord Carrington was said to have given to the Bishop, he himself had not had them first hand from the Secretary of State. It would be important to hear Ian Smith out patiently, and give factual answers to his questions. Only Lord Carrington himself could do this.

Another way to encourage Ian Smith to come across would be by the promise of a development fund for Rhodesia after independence, along the lines of the Kissinger proposal. Ian Smith would need to feel that he himself had personally secured some such fund. Although the Rhodesian economy was not too bad, David Smith knew that investment from abroad would not be forthcoming until there had been a settlement; the message had come through clearly from otherwise sympathetic Swiss bankers he had talked to in Zurich on his way to London.

David Smith also said that it would be useful if we could make a concession to the Salisbury team on the question of unamendable aspects of the Constitution. However blinkered this view might seem, the Salisbury team's lawyers wanted the

---

1 Helms sent two of his aides to the Conference as he did not trust the US State Department's policy on Rhodesia.

possibility of amendments by 100% votes. Lord Carrington said he thought we could do this; we had been under the impression that our present proposals were more helpful. Mr David Smith said that we should not underestimate the intelligence of Mr Anderson, though he had begun to behave oddly since he had come to London. Previously he had been a moderate.

G.G.H. WALDEN

No. 78

Minute from Mr Barltrop to Mr Johnson, 19 September 1979
Confidential (FCO 36/2509)

Nigeria and the Commonwealth

1. Over lunch today with Mr Emanuel Oba, the Nigerian High Commissioner in Lusaka who is in London to cover the Rhodesia talks and who is an old friend of mine from Addis Ababa days, I reverted to a conversation which I had with him in the corridors during the Lusaka CHGM about the Nigerian Military Government's implied threat to leave the Commonwealth if the outcome of the discussions on Rhodesia were not in their view satisfactory (see Lusaka tel. 829 para 16 of 3 August and attached extract from the provisional record).[1]

2. Mr Oba said that Commissioner Adefope had gone to Lusaka with a brief on Rhodesia containing contingency instructions approved by the Supreme Military Council that, in the absence of satisfactory progress over Rhodesia, he should announce at the end of the meeting that Nigeria was leaving the Commonwealth. Following the agreement reached on the Rhodesian formula on the Sunday (5 August), the Commissioner had sent a telegram to Lagos that evening informing his government of it and, I gather, seeking authority in the light of it not to go ahead with the announcement of Nigeria's withdrawal. The telegram from Lagos conveying this authority arrived at the Nigerian High Commission at 3 p.m. on the Tuesday afternoon, only 2 hours or so before the meeting ended. Mr Oba made it clear that the arrival of this telegram was greeted with great relief within the Nigerian delegation. He added, in the course of some further comments, that there were those in the Military Government who had for some 5 years been pressing for Nigeria to leave the Commonwealth; and officials in the Ministry of External Affairs had at one stage had to produce a considered paper setting out the pros and cons of continued Commonwealth membership. The tangible benefits cited in the paper had greatly outweighed the disadvantages, but it had even so not been an easy task to dissuade the 'hawks' from pressing their arguments to a conclusion.

3. You may like to know that, in the course of some general conversation about the Nigerian internal scene, Mr Oba remarked that the emergence of Shehu Shagari as President designate was generally welcomed by civil servants—he was for most of them very much the preferred candidate. So far as Anglo-Nigerian relations were concerned, he thought that Alhaji Shagari would personally be in favour of

---

1 Not printed.

good relations with Britain. He implied however that his own natural inclinations would probably be subject to some political constraints. Mr Oba, incidentally, spoke warmly of the newly-arrived Nigerian High Commissioner in London, Mr Yolah. He added that he was one of a minority of senior Nigeria civil servants who were genuinely de-tribalised.

R.A.R. BARLTROP

No. 79

Minute by Rhodesia Department, 19 September 1979
Restricted (FCO 36/2437)

Record of a Bilateral Meeting between the British and Nkomo/Mugabe Delegations at Lancaster House on 18 September 1979 at 4.00 p.m.

Present:

Lord Carrington	Mr Nkomo
Sir I. Gilmour	Mr Mugabe
Mr Luce	Mr Msika
Sir A. Duff	Mr Mlambo
Mr Day	Mr Barron
Mr Byatt	Mr Mubako
Mr Fifoot	Mr Tungamirai
Mr Renwick	Mr Sibanda
Mr Powell	and other members of the Patriotic Front delegation
Private Secretary	
Mr Barlow	
Mr Lyne	
Mr Layden	
Mr Richardson	

1. *The Secretary of State* proposed that the meeting should consider which issues in the constitution needed to be discussed first by the principals on each side, and which could be remitted in the first place to experts, who would report back in due course.

2. *Mr Nkomo* expressed doubts about the basis on which bilateral meetings would be held: would the British be frank, or would they be continually reserving their position because they thought particular proposals would cause difficulty for Bishop Muzorewa? It was agreed that frank discussion could take place in bilaterals, but that any agreement reached would have to be considered later in plenary.

3. It was then agreed that the chapters on the State of Zimbabwe, Citizenship, the Declaration of Rights, Finance and the Ombudsman could be dealt with in the first

instance by experts. So too could the Patriotic Front's draft Order in Council. The other chapters would need to be discussed between principals.

4. There followed a discussion of whether there should be a constitutional head of state or an Executive President. *Mr Nkomo* argued for a directly-elected Executive President because: the trend in Africa, except South Africa, was to have Executive Presidents; in African communities a head of state had to have power; and the holder of the central office of the state must be elected by the whole people. *Sir I. Gilmour* accepted that the trend in Africa was in that direction, but pointed out that a non-executive President would not be completely without powers: he would have certain important functions such as appointing the Prime Minister. The crucial objective to setting up an Executive Presidency in Rhodesia was that such a system worked satisfactorily only in a two-party or single-party system. If there were more parties, all putting up candidates for the Presidency, the successful candidate might well have the support of only a quarter or a third of the electorate. The recent elections in Nigeria were an example of the problems which could arise. The new Zimbabwe would be starting out as a deeply-divided country. A process of reconciliation was needed. Under the system proposed by Britain, the leader of the successful party in an election would have to seek accommodation with other parties in order to form a government. The vital process of reconciliation would therefore be advanced. A national leader for all the people was more, not less likely, to emerge under the system envisaged in the British proposals.

5. *Mr Nkomo* said that the British parallel was not exact, since the special position of the Monarch would have no equivalent in Zimbabwe. *Mr Mugabe* said that under the system proposed by the UK the man at the top would not have effective control of the machinery of government: power would lie with the Prime Minister. This would be divisive. An elected President would not necessarily command the support of only a minority of the electorate—this would depend on how many votes he could attract. *Sir I. Gilmour* commented that, from the British point of view, a constitutional head of state was less important than the establishment of the Prime Ministerial form of government. *Mr Mugabe* replied that the African tradition was for the top man to have the power. He gave the example of the King of Swaziland, who was intended to be a constitutional ruler, but after independence had formed his own party, won an election and become an Executive King.

6. In the course of much further discussion, *Mr Tungamirai* pointed out that in a multi-party system, a Prime Minister might be hamstrung by divisions in parliament, whereas an elected President could always get things done. *Sir I. Gilmour* countered that the danger with an Executive President was that he was so much more powerful than the legislature that the process of coalition-forming was often unnecessary: the President just took control, as had happened in certain other African countries.

7. *Mr Barron* suggested that the position of the 2 sides might be reconciled by the experts. In the Patriotic Front proposals the Vice President had the job of organising the House of Assembly. Perhaps he could fill the Prime Ministerial role by which the British set such store. *Lord Carrington* replied that he did not think that the position were readily reconcilable. The British Government continue to prefer its proposal.

8. It was agreed that the meeting would adjourn so that each side could consider the other's arguments; and that there would be a further bilateral meeting at 3.00 pm the following day.

No. 80

Minute by Rhodesia Department, 20 September 1979
Restricted (FCO 36/2437)

Record of a Bilateral Meeting of the British and Salisbury Delegations at Lancaster House at 10.30 a.m. on 19 September 1979

Present:

Lord Carrington	Bishop Muzorewa
Sir I. Gilmour	Dr Mundawarara
Mr Luce	Mr Ian Smith
Sir M. Palliser	Mr David Smith
Sir A. Duff	Rev N. Sithole
Mr Day	Mr Nyemba
Mr Byatt	Chief Kayisa Ndiweni
Mr Fifoot	Mr Bafanah
Mr Renwick	
Mr Powell	
Private Secretary	
Mr Barlow	
Mr Lyne	
Mr Richardson	

1. *The Secretary of State* explained in detail the basis of the British government's policy towards Rhodesia since it had taken office on 3 May. The government fully recognised the political progress which had been achieved in Rhodesia and the sacrifices which had been made to get the country to its present position. But if they had proceeded to grant Rhodesia independence and lift sanctions immediately on taking office, they would have done so with no international support whatever. The consequence for British interests would have been disastrous, and Rhodesia would not have benefitted. Indeed the war would have intensified.

2. Instead, the government decided to embark on a process of consultation with its friends and partners, the outcome of which had already been described in detail to the Salisbury government. This had been followed by the Lusaka conference, at which the atmosphere was remarkably constructive and had suggested that there was now conviction of the need to try for a settlement involving all the parties. Britain had agreed at Lusaka to work for a new constitution for Rhodesia which would differ in two major respects from the present arrangements, and it was a logical consequence of this that if there were agreement by both sides on a new constitution, the parties should contest an election on that basis—but under British, not UN auspices. At every step along the way we had kept the Bishop and his colleagues fully informed.

3. Our constitutional proposals, which were the proposals of *all* the British government, had been recognised as fair and reasonable by the United States, the Commonwealth and Europe. What would happen if the Bishop's government failed to accept them? Even supposing that those who were now trying to mislead them were right, and British economic sanctions lapsed in November, would that get them international recognition and the investment they needed? How could the Prime Minister recommend to Parliament that sanctions be lifted if her own constitutional proposals had been rejected?

4. In any case, sanctions would not lapse automatically even if Section 2 of the Southern Rhodesia Act 1965 did lapse in November. Direct trade between Britain and Rhodesia and the transfer of funds to Rhodesia would still be prohibited unless the government took positive action which would require the support of Parliament and, failing that, the prospect of motion of censure. To lift the present exchange controls would be subject to negative procedure in Parliament in any case.

5. The present situation in the conference was that the Patriotic Front did not yet look as if they were going to walk out in a way which would be demonstrably unreasonable. Some of them at any rate really wanted a settlement. The Salisbury delegation would do well to consider what their position would be if in the end the Patriotic Front accepted a fair constitutional settlement and they refused it.

6. *Bishop Muzorewa* acknowledged that it was fair to say that Britain had been frank with them throughout, however much they disagreed with our policy. There was only one point on which we had been unfair—he thought we had agreed to discuss our constitutional proposals with them before disclosing them to others.

7. Asked by *Chief Ndiweni* how we intended to stop the war if they accepted our proposals, the *Secretary of State* said that the war would stop automatically if there were an all-party agreement. The Front Line [Presidents] would not support the Patriotic Front if they lost a fair election. But if—and we had always said no-one should have a veto—the Patriotic Front refused to accept a reasonable solution which was accepted by Salisbury, we could then maintain to our friends and allies that they now had a proper constitution, had already had a fair election amongst themselves, and were a legitimate government worthy of recognition. The Patriotic Front might well go on fighting, but with diminished support, while Rhodesia could hope to attract the international investment she needed.

8. *Mr [Ian] Smith*, referring to what Lord Carrington had said about British interests, said Rhodesia interests should be paramount in this situation. Their lives were at stake. All the countries giving us advice were dictatorships. Britain should have tried to get agreement with Rhodesia on certain broad principles in advance of the conference, and they had been 'led to believe' that this was what had been accepted. He wanted to avoid a public confrontation. Lord Carrington was wrong to suggest that some of the Rhodesian side were merely out to resist all change. There were more constructive than that—they hoped to convince the British side that they were right. In any case, there was a strong chance that the United States would remove sanctions, and that would solve Rhodesia's problem. He was not impressed by talk about the consequences of failure of the conference—he had heard it all before. The concessions Britain was asking for would interfere with the rights secured for whites in the present constitution. It was the long term that concerned him. If the British

proposals were contrary to vital Rhodesian principles, the delegation would have to oppose them.

9. *Mr Sithole* said that we should bear in mind the different meanings which members of their delegation might attach to the word 'our'. To Mr Smith, 'our interests' might mean those of the whites. To him, 'our interests' meant primarily those of the black majority. *Mr Nyemba* said that the Rhodesian delegation should come to terms immediately. They should not cling to what they had repeatedly been told was not good enough. The 1979 constitution had not brought peace.

10. *Mr Mundawarara* asked if any radical changes in the British proposals would have to be referred back to the other countries who had been consulted about the proposals as they originally stood. *The Secretary of State* said that we might be open to reconsideration of details. But we were satisfied that what we had now proposed was fully within the terms of the Lusaka declaration.

11. *Chief Ndiweni* pleaded that the country should not have to go through another election.

12. *Sir I. Gilmour* urged Mr Smith to consider whether the whites should not put their faith in constitutions but in political arrangements. Many people would say it was ludicrous for 3% of the population to have 20% of seats in Parliament. It would put the whites in an extremely strong position to forge political alliances with the black parties in Parliament.

No. 81

Lord Carrington to Sir L. Allinson (Lusaka) 20 September 1979, 9.55 a.m.[1]
Tel. No. 777 Confidential, Immediate (FCO 36/2437)

My Tel. No. 772: Rhodesia: Constitutional Conference.[2]

1. On the morning of 19 September there was a bilateral meeting with the Salisbury delegation; and in the afternoon with the Patriotic Front.

2. During the morning meeting I reaffirmed a number of points which I had already made at my earlier meeting with Mr Smith and others on 14 September (see Para 5 of my telno 765). I emphasised that constitutional change to remove the white blocking power and to permit political control over the senior public service appointments was indispensable if Parliament was to be persuaded to grant Rhodesia independence and lift sanctions. I explained the figures for white representation which we had in mind and the majorities which would be necessary for constitutional change. I repeated that positive action on the Government's part was required to lift the bulk of the sanctions against Rhodesia, and that this would require the approval of both

---

1 And to Immediate Mirimba, Salisbury, Nairobi, Maputo, Gaborone, Dar es Salaam, Luanda, Lagos, Washington, Pretoria, Addis Ababa, Monrovia, Canberra, Ottawa, Wellington; Information Immediate UKMIS New York; Priority Abidjan, Dakar, Kinshasa, Khartoum, Tokyo, EEC Posts, Kingston, Bridgetown, Dacca, New Delhi, Singapore, Georgetown, Maseru, Freetown, Port Louis, Mbabane, Port of Spain, Kampala, Lilongwe, Valletta, Banjul, Colombo, Accra, Kuala Lumpur, Nicosia, Castries, Oslo, Stockholm, Lisbon, Madrid, Manila, Tehran, Bucharest, Caracas, Athens; Info Saving Suva, Port Moresby. Honiara, Nuku'alofa, Victoria, Tarawa.

2 None of the telegrams referenced in this document are printed.

Houses of Parliament. I urged the Salisbury delegation to agree to the constitutional changes proposed. Agreement on this basis followed by free and fair elections in accordance with the Lusaka Agreement would lead to legal independence and the lifting of sanctions.

3. With the Patriotic Front we continued our discussion on points arising from our constitutional summary. On the composition and functions of the public service commissions, the Patriotic Front argued that these provisions could only be determined once the composition of the actual public service at independence was known. We replied that our concern was to ensure that the future elected government would be in a position to exercise effective control over the civil service and defence forces and to promote Africanisation: but that the composition of those forces was for the future government to decide. It could not be pre-judged in advance of the elections.

4. The Patriotic Front maintained their objections in principle to white minority representation. I emphasised that such an arrangement was in our view fundamental to a settlement. In discussion, you should not suggest that either the principle of temporary white representation, or the figures we have put forward, are negotiable by either side: you should draw fully on the arguments set out in my telno 769 and 776.

5. Please note that in my telno 772 the date in para. 1 line 1 should be 18 and not 19 September. Error regretted.

No. 82

Minute from Mr Renwick to Mr Walden, 21 September 1979
Confidential (FCO 36/2507)

Rhodesia: US Senate

1. I agreed with Mr Lake and Mr Moose the following press guidance for use if necessary by the State Department spokesman today:

'An FCO official discussed with a US Embassy official on 19 September the progress being made towards agreement on the Constitution at the Rhodesia Conference. In the course of that discussion he indicated that some members of the Salisbury delegation might be more reluctant to accept the changes which would render an agreement possible because they believed they had assurances [from Senate staffers] that the Senate would move to lift sanctions by 1 October.'

2. This is an accurate account of this part of the daily background briefing to Mr Lanpher—except for the phrase in square brackets. It was the US Embassy who raised and expressed indignation about Mr Carbaugh and Mr [James] Lucier:[1] their activities were not our affair. Mr Lake said that he realised the report was inaccurate. But Mr Vance would be relieved that we had found a way to help him. He was worried because the vote in Congress might be very close and he did not want to have

---

1 While working for Senator Helms, Lucier and Carbaugh were criticised by the US media for apparently profiting from private foundations they had set up with Helms, and were accused of meddling in foreign policy on Helms' behalf, particularly when both attended and attempted to influence the Lancaster House talks between Britain and Rhodesia. For more detail on this, including Carbaugh's attempt to undermine Mrs Thatcher's trust in Lord Carrington, see Charles Moore, *Margaret Thatcher: The Authorised Biography*, Vol. I, *Not For Turning* (London: Allen Lane, 2013), p. 501.

Congress under-cutting our efforts. I told Mr Lake how matters now stood in the Conference: we hoped that we were on the way to an agreement which would enable both of us to lift sanctions.

R.W. Renwick

No. 83

Lord Carrington to Sir L. Allinson (Lusaka), 22 September 1979, 11.45 a.m.[1]
Tel. No. 781 Confidential, Immediate (FCO 36/2437)

My Tel. No. 778: Rhodesia: Constitutional Conference.[2]

1. Further bilateral meetings were held on 21 September with the Salisbury Delegation and with the Patriotic Front. Various members of the Salisbury delegation asked for clarification of certain points on our proposals and sought to discover whether there was any possibility of eroding our insistence that the proportion of white seats should be no more than twenty per cent and that for constitutional amendment seventy-five percent: and on governmental control over the armed forces and public services. Mr Ian Smith asked what assurance there would be that if agreement was reached on a constitution sanctions would automatically be lifted. It was explained to him that our intention was that the conference would end with agreement on a constitution and on the arrangements for elections to bring it into effect. The question of the lifting of sanctions would depend on the nature of the interim arrangement.

2. At the meeting with the Patriotic Front there was a lengthy and tough discussion of the provisions for defence. The Patriotic Front continue their efforts to insist on discussion of the arrangement for the armed forces before independence. We maintained our position that agreement on the constitution had to come first. The Patriotic Front also resisted any commitment to pay the pensions of civil servants of the present regime.

3. In the evening, Bishop Muzorewa's delegation formally announced that they accepted the main points of principle of the British proposals for constitutional change. This decision had been taken after a ballot of the delegation in which the voting was eleven to one in favour of acceptance (the dissenting vote being that of Mr Ian Smith). This acceptance was contingent on satisfactory detailed arrangements being drawn up and also on agreement on the subsequent process of implementation.

4. The Secretary of State has announced that he will be away from the conference to attend the UNGA on Monday, Tuesday and Wednesday. The Chairman will therefore be Sir I. Gilmour. Bilateral meetings will resume on Monday.

---

[1] And to Immediate Mirimba, Salisbury, Nairobi, Maputo, Gaborone, Dar es Salaam, Luanda, Lagos, Washington, Pretoria, Addis Ababa, Monrovia, Canberra, Ottawa, Wellington; Information Immediate UKMIS New York; Priority Abidjan, Dakar, Kinshasa, Khartoum, Tokyo, EEC Posts, Kingston, Bridgetown, Dacca, New Delhi, Singapore, Georgetown, Maseru, Freetown, Port Louis, Mbabane, Port of Spain, Kampala, Lilongwe, Valletta, Banjul, Colombo, Accra, Kuala Lumpur, Nicosia, Castries, Oslo, Stockholm, Lisbon, Madrid, Manila, Tehran, Bucharest, Caracas, Athens; Information Saving Suva, Port Moresby. Honiara, Nuku'alofa, Victoria, Tarawa.

[2] Not printed.

No. 84

Sir A. Parsons (UKMIS New York) to Lord Carrington, 24 September 1979, 10.58 p.m.[1]
Tel. No. 1098 Immediate, Confidential (FCO 36/2459)

Following from Private Secretary
Secretary of State's call on Dr Waldheim: Rhodesia

1. Lord Carrington outlined the stage the Conference had reached, stressing the importance of the Lusaka Agreement, which had put Britain in a stronger position than during the period of the AAP. Dr Waldheim said that it was clear from his conversations with President Nyerere that the Tanzanians accepted that the UK must exercise its responsibilities. He had found Kaunda somewhat less outspoken than Nyerere about the Patriotic Front, though he had taken a similar line.

2. Lord Carrington said that the interim arrangements contained the seeds of trouble, and some people might make subjective judgements on the arrangements we might propose. It would be important to remember that our proposals would be based on a compromise between the divergent positions of the two parties. The interval before elections must be as brief as possible. (Dr Waldheim agreed.) Difficult issues would have to be left until after the elections. Anyone who wanted to opt out of the negotiations would no doubt claim that whatever we decided on the interim arrangements was unfair. But we were determined that the final decision should be ours after listening to both sides.

3. Dr Waldheim asked about the role of the United Nations. He was happy to see that the Commonwealth would play a role, and had no wish to push for UN involvement. Though the Patriotic Front now wanted this after having first opposed it. Lord Carrington stressed that the Lusaka Agreement, with its provision for Commonwealth observers, was our lifeline and that we could do nothing to undermine it. If we moved away from it we would lose people in the process. Dr Waldheim stressed that he was not keen to involve the UN: he had enough trouble elsewhere. They should not reopen old dossiers of proposals which had proved too complicated. But the UN were ready to help in any way if they were needed.

4. Lord Carrington also spoke briefly to the President of the General Assembly, Salim (Tanzania) about Rhodesia. Salim said that he would do his best to defer any debate on Rhodesia until the end of the year. In the light of his experiences at the Geneva Conference on Rhodesia, he thought an early debate would be a mistake. He was currently thinking in terms of November, and would talk to the Chair of the Fourth Committee on these lines. Salim undertook to do what he could to make things less difficult for us at the UN.

---

1 And Information Priority to Washington, Nairobi, Dar es Salaam, Lusaka, Pretoria, Maputo, Lagos, Luanda.

No. 85

Lord Carrington to Sir L. Allinson (Lusaka), 25 September 1979, 6.37 p.m.[1]
Tel. No. 787 Confidential, Immediate (FCOA 36/2437)

Rhodesia: Constitutional Conference

1. Further bilateral meetings between officials took place in the morning and afternoon of 25 September. The session with the Patriotic Front was devoted almost entirely to the question of citizenship. The Patriotic Front demanded that the incoming government after independence should have the power at its discretion to confirm or withdraw citizenship granted to post-UDI immigrants. They admitted that this was to enable unacceptable elements to be weeded out. We stressed we favoured provisions which would lead to a reconciliation between the two sides engaged in the conflict.

2. With the Salisbury delegation discussion continued on the size of the assembly, the composition and powers of the Senate, the voting arrangements for the white minority and other more detailed aspects of the constitution affecting the executive and the legislature.

3. In discussing the new proposals for white minority representation put forward by the Patriotic Front (my telegram number 533 to UKMIS New York)[2] you should say that it is encouraging that this step towards an agreement has been taken. The conference has made good progress and we hope that agreement on the constitution will be attainable. But there are still important points on the constitution on which the Patriotic Front have not accepted our proposals, even in principle (see, for example, para. 1 above). These difficulties will have to be resolved. We shall then be ready to consider the arrangements for implementing the constitution—the key element in which is acceptance of the agreement of Lusaka that elections should be supervised under our authority.

No. 86

Letter from Mr Walden to Mr Alexander (No. 10), 27 September 1979
Confidential (FCO 36/2513)

Dear Michael,

You asked if we would like to suggest a message which Colonel van der Post could pass to the South Africans. The Secretary of State thinks that this is a good idea. We suggest the following:

'We are now very close to agreement with the Salisbury delegation on the Constitution. We must keep up the momentum. If Muzorewa is in a position to say that he has agreed on a Constitution with us, and can accept elections under our authority, we shall be on the verge of a successful outcome to the Conference.

---

[1] And to Immediate Mirimba, Salisbury and certain other posts; Priority Abidjan and certain other posts; Information Immediate UKMIS New York; Information Saving Suva, Port Moresby. Honiara, Nuku'alofa, Victoria, Tarawa.
[2] Not printed.

Muzorewa himself will go back to Rhodesia in a position of some strength as the promoter of a settlement which will lead rapidly to legal independence and the early lifting of sanctions. We have strong indications from the Zambians that they want a settlement.'

Yours ever,
G.G.H. WALDEN

No. 87

Minute from Mr Manning to Mr Renwick, 27 September 1979
Unclassified (FCO 36/2438)

Rhodesia Conference: Entertainment

1. Following his lunch with Messrs [David] Smith and Cronje yesterday, Mr Luce is very conscious that delegates to the Conference are finding the atmosphere claustrophobic especially at weekends. He feels that this could have a bad effect on the future of the Conference as it seems likely to continue for several weeks and would like consideration given to the possibility of organising more entertainment, social functions and possibly outings for delegates to relieve the problem of boredom. For his own part he would be prepared to organise, for example, a visit to Rockingham Castle in Leicestershire (the property of a cousin). If this was considered desirable he thinks that something on these lines involving getting away from London might be helpful.

2. Mr Luce would be interested in your views.[1]

K.Q.F. MANNING

1 Ms Spencer minuted on 2 October: 'Discussed with Mr Renwick. The liaison officer with the Salisbury delegation is floating this suggestion with them and will let me know the upshot. Spoken to Miss Walker.' Ms Olivia Rosalyn Walker was Assistant Private Secretary to Mr Luce.

No. 88

Lord Carrington to Sir L. Allinson (Lusaka), 28 September 1979, 8.05 p.m.[1]
Tel. No. 796 Confidential, Immediate (FCO 36/2438)

My telno 792: Rhodesian Constitutional Conference.[2]

1. At bilateral meetings with both delegations at official level on 28 September, we completed the detailed consideration of our constitutional proposals. The outstanding points of difference which emerged in the course of these discussions will be considered in further plenary and bilateral meetings on 1 and possibly 2 October. After that we propose to table in plenary a full version of the Constitution we will be prepared to commend to Parliament. This, inevitably, will not in some respects meet

1 And Immediate Priority to other posts; Information Immediate to UKMIS New York; Info Saving to Suva and other posts.
2 Not printed.

the requirements of either side. But it will, indisputably provide for genuine majority rule and we hope that both sides will be able to agree to it. Executive, Parliament, the judicature, the defence forces, finance and the Ombudsman with the Salisbury delegation: the Declaration of Rights and the Executive.

No. 89

Minute from Lord Carrington to Mrs Thatcher, 28 September 1979[1]
PM/79/83 Confidential (PREM 19/112)

Rhodesia: The Pre-Independence Arrangements

1. We are now close to agreement with Bishop Muzorewa and his delegation on a full description of the independence Constitution. I intend to table this in the Conference next week and to wind up discussion of the Constitution (apart from legal drafting) as quickly as I can.

2. The Patriotic Front will resist our proposals and may try to prolong the discussion. But they have accepted that 20% of the seats in the House of Assembly should be reserved to the white community. The unaccustomed moderation up to now shows the extent of the pressure they are under from the Front Line states. The indications still are that the Zambians want a settlement. Nkomo would also like one, but will find it difficult to accept our terms and to produce plausible reasons for breaking with Mugabe.

3. It is probable that the Patriotic Front will come near enough to acceptance of our Constitution to enable us to go on to the next stage of the Conference in the week beginning 8 October. This must be based on our proposals for the pre-independence period. These proposals should be designed to meet a situation in which we have all-party agreement to proceed to elections and independence; but they should at the same time be adaptable for use if we are going ahead with the Salisbury government alone.

4. Our objective should be to devise a plan for elections which would:
(*a*) help Muzorewa as much as possible and therefore be acceptable to him;
(*b*) win the widest possible international recognition for Rhodesia (and safeguard our position in international law);
(*c*) enable us to demonstrate, if the Patriotic Front refuses to participate, that they have been given a fair chance to do so.

5. Our aim when discussion of the pre-independence arrangements begin in the plenary sessions should be to get the Bishop to make a statement in the Conference on the following lines:
(*a*) he had agreed the independent Constitution to be elected by the British parliament;
(*b*) the illegal declaration of independence had been nothing to do with him;
(*c*) he had already won elections in which 1.8 million people had participated.
But
(*d*) In the interest of attracting international recognition for his country, *he was*

---

[1] The Private Secretary minuted on 3 October: 'Discussed between PM & F.C.S.'

prepared to accept the agreement by the Commonwealth Heads of Government that new elections should be held and that these should be supervised under the British government authority.

6. Such a statement would put the Bishop in the best possible position *vis-à-vis* the international community. The only new element in it is 5 (*d*). In private discussion he has assured us that he can accept this.

7. We should work for an arrangement which will enable us to declare that the state of rebellion has ended and that legality has been restored *before* independence. If legality has *not* been restored by November, we shall be in great difficulty over Section 2 of the Southern Rhodesia Act. The attraction for Bishop Muzorewa in a *return to legality before independence* is that it *would enable us to lift sanctions forthwith* and thus give him a considerable advantage in the elections. The lifting of sanctions would encourage the whites and help to ensure their co-operation. We must ensure that the Salisbury parties understand that, if the removal of sanctions is to be of maximum benefit to them, it must be conditional on their having accepted an independence Constitution and arrangements for the transition to independence which are internationally defensible. The *legislative* steps for effecting a return to legality as summarised at Annex A. The subsequent provision for elections and an independence constitution will require an Act of Parliament.

8. The basis for a return to legality before independence likely to carry most conviction with the international community and exert most pressure on the Front Line States' support for the Patriotic Front, would be to make interim 'colonial' arrangements, under the authority of a British Administrator, (or 'Agent' which may be a more acceptable title in Rhodesia), who would have full legislative and executive authority for the administration for a limited period (the aim would be to conduct the election and proceed to independence within at most 12 weeks). In practice the Administrator would confine his activities very largely to what was strictly necessary for the electoral process (including the supervision of the police). The present government would stand aside, with Bishop Muzorewa concentrating on the electoral campaign. The administration of the country would be carried on by Rhodesian civil servants (under the authority of the Administrator); but the formal legal position would need to be a vesting of authority in the UK or its appointee. The incentive for the Rhodesians would be:

(*a*) British economic sanctions would be removed immediately the Administrator took over;

(*b*) The arrangement would put pressure on the Front Line Presidents *either* to push the Patriotic Front into agreeing a ceasefire and participating in the elections *or* to diminish their support for them.

The Patriotic Front will try to negotiate with us the arrangements for control over the administration etc., but we should take firmly the line that this is our business.

9. Bishop Muzorewa is prepared to agree to a plan of this kind (you may wish to see the enclosed record of his talk with the Lord Privy Seal)[2]. Apart from the immediate lifting of sanctions, it has for him the great advantage that it would be the present civil service and the police force who would be administering the elections. The plan would maintain *momentum* towards the settlement. It would put the

---

2 Not printed.

Bishop—as the man who had negotiated the basis for legal independence and who had already achieved the lifting of sanctions—in a very strong electoral position.

10. The Patriotic Front would be in a difficult position. They would not want to participate in elections on any terms which did not give them a major say in their administration, and possibly would refuse to do so. But a return to legality on this basis, especially if the Patriotic Front had, even conditionally, accepted the independence Constitution, would largely under-cut their arguments about the *legality* of the pre-independence regime, even if they continued to dispute its impartiality. (They would continue to argue that elections held within the existing administration and security forces in place would put them at a disadvantage; and that there should be some neutral force.)

11. *Vis-à-vis* the Commonwealth, the elections would manifestly be held under our authority. There could be no guarantee that we would get full Front Line support. But the 'respectable' international community would find it harder to see anything wrong with this plan—provided they could be assured of our involvement as impartial supervisors. If the Patriotic Front refused to co-operate, we could still proceed immediately with the return to legality, the lifting of sanctions (despite resisting in the Security Council) and the arrangements for the elections in which we would keep open the offer to the Patriotic Front to participate. But the difficulty in that case is that we would be in effect responsible for the Rhodesian Army's actions in the continuing war. We would be able to say at every stage that we were acting in complete accordance with the Lusaka communiqué (and it is this which is worrying the Patriotic Front). With sanctions already lifted, the Bishop would have the best possible chance of achieving a high turn-out in the elections, and of winning them.

12. We have begun to prepare the ground with some of the white members of Muzorewa's delegation—in particular David Smith. We shall be in touch with General Walls, whose co-operation will be essential. We shall also have to carry the South Africans with us.

13. As part of the plan, we shall need to propose:

(*a*) a ceasefire, and

(*b*) the disengagement of the forces.

Commonwealth and other observers would be invited to witness the elections.

14. What are the main disadvantages of this plan?

15. *If the Patriotic Front participates,* the main difficulty will be in <u>maintaining the ceasefire</u>. A small military <u>'third force'</u> might well be necessary to monitor it. Any such force would have to be acceptable in Salisbury. A *small* Commonwealth force composed of acceptable elements would have the effect of driving a further wedge between the Patriotic Front and the Commonwealth governments supporting them and might well prove to be a *sine qua non* for Kaunda's support. But *we should not put forward any such ideas without Muzorewa's prior agreement*. It will be very difficult in practice to devise an agreement for the separation of forces which would not put one side or the other at a disadvantage. There would be no point in putting forward proposals in this area which would be unacceptable to the Rhodesian military commanders. We are exploring the possibilities with General Walls.[3]

---

3 Mrs Thatcher minuted against this paragraph: 'Am very worried about this proposal. Think it impossible for Muzorewa to accept and for the Parliamentary Party.'

16. *If the Patriotic Front do not participate*, we should be engaged, with the Rhodesian administration, in supervising elections with the war continuing.[4] But Muzorewa has said that he will accept elections; and we will have to be prepared to fulfil the commitment in the Lusaka communiqué. We should need to show that our supervision of the elections is effective, and if the war continues our supervisors could be at some risk. The Front Line States might continue to support the Patriotic Front—though this plan would give us the basis on which to try to persuade some of them at least that they should no longer do so. We should be legally responsible for the activities of the Rhodesian administration as a whole and our responsibility under international law for the Rhodesian military would be irrefutable. We should have to get General Walls to give us a firm assurance that, for the period required to organise the elections, military activity by the Rhodesian forces *vis-à-vis* Zambia and Mozambique would be restricted to defence from inside Rhodesian frontiers.[5] But our responsibility would last only for a strictly limited period (in this case less than the 12 weeks envisaged in the main plan).

17. We should have to reckon with resistance at the United Nations to the lifting of sanctions on the basis of a return to legality without the Patriotic Front. We have prepared an argument that, with a return to legality, sanctions will lapse. This is not an argument which will be generally accepted in the event, without participation of the Patriotic Front, of either a return to legality or of the granting of legal independence. In the event of a temporary return to dependent status, it may be argued by others that sanctions ought not to be lifted until after elections have been held; or that they should only be suspended pending the elections. *But if we do not get rid of sanctions before an election without the Patriotic Front's participation, we may find it even more difficult to get rid of sanctions after it.* There would therefore be advantage in going straight to the lifting of sanctions from the outset, provided we have a fully defensible interim arrangement. This would have most effect on the situation inside Rhodesia.

18. Sir Ian Sinclair (the FCO legal adviser) advises me that a full-scale return to legality would give us respectable arguments to deploy in the Security Council. The lifting of sanctions before granting legal independence can only be justified on the basis of our being seen to assume direct responsibility and authority for Rhodesia in the interim period before independence.

19. The main resistance to return to legality on these terms is likely to come from Ian Smith, who will try to insist that the present government should remain in office.[6] It would be very difficult to devise pre-independence arrangements on this basis which would have much chance of attracting international support, even if we appointed a British Election Commissioner to work alongside the existing government. This arrangement would carry little conviction with the Front Line States. President Kaunda would be unlikely to put any pressure on Nkomo to participate. Even if the Election Commissioner was able to claim that the police would act under his authority, it is unlikely that anyone, with the probable exception of the Americans, would follow our example in lifting sanctions in these

---

4 'If the P.F. do not participate there is little point in further elections.'
5 'Not possible if Mozambique build-up continues.'
6 'Not only from him. But from all those who feel that we are going to an unstable situation.'

circumstances; and we should find ourselves isolated or with very little support at the United Nations.

20. If we cannot secure the agreement of the Salisbury delegation to a return to legality on terms which offer good prospects of attracting international support, we should still want to do our best to say that we were complying with the Lusaka communiqué and were prepared to exercise supervision over the electoral process.[7] But without a return to legality sanctions could not formally be lifted before independence and we should have to consider how to deal with the situation arising from the probable lapse of Section 2 of the 1965 Act before that date.

Conclusions

21. In relation to the pre-independence arrangements, as over the Constitution, we must retain the initiative. The Patriotic Front will be able to direct the course of discussion over the interim period towards their proposals for transitional Councils, etc. unless we proceed on the basis of a firm British plan. We will gain most political advantage, and so will the Rhodesians, from a plan for the interim which involves the acceptance by the Rhodesians of a return to dependent status under British authority. This would cause the most difficulty for the Patriotic Front. Next in order of feasibility, but much less attractive to the Salisbury parties and to us, would be to proceed to independence *without* a preliminary return to legality.

22. If we can get the Salisbury delegation to agree to return to legality with a British Administrator we should <u>work hard to get American support</u>[8] for this approach; a return to legality would enable them to lift sanctions too. This would do a great deal to promote stability and confidence in Rhodesia.

23. We should meanwhile press ahead with completion of the full independence Constitution, with a view to enacting it in late October/early November. The Rhodesians should begin work on plans for the elections.

24. In the Conference, if agreement has been reached on the independence Constitution (however reluctantly by the Patriotic Front) we should begin to indicate our ideas with a brief statement on the lines set out at Annex B. The objectives of such a statement would be:

(*a*) to make clear we are not prepared to accept the Patriotic Front's ideas on the pre-independence arrangements;[9]

(*b*) to indicate our intention to fulfil the commitment in the Lusaka communiqué;[10]

(*c*) to open the way for Bishop Muzorewa to state that he is prepared to accept elections held under our authority.[11]

---

7 Mrs Thatcher placed a tick against the second half of this sentence.
8 'We should need American support before.'
9 Mrs Thatcher placed a tick against this paragraph.
10 'Provided there is a cease-fire.'
11 'Provided there is a cease-fire.'

Annex A[12]

Procedure for Bringing Rhodesia to Independence with a Return to Legal Dependent Status

1. The Government takes an <u>Order</u> in Council under Section 2 of Southern Rhodesia Act 1965, appointing an Administrator with full powers and suspending <u>or amending</u> the 1961 Constitution.[13]

2. The administrator arrives in Rhodesia and assumes his functions. The local administration complies with his directions.[14]

3. The United Kingdom's Permanent Representative informs the Secretary Council that legal administration has been restored in a Rhodesia and rebellion has come to an end. [We therefore regard the sanctions resolutions as having lapsed.]

4. The British Government makes an Order in Council revoking all sanctions orders under the 1965 Act. This requires a resolution of both Houses within twenty-eight sitting days, but may come into operation beforehand. Other sanctions enforcement measures are revoked by administrative action and/or statutory instruments under other legislation (none is subject to Parliamentary procedure except the Exchange Control orders, which are subject to negative resolution).[15]

5. Parliament approves both Orders in Council.

6. Introduction and passing of a short enabling Act to provide for the asking of Orders in Council in respect of (*a*) elections[16] (*b*) the independence Constitution (*c*) transitional provisions on independence (NB this cannot be done by Orders under the 1965 Act).

7. Orders in Council are made under the Act.

8. Elections.

9. Introduction and passing of the Independence Bill. (The Act at 6 could provide for independence to be granted by Order in Council on date to be fixed following elections. But it will be strongly argued that Parliament should grant independence only after the elections have taken place. And Act will in any event be required to deal with consequential matters in UK law.)

10. Rhodesia becomes independent.

---

12 Mrs Thatcher wrote at the top of the page: 'The British Administrator would normally have an Advisory Council. Can that not be the existing 'govt' augmented by Nkomo and Mugabe if they take part in the elections [?]' M.T.
13 'Can't amend by order.'
14 'Under what law? Surely we shall have to accept the existing state of the law there.'
15 'Arrangements over Rhodesian borders?'
16 'Under what law?'

Annex B

Constitutional Conference
Outline of Proposals for Implementing the Independence Constitution

1. The independence Constitution will give the government the power to execute its policies within the law.[17]

2. The elected government will be chosen by the people of Rhodesia in fair elections, in which all parties will be free to participate.

3. Under the independence Constitution the elected government will be in a position to carry out the policies on the basis of which it has been elected.

4. The services of the State[18] will be at its disposal in doing so. The elected government will have the power to make changes in those services, as specified in the Constitution.

5. Until the elected government takes office, nothing should be done which prejudices or pre-empts the freedom of choice of the people of Rhodesia.

6. The election of the House of Assembly, which is the first step in the implementation of the independence Constitution will take place in the following conditions:

(*a*) the administration of the election will be scrupulously impartial as between one party and another;

(*b*) peaceful political activity will be freely conducted; and

(*c*) all parties will have free and uncensored access to all the public media.

7. It will be for Britain, as the constitutionally responsible authority, to ensure that these requirements are met.[19]

8. In accordance with the agreement in the Lusaka communiqué, the elections will be supervised under the authority of the British Government.

9. There will be a ceasefire and a disengagement of the military forces on either side during the election campaign.

10. There will be provision for the exercise of the right of vote by citizens of Rhodesia who are absent from the country.[20]

11. There will be provision for all those citizens of Rhodesia who wish to do so to return.

12. A British Administrator/Election Commissioner will supervise the conduct of the election.

13. Commonwealth observers will be present to witness the manner in which that authority is exercised.

---

17 'What law? What about all the Acts the existing govt has passed?'
18 'i.e. the Security Forces—the Police and the Civil Service.'
19 '—using General Walls?'
20 'And how do they prove citizenship [?]'

No. 90

Minute from Mr Day to Sir A. Duff, 1 October 1979
Confidential (FCO 36/2438)

Rhodesia

1. Our objective for Rhodesia since May has been to achieve a return to legality with wide international acceptance.

2. How far have we gone along this road, and where do we go from here?

Constitution

3. Our first aim has been to reach agreement with the parties concerned on an Independence Constitution. We are within sight of an agreement on this with the Muzorewa delegation. We plan to table, shortly, a full summary constitution that the Bishop will accept. The Patriotic Front delegation will protest strongly. They will argue (with some justification) that we have paid insufficient attention to their views; that our full proposals are the result of collusion with the Bishop; that on a number of issues (i.e. dual citizenship) we have totally disregarded their arguments—which have Front Line support. However, at the end of the day, the Patriotic Front seem likely to accept the Constitution, reluctantly, and with bad grace.

4. The Front Line States will have some sympathy for the Patriotic Front's view that they have been bounced. We shall then, by this stage, have used up some of the credit that we earned in Lusaka. This will make it more difficult for us to secure the maximum international support for the eventual settlement.

Pre-Independence Arrangements

5. The next stage will be the pre-independence arrangements. The Patriotic Front have tabled their ideas. Salisbury have made no proposals. We are still working on our plans.

6. If we are to maintain wide international backing for our plans for an overall settlement, we must at least *appear* to pay heed to the views of the Patriotic Front. If we ride roughshod over them—as we have tended to do over the Constitution—it will be increasingly difficult for us to carry the Front Line, and other non-aligned opinion with us. This is important. We should avoid, if we possibly can, a situation in which the only people who back the eventual solution are our NATO and EEC partners. We need a wider spectrum of support if our national and international interests are not to suffer considerably.

7. We cannot accept the Patriotic Front pre-independence proposals. We are committed to a ceasefire and disengagement rather than integration of forces. We can probably get away with this. Where the Patriotic Front and others would part company from us is if we allowed the Muzorewa government to remain *in situ* during the interim period. This does *not* feature in our plans. The next most sensitive issue will be the continuance in office in Rhodesia of all existing military, judicial and civil service personnel. There is no alternative to this. But we must position to argue convincingly to the Patriotic Front and others that all these services will be under the effective control of HMG throughout the interim period. And, where necessary, we must be prepared to exercise that control.

8. Our present plans place all executive and legislative power in the interim period in the hands of a British Administrator. The Patriotic Front envisage the establishment of a Transitional Council. Such a Council could add to the problems of the Administrator. However, we already envisage some liaison arrangements between the Rhodesian and Patriotic Front Security Commanders in respect of military matters. We should not rule out some similar liaison on civilian affairs. Any such Council would have to be purely advisory. Ultimate authority must rest with the Administrator. However, such an arrangement would enable us to demonstrate that we had not wholly ignored the proposals of the Patriotic Front—and would thus make it more difficult for international opinion to withhold their support from an eventual settlement.

Tactics

9. A general word on tactics. Over the Constitution we left ourselves virtually no negotiating flexibility with the Patriotic Front. We should avoid this, if possible, in the discussions on the pre-independence arrangements. One example. We shall have to agree on the period allowed before elections. The Patriotic Front will want time to organise their political machine inside Rhodesia. We and the Bishop will want to get it over with as soon as possible. If we and the Bishop agree that the process will probably take 12 weeks, let us (in agreement with him) first propose 8 weeks and thus be able to 'concede' up to 12 weeks to the Patriotic Front in due course. This will place us on a far better posture with international opinion than rigid adherence to our initial suggestion. There may well be other aspects of our plans which could be handled similarly.

Conclusion

10. In our search for a settlement, we must not lose sight of the importance for us—and Rhodesia—of a 'wide international acceptance'. We must carry the Bishop with us all the way to legal independence. This is bound to limit the scope for compromise. But we must not let him and his delegation prejudice unduly the achievement of our second and equally important objective.[1]

D.M. DAY

---

1 Sir A. Duff minuted on 1 October: 'Some of this has been overtaken by the discussion with the Prime Minister this evening. But Mr Day puts his finger on a number of difficult points in both the strategy and the tactics.'

No. 91

Lord Carrington to Sir L. Allinson (Lusaka), 2 October 1979, 3.30 p.m.[1]
Tel. No. 799 Confidential, Immediate (FCO 36/2439)

Rhodesia: Constitutional Conference
1. You will be receiving in the Verbatim Series the text of the full proposals for the Independence Constitution which I expect to table at the Conference at 1500Z on 3 October. You should give a copy to the government to which you are accredited as soon as possible thereafter, speaking as indicated below. You may subsequently distribute copies of the document as you think fit.
Points to Make
2.
(*a*) We have now had over three weeks of discussions with the Salisbury and Patriotic Front Delegations on the basis of the proposals we tabled on 12 September. It has not been possible to reach complete agreement with either side on the shape of the Independence Constitution, though the Salisbury Delegation's agreement in principle with our proposals and the Patriotic Front's agreement to the principle of Special Representation in Parliament for the white minority showed a willingness by both sides to Compromise.

(*b*) The proposals we are now putting forward necessarily represent a compromise between the different requirements of the two sides. They provide for a genuine majority rule. They make special provisions for a limited period, for the white minority. But that minority will not by themselves be able to block amendments to the Constitution. The proposals are firmly within the framework unanimously agreed by Commonwealth Countries at Lusaka. I am convinced that they will be widely acceptable internationally. I hope both parties at the conference will be able to accept them. But it is with the British Parliament that the constitutional responsibility for granting independence rests, as was agreed at Lusaka. If the parties are not able to agree, it is for us to take the responsibility of making clear what we believe is fair and reasonable and what we would be prepared to commend to the British Parliament as a reasonable basis for Independence.

Further points to be made in discussion as necessary
3.
(*a*) *The State*. No problem here—both sides agree.

(*b*) *Citizenship*. The Patriotic Front have held out for a formula which would allow the incoming government to vet all those who have become citizens of Rhodesia, black and white, since UDI, and deprive of citizenship anyone considered to be politically undesirable. We cannot accept this and it is not reflected in

---

1 And to Immediate Mirimba Salisbury, Nairobi, Maputo, Gaborone, Dar es Salaam, Luanda, Lagos, Washington, Pretoria, Addis Ababa, Monrovia, Canberra, Ottawa, Wellington, Peking, Moscow, Prague, Abidjan, Dakar, Kinshasa, Khartoum, Tokyo, EEC Posts, Kingston, Bridgetown, Dacca, New Delhi, Singapore, Georgetown, Nassau, Freetown, Port Louis, Mbabane, Port of Spain, Kampala, Lilongwe, Valletta, Colombo, Accra, Kuala Lumpur, Nicosia, Castries, Oslo, Stockholm, Lisbon, Madrid, Manila, Tehran, Bucharest, Caracas, Athens, UKMIS New York, La Paz, Kuwait; Saving for information to Suva, Port Moresby, Honiara, Nuku'alofa, Victoria, Tarawa, Banjul.

our proposals which, here and throughout, are designed to promote conciliation rather than recrimination. We have also insisted on a formula which will allow those deprived of citizenship by the illegal regime for such reasons as 'disloyalty' to be reinstated as citizens. The PF have also opposed dual citizenship. But this is a normal feature of Independence Constitutions. We have therefore included provision for it. The elected government could, of course, decide that some restriction in time should be placed on the exercise of this right.

(c) *Declaration of Rights*. Most of the provisions under this heading are common form. They are designed to give protection against the arbitrary exercise of power to all the citizens of Zimbabwe. On Part V (Freedom from deprivation of property) the Salisbury Delegation's proposals (based on their existing constitution) would have made it virtually impossible for the elected government to acquire land for resettlement purposes as well as making over-generous provision for compensation. The PF have opposed our own proposals in this area as restricting the government's freedom of action. Our proposals ensure the government's ability to develop its policies in the important area of land use, while assuring citizens of adequate compensation for any compulsory expropriation. The provision for remitability is appropriate in the circumstances—a similar provision was made in Kenya and in Zambia at Independence.

(d) *The Executive*. The PF (particularly Nkomo) argued strongly for an Executive Presidential System. But we believe that a Constitutional President, who would be above party controversy, will be more likely to provide a basis for reconciliation in the wake of conflict and is more suited to a situation where there are a number of competing parties. The provision will be amendable, given a sufficient majority in parliament. On the Public Service, Police and Armed Forces, our proposals give the Prime Minister power to appoint Ambassadors, Permanent Secretaries, the Secretary to the Cabinet, the Commissioner of Police and the Commanders of the defence forces after consultation with the relevant commissions, whose recommendations he will be free to accept or reject as he sees fit. (Under the Salisbury Delegation's proposals, the Independent Commissions would have made all the appointments.) Other appointments will be made by the Commissions, subject to any general policy directions from the Government designed to produce better representation of the different sections of the community in the public services, i.e. Africanisation (The PF would have preferred to make no reference to 'reverse discrimination'; but we think it essential to permit this in view of the present imbalances in the Rhodesian Services.) The PF have said they cannot form a judgement on our proposals on the Police and Defence Forces until they know the composition of these forces at Independence. Our view is that the Constitution will provide the mechanism by which the Police Force and Defence Forces are directed and administered: matters relating to their composition will be for the elected government to decide. We have agreed that agreement on the Independence Constitution may be contingent on subsequent agreement on the arrangements for putting it into effect: but we must see agreement on the Constitution first.

(e) *Parliament*. This was the area of greatest difficulty for both sides, and the willingness of both to compromise here has been the most encouraging feature of the Conference so far. The Salisbury side have agreed to the removal of the white blocking mechanism—under our proposals, the whites will have 20 out of 100 seats, and 70 votes will be required for the amendment of the principal provisions of the Constitution. The PF have agreed to the principle of special white representation, and to this percentage of white seats. Despite repeated representations by some members of the Salisbury delegation, we have not been prepared to accept any change in these figures. We propose that the constitutional provisions relating to white representation shall be amendable only by a unanimous vote of the membership of both Houses of Parliament for the first seven years after Independence. We believe that in the circumstances of Rhodesia (a larger and more settled white population than in comparable countries) the whites' agreement to give up their blocking mechanism: and the need to encourage as many whites as possible to stay and contribute to the prosperity of Zimbabwe, which will be in the interests of all its citizens, black and white) our proposal is reasonable. We also propose that the substantive provisions of the Declaration of Rights shall be similarly protected for ten years. These provisions are designed to protect all the citizens of Zimbabwe against the arbitrary exercise of power. They entrench basic human rights. The PF expressed reservations about the composition and delaying powers of the Senate. The essential point in this regard is that the Senate will have no powers, except to impose a very limited delay on legislation.

(*f*) *The Judicature*. Our objective has been to widen the qualifications. The Prime Minister is given a say in the appointment of the Chief Justice. The independence of the Judicature is fully protected.

(*g*) *The Defence Forces*. The Prime Minister is given power to appoint and dismiss Service Commanders, and to give them general directions. This gave great difficulty to the Salisbury Delegation. But we consider it essential in the interests to provide for adequate political control over the Armed Forces.

(*h*) *Finance*. Most provisions here are common form, and gave no difficulty. The provisions on pension rights of public officers gave trouble to both sides. We consider it in the interests of good government in Zimbabwe that the Constitution should guarantee the pensions of public servants.

(*i*) *Ombudsman*. Common form provisions.

4. If asked what we propose to do about the interim arrangements, you should say that the first task is to reach agreement on the Independence Constitution. We will then go on to deal with the arrangements for implementing it. In that regard we must first seek acceptance that, as agreed at Lusaka, new elections should be supervised under the British Government's authority.

5. In general you should emphasise that the proposals we put forward at the beginning of this conference were formulated after extensive consultation with Commonwealth and other governments concerned and with the parties. If it had been possible for the parties themselves to agree on other arrangements, we would have been prepared to consider these. But to the extent that this is not possible, it is for the British Government to make clear what it is prepared to commend to the British Parliament. We have done this on the basis which, indisputably, provides for genuine majority rule. It also offers reasonable reassurance to the members of the minority community for the first years after independence. We have not been prepared to depart from the original proposals in discussion with the Salisbury delegation. For

the same reason it has been difficult to depart from them in discussion with the Patriotic Front. The proposals we are now making are fully compatible with those we put forward on 12 September (and with the Statement of Principles which was made on 14 August). Discussion on the Constitution has now reached a point at which decisions are needed, before the Conference can move on. We recognise that what we have proposed does not meet the requirements of either side. As we said at the outset of the Conference, there will be a need for compromise on both sides if agreement is to be reached which will enable the people of Rhodesia to resolve their difficulties by political means: which will lay the foundations for a truly multi-racial society and genuine majority rule: and which, if accepted, could provide also a basis for bringing an end to the war.

No. 92

Summary record of a bilateral meeting between the British and Patriotic Front Delegations at Lancaster House, 2 October 1979, 10 a.m.
Confidential (FCO 36/2439)

Present:

Secretary of State	Mr Nkomo
Lord Privy Seal	Mr Mugabe
Mr Luce	and members of the Patriotic Front delegation
and officials	

Declaration of Rights

The Patriotic Front reiterated their reservations about the inclusion in part (i)—the right to life—of a derogation covering the defence of property. Many people in Rhodesia were too ready to shoot 'natives' for trespassing on their property. *The British side* pointed out that this was a common form provision. Under it, the Courts would still have to determine whether, in any given circumstances, the taking of life had been 'reasonably justifiable'. *The Patriotic Front* said that in any cases where it was justifiable, it would be covered by the derogation of referring to the prevention of crime. *Mr Fifoot* agreed to look again at this provision.

The Patriotic Front were not yet able to discuss their reservations on section (iii) relating to forced labour.

There was a long discussion on section (v)—protection from arbitrary deprivation of property. After Mr Fifoot had explained British thinking on this, *Mr Mugabe* said the PF were not opposed in principle to the right of private property, and wanted it to be guaranteed by the constitution. But this should not prevent the State from acquiring movable and immovable property in the public interest under the law. They did not agree that compensation should be guaranteed. The Government should decide in the national interest whether in any particular case compensation was due. The distribution of land in Rhodesia was thoroughly inequitable. Africans had been deprived of property by arbitrary Government action without compensation over a period of many years—why should the new 'owners' receive compensation if the Government wanted to restore it? The British proposal sought to entrench a historic situation of grave injustice. If the PF were to accept the idea of guaranteed compensation, which was repugnant in principle how did the British side propose that they should raise the money?

The British side said it would be impossible to take into account the whole history of land apportionment in Rhodesia in formulating the relevant provision of the Declaration of Rights. The provision suggested would not prevent the Government from implementing a policy of redistribution of under-developed or underutilised land. *Mr Luce* referred to the Kenyan precedent. It would be open to the Government to ask other countries and multi-lateral agencies to help them finance such a scheme.

Mr Nkomo suggested that an introductory phrase should be inserted at the beginning of section (v) stating the basic principle that 'the land belongs to the people'. *The Secretary of State* recalled that the Liberal Party had in the past used an anthem whose key line was 'God gave the land to the people'. But the party had found this very difficult to interpret in practical terms. *Mr Mugabe* hinted darkly that the PF would have no such difficulty. *Mr Nkomo* repeated that they could not agree to a provision along the lines proposed without such an introductory statement, and without concrete British proposals on financing a compensation scheme.

On section (viii)—freedom of conscience—the PF repeated their concern that the common form provision allowing religious communities to give religious instruction in schools run by them should not be so drafted as to permit racially-segregated schools. *Mr Day* said that the provision the British side had in mind would refer specifically to religious communities. There would be no reference to ethnic or racial groups. Since religion spanned the various ethnic groups in Rhodesia, he did not think any such problem would arise.

There was inconclusive discussion about public or private institutions which might in effect perpetuate racial segregation by imposing high charges for the services they provided. The British side maintained that it would be impossible to prevent this by any general provision in the Declaration of Rights.

[The Secretary of State withdrew at this point.]

Mr Mugabe asked whether section (xii) on freedom from discrimination would strike down the discriminatory provisions for special minority representation in Parliament. *Mr Fifoot* explained that it would not. The PF asked about a British proposal that existing discriminatory legislation should for a period be protected from challenge under the Declaration of Rights. Mr Fifoot recalled that he had intended to let the PF examine Volume 8 of the 1974 Rhodesian revision of the Statute Book, which contained certain discriminatory legislation which the Government might consider beneficial to blacks and hence would not necessarily wish to see invalidated by the Declaration of Rights until there had been time to study it and consider how its beneficial provisions (if any) should be preserved or replaced. He undertook to let the PF see it later that day. *Mr Mugabe* said the Patriotic Front were against keeping existing discriminatory legislation in force. *The Lord Privy Seal* agreed with this in principle.

Mr Mugabe asked when the PF could see the detailed British proposal on the Declaration of Rights.

Mr Day replied that it would be available within a few days.

Mr Silundika proposed the inclusion of rights to work and to education. This was not pursued.

The PF strongly opposed the British proposition that the main principles of the Declaration of Rights should be amendable only by a 100 per cent vote of the House of Assembly for 10 years, and that unanimity would also be required to amend the derogation from these basic principles so as further to limit the rights concerned. The proposal was unacceptable, unprecedented and counter-productive. It sought to secure those who were secure already—the white minority. In effect, it continued the white blocking mechanism under another guise. *Mr Nkomo* argued strongly that such entrenchment of the Declaration of Rights would perpetuate such existing injustice in Rhodesia.

The British side said that the Declaration of Rights would protect all citizens, not only the whites; that the entrenched provisions were basic human rights which should surely be universally acceptable; that their entrenchment was necessary in the interests of securing an agreement among all the parties to the present conflict; and that the special entrenchment would be for a limited period only. *Mr Nkomo* questioned whether the British side were in fact trying to secure agreement by all parties: were they not simply trying to achieve a situation in which they could say 'this is the best we could get. Take it or leave it'? The 100 per cent rule was an unprecedented and unacceptable limitation of the sovereignty of the Zimbabwe Parliament. It would not help reconciliation, but the reverse. *The Lord Privy Seal* observed that this discussion could not usefully be taken further until the Patriotic Frond had seen the full text of the British proposals.

Order in Council

In answer to a question from Mr Baron, *Mr Fifoot* said the British side envisaged that the Order in Council conferring independence would provide that those holding various public offices the day before independence would continue to hold them immediately afterwards. The Government could then, of course, make senior appointments in accordance with the proposed constitution. The question of who would be in the various offices on the day before independence would have to be discussed, with other interim arrangements, later.

No. 93

Lord Carrington to Sir L. Allinson (Lusaka), 2 October 1979, 8.15 p.m.[1]
Tel. No. 801 Confidential, Immediate (FCO 36/2439)

Rhodesia: Constitutional Conference

1. At a bilateral meeting with the Patriotic Front on the morning of 2 October they concentrated on the provision in the Declaration of Rights section of the British proposals for protection from arbitrary deprivation of property. They argued that this should not prevent the elected government from redistributing land (which had

---

[1] And to Immediate Mirimba Salisbury and certain other posts; Priority Abidjan and certain other posts; Information Saving Suva, Port Moresby, Honiara, Nuku'alofa, Victoria, Tarawa.

never been our intention). They criticised the proposal that the main provisions in the declaration of rights should be amendable only by a 100 percent vote in the House of Assembly for ten years as a restraint on the sovereignty of Parliament.

2. In reply I and the Lord Privy Seal pointed out that the provisions we were proposing were common form in independence constitutions. There was a problem on land distribution in Rhodesia which the elected government would have to tackle. Our proposals would not prevent the government from implementing a fair policy of land resettlement. The entrenchment of the main principles of the Declaration of Rights was justified by the fact that these rights were widely accepted internationally: the need to re-assure everyone that their rights will be respected seemed to us self-evident in view of the history of the conflict.

3. A plenary session requested by the Patriotic Front was held in the afternoon, so that, they could report to the Conference as a whole what points of difficulty remained between them and us. The Salisbury delegation said that they had accepted in principle the British proposals tabled on 12 September and had nothing more to say until further details were made available. I said that I would consider all the points which had been made in bilateral meetings by both sides, and would table as soon as possible a further paper containing a full description of the sort of constitution we would be prepared to recommend to Parliament as a basis for independence. We expect to table our full constitutional proposals in a plenary session on the afternoon of 3 October. It will then be for both delegations to decide whether they can accept them.

No. 94

Letter from Mr Lyne to Mr Alexander (No. 10), 3 October 1979
Confidential (PREM 19/112)

Dear Michael,
Rhodesia: The Independence Constitution
I enclose a copy of the full proposals for the Independence Constitution which, subject to any final suggestions by Bishop Muzorewa, Lord Carrington proposes to table at a plenary session of the constitutional conference on third October.[1]

The document follows closely the pattern of the proposals which we tabled early in the conference, and represents a very wide measure of agreement with the Salisbury delegation, whom we have consulted at every stage. Its purpose is to act as a comprehensive guide from which the legal draughtsmen can prepare the final text of the constitution, basing themselves closely on the present Constitution, subject to the changes we have negotiated. It deals with the main points in dispute at the Conference in the following ways:

(*a*) *Citizenship:* We provide that all those who have citizenship immediately before Independence should be confirmed as citizens thereafter. This runs counter to

---

1 Not printed. Mr Alexander minuted to the Prime Minister on 3 October: 'I have detached the constitution but you may like to see this letter.'

the Patriotic Front's views. They contend that citizenship should not automatically be granted to those who entered Rhodesia after November 1965. The result would be that many thousands of people would find their status in doubt while investigations were conducted to determine who should and should not be granted citizenship. We have rejected these arguments. Despite Patriotic Front objections, we have retained the provision for dual citizenship (this has no implication for the position under our own law). We have agreed with the Salisbury delegation that those who have forfeited or been deprived of their citizenship since 1965 should be allowed to resume it on Independence.

(b) *Declaration of Rights:* We have reached a compromise with the Salisbury delegation on the question of the compulsory acquisition of agricultural land for settlement. This will be allowed where the land is not fully utilised, where a court order has been obtained and adequate compensation has been agreed. Provision for preventive detention has been taken out of the body of the Declaration of Rights and included in the savings for periods of emergency. The protective provisions of the Declaration of Rights will be amendable only by unanimous vote of the House of Assembly for ten years. This gives added protection to the whites and others, but it is contested by the Patriotic Front who argue that it interferes with the sovereignty of Parliament and the legitimate areas of government policy such as land settlement. We should take the line that the Declaration protects the rights of all citizens, not just the minority, and is fully justiciable.

(c) *The Executive:* We have not accepted the Patriotic Front argument that there should be an Executive President.

(d) *Senior Appointments:* The Prime Minister of independent Zimbabwe will have the final say on senior appointments. But we have agreed that, in normal circumstances, recommendations would come forward from the appropriate Commission or selection board and that, where the Prime Minister decided instead to put forward a candidate of his own choice, Parliament would be informed. This is to reassure the public services that arbitrary changes will not be made. In the case of the Chief Justice, since he would have security of tenure once appointed, we have provided that if the Prime Minister decided not to accept the candidate recommended by the appropriate Commission, then Parliament must be informed before the appointment is made. Before deciding to change a Service Commander or the Police Commissioner the Prime Minister would be required to consult the Cabinet (and the matter would be subsequently reported to Parliament).

(e) *The Commissions:* All appointing bodies would be required to select the most efficient and suitable candidate for a post, but would also be subject to a general direction from the President to achieve a suitable representation of different sections of the population. This would permit a policy of gradual Africanisation.

(f) *Parliament: Our* proposals here provide for 20% of the seats in the House of Assembly to be reserved to the white community. This would be amendable only by a unanimous vote in the House of Assembly for seven years; and would be carried forward thereafter, subject to the normal procedure for constitutional amendment. The majority required to amend any clause of the Constitution has been confirmed at 70%. The Senate has been made more representative by an increase in its size

(Muzorewa attached particular importance to this); and its delaying power for ordinary legislation has been reduced.

(g) Pensions: These are protected under the Constitution by providing that any public officer has the right to a pension at the most favourable rate applying during his period of service. The right to remit pensions abroad is also guaranteed. The Patriotic Front can be expected to react strongly against this on the grounds that it is unreasonable to expect the new State to pay the pensions of servants of the illegal regime. Both sides have, for different reasons, pressed HMG to guarantee public service pensions. We have refused on the grounds that we have never done so for a local colonial service and cannot accept expenditure on the scale involved, even on a contingency basis, as a fair charge on the British taxpayer.

These proposals are based on those which we put to the Salisbury administration in August. The Salisbury delegation have also agreed to some shortening of the Constitution. In other respects we have been able to take account of their concerns, for instance by providing that if the Prime Minister selects an outsider for a senior appointment, the matter will be reported to Parliament. Lord Carrington intends to present the proposals to the Conference as the Constitution which the British Government is prepared to invite Parliament to enact. He will invite both sides to let him know whether they can accept the proposals by next Monday, so that the Conference can move onto the next phase of its business. The Patriotic Front are likely to protest that they are being stampeded and may produce proposals of their own. Lord Carrington proposes to take the line that we would have been willing to accept alternative proposals on which both sides could agree; but it has become clear that there is no basis for such agreement and, after a month of discussion, we must ourselves lay down what we believe to be the basis for solution.

It is not clear whether the Patriotic Front will accept a Constitution on these lines. They will strongly criticise the provisions for citizenship, pensions, land for agricultural settlement and the entrenchment of the Declaration of Rights. But they could find themselves in considerable difficulty if the Conference breaks down on their rejection of constitutional proposals which, to any reasonable observer, mark an enormous advance on any previous attempt to achieve a constitutional settlement for Rhodesia.

I am sending a copy of this letter and enclosure to the private secretaries of members of OD, and to the Private Secretary of the Attorney General.

Yours ever,
RODERIC LYNE

No. 95

Minute from Mr Manning to Mr Gomersall, 4 October 1979
Secret (FO 36/2439)

Rhodesia

Mr Luce would like to bring to the Lord Privy Seal's attention two points [. . .][1]

(i) There are clear differences of approach between ZANU and ZAPU. We should not miss the opportunity to work on ZAPU especially through personal contact with delegation members including Nkomo himself with a view to making them realise that we are genuinely interested in including them in a final settlement.

(ii) Recent reports suggest that the Bishop and other members of his delegation are prepared to agree that the Bishop should stand down during the pre-election period. In the circumstances it seems unnecessary that we should provide for the Bishop to continue in power when by doing so we should surely reduce the possibility of arriving at any agreement which would include ZAPU.

K.Q.F. MANNING

1 A phrase is here omitted.

No. 96

Minute from Mr Renwick to Sir A. Duff, 5 October 1979
Confidential (FCO 36/2613)

Rhodesia: British Governor or Administrator

1. You asked for some further suggestions. Whoever occupies this post will have to be of sufficient stature to:

(*a*) impress the Rhodesians

(*b*) secure the full confidence of Bishop Muzorewa

(*c*) deal with the Rhodesian military.

2. Although either Lord Home[1] or Lord Boyd would fill the post admirably, they are declared supporters of the internal settlement and the choice of either of them would produce strong reactions elsewhere in Africa. It would be argued that we were not giving the Patriotic Front a fair chance.

The candidates we suggest, therefore, are:

(*a*) Lord Soames

(*b*) Sir John Hunt

(*c*) Sir John Paul (former Governor of the Gambia, British Honduras, the Bahamas)

(*d*) Lord Elworthy[2]

(*e*) Sir Maurice Dorman.[3]

R.W. RENWICK

1 The former Prime Minister and Foreign Secretary (Alec Douglas-Home).
2 Samuel Charles Elworthy, former Marshal of the UK Royal Air Force.
3 Governor-General of Sierra Leone, 1962-64; and Governor-General of Malta, 1964-71.

No. 97

Lord Carrington to Sir L. Allinson (Lusaka), 6 October 1979, 1.10 p.m.[1]
Tel. No. 820 Confidential, Immediate (FCO 36/2439)

Your telno 1048 and UKMIS New York telno 1203 (not to all): Rhodesia Conference.[2]

1. You and the other posts to whom this telegram is addressed should at your discretion make the following points to the governments to which you are accredited.

2. From the beginning of this Conference I have said that agreement of the Constitution will be conditional on the arrangements for implementing it. I made this clear in the Conference on 12 September and repeated this statement when I presented the Independence Constitution to both delegations on 3 October ('We now need to know whether both delegations can accept such a Constitution. Agreement to do so will be subject to subsequent discussions of the arrangements to bring that Constitution into effect. The key element in that regard is acceptance by both delegations that elections should be held in which all parties have a chance to participate freely and that those elections should be supervised under the British Government's Authority').

3. Bishop Muzorewa has now announced not only his acceptance (despite strong resistance from Mr Ian Smith) of the Independence Constitution but also his delegation's acceptance that elections should be supervised under the British Government's authority. He has made that agreement conditional on satisfactory arrangements for implementing the Constitution: and it is open to the Patriotic Front to do exactly the same. But we cannot agree that the Patriotic Front should refuse to accept those parts of the Constitution which do not fully meet their wishes, thereby enabling them to re-open negotiation on the Constitution at a later stage. We have to negotiate in good faith with both sides. We cannot ask Bishop Muzorewa and his delegation to agree to constitutional proposals which have been the subject of lengthy discussions between us (as with the Patriotic Front) and which have involved major concessions by the Salisbury delegation and then seek to ask them for further concessions on the agreed Constitution at a later stage. We have no intention of proceeding in this way.

4. The Patriotic Front have argued from the beginning that if they agreed to the Constitution, Bishop Muzorewa and his delegation would return to Salisbury and implement it without discussion of the pre-independence arrangements and without allowing them to participate in elections. You should point out that Bishop Muzorewa's acceptance of new elections makes nonsense of this argument. If the Patriotic Front accept the Independence Constitution, it will be possible to go on to discuss the arrangements for the elections. You should make clear as appropriate to those concerned that we consider that at this stage of the Conference the Salisbury

---

[1] And to Immediate Nairobi, Maputo, Gaborone, Dar es Salaam, Luanda, Lagos, Washington, Pretoria; Priority Addis Ababa, Monrovia, Canberra, Ottawa, Wellington, Peking, Moscow, Prague, Abidjan, Dakar, Kinshasa, Khartoum, Tokyo, EEC Posts, Kingston, Bridgetown, Dacca, New Delhi, Singapore, Georgetown, Nassau, Freetown, Port Louis, Mbabane, Port of Spain, Kampala, Lilongwe, Valletta, Colombo, Accra, Kuala Lumpur, Nicosia, Castries, Oslo, Stockholm, Lisbon, Madrid, Manila, Tehran, Bucharest, Caracas, Athens, UKMIS New York, La Paz, Kuwait; Information Immediate Mirimba Salisbury; Information Saving Suva, Port Moresby, Honiara, Nuku'alofa, Victoria, Tarawa and Banjul.

[2] Not printed.

delegation have done as much as we could possibly ask them to do: and that it is now for the Patriotic Front to make a positive response.

5. In order to support the efforts of the moderate white leaders to deal with expected attempts by Mr Ian Smith on his return to Salisbury today to mobilise resistance to our constitutional proposals and elections, I have this morning given an interview to Rhodesian television. The interview makes clear that we will now proceed to discussion of the interim arrangements; you should emphasize that we are looking for an agreement which will bring an end to the war. The text is in MIFT.[2] You can at your discretion explain to the governments to which you are accredited the purpose of this interview. The text of a statement by the FCO spokesman is in my second IFT.[2]

No. 98

Minute from Sir A. Duff to Mr Walden, 6 October 1979
Confidential (FCO 36/2507)

1. The US Ambassador brought round to me yesterday afternoon the attached instruction he had received from Mr Vance.

2. I said that, as recognised in the last sentence of the instruction, we did indeed feel it difficult at this stage to make any public appeal. Anything we said would be likely to be misunderstood. We were doing what we could privately with the Salisbury Government; but, I pointed out, we were just entering a stage in the negotiations where the cooperation of the Rhodesian military would become important to us, and it was therefore very necessary to be circumspect over anything which affected them or their task of protecting the country. I added that, in reply to the Mozambican approach which had been made to both the Americans and ourselves, we were simply taking the line that we were sympathetic with the Mozambican problem—but the only real solution was to get a firm settlement and an end to the war.

A. DUFF

ENCLOSURE IN No. 98

Message from Secretary of State Vance to Lord Carrington

I suggest that you inform Peter Carrington as soon as possible of our concern that continued high level of military action will jeopardize the Lancaster House negotiations. I believe that Machel's willingness to maintain real pressure upon the Patriotic Front may be reduced if military actions directed at Mozambican targets, including civilian infrastructure, continue. A cease-fire must include all parties. In my meetings today with Foreign Ministers Mkapa and Chissano[1] I have urged that Patriotic Front show military restraint during this sensitive period. As you may know, I have instructed Davidow in Salisbury and Edmondson[2] in Pretoria to make a serious

1 Mr Joaquim Alberto Chissano, Mozambique Minister of Foreign Affairs, 1975-86.
2 Mr William Brockway Edmondson, US Ambassador to South Africa, 1978-81.

appeal for restraint. The British may wish to follow up with an appeal to both sides. I understand that they have felt inhibited in doing so because of the negotiations, but we have found it necessary to proceed in any case.

No. 99

Minute from Mr Renwick to Sir A. Duff, 8 October 1979
Secret and Personal (FCO 36/2439)

Rhodesia
1. At the Secretary of State's meeting this morning, we were asked to explore the idea that, if the Patriotic Front do not agree to participate in elections on the terms we propose, we should proceed to enact the independent Constitution and lift sanctions on the understanding that the Salisbury government would implement the Constitution. We shall be submitting papers about the legislative action which would be necessary and the legal and international implications. You may however find it useful to have some preliminary comments.

2. Such a course would enable us to normalise our relations with Rhodesia and get rid of our constitutional responsibility. But it will raise considerable difficulties in relation to the parliamentary procedures in Salisbury. If we lifted sanctions before the new Constitution was adopted by the Salisbury Parliament, there would be no guarantee that it would be implemented. The parliamentary procedures in Salisbury are likely to take five or six weeks after the conclusion of the Conference. We should be in difficulty over our sanctions legislation in the meantime—though it *might* be possible to allow Sanction 2 of the Southern Rhodesia Act to lapse, while keeping *other* sanctions in force until the Constitution had been approved. The course we now have in mind will cause some concern to Bishop Muzorewa who had been hoping that by a means of a return to legality that we would be able to act faster and short-circuit the procedure in the Salisbury Parliament (though it will enable him to remain in charge of the government in the interim).

3. It will be strongly argued in Parliament here and in Africa that neither the fifth principle nor the Lusaka agreement will have been fulfilled. We are unlikely therefore to be able to proceed in this way without considerable damage to our interests elsewhere. The majority of Commonwealth governments will not accept an outcome which, in their view, will not correspond to the Lusaka agreement. The United States probably would move to lift sanctions; but it is doubtful whether we will be able to persuade many other governments to follow suit. It will, furthermore, be argued that it will not be possible to implement the new Constitution with an election. In these circumstances we could hope to attract very limited international support, particularly as those supporting us would be likely to have to pay a penalty elsewhere in Africa.

4. The only way in which we are likely to be able to lift sanctions before elections and get a fair number of other western governments to follow suit is by a return to legality. It would be more difficult for our western partners to continue to impose sanctions against a country which was part of our dominions and had accepted our authority. We should not underestimate the effect on the international community

and in Africa of the *formal* assumption by us of the 'de-colonising authority' for the period which would be necessary to enable elections to be held. But, as the Secretary of State has pointed out, this would involve us in greater formal responsibility—for however limited a period—in a situation in which Rhodesia is at war.

5. If we decide on a different approach, we shall at least need to try to attract more international support than is likely to be forthcoming than if we proceed as in paragraph 1 above. It might be possible to do so by making the granting of independence and the lifting of sanctions conditional not only on the implementation of the Constitution but on the conduct of elections to implement it; or, at the least, on a referendum to demonstrate that is acceptable. Either course would under-cut the arguments in relation to the fifth principle. It would be open to us to leave it to the Rhodesians to organise the elections or referendum and for us simply to observe the outcome. But to dispense with elections or any demonstration of acceptability would put us in a very difficult position in terms of securing international support. The Patriotic Front would then claim that we were proceeding, as they had always said we would, to agree the Constitution with Muzorewa and then simply to implement it. It is, furthermore, probably unnecessary. Bishop Muzorewa and his government are at present committed to the idea that, if we are to proceed with them alone, there will have to be elections or a referendum. It would be prejudicial to their chances of securing wider international recognition and to our prospects of helping them do so if we abandoned that requirement.[1]

R.W. Renwick

No. 100

Minute from Mr Burgess to Ms Spencer, 8 October 1979
Restricted (FCO 36/2410)

Attack on Members of the ZAPU Delegation

1. I was alerted by the Resident Clerk at approximately 3.30 this morning to the fact that two members of the ZAPU delegation were then giving statements in Lime House Police Station after having been attacked by a party of white youths. In subsequent telephone conversations with the police on duty at Lime House at that time, and with Chief Superintendent Simpson, who has taken over the case this morning, I obtained the following facts:

(*a*) The people concerned are:

(i) Joseph Masuku (34), who describes himself as Head of ZAPU broadcasting 'in Rhodesia'. He is staying at the Metropole Hotel.

(ii) Herbert Musikivanku (41), who describes himself as Legal Adviser to the ZAPU delegation. He is normally resident in London and is currently staying at the Metropole Hotel with the rest of the delegation.

(*b*) The two are related as uncle and nephew and had been visiting a friend, Mr

---

1 Sir A. Duff minuted on 8 October: 'I think we must strive for elections with some form of British supervision. But we should examine the possibility of enacting the Constitution, dissolving the Rhodesia Parliament, lifting sanctions, and then having elections.'

Alex Osomo, in the East End yesterday evening. They left Mr Osomo's house at about 9.30pm and claimed that they were waiting at a bus stop when a car drew up containing 4 or 5 white youths, aged about 20. The youths apparently got out of the car, taunted them in racial terms and then attacked them with bricks. Mr Masuku was knocked to the ground and lost consciousness for a short while.

(*c*) The victims were taken to the London Hospital where they received treatment. Mr Masuku's injuries were sufficiently serious for the hospital to want to keep him overnight for observation but he discharged himself. Mr Musikivanku was less seriously injured. They were taken back to the hotel by the police.

(*d*) At Lime House Police Station, they gave signed statements which referred, understandably, to the racial nature of the attack. Both said in their statement that they did not want publicity for the incident.

2. Superintendent Simpson is aware of the delicate nature of this incident and promised to inform me of any developments. He is not very optimistic about catching the culprits as the victims were only able to give vague descriptions and did not recall the car number. He said that a senior member of his staff would probably visit the victims at their hotel later today.

3. I have spoken to Mr Singleton, the ZAPU Liaison Officer, who has nothing to add to the above.

4. *For News Department*: If asked News Department should say that we are aware of the incident, but so far have not received any representation from the ZAPU Delegation. Police enquiries are continuing. [If appropriate] We have absolutely no reason to believe that the attack was in any way connected with the Constitutional Conference.

A.R.F. BURGESS

No. 101

Minute from Sir A. Duff to Lord Carrington, 8 October 1979
Secret (FCO 36/2613)

May I offer two thoughts before you see the Prime Minister tonight and tell her of your decision not to put a Governor into Rhodesia in the event of the Patriotic Front walking out of the Conference.

(a) There are (I think) several ways in which we could deal with this situation and the trick will be to find the one that is likely to attract the most Western support. I hope therefore that we can leave open, for the time being, the question of what we actually do, until we have had time to study it further.

(b) Given that we want to work genuinely for an agreement on the pre-independence arrangements, it is important to keep Muzorewa and his delegation hooked on their undertaking to hold elections, with all the difficulties that implies for them both practical and political. They are so hooked at the moment, and they think that they will have to have elections even if the PF do not participate. It would be disastrous if word got back to them (e.g. from Blackpool)[1] that actually they might not have to

---

1 The Conservative Party Conference was taking place in Blackpool on 9-12 October 1979.

go through with elections and all that, if the PF walk out. I very much hope therefore that you can persuade the Prime Minister that it is important to keep absolutely quiet about what we might do in the event of the Conference breaking up.

A. DUFF

No. 102

Lord Carrington to Sir L. Allinson (Lusaka), 9 October 1979, 5.35 p.m.[1]
Tel. No. 829 Confidential, Immediate (FCO 36/2439)

My telno 822: Rhodesia: Constitutional Conference[2]

1. In a short plenary session this morning, I welcomed the fact that, in the Constitutional proposals they tabled yesterday, the Patriotic Front had accepted our proposals for the legislation and the executive. But I could not agree that we should re-open other major issues, such as citizenship, land and the declaration of rights. I asked the Patriotic Front to reconsider their position in the light of my comments and to give me a definite reply on 11 October as to whether they can agree to the independence Constitution, subject to agreement also on the arrangements for implementing it.

2. The text of my statement is being sent to you in the Verbatim Series. You may draw on it as appropriate. In doing so you should draw attention to the fact that I have dealt with the Patriotic Front argument that the white representatives in Parliament might form a coalition to frustrate the wishes of the African majority. In relation to land settlement, I made it clear that, in the event of an agreement, there would be likely to be international financial assistance, including the possibility of assistance for land development projects, you may add that we should be ready to contribute bilateral aid and development projects (and, for your own information, we are considering what we could do to help with projects connected with African land settlement).

3. There can be no question of our meeting the Patriotic Front's point on citizenship. The proposition that the incoming government should scrutinise all those, black and white, who have become citizens of Rhodesia since 1965 and deprived of their citizenship any of whom they disapprove on political grounds would not be acceptable to any British Government.

4. The position now reached in the Conference is that Bishop Muzorewa has accepted our Constitutional proposals (subject to satisfactory arrangement to implement the Constitution): and that new elections should held and supervised under our authority. He accepted a cease-fire at the out-set of the Conference. The Patriotic Front have not yet agreed on any of these points.

[1] And to Immediate Mirimba, Salisbury, Nairobi, Maputo, Gaborone, Dar es Salaam, Luanda, Lagos, Washington, Pretoria, Addis Ababa, Monrovia, Canberra, Ottawa, Wellington, Peking, Moscow, Prague; Priority Abidjan, Dakar, Kinshasa, Khartoum, Tokyo, EEC Posts, Kuwait, Kingston, Bridgetown, Dacca, New Delhi, Singapore, Georgetown, La Paz, Nassau, Freetown, Port Louis, Mbabane, Port of Spain, Kampala, Lilongwe, Valletta, Banjul, Colombo, Accra, Kuala Lumpur, Nicosia, Castries, Oslo, Stockholm, Lisbon, Madrid, Manila, Tehran, Bucharest, Athens; Information Immediate UKMIS New York; Information Saving Suva, Port Moresby, Honiara, Nuku'alofa, Victoria, Tarawa, UKDEL NATO.
[2] Not printed.

5. Following Mr Ian Smith's return to Salisbury, the Rhodesia Front MPs issued a statement on 8 October expressing support for his reservations about the independence Constitution. It is never wise to under-estimate Mr Smith. Any attempt to re-open the question of the independence Constitution would play straight into his hands and put Muzorewa in an impossible position. There can be no doubt that the Constitution we have put forward will produce genuine majority rule and give the elected Government effective control over the Army, the Police and the Services of the State. The Patriotic Front are not disputing this. They have accepted our proposals on the Executive and Legislature and are now arguing about secondary points. We hope that on 11 October the Patriotic Front will be able to agree to the independence Constitution, thereby enabling us to proceed to discuss the arrangements for implementing it. We shall not be prepared to move to that stage until there is agreement on the Constitution. The Patriotic Front have stated their main concern as being that, if they accept the Constitution, the Salisbury delegation may simply return home and implement it. Their concern on this point has been met by Muzorewa's statement that he is prepared to accept new elections.

6. For your own information we believe that there is a good prospect of the Patriotic Front agreeing to the Constitution. There have been indications, particularly from ZAPU, that they accept that the Constitution we have proposed represents an effective transfer of power.

7. Please give copies of this telegram and my statement to your US colleague.

No. 103

Lord Carrington to Sir L. Allinson (Lusaka), 11 October 1979, 6.20 p.m.[1]
Tel. No. 831 Confidential, Immediate (FCO 36/2439)

Rhodesia: Constitutional Conference

1. When the Conference resumed in Plenary Session this afternoon I asked the Patriotic Front delegation whether they could now accept our Constitutional proposals. They made a statement that a wide measure of agreement on the independence Constitution had been reached but saying that they had to reserve their position on 'such major issues as land, the inalterability of the Declaration of Rights insofar as it affects land and pensions and the provision relating to the four principal institutions of government (the Army, the Police, the Public Service and the Judiciary)' they urged the Conference to proceed without delay to discuss all the issues under the transitional arrangements and said: 'If we are satisfied beyond doubt as to the vital issues relating to transitional arrangements,

---

[1] To arrive Deskby 2100Z Lusaka; and to arrive Deskby 2100Z Immediate to Maputo, Gaborone, Dar es Salaam, Lagos, Monrovia; and Immediate to Mirimba, Salisbury, Nairobi, Luanda, Washington, Pretoria, Addis Ababa, Monrovia, Canberra, Ottawa, Wellington, Peking, Moscow, Prague; Priority Abidjan, Dakar, Kinshasa, Khartoum, Tokyo, EEC Posts, Kuwait, Kingston, Bridgetown, Dacca, New Delhi, Singapore, Georgetown, La Paz, Nassau, Freetown, Port Louis, Mbabane, Port of Spain, Kampala, Lilongwe, Valletta, Banjul, Colombo, Accra, Kuala Lumpur, Nicosia, Castries, Oslo, Stockholm, Lisbon, Madrid, Manila, Tehran, Bucharest, Athens; Information Immediate UKMIS New York; Information Saving Suva, Port Moresby, Honiara, Nuku'alofa, Victoria, Tarawa, UKDEL NATO.

there may not be need to revert to discussion on the issues we have raised under the Constitution'.

2. I sought to give them reassurance on the question of land by making a statement, the text of which you will be receiving in the Verbatim Series (067/79) and on which you should draw freely (instructions and guidance on this are going to Front Line Posts). Mugabe, who has been taking a much harder line than Nkomo confirmed that the Patriotic Front reserved their position on all the issues in paragraph one above. I pointed out that several of these had nothing whatsoever to do with the interim arrangements.

3. There was then an adjournment during which I discussed the precise meaning of their statement in private with Mr Nkomo and Mr Mugabe. When the session resumed I explained that following my conversation with Mr Mugabe and Mr Nkomo it was clear that the Patriotic Front were making reservations on a number of issues which as they stated, were of major importance. I had tried to be of assistance on the question of land and hoped that Mr Mugabe and Mr Nkomo would read my statement carefully. It was necessary to reiterate what had been said at the beginning of the Conference. Discussion should proceed on a step by step basis to avoid a repetition of what had happened in Geneva. It had been agreed to deal with the Constitution first, and to reach agreement on it subject to the satisfactory interim arrangements. Consequently it was not possible to accept the reservations contained in Mr Nkomo's statement. This would mean that major questions would remain on the table after discussions of the Interim Arrangements. There was therefore now no alternative but to adjourn the Conference. When the Conference met again it would discuss the Interim Arrangements. In the meantime I needed to know whether Mr Mugabe and Mr Nkomo would accept the British proposals, and hope to receive a response in the near future.

4. Mugabe said that there would be no change in the Patriotic Front's position. Nkomo however, may still be looking for a compromise. The Conference has not at this stage 'broken down' though there will be no more plenary sessions until Monday, before this we hope to have a positive response from the Patriotic Front on the Constitution. We are not prepared to open discussion with the Patriotic Front of the arrangements for implementing the Constitution until we have that agreement.

No. 104

Letter from Mr Lyne to Mr Alexander (No. 10), 11 October 1979
(PREM 19/113)[1]

Dear Michael,

Rhodesian Constitutional Conference

At this afternoon's session of the Conference, the Foreign and Commonwealth Secretary asked the Patriotic Front whether they were now in a position to accept the Constitution, subject to agreement on the interim arrangements. In a prepared

---

1 Mr Alexander minuted to the Prime Minister: 'I also attach the statement made by Lord Carrington on the land question.'

statement (copy enclosed)² Nkomo replied that the Patriotic Front reserved their position on major issues and wanted to keep open the possibility of reverting to them.

Lord Carrington then saw Nkomo and Mugabe privately, but they declined to lift their reservations. When the Conference resumed, Lord Carrington therefore said that the British Government could not accept the Patriotic Front's reply as a sufficient basis to allow discussion to move onto the next item: and that he had no alternative but to adjourn the session. When the Conference met again, it would be to discuss the interim arrangements. The Patriotic Front should let him know before then whether they could accept the Constitution.

Although Lord Carrington set no date for the next meeting, he made it clear that it would be in the near future (we have in mind Monday)

There were clear signs of strain between ZAPU and ZANU at today's session. Nkomo appears to be looking for a way out, while Mugabe seems determined not to accept the points in the Constitution covering land and pensions, as well as maintaining general reservations about the Army, Police and Public Service.

There is a possibility that ZAPU will look for a way out of the dilemma. But, if we have to face a breakdown of the Conference, we will, in Lord Carrington's view, have a fully defensible position, and we would lose the support of Bishop Muzorewa and his delegation if we give way on this issue.

Yours ever,
RODERIC LYNE

2 Not printed.

No. 105

Handwritten note from Mr Alexander (No. 10) to Mrs Thatcher, 11 October 1979
(PREM 19/113)

Prime Minister (did not see)¹

I have passed on to the Foreign Secretary's office a message from the South Africans, received by Col. van der Post, to the effect that we should not take Mr Smith's statements too seriously. They believe that they can 'contain' him.

Since Col. van der Post had begun to feel a little out of touch the Foreign Secretary has kindly agreed to give him a briefing on his return from Blackpool on Thursday.

1 Words in brackets added later by Mr Alexander.

No. 106

Lord Carrington to Mr Leahy (Pretoria), 12 October 1979, 6.10 p.m.[1]
Tel. No. 380 Restricted, Immediate (FCO 36/2513)

Your telno 689: Rhodesia[2]

1. The South African Embassy delivered this morning the following message from the South African Government about Rhodesia:

'The South African Government is profoundly disturbed at the latest turn of events at the Lancaster House Constitutional Conference on Zimbabwe/Rhodesia. The conference, originally scheduled to last two weeks, has now dragged on for five, and the delay is due to the publicly proclaimed intransigence of one of the parties, the Patriotic Front. The momentum gained by the tabling of the constitutional proposals of the United Kingdom and their subsequent acceptance by Bishop Muzorewa has been dissipated by failure to deal decisively with the refusal of the Patriotic Front to give an unqualified acceptance of the proposed constitution. Despite the clear prior statement by the United Kingdom Government that the constitution as tabled was not negotiable and was presented on a take-it or leave-it basis, the Patriotic Front have repeatedly been afforded additional time to reconsider their rejection of the constitution as it stands. This has had no effect on their position, as was confirmed yesterday, but the reaction of the United Kingdom Government has been to announce another postponement, despite the statement at the Conservative Party Conference on the previous day by the Secretary of State for Foreign and Commonwealth Affairs that:

"I say to those who . . . appear to think that we should talk on and on and on about everything, without getting agreement to anything, that a time had to come when a decision would be taken on the principal issues at stake."

The South African Government believes the following facts to be relevant and important at this juncture:

Firstly, agreement to the United Kingdom draft constitution was a courageous act by the delegation of Bishop Muzorewa. There is no doubt that it was a controversial decision not lightly taken, which could have caused the disintegration of his delegation. Deep-seated differences of opinion could easily have frustrated acceptance.

Secondly, that Bishop Muzorewa's acceptance was predicated upon the assumption that the same rules would apply to the Patriotic Front delegation and that, having accepted the constitution, he was entitled to believe that his government had done all, if not more, that could be expected of it. Therefore there was no justification for the continued imposition of sanctions.

Thirdly, that the malaise surrounding developments concerning the attitude of the Patriotic Front is leading to a climate of cynicism, uncertainty, frustration and distrust in Zimbabwe/Rhodesia itself. Decisiveness, particularly as regards the lifting of sanctions is of vital importance at this crucial period, when many white Rhodesians, whose experience and technological proficiency is so urgently required in Zimbabwe/Rhodesia, are making up their minds either to stay or leave.

---

1 And Immediate to Mirimba, Salisbury. Both Deskby 1830Z.
2 Not printed.

Fourthly, that every moment of delay encourages the armed conflict in Zimbabwe/Rhodesia, jeopardising the eventual recovery and reconstruction of the country. The toll of human life is appalling.

Fifthly, that the absence of the Prime Minister from his country for five weeks contributes to the confusion and the feeling of insecurity in the country, and is having a negative effect on orderly administration. Bishop Mozorewa [*sic*] stands in a special relationship to his people and they require his leadership.

Finally, that the present uncertainty is playing into the hands of the enemies of peace, stability and orderly progress in the region and is being exploited by them. The consequences for the whole southern African region could be catastrophic, with violence spreading like cancer from one country to the next, and with incalculable danger to the survival of democracy in the region and harm to the strategic interests of the West and the democratic leaders of Africa.

The South African Government therefore urgently requests the Government of the United Kingdom to take the steps necessary to remove the uncertainty from the present situation. In particular the South African Government urges the Government of the United Kingdom to remove sanctions without delay as the minimum step required to restore essential confidence in the future of Zimbabwe/Rhodesia and avoid further deterioration in the situation.'

2. Please see my immediately following telegram.[3]

---

3 No. 107.

No. 107

Lord Carrington to Mr Leahy (Pretoria), 12 October 1979, 6.11 p.m.[1]
Tel. No. 381 Restricted, Immediate (FCO 36/2513)

MIPT: Rhodesia[2]

1. Unless you see objection, please tell Fourie that recent South African public statements about our handling of the Rhodesia Conference have not gone down well here. It is not helpful in the middle of this conference to have the South African Government publicly urging us to go it alone with Muzorewa. Nor is it helpful to have them threatening military intervention in Rhodesia.

2. You should go on to make the following points. There is no question of changing our proposals for the independence constitution. But as the South Africans well know, we are trying to bring the Lancaster House Conference to an outcome which will provide the best start we can achieve for the newly independent Rhodesia. This means, *inter alia*, seeking maximum western support for independent Rhodesia. In order to obtain this we have to be able to demonstrate that we have given the Patriotic Front every reasonable chance during the conference. We certainly do not mean to delay indefinitely. We are just as concerned as they are to move ahead as quickly as possible, consonant with our objective. But

---

1 And Immediate to Mirimba, Salisbury. Both Deskby 1830Z.
2 No. 106.

we are playing this hand, not the South Africans, and they really must allow us to judge how to do it.

3. For your own information, if the Patriotic Front do not (not) give a positive response on the constitution, it will be necessary to carry forward discussion of the interim arrangements and the implementation of the constitution without them. If pressed by Fourie you may hint at this, but you should be careful not to give him a quote for Pik Botha's subsequent use in public.

4. It is no less important to the South Africans than to ourselves and Bishop Muzorewa that we should bring this conference to a conclusion in a manner which offers some prospect of reducing support for the Patriotic Front if, as is probable, all or part of the Front are unwilling to participate in elections on our terms. Otherwise the likelihood is that, whatever happens about sanctions, the war will be intensified and the Rhodesians will not be able to cope with the military situation. In other words the danger of the South Africans being left with a major problem on their hands will not be solved simply by the lifting of sanctions.

5. We have kept the South Africans very closely informed about the conference and will continue to do so. We fully understand their concern about the security of the region: and, like them, we are working for the establishment of a moderate and more stable government in Rhodesia. But we hope they will adopt a constructive attitude towards our efforts to bring Rhodesia back into the International Community with the widest possible acceptance.

No. 108

Lord Carrington to Sir L. Allinson (Lusaka), 12 October 1979, 11.45 a.m.[1]
Tel. No. 833 Confidential, Flash (FCO 36/2523)

Rhodesia: President Kaunda's Message

1. Like you we are concerned that Chona is seriously mis-representing to President Kaunda the course of discussions at the conference. The President's message indicates that Chona is still fighting over points which the Patriotic Front (particularly ZAPU) have already conceded.

2. You should therefore arrange to deliver the message in MIFT to Kaunda personally. In doing so you should add the following comments on the detailed points in Kaunda's message:

(*a*) *Presidency*. It will be open to the people of Rhodesia to move to an Executive Presidency if they wish to do so. In the proposals they put forward on 8 October the Patriotic Front accepted a 'constitutional' Presidency;

(*b*) and (*c*) *Declaration of Rights*. We shall be ready to provide technical assistance for land settlement schemes and capital aid for agricultural development projects and infrastructure. If an agricultural development bank or some equivalent institution were set up to promote agricultural development including land settlement schemes, we should be prepared to contribute to the initial capital (though the

---

1 And to Immediate Washington, Dar es Salaam, Pretoria, Gaborone, Maputo, UKMIS New York, Lagos.

costs would be beyond the capacity of any individual donor country and we cannot commit ourselves to a specific share at this stage). We should be ready to help independent Zimbabwe to obtain international assistance in this as in other areas. There is however, no possibility of establishing an international fund to underwrite the pensions of Rhodesian public servants;

(*d*) *Coalition.* We have made provision that the party representing the majority of whites should not be able to form a coalition with any single party except that which has the largest number of seats elected on the common roll. The President would be expected to call on the leader of the largest African party to try to form a Government. But it will be necessary for any party which seeks to form a government either to win a majority of seats in the House of Assembly or to form a coalition;

(*e*) *The Unanimity Rule.* Making the main protective provisions of the Declaration of Rights (and those concerning white representation) amendable only by unanimous vote by the House of Assembly in a number of areas was essential, in view of the history of the conflict in Rhodesia, to give adequate protection to all the people of Rhodesia against the arbitrary exercise of power. It is a temporary provision to allow confidence to be re-established and to protect the rights of all the citizens of Zimbabwe, black or white;

(*f*) *Linkage.* We have made clear from the beginning of the conference that each delegation's acceptance of the constitution will be contingent on agreement on the arrangements for implementing it. Bishop Muzorewa has made his acceptance of the independence constitution contingent on that point and it is open to the Patriotic Front to do exactly the same. What we cannot accept is that either side should reserve the right to reopen negotiation on the constitution after we have moved on to discuss the pre-independence arrangements. Otherwise, we should be in danger of losing all the gains which have been achieved in five weeks of difficult negotiations. We were unable to accept the statement made by the Patriotic Front at the plenary session on 11 October precisely because it entered reservations on major issues on the constitution and kept open the possibility of re-opening them at a later stage.

3. You will be receiving further guidance by immediate telegram on the point now reached in the conference.

No. 109

Lord Carrington to Sir L. Allinson (Lusaka), 12 October 1979, 11.46. a.m.[1]
Tel. No. 834 Confidential, Flash (FCO 36/2523)

MIPT: Rhodesia[2]

1. Following is text of reply from the Prime Minister to President Kaunda:
'Dear Kenneth,
Thank you for your helpful and constructive message. I was particularly grateful for your assurance of continuing support in the difficult task ahead. I can assure

---

1 And to Immediate Washington, Dar es Salaam, Pretoria, Gaborone, Maputo, UKMIS New York, Lagos.
2 No. 108.

you that our aim is a settlement involving all the parties, which will bring peace to Rhodesia and to Zambia, in accordance with the principles we agreed on at Lusaka.

I was heartened by your welcome for the independence constitution which we have tabled. It has gone a long way to meet the Patriotic Front's requirements and it has therefore been no easy task to secure the Salisbury Delegation's acceptance of it. Both sides have been willing to compromise and we are appreciative of that. But there can be no further changes. In these weeks of intensive negotiations we have thoroughly examined all these issues and are quite confident that our constitution represents the only basis on which agreement is possible.

At the session of the conference on 11 October the Patriotic Front reserved their position on major issues and kept open the possibility of reverting to them at a later stage. This is not compatible with our agreement at the beginning of the conference that, before moving on to discuss the interim arrangements, we would need to have agreement on the constitution itself, contingent of course to subsequent agreement on the interim arrangements. We have made clear that the next meeting of the conference will be to discuss the interim arrangements and we hope that they will let us know in the very near future that they can accept the constitution, subject to satisfactory interim arrangements.

I am asking my High Commissioner to explain to you the position on the specific points which you raise on the constitution.[3] In particular, we here are deeply conscious of the immense importance of the question of land. But the point is, as I am sure you yourself understand, that it is of real significance to both sides. It is natural that the subject should arouse strong emotions on both sides. We are all conscious of that. But what we have done, in our constitution, is to make it possible for the new government to acquire underutilised land compulsorily—as well of course as being able to buy land from farmers who want to leave. What we have *not* been able to do is to agree that compensation should necessarily be payable. I am sure you understand that. Once Rhodesia is independent, investment funds, and aid money too, will begin coming in and I am sure in my own mind that finding money for a sensible scheme of land redistribution will not be a real problem. We would help with this—within the limits of our financial resources.

You raise the question of Rhodesian raids into neighbouring countries. Since issuing invitations to the constitutional conference, we have pressed both sides to accept a cease-fire. Bishop Muzorewa has expressed a readiness to agree to this. I think that it is a tragedy that the fighting has continued during the conference. Once we have agreement on the constitution, we shall be renewing our efforts to achieve a ceasefire and elections in which all parties can participate. I hope that you will support us in this.

Let me repeat in conclusion how grateful I am for your advice and support. I know that you are as anxious as I am to see the conflict ended. You have personally made great efforts, at the Heads of Government meeting and since, to make a settlement possible. The conference has reached a difficult point, but I can assure you that we are doing all we can to reach a lasting settlement and to bring about reconciliation.'

2. Please see MIPT.

---

3 In tel. No. 1083 of 13 October (FCO 36/2523), Sir L. Allinson reported that he had delivered the Prime Minister's letter and spent nearly an hour and a half with President Kaunda that evening. 'He was in friendly and philosophical mood. Mark Chona however made some sharp interventions arguing the Patriotic Front case uncritically.'

No. 110

Letter from Mr Lyne to Mr Alexander (No. 10), 12 October 1979
Secret (FO 36/2480)

Dear Michael,

I enclose a paper which examines the possible consequences of events in Rhodesia following the Constitutional Conference; and their implications for British policy. Lord Carrington has seen and approved an earlier draft of this paper (to which minor amendments have since been made).

Yours ever,
RODERIC LYNE

ENCLOSURE IN NO. 110

Rhodesia: Wider Implications

1. Given that no basis exists for a comprehensive settlement involving the Salisbury parties and both wings of the Patriotic Front, there appear to be three ways in which the situation in and around Rhodesia might develop following the Constitutional Conference:

(*a*) *If Bishop Muzorewa continues in Government without a broad measure of international support* the war will continue unabated. The Front Line States will continue to support the Patriotic Front and to provide them with bases. The more radical non-front line OAU States will encourage them in this. Moderate members of the OAU will be unable to resist this trend, because they will see no advantage for themselves in backing the side which appears to rely largely on South African support for its survival. Rhodesian raids into Zambia and Mozambique will continue. The Soviet Union and its allies will respond to requests for further military assistance to resist these raids and will provide the Patriotic Front with more weapons and equipment. It is unlikely that Cuban or other non-African surrogate troops will be involved, but the possibility of Ethiopian involvement cannot be ruled out. Although Congress might force the US Administration to follow us in lifting sanctions, Rhodesia would be unlikely to attract foreign investment and credit on favourable terms.

In these circumstances, a severe decline in white morale would be likely by mid-1980 (the Rhodesians already fear that many middle-ranking officers and public servants may take their accrued pension rights and leave in April unless there is a marked improvement in the situation by then). This in turn would generate a failure of black confidence in the Bishop's government, with the risk that Sithole, Chikerema and others might begin to think again of allying themselves with one wing or the other of the Patriotic Front.

This could face the South African government with a choice between direct intervention in the war in support of the Rhodesian government, or allowing it to disintegrate and making the best of the resulting debacle by evacuating the remaining white population.

(*b*) *If Bishop Muzorewa establishes a government with broad Western support,* there will, however, be a good prospect of Rhodesia attracting enough international aid and commercial credit and investment to enable the government to restore the economy and reinforce both white and black morale. In that case, the security forces should remain in a high state of efficiency. There may be defections from the Patriotic Front, and they will find recruitment more difficult. ZAPU's military capability is already smaller than ZANU's and Kaunda may feel emboldened to restrict the facilities he offers them if they appear to be losing ground. There will be some prospect of encouraging the more moderate OAU States to move towards establishing relations with the Muzorewa government.

(*c*) *If the Patriotic Front splits, and ZAPU agrees to a separate ceasefire and to take part in elections*, ZANU will continue fighting after independence, with Mozambican support. In this case, the restoration of normal relations with Zambia and Botswana will put the new government in a good position to contain ZANU activities at a tolerable level. The Soviet Union might try to switch its support to ZANU in these circumstances. But it would be on very weak ground in doing so. In other respects the situation would develop very much as in case (*b*) above, but more rapidly and more favourably for Rhodesia.

2. *South Africa's* role in any of these situations will be of crucial importance, especially in Case (*a*). Mr P.W. Botha's present policy is to remove the more offensive features of apartheid at home, while also trying to establish a 'constellation' of friendly States in Southern Africa, to include not only the 'independent' homelands, but also Rhodesia and Namibia and even Botswana, Malawi and Zambia. There are already indications that his government is considering, both privately and publicly, the possibility of direct intervention in Rhodesia in order to forestall the establishment of a Patriotic Front government there. Whether they would actually do so is uncertain. If they did, there would be strong and probably irresistible international pressure for mandatory UN action against South Africa (which would cause severe damage to British economic interests there). This consideration might lead them to decide against such a course. But if Bishop Muzorewa's government collapses, they might well feel that they should cut their losses in the region. They would probably decide also to impose an internal settlement in *Namibia* and perhaps to accelerate their *nuclear programme*. They would end their present economic co-operation with Zambia and Mozambique. There would be no prospect of a rapprochement with Angola. Zaire would be left exposed and vulnerable. The net result would be further international isolation of South Africa and its immediate neighbours and, probably, encouragement for the emergence of more radical regimes further north.

3. Developments of this kind would be of great concern to the *Americans*. They will see them as likely to create openings for the Soviet Union to entrench and expand its political and military position not only amongst its present clients in Africa but in countries, like Zambia and Nigeria, which up to now have not been particularly receptive to Soviet advances. They will be very reluctant, therefore, to support any moves which they see as tending to increase these risks. Similar considerations are likely to influence our other *NATO* and *EEC* partners. They will be reluctant to follow any policies in Southern Africa which they will see as providing the Soviet Union and its allies with opportunities to strengthen their position not only in Africa but elsewhere in the Third World.

4. In relation to Rhodesia, *we ourselves* share the South Africans' wish to see the emergence there of a moderate government, since this offers the best prospect of avoiding an exodus of the white population, re-activating British economic interests there, and staving off the creation of another focus of radical pressure on our African policies. But it is important that such a government should have a good chance of long term survival and that we should try to avoid or minimise a sharp polarisation in Southern Africa which could do severe damage to British and Western interests. The economic interests which might be at risk are listed in an Annex.[1] First among these is of course our trade with Nigeria.

5. Our best chance of pursuing and achieving all these objectives will be in continuing to work for an outcome to the Constitutional Conference which will as far as possible undercut international and especially Front Line support for the Patriotic Front and offer hope of de-escalating the war in either of the ways suggested at (*b*) or (*c*) above. The prospects both for us and for Rhodesia will, however, be much poorer if the Conference ends and independence is granted in circumstances which do not attract Western support for Bishop Muzorewa's government and the situation develops as in (*a*).

[1] Not printed.

No. 111

Handwritten note from Mr Alexander (No. 10) to Mrs Thatcher, 12 October 1979
(PREM 19/113)

These two texts (from the SA Govt & from Bp. Muzorewa) were delivered to-day.[1] The Foreign Secretary is not taking them too tragically. He has spoken to the Bishop & told him he understands and sympathises with the Bishop's position.

The S. African message is not v. surprising. Col van der Post spoke to Mr P.W. Bother [*sic*: Botha] last night: Mr Bother was 'reassuring' & said that he would keep Mr Smith 'under control.[2]

[1] Not printed.
[2] Mrs Thatcher minuted: 'I agree the Conference is dragging on far too long.'

No. 112

Lord Carrington to Sir N. Henderson (Washington),
14 October 1979, 12.35 p.m.[1]
Tel. No. 1406 Secret, Immediate (FCO 36/2540)

Rhodesia

1. Following is text of a message from Secretary Vance conveyed to me this morning by US Ambassador:

Begins:

I hope you will let us know if there is anything else we can do to help gain agreement on constitutional proposals. I have requested Ambassador Brewster to back up your October 11 statement by indicating privately to Front Line representatives that we believe a multi-donor effort would be appropriate to assist in the agricultural and economic development of an independent Zimbabwe within the framework of a wider development concept for Southern Africa as a whole and we would be prepared to cooperate in such an effort. We cannot of course make a specific commitment and will point out that this effort would be contingent both on reaching a successful outcome at Lancaster House and on gaining Congressional support for the concept at a time of severe budgetary constraint.

We also want to be helpful now in looking ahead at transition arrangements. We understand how thorny they will be, since it will be very important that they strike a balance between workable simplicity and yet sufficient guarantees that each of the parties can compete fairly in elections. Without the latter, western interests in Africa could be seriously damaged.

I understand that Tony Lake will be going to London at some point in the coming days to discuss transition issues. This would be useful to us, although we would want it to be at a time when such meetings would not interfere with your officials' work at Lancaster House. In particular, it would be useful to get the FCO's thinking on three issues:

(*a*) While we understand and sympathise with the need to have a short and uncomplicated transition period, we believe that it should be sufficiently long to give a fair opportunity for the external parties to become engaged. We have no precise timelines in mind, but believe a period in the range of four to six months might be acceptable to the parties and yet short enough to be manageable.

(*b*) It will be important to provide adequate assurances that law and order will be fairly maintained during the transition. An outside Commonwealth force might be acceptable to the parties, in addition to Commonwealth observers.

(*c*) We shall also have stay in close touch on our respective positions on sanctions. If the Orders in Council are allowed to expire mid-November before a settlement is reached, there would be important implications for our position.

You continue to have our support and admiration. Cy.

Ends

---

1 And Immediate to Lusaka, Dar es Salaam, Gaborone, Maputo, Luanda, Lagos; Priority to UKMIS New York. Deskby 14 October 1400Z to all addressees except Washington and UKMIS New York.

2. US Ambassador has been authorised to draw on above in 'briefing privately' Zambian and Tanzanian High Commissioners, and other Front Line representatives as considered appropriate.

No. 113

Minute from Mr Renwick to Sir A. Duff, 15 October 1979[1]
Secret (FCO 36/2540)

Rhodesia: Mr Vance's Message

1. The Americans have made representations to the front-line states in support of the proposals we have put forward for the independence Constitution. Mr Vance's conditional offer of assistance for agricultural development is a helpful response to the Secretary of State's statement on 11 October.

2. Mr Vance's message, however, puts forward suggestions for the interim period which are not in line with our ideas and would not be negotiable with the Salisbury delegation. (The references to arrangements which 'might be acceptable to the parties' appear to have only the external parties in mind). It would seem best to put our views on record in reply before discussions begin with US officials. We do not envisage a long period for the interim. A Commonwealth force will not be acceptable in Salisbury. We should not lead the Americans to believe that if agreement breaks down on the positions at present adopted by the parties, it will be possible to renew sanctions in November.

3. I *submit* a draft reply to Mr Vance[2]. This might also serve as a note for the Secretary of State's meeting with Ambassador Brewster.

R.W. RENWICK

1 Also sent to Mr Walden.
2 Not printed. See No. 114 for final version.

No. 114

Lord Carrington to Sir N. Henderson (Washington), 15 October 1979, 4 p.m.
Tel. No. 1411 Secret, Immediate (FCO 36/2540)

My telno 1406: Rhodesia[1]

1. Please pass the following reply from me to Mr Vance:
Begins.
Thank you for your message which was passed to me by Kingman Brewster on 14 October. I am most grateful for the action you have taken with the Front Line states in support of our proposals for the independence constitution: and for the indications you are giving to the Front Line Governments that you would be prepared to cooperate in international assistance for agricultural development. I hope that this,

1 No. 112.

together with my statement of 11 October, will help the Patriotic Front to accept the Independence Constitution and enable us to carry forward the discussions about the arrangements for implementing it with both delegations.

I am glad that Tony Lake will be coming to London for discussions on the interim arrangements, but on the points you raised in your message I thought it would be useful to let you know my views.

It is now clear that, however the discussion of the interim arrangements comes out, the only basis on which we shall be able to get the parties to agree is likely to be one that involves the British Government in assuming a very large measure of responsibility for that period: and the longer the period, the less likely it is that a cease-fire will hold. A period of 4-6 months is in my view too long. I do not envisage our assuming responsibility for a period of more than, at most, three months. This would be adequate for the external parties, who already have a very considerable presence in the country, to prepare for the elections. (As you may have seen, President Machel appears to share these views).

I very much doubt if a Commonwealth Force will be acceptable to the parties. One of the unfortunate elements in the whole situation is the extreme hostility manifested by many Commonwealth Governments towards Muzorewa. The Salisbury Delegation consider that most Commonwealth Governments are already politically committed against them and could not be brought to agree a Commonwealth Force.

Our objective is to achieve a settlement which will enable the Patriotic Front to participate in elections supervised by us and will thereby bring an end to the war. But the position at present reached in the Conference is that Bishop Muzorewa and his delegation have accepted the Independence Constitution, and have also accepted that elections should be held under our authority. I would be misleading you if I led you to believe that, in these circumstances, there is any prospect of Parliament retaining sanctions against Rhodesia after mid-November. I saw Nkomo and Mugabe again this morning. They were still not able to say that they accepted the Independence Constitution, subject to agreement on the interim arrangements. I cannot hold up any longer discussions with the Salisbury Delegation, who have now been waiting a week. I shall, therefore, have to continue the discussion of the pre-independence arrangements with them, hoping that the PF will shortly join in. In any event it will be my objective to work out pre-independence arrangements which would enable the Patriotic Front to participate in free elections on the basis of that Constitution: and that these would be supervised under the British Governments authority, as was agreed at Lusaka. We shall therefore be continuing our efforts to reach an agreement in which the Patriotic Front will be able to participate.

Ends.

2. As you will realise, the content of this message is particularly sensitive. It is intended for Mr Vance personally. I should be grateful if you would ensure that this is made clear in delivering it to him.

No. 115

Meeting between Lord Carrington and the leaders of the Patriotic Front, 15 October 1979, 11.30 a.m.
Restricted (FCO 36/2439)

Present:

Lord Carrington	Mr J. Nkomo
Sir A. Duff	Mr R. Mugabe
Mr R.J. Lyne	Mr E. Tekere
	Mr J. Msika

Lord Carrington said that the position as he had left it on Thursday 11 October was that there needed to be agreement next stage.[1] He had made clear the Government's readiness to help over finance for land transfer; the Americans had since said that they would also be prepared to contribute. The British Government could go no further. He had therefore asked the Patriotic Front to reflect. *Mr Mugabe* said that Lord Carrington had observed that all parties would have to do some thinking. *Lord Carrington* said that his position was unchanged. *Mr Nkomo* asked what the Americans had said. *Lord Carrington* and *Sir A. Duff* replied that the Americans had told the Front Line States that they were willing to help on the land question.

Mr Nkomo said that the Patriotic Front had come at Lord Carrington's invitation to hear his views. *Lord Carrington* asked if the Patriotic Front had changed their minds over the weekend, and whether they were prepared to accept the Independence Constitution.

Mr Mugabe said that the British were asking the Patriotic Front to make all the concessions. The question of land was vital. It was what the Patriotic Front were fighting for. Acceptance of the British proposals would lose them their support. The Patriotic Front had their own 'Blackpools' to think about. The British Government had arranged for transfer in Kenya.

Lord Carrington replied that he had tried to meet the Patriotic Front's problem in his statement on land (from which he quoted again). He could not go further. The Americans had made a similar offer. *Mr Nkomo* said this was beside the point. The problem was how to develop the new country of Zimbabwe. *Sir A. Duff* said that an independent Zimbabwe would receive aid and investment in the normal way from other countries: some of this could be used for land resettlement, as had happened in Kenya. *Mr Nkomo* said the Kenyans had come out of their Constitutional Conference with a pledge from Britain to pay off the farmers. *Sir A. Duff* said that this was not true. For 15 years after independence the Kenyans had used part of their aid flow to effect land transfer.

Lord Carrington proposed that Zimbabwe should do the same, and repeated that the British Government could go no further on land. *Mr Nkomo* asked if the British Government were now up against the wall. They should realise that this was a very

---

1 No. 103.

serious situation. *Lord Carrington* said that we were trying to compromise between two opposing points of view. *Mr Nkomo* said that this was not the point. The war in Zimbabwe was basically about land. A large section of the country was now occupied by the Patriotic Front. It had been decided at Lancaster House that the British should withdraw from the situation. *Lord Carrington* interjected that the Salisbury Delegation would not agree to the expropriation of land without compensation: this was a reality.

Mr Nkomo said that the British had not moved, but were throwing the problem back at the Patriotic Front. They were asking the Patriotic Front to do what an independent government would do naturally—i.e. to work out development schemes. The British were not putting forward a scheme of their own or making any concrete offer. *Sir A. Duff* said that it was not for us to say how the post-independence Government should decides on its policies. *Lord Carrington* read for the second time an extract from his statement in the Conference on land. *Mr Nkomo* said that the British Government would in any case be contributing to a land fund: what they should deal with now was the question of how to get the land back. Who would buy the land? *Sir A. Duff* said that we would provide funds to help with the purchase of land: but the way this was put into effect would have to be discussed between the British Government and the post-independence Government in Zimbabwe. *Mr Nkomo* suggested that the Government should work out a land fund scheme. *Mr Mugabe* said that we should combine with the Americans on this, to put together a package similar to that in the Anglo/American Proposals. *Lord Carrington* said the Anglo/American Proposals package had been a total disaster: nobody had wanted to subscribe to it. *Mr Mugabe* said there had at least been a definite plan in the Anglo/American Proposals: there was now no plan, but only a vague idea.

Mr Nkomo said that the Patriotic Front had expected Lord Carrington to 'come up with something'. *Lord Carrington* replied that we had made our offer, and that he must now ask the Patriotic Front if they accepted the Constitution. *Mr Nkomo* said Lord Carrington should not put this question now: this was not what they had come to the meeting for. *Lord Carrington* reminded Mr Nkomo that he put the question when tabling the independence Constitution on 3 October: that he had since asked for an answer on several occasions, and could not put the time off for a decision any longer. He would now have to go ahead to discuss the interim arrangements with the delegation which had accepted the Constitution. *Mr Mugabe* replied that the Patriotic Front would not proceed, and would not be intimidated into accepting objectionable proposals. *Lord Carrington* repeated that he would begin discussion on 16 October with the delegation which had accepted the Constitution. If the Patriotic Front had not accepted the Constitution, there was nothing to talk about. He had made it clear from the outset of the Constitutional Conference that discussion of the pre-independence arrangements could not take place until that on the Constitution had been concluded.

Mr Mugabe described this as very poor tactics. *Mr Nkomo* echoed his statement and asked if Lord Carrington would use the Police to keep the Patriotic Front out of the Conference on 16 October. Was the British Government turning them out? *Lord Carrington* said that this was not the case.

Mr Tekere reverted to the land question. It was unrealistic of the British Government to press forward and seek a further concession from the Patriotic Front. The principle of compensation was unacceptable and could not be explained to the

Patriotic Front's own people. Now the British were talking about going ahead with those who had accepted the Constitution but their document was not a good instrument with which to place a Government securely in power. If it was used for the basis of a Government led by Bishop Muzorewa, he would crumble, as it did not represent the feeling of the people of Zimbabwe. *Sir A. Duff* said that Mr Tekere had made it clear that he did not accept the principle of compensation and did not think that the Independence Constitution was good. *The Patriotic Front representatives* indicated that they did not accept this summary of their position.

Mr Msika accused Lord Carrington of using intimidatory tactics. He had asked the Patriotic Front leaders to call. They would now have to go back to their delegation to discuss the matter. Until they had done so it was not for Lord Carrington to tell them that he was going ahead. The British statement on land was meaningless as it did not accept that there were two separate issues involved, of land transfer and land development respectively. It was not proper for the British Government to intimidate the Patriotic Front. The British Government should state their case and the Patriotic Front would come up with a decision on it. *Lord Carrington* replied that he could go no further on land. It was time to face the facts.

Mr Nkomo said that in that case the British should send their Constitution in an envelope to the Patriotic Front in Maputo and Lusaka, and should tell them that this was the Law of Moses. If the SALT negotiations had been conducted like this, agreement would never have been reached. Lord Carrington was dealing with the Patriotic Front like school boys. *Mr Mugabe* rose, saying that the British should proceed with their discussion on the interim arrangements.

The meeting lasted 35 minutes.

No. 116

Lord Carrington to Sir L. Allinson (Lusaka), 15 October 1979, 3.43 p.m.[1]
Tel. No. 838 Confidential, Immediate (FCO 36/2439)

MIPT: Rhodesia[2]

1. It is still uncertain how the Patriotic Front will now decide to play their hand. ZAPU may wish to give a more positive indication of their attitude on the Constitution and proceed to the next stage of the Conference on that basis. ZANU will be very reluctant to do so. Unless they see objection, posts in the Front Line States and Lagos should speak to the governments to which they are accredited on the lines set out below. Other posts may draw on this telegram and MIPT at their discretion.

---

1 And Flash to Maputo, Gaborone, Dar es Salaam, Luanda (Deskby 1700Z), Lagos (Deskby 1700Z); Immediate to Mirimba, Salisbury, Nairobi, Luanda, Lagos, Washington, Pretoria, Addis Ababa, Monrovia, Canberra, Ottawa, Wellington, Peking, Moscow, Prague (all Deskby 1700Z); Priority Abidjan, Dakar, Kinshasa, Khartoum, Tokyo, EEC Posts, Kuwait, Kingston, Bridgetown, Dacca, New Delhi, Singapore, Georgetown, La Paz, Nassau, Freetown, Port Louis, Mbabane, Port of Spain, Kampala, Lilongwe, Valletta, Banjul, Colombo, Accra, Kuala Lumpur, Nicosia, Castries, Oslo, Stockholm, Lisbon, Madrid, Manila, Tehran, Bucharest, Athens; Information Immediate UKMIS New York (Deskby 1700); Information Saving Suva, Port Moresby, Honiara, Nuku'alofa, Victoria, Tarawa, UKDEL NATO.
2 Not printed.

2. You should emphasise that, if the Patriotic Front can accept the Independence Constitution, the door is open to them to join in the discussions on the pre-independence arrangements. We hope that they will do so, if the Patriotic Front do not accept the Constitution in time to enable them to participate in the negotiations on its implementation, when they begin tomorrow, it will still be my objective to work our pre-independence arrangements which would enable the Patriotic Front to participate in free elections on the basis of the new Constitution, as was agreed at Lusaka. In short, we are still aiming for an agreement involving the Patriotic Front which will enable the parties to the conflict to settle their differences by political means and the people of Rhodesia to choose for themselves the government they wish to operate the Independence Constitution. We have no intention of doing anything at this state [*sic*] which could fore-close that possibility.

3. I shall want to be in touch with the governments of the Front Line States in the next few days about the proposals for the pre-independence arrangements which we shall be developing in the Conference. You will be receiving further instructions on this shortly.

4. For your own information only, at this stage, I may, depending on the situation in the Conference, wish to ask Mr Richard Luce to visit the Front-Line States and Lagos in the next few days to begin to explain to the Front Line presidents the arrangements we have in mind for the pre-independence period. In that case, Mr Luce would visit Lusaka, Dar es Salaam, Maputo, Gaborone (not necessarily in that order) and return to London via Lagos. He would be accompanied by Mr Day. It would probably not be practicable for him to visit Luanda on this occasion, and Mr Byatt would be asked to speak on my behalf to the Angolan Government.

5. It would therefore be helpful to have your advice (but without making an approach to governments at this stage) about the likely availability of the presidents concerned in the period between 15 and 25 October.

(Lagos) is President Shagari likely to be available in the week beginning 22 October?

No. 117

Minute from Mr Walden to Mr Renwick, 15 October 1979
Confidential (FCO 36/2540)

Call by the American Ambassador

Mr Brewster discussed Rhodesia with Lord Carrington this afternoon. The Secretary of State described the current background. We were about to lose Salisbury if we were not careful. The Patriotic Front had seen him today, but had prevaricated. Nkomo might accept the Constitution, but he was not sure about Mugabe. If we began discussing the interim with the Salisbury parties alone, it would still be open to the Patriotic Front to join in. We could hardly be accused of rushing them after six weeks.

Lord Carrington said he would like to comment candidly on Mr Vance's message. Reading between the lines, his impression was that the Americans thought that he had only one customer to satisfy: the Patriotic Front. In fact he had two customers: one already in possession with an election and a 64% turnout behind it, and with a certain political support in this country; and the Patriotic Front. On the pre-election arrangements, we had decided that brevity and simplicity were essential, not least to maintain the ceasefire. The AAP was unworkable, and there was no question of a UN force. Moreover, the Commonwealth were loaded against the Bishop, and a Commonwealth force would not be possible either.

Mr Brewster said that he did not think that the length of the interim period was a very strong point, and he understood Lord Carrington's argument. The important thing was that neutral countries should not say the arrangements were unfair. This was the only motive behind American recommendations. He himself was relaxed about the disappearance of the UN force. But he hoped there would be no problem about Commonwealth observers, as distinct from a Commonwealth force. Lord Carrington said that the UK could not of course be involved militarily, but he thought we could possibly work out arrangements in which we could help. Mr Brewster asked about Muzorewa's role during the run-up period. Would we have a sort of British regent like Lord Carver? Lord Carrington indicated that our minds were moving in that direction. Mr Brewster said that the main concern of the Americans was that the arrangements should not appear to have been rigged up for the Bishop. Lord Carrington said that we were not thinking of rigging anything but commented that the Bishop had won elections. Mr Brewster said that a lot of people, including some members of the White Commonwealth, would be unhappy if the Bishop were to be treated as an incumbent during the election period, rather than simply as a candidate.

Lord Carrington said that we had not recognised the Bishop's government but there would be no chance of success in the conference at all if we rubbed his nose in this too much. We would not recognise him as an office holder, but could not stop him calling himself whatever he wanted. Our main concern was that the elections should be free and fair. There could be some sort of electoral commission on which all parties could be represented. Mr Brewster reiterated that it was important that the Bishop should be seen as no more than an electoral candidate. He should not for example sit in his Prime Ministerial office during the campaign.

Summing up, Mr Brewster said that the main points of concern for the Americans were the Bishop's status during the pre-election period, and the question of observers or an international force. The length of the interim period was a secondary issue.

G.G.H. WALDEN

No. 118

Lord Carrington to Sir L. Allinson (Lusaka), 17 October 1979, 4.40 p.m.[1]
Tel. No. 844 Confidential, Immediate (FCO 36/2440)

Rhodesia: Constitutional Conference

1. At a meeting with Bishop Muzorewa and his delegation this afternoon we discussed arrangements for elections in which all parties of the Conference would be able to take part. The Salisbury delegation made it clear that they accept the principle of such elections, and the presence of Commonwealth observers. A certain amount of common ground was identified, though no decisions were taken which could make it difficult for the Patriotic Front to rejoin the discussions. On the lifting of sanctions we explained that this was linked to the legal status of Rhodesia.

2. The Patriotic Front have not yet approached us, but we hope that they may be preparing to make a statement which would enable them to rejoin the discussions in the near future. You should make it clear that we are doing nothing which could foreclose the possibility of them participating or could make it difficult for them to do so.

---

[1] And to Immediate Mirimba, Salisbury, Nairobi, Maputo, Gaborone, Dar es Salaam, Luanda, Lagos, Washington, Pretoria, Addis Ababa, Monrovia, Canberra, Ottawa, Wellington, Peking, Moscow, Prague; Priority Abidjan, Dakar, Kinshasa, Khartoum, Tokyo, EEC Posts, Kuwait, Kingston, Bridgetown, Dacca, New Delhi, Singapore, Georgetown, La Paz, Nassau, Freetown, Port Louis, Mbabane, Port of Spain, Kampala, Lilongwe, Valletta, Banjul, Colombo, Accra, Kuala Lumpur, Nicosia, Castries, Oslo, Stockholm, Lisbon, Madrid, Manila, Tehran, Bucharest, Athens; Information Immediate UKMIS New York; Information Saving Suva, Port Moresby, Honiara, Nuku'alofa, Victoria, Tarawa, UKDEL NATO.

No. 119

Letter from Mr Lyne to Mr Alexander (No. 10), 17 October 1979
Confidential (PREM 19/113)

Dear Michael,

Rhodesia: Pre-Independence Period

I enclose a paper describing our proposals for the pre-independence period in Rhodesia.

Lord Carrington proposes to carry forward our discussions with the Salisbury Delegation on the basis of this paper, and to seek Bishop Muzorewa's agreement to it.[1]

Yours ever,
RODERIC LYNE

---

[1] Mr Alexander minuted to the Prime Minister: 'I think this paper takes account of most of the points you made at Chequers and yesterday. Agree?' Mrs Thatcher replied: 'Yes.'

Enclosure in No. 119

Rhodesia: The Pre-Independence Period

1. On a date to be agreed, by an Order in Council of the Southern Rhodesia Act of 1965, executive authority in Rhodesia will be vested in a Governor who will be British.

2. There will be no Parliament in Rhodesia in the pre-election period to act as the legislative authority. This authority will therefore have to be vested formally in the Governor.

3. The Governor will be appointed by the British Government. He will have a small British staff, and Election Commissioner, a military adviser and a police adviser.

4. At the end of the Conference and before the Governor arrives, Bishop Muzorewa would return to Rhodesia and resume control of the Government. He would *if necessary* arrange for the new Constitution to be approved by the Rhodesian Parliament by a rapid procedure; and in any case for Parliament to be dissolved to enable new elections to be held. He would invite us to appoint a British Governor to enable elections to be held under our authority.

5. The Governor would then proceed to Rhodesia. From his arrival, he would be *formally* responsible for the administration of the country. (For a short period after his arrival, Bishop Muzorewa and his principal Ministers would deal with day to day business in matters which did not relate to the holding of elections and a ceasefire.) From this point Rhodesia would have returned to legality as a British dependent territory and sanctions would be lifted.

6. Bishop Muzorewa and his Ministers, and all other political leaders, would thereafter commit themselves to the election campaign. Bishop Muzorewa would not be asked to resign. The Governor would not take action to divest him of his office. But the Governor would become directly responsible for the day to day administration of the country, acting through the Permanent Secretaries, for such time as was necessary to enable elections to be held.

7. The Governor's instructions would require him to do all things necessary to secure compliance with the conditions for free elections. In particular, he would ensure that during the election campaign:

(*a*) the administration of the election is scrupulously impartial as between all the political parties;

(*b*) peaceful political activity is freely conducted;

(*c*) all parties will have free and uncensored access to all the public media.

8. The Governor's Election Commissioner and supporting staff would assist him in carrying out these functions. Commonwealth observers would be present during the election.

9. The Governor would appoint an Election Council, under the chairmanship of his Election Commissioner, on which parties taking part in the election would be represented. The Council and its individual members would be able to offer advice and make representations to the Governor on any matter concerning the elections.

10. The existing civil police would be responsible for the maintenance of law and order, under the authority and supervision of the Governor and his police adviser and supporting staff.

11. There would be agreement between the opposing forces regarding a ceasefire

and disengagement of their respective forces. A Ceasefire Commission under the chairmanship of the British military adviser would be established to assist with the oversight of the ceasefire on which the commanders of the opposing forces will be represented and would be answerable to the Governor.

12. The elections would be held on a date to be decided by the Governor, after consultation with the parties participating in them. Immediately thereafter the independence government would be established and Zimbabwe would become independent.

No. 120

Letter from Mr Alexander (No. 10) to Mr Walden, 17 October 1979
Secret (FCO 36/2513)

Dear George,

As you know the South African Foreign Minister, Mr Pik Botha, called on the Prime Minister at 6 p.m. this evening. I enclose a record of the discussion. I should be grateful if you could give the record an even more limited distribution than that normally accorded to records of Prime Ministerial conversations.

Yours ever,
MICHAEL ALEXANDER

ENCLOSURE IN No. 120

Record of a Discussion between the Prime Minister and the Foreign Minister of South Africa, Mr Pik Botha, at 10 Downing Street on 17 October at 1800

Present:

Prime Minister	Prime Minister Mr Pik Botha
Foreign and Commonwealth Secretary	H.E. Dr Dawid de Villiers
Mr M. O'D B. Alexander	

After an exchange of courtesies, *Mr Botha* said that he had been asked by his Prime Minister to say that he very much hoped it might be possible to arrange a meeting between himself and the Prime Minister at an opportune moment. Mr P.W. Botha considered that it would be extremely useful for the two Prime Ministers to be able to discuss their common problems and get to know each other better. The *Prime Minister* recalled that she had met Mr P.W. Botha when he was the South African Defence Minister. She said that it would be virtually impossible to meet Mr P.W. Botha in the months immediately ahead. Her diary was already overcrowded. *Mr Botha* made it clear that his Prime Minister was thinking of a visit to London rather than of a visit by Mrs Thatcher to South Africa. He did not attempt to pursue the matter further.

Mr Botha said that his Prime Minister had asked him to make clear how grateful he was for the Prime Minister's response to his initiatives in South Africa. Mr P.W. Botha's ambition was to bring the leaders of the black and the Asian communities to share his vision of Southern Africa. This was based on a belief that South Africa could and should play a bigger role in the social and economic development of the entire region. The region contained 40 million people. It possessed a good infrastructure and a large internal market. It was in every sense the most highly developed region in Africa. It had enormous resources of gold and other minerals, of the various metals and of water. South Africa's knowledge and expertise e.g. in the areas of agriculture, treatment of disease, and industry was tailored to the African situation. The region was one of great importance. Given the chance, the present South African Government aimed to show the other African countries that co-operation with them would be worth seeking. Within South Africa the Government's objective was to convince the whites that the blacks were their natural partners. If Mr P.W. Botha's policies succeeded, the result would be a solid and stable region in Southern Africa which it would be easier for the West to support.

The *Prime Minister* said that she needed no convincing about the importance of South Africa. She considered that Mr P.W. Botha's efforts had not received enough recognition in the West. His recent initiatives were part of a continuing process. The setbacks he had encountered in the recent by-elections had underlined how courageous his policies were. The *Foreign and Commonwealth Secretary* said that he agreed with the Prime Minister. Mr Botha's point about making it easier for Western Governments to support South Africa was of particular importance. The greater the movement to which they could point within South Africa, the better.

Mr Botha said that despite the difficulties, the South African Government had the will to complete their programme. But they would be unable to do so if the Marxists won in Zimbabwe/Rhodesia. The *Prime Minister* said that everyone would be lost if the Marxists won. It was essential to have moderate Governments, supported by the white population, in both Zimbabwe/Rhodesia and in Namibia. Britain's objective was to achieve a lasting solution in Zimbabwe/Rhodesia of the type secured in Kenya. This would allow the country to flourish, would give the neighbouring countries a better chance and would make co-operation with South Africa easier. We would try to get others to share our view of the situation in the region as a whole. A constitutional settlement supported only by South Africa and the United Kingdom would leave Zimbabwe/Rhodesia isolated. There had been two aspects of Bishop Muzorewa's Constitution which had had to be rectified because they had no parallel in any other Constitution granted by Britain. Both points had been put right. There was now a Constitution which was in all respects similar to those we had granted to many other countries on gaining independence. Britain recognised that what Rhodesians wanted was an end to the war: we intended to offer the ballot in exchange for the bullet. Great difficulties remained and progress at the Conference had been too slow. Bishop Muzorewa had been away from Salisbury too long. None the less we were on course. The *Foreign and Commonwealth Secretary* added that it was essential that Britain should be seen to be being reasonable in the conduct of negotiations. As it was he had already been accused by many of attempting to wreck the Conference.

Mr Botha said that it was important that Bishop Muzorewa's position should not be weakened. There was no-one in Rhodesia who would look after his interests. His power base lay in his link with the Security Forces. If this were to be severed, the Bishop would be a laughing stock in the country. Access to the levers of power was what mattered in African politics. Looking further ahead, Mr Botha said that he was concerned about the possibility that Mr Nkomo would be allowed to participate in the elections even though he had not accepted any agreement in London. If this happened, Mr Nkomo would have a platform that would enable him to destroy Bishop Muzorewa. He would say that he had sought a better agreement in London but that the Bishop had sold out to the British. The *Prime Minister* said that there was force in Mr Botha's point but that in our view Mr Nkomo should not be allowed to participate in the election unless he accepted the Constitution. As regards Bishop Muzorewa's position, the aim would be for him to return to Salisbury with definite achievement e.g. the lifting of sanctions and the return to legality, to his credit.

Mr Botha said that South Africa had a military presence in Rhodesia at the Bishop's request. This consisted of equipment rather than men. South Africa was also giving financial support to the tune of some 40 million rand per month. It they were to decide to end their presence, they would wish to do so soon. South Africa could not afford a repetition of what had happened in Angola where they had appeared to capitulate under external pressure. (It had evidently been Mr Botha's intention at this point to describe the alternative course of action which South Africa might pursue if the situation deteriorated and they decided not to withdraw. However, in the event the conversation took a different direction and he never returned to the point.)

The *Prime Minister* expressed the hope that South Africa would not decide to pull out of Rhodesia. The *Foreign and Commonwealth Secretary* said that it was entirely reasonable for Bishop Muzorewa to have purchased the South African equipment. If there were a British presence in Zimbabwe/Rhodesia during the interim period, no questions would be asked about the equipment.

Mr Botha said he was concerned that the United States Government might try to exert pressure on the British Government. The *Prime Minister* said he need have no concern on that score. We would do our best to bring the Americans along and would remind them of our extensive experience in the problems of the region. The *Foreign and Commonwealth Secretary* said that he did not believe the American Government could afford not the follow HMG's line. *Mr Botha* referred to intercepts available to the South African Government of President Nyerere's conversations with colleagues. President Nyerere's interpretation of what he had been told by the Americans did not altogether square with the Prime Minister's view. It was of course possible that President Nyerere had misunderstood what the Americans were saying. The *Secretary of State* said that he thought President Nyerere was probably wide of the mark. The only worry was that the Americans might not regard the interim arrangements as fair. But they could probably be brought round.

At the end of the conversation *Mr Botha* reverted to his Prime Minister's vision of the development of Southern Africa as a whole. He said that Mr P.W. Botha intended to have a meeting with South African industrialists and financiers on 22 November at which he would be seeking financial support for his grand design. The meeting ended at 1835.

No. 121

Sir A. Parsons (UKMIS New York) to Lord Carrington, 18 October 1979, 6.45 p.m.

Tel. No. 1284 Confidential, Priority (FCO 36/2550)

Rhodesia

1. Rhodesia has been the main subject raised with Mr Hurd during his UN calls. Apart from the Nigerian initiative in the Sanctions Committee (my Tel. No. 1280)[1] there is no sign of mounting pressure. Salim (Tanzania) was relaxed and helpful. He confirmed that it was still the intention to leave the Rhodesia debate in the Fourth Committee until the end of the agenda i.e. towards the end of November. He said that it would be irrelevant to hold this debate while the Lancaster House Conference was in progress. He had no complaint or criticism of your handling of the Conference.

2. Waldheim's attitude was similar. He confined himself mainly to asking questions. He was obviously preoccupied with what would happen in the UN if things went wrong. He made clear that he had no wish for UN involvement in the transitional period. He believed that Commonwealth participation would be best. Neither he nor Salim nor anyone else raised difficult questions such as the lifting of sanctions.

1 Not printed.

No. 122

Meeting between Lord Carrington and the co-leaders of the Patriotic Front, 18 October 1979, 2.15 p.m.

Confidential (FCO 36/2440)

Present:

The Right Honourable	Mr J. Nkomo
Lord Carrington KCMG MC	Mr R. Mugabe
Sir Ian Gilmour MP	plus two members of the Patriotic
Sir A. Duff	Front Delegation
Mr R.M.J. Lyne	

Mr Nkomo handed over the attached reply to Lord Carrington's statement in the Constitutional Conference on 9 October.[1]

Lord Carrington said that he took the statement to mean that the Patriotic Front accepted the Independence Constitution subject to agreement on the interim arrangements, though they had expressed the point in different words. *Mr Nkomo* replied that the statement was worded as the Patriotic Front had meant it to be worded and

1 Not printed.

was clear. *Lord Carrington* proposed that there should be a plenary session of the Constitutional Conference on 19 October at which the Patriotic Front would make their statement for the record: the Conference could then go on to discuss the interim arrangements. *Mr Mugabe* and *Mr Nkomo* assented.

Mr Mugabe remarked that, according to the newspapers, the British Government had distributed their plan for the interim arrangements. *Lord Carrington* said that the newspaper reports were speculative. In the meetings held with the Salisbury Delegation in the absence of the Patriotic Front, we had exchanged views on the interim arrangements, some of which had been reflected in the press. Some of the press accounts were garbled and the British spokesman had tried to correct them. Nothing had been decided yet on the interim arrangements. However, we had a clear idea of what both the Salisbury Delegation and the Patriotic Front wanted.

Mr Nkomo enquired about the visit of the South African Foreign Minister. *Lord Carrington* said that it was not entirely clear why Mr Botha had decided to come, especially as he had sent Mr Anthony Hamilton[2] as a personal emissary to see Lord Carrington on the previous day. The South African Government faced a difficult situation in Namibia and were also in some trouble domestically: this had perhaps made them jumpy about the Rhodesia Conference.

In conclusion, *Lord Carrington* said that he was very glad that the Patriotic Front were rejoining the Conference; and that there was a need to get a move on.

The call lasted 15 minutes.

2 Former South African diplomat.

No. 123

Letter from Mr Tomlinson to Mr Pattison (No. 10), 18 October 1979
Unclassified (FCO 36/2565)

Dear Mike,

Mr Luce's Tour of the Front Line States

The Secretary of State considers that at the present stage of the Constitutional Conference on Rhodesia it is important that an envoy should be sent to make contact with the leaders of Front Line States. To this end he proposes that the Parliamentary Under-Secretary of State, Mr Luce, should make a tour including visits to Zambia, Mozambique, Tanzania, Botswana, Angola, Nigeria and Liberia between 19 and 26 October. He will be accompanied by one official and a Private Secretary.

I should be grateful to receive the Prime Minister's approval for this tour.

I am copying this letter to Murdo Maclean (Government Whip's Office) and to Barry Hilton (Cabinet Office).

Yours Sincerely,
S.E. Tomlinson

No. 124

Minute from Mr Renwick to Sir A. Duff,
18 October 1979
Confidential covering Secret (FCO 36/2540)

Rhodesia: Consultations with the Americans

1. In your talks with Mr Lake tomorrow, you may wish to emphasise that our tactics over the discussions on the Constitution were firm from necessity: if we had made changes to the document we laid down on 3 October we would have lost the agreement of the Salisbury delegation. There is a disconcerting tendency among almost everyone not engaged in the negotiations to believe that we are negotiating only with one side (the Patriotic Front) and that the Salisbury delegation can somehow be taken for granted. This has never been the case in previous negotiations; and it is certainly not the case on this occasion. It is equally unreasonable to ostracize Muzorewa. In the negotiations so far the Bishop and his Ministers have stood up to Ian Smith and succeeded in isolating him.

2. The interim arrangements are going to be much more difficult. But we are proceeding on the basis that we will have to assume direct responsibility. That being so we are not prepared to enter into such a commitment for an extended period (or to have others telling us for how long or how we should exercise the responsibility they are calling on us to assume). In other words we cannot have President Nyerere and others deciding the terms of the interim any more than we could have them or Mr Chona trying to write the Rhodesian Constitution.

3. We are determined to create conditions for *elections* in which the Patriotic Front will be able to take part with a fair chance of winning if they can command enough popular support. There will be an Election Commissioner with supporting staff. All the parties participating in the election would be represented on the election council. They would have free access to the media and complete freedom to campaign. We will supervise the entire election process. We do not believe that there was a great deal wrong with the way the Rhodesians ran their last elections so far as the mechanics were concerned. The valid criticisms of those elections was that it was not possible for anyone to put the opposing case (to say nothing of the Constitution on which they were based).

4. We are not prepared to get involved in attempts to 'integrate' *the forces* before elections are held. This will be an impossible task until the people of Rhodesia have made the basic political choice. Nor is it possible to replace the existing police force: there is no practical alternative to our bringing the police under our supervision. There will need to be negotiations on a cease-fire and the dis-engagement of the forces. There will also need to be arrangements for monitoring the cease-fire. There is no hope of the Salisbury delegation agreeing to a UN peace-keeping force (or of the UN providing one). Particularly in view of Mr Ramphal's recent statement, there is no prospect of them agreeing either to a Commonwealth peace-keeping force. Nor do we believe a peace-keeping force to be a necessary or practicable concept on the sort of time-scale we envisage. But there will be a need to monitor the cease-fire and for a cease-fire commission to

supervise the monitoring (you may want to begin to open up some of the ideas in the attached paper[1] on the cease-fire).

5. The essential question in this period is that of *the political structure*. We do not believe that a 'transitional government' would be workable or compatible with our intention to assume responsibility in this period. It will therefore be our intention to appoint a British Governor who would supervise the work of the administration. Bishop Muzorewa and his Ministers would commit themselves to the election campaign (as soon as there had been a hand-over to the Governor).

6. *Sanctions* will be lifted at the moment Rhodesia returns to its lawful status as a British dependent territory for the period necessary for elections to be held. This would be effected by an Order in Council under the 1965 Act. We would then state in the Security Council that the rebellion had ended; that Rhodesia was no longer in a state of illegality; and that the consequent measures (i.e. sanctions) were therefore being terminated. Our legal advisers will be prepared to give full memorandum of explanation to the State Department legal advisers. We would call on our allies to cease forthwith to apply sanctions against a part of Her Majesty's dominions which had now accepted the lawful authority of a British Governor.

7. You will want to make clear to Mr Lake that, in a situation which the Patriotic Front participate, the British Governor would exercise direct control over the administration. If the Patriotic Front do not participate, we would have to consider what should be done. In those circumstances there would still be a return to legality and consequently the lifting of sanctions. But the British Government would be concerned not to get directly involved in a continuance of the war.

R.W. Renwick

1 Not printed.

CHAPTER III

The Pre-Independence Arrangements
October – November 1979

No. 125

Lord Carrington to Sir L. Allinson (Lusaka), 19 October 1979, 4 p.m.[1]
Tel. No. 853 Confidential, Immediate (FCO 36/2440)

Rhodesia: Constitutional Conference
1. When the conference resumed in plenary session this morning the Patriotic Front made their statement (text in my telno 849).[2] I then welcomed the fact that all delegations had now agreed to the Independence Constitution, subject to satisfactory arrangements for the interim period.

2. I said that the task now was to provide for elections to enable a legislature and executive to be constituted in terms of that Constitution. I proposed that the various problems should be tackled step by step, starting with arrangements for the elections themselves which should be based on the provisions of the Lusaka Agreement, i.e. they must be free and fair, and properly supervised under the British Government's authority with Commonwealth observers present. I invited delegations to state their positions and asked them first whether they were prepared to accept elections as described in the Lusaka Agreement.

3. Bishop Muzorewa said that his country had recently organised elections which all objective observers had agreed were free and fair. He was however prepared to agree to fresh elections, in order to permit those who had felt themselves unable to take part in April to do so now. But the proposals for the interim period which the Patriotic Front had tabled earlier in the Conference were not acceptable.

4. I then explained how we envisaged elections. The interim period would have to be long enough for free and fair elections to be organised. However, the aim would be to bring Rhodesia to independence as soon as possible and there was a danger that ceasefire arrangements would break down if the period was too long. We therefore hoped elections could be held within approximately 2 months. The prerequisites for free and fair elections were that they should be impartially administered, that

---

[1] And to Immediate Mirimba, Salisbury, Nairobi, Maputo, Gaborone, Dar es Salaam, Luanda, Lagos, Washington, Pretoria, Addis Ababa, Monrovia, Canberra, Ottawa, Wellington, Peking, Moscow, Prague; Priority Abidjan, Dakar, Kinshasa, Khartoum, Tokyo, EEC Posts, Kuwait, Kingston, Bridgetown, Dacca, New Delhi, Singapore, Georgetown, La Paz, Nassau, Freetown, Port Louis, Mbabane, Port of Spain, Kampala, Lilongwe, Valletta, Banjul, Colombo, Accra, Kuala Lumpur, Nicosia, Castries, Oslo, Stockholm, Lisbon, Madrid, Manila, Tehran, Bucharest, Athens; Information Immediate UKMIS New York; Information Saving Suva, Port Moresby, Honiara, Nuku'alofa, Victoria, Tarawa, UKDEL NATO.
[2] Not printed (but see No. 122).

there should be peaceful political activity and no intimidation, and that all participants should have free and uncensored access to the media. As agreed at Lusaka, responsibility for ensuring that those conditions were met would rest with the British Government. We were ready to appoint an Election Commissioner with supporting staff to supervise the detailed organisation of the election. Supervision was our responsibility and there was no question of the UN being invited to undertake the task: Commonwealth observers would provide an international element. It would be vital to have a ceasefire, arrangements for which should be worked out between the two sides. In order that parties should be able to satisfy themselves that the conduct of elections was fair and impartial we propose an election council, with the Election Commissioner as Chairman, which would consider complaints brought to its attention by the parties and on which all parties would be represented. The Council would not have executive authority, but the Commissioner would decide whether to follow up complaints. In view of our aim to proceed to elections as quickly as possible, full voter registration was not practical, nor was the delimitation of constituencies. There would have to be a party list system on a regional basis. The choice of Commonwealth observers would be for negotiation between the parties and with the Commonwealth.

5. Invited to express preliminary views, the Patriotic Front said that they accepted the need for elections but could not comment further until they had seen our proposals on paper. Nor would they be able to judge the proposals for elections in isolation. They would need to see plans for the interim period as a whole. I agreed to circulate a document setting out proposals for implementing the Independence Constitution to delegations as soon as possible.

No. 126

Message from Mr Renwick to Mr Manning, 19 October 1979
Confidential (FCO 36/2565)

Message from Robin Renwick in Paris: Rhodesia

1. Mr Luce may well find that some at least of the front-line Presidents try to push him on to the defensive and to start laying down conditions of their own for the interim. The best form of defence will be counter-attack. The sort of points worth making might be:

(*a*) We have constantly been urged to exercise our responsibility as the decolonising power. That is precisely what this Government intends to do.

(*b*) We have to form our own judgement of the way in which to do this. What is being described to the front-line Presidents is *a real plan* which we fully intend to put into effect—not theoretical proposals which are incapable of application (like some previous schemes).

(*c*) We believe that the Rhodesian Army Commanders will accept the authority of a British Governor. The police will act under his supervision and that of his police advisers.

(*d*) It is no use looking for a longer and more complicated transition. We are prepared to carry out our responsibility but not if it is made impossible or unworkable for us to do so.

(*e*) We will guarantee that all parties participating in the election will do so with the same chance of success. Commonwealth observers will be present to ensure that this is the case. We have in many other of our dependent territories transferred power to parties which have opposed us in the past.

(*f*) With the armed forces acting under our authority this means that if the PF participate there will be an end to the war for neighbouring countries. We would want the process of bringing back the refugees to start as quickly as possible.

2. The point to emphasise throughout is that we fully intend to put this plan into effect. Mr Smith will do everything he can to stop us and we do not believe that he will be able to do so. But to be successful it requires the front-line Presidents to support us and to insist that the PF must be prepared to put their political standing to the test in an election held under our authority. [If they are not prepared to do so we will not be able to hold up the decolonising process on that account].

3. What Mr Luce needs to try to do is to impress on them that it is going to happen, that it is a *practical* plan and not just another version of the Anglo/American proposals.

No. 127

**Lord Carrington to Sir N. Henderson (Washington),
20 October 1979, 3.20 p.m.**[1]

Tel. No. 1467 Immediate, Confidential (FCO 36/2540)

Rhodesia

1. Duff, Day and Fifoot went over the ground comprehensively yesterday with US Ambassador, Lake, Miss Spiegel[2] and Lanpher[3].

2. Lake confirmed that the US regarded the constitution that we had ended up with as eminently reasonable and that it had their full support. The US Government were anxious to continue to give us their full backing. It was however important for them that any proposals that we put forward for the pre-independence period should be as reasonable, fair and satisfactory as were our proposals for the constitution. The US Administration were concerned at the likely reactions, not only of the Congress but also, in the pre-presidential election period, of important domestic constituencies such as the black vote. The Administration's attitude would not be wholly or even primarily influenced by the attitude of the Senate. Furthermore the Administration would need to consider the implications for US foreign policy as a whole of the attitude that they adopted towards our proposals for the pre-independence period. We drew attention to the often overlooked fact that we were negotiating with two totally opposed sides, one of which was in possession. The agreement of the latter had therefore to be obtained but we had pushed them a long way. Much of the world appeared to consider only the Patriotic Front.

1 And for Information to UKMIS New York, Pretoria, Lusaka, Maputo, Dar es Salaam, Gaborone, Luanda, Lagos, Ottawa, Canberra, Wellington, Paris.
2 Ms Marianne Spiegel, US State Department.
3 Mr Edward Lanpher, First Secretary, US Embassy in London.

3. In discussion on the pre-independence arrangements we gave Lake a full account of our views on the procedure for the elections. It was our intention that, in accordance with Lusaka, these would be supervised under British Government authority with Commonwealth observers. We would propose to appoint a British election Commissioner who would be responsible for the supervision of all election arrangements from the printing of the ballot papers to the actual polling. The organisational arrangements for the election would have to be in the hands of the Rhodesian Administration. This would in practice mean the election directorate which had been responsible for the April elections. We also envisaged the creation of an electoral council on which all the parties taking part in the elections would probably need to be represented. This would provide a status for the Patriotic Front. The precise composition of this council would be a matter for the Election Commissioner himself to decide. The Commissioner would be responsible for ensuring that all political parties participating in the election were able to conduct their campaign without intimidation or harassment. They would have to be given free access to the media. It would be up to the Election Commissioner to ensure fair play.

4. In reply to questions we explained that we would not necessarily envisage British election staff being present at all polling booths on election day or days. We would however need to put a considerable number of staff on the ground during the actual period of the elections. To some extent the process would be self-policing in that the parties would themselves be keeping careful watch on each other and would know that they had, in the Electoral Council a body to which they could take complaints. The Council would not however have any executive role. Decision and action would rest with the Election Commissioner.

5. We confirmed that we would expect Commonwealth observers to be present during the electoral process. They would no doubt wish to be in the country during the immediate run-up to the election as well as the election itself. The precise arrangements for this and the composition of the Commonwealth observer group were matters for further discussion.

6. Given the distrust and suspicion of each side for the other, there was no hope of any joint political arrangements being agreed for the pre-independence period. Let alone the complications of a transitional constitution and transitional government such as the Patriotic Front envisaged. In our view, the only sensible thing, unwelcome as it was to us, was to bring Rhodesia under British Authority and leave it to the British to see fair play. British authority during the period up to independence would be asserted by the appointment of a governor with full executive and legislative authority. The existing public service would remain in being and the Governor would assume responsibility for the day to day administration of the country using the existing administrative machinery. Once the Governor had arrived he would conduct the administration of the country through the secretaries of the ministries, and the defence force commanders and the commissioner of police would report direct to him. Muzorewa and his Ministers would concentrate on the election campaign. The US Ambassador and Lake were insistent that, if our arrangements were to be regarded as fair to both sides, Muzorewa and the Ministers must play no part in the administration of the country. Lake suggested that it might make the re-assertion of British authority more evident if British personnel were attached to all ministries.

We said that we had not ourselves been thinking on these lines. In practice (although we did not say so to Lake) this is unlikely to be a starter. We explained however that there would be British supervision of the police force, which would mean the appointment of a number of British police liaison officers at various levels.

7. We explained that our present thinking was that the elections should be held on a party list system based, as the April elections, on regional lists. Since we were thinking of an election taking place within 2-3 months of the end of the Conference (not 3-4 months as Lake had imagined) there would be no time for a registration of voters and a delimitation of constituencies. We realised that this created problems e.g. what arrangements should be made for those in ZANLA and ZIPRA camps outside Rhodesia to vote? How could we decide for which of the regional lists they should cast their vote? However we would have to accept a number of inconsistencies and difficulties for the sake of a short election campaign, and in what was essentially a rough and ready solution to a difficult problem.

8. We made it clear that we were not thinking of any kind of UN peacekeeping force. This would be totally unacceptable to Muzorewa. The present Commonwealth attitude of implacable hostility to Muzorewa, recently reinforced by the Commonwealth Secretary-General's statement of 15 October, made it unlikely that even a Commonwealth force would be acceptable. The Americans pressed us on some form of observation, supervision or monitoring of the cease fire. If a Commonwealth force were ruled out could there not perhaps be a group of observers or monitors drawn from selected Commonwealth countries? We said that, if it were necessary to introduce any kind of monitoring arrangements in the context of the ceasefire, this would have to be a fairly modest arrangement. In reply to a question from Brewster, we made it clear that the Commonwealth observers would be concerned only with the election process and not with the cease-fire.

9. Lake raised a number of detailed questions about the implementation of the cease-fire, dealing with such matters as the responsibility for investigating breaches, what would happen if there were a major infringement of the cease-fire provisions, whether ZANLA and ZIPRA units would be allowed back into Rhodesia with their weapons etc. We acknowledged that these were important and difficult issues to which we as yet had no precise answers. They were matters that would have to be discussed at the appropriate stage between the military authorities on both sides. There were a number of options that could be considered ranging from the withdrawal of all existing forces to their present bases (i.e. ZANLA and ZIPRA to return to Mozambique and Zambia and the Rhodesians to withdraw into Rhodesia), to the allocation of certain areas within Rhodesia to the forces of the two sides. We made it clear that there was no possibility of our getting the Rhodesian security forces to accept restrictions on investigative patrolling in areas allocated to them.

10. Brewster reverted to the monitoring issue on several occasions. This is clearly a matter to which the Americans attach considerable importance. We were also asked whether we saw a continuing role for any monitoring group after independence to ensure that whatever government emerged did not act in an arbitrary way against its former opponents. We said that we saw little if any prospect of any such residual presence.

11. Lake asked how we were dealing with questions about aid, and in particular our attitude towards the Zimbabwe Development Fund. We explained that we

no longer regarded the Zimbabwe Development Fund as an active issue. If asked, we were saying that when the idea was originally launched, we found remarkably little enthusiasm for it amongst other governments and would not expect any more favourable reaction now. We had indicated that we were ready to help with assistance to economic and agricultural development (the Secretary of State's Statement of 11 October) and that we would do our best to encourage other governments to assist the new Government of Zimbabwe in this way. Lake explained that US assistance would probably be under the umbrella of existing US fund for regional development in Southern Africa. We made it clear that we were not thinking in terms of a regional fund as such. Our assistance would take the form of bilateral aid plus involvement in any multilateral assistance through e.g. The World Bank or the EEC.

12. Lake was understandably interested in the present position on sanctions. We explained that, although certain sanctions would lapse if Section 2 of the 1965 Southern Rhodesia Act were not renewed in mid-November, other sanctions legislation would require formal government action before it could be repealed. There was a possibility that Section 2 might lapse whilst the other sanctions remained in force. This might give us at least some partial and temporary cover in the United Nations. However political pressure for the total lifting of sanctions was considerable, if not irresistible, and we were fast approaching a situation in which all sanctions were likely to be lifted.

No. 128

Lord Carrington to Sir N. Henderson (Washington), 20 October, 4.45 p.m.[1]
Tel. No. 1468 Immediate, Confidential (FCO 36/2540)

MIPT[2]
Rhodesia

1. At the end of our meeting, we pointed out that although we were trying hard for an all party solution, the Patriotic Front might not participate and we therefore all had to face the possibility of a situation in which we were left with Muzorewa who had done all that had been asked of him. We had always said that no-one would have a veto of the outcome of the Conference. We should therefore be honour bound in such circumstances to go for a settlement with Muzorewa alone, lifting sanctions and granting independence. We would expect our friends to support us and to support Rhodesia. We would have to accept some damage elsewhere in Africa. Other Western countries who recognised Rhodesia in such circumstances would not suffer the same repercussions.

2. The Americans admitted that the compulsion to recognise Rhodesia in such a case would be very strong, especially if the Conference had in fact given the Patriotic Front a fair opportunity to participate: but the President would obviously have to consider US interests and his political situation. Much would depend on whether they felt comfortable enough with what was on the table to argue with their friends

---

[1] And for Information to UKMIS New York (Personal for Ambassador).
[2] No. 127.

in Africa and elsewhere. They were concerned about the problems that would follow on independence granted without the participation of the Patriotic Front. The war would proceed and we might find ourselves with some form of commitment to the independent Zimbabwe. When pressed however they agreed that in the circumstances we were discussing (an independent Zimbabwe with adequate Western support) there was a fair chance that the Rhodesians would gradually get on top of the war, and that support for it would diminish.

3. For Washington only. They concluded that it was important to stay in close touch, in order to understand each other's perceptions and minimize the risk of political embarrassment.

No. 129

Record of a private meeting between Sir I. Gilmour and Bishop Muzorewa at the Ferry House,[1] 21 October 1979
Secret (FCO 36/2440)

The *Lord Privy Seal* said that the fundamental point was whether the international community would recognise as free and fair an election held under the control of Bishop Muzorewa and the Salisbury Government. Even our closest allies would not do so. We had not let the Bishop down yet. But although we would if necessary be prepared to move ahead unilaterally with him and support him, we could not bring others with us unless the elections were demonstrably under our authority. If this were not the case, the outcome would be no better than after the April elections. *Bishop Muzorewa* said that he understood our view, but that beneath the superficial dimension of international acceptability was a deeper problem of how to preserve democracy and freedom in Rhodesia: we were like eminent surgeons summoned to operate on a famous patient. Of course we were doing our best to save him, but if the knife went too deep it could have fatal consequences. We should operate very judiciously. The appointment of a Governor would be seen as a dismissal of his government, which would thereby lose much of its credibility, whatever nice formulae were used to pretend otherwise. He did not see why a government of national unity elected by a vast majority of the people should undergo this. It would be appropriate if Mr Smith were still in power, but they had removed him.

The *Lord Privy Seal* said that the appointment of a Governor for the first time was necessary because Mr Smith had perverted Rhodesia's natural evolution and created deep suspicion of the Rhodesian Front. We were already going to the limits of credibility by proposing to retain the existing police and armed forces; it was not within our power to convince the world that an election would be fair unless the Bishop stood aside. *Sir A. Duff* said we realised that this was a personal decision for the Bishop. The *Lord Privy Seal* said there was no question of our asking for more. By standing aside he would achieve the immediate lifting of sanctions, independence and support from the democratic world. *Bishop Muzorewa* queried the attitude of our

1 Private residence of the Lord Privy Seal.

allies. The *Lord Privy Seal* said that the US Administration had reservations about our proposals for elections but that the question of who controlled the country in the interim period would be the litmus test for them. *Bishop Muzorewa* said that in addition to the problems which would arise if the government were 'sacked', he also doubted the move on practical grounds. Would the Governor respond to renewed guerrilla penetration if necessary by authorising pre-emptive attacks? Concern for Rhodesia's international image could not override her security. The *Lord Privy Seal* said that without a ceasefire there would be no agreement. We should be able to count on help from the Front Line Presidents, but in the worst event the Governor might have to declare that elections could not be held. If military actions of that kind had to be taken, it was surely in the Bishop's interest that the Governor and not he himself be responsible. It was important that General Walls should have confidence in the Governor, and we in the good sense of the security forces.

Bishop Muzorewa said the positions of the three delegations were far apart. He invited Lord Carrington to table the UK proposals as they stood and saw no harm in disagreement provided there remained an atmosphere of trust and communication between the Salisbury and UK delegations. He thought however that discussion in plenary with the Patriotic Front could seriously jeopardise this relationship. *Sir A. Duff* said that some discussions in plenary was inevitable. *Bishop Muzorewa* said that a majority of his delegation—and a fair cross-section were opposed to the UK proposal for a Governor with full powers—though for different reasons. For the Africans it was a question of their credibility in new elections. He would reflect further, but it would be difficult for him to persuade his delegation to swallow the pill unless it was demonstrated that there was no alternative. *Sir A. Duff* said that we too had thought and talked about it a great deal but could see no other way.

No. 130

Lord Carrington to Sir L. Allinson (Lusaka), 22 October 1979, 12.48 p.m.[1]
Tel. No. 858 Confidential, Immediate (FCO 36/2440)

My telno 492 to Canberra: Rhodesia Pre-Independence Arrangements.[2]

1. We shall be tabling in the Conference this afternoon the paper in MIFT,[2] which contains our proposals for implementing the Independence Constitution. You will be receiving by immediate telegram the text of the statement which the Secretary of State will make in tabling this paper.

2. You should hand over the statement and the paper to the government to which you are accredited. In doing so you should make the following points.

---

1 Deskby Lusaka 1400Z.; and Immediate to Mirimba, Salisbury, Gaborone, Lagos, Pretoria, Dar es Salaam (all Deskby 1400Z), Nairobi, Maputo, Luanda, Washington, Pretoria, Addis Ababa, Monrovia, Canberra, Ottawa, Wellington; Priority Abidjan, Dakar, Kinshasa, Khartoum, Tokyo, EEC Posts, Kuwait, Kingston, Bridgetown, Dacca, New Delhi, Singapore, Georgetown, La Paz, Nassau, Freetown, Port Louis, Mbabane, Port of Spain, Kampala, Lilongwe, Valletta, Banjul, Colombo, Accra, Kuala Lumpur, Nicosia, Castries, Oslo, Stockholm, Lisbon, Madrid, Manila, Tehran, Bucharest, Athens; Information Immediate UKMIS New York; Information Saving Suva, Port Moresby, Honiara, Nuku'alofa, Victoria, Tarawa, UKDEL NATO.
2 Not printed.

3. The essential step in implementing the Independence Constitution is the holding of free and fair elections in which all parties will be able to participate. These will take place as soon as possible.

4. Our proposals provide that a Governor appointed by HMG will assume executive and legislative authority until elections are held. All political leaders would devote themselves to the election campaign. It will be our responsibility to ensure that the administration of the country during the election, is impartial, in full accordance with the agreement at Lusaka that elections should be supervised under the British Government's authority.

5. The elections will be supervised by the British Election Commissioner and his staff to the full extent necessary to ensure that the process is fair to all the parties participating in them. The Election Council will provide a forum in which all parties can express their views on the conduct of the elections. But the supervision of the election is the British Government's responsibility and will be exercised through the Election Commissioner.

6. A cease-fire will be essential if arrangements on these lines are to be put into effect.

7. These proposals will allow elections to be held as soon as possible, under fair and impartial control, which will do nothing to prejudice the decisions of the future elected government.

8. It will be extremely difficult to secure the Salisbury delegation's acceptance of these proposals, which require them to accept the restoration of British authority. We believe that the only way to ensure that the Independence Constitution is put into effect on the basis of free and fair elections is to take charge ourselves. Britain has constantly been urged to carry out its responsibility as the de-colonising power. That is precisely what the present Government intends to do.

9. If there is a disposition to hark back to elements of earlier schemes, you should emphasise strongly that what we are now proposing is a real plan which we fully intend to put into effect-not theoretical proposals which are incapable of application. There will be strong opposition to our proposals from both sides. The Patriotic Front are being offered a fair chance to put their political standing to the test in elections which we will be prepared to supervise to the full extent necessary to ensure that they are completely fair as between the parties. If these proposals are accepted they will bring peace to the people of Rhodesia and to the neighbouring countries. We look to other governments to support our efforts to secure their acceptance.

10. In reply to questions you should say that:

(*a*) The elections must be held as soon as possible, the two months is all that is required to enable the parties participating in them fully to explain their policies to the people of Rhodesia. It will be extremely difficult to maintain a cease-fire for a longer period in the absence of a political decision about the future Government:

(*b*) It is not practically possible to replace the existing Rhodesian police force (or the civil service). But both the police force and the civil service will be responsible to him [the Governor]. There will be police advisers to carry out the task of supervision:

(*c*) (If asked about the status of Bishop Muzorewa and his ministers during the interim period.) We expect all political leaders, both the members of the present government and the Patriotic Front leaders, to devote themselves to the election campaign. The Governor will be responsible for the govt of the country. (You should not be drawn beyond paras 6, 10 and 11 of the Paper in MIFT, in response to questions as to whether Bishop Muzorewa and his Ministers will 'cease to be Ministers'):

(*d*) The Constitution of the country during the interim period will be provided by the Order in Council appointing the Governor. He will have full Executive and Legislative powers. The Salisbury Parliament will be dissolved.

(*e*) The UK Parliament will enact the Independence Constitution. There is no need for any other legislative action. If the Salisbury administration decide to put the Constitution through their Parliament, that is their affair. The Governor will not take up his post until the Salisbury Parliament has been dissolved.

(*f*) Negotiations on a cease-fire will take place between the parties, under our Chairmanship.

(*g*) Rhodesia is a British responsibility. There is no question of a UN peace-keeping force (nor is it likely that the UN could provide one). What is required is not a peace-keeping force, but a cease-fire. There will need to be arrangements to supervise the cease-fire.

(*h*) There is no question of trying to integrate the opposing forces during the interim period. It will be for the elected government to decide the future structure of the security forces. During the cease-fire the Rhodesian security forces will be under the Governor's authority.

(*i*) In answer to further questions about the elections themselves, you should say that we propose to enact the Constitution in time to allow relevant parts to be brought into operation as the basis for the elections. Since the elections will be held as soon as possible, full registration of voters and delimitation of constituencies will not be feasible. The elections will be held on a party list system.

(*j*) If asked at what stage in our proposals sanctions would be lifted, you should say that we need to consider the reactions of the parties to our proposals before deciding on any consequential action.

No. 131

Minute from Mr Renwick to Sir J. Graham, 24 October 1979[1]
Confidential (FCO 36/2480)

Rhodesia: Future Policy

1. As the Secretary of State requested, I *submit* papers dealing with the related problems of:

(*a*) our tactics in the Conference

(*b*) sanctions

(*c*) proceeding towards independence with Muzorewa alone.

2. Our main objective in the next few days must be to get Muzorewa's agreement to the interim arrangements and that the Salisbury Parliament will be dissolved,

---

1 Also sent to Mr Walden.

thereby committing him to elections and avoiding the dangers of the Rhodesian Front upsetting the agreement we have reached on the Constitution. If we can get this far, we should then exert maximum pressure on the Patriotic Front also to agree to the political arrangements for the interim. We should avoid opening negotiations on the military arrangements until that agreement has been achieved.

3. Unless we are prepared:

(*a*) to lift sanctions without any legal cover; or

(*b*) to grant independence forthwith without elections,

we shall have to proceed on the basis of effecting a return to legality. We should seek at every stage to approximate our actions as closely as possible to the Lusaka agreement and to hold open as long as possible the possibility for the Patriotic Front to participate. If we have the agreement of the Salisbury delegation we should be prepared to set in train the process of a return to legality in November. If the Patriotic Front do not participate, the Governor would be given more limited powers; the elections would be held as soon as possible; and legal independence would be granted thereafter.

4. No settlement without the Patriotic Front is likely to attract very much support in the international community. But the alternative of allowing sanctions to lapse and not doing anything to legalise the situation would leave us in a very difficult situation. To cut the present Government loose on the basis of legal independence forthwith would be liable to attract less international acceptance than the course we are recommending.

R.W. Renwick

Enclosures in No. 131

Rhodesia Conference: Future Tactics and Sanctions Legislation

1. The Secretary of State has asked to see a paper setting out options for our future tactics.

2. The three main problems are:

(*a*) how to bring the Conference to a conclusion;

(*b*) how to deal with sanctions;

(*c*) what proposals to make for a 'Muzorewa only' situation.

Future Tactics at the Conference

3. The Patriotic Front are determined not to walk out of the Conference. They are likely to try to spin out negotiations on the interim period in the hope that international (particularly Commonwealth) pressure will build up against us.

4. We must give the Patriotic Front a fair opportunity for discussion in plenary sessions, though protracted discussion of the interim arrangements is unlikely to be profitable. In any event we cannot proceed until we have the Salisbury delegation's support for our proposals.

5. If the Salisbury delegation are brought to accept these we will have nothing to gain from delay:

(*a*) we should find ourselves pushed up against the deadline of 15 November for renewal of Section 2 of the Southern Rhodesia Act (1965);

(*b*) the Patriotic Front will not be brought to the point of taking decisions on the interim unless they are under pressure not to exclude themselves from the process.

6. The Secretary of State has asked us to plan on the assumption that he will not wish to move an Order to renew Section 2 (though it would be possible to renew Section 2 on the grounds that we need its general powers, but in doing so to make it clear that we are amending the relevant sanctions Orders so that they would expire at the end of one or two months unless renewed).

7. If Section 2 is allowed to lapse, this would not mean the expiry of all sanctions. Direct trade with Rhodesia would still be prohibited and financial transfers would remain blocked by the exchange control machinery. But indirect trade e.g. via South Africa, would become possible and there would be no legislative obstacle to British oil companies supplying Rhodesia via South Africa. In practice an interval of more than about two weeks between the lapse of Section 2 and the lifting of other sanctions would be very hard to justify. But it would give some room for manoeuvre between 15 November and the end of the month if negotiations in the Conference were at an advanced stage.

8. There will be danger in allowing Section 2 to lapse if the Salisbury Parliament has not by then been dissolved, leaving open the possibility that the Rhodesian Front might block the independence Constitution (though a good deal of the sanctions legislation would still be in force and we could in the worst case take powers to continue sanctions). As it becomes apparent that we do not intend to renew Section 2, we shall run into accusations that our conduct at the Conference is related to the sanctions deadline. If we do not table an Order for renewal in the first week of November, it will soon be concluded that we do not intend to renew sanctions (though it would begin to give guidance to the effect that most sanctions would not automatically expire on 15 November). In terms of the tactical handling of the Conference, there will be much to be said for delaying to the last possible moment revealing a decision not to renew Section 2.

9. If sanctions are allowed to lapse, we shall be in flagrant breach of our international obligations if we have not (*a*) granted legal independence or (*b*) effected a return to legality. To grant legal independence to the present government in advance of new elections would deprive us of almost any support in the international community. These considerations point to the need, if we can achieve agreement with the Salisbury delegation before then, to effect the return to legality in mid-November or soon as possible thereafter. If, furthermore, the Salisbury delegation have accepted our proposals for the interim, they will not themselves be prepared to accept a long delay in the process of implementing them. Before revealing a decision not to renew Section 2, *we should get a firm commitment from Bishop Muzorewa* (*a*) *that he will accept our proposals* (*b*) *that he will dissolve the Salisbury Parliament.*

10. In terms of the Conference, if the Salisbury delegation have accepted by the first week of November, we must try to bring the Patriotic Front to take the decision to accept the political arrangements we have proposed for the interim, subject to agreement on the arrangements for a cease-fire. We should insist that the military negotiations should not be engaged until there is political agreement on the interim. We should exert maximum pressure through messages to the front-line Presidents, etc.

11. By 7 November, we should bring the Enabling Bill before Parliament. If Section 2 lapses, this must become law by 15 November. We would tell the front-line Presidents and others that the Bill is designed to ensure that the Government has the power to provide for the new Constitution and the arrangements for elections. This is fully consistent with our desire to reach a settlement involving the Patriotic Front. We would urge them to exert pressure on the latter to participate. It would be realised, however, that the introduction of the Bill implied that we were not seeking to renew Section 2.

12. The next stop would be to make clear our intention to make the Order in Council appointing the Governor. We should then be in a position to argue before the lapse of Section 2 that we were on the verge of bringing Rhodesia back to the legal status of a British dependent territory. We would still be urging the Patriotic Front to agree to a cease-fire and to participate.

13. If the Patriotic Front were still participating in negotiations in a positive spirit (having accepted interim arrangements and begun negotiations on a cease-fire) we could use the arguments in paragraph 12 above as justification for allowing Section 2 to lapse, on the grounds that an agreed solution was now very close, while deferring the removal of the remaining sanctions for a limited period.

14. As soon as we had achieved:

(*a*) the enactment of an Order in Council appointing a Governor;

(*b*) statements by Bishop Muzorewa and General Walls that they were ready to accept the Governor's authority;

(*c*) the dissolution of the Salisbury Parliament;

we would have a case to go to the Security Council and argue that legality was in the process of being restored.

14. [*sic*] In the absence of participation by the Patriotic Front there would be strong reactions in Africa and our argument will be strongly contested in the Security Council. (But our position would be better than if we simply allowed Section 2 to lapse.) We would be looking for a measure of support at least from the French and Americans and the US Congress would move to lift sanctions. We would continue to make clear that we were still trying for a solution involving the Patriotic Front. We would state that the return to legality was designed to facilitate this and not preclude it; but we could not allow the Patriotic Front to decide unilaterally that Rhodesia should remain in a state of illegality.

15. It will probably be best to proceed on the basis of an Order in Council appointing a Governor with the executive and legislative powers. This would be the best basis on which to secure some international support for the lifting of sanctions. We would argue that we were keeping open the possibility of Patriotic Front participation in the elections.

16. If, however, it became clear that the Patriotic Front would not participate in the elections and that the war would continue, it would be open to us to state that in that event we were not prepared to accept any direct responsibility for the war. The Governor, therefore, would act broadly in accordance with the arrangements in the 1961 Constitution. He would reserve to himself powers to deal with all matters affecting the elections and foreign affairs; but Bishop Muzorewa would be invited to form a care-taker government to deal with the day to day administration. We should

not, however, move to this stage so long as the possibility remained of the Patriotic Front participating. We should make clear from the outset that if the Patriotic Front did not participate, the Governor would exercise more limited powers.

Rhodesia: Proceeding to Independence without the Patriotic Front

1. If the Conference breaks down on a refusal by the Patriotic Front to accept the pre-independence arrangements, our objective will be to lift sanctions and grant Rhodesia independence on a basis which will:

(*a*) limit so far as possible the damage to our interests elsewhere;

(*b*) attract as much support as we can from other countries for the action we take and for Rhodesia.

2. We shall have little hope of achieving these objectives if we are in breach of our international obligations at the point at which we lift sanctions. In view of the parliamentary situation, we shall not be able to defer the lifting of sanctions until after elections have been held and legal independence has been granted.

3. One possible response to a Patriotic Front refusal to participate in elections under our authority would be to take action forthwith to bring Rhodesia to independence on the basis of the new Constitution, leaving it to the Rhodesian authorities to organise the elections and make the other arrangements needed to bring the Constitution into effect. We could argue that in these circumstances it would be pointless to hold new elections with the same parties participating and in the absence of a ceasefire, but such a course would be likely to attract very little international support. It would be represented as legalising the illegal regime. It would be criticised as being incompatible with the Lusaka agreement and as not fulfilling the Fifth Principle. The Patriotic Front would claim that it had always been our intention to implement the Constitution with Muzorewa alone. It would not be possible to take the necessary legislative action before sanctions lapsed.

4. If we lift sanctions *before* either independence has been granted or there has been a return to dependent status, we shall be in formal breach of our international obligations, and will have no case to argue in international law. This would put us in an extremely difficult position in the Security Council; and would certainly result in reprisals against us in Africa. The Congress might oblige the US Administration to lift sanctions; but it is questionable whether the Administration itself would support us. We would still be left with formal constitutional responsibility for Rhodesia. The need is for an arrangement which will (*a*) allow sanctions to be lifted before independence, (*b*) provide for elections to be supervised under the British Government's authority.

5. Our current planning assumes, therefore, that there will be a return to *legal dependent status* under a Governor appointed by the British Government. We would make constitutional provision for a re-assertion of British authority in Rhodesia, the Rhodesian administration would act in compliance with these provisions and we would then lift sanctions, arguing that the rebellion had come to an end and the basis for the mandatory resolutions on sanctions had fallen away. Elections would be held under our authority and independence would be granted on the basis of the new Constitution.

6. This course should offer us a reasonable prospect of attracting American and

some other Western support at the United Nations and elsewhere. It would not attract much African support, but there would be a prospect of limiting the damage to our interests elsewhere in Africa. Some moderate African Governments might begin progressively to normalise their relations with Rhodesia.

7. This approach would also enable us to claim that we were doing our utmost to fulfil the Lusaka agreement; and that we had left a way open for the Patriotic Front to participate in the elections up to the last possible moment. Provided that our authority was seen to be accepted, both Western and some African Governments would see force in the argument that sanctions should not continue to be applied against a part of our dominions which had accepted our authority. *To carry real conviction with the international community, the most effective course would be to proceed with the appointment of a British Governor with executive and legislative authority*. No one would then be able to contest the 'reality' of the return to legality or that elections really were being held under our authority. It would be possible to conduct the elections on a short timescale (the Rhodesian authorities have proposed that, if they reach agreement with us by mid-November, it would be possible to hold elections by the end of the year). General Walls would be prepared to give an undertaking in relation to cross-border raids in this period. But the serious disadvantage of this course, if we are proceeding without the Patriotic Front, is that it would involve us in a measure of responsibility for the war, which would be conducted under our direct authority.

8. A possible solution in this situation would be to effect a return to legality on a basis approximating as closely as possible to the situation which prevailed before the illegal declaration of independence. Sir Humphrey Gibbs, if he could be persuaded to take this on, might be re-appointed as Governor (but he is now 77 and is not really up to the job). The Governor would appoint Bishop Muzorewa to form a caretaker Administration on the basis of ministerial functions approximating to those in the 1961 Constitution. Mr Ian Smith and Mr Van der Byl, as signatories of the illegal declaration of independence, would not be re-appointed. The elections to bring the new Constitution into effect could still be held under the supervision or at least the observation of a British Election Commissioner. The Governor could be given reserved powers for all matters relating to the conduct of the elections and foreign affairs in the period before the elections were held. Such a solution would have some presentational advantages; but it would certainly be represented that Sir H. Gibbs was a figure-head.

9. Alternatively, we could appoint a British Governor, with legislative and executive authority, but with the proviso that he would act on the advice of Ministers (who would be appointed by Bishop Muzorewa) *except* in the exercise of certain reserved powers. The reserved powers could include all matters relating to the conduct of the election and to foreign affairs. Arrangements of this kind are well-precedented in colonies proceeding to independence. Bishop Muzorewa would agree in advance that he would not appoint Mr Ian Smith and Mr Van der Byl as Ministers.

10. Whichever of these courses was adopted, we should need to explain our reasons for departing from the proposals we put forward in Conference. We could seek to do so by making a statement on the lines of the attached draft.

11. If arrangements of this kind are made, elections to bring the new Constitution into effect under British supervision will still be important in terms of carrying

international opinion with us when independence is granted. There is a risk that a new election held so soon after that in April, and under the threat of Patriotic Front intimidation, will not result in a high turn-out (though in reply to criticism, we should point out, for example, there was only 35% poll in the recent elections in Nigeria). But General Walls and senior Rhodesian officials accept that a new election will be necessary and consider that it will be possible to hold a reasonably successful one. The alternative possibility of a referendum on the Constitution would be likely to produce a positive result. It would enable us to claim that there had been a demonstration of acceptability. But it would not be compatible with the terms of the Lusaka agreement. It would not enable us to hold open to the same extent the possibility of Patriotic Front participation. It would encounter strong resistance from some of their internal parties; and a partial election at any rate will be necessary to bring the new Constitution into effect. There are strong arguments, therefore, for proceeding with an election; and it would be much harder to receive a measure of international support if we are not prepared to do so.

Draft of a possible statement

Rhodesia: Implementation of Independence Constitution

1. The British Government has made clear, in the proposal for implementing the independence Constitution for Zimbabwe which it placed before the Constitutional Conference at Lancaster House on 22 October, that it is prepared to exercise its constitutional responsibilities to bring Rhodesia to independence by appointing a British Governor with full executive and legislative authority. The Governor's instructions will require him to be all things necessary to secure compliance with the conditions for free and fair elections. He will be responsible for the administration of the country during the election campaign. The Commanders of the Security Forces will be responsible to the Governor who will supervise the civil police in the maintenance of law and order.

2. Bishop Muzorewa's delegation have accepted these proposals. To the British Government's regret, the Patriotic Front have not. [They have declared their intention of continuing the war, and have withdrawn their acceptance of the independent Constitution.]

3. The British Government has an obligation to implement the Constitution which it has said it is prepared to commend to the British Parliament as the basis for independence. The Rhodesian party other than the Patriotic Front which were represented at the Constitutional Conference have called on Britain to do so and have expressed their willingness to return to legal dependent status as part of Her Majesty's Dominions to enable elections to be held for the purposes of the new Constitution.

4. The British Government is not in these circumstances prepared to assume a responsibility for that administration of Rhodesia which would imply also an assumption of direct responsibility for the conduct of the war. In the absence of a ceasefire, and given the refusal of the Patriotic Front to accept an assumption of British responsibility on the terms offered to the Constitutional Conference, the British Government therefore propose to return Rhodesia to legal dependent status and to implement the Constitution of Zimbabwe, on a basis approximating to that

which prevailed in Southern Rhodesia before the illegal declaration of independence. To this end they will appoint a Governor, who will have reserved powers in relation to foreign affairs and all matters concerning the elections.

5. The elections will be supervised by a British Election Commissioner. Bishop Muzorewa will be asked to form a caretaker government to deal with the day to day administration of the country in the period before the elections are held.[1]

---

1 Sir J. Graham minuted, on 24 October, that he preferred the solution proposed in para 8 of the second paper—the appointment of a British (or a non-Rhodesian) Governor with reserved powers, sticking as close as possible to the Lusaka procedures. But the difficulties of this course, and his fear that retaliation would not be confined to the African states but could spread through the Middle East and perhaps elsewhere (Libya, Iraq, Iran), argued strongly for a real and continued effort to get the Patriotic Front to agree. He added: 'I foresee great difficulty in persuading anybody to take on the job!'

No. 132

Lord Carrington to Sir N. Henderson (Washington), 25 October 1979, 8.20 p.m.[1]
Tel. No. 1510 Immediate, Confidential, (FCO 36/2540)

Rhodesia: Consultations with the Americans

1. On 22 October we gave a full explanation of our proposals for the interim period to the US Embassy and expressed the hope that the Americans would take action in support of them. We explained that our objective in the next stage of the Conference was to seek agreement on the general arrangements we had put forward for the interim period. This could be subject to subsequent agreement on the arrangements for a cease-fire and its supervision. The negotiation of a cease-fire will be the last and most difficult task before the Conference. There will be much greater chance of success if a further measure of political agreement has been reached before those negotiations are engaged. We would be ready to seek to arrange negotiations under our chairmanship between the military commanders on both sides once agreement has been reached on the arrangements for elections and the administration of the country in the interim. We added that we could not agree (and there would be no prospect of the Salisbury Delegation agreeing) to arrangements going well beyond the Lusaka Agreement e.g. a UN or Commonwealth peace-keeping force and UN or Commonwealth supervision of the elections.

2. The US Embassy informed us this morning that Mr Vance has approved instructions to US Embassies in the Front-Line States and Nigeria to support our proposals for the interim in the terms set out below. The State Department would take the same position publicly, except for the sentences in brackets.

---

1 And to Immediate Mirimba, Salisbury (Deskby 26 October, 0900z.), Nairobi, Maputo, Gaborone, Dar es Salaam, Luanda, Lagos, Lusaka, Pretoria, Addis Ababa, Monrovia, Canberra, Ottawa, Wellington; Priority Abidjan, Dakar, Kinshasa, Khartoum, Tokyo, EEC Posts, Kuwait, Kingston, Bridgetown, Dacca, New Delhi, Singapore, Georgetown, La Paz, Nassau, Freetown, Port Louis, Mbabane, Port of Spain, Kampala, Lilongwe, Valletta, Banjul, Colombo, Accra, Kuala Lumpur, Nicosia, Castries, Oslo, Stockholm, Lisbon, Madrid, Manila, Tehran, Bucharest, Athens, Maseru; Information Immediate UKMIS New York; Information Saving Suva, Port Moresby, Honiara, Nuku'alofa, Victoria, Tarawa, UKDEL NATO.

(*a*) We believe that the principles put forward in the British proposals offer a positive framework for the pre-independence arrangements.

(*b*) The United States supports the assertion of UK authority in Salisbury in order to bring the independence Constitution into force. The principle of British authority over the elections, as recognized in the Lusaka communique, is a positive one.

(*c*) We urge the parties to the conflict to work closely with the British Government in working out satisfactory agreements on management of the elections and a cease-fire that are fair to all.

(*d*) Agreement on transition arrangements, as on the Constitution, will require real compromise on both sides. (Just as concessions have been asked of ZAPU and ZANU, Salisbury also has been asked to make concessions—such as assumption of all legislative and executive authority by a UK Governor.)

(*e*) Significant progress has been made at Lancaster House: and we believe a settlement is possible if the parties continue to seriously seek arrangements that will be fair to all. (We appreciate the Front-Line's continuing efforts to help assure that this hope for peace will not be destroyed by unrealistic demands for predominance on either side.)

3. My thanks have been passed on to Mr Vance through the US Ambassador. Unless you see objection please make clear to the State Department we are grateful for the action they are taking and that we hope that the US State Department spokesman will indicate clearly that the US Government support our proposals.

4. Posts in the Front-Line states and Lagos should consult with their US colleagues. For their guidance we have explained to the Americans that we shall not be prepared to agree to an interim period significantly longer than the two months we have proposed. It is the British Government which has to undertake direct responsibility for Rhodesia in this period and we shall not be prepared to do so for longer than is necessary to enable all the parties to campaign and put their case freely to the people of Rhodesia. We do not believe that a longer period is compatible with the preservation of the cease-fire or with the requirement that all the parties should commit themselves to the election campaign leaving us free to conduct the administration of the country on a caretaker basis until the people of Rhodesia have been able to decide their political future.

No. 133

Minute from Mr Renwick to Mr Walden, 25 October 1979[1]
Confidential (FCO 36/2540)

Rhodesia: Consultations with the Americans

1. Following up Sir A. Duff's talks with Mr Lake on 19 October, I gave the US Embassy an explanation on 22 October of the transitional proposals we were tabling in the Conference and expressed the hope that we would get their support. The attached reply[2] has been approved by Mr Vance. If the Secretary of State agrees,

[1] Also sent to Sir J. Graham.
[2] Not printed.

I will ask the Americans to instruct their posts in Africa—as they have offered to do—to support our proposals on the interim. The State Department spokesman will be prepared to make a statement to that effect.

2. I have explained to the Americans that our intention—as they have been aware from the outset of the Conference—is to seek agreement on the general proposals for the interim, before going on to tackle the question of the cease-fire and arrangements for supervising it. The Americans accept that this is a sensible approach and is likely to be the only way to get agreement. Agreement on the interim proposals could of course be conditional on both sides on the subsequent arrangements for the cease-fire. When we come to that point, the Americans will attach importance to some arrangement for monitoring the cease-fire. I have made clear to them the difficulties about UN and Commonwealth involvement. I have explained that we envisage a cease-fire Commission under the chairmanship of the Governor's military adviser, on which the Commanders on both sides would be represented. I have no doubt that it would help greatly to get American support at that stage if we were able to indicate that we will be prepared to play a role in the monitoring of a cease-fire.

R.W. RENWICK

No. 134

Lord Carrington to Sir L. Allinson (Lusaka), 26 October 1979, 4.20 p.m.[1]
Tel. No. 876 Confidential, Immediate (FCO 36/2440)

Rhodesia: Constitutional Conference

1. At a plenary meeting on 26 October the Patriotic Front tabled two papers on the interim period (texts being telegraphed separately). In these papers the Patriotic Front seek to insist on a UN peace-keeping force, a UN police force and UN supervision of the elections.

2. In response, I made clear that the British Government are not prepared to go beyond what was agreed at Lusaka. It was agreed that it was the British Government's responsibility to bring Rhodesia to independence and that the Government formed under the Independence Constitution 'must be chosen through free and fair elections, properly supervised under British Government authority, and with Commonwealth Observers'. It would be for the British Government to supervise elections: there was no question of UN or other supervision.

3. Mr Nkomo said that in view of my statement it would be necessary for the Patriotic Front to appeal to the Commonwealth. I replied that the Patriotic Front could communicate with anyone it pleased. I had taken part in the conclusion of the Agreement at Lusaka and I would not be prepared to depart from that Agreement.

---

1 And to Immediate Mirimba, Salisbury, Nairobi, Maputo, Gaborone, Dar es Salaam, Luanda, Lagos, Washington, Pretoria, Addis Ababa, Monrovia, Canberra, Ottawa, Wellington, Peking, Moscow, Prague; Priority Abidjan, Dakar, Kinshasa, Khartoum, Tokyo, EEC Posts, Kuwait, Kingston, Bridgetown, Dacca, New Delhi, Singapore, Georgetown, La Paz, Nassau, Freetown, Port Louis, Mbabane, Port of Spain, Kampala, Lilongwe, Valletta, Banjul, Colombo, Accra, Kuala Lumpur, Nicosia, Castries, Oslo, Stockholm, Lisbon, Madrid, Manila, Tehran, Bucharest, Athens; Information Immediate UKMIS New York; Information Saving Suva, Port Moresby, Honiara, Nuku'alofa, Victoria, Tarawa, UKDEL NATO.

4. Mr Mugabe said he could not understand why the Conference should consider itself bound by the Lusaka Communique. It should be open to the Conference to 'enhance' the Lusaka Agreement. I said that the question of the British Government's responsibility and of our supervision of elections were for us matters of principle and we would not be prepared to depart from them. The British Government had accepted its responsibility to bring Rhodesia to independence. We were ready to appoint a Governor with full powers and an Election Commissioner to carry out this responsibility. We had ourselves consulted several Commonwealth Governments within the last few days, and none of them had questioned this point.

5. It is important that there should be no misunderstandings of our position by the government to which you are accredited. You should take any action you think necessary to ensure that this is so. You should emphasise that Britain is prepared to carry to the full its responsibility to bring Rhodesia to independence, as our proposal to appoint a Governor and the extent of his powers clearly demonstrates. You should draw at your discretion on FCO telno 851 to Lusaka.[2]

2 Not printed.

No. 135

Minute from Mr Luce to Lord Carrington, 26 October 1979
Confidential (FCO 36/2565)

Visit to Africa: 19-25 October

1. I saw Presidents Kaunda, Nyerere and Shagari (Nigeria) and the Foreign Ministers of Botswana, Mozambique, Angola and Liberia.

2. My tour served two main purposes:

(*a*) to demonstrate to the governments concerned that we valued their cooperation and wished to keep in close touch with them;

(*b*) to explain our proposals for the pre-independence period and to persuade them that these arrangements were sound and merited their support.

Reception

3. I was welcomed everywhere with friendship and courtesy. All those I saw expressed satisfaction that agreement had been reached on the Constitution. No-one sought to re-open constitutional issues; nor did they question that the Constitution provided for genuine majority rule.

Attitudes to Pre-Independence Arrangements

4. Attitudes towards the pre-independence arrangements were not fully informed. There was a general recognition (and admiration) of the determination of the Government to assume full authority for the decolonising process. Everyone hoped that we would succeed. There were, however, some reservations about our proposals, which were expressed, with varying degrees of emphasis, in all capitals. These related to

(*a*) *The duration of the pre-independence period*

No-one thought two months sufficient for the Patriotic Front to organise their campaign. We will not get Front Line support for this. Even three months will be hard to sell.

(b) The control of the Security Forces

The preservation, intact, of the present Rhodesian Security Forces was regarded as likely to favour Muzorewa and to prejudice the chances of a genuinely fair election. There were doubts as to the ability of the Governor to control effectively the activities of the Security Forces, and of other elements of the existing administration.

(c) The Cease-Fire

There are anxieties about the maintenance of the cease-fire in the absence of any peace-keeping or monitoring force. Shagari and Jorge[1] thought that there was a case for some kind of Commonwealth Force.

(d) Electoral Register

The lack of an electoral register casts doubts, in some minds, about the integrity of the election process.

Relations with the Patriotic Front

5. Several of those to whom I spoke stressed that it was not helpful if they were made to appear, publicly, to be pressurising the Patriotic Front. However, if we could convince the Front Line leaders that our pre-independence proposals were genuinely fair, they would do their best to help us to find a satisfactory settlement.

Appointment of Governor

6. We still have a lot of convincing to do. The stature and personality of the Governor will be very important. There will be a greater disposition to accept our pre-independence plans, even those unattractive to the Patriotic Front, if the Governor is someone who inspires confidence. This point was made specifically to me by Kaunda. An early announcement of the Governor's appointment might therefore be helpful.

Sanctions

7. The sanctions issue was only raised by the Liberian Foreign Minister[2], This does not imply that it is not regarded as important. The non-renewal of Section 2 in mid-November, in the absence of a settlement at Lancaster House, will make it more difficult to keep the understanding and support of the Front Line. The way in which we handle and present this in the Conference and with the Front Line will be most important.

Further Contact

8. Continued personal contact with key African leaders will pay dividends. They regard such visits as evidence of our determination to find a just settlement and of our desire to take their views into account, even if we do not necessarily agree with them. Our main targets should be Kaunda, Nyerere and Machel. A further brief visit to at least these three could be valuable if it looks as if we are heading for a deadlock in our negotiations with the Patriotic Front.

RICHARD LUCE[3]

---

1 Mr Paulo Teixeira Jorge, Foreign Minister of Angola, 1976-84.
2 Mr (Charles) Cecil Dennis.
3 Signed by his Private Secretary, Keith Manning, in the absence of the Minister.

No. 136

Lord Carrington to Sir L. Allinson (Lusaka), 27 October 1979, 4.35 p.m.[1]
Tel. No. 880 Unclassified (FCO 36/2440)

Rhodesia: Constitutional Conference

1. At a plenary meeting on the morning of 27 October the Lord Privy Seal took the Chair in my absence on a visit to Norway. He began by making a statement commenting on the Patriotic Front papers tabled on the 27 October about interim arrangements (Text in MIFT).[2]

2. In response to the Chairman's opening statement, Mr Mugabe questioned the usefulness of the Conference. The Lord Privy Seal observed that the usefulness of the Conference was self-evident. A great deal of progress had been made. This was the result of concessions by both sides. Britain as the constitutionally responsible authority had to make proposals. Our room for manoeuvre was limited by the need to reach agreement with both sides. Mr Mugabe said that our proposals favoured the illegal regime, which had committed treason. Mr Nkomo said that without an international force a cease-fire would break down. The Patriotic Front would not allow Britain to organise a massacre of its people.

3. Bishop Muzorewa said that he strongly resented the suggestion that he had committed treason. His administration had nothing to do with UDI. He then read out the statement in my second MIFT[3] accepting our proposals for the interim period. Sithole spoke in similar terms: The Patriotic Front did not appear to realise that the regime which had been responsible for UDI had been replaced. The principle of one man one vote was no longer an issue.

4. The Chairman said that the Conference had now been in progress for several weeks. He proposed a further meeting in the afternoon to discuss arrangements for the elections. The Patriotic Front insisted on an adjournment to enable them to respond to Bishop Muzorewa's statement.

---

1 Deskby 280800Z to Oslo. And to Immediate Mirimba, Salisbury, Nairobi, Maputo, Gaborone, Dar es Salaam, Luanda, Lagos, Washington, Pretoria, Addis Ababa, Monrovia, Canberra, Ottawa, Wellington, Peking, Moscow, Prague; Priority Abidjan, Dakar, Kinshasa, Khartoum, Tokyo, EEC Posts, Kuwait, Kingston, Bridgetown, Dacca, New Delhi, Singapore, Georgetown, La Paz, Nassau, Freetown, Port Louis, Mbabane, Port of Spain, Kampala, Lilongwe, Valletta, Banjul, Colombo, Accra, Kuala Lumpur, Nicosia, Castries, Oslo, Stockholm, Lisbon, Madrid, Manila, Tehran, Bucharest, Athens; Information Immediate UKMIS New York; Information Saving Suva, Port Moresby, Honiara, Nuku'alofa, Victoria, Tarawa, UKDEL NATO.
2 Not printed.
3 Not printed; but Bishop Muzorewa's acceptance of the interim arrangements included agreement that his own government would stand aside during the interim period.

No. 137

Lord Carrington to Sir N. Henderson (Washington), 29 October 1979, 9.59 a.m.[1]

Tel. No. 1527 Immediate, Confidential (FCO 36/2540)

Rhodesia

1. Unless you see objection please pass the following message from me to Mr Vance. Begins:

Dear Cy, I am very grateful for the action you have taken to support our proposals to bring the independence Constitution for Rhodesia into effect. They have now been accepted by Bishop Muzorewa, despite strong resistance from Ian Smith. This was not an easy decision for the Bishop or his delegation: our proposals involve him relinquishing power and accepting a British Governor with Executive and Legislative authority. He has dealt courageously with resistance from members of his own delegation: and he has in my judgement now been pushed as far as it will be possible for him to go.

Richard Luce has been in Africa to give a full explanation of our thinking to the Front-Line Presidents. His reports, which I have arranged for your embassy to receive, have been reasonably encouraging. The proposal that we should assume direct responsibility for Rhodesia through the appointment of a Governor for the period to enable elections to be held has been generally welcomed.

I am emphasising to the Patriotic Front that our proposals offer them a perfectly fair chance to put their political support to the test in elections which we shall be prepared to supervise to the full extent necessary to ensure that all the parties participating in them are able to do so on an equal basis. During the interim period the security forces, the police and the civil service will be under the Governor's authority and responsible to him. The appointment of an election commissioner and his staff will enable us to supervise the conduct of the elections at all levels. These proposals are fully in accordance with the Lusaka Agreement. We shall not, however, be able to accept arrangements which go well beyond the scope of what was agreed at Lusaka or which would deny us the authority to exercise our responsibility.

If we can secure acceptance of our proposals for the elections and the administration in the interim period, we can move on to discussions on the cease-fire and the arrangements for maintaining it. We remain of the view that it will be necessary to tackle this very difficult problem once agreement has been reached on the general proposals for the interim period.

With Muzorewa's acceptance, there is no doubt that it will be possible to put this plan into effect. The proposals offer the only practical possibility to enable elections to be held in which both sides could participate. That is the key to the end of the war.

I am concerned about the Zambian attitude. The Prime Minister has just received another message from Kaunda, to which she will be replying. If Kaunda can be persuaded to support us, a peaceful settlement will be within our grasp. I am disturbed by the air of unreality about Kaunda's thinking, his tendency towards uncritical

---

[1] And Immediate to Lusaka, Lagos, Gaborone, Maputo, Dar es Salaam and UKMIS New York.

support of the Patriotic Front and a failure to realise that we have a real opportunity to bring about both of his major objectives—peace and genuine majority rule. It would be very helpful if you could make a further effort with the Front-Line States generally and with Kaunda in particular to impress upon him the sincerity of our intentions and our determination to ensure that the Patriotic Front will be given a fair chance in the elections, if they are prepared to participate.

Ends.

2. You may pass to the State Department the text of Kaunda's message in Lusaka telno 1154[1]. We will be telegraphing in due course the text of the Prime Minister's reply.

1 Not printed.

No. 138

Lord Carrington to Sir L. Allinson (Lusaka), 30 October 1979, 11.05 a.m.[1]
Tel. No. 888 Immediate, Confidential (FCO 36/2523)

My tel No. 351 to Dar es Salaam: Rhodesia[2]
Following is text of message to President Kaunda:[3]
Dear Kenneth,

Thank you for talking so fully to Richard Luce on 20 October and for your subsequent letter about the Rhodesia Conference which reached me on 27 October.

2. I agree with most of the points you make in your letter and in particular that we are closer now to a solution than we have ever been before. There are one or two points on which we take a different view. These may not be important in relation to the area of agreement between us, but I would like to explain why.

3. You are concerned that two months may not be enough to arrange for the holding of elections. I cannot believe that any of the parties will need more than two months to state their case to the electorate, and this is what is essential. It is Britain which will have to take direct responsibility for Rhodesia in this period. We will only be prepared to do so under conditions and for a period in which we can be confident that we will be able to carry out that responsibility. What is required is not a complicated transitional structure, which would render it impossible for us to carry out our responsibility, but for the people of Rhodesia to be enabled to decide for themselves, what government they want in fair elections. The longer the interim period lasts before the people of Rhodesia have been given the chance to decide their political future for themselves, the greater will be the risk of a break-down of the cease-fire. It is very much in the Rhodesian people's interests and in those of the people of the neighbouring countries that they should be given the opportunity as soon as possible. We shall not be prepared to transfer power to any party which has not won it through fair elections.

1 And for Information Immediate to UKMIS New York, Washington and Canberra.
2 Not printed.
3 Message sent by the Prime Minister.

4. The registration of voters would be likely to take much longer then the six months you envisage. This would be too long to wait to resolve a problem which is of extreme and growing urgency. We have no doubt that it will be possible, as it has been in other countries, to carry out a fair election without prior registration, provided there are adequate safeguards against double voting and other mal-practices.

5. I entirely agree that an effective cease-fire must be an essential part of any agreement on the arrangements leading to independence. The essential ingredient in this will be the political will of the parties themselves to observe the cease-fire and to stand by the result of the elections, whatever it may be. I do not share your interpretation that at Lusaka there was agreement to an international force. But when we reach that stage of the negotiations we shall be ready to arrange discussions about a cease-fire between the military commanders on both sides: and this must include effective arrangements for its observance.

6. What we must seek in the next phase of the conference is the agreement of both sides of the general structure of the interim period—namely the re-assertion of British authority, a Governor with full executive and legislative authority exerting direct control over the administration, and the arrangements for elections. The proposals we have put forward involve major concessions by Bishop Muzorewa. He and his colleagues have agreed to relinquish power to enable new elections to be held under our authority. This has involved very difficult decisions for him, in the interests of achieving international recognition and the prospect of a peaceful settlement. There is no doubt, therefore, that unlike some previous efforts to reach a settlement, we are in a position to put these plans into effect. If they are accepted by both sides, it will be possible to proceed to the final phase of the conference, which must concern itself with the negotiations for a cease-fire. I have no doubt that it will be very much easier to resolve the difficulties which are likely to arise in that phase of the negotiations on the basis of prior agreement by both sides on the acceptance of British Authority and our general proposals for the interim period.

7. I very much hope that the Patriotic Front will accept the sincerity of our intentions and our determination to ensure the impartiality of the election process. In that event a solution will be within our grasp. In view of all this would mean for the people of Rhodesia and for Zambia, I hope that you will be prepared to use your influence to persuade the Patriotic Front too of the need for compromise.

No. 139

Lord Carrington to Sir D. Tebbit (Canberra), 30 October 1979, 8.06 p.m.[1]
Tel. No. 526 Immediate, Confidential (FCO 36/2531)

Personal for High Commissioner.
MIPT[2]
Following is text of message from Prime Minister to Mr Fraser.
Begins:
Thank you for your message about Rhodesia. I am grateful for what you say about the extent of what has been achieved so far in the talks at Lancaster House. We really have made progress and I only hope we can keep it up. I am also grateful for your suggestion that you are prepared to do whatever you can to help.

As you will know, we put forward our proposals for the pre-independence arrangements on 22 October. These involve the assumption by Britain of direct responsibility for Rhodesia in this period. We are taking action to give effect step by step to the agreement we reached at Lusaka. But we will only be prepared to do so under conditions and for a period in which we can be confident that we will be able to carry out that responsibility. We will not be able to agree to arrangements which go well beyond what was agreed at Lusaka—still less to any attempts to re-interpret or re-formulate that agreement—or which would render the task of supervising the administration impossible for us.

It is central to our conception that in the interim period the Governor should be responsible for the day to day administration. The role of the political leaders in this period would be to commit themselves to the election campaign and not to seek to set up parallel administrations of their own or to impede the Governor in his task. There will be an Election Council on which all parties will be represented. The longer the interim period lasts before the people of Rhodesia are given the chance to decide their political future for themselves, the greater will be the risk of a break-down of the cease-fire. We will not be prepared to assume responsibility for the administration of Rhodesia for longer than is necessary to enable elections to be held in which all the parties will be able to participate with equal chances of success.

Bishop Muzorewa has announced his acceptance of our proposals. I am sure you will realise that this was a very difficult and painful decision for him. He is being asked to relinquish power, to entrust both executive and legislative authority to a British Governor, and to go through elections for the second time in 9 months, this time with Patriotic Front participation: and he has agreed to do so. There is a tendency to imagine that we are engaged in negotiations only with the Patriotic Front: and that there is no need to take account of the views of the Salisbury delegation. This is not the case. Bishop Muzorewa has now been pushed as far as possible in this negotiation. We shall not be able to require him to do more.

It is essential to our strategy in this phase of the Conference that we should first seek agreement on the general proposals we have put forward for the interim period. If these are accepted, we will be able to proceed to the final phase of the Conference.

---

1 To reach Canberra Deskby 310001Z. Variants were sent to other Commonwealth leaders: see Nos. 141 and 142.
2 Not printed.

This will involve negotiations between the commanders on both sides, under our chairmanship, on a cease-fire and its observance.

You raise the question of the status of the Rhodesian armed forces and of the forces controlled by the Patriotic Front. The Rhodesian security forces in this period will be under the authority of the Governor who will have a senior British officer as his military adviser. The police will be supervised by the Governor, who will have a police adviser and supporting staff. The commanders of the Patriotic Front will also be responsible to the Governor, in relation to the maintenance of the cease-fire. There will be a cease-fire commission, under the chairmanship of the Governor's military adviser, on which the commanders of both sides will be represented. The responsibility for dealing with breaches of the cease-fire will in the first instance rest with them. There will also need to be arrangements for monitoring the ceasefire. Some Commonwealth participation in this could be valuable and I am grateful to you for your readiness to help. We shall be asking Sir Donald Tebbit to pursue this with you. Bishop Muzorewa will not, however, be prepared to accept any role in relation to supervision of the ceasefire for governments which are already committed to support the Patriotic Front.

As regards the electoral process, we agreed at Lusaka to accept Commonwealth observers and will, of course, make arrangements for them to be able to witness the elections.

I agree with you that we are closer now to a break-through than ever before. The difference between the plan we have put forward and previous proposals which had been made for a settlement is the very important one that we are in a position to put this plan into effect. We hope that the Patriotic Front will agree to participate and we shall be intensifying our efforts to get them to do so. It will not, however, be possible to put into effect some other plan: and it would be fatal to the chances of success if the Patriotic Front were led to believe that it may be.

I would like to make one final point. Bishop Muzorewa has accepted the Independence Constitution. He is prepared to hand over power to a British Governor, and he is ready to face new elections. In these circumstances I would be misleading you if I led you to believe that the British Government would consider it reasonable for Rhodesia to remain in a state of illegality if the Patriotic Front were not prepared to put their political support to the test in elections under our authority. I hope very much that they will participate. We shall be continuing our efforts to get them to do so.

Ends.

No. 140

Minute from Mr Lyne to Mr Renwick, 30 October 1979
Secret and Personal (FCO 36/2441)

Meeting Between the Secretary of State and Mr Nkomo

As you know, Mr Nkomo met Lord Carrington at Ovington Square[1] from 6.30 pm to 7.30 pm this evening. Other than himself, no one else was present. Nkomo began with a long, detailed and moderately-phrased presentation of his current position on our proposals. He stressed the need for Patriotic Front representation on some form of Governing Council. The Patriotic Front accepted the Governor but saw some such relationship, with the British included on the Salisbury side, Nkomo could tell Lord Carrington unofficially that the Patriotic Front were prepared to move to 4/4 position with the British outside (as Chairman?). He also complained about the shortness of the interim period, though he said he understood the reasons why we were opposed to a six month interim.

Nkomo's main worry however was the continuation of the war after any elections. We should try to understand that position on the ground. The Patriotic Front forces were widely scattered over the country. They had arms caches, including all types of weapons, in caves and elsewhere. It would take a long time for word to get through about a ceasefire. Some of his own men would recognise his voice on radio, but not everyone. In his only indirect criticism of Mugabe and ZANU, Nkomo said that some people said that ZANU would not observe the ceasefire. We had to recognise the reality that had developed during the war.

It was no good our saying that the Governor in Salisbury would oversee the ceasefire. How could Nkomo persuade his men, who had their pride as fighters, to 'jump into the fire to put it out'? How could he persuade them that their security would be guaranteed by the Governor using the Salisbury forces? He understood our reasons for declining a UN presence; the Patriotic Front itself had only come round to a UN force late on in the discussions of the Anglo/American Proposals. But some international force, e.g. based on the Commonwealth, would be essential. Otherwise everything could easily go up in smoke. We must take account of the attitudes which had developed during the war. (Later in the discussion Nkomo referred indirectly to the need to gather Patriotic Front forces together in specific locations if the ceasefire was to work.) He implied that the Patriotic Front forces were to be disarmed; Lord Carrington denied this, and Nkomo commented that this showed how necessary it was for us to put our full proposals on the table.

Mr Nkomo also stressed the problem of his personal security. When he had mentioned to his wife on the telephone that he might go back to Rhodesia to fight an election, she had been very concerned. How was it possible to entrust his security to the sort of people who had wrecked his house in Lusaka in an attempt to assassinate him?[2] (Lord Carrington indicated later on in the conversation that he fully understood this problem and agreed that the Governor would have to pay special attention

1 Private home of the Foreign Secretary.
2 On Good Friday 1979, Rhodesian Security Forces had crossed into Zambia bound for Lusaka in an attempt to assassinate Nkomo. The mission was codenamed Operation Bastille.

to the personal security of the leaders of all the parties. Though we had not discussed the issue in detail he thought it might be possible to make provisions for Nkomo's bodyguards, and perhaps for the Special Branch people who had been protecting him in London, to do so in Rhodesia).

In restating the British position, Lord Carrington stressed the difficulty we had had in persuading the Salisbury Delegation first to amend the Constitution, and secondly to accept new elections, temporarily relinquishing power in the process. Many people imagined that we were negotiating simply with the Patriotic Front and forgot that we had to deal with the Salisbury side too. He fully understood Nkomo's problems; but we had our own. Nkomo might not like to hear this said, but the Bishop considered that he had won a fair election. There was no alternative to relying on the present police force, and it would be misleading for him to suggest otherwise. Lord Carrington dismissed a suggestion by Mr Nkomo that the Patriotic Front had a trained police force too.

Nkomo (with some irritation) refused to take cognisance of the position of the Bishop or the blacks on the Salisbury Delegation, though he recognised that the whites had been obliged to make concessions. (Nkomo here made an oblique reference to his negotiations with Mr Smith in the past.) He insisted that if we continue our present path, the Rhodesian people would see the arrival of a white Governor as a move to legitimise a white government exercising power through white-dominated security forces, and as a means of removing sanctions. It was clear from General Walls' performance on television last night that he felt he would have a licence under our proposals to recruit whites abroad to finish off the guerrillas.

He returned again to his personal security, recalling that whatever the protection, a number of whites would be gunning for him as the man accused of shooting down the Viscount. He appealed as he had done in the Conference this morning, to Lord Carrington to give very careful consideration to what he and Silundika had said about the conditions for the elections. This was a very serious problem and could only lead to a continuation of war if we continued in our present course. Lord Carrington emphasised that his role as Chairman gave him very little room for manoeuvre. Nobody would be fully satisfied with the outcome of the Conference. Nkomo must accept that he was determined to achieve free and fair elections. He must also feel able to come and see Lord Carrington again whenever he wished. Without replying directly, Nkomo said that it was not easy for him to see Lord Carrington in this way; he would always be suspected of letting his partners down, whatever he did.

R.M.J. LYNE
PP (G.G.H. WALDEN)

No. 141

Sir H. Smedley (Wellington) to Lord Carrington, 31 October 1979, 4.41 a.m.
Tel. No. 362 Confidential, Immediate (FCO 36/2531)

MIPT: Rhodesia[1]

1. Mr Muldoon[2] asked me whether PM's message[3] was specific to him or in common form to other Commonwealth PMs. I said my instructions did not tell me this. However cautious phraseology of sentence he had questioned suggested to me that it was also being used for recipients less in sympathy with British position than himself. Grateful immediate guidance.

1 Not printed.
2 Mr, later Sir Robert David Muldoon, Prime Minister of New Zealand, 1975-84.
3 Identical in most respects to No. 139.

No. 142

Lord Carrington to Sir H. Smedley (Wellington), 31 October 1979, 3.30 p.m.
Tel. No. 257 Confidential, Immediate (FCO 36/2531)

Your Tel No 362: Rhodesia[1]

1. The Prime Minister has also sent messages over the past two days to the Presidents of Zambia, Tanzania, Botswana and Nigeria and to the Prime Ministers of Canada and Australia. The messages were not identical but all sought further to explain our thinking on the present discussion of the interim arrangements and to obtain support for our proposals.

1 No. 141.

No. 143

Minute from Mr Day to Mr Walden, 31 October 1979
Confidential (FCO 36/2613)

Meeting with Lord Soames

1. I saw Lord Soames this afternoon for an hour and a half. I explained to him the present position that had been reached at Lancaster House making it clear that it was not yet certain whether we would reach an agreement involving all the parties concerned or whether we would have to go ahead in a Muzorewa only situation.[1] However, on the assumption that there was a return to legality and Patriotic Front participation in elections, we went over a great deal of ground covering:

1 On the same day, Mr Day minuted to Mr Renwick that the PUS was seeing Sir John Paul on 2 November to offer him the post of Governor 'in a Muzorewa only situation'. The minute was titled: 'Governor Mark II'.

(*a*) the role of the Governor as the ultimate executive and legislative authority in Rhodesia;
(*b*) the timing and arrangements for the elections;
(*c*) our present thoughts on the ceasefire and the relationship between the Governor and the Rhodesian security forces and the forces of the Patriotic Front;
(*d*) the present legislative timetable relating to the Enabling Bill and a subsequent Independence Bill;
(*e*) our present thoughts on sanctions and the action contemplated in the United Nations;
(*f*) the staff that would be supporting the Governor including the arrangements that we have already made for a Police Adviser, an Election Commissioner and his deputy, a Military Adviser and political staff.

2. Lord Soames asked a number of highly pertinent questions about the election arrangements, the ceasefire, his relationships with political leaders and public servants and the nature of his authority over the security forces and the police. We also discussed the extent to which Lord Soames should, when his appointment is announced, become involved in meetings with the press. His own inclination, which I said I shared, was that he should not engage in any concentrated press activity. However, it would no doubt be desirable for him to make some statement in this country at the time of his appointment and some further statement to the people of Rhodesia shortly after his arrival in Salisbury.

3. I have arranged to keep in close touch with Lord Soames as the situation develops. We are arranging for him to receive regularly copies of relevant telegrams and papers. His Private Secretary will also be in touch with Miss Spencer about a number of administrative arrangements.

4. Lord Soames would intend to take his own Private Secretary and PA with him together with a member of his personal staff. Miss Spencer will be tying up these arrangements with Personnel Services Department.

D.M. DAY

No. 144

Extract from the conclusions of a meeting of the Cabinet, 1 November 1979[1]
CC(79) 19th Conclusions Secret (CAB 128/66)

Limited Circulation Annex

Minute 2

The Foreign and Commonwealth Secretary said that Bishop Muzorewa had now accepted our proposals for the transition to independence. It was a major concession for him to have agreed to the Rhodesian Parliament being dissolved, and to himself and his Ministers ceasing to exercise their functions during the election period. No more could be expected. The Patriotic Front remained opposed, formally to the whole of our proposals, particularly strongly to the shortness of the transitional period and to the role proposed for the existing police force. It might be possible for them to be brought to overcome their objections; but it was possible that Mr Mugabe and (more reluctantly) Mr Nkomo would walk out of the Lancaster House Conference. In these circumstances the Foreign and Commonwealth Secretary intended to table our proposals in definitive form on 2 November and to call for the Front's reply by 5 November. Only if they agreed would the Conference move on to consider arrangements for a ceasefire, which would be the most difficult problem of all. If the Front withdrew, we would carry out our transitional plan in agreement with Bishop Muzorewa. We could not then expect much general international support. But at least some of our European Economic Community partners should be with us; the United States Congress would certainly be sympathetic; and it was to be hoped—though it was not certain —that the United States Government would also support us. Meanwhile urgent action needed to be taken in Parliament here, given that Section 2 of the Southern Rhodesia Act 1965 (and thereby sanctions on indirect trade with Rhodesia) would lapse on 15 November. A renewal of the Section 2 sanctions could be passed through the House of Commons only on the basis of Opposition support (and perhaps not at all in the House of Lords): given the views of many in the Government's supporters and the willingness of Bishop Muzorewa to accept the Government's proposals, that course would not be politically tolerable. An interim Enabling Bill would need to be passed before 15 November, under which

[1] The following were present: The Rt Hon Margaret Thatcher MP, Prime Minister; The Rt Hon William Whitelaw MP, Secretary of State for the Home Department; The Rt Hon Lord Hailsham, Lord Chancellor; The Rt Hon Lord Carrington, Secretary of State for Foreign and Commonwealth Affairs; The Rt Hon Sir Geoffrey Howe QC MP, Chancellor of the Exchequer; The Rt Hon Sir Keith Joseph MP, Secretary of State for Industry; The Rt Hon Francis Pym MP, Secretary of State for Defence; The Rt Hon Lord Soames, Lord President of the Council; The Rt Hon James Prior MP, Secretary of State for Employment; The Rt Hon Sir Ian Gilmour MP, Lord Privy Seal (Items 1-3); The Rt Hon Peter Walker MP, Minister of Agriculture, Fisheries and Food; The Rt Hon Michael Heseltine MP, Secretary of State for the Environment; The Rt Hon Nicholas Edwards MP, Secretary of State for Wales; The Rt Hon Humphrey Atkins, Secretary of State for Northern Ireland; The Rt Hon Patrick Jenkin MP, Secretary of State for Social Services; The Rt Hon Sir Norman St John-Stevas MP, Chancellor of the Duchy of Lancaster; The Rt Hon John Nott MP, Secretary of State for Trade; The Rt Hon David Howell MP, Secretary of State for Energy; The Rt Hon Mark Carlisle QC MP, Secretary of State for Education and Science; The Rt Hon John Biffen MP, Chief Secretary, Treasury; The Rt Hon Angus Maude MP, Paymaster General; Mr Paul Channon, Minister of State, Civil Service Department (Item 8). The following were also present: The Rt Hon Norman Fowler MP. Minister of Transport; The Rt Hon Michael Jopling MP, Parliamentary Secretary, Treasury. Secretariat: Sir Robert Armstrong; Mr M.D.M. Franklin (Items 2-4) Mr R.L. Wade-Gery (Items 2-4) and five others.

the British Government could by Order appoint the Governor, promulgate the new Constitution and briefly maintain sanctions on direct trade with Rhodesia in order to protect our position at the United Nations until legality was restored following the Governor's arrival. Later in November a second Bill would be necessary under which independence would be conferred at the end of the transitional period.

The Prime Minister, summing up the discussion, said that the Cabinet endorsed the Foreign and Commonwealth Secretary's policy and proposals. The Parliamentary and public handling of these proposals, which were likely to be very controversial, would be difficult and contentious, and would require the utmost care and attention. She and the Foreign and Commonwealth Secretary and the Lord Privy Seal would offer to brief the Leader of the Opposition and Shadow Foreign and Commonwealth Secretary on Privy Counsellor terms at a meeting on 2 November.[2] On 5 November Rhodesia would be considered by the Defence and Oversea Policy Committee; and the Government's Parliamentary supporters would be briefed. Notice of the Enabling Bill would be given on that same day; the Bill would then be tabled on 6 November and arrangements made for a Second Reading debate on 8 November.

This would entail a change of Parliamentary business from that proposed by the Chancellor of the Duchy of Lancaster earlier in the meeting, and therefore a revised business statement. Despite the tightness of the timetable, it should be possible for the Bill to be considered by the House of Lords on 12 November and receive the Royal Assent by 14 November.

The Cabinet—

Took note, with approval of the Prime Minister's summing up of their discussion.

No. 145

Memorandum by Lord Carrington for the Cabinet Defence and Oversea Policy Committee, 2 November 1979
OD(79)38, Confidential (CAB 148/183)

Rhodesia

1. Both sides at the constitutional conference have accepted the Independence Constitution, subject to satisfactory arrangements for the pre-independence period.

2. We have tabled proposals for an interim period of two months between a cease-fire and the holding of elections. During this period Rhodesia would be administered by a British Governor. The Governor would work through the existing civil service. The police and defence forces would be under his authority. Bishop Muzorewa and his Ministers would not exercise their ministerial functions, but would devote themselves to the election campaign. A British Election Commissioner and staff would supervise the conduct of elections.

3. There are risks in direct British involvement, but no other solution is likely to convince international opinion that the arrangements for elections would give a fair chance to both sides. The appointment of a Governor and the consequent return to

---

[2] It took place on 6 November: see No. 148.

legality by Rhodesia will be crucial to a legal position on the lifting of sanctions. I have however made clear that our present proposals relate to a situation in which there is prior agreement on a cease-fire. If the Patriotic Front refuse to take part in the elections and the war continues, we should still need to affect a return to legality in order to sustain our legal case on sanctions and obtain some international support for a settlement with the internal parties alone. But the task of the Governor in that event might be limited to the organisation of elections and the conduct of external affairs. Elections would be held in December. Our involvement would be limited to five or six weeks.

4. Bishop Muzorewa's delegation have accepted our proposals. Negotiations continue with the Patriotic Front. We have kept the front-line Presidents fully informed, but they will be reluctant to break with the Patriotic Front. Introduction of the Enabling Bill into the House of Commons next week will bring it home to the Patriotic Front that progress towards independence, with or without them, has begun. The odds are that Mugabe will not accept the interim arrangements, though Nkomo is hedging his bets. My intention is to confront the Patriotic Front with the need for a decision in the week beginning 5 November.

5. If the Patriotic Front accept our proposals, there will be negotiations on a cease-fire. These will be very difficult. No ceasefire arrangement will be without some limited provision for monitoring it. The Rhodesians will accept this provided that it is under British auspices. We may therefore need to provide a limited number of UK military observers together with elements from Commonwealth countries acceptable to the Salisbury administration (Australia, New Zealand, Kenya and Fiji).

6. Bishop Muzorewa has agreed to remain in London until 9 or 10 November. If by that point negotiations with the Patriotic Front have floundered, my intention is to make the Order in Council appointing the Governor in the week beginning 12 November, arrange for elections to be held on 17-19 December and bring Rhodesia to independence before the end of the year. If on the other hand, negotiations on a ceasefire are taking place we shall have to think in terms of elections in January.

7. We have always recognised that a settlement with the Salisbury parties alone will not get much international support. But provided the Patriotic Front are seen to have been offered a fair chance *and that we are prepared to go through with the appointment of a Governor*, there are reasonable prospects of being able to carry the French, the Americans (though with many hesitations) and some others with us. There will be damage to our interests, in particular in Zambia and Nigeria and possibly elsewhere. But the consequences will be no less serious if we do not take this opportunity finally to discharge our responsibility to bring Rhodesia to independence.

8. Talks with the Salisbury delegation on the position regarding pre-UDI debts and liabilities are progressing satisfactorily.

9. Attached at Annex A is a note on Sanctions and Legislation. Questions and answers on legislation are at Annex B.

ANNEX A

Rhodesia: Sanctions and Legislation

1. Our aim at the Constitutional Conference is early agreement on a return to legality which will justify the lifting of sanctions. Legality would be restored with the arrival in Salisbury of a British Governor and the acceptance of his authority.

2. Bishop Muzorewa has accepted our proposal for a Governor. We shall be trying to bring matters to a head with the Patriotic Front over the next week. We must reckon with the possibility that negotiations will not finish in time to allow us to get a Governor to Rhodesia by 15 November.

3. My recommendation nonetheless is that Section 2 of the Southern Rhodesia Act should be allowed to lapse. Bishop Muzorewa has agreed to all that we have asked of him. It would not be understood in the party and the country generally if we were to extend the sanctions provisions under Section 2. Bishop Muzorewa has agreed to dissolve the Salisbury Parliament, thereby enabling us to make the Order in Council appointing the Governor before 15 November and to *inform the Security Council that legality will be restored with the Governor's arrival*. Other sanctions, not covered by Section 2, including the prohibitions on direct trade and the transfer funds would remain in force until the Governor's arrival. If we are proceeding without the Patriotic Front, we shall come under strong pressure at the United Nations. Our aim will be to achieve as many abstentions as possible on resolutions directed against us. But it is likely that we shall have to veto resolutions seeking to reaffirm sanctions.

4. We shall need legislative cover to enable us to enact the Independence Constitution and introduce parts of it before independence and to allow elections to be held in Rhodesia. I therefore propose to introduce an Enabling Bill into Parliament on 6 November to provide these powers. This will also enable us to appoint a Governor under powers which otherwise would lapse with the non-renewal of Section 2 (a copy of the Bill is attached).[1] Introduction of the Bill will be taken as a signal that we do not intend to renew Section 2 and this could give rise to attempts at pre-emptive action at the UN. This will, however, depend on whether the Patriotic Front are still at the negotiating table, in which case the reactions will be muted.

5. The Enabling Bill will need to have the Royal Assent by 14 November if we are to avoid the lapse of the general powers conferred by Section 2. The Chief Whip has agreed to find the Parliamentary time.

6. A number of further Orders will be required to deal with the consequences of lifting sanctions. These are in preparation. I propose to introduce an Independent Bill in the second half of November, which would confer on the Government power to grant independence to Rhodesia by Order in Council after elections and the formation of a new Government.

---

1 Not printed.

ANNEX B

Questions and Answers on Rhodesia Legislation

1. *What is Section 2?*

Section 2 of the Southern Rhodesia Act 1965 gave the Government powers to make Orders in Council in Relation to Rhodesia including Orders of a constitutional nature and Orders applying sanctions.

2. *What happens when Section 2 expires?*

Section 2 expires automatically on 15 November unless renewed by Parliament. It can be renewed only for a year at a time. If it lapses, the Government loses the general power to make Orders in relation to Southern Rhodesia (but the sanctions Orders could be replaced under the United Nations Act, 1946). Some, but not all, sanctions would also lapse.

3. *Why not all sanctions?*

Because many sanctions are applied under other legislation, for instance the Import, Export and Customs (Powers) Defence Act, the Exchange Control Act and (with regard to dependencies) the United Nations Act. These sanctions can be revoked by the Government at any time by Order or administrative action. Sanctions on financial flows are *not* covered by Sanction 2 and those on direct trade are double banked, i.e. are made both by Section 2 and Export/Import control.

4. *Why does the Government need new powers in relation to Rhodesia?*

The powers under the Southern Rhodesia Act are not sufficient to allow the Government to make a new constitution for Rhodesia or to arrange elections for a republican constitution there. We shall need to do both very shortly if there is agreement at the Constitutional Conference. We therefore need an Enabling Bill.

5. *But why all the hurry to get it through by 15 November?*

Sufficient progress has been made at the Constitutional Conference to bring a return to legality in Rhodesia very close. It would thus be hard for the Government to justify renewal of Section 2 on 15 November. But if Section 2 lapses, it is not just the sanction orders which go, so too do certain constitutional orders and the power to make constitutional arrangements for the interim period until independence. Moreover, certain of the orders under Section 2 are of direct interest to individuals, e.g. those concerning marriage and divorce. The Enabling Bill will carry these Orders forward.

6. *What is the time-table envisaged?*

The Bill would have its first reading on 6 November, pass all its stages in the Commons on 7 and 8 November. If it does not go to the Lords on 8 November, it should be taken there on 12 November. It must receive the Royal Assent not later than 14 November.

7. *Why was not the Bill introduced earlier?*

A decision on introducing the Bill had to depend on progress at the Constitutional Conference. We are only now reaching the point at which it is appropriate to introduce legislation.

8. *Will not introduction of the Bill expose the Government's intention not to renew sanctions?*

This would in any case be apparent this week from the Government's failure to introduce a resolution to extend Section 2. The Bill may be controversial, though we shall argue that its basic purpose is to provide the powers to implement a settlement speedily and that other sanctions will remain in force until the arrival of the Governor in Rhodesia.

9. *What other legislation will be needed?*

The main legislation will be an Independence Bill to bring Rhodesia to legal independence. The intention is to introduce this in the second half of November and make it law by mid-December. We propose that the Bill would give power to set the date of independence by Order in Council once elections had been held.

10. *Is that all?*

A number of Orders in Council will be laid this month. These will be needed to appoint a Governor, make the Independent Constitution, and deal with the consequences of the lapse of sanctions. Some of them will require affirmative resolutions.

11. *When will other sanctions be lifted?*

Sanctions not covered by Section 2 will be lifted as soon as legality is restored in Rhodesia. This will be on the arrival of a British Governor and acceptance of his authority.

No. 146

Extract from the minutes of a meeting of the Cabinet Defence and Oversea Policy Committee, 5 November 1979[1]
OD(79) 12th Meeting, Secret (CAB 148/183)

1. Rhodesia

The Committee considered a memorandum by the Foreign and Commonwealth Secretary (OD(79) 38) describing the situation and prospects at the Lancaster House Conference, to which were annexed proposals on sanctions and on legislation.[2]

The Foreign and Commonwealth Secretary said that the Patriotic Front seemed to be delaying their final reply to his proposals for the transitional period. If they accepted these, the Conference would move on to discuss arrangements for a cease-fire; and we should meanwhile appoint a Governor who might arrive in Salisbury about 19 November and make early arrangements for elections to be held after a 2 month campaign, i.e. in late January 1980. If the Patriotic Front rejected his

---

1 Present were: The Rt Hon Margaret Thatcher MP, Prime Minister; The Rt Hon William Whitelaw MP; Secretary of State for the Home Department; The Rt Hon Lord Carrington, Secretary of State for Foreign and Commonwealth Affairs; The Rt Hon Sir Geoffrey Howe QC MP, Chancellor of the Exchequer; The Rt Hon Francis Pym MP, Secretary of State for Defence; The Rt Hon Lord Soames, Lord President of the Council; The Rt Hon Sir Ian Gilmour MP, Lord Privy Seal; The Rt Hon John Nott MP, Secretary of State for Trade. The following were also present: The Rt Hon Sir Keith Joseph MP, Secretary of State for Industry (Item 2); The Rt Hon Humphrey Atkins MP, Secretary of State for Northern Ireland (Item 3); The Rt Hon Norman St John-Stevas MP, Chancellor of the Duchy of Lancaster (Item 1); The Rt Hon Angus Maude MP, Paymaster General (Item 4); The Rt Honourable Michael Jopling MP, Parliamentary Secretary, Treasury; Mr K.R. Stowe, Northern Ireland Office (Item 3). Secretariat: Sir Robert Armstrong; Mr R.L. Wade-Gery; Mr R.M. Hastie-Smith. The other items discussed were Export Credits for South Africa (Item 2), Northern Ireland: Political Development (Item 3) and Planned reductions in BBC External Services (Item 4).
2 No. 145.

proposals, the Government would have to go ahead without them; a different type of Governor would be appointed, and he would arrive in Salisbury rather earlier, and elections would be held by about 19 December. In either case, the intention would be that the security forces should conduct no operations outside Rhodesia during the transitional period, although if the Patriotic Front were refusing to take part, there would be no cease-fire and the war inside Rhodesia would be continuing. It was necessary to press the Patriotic Front for an early decision if the co-operation of the authorities in Salisbury was to be retained; but it would be a mistake to go so fast that he could fairly be described as behaving unreasonably by e.g. President Kaunda of Zambia or President Nyerere of Tanzania, who might both visit London within the next few days. It was to be hoped that the Conference would not break up before Parliament had been able to pass a new Enabling Bill which would be needed by 15 November when Section 2 of the Southern Rhodesia Act 1965 would lapse. Sanctions against indirect trade would be allowed to lapse with Section 2, although in order to protect the Government's position at the United Nations, sanctions against direct trade (which did not depend on Section 2) would be briefly retained until legality had been restored following the arrival of the Governor. The enabling bill was required in order to provide power to make the arrangements for the transitional period and to preserve legislative continuity for certain technical purposes. It had to be recognised that the Government would be criticised internationally both for not renewing sanctions on indirect trade under Section 2 and for going ahead without the Patriotic Front if that proved necessary. In that event some damage to British economic and other interests in Africa—notably Zambia and Nigeria —would be unavoidable.

In discussion it was agreed that it would be impossible to renew Section 2 of the 1965 Act, not only because of parliamentary opposition from the Government's supporters but also because it would be dishonourable to renew sanctions against Bishop Muzorewa's Government after they had accepted both the new constitution and the transitional arrangements we had proposed. It was noted that damage to British commercial interests, particularly in a major market like Nigeria, would be very unwelcome given present economic difficulties; but that there was a point beyond which the Government could not go to accommodate the Patriotic Front's views without losing the support of the Salisbury authorities. Bishop Muzorewa might perhaps be persuaded to accept an electoral period of 10 weeks (if the Patriotic Front were taking part), which with the time before elections could be called might amount to almost 3 months in all; but he could not be expected to go further than that. It was recognised that in terms of the security situation there were dangers in resuming direct rule and holding elections under British auspices.

But for United Nations and other reasons it was essential to create a legal government; Bishop Muzorewa now saw fresh elections as a means of increasing international support for his regime; and General Walls was confident that the situation on the ground could be contained during the transitional period.

In further discussion, the difficulties of the parliamentary timetable for the proposed Enabling Bill were noted. The Opposition seemed unlikely to be co-operative. It was agreed that consideration of the Bill in the House of Commons must be completed before 12 November, and that consideration in the House of Lords must end in time for Royal Assent to be given not later than 14 November.

The Prime Minister, summing up the discussion, said that the Committee congratulated the Foreign and Commonwealth Secretary on his handling of the Rhodesia issue so far and endorsed his paper OD(79) 38. In spite of the danger of the conference breaking down and of unwelcome damage to British economic and other interests in Africa, the Committee agreed that there was no effective alternative to proceeding as now proposed. The Enabling Bill would need very careful handling in Parliament. Notice of it should be given to the Table Office on the evening of 6 November, and a Money Resolutions and procedure motions would need to be tabled by 10.00 pm that evening. The Bill should be formally introduced on 7 November. The Chancellor of the Duchy of Lancaster would need to make a revised Business Statement that afternoon; that should be preceded by a statement by the Lord Privy Seal. She herself would need to consider further how to handle any questions in Parliament on the afternoon of 6 November; it might be possible to say no more than that a statement would be made on 7 November. Consideration of the Bill in the House of Commons could then be completed in a single session on 8 November, which would if necessary continue without a break into 9 November when it would need to displace Private Members' business. The Chancellor of the Duchy of Lancaster should not make, but should be free to respond (if it seemed advantageous to do so) to a request to remove Private Members' business from 9 November to 12 November, in which case the Bill could be taken through all its stages in two separate House of Commons sittings on 8 and 9 November. If necessary 12 and 13 November would then be available for House of Lords consideration. The first Orders would need to be made under the Bill on 14 November; this could if necessary be done immediately following Royal Assent.

The Committee—

1. Took note with approval of the Prime Minister's summing up of their discussion.

2. Invited the Foreign and Commonwealth Secretary, the Lord Privy Seal, the Chancellor of the Duchy of Lancaster and the Chief Whip to be guided accordingly.

No. 147

Minute from Mr Renwick to Mr Day, 5 November 1979[1]
Secret and Personal (FCO 36/2441)

Rhodesia: Mr Nkomo

1. At his meeting tomorrow with Mr Nkomo, the Lord Privy Seal will need to approach cautiously—but in the end to address himself directly to—the possibility of Nkomo participating in a settlement without Mr Mugabe. Mr Nkomo may be in a mood for this. There is dis-satisfaction in ZAPU with Mr Mugabe and his tactics; and a realisation that ZANU are likely to contest the elections separately and that ZANLA will not observe the ceasefire. Mr Nkomo also probably hopes that he may get better terms for a cease-fire if he is negotiating on his own. This is partly illusory, but there are ways in which our proposals could be dressed up for his benefit. The Lord Privy Seal will, however, want to bear in mind that the Rhodesian

---

1 Also sent to Mr Manning.

military commanders will resist any *formal* 'equality of status' as between ZIPRA and the Rhodesian security forces, as well as joint patrolling. General Walls accepts that ZAPU must be allowed to join in if they want to do so. He is not prepared to buy them in. But our cease-fire arrangements do offer a role for ZIPRA. If they are prepared to concentrate their forces, it will be possible to avoid clashes with the Rhodesian security forces, who would devote their attention to ZANLA.

R.W. RENWICK

No. 148

Note by Mr Whitmore (No. 10) of a meeting held in the Prime Minister's Room in the House of Commons, 6 November 1979, 9.30 p.m.
(PREM 19/114)

Present:

Prime Minister	The Rt. Hon. James Callaghan, MP[1]
Lord Privy Seal	The Rt. Hon. Peter Shore, MP[2]
Mr C.A. Whitmore	The Rt. Hon. John Morris, QC MP[3]

Mr Callaghan said that he and his colleagues were grateful to the Prime Minister for being ready to see them to discuss the draft Enabling Bill on Rhodesia which she had sent him earlier in the day. He was bound to tell the Prime Minister that he saw no prospect of the Government proceeding on the bill in the way they were proposing. He said this not because he wished to oppose what the Government wanted to do just for the sake of opposition; on the contrary, he wished to be helpful in what he knew were difficult circumstances and to see the bill go through quickly. But he thought that the Government's judgement was wrong on both procedural and political grounds. It was a procedural mistake to ask the House of Commons to consider the Enabling Bill when it had had no report on the progress of the Lancaster House conference presented to it. In similar circumstances in the past it had been the practice for the Government to publish a White Paper setting out the proposed constitution for the territory that was about to become independent before the House was asked to pass the necessary legislation. The Government was now asking the House to pass a bill which would subsequently allow the Government to make a constitution by Order in Council, but the House had no knowledge of the provisions of the constitution. He urged the Government to publish a White Paper on the draft constitution in the form in which it had been agreed so far at the Lancaster House conference. Members of the House should then be allowed to reflect and consult before they were asked to pass the Enabling Bill. He had to warn the Government that the Labour Party would take it very amiss if the Government went ahead with its plans to make a statement the following day and to pass the bill through all its stages on Thursday.

1 Leader of HM Opposition, the Labour Party.
2 Shadow Secretary of State for Foreign and Commonwealth Affairs.
3 HM Opposition spokesperson on Legal Affairs and Shadow Attorney-General.

The *Prime Minister* said that it should be borne in mind that the way in which the new constitution for an independent Rhodesia had been drawn up was very different from the circumstances in which constitutions for other dependent territories had been arrived at. The *Lord Privy Seal* said that he understood the procedural point which the Leader of the Opposition was making but the fact was that the constitution was no longer controversial. It had now been agreed with both Bishop Muzorewa's delegation and the Patriotic Front, subject to agreement being reached on the pre-independent arrangements, and our allies and the Front Line states had had nothing but good to say about it. Moreover, its provisions had been widely known for some time. The constitution was not yet cast in legal terms but he was ready to arrange for it to be published, as it stood at present, the following afternoon.

Mr Callaghan said that he believed that the bill was also premature in political terms. The House was bound to ask why the bill was needed now when the detailed transitional arrangements for Rhodesia had still to be agreed at Lancaster House. He thought that by proceeding with the bill at this stage the Government might find that the effect on the conference was adverse. If the Government tried to take the bill on Thursday, as they were planning to, and there was an enormous row in the House, what impact would this have on Lancaster House? He believed that the Government would have a much better chance of getting the bill through with less difficulty if it was taken on Monday of the following week and not Thursday.

The *Prime Minister* said that the bill was needed on Thursday because the proceedings at Lancaster House were on a razor's edge. The Government had delayed introducing the bill to the last possible moment in order to get as much agreement as possible at the conference but they had to move now. The bill did two things. First, it would give the Government powers, which it did not have under the 1965 Act, to make a new constitution, to arrange elections and to appoint a governor with legislative and executive powers. These provisions were constructive and forward looking. Second, the 1965 Act would expire on 15 November, and the new bill would carry forward those Orders which needed to be continued but which would otherwise lapse. This meant that the Government had to have the new bill enacted by midnight on Wednesday 14 November. If there was a gap between the expiry of the 1965 Act and the coming into force of the new bill, unforeseeable legal difficulties might arise. If the Government had a guarantee that the Commons would complete all stages of the bill by Monday so that the bill could go to the Lords on Tuesday, it could accept that timetable. But nobody could in practice give such a guarantee. It was for these reasons that the Government proposed to take the bill through all its stages in the Commons this week.

Mr Shore said that the only constraint on the Government at present was the imminent expiry of the 1965 Act. It did not seem to him that there was any hurry about giving the Government the powers it needed for other purposes such as the appointment of the governor and the holding of elections. The House would want a major debate on the constitution and the transitional arrangements in due course, and there was no need to face it with the abrupt timetable the Government was seeking to follow. The reaction of the house was bound to be strong. *Mr Callaghan* added that the Lord Privy Seal was bound to be asked during his statement the following day what the Government proposed to do about sanctions, and his answer would largely determine how easily the bill got through the Commons.

The *Prime Minister* said that she wished to emphasise that the bill was only an enabling one. It did not of itself make provision for the constitution. That would require an Order subsequently and there would no doubt be a debate on it. Given that the bill did no more than carry forward certain existing powers and give the Government new powers which were needed to implement pre-independence arrangements which had been agreed at the conference, it was difficult to see why the Opposition should object to it. She urged them to think of the consequences for the conference if the Government did not get the bill [passed]. The overriding objective was to keep both sides at Lancaster House and to try to bring them to an agreement. With this in mind the Government was obliged to stick to its plan to take the bill through all its stages in the Commons on Thursday.

No. 149

Mr Brown (Lagos) to Lord Carrington, 6 November 1979, 7 a.m.[1]
Tel. No. 937 Secret, Immediate (FCO 36/2509)

Rhodesia Conference—Nigerian Attitude.

1. With the continuing lack of Foreign Minister and difficulties of access to the President there has been no opportunity since the visit of Mr Luce of explaining our policies at the highest level. However we have continued to supply full texts to all concerned and are doing everything we can at official level and through other channels (the Americans are also helping) to emphasise the validity and reasonableness of our proposals, the major concessions made by Muzorewa and the closeness of a real solution, etc.

2. The indications we have had of the new government's attitude have been relatively favourable. We have been told by officials that the President last week was generally happy with the way things were going and admired your handling of the conference; it is perhaps significant that the previous hostile tone of the press has been little in evidence in recent weeks. Reporting from London has been reasonably objective and apart from a couple of lapses by the 'Daily Times' there has been little hostile comment and indeed little editorial comment of any kind. However there has been reporting of hostile statements and press comment from e.g. Lusaka and Dar es Salaam.

3. It seems likely that the President is still concerned about the military arrangements: But I would expect him to be somewhat reassured by the indication that the Patriotic Front military leaders will be represented on a military commission, with presumably the same status as the government forces. He would clearly prefer to see a Commonwealth 'peace-keeping force'. He might be appeased by the involvement of Commonwealth officers in monitoring the cease-fire, although the choice of states envisaged might be criticised here (I think the inclusion of India would be helpful).

---

1 To reach FCO Deskby 1130z, Repetition to Luanda referred for departmental decision; repeated Immediate to Dar es Salaam, Lusaka, Maputo, Gaborone, Luanda, Washington, UKMIS New York.

4. The President's principal concern, which he expressed publicly during the weekend, appears to be the shortness of the pre-election period. This does not mean that he supports the Patriotic Front's demand for six months (in talking to a member of Chancery a senior MFA official was critical of Nyerere's public support for six months, and said the Nigerians has been pressing the Patriotic Front to accept a shorter period).

My guess is that Shagari would be reasonably happy if the present two months after the establishment of the cease-fire could be extended to three months but even two weeks more would be a help and might enable Nigeria to continue to give support at Lancaster House and to use their influence with the Front Line States (although I doubt whether this amounts to much) in a helpful way.

5. Nigerian reaction to a break-down of the conference will depend very much on circumstances. If we succeed in winning over Nkomo (and therefore presumably Kaunda) leaving Mugabe (and possibly Nyerere and Machel) outside then I would expect the Nigerian reaction to be fairly muted: in fact they would be privately delighted because this would be their own preferred solution (viz. the Garba[2] initiative last year). However if the Patriotic Front as a whole remained outside the settlement, with the backing of the Front Line States, and we went ahead to legitimise the present administration, then I would expect Nigeria to join the Front Line States in strong condemnation and in specific action against us e.g. breach of diplomatic relations and perhaps the resumption of the embargo on British contractors. However successful we might be in persuading influential Nigerians individually that our proposals are reasonable and that we cannot allow the Patriotic Front to exercise a veto, they would be critical of us for our 'brinkmanship' or 'blackmailing' tactics and for not allowing even more time to resolve the problem by discussion and negotiation. Given the strong line taken by the military administration and the relatively weak position of the civilian government at the present time (it has cut a poor figure with the Senate failing to approve merely half of the Ministers submitted by the President), there is little chance that they would stand out against a generally hostile American tide. Nevertheless our assessment is, at this point, that the Nigerian Government would not apply the wide ranging economic sanctions against us which were under consideration in June and July by their predecessors. Any commercial measures they took would probably be temporary and their results of a kind to inflict some damage but which we could live.

6. I have just been informed that I have an appointment with Professor Abubakar,[3] Defence Minister and acting Foreign Minister, tomorrow at 0900Z.

---

2 Major General Joseph Nanven Garba, Nigerian Foreign Minister, 1975-78.
3 Professor Iya Abubakar, Nigerian Minister of Defence, 1979-82.

No. 150

Lord Carrington to Sir N. Henderson (Washington), 6 November 1979, 10.06 p.m.[1]
Tel. No. 1584 Confidential, Immediate (FCO 36/2441)

Rhodesia

1. The Salisbury Delegation accepted yesterday the full proposals we have put forward for the pre-independence period. The Patriotic Front are at present engaged in a filibuster.

2. At your discretion you should explain to the governments to which you are accredited the position reached in the Conference and that decisions on the pre-independence period will have to be taken this week. You should make the following points:

(*a*) If the Patriotic Front agree to our proposals for the interim arrangements, we will proceed immediately to discussions on a cease-fire:

(*b*) We will be proposing that the cease-fire should come into effect within fourteen days after agreement is reached (a longer period would be unacceptable and would prejudice the bringing into effect of a genuine cease-fire):

(*c*) We will be proposing that the military commanders on both sides should appoint representatives to a cease-fire commission, under the Chairmanship of the Governor's Military Adviser. The Patriotic Front forces, like the Rhodesian Security forces, will be responsible to the Governor for the preservation of the cease-fire. We do not envisage any other role for either side's forces in this period:

(*d*) Arrangements will be made under United Kingdom auspices, with the participation of some other Commonwealth Governments for the monitoring of the cease-fire. (For your own information the Australian, New Zealand, Kenyan and Fijian governments have agreed to participate in monitoring arrangements under our auspices.) All Commonwealth countries will be invited to send observers to the elections. But the Salisbury Delegation will not be prepared to accept the participation in the cease-fire monitoring arrangements of any countries which are committed to support the Patriotic Front.

3. If you are asked about the length of the interim period at your discretion you may point out that we envisage two weeks to bring a cease-fire into effect and the elections being held two months after that. (The overall length of the period will therefore be close to three months). A two month period for the elections is fully adequate to enable the parties to put their case to the people. The Patriotic Front already claim to be the sole representatives of the people of Zimbabwe and to have the support of a great majority of the people inside the country. Muzorewa, however, appears to be readier to put his political support to the test in elections than the Patriotic Front. A longer interim period will not be acceptable to us because:

---

[1] And to Immediate Canberra, Ottawa, Wellington, EEC Posts, Lisbon, Oslo, Madrid, Tokyo, Athens, Berne, Vienna; Information Immediate UKMIS New York, Nassau, Dacca, Bridgetown, Nicosia, Suva, Georgetown, New Delhi, Kuala Lumpur, Port Louis, Freetown, Singapore, Colombo, Port of Spain, Port Moresby, Lagos, Algiers, Luanda, Gaborone, Yaounde, Cairo, Addis Ababa, Libreville, Banjul, Accra, Abidjan, Nairobi, Maseru, Monrovia, Tripoli, Lilongwe, Rabat, Maputo, Dakar, Victoria, Mogadishu, Khartoum, Mbabane, Dar es Salaam, Tunis, Kampala, Kinshasa, Lusaka.

(a) It is the British Government which will have to assume direct responsibility for Rhodesia throughout this period:

(b) The risks of a break-down of a cease-fire will be much greater if there is a protracted period of political uncertainty:

(c) A longer period would result in the Patriotic Front and other leaders devoting themselves to create a parallel administration rather than committing themselves to the election campaign.

4. You should leave the government to which you are accredited in no doubt that it is essential that decisions should be reached on the pre-independence period in the next few days. The timing of this is not related to the question of sanctions and Section 2 (nearly all UK sanctions do not in fact depend on Section 2) but to the time-scale of the Conference. The Salisbury Delegation will not be prepared to remain in London much longer unless we can move on to negotiations on a cease-fire. It will not be possible to reach agreement on some other basis than the one we have proposed. In particular we will not be able to agree to a six-month interim period as proposed by Nyerere.

No. 151

Letter from Mr Lyne to Mr Alexander (No. 10), 7 November 1979
Confidential (PREM 19/114)

Dear Michael,

Rhodesia

If the Constitutional Conference breaks [down] within the next week, as a result of the Patriotic Front's failure to accept our proposals for the pre-independence arrangements, it will be important to have demonstrated to the leaders of moderate African opinion that we have done our utmost to reach a settlement on terms which are fair to the Patriotic Front. If they are themselves prepared to associate themselves with our approach in the Conference, this may also encourage them subsequently to support, or at least not to dissent publicly from, a subsequent decision by us to go ahead without the Patriotic Front.

It would help to achieve these objectives if the Prime Minister sent a personal message to selected African Presidents and to King Hassan of Morocco in terms of the enclosed draft.[1] If the Prime Minister agrees, we will arrange to have this sent by telegram to the posts indicated.[2]

Yours ever,
RODERIC LYNE

---

1 Not printed.
2 Mr Alexander minuted to the Prime Minister: 'Agree text?' Mrs Thatcher replied: 'Yes.'

No. 152

Sir A. Parsons (UKMIS New York) to Lord Carrington, 8 November 1979, 11.05 p.m.[1]
Tel. No. 1483 Immediate, Confidential (FCO 36/2550)

My telno 1457 and your telno 769:[2] *Fourth Committee Debate on Rhodesia*

1. I met yesterday the chairman of the Fourth Committee, Ambassador Boya of Benin.[3] I stressed to him our view that a debate this week in the Fourth Committee was undesirable: The Lancaster House Conference was at a crucial stage. I rubbed it in pretty hard. Boya confirmed that he had at the request of the Patriotic Front and various African delegations agreed that the Fourth Committee should meet today on Rhodesia. He said, with some justification, that since the rest of the agenda was completed he was not in a position to refuse this request. He said however that he fully understood our concerns, that he would talk to the Patriotic Front again and try to ensure that the debate would be adjourned as soon as possible after the Patriotic Front had made their statement (i.e. the scenario Salim had given me on 6 Nov).

2. This was as helpful a reply as we could have expected. I told Boya that we would not be making any substantive statement today.

3. Chinamano duly delivered the Patriotic Front statement (copy by bag) in the Fourth Committee this morning. He claimed credit for the Front's conduct of the negotiations, criticised us for favouring the Smith/Muzorewa regime and them for acquiescing sheepishly in whatever we proposed. But he did so in comparatively moderate terms, indeed one of his criticisms was that you appeared to be acting as a mediator between the Patriotic Front and the Smith/Muzorewa regime rather than as a decoloniser. He said that his purpose was not to embarrass us, but to ask for a UN expression of interest in a solution that would bring lasting peace to Rhodesia. He called upon members of the UN to assist the UK to devise satisfactory transitional arrangements, but did not want acrimonious debate in the Fourth Committee. He did not mention sanctions.

4. After it had been agreed that the statement should be circulated in full as a committee document, the Chairman proposed adjournment. When the Soviet Union asked that a date for resumption should be fixed, he declined. The debate is unlikely to be resumed before the end of next week.

---

1 To arrive in the FCO Deskby 9 November 0900z; and information Priority to Washington.
2 Not printed.
3 Mr Sentonji Thomas Boya, Permanent Representative of Benin to the UN.

No. 153

Minute from Mr Gomersall to Mr Walden, 8 November 1979
Secret and Personal (FCO 36/2441)

Rhodesia: Mr Nkomo

The Lord Privy Seal had a private meeting with Mr Nkomo on 6 November. In the course of the conversation, which lasted over two hours. Mr Nkomo made clear his essential concerns about the military arrangements, but did not offer any new openings.

Mr Nkomo took the line throughout that ZANU had to be contained. The Patriotic Front alliance was important for him. 'Robert', despite his hard image and mistaken tactics in the Conference, was 'not a brute'. Nkomo had never seen him so keen to reach a settlement. Though he Nkomo, badly wanted an end to the war he could not accept a settlement at any price. It depended on how he, and we, handled others. If we acted crudely he would be destroyed and the chances of peace bungled. ZANLA would be much more dangerous outside than inside a settlement.

Mr Nkomo returned insistently to the need to 'do something about' paragraph 13 of the interim paper. He could not accept that the Rhodesian forces would become the legal forces under the Governor, and the guerrillas as 'extra-legal force'. His boys had to have a settlement which gave them a feeling of acceptance. If the British Government could do something about that, Mugabe might well accept our interim proposals. There was a core of well-intentioned people who would stand up and be counted, but who were holding back at present because they feared that our interim proposals would lead to a much bloodier conflict. On paragraph 13, Nkomo put forward the following ideas:

(*a*) That we freeze the forces on both sides;

(*b*) That we should establish the nucleus of an integrated army under the Governor (he suggested 2-3 companies of the cream of each, leaving the rest outside to undergo training);

(*c*) 'some form of structure' under the Governor that would give status to the Patriotic Front.

The Lord Privy Seal emphasised repeatedly that these issues could be discussed in the Conference if the Patriotic Front would agree conditionally on our interim proposals, but Nkomo said this was not possible because he could not sell paragraph 13 to his supporters. This was closely linked with his anxiety over what would happen after independence under the British proposals. If Muzorewa won and Walls remained in power, his men could meet the same fate as Sithole's auxiliaries. It was no good reassuring him that he or the international community would not countenance such action—or South Africa would not be mad enough to launch an invasion-because his men would be dead by then. All the parties needed confidence in the intentions of the others after independence and this could only be built up during the interim period.

Nkomo also proposed that Britain should provide the entire electoral staff and keep the organisation out of the hands of the Rhodesian Civil Service. Elections organised by Pope-Simmonds[1] and the Rhodesia Election Directorate, even under our close supervision, would not be fair.

The Lord Privy Seal explained the purpose of the Enabling Bill which would be introduced into Parliament on 7 November. The decision not to renew the Order in Council under Section 2 should be seen as a matter of domestic politics: the vast bulk of sanctions would remain. Nkomo said that this would be difficult for his supporters to understand: they would see it as encouraging a bilateral settlement and as contrasting badly with President Carter's resistance to Congress.

S.J. GOMERSALL

1 Mr Eric Pope-Simmonds, Rhodesian Registrar-General of Elections.

No. 154

Minute by the Rhodesia Department, 8 November 1979
Confidential (FCO 36/2523)

Discussion between the Foreign and Commonwealth Secretary and President Kaunda: 8 November

Lord Carrington had a private discussion for three-quarters of an hour with President Kaunda *en route* from the airport to London. President Kaunda was in a calm and good-natured mood. The main points to arise were as follows:

(*a*) *Lord Carrington* explained that while it was easy to find fault on numerous details with the British proposals for a settlement, they represented the best compromise available and the only course which we considered likely to be effective. *President Kaunda* expressed concern about the short duration of the interim period. *Lord Carrington* explained why we wished to move as rapidly as possible to independence, and pointed out that in addition to the two calendar months allowed for the pre-election period there would be an additional two weeks to bring the ceasefire into effect, bringing the overall period near to three months.

(*b*) *President Kaunda* asked about Bishop Muzorewa's position during the pre-election period. *Lord Carrington* said that Bishop Muzorewa would not be running the Government. It did not matter what title he gave himself; as far as we were concerned he could use whatever title he wished: we had never formally recognised him as Prime Minister. Muzorewa had made a tremendous concession in agreeing to give up executive authority during this period. In reply to a question from the President, Lord Carrington said that if Muzorewa needed to use air force planes during the pre-election period similar facilities would be afforded to Nkomo and other party leaders.

(*c*) In reply to a question from the President about security forces and police, *Lord Carrington* stressed that the different forces would be represented on the Ceasefire Commission. He realised that it was not an ideal solution to have to use existing police force, but this was the only way of achieving the necessary result. The activities of the police and security forces during the pre-election period would come under the scrutiny of the international observers and world press and of the Election Council; and there would of course be British military and police advisers.

(d) *President Kaunda* enquired about the prospective Governor and whether he would have a chance to meet him during his visit to London. *Lord Carrington* said that we had a very senior political figure in mind, but could not put him forward until the Patriotic Front had agreed to the interim proposals.

(e) *Lord Carrington* explained the Government's reasons for putting forward the Enabling Bill, and described the present position over sanctions. There was no complaint from President Kaunda about sanctions.

(f) *Lord Carrington* explained that there was a risk of losing the Salisbury Delegation if we allowed the Patriotic Front to filibuster much longer. We had persuaded Salisbury to make major concessions, to place their trust in us and to accept a compromise. It was now up to President Kaunda to persuade the Patriotic Front also to compromise. Lord Carrington had the personal impression that Robert Mugabe was taking a harder line over acceptance of our proposals that Joshua Nkomo.

(g) *President Kaunda* said that he was consciously separating the Rhodesian raids into Zambia and Mozambique from the business of the Conference and had not come to London to create trouble about the raids.

(h) *Lord Carrington* referred to the Rhodesian interruption of maize supplies to Zambia. President Kaunda did not react strongly.

No. 155

Memorandum from Lord Walston to Lord Carrington, 8 November 1979
(FCO 36/2441)

Meeting with Mr and Mrs Mugabe, 7 November 1979

My wife and I lunched quietly with Robert and Sally Mugabe yesterday, November 7th, at their invitation. We talked very freely and frankly about the present state of negotiations, and the following are our impressions.

We were confirmed in our belief that Mr Mugabe is an honest man, and that the views he expressed were sincerely held and not negotiating points. While he may well expect some of the conversation to be passed on [to] the FCO, we are sure he was not speaking with that in mind. To understand Mugabe's approach, one has to recognise that his thinking and attitudes are based on the deep-rooted conviction that the British Government is negotiating with what is still a rebel regime, and that any moves in the past few years towards a settlement have been brought about only by the Patriotic Front's activities.

In addition, Mugabe has a distrust of Lord Carrington and some other political figures. We hope we may have had some influence in allaying these fears at least so far as the Foreign Secretary is concerned. However, we would urge some informal personal contacts. The rushing through of today's Bill will not make the matter easier.

Apart from the fact that he undoubtedly wishes for a peaceful settlement, our main impression was that Mugabe had grave doubts about the openness of the British side in negotiations. While he accepted that HMG was very anxious to achieve a settlement, he believes that they are strongly in favour of Muzorewa, and are working to ensure that he is head of the next Government.

He is adamant in maintaining that the Patriotic Front needs more than two months in which to prepare for elections. We would be very much surprised if he would settle on the basis of two months, even from the cease-fire. He specified that a total period of six months was necessary to effect a cease-fire and prepare for an election, adding the argument that what had taken thirteen years to achieve would lose nothing by taking a further thirteen weeks. He also spoke very strongly (and persuasively) concerning the supervision of the elections, and in particular the control of the police and the armed forces.

His view is that both of these and the civil service are, at the moment, under the control of the officers and officials who have been loyal to Smith from the beginning of UDI, and their loyalties and their prejudices have not and will not change. Even a strong Government (and he was surprisingly unconcerned as to who the Governor might be) would not be able to control them. Their influence at all levels, and especially at the grass roots, would be very great, and strongly adverse to the Patriotic Front. He also made the point that, should the Patriotic Front win the election, but the armed forces did not comprise an equal number of Patriotic Front forces, the risk of a military coup against the newly-elected Government would be great, and the new Government would have no forces with which to counter this. (On reflection, it passed through our minds that the reverse of this situation might not be entirely absent from his thoughts.)

He was not particularly concerned with the size of the armed forces, but was insistent that whether they were 4,000, 10,000 or 20,000, they should consist of equal numbers of the present Rhodesian forces and those of the Patriotic Front. Although this was not mentioned, it has occurred to us that unless Patriotic Front forces were incorporated in some new military organisation, it would be very difficult to prevent roving bands of terrorists operating in remote parts of the country. The demobilisation of any forces, and particularly guerrillas, is notoriously difficult. It would be far easier to cope with this problem if they were brought under the control of a new military command and demobilised in stages.

He agreed that Machel was a key figure in the situation, but stated that there was no threat from Russia or Cuba. China, he said, was his friend and Mozambique's also. Only if South Africa entered the conflict might the situation change. The present raids into Mozambique from Rhodesia were of no great significance.

The only mention of Nkomo was when we specifically asked Mugabe about his relations with him. He said they were satisfactory, and they were in continuous consultation with each other in all key problems. He said further that Nkomo and he had in April completed plans for future combined operations of the two forces, and these would have been put into action had the talks not started.

Finally, we gained the impression that while he hoped the talks would succeed and the fighting would stop, he was not prepared for a peaceful solution except under the right conditions, and would continue the armed struggle if he could not get satisfaction on the outstanding points. He also made it clear when the message was given to him that 'negotiating time was running out' that he would not be rushed into accepting proposals he considered required more detailed examination and agreement. There were many important details, such as the immediate future of the civil service, which had to be agreed upon before it could be said that the talks had succeeded.

We are checking with Mugabe on his views concerning the command of the armed forces, and will let you know those as soon as we have heard from him.

No. 156

Minute from Mr Day to Sir M. Palliser, 8 November 1979[1]
Secret (FCO 36/2514)

South Africa and Rhodesia

1. The South Africans are deeply involved militarily in Rhodesia. Military supplies have to come in via South Africa. South Africa provides on loan a considerable quantity of military equipment (aircraft, helicopters etc). South African crews fly aircraft on combat missions within Rhodesia and over neighbouring countries. South African ground forces are stationed in Rhodesia and are engaged in military operations.

2. During the South African Foreign Minister's talk with the Prime Minister on 17 October[2] Mr Botha referred to South Africa's military presence in Rhodesia and alleged that this consisted of equipment rather than men. Mrs Thatcher expressed the hope that South Africa would not decide to pull out of Rhodesia. The Secretary of State said that, if there were a British presence in Rhodesia during the interim period, no questions would be asked about the equipment.

3. We can get away with the continuing use of South African military equipment in Rhodesia. The continued presence of South African military personnel, in any numbers and in formed units, during the period of direct British rule will be highly embarrassing and potentially extremely damaging to our international reputation. The involvement of the South Africans within Rhodesia will already be known to, or at least suspected by, a number of governments. The United States Government are already asking questions (Washington telegram No 3581 attached)[3]. If there is a full agreement at Lancaster House, and given the presence in Rhodesia of large numbers of official observers from the Commonwealth and elsewhere, not to mention the international press, the chances of the presence of South African units being kept quiet are remote, if not non-existent. A similar, if lesser, risk exists if we go ahead with the internal parties alone.

4. Neither the Rhodesians nor the South Africans will welcome the thought that operational South African units should be removed from Rhodesia whilst a British Governor is in charge. Mr Botha may believe that he obtained an assurance from us that we would turn a blind eye to the presence of South African units. General Walls will be extremely sensitive to any suggestion that the Security Forces should be disadvantaged. Whatever ceasefire arrangement the Patriotic Front may agree to, there is little doubt that ZANLA, at least, intend to persist in guerrilla activity. We therefore need to approach this issue with great delicacy. Otherwise we risk losing Salisbury.

5. The most effective way of tackling this would be for the Secretary of State to

---

1 Also sent to Mr Walden.
2 No. 120.
3 Not printed.

see General Walls. He could confirm that we have no intention of disadvantaging the Rhodesian Security Forces and that we understand the need for him to rely on South African equipment. We also accept that in certain cases it may be necessary for some South African military personnel to remain in Rhodesia, discreetly, to provide specialist assistance. On the other hand, the continued presence of formed operational South African units in Rhodesia during the period of British rule could cause us serious difficulties. We are sure that General Walls (and the South Africans) would understand this. We hope therefore that arrangements will be made to ensure that there is no risk of embarrassment to us during the period in which the Governor is in charge.

D.M. Day

No. 157

Letter from Mr Alexander (No. 10) to Mr Walden, 8 November 1979
Confidential (FCO 36/2523)

Dear George,

President Kaunda's Visit

As you know, President Kaunda has had a tête-à-tête meeting with the Prime Minister, followed by a working dinner here this evening. I shall not be doing a formal record of the discussions since no-one sat in on the tête-à-tête and since the Prime Minister decided against having a note taken during the meal.

In fact, there was little detailed discussion during either part of the talks with President Kaunda. President Kaunda said that he had come to listen. Apart from the efforts to create a favourable atmosphere, the Prime Minister and the Foreign and Commonwealth Secretary both concentrated on getting across to President Kaunda and his colleagues that the Lancaster House Conference had arrived at the moment of decision. They said that much progress had been made at the Conference and that agreement was now within reach. The Conference could not be allowed to drag on much longer: further delay would only result in Bishop Muzorewa's delegation being lost. HMG had made proposals which seemed to it to lie between the positions of the two parties. It might be that the proposals would seem unfair to both sides but this was inevitable in the circumstances. Bishop Muzorewa's delegation had accepted the proposals. We now awaited the verdict of the Patriotic Front. We hoped that they would say 'yes' and that they would do so soon. We very much hoped that President Kaunda would bring his influence to bear on the Patriotic Front to reach an early and favourable decision.

The Foreign and Commonwealth Secretary stressed that he recognised that it would not be easy for Mr Nkomo to reach such a decision. In order for him to do so it would be necessary for him to trust the United Kingdom. HMG had throughout the Conference attempted to be fair and were determined to be equally fair during any interim period. At one stage President Kaunda said in response to the Foreign and Commonwealth Secretary, that it was because he trusted HMG that he had come to London to try to help to secure an agreement.

It was striking throughout the evening's discussions how little attention was focussed by President Kaunda and his delegation on the problems we had been led to expect them to raise, e.g. the length of the interim period and the question of a Commonwealth force. Instead, they seemed to be principally preoccupied with the question of the status of Bishop Muzorewa and of the Patriotic Front leaders during the interim period and the election campaign. They were concerned about the advantage Bishop Muzorewa would derive from appearing to be Prime Minister even if he were not in fact carrying out the duties of the office. The Foreign and Commonwealth Secretary promised that all the political leaders participating in the election would enjoy equal status. He said that they would, for instance, certainly have the use of government aircraft. One of the Governor's principal functions would be to ensure that all the participants in an election were treated similarly.

There was some discussion of the kind of result from an election which would be most likely to lead to stability in the early stages of Independence. The Foreign and Commonwealth Secretary said that it might be no bad thing if the result was that no-one won the majority. The resulting need for accommodation between the various parties might make a reconciliation between the warring factions easier. President Kaunda dissented strongly from this view. He considered that the best, and indeed the only, hope for the country was that an outright victor would emerge. A coalition government would be extremely weak. Only a government with a clear majority would be able to give the direction required. There was general agreement in this context that Mr Nkomo was the most charismatic figure among the various political leaders at present on the scene.

In the course of discussion on subjects other than Rhodesia, President Kaunda expressed considerable concern about the developing situation in Zaire. He thought President Mobutu's[1] situation was not strong and that the insurgents who had previously tried to overthrow his regime from outside were now infiltrating into the country. President Kaunda expected that when the next upheaval came it would be very serious. He evidently regarded with a good deal of dismay the prospect of being bordered to both north and south by unstable regimes. He spoke favourably, however, of President Santos of Angola. He expected President Santos to continue President Neto's policy.

At the end of the discussion it was agreed that President Kaunda and his party would call again at 1030 tomorrow. The Prime Minister expressed the hope that an answer from the Patriotic Front might be forthcoming in the course of the day. She said that the decision for the Patriotic Front would not get any easier by being delayed.

I am sending a copy of this letter to Martin Vile in the Cabinet Office.

Yours ever,
MICHAEL ALEXANDER

---

1 Mr Joseph Desire Mobutu, President of Zaire, 1971-97.

No. 158

Lord Carrington to Sir N. Henderson (Washington), 9 November 1979, 8.17 p.m.[1]
Tel. No. 1614, Immediate, Secret (FCO 36/2540)

Personal for Ambassador
Rhodesia
1. The US Ambassador called on the PUS on 9 November to discuss Rhodesia.
2. After Sir M. Palliser had outlined the reasons for which the British Government had decided that it could not take positive action to continue sanctions after 15 November, Brewster said that, speaking personally, he thought it would be in the interests of progress in the Lancaster House Conference for the President to announce on 15 November that he proposed not to lift sanctions as long as the talks were continuing. If the President did not continue sanctions after 15 November, there was no way in which they could be reimposed. The Salisbury Parties might then become less 'tractable' and the Patriotic Front would be less inclined to stay in the talks.
3. Sir M. Palliser said that in that case we would attach great importance to the President's making a public statement that sanctions would be lifted as soon as the Governor arrived in Rhodesia and legality was restored. If the President continued sanctions without making such a statement, it would look as if the Administration had reservations about our proposals. Brewster agreed, and said he would convey this to Washington. He agreed also to make contact again on 13 November about the merits of continuing US sanctions after the 15th. It was still very important to ensure that if the Patriotic Front got off the train, it was seen to be their fault.
4. Brewster also raised the question of South African involvement in Rhodesia. He accepted that the security forces would have to go on using South African equipment. But the presence of extra-territorial forces in Rhodesia after the installation of a Governor would be 'very prejudicial'. Sir M. Palliser agreed.

1 And for information Immediate to UKMIS New York; Priority Pretoria.

No. 159

Minute from Mr Lyne to Mr Renwick, 9 November 1979
Confidential (FCO 36/2523)

Zambia/Rhodesia
Following Lord Carrington's singularly unproductive meeting with President Kaunda at 6.45 pm this evening (at the President's 'urgent' request) Mr Luce passed an oral message on Lord Carrington's behalf to the Zambian President. Having tried and failed to get hold of a Minister or other senior member of the President's party, Mr Luce told President Kaunda's Private Secretary on the telephone that the British Government were looking to the President to assist us in the process of trying to bring about a Rhodesian settlement. If we could persuade all the parties to join in

we could at last master the problem. Lord Carrington therefore hoped that President Kaunda would take every opportunity to persuade Mr Nkomo to accept an agreement. We were all looking to Kaunda to give the lead. This could be the turning point in the Conference.

The Private Secretary said that he had taken the message.

R.M.J. LYNE

No. 160

Letter from Mr Lyne to Mr Alexander (No. 10), 9 November 1979
Confidential (FCO 36/2523)

Dear Michael,
Prime Minister's Meeting with President Kaunda: 10 November
I have sent you the reply given today by the Patriotic Front to our proposals for the pre-independence arrangements. This takes us no further forward. It consists to a large extent of a re-statement of their opening position. It will not be possible to reach agreement on this basis.

On the points we can 'offer' President Kaunda, the Prime Minister may wish to emphasise that, if the Patriotic Front can agree to our general proposals:

(*a*) we envisage a *Ceasefire Commission* on which the Commanders of the forces on both sides would be represented. The Patriotic Front forces would have 'status' (arrangements would need to be made for their housing, food, etc.) and would be responsible to the Governor for the maintenance of the cease-fire.

(*b*) to meet some of the concerns expressed by the Front Line Presidents we envisage a *monitoring force* under United Kingdom auspices, to which certain other Commonwealth Governments have already offered to contribute (Australia, New Zealand and Fiji; we have also approached Kenya and may approach Malaysia). This will not be an intervention force (which could easily find itself involved in clashes with the Patriotic Front). Its purpose will be to monitor and control the cease-fire and to help to exercise a stabilising influence when the result of the election is known.

(*c*) with regard to the status of the parties and their leaders during the election campaign (about which Kaunda has expressed great concern), we should emphasise that they will all be represented on the *Election Council* and will all campaign on the same basis.

This really is as much as we can offer the Patriotic Front or President Kaunda. The Prime Minister will wish to emphasise once again to President Kaunda that the key to peace is in his hands. (On behalf of Lord Carrington, Mr Luce sent him an oral message this evening to this effect)[1]. We are doing everything we can to give effect to the Lusaka agreement. A settlement is obtainable on this basis; but not on some other basis. We are in a position to put these plans into effect. We are closer to a solution than ever before; but we can only succeed if President Kaunda decides to support us. The Prime Minister may also wish to indicate that we believe that

1 No. 159.

Mr Nkomo is showing considerably more interest in a settlement than Mr Mugabe; and that it would be a tragedy if the latter's intransigence caused the chance of a settlement to be lost.

R.M.J. LYNE

No. 161

Sir N. Henderson (Washington) to Lord Carrington, November 1979, 1.30 a.m.[1]

Tel. No. 3664 Immediate, Confidential (FCO 36/2540)

Meeting with Secretary of State Vance about Rhodesia

1. On my return from London today I saw Vance to give him your mind on how the Conference is going and on how the US Government might help at this difficult juncture. Vance, who is very preoccupied at the moment with the Iranian hostage problem[2], said that he was eager to know exactly what you felt on Rhodesia.

2. Giving a general account of where the Conference stands at the moment and the impasse that has been reached because of the Patriotic Front's prevarications, I said that your underlying problem lay in maintaining sufficient momentum and in keeping up the pressure on the Patriotic Front without giving grounds for people to say, should the Conference break down, that this had been due to lack of patience at a late stage when so much had already been achieved. Although the Patriotic Front were being very negative, as I had been able to witness myself at the meeting yesterday, it was necessary to bear in mind that they had shown similar prolonged intransigence over the first part of the Conference only to turn round suddenly and accept the proposed constitution. It could not therefore be ruled out that they would come round over the transition arrangements. But there was no doubt that at the moment you saw great difficulties. Moreover the Conference just could not be allowed to drag on indefinitely. Apart from the need for us to hold the initiative there was a danger that if it went on interminably you would lose Muzorewa and the Salisbury Delegation. I had just heard that some of the delegation were being sent home. I stressed to Vance what a very long way we had travelled since the spring. It was quite untrue to suggest, as the Patriotic Front were now trying to do, that everything had been cooked up with Salisbury who had made no concessions and that it was only they, the Patriotic Front, who were being forced to yield. The proposed constitution would provide for majority rule, no white blocking vote, for the police and army under black rule. Ian Smith had been smashed. Muzorewa had had to accept handing over power to a Governor, notwithstanding the fact that he had been elected by 64 per cent of the electorate and the Rhodesian Parliament, elected in May, would be abolished. (I pointed out that Mugabe had been elected by three people not 1.8 million.)

---

1 Deskby to the FCO 11 November 1000z; and for information to Dar es Salaam, Maputo, Lusaka, Gaborone, Luanda, Lagos, Pretoria, UKMIS New York, Paris, Oslo, Lisbon.

2 On 4 November 1979, US Embassy staff in Tehran were taken hostage after a group of armed pro-Iranian Revolution students took over the embassy. The hostages were held for 444 days, and finally released on 20 January 1981.

3. The question in your mind now was whether the Patriotic Front wanted elections or not. There was a difference between Mugabe and Nkomo. The latter must have difficulty deciding. He might well do badly in the elections: But his position would also be difficult if the war went on and if he had no chance of getting into power by peaceful means. On the basis of the evidence so far it was difficult to say that Kaunda's presence in London had had a beneficial effect upon Nkomo. The immediate issue was what further pressure could be exercised now quickly to induce Nkomo at least to agree to something reasonable on the transition. Vance said that he appreciated the reasons against a long transition but commented that two months seemed 'a short time'. It would be a pity if the Conference were to break down over what appeared to be simply a question of timing. I described our views on the length of the transition period and said that the basic question remained whether the Patriotic Front's view on this subject was a fundamental objection or simply part of their policy to spin out the Conference for as long as possible.

4. Vance asked about the presence of the South African troops in Rhodesia. He said that a US mercenary had reported in detail on their presence and that an article would be appearing in the *Washington Post* on 13 November describing this. Vance suggested that it would be difficult if we were to countenance the presence of such troops during the transition.

5. I said that I could tell him for his own information that you had had a discussion about this with General Walls. Your view was that there should not be South African units operating in Rhodesia but that this was different from South Africans volunteering themselves to serve with Rhodesian units. Vance said that according to American information there were four companies of South Africans in Rhodesia.

6. We then had a general discussion in which others who were present, (Vest, Moose, Lake and Hare[3]), took part, about your intentions regarding the arrival of the Governor in Salisbury, what his powers would be and what would happen to the forces of the two sides during the transition period. Obviously the question of the positioning of the troops worried them and I said that my understanding was that the troops on both sides would come under the Governor and that they would have to stay put.

7. They also expressed great interest in the proposals for a cease-fire monitoring force composed of contingents from Commonwealth countries, and they seemed favourably impressed by what I was able to tell them. I took the opportunity of explaining what we were thinking of as regards this and the cease-fire commission though these were subjects of course for the third stage of the conference.

8. Reverting to the present impasse in the Conference and the various objections raised by the Patriotic Front regarding timing, registration etc., Moose and Lake, with Vance's encouragement came forward with a number of suggestions. The first was based on their belief that there was little to be done at this stage by hammering on at Nkomo and Mugabe. The only way to get them to move was to exert pressure on the Front Line States and get them, particularly Machel and Nyerere, to lean on the Patriotic Front leaders as they had done at the critical stage of the negotiations on the proposed constitution. But if we were to do this successfully we would have to

---

3 Mr Paul Julian Hare, Director of the Office of Southern African Affairs, US State Department, 1979-81.

dress it up as a new package. This was important psychologically at this moment of the Conference. Would it not be possible for us to show some readiness to be flexible on timing and to reveal our hand a bit more to the Front Line Presidents about our intention to keep troops concentrated and to make provision for a Commonwealth cease-fire monitoring force? As an extension of this idea the suggestion was also made that we should deliberately merge stages two and three of the Conference. We were stuck on stage two: why not therefore go on to stage three? Our flexibility on that might help to unblock the problems on the transition stage.

9. I said that I thought that your reaction to these ideas would be as follows. Firstly that you had deliberately decided to handle the Conference step by step, even though final agreement to one stage could be conditional upon agreement on the subsequent stage. This procedure had worked well as regards the constitution. (Vance interjected to say that it had worked brilliantly.) The idea of an improved package seemed to me to leave out of the account the very considerable moves towards the ideas of the Patriotic Front that had already been made by you. There was not really a great deal more room for further packages. In any case it was extremely inexpedient to give any encouragement to the idea that whole areas of the subject could now, after nine weeks of the Conference, be opened up as a result of pressure by one side. It was an article of your faith that the momentum must be maintained and that no encouragement could be given to the Patriotic Front to think that the Conference could be endlessly drawn out by discussion or this or that point. On the issue of the length of the transition time we were not prepared to start negotiating about this, partly because this would lead to prolonged and fruitless argument but also because it was pointless. The time that we were envisaging, which was two months plus, was plenty of time for the people of Rhodesia to know who the parties and candidates were. It was absurd for Nkomo to pretend that he needed a lot more time to become known to the electorate. He was already well known to everybody in Rhodesia.

10. The State Department officials insisted that we should really give thought to a fresh approach to Machel and Nyerere. They thought that they might well hold the key.

11. I said I would of course report what I had heard, but I must make one final and important observation regarding the US attitude. You were grateful for the support that Vance had given. Solidarity was essential. But the one thing that could make the negotiation harder and more prolonged would be if countenance were given to the idea that the US favoured some of the points such as timing that the Patriotic Front were insisting upon. I knew the US Government had been extremely careful not to give any false impression on this but I did want to emphasise the point. There was another aspect to this. What would also undermine your negotiating position would be if the Front Line States or Patriotic Front believed that in the event of the Conference failing, of the appointment of a Governor and of elections being held without the Patriotic Front and with the guerrilla war continuing, the US Government might not be prepared to recognise the new government that was elected by those elections on the basis of the proposed new Constitution. If the African leaders thought that the United States Government might hesitate in this way this would give them enormous encouragement to hold out against coming to terms. Vance's reaction to this was to say that he did not wish or intend to do anything that might impede the progress of the Conference. I thought he was careful however to avoid saying what he would do

in the hypothetical case I have just described. I left Vance in no doubt that we would be looking to our friends for support in such circumstances: the Governor would mean legality. I must reiterate that Vance is unhesitating in his admiration for what you have achieved and his backing for your attempts to reach a fair agreement.

12. Please see MIFT.[4]

[4] No. 162.

No. 162

Sir N. Henderson (Washington) to Lord Carrington, 10 November 1979, 1.35 a.m.[1]

Tel. No. 3665 Immediate, Confidential (FCO 36/2540)

Talk with Secretary of State Vance about lifting of Rhodesian sanctions: Please see MIPT[2]

1. During my talk today with Vance I said I wanted to explain our intentions about sanctions and to why we did not consider positive action by the Security Council necessary to bring to an end the situation that led to the imposition of sanctions. This subject would come easily to him with his legal training. There was not only the question of precedent, (and I described what had happened over the Palestine and Korean resolutions of 1948 and 1950, as well as subsequent Rhodesian resolutions) but there was also the very important practical point that if you took the line that the Security Council itself must decide whether a situation that gave rise to some action was over or not this would mean that one permanent member, by use of the veto, could claim that some action must be continued in perpetuity. One of the State Department officials said that the Rhodesia case was the only one in which sanctions had been applied under Chapter VII and he suggested therefore that there could not be a precedent for it. I asked Vance whether he knew of any example in which a resolution based on a threat to or a breach of peace under Chapter VII had been positively brought to an end by a Security Council decision saying that impairment to peace no longer existed. He said he could not.

2. But officials went on to ask whether, even if a terminating resolution might not be legally required, there might not be something to be said for having one if all parties to the London Conference reached agreement about the Constitution, elections, etc. I said that I was not an expert on this matter but I really did not think that we would want to get involved in the rigmarole of a protracted Security Council debate about the situation in Rhodesia. There might well be a lot of raking up of the past and suggested breaches of sanctions by one or other party since the original Security Council resolution. When legality was restored we would lift sanctions and would expect others to follow suit immediately. This was essential because otherwise people would be applying sanctions against us. Vance's response on this was that he was still wrestling with the problem. His advisors had told him that the legal argument was split fifty-fifty.

[1] Deskby to the FCO 11 November 10.00z; and for information to Dar es Salaam, Maputo, Lusaka, Gaborone, Luanda, Lagos, Pretoria, UKMIS New York, Paris, Oslo, Lisbon.
[2] No. 161.

3. We then came on to discuss the rather different question of what the Administration was going to do about US sanctions. He said that the Administration would have two choices on 15 November, when the President is required to make a determination. These were:

(*a*) to continue US sanctions while the negotiations in London were going on: and

(*b*) to continue US sanctions until legality was restored to Rhodesia.

I said that it would be unacceptable to the UK for the United States to maintain sanctions against Rhodesia once the Governor was there because if they did that they would be maintaining sanctions against the UK.

4. On the subject of the Presidential Determination on 15 November, I referred to the language used in the Determination in June which raised certain difficulties for us and asked Vance whether he would give us advance notice of what they intended to do and let us see the text of what the President was going to say. Vance undertook to do so.

No. 163

Minute from Mr Powell to Mr Walden, 11 November 1979
Secret (FCO 36/2441)

Rhodesia: Meeting with Mr Nkomo

1. Mr Renwick and I saw Mr Nkomo for a couple of hours today. Mr Chambati was also present. Nkomo was in a forthcoming mood. He had received a copy of the paper which the Prime Minister handed to President Kaunda.

2. We emphasised the Government's determination to put its proposals into effect and the need for a decision very soon by the Patriotic Front. Nkomo appeared to realise that matters could not be delayed (I understand that President Kaunda told Mr Luce this morning that he agreed that cease-fire talks must start not later than Wednesday or Thursday). He talked throughout on the assumption that if he decided to accept our proposals, the bulk of ZANU would do so too.

3. Nkomo rehearsed his argument for a *Governing Council* but without much conviction. He appeared satisfied with the point that all political leaders could have access to the Governor. On the *election* his main concern was that the election administration should be hived off from the remainder of the government machine (though he was at pains, on this point and others, to emphasise that he was not asking for particular individuals to be removed). Electoral officials should be under the supervision of the Election Council, which would include representatives of both sides, and exercise effective control over the elections. The impression he gave was that the first part of this proposition—i.e. the separate election administration—was what really mattered. On the *status of Bishop Muzorewa* and his Ministers, Nkomo accepted that we could not humiliate them. He took the point that whatever residual advantage they might derive from their titles would be balanced by the Patriotic Front's advantage of being in opposition. He appeared satisfied that the PF leaders would be allowed their own *bodyguards*.

4. On the *police*, Nkomo said he personally accepted that the existing force would continue as the Governor's police and would act impartially. But there was a

presentational problem vis-à-vis his forces. There should be a role for 'some' Patriotic Front police to help maintain law and order. He did not, however, press the point.

5. Most of the discussion centred on the *cease-fire* and *status of forces*. He had obviously found the formulation in the paper which the Prime Minister gave to President Kaunda helpful. When we mentioned the need for Patriotic Front forces to assemble at pre-determined places, he raised no objection. Nor did he rise when we said that there might be some circumstances in which the Governor would need to use General Walls' forces. He did not mention the idea of a Commonwealth peace-keeping force. But the one point he could not, he said, agree on was the unequal status in our proposals (paragraph 13) of the Patriotic Front and Salisbury forces. Unless PF forces were brought under the Governor's authority it would look as though the PF's forces had surrendered. He could never persuade them to accept that. The regime's forces appeared in paragraph 13 on the machinery of government. The PF's forces must appear there too.

6. Nkomo advised strongly that we should omit the words 'rehabilitation' and 'ex-combatants' from the section of the paper dealing with refugees. They were a red rag to the Patriotic Front.

7. We touched briefly on the length of the interim period. Nkomo said that four months would be needed. We said that there was no chance of going beyond the time-scale mentioned by the Prime Minister to Kaunda, i.e. 2 weeks for the cease-fire to come into effect plus 8/9 weeks for the elections.

8. Nkomo is still probing to see if there is any more to be had from us. We gave him no reason to think that there would be. The main point of substance is the status of his forces. We cannot change the text of our paper since this would lead to immediate trouble with the Salisbury delegation. But there may be scope on this and some of the other points for a carefully prepared question and answer exchange in a plenary (i.e. 'Will the Patriotic Front's forces also be required to comply with the Governor's directions?' 'Will the machinery to supervise the elections be separate from the other machinery of government?') on the basis of which he could accept our proposals, subject to satisfaction on a cease-fire. The paper given to President Kaunda could be turned into the answers.

9. There seems no point in a further plenary session of the conference until the Patriotic Front have taken their decision. The most profitable way forward is likely to be to continue to work on ZAPU. Mr Nkomo has asked to see Mr Renwick and me again tomorrow morning. Thereafter we may need a full bilateral. We should be ready to offer Nkomo and Mugabe a meeting with the Secretary of State.

10. This was the moderate presentation of Nkomo's position. If he asks for no more and can carry the Patriotic Front there is a chance of agreement. But we may well find his attitude less forthcoming once Mugabe returns. If [he] steps up his demands again, there is nothing more we can offer him.[1]

C.D. POWELL

---

1 On 12 November Mr Lyne minuted: 'Secretary of State. You have already had an oral account of this.'

No. 164

Minute from Mr Walden to Mr Renwick, 12 November 1979
Confidential (FCO 36/2523)

Secretary of State's Meeting with President Kaunda

As you know, Lord Carrington had a brief meeting with President Kaunda after the plenary session on Saturday morning, and before Kaunda saw the Prime Minister later that day.

Kaunda said that he had spoken again to the Patriotic Front, and was sure that Nkomo wanted a settlement. He was much less sure about Mugabe, but thought that Nkomo was the central figure. Having asked everyone else (including the LPS) to leave the room, Kaunda told Lord Carrington in a stage whisper that Tongogara was on Nkomo's side. He elaborated on the position in ZANU on the lines of what he later repeated to the Prime Minister (see Mr Alexander's record).

Lord Carrington made a point of telling Kaunda that the Prime Minister would give him a list of issues on which we had shown flexibility during the negotiations. He also stressed the urgency of the situation, warning the President that the entire Salisbury delegation might go home very soon if we did not get agreement.

G.G.H. WALDEN

No. 165

Minute from Mr Day to Ms Spencer, 13 November 1979
Confidential (FCO 36/2613)

Rhodesia: Lord Soames

1. Lord Soames telephoned this morning to say that he was sending a minute to the Secretary of State about our cease-fire paper, a copy of which had been sent to him. He thought that the paper skated around a number of the difficult issues, and he feared that he, as Governor, would face a whole range of difficult problems and decisions unless the arrangements for the cease-fire were far more watertight. I explained to Lord Soames that our paper was not intended to be a final document. It would be the outline of proposals for a cease-fire that we would put to the Conference if and when we got to that stage. Many details would need to be filled-in in the light of the discussions with the parties concerned. It still seemed improbable to us that an agreement would be possible with the Patriotic Front, or at least with both elements of the Front. If, however, it emerged that a full agreement were possible, we would certainly need to table at the next stage a fuller and more detailed cease-fire plan.

2. Lord Soames was also worried about the logistic support that would be available to him and to his senior advisers. General Walls had told him that the Rhodesian Security Forces would not be able to make any transport available to the Governor, the Election Commissioner, the Military Adviser, etc. He hoped,

therefore, that he would not find himself in a situation in which we had a perfectly good plan, but could not implement it effectively for lack of logistic support. I acknowledged that the question of transport was a difficult one, but that we did not consider it insuperable. We would expect the Rhodesian authorities to make all necessary arrangements in respect of the Election Commissioner and his staff. We were discussing with the Ministry of Defence how best to make arrangements for the logistic support for the monitoring group, should we actually reach that stage. There would certainly be no excess of transport, etc., but we believe that we could make adequate arrangements.

3. Lord Soames thought that before the end of the Lancaster House Conference we should make it clear that if, during the pre-independence period, any of the parties to the agreement flagrantly broke their undertakings in respect of the cease-fire, adherence to the Constitution, or any similar matter, the Governor would have the right to exclude them from the election. Lord Soames said that he had mentioned this thought to the Secretary of State. I said that it had been made clear that anyone taking part in the election must be required to abide by the Constitution and any other agreements, e.g. the cease-fire, that had been concluded in London. If these undertakings were not fulfilled, then the party would have excluded themselves from the process leading to independence. Lord Soames will, I think, wish this to be spelt out again and more clearly before the Conference comes to an end.

4. Finally, Lord Soames enquired about the timing of the Governor's arrival. He would find it extremely difficult to leave the UK before November 20. I said that I thought that in the circumstances in which we envisaged his departure, he would not be required to move earlier than that. Miss Spencer was discussing this with you.[1]

D.M. DAY

1 Ms Spencer wrote in the margin that she had discussed with Jim Buckley, Lord Soames' Private Secretary. This was dated 14 November 1979.

No. 166

Letter from Mr Alexander (No. 10) to Mr Lyne, 14 November 1979
(PREM 19/114)

Dear Roderic,

Call by Mr Sule

As you know, the special representative of the President of Nigeria, Mr Sule, called on the Prime Minister this afternoon. The letter he bore, of which I enclose a copy, was, as in the case of Mr Nguza, simply a letter of introduction.[1] The Prime Minister handed over the signed copy of the draft enclosed with George Walden's letter to me of 13 November.[1]

I do not think there is any need to record the conversation between Mr Sule and the Prime Minister: it has in any case largely been overtaken by events. The Prime

1 Not printed.

Minister told Mr Sule where matters stood; Mr Sule told the Prime Minister about the immense importance of a successful outcome to the Conference and of his determination to do everything he could to bring the parties together.

It may, however, be worth noting that Mr Sule laid a great deal of stress on relations between Nigeria and Great Britain and upon the potential significance for them of a breakdown in the Rhodesia talks. He said that Britain was a country that the Nigerians held particularly dear. Moreover, the two countries had many mutual interests. It was essential that the outcome of the Lancaster House Conference should not tarnish Britain's reputation. There was a danger that failure of the Conference would affect Britain's relations with Nigeria. This would be against the wishes of the Nigerian Government but might be inevitable. Therefore the Conference must not fail. Mr Sule made it clear that for Nigerian purposes, an agreement with one party to the Conference would constitute a failure. There must be no bilateral deal.

As I was taking Mr Sule to the door, I told him of the critical point reached in the Conference and of the fact that developments this evening were likely to be crucial. Mr Sule said that he hoped there was no question of HMG issuing an ultimatum. I said that HMG, of course, did not issue ultima in negotiations of this kind. Mr Sule said that he was glad to hear this. He then volunteered that he would try to see the Patriotic Front this evening to urge them to be reasonable.

MICHAEL ALEXANDER

No. 167

Letter from Mrs Thatcher to President Shagari of Nigeria, 14 November 1979
(FCO 36/2509)

Dear Mr President,

Many thanks for your message of 5 November,[1] which has encouraged me to feel that there is a great deal of common ground between us in our approach to the Rhodesia problem. I note that you still feel that the period we envisage for the electoral process is too short. The British Government has always taken the view that the independence constitution should be implemented as soon as is consistent with the holding of free and fair elections. Their starting point was that the election period need not last more than four to six weeks. But they have taken account of the strongly held views that it should be longer, in eventually deciding that it should run from two months from the date when a cease-fire becomes effective. It will take up to two weeks to bring the cease-fire into effect. The election will be held eight or nine weeks after the cease-fire comes into effect.

I entirely agree with you that provisions should be made against possible breaches of the cease-fire. For this reason, we shall be putting forward proposals in the Conference for a Commonwealth monitoring force, to which a number of other Commonwealth countries have now agreed in principle to contribute. This will provide all parties with reassurance that the maintenance of the cease-fire will

---

1 Not printed.

be impartially observed and controlled. With the agreement of the parties and of the contributing countries, this force would play a stabilising role in resolving military questions which could arise after elections and before independence.

Following intensive discussions with President Kaunda, I gave him a paper which sets out fully our views on the way ahead. I am asking our High Commissioner to give you a copy of this paper for your strictly personal information.

I am convinced that we now have a set of proposals for the interim period which will be fair to all parties. I very much hope that the Patriotic Front will agree to participating in the elections.

WITH BEST WISHES,
M[ARGARET] T[HATCHER]

No. 168

Minute from Mr Lyne to Mr Renwick, 14 November 1979
Confidential (FCO 36/2441)

Bishop Muzorewa

Lord Carrington spoke briefly to Bishop Muzorewa on the telephone this evening, following the meeting at Lancaster House.

Lord Carrington said he had a hunch that the Patriotic Front would agree to the British proposals at tomorrow morning's Plenary. But if they did not do so, Cabinet would have to consider the matter immediately afterwards. We would certainly know where we stood tomorrow. He appreciated that the time taken to reach the point of decision had caused problems for Bishop Muzorewa, and he understood that officials of the Salisbury delegation would be discussing the timing and presentation of Muzorewa's return to Salisbury with you tomorrow. Bishop Muzorewa said that he wanted to depart as soon as possible, but not at a time when this would be embarrassing for the British Government.

Lord Carrington told Bishop Muzorewa that he hoped to see him tomorrow or the day after.

R.M.J. LYNE

No. 169

Mr Leahy (Pretoria) to Lord Carrington, 14 November 1979, 4.05 p.m.[1]
Tel. No. 852 Immediate, Confidential (FCO 36/2514)

Mirimba Salisbury telno 891:Rhodesia[2]

1. The South Africans profess to believe that with every week that slips by Muzorewa is losing more and more of the black electorate to the Patriotic Front. Moreover they think he has been out of the country so long he does not realise the extent of this himself. What their evidence for this shift in opinion is I do not know, but to judge by paragraph 8 of Mirimba Salisbury telegram No. 809 of 27 October there is some support for this view in Rhodesia itself. Pik Botha told me recently (my telno 801)[2] that in his view the PF were spinning things out at Lancaster House in order to be sure of winning the eventual elections; and he seemed to think that by this time Nkomo was already a winner. He also emphasised the continuing heavy cost to South Africa of underpinning Muzorewa. Even allowing for his habitual exaggeration, have no doubt that he would regard any extension of the interim period as putting the final nail in Muzorewa's coffin. What is worse he is quite capable of saying so publicly.

2. If, therefore, any extension of the interim period should be contemplated, we shall need to explain the reason in advance to the South Africans, for the time being they are displaying reticence in public about the course of negotiations, but this could be the issue which would cause them to break their silence. Whether or not this would necessarily be unhelpful to you in the wider context of dealing with the criticisms from the other side is another matter which only you can judge.

No. 170

Minute from Mr Luce to Lord Carrington, 15 November 1979
Confidential (FCO 36/2509)

Relations with Nigeria

1. On 24 October I called on President Shagari. This morning I met the President's personal emissary, Alhaji Maitama Sule.

2. I have been very struck by their demeanour and manner. Both men are singularly calm, thoughtful and moderate. They went to some lengths to explain the importance which they attach to relations with Britain and indeed the real affection they feel for us. I think both were sincere in this. The President's emissary told me that Nigerians regarded relations with Britain as more important than with any other country.

3. In addition to the warmth described above I have been impressed by the moderate views expressed to me both by the President and by his emissary. The latter told me this morning that while he was neither a capitalist nor a socialist he believed that

---

1 And Information Priority to Lusaka, Dar es Salaam, Maputo, Gaborone, Luanda, Washington, UKMIS New York, Lagos.
2 Not printed.

for good or ill Nigeria was and must remain a capitalist country. He hoped that by following the system of free enterprise, by encouraging both domestic and foreign investment, Nigeria be able to emulate the successful examples of developed capitalist countries such as the US, Japan and West Germany.

4. I think we must not underestimate the change that has taken place in the Nigerian Government since 1 October. The new Nigerian leaders are far more disposed than their predecessors to cultivate good relations with us. The fact that their advent to power coincides with the likely removal of the single most difficult obstacle to good relations between us (i.e. Rhodesia) presents, I believe, a unique opportunity to put our relations on a better footing and keep them there. I think that during the next few months we should plan to maintain and extend our contacts with Nigeria (we are fortunate in having an intelligent and sympathetic High Commissioner here in London) and seek the best ways of exploiting the opportunity which presents itself.

5. We should certainly consider the possibility of a visit to Lagos by you or the Lord Privy Seal in the early part of next year. We should also try to involve the Nigerians more in our approach to matters of common concern—Southern Africa, energy, North/South dialogue. I think we have a chance to establish genuinely close and friendly relations and that it will be very much in our interests to seize it.

RICHARD LUCE

No. 171

Lord Carrington to Sir L. Allinson (Lusaka), 15 November 1979, 2.42 p.m.[1]
Tel. No. 947 Confidential, Immediate (FCO 36/2441)

Rhodesia Conference

1. In the Conference this morning the Patriotic Front agreed to the proposals we have put forward for the interim period, subject to a successful outcome of the negotiations on a cease-fire. I undertook to add a reference to the Patriotic Front's forces to paragraph 13 of our paper, in the following terms: 'The Patriotic Front's forces will also be required to comply with the directions of the Governor.'

2. We will be tabling in the Conference tomorrow proposals for the cease-fire. The negotiations will be extremely difficult. No effective cease-fire will be possible on the basis of the forces being 'frozen' in their present positions: they are interlocked throughout Rhodesia. The Prime Minister has explained to President Kaunda and we have explained to the Patriotic Front that it will not be possible to deploy the

---

[1] And to Mirimba, Salisbury, Nairobi, Maputo, Gaborone, Dar es Salaam, Luanda, Lagos, Washington, Pretoria, Addis Ababa, Monrovia, Canberra, Ottawa, Wellington; Priority Peking, Moscow, Prague, Dakar, Kinshasa, Khartoum, Tokyo, EEC Posts, Kuwait, Kingston, Bridgetown, Dacca, New Delhi, Singapore, Georgetown, Freetown, Port Louis, Port of Spain, Lilongwe, Valletta, Banjul, Colombo, Accra, Kuala Lumpur, Nicosia, Oslo, Stockholm, Lisbon, Madrid, Athens, Mbabane, Abidjan; Information Immediate UKMIS New York, UKMIS Geneva; Information Saving Nassau, Maseru, Castries, Suva, Port Moresby, Honiara, Nuku'alofa, Victoria, Tarawa, UKDEL NATO, Sofia, Budapest, Bucharest, East Berlin, Belgrade, Cairo, Algiers, Tunis, Tripoli, Rabat, Tehran.

Monitoring Force unless the Patriotic Front are prepared to assemble their forces at pre-determined places, where arrangements will be made for their security, accommodation and other agreed requirements. It will also be essential to the preservation of a cease-fire that there should be effective arrangements, in agreement with the Botswana, Zambia and Mozambique governments for the avoidance of cross-border incidents and infiltration. This will involve some cross-border monitoring or—at least—liaison arrangements.

3. All these elements will be very difficult to negotiate. But it will be essential to the prospects of success in the Conference to use the momentum which has now been achieved to try to bring the cease-fire negotiation to a conclusion as quickly as possible.

4. We have been grateful for the action taken by the Americans and by some of our other allies in the Front-Line states. The Australian and New Zealand and Fijian offers of participation in a Commonwealth Monitoring force made a major contribution in helping the Conference forward to this stage. All posts to which this telegram is addressed should at their discretion impress on the governments to which they are accredited the need over the next few days for the strongest possible international support for our efforts to complete the settlement. We shall be wanting to ask the Americans, European and Old Commonwealth governments in particular to support our efforts in persuading the Botswana, Zambian and Mozambique Governments to help in resolving the problems of the cease-fire.

CHAPTER IV

Negotiations on the Cease-Fire and the Return to Legality

November – December 1979

No. 172

Mr Leahy (Pretoria) to Lord Carrington, 15 November 1979, 3.30 p.m.[1]
Tel. No. 856 Immediate, Confidential (FCO 36/2514)

My telno 852: Rhodesia[2]

1. Pik Botha summoned me for another session of doom and gloom this afternoon. Even the news which was telephoned through to me during our meeting that the Patriotic Front had this morning agreed to our proposals for the interim arrangements and that the ceasefire discussions would be starting immediately failed to lighten his mood.

2. As foreshadowed in my TUR, the burden of Mr Botha's remarks was that, according to reliable information available to the South Africans, Bishop Muzorewa now only enjoyed the support of between 35% and 40% of the electorate and every week that went by he lost another 2%-3%. From what he (Botha) had heard from London it might take as much as two weeks before the ceasefire was negotiated: This in turn would delay the arrival of the Governor and also the date of the elections. The way things were going he would take a bet with me that the elections would not in fact take place until April. It was easy for me to say that we intended to get the ceasefire discussions over quickly; we had said the same thing about the Conference itself and it had now dragged on for well over two months.

3. Mr Botha went on to say that we perhaps had a different assessment of Muzorewa's chances. In general he could not help wondering whether we were still 'on the same wave-length'. He did not wish to suggest that we had been guilty of bad faith, but when he was in London he had understood that we intended to get the Governor to Salisbury by the middle of November. The repeated delays at Lancaster House meant that Nkomo was now winning all along the line. He was opening offices 'everywhere' and had 'enormous' sums of money at his disposal. He had completely out-played Muzorewa, who had stayed in London far longer than he should have done against his (Botha's) advice. Even now it was not known when Muzorewa would return.

---

[1] And for Information Priority to Mirimba Salisbury, Lusaka, Dar es Salaam, Maputo, Gaborone, Luanda, Washington, UKMIS New York, Lagos.
[2] No. 169.

4. Mr Botha said he did not doubt our good intentions, but unfortunately intentions did not win elections. It was organisation that won elections and the man who had the organisation was Nkomo. South Africa could not afford to go backing a losing horse and paying out Rands 40 million a month for this purpose. There was no point in going on supporting the Bishop and incurring the wrath of Nkomo at the same time. His (Botha's) position in the Cabinet was becoming 'embarrassing'. He intended, therefore, to put these views to the Cabinet next Tuesday and to suggest that the time had come for SAG to reconsider their attitude. If between now and then I would like to give him our considered reactions to what he had said he would be glad to have them.

5. I told Mr Botha that I would report what he had said. I had hoped that the news that I had just given him would be encouraging and was sorry to see that it was not. I saw no reason why the ceasefire discussions should go on for another two weeks or why the Governor's arrival in Salisbury should be long delayed. We might well have a different assessment from him of Muzorewa's electoral chances. Nor was it fair to suggest, as he had done earlier, that the British Government, unlike the SAG, did not mind too much what happened in Rhodesia as long as they got the problem off their hands. Mr Botha intervened to say that he did not mean to put it as strongly as that, but it was only natural that South Africa should be more concerned with a country on its doorstep than was the United Kingdom at a distance of 6000 miles. I said we had demonstrated at Lancaster House that we were concerned with the quality of the agreement we got on Rhodesia, as well as with its timing. Mr Botha replied that the upshot of what was now happening was that although we did not intend it we would be creating in Rhodesia not peace but rather the beginning of a large-scale conflict in Southern Africa.

6. I am sorry once again to be burdening you with Pik Botha's moody prognostications. I do not exactly enjoy them myself, but it is, I think, important to go on trying to calm him down and reassure him. The personal message which you sent him in Namibia had a good effect, and if you could see your way to doing the same thing now on Rhodesia it would help him if, as he says, he feels obliged to raise the matter in Cabinet next Tuesday. The two important points to cover in such a message would be our latest forecast of the timing of the Governor's arrival in Salisbury and our assessment (which Mr Byatt may be able to provide) of Muzorewa's electoral standing. If in this context you could add anything about the possibility of the likely cohesion or lack of cohesion between Mugabe and Nkomo during the election campaign, so much the better, but this may be either too speculative or too delicate.

7. At one point Mr Botha asked me whether the British Governor would 'recognize' the loans South Africa had made to Rhodesia: I treated this as a rhetorical question, but it is interesting that he spoke of loans rather than grants.

No. 173

Mr Leahy (Pretoria) to Lord Carrington, 16 November 1979, 11.30 a.m.[1]
Tel. No. 860 Immediate, Confidential (FCO 36/2514)

My tels Nos. 856[2] and 858:[3] Rhodesia

1. The South Africans are clearly in [the] process of convincing themselves that the man they have put their money on, Muzorewa, is going to lose the election and that another hostile, Marxist regime will come to power on their borders. Given their view of the threat to their survival from the 'total communist onslaught', this is for them an appalling prospect, all the more so because in South Arica itself they have become used over 30 years to the certainties of one-party government. Their practice, as we have seen in the face of the equally abhorrent danger of a SWAPO victory in Namibia, is to back their chosen group and not to risk an election until they can be certain that their men will win. Confronted now by the unexpected turn of events in Rhodesia—they have probably been banking on a failure to reach a comprehensive agreement at Lancaster House, just as they earlier assumed that the Lusaka Conference would fail—what can they do about it?

2. There was a hint in what Pik Botha said to me yesterday that they might try to move closer to Nkomo. They have had contact with him in the past. The way Pik Botha talks about him suggests he regards him as a greater threat than Mugabe. Nevertheless whether they should consider taking out some re-insurance with Nkomo by giving him financial encouragement to break away from Mugabe is a question they may be asking themselves. They might try to do this at the same time as continuing to prop up Muzorewa. But Nkomo might of course insist that they drop their support for Muzorewa.

3. An alternative might be for the South Africans to try to prevent the elections ever happening by covert sabotaging of the ceasefire agreement. It does not need much imagination to see that there are ways in which this could be done. Moreover it would happen at a time when sanctions had already been lifted.

4. What I do not think the South Africans will do, at least not at this stage, i.e. before the elections, is to undertake overt military intervention in Rhodesia. I would not rule this out after the elections if the 'wrong side' won, but even then this would be a traumatic decision for them to take after their Angola fiasco a few years back. Moreover they have committed themselves to a special debate in Parliament first.

---

1 And for Information Priority to Mirimba Salisbury and Washington.
2 No. 172.
3 Not printed.

No. 174

Lord Carrington to Mr Leahy (Pretoria), 17 November 1979, 12.19 p.m.
Tel. No. 479 Immediate, Confidential (FCO 36/2514)

Your telno 856: Rhodesia[1]

1. Please transmit the following message from me to Pik Botha.
BEGINS
'Dear Pik,
We have moved into the final phase of the Rhodesia Conference. It has taken longer to get to this point than, ideally, either of us would have wished. As Bishop Muzorewa knows, I am surprised that we have succeeded in getting this far. I know that you are anxious about the way things will turn out, and are keen that we should reach a conclusion soon.

But in my view, by securing agreement on the pre-independence arrangements, on the terms which we put forward, we have placed ourselves in a strong position.

As I told the Conference this morning, I am determined to sustain the momentum so that we can move rapidly through the ceasefire negotiations. John Leahy will have shown you the proposals I have tabled on the ceasefire. An essential element is that we shall be requiring the Patriotic Front forces to assemble within a very short period. We have agreed that they will be required to comply with the directions of the Governor: but I have made it very clear that their status cannot be the same as that of the existing security forces.

I have acknowledged in public that it will not be at all easy to reach agreement on the ceasefire. We cannot allow this phase of the negotiations to be dragged out, and I think the next few days will show whether we are continuing to make progress. I hope that we shall have your support during this critical period, and that we can continue to keep closely in touch.

I am very glad that you were able to send a delegation to the Namibian talks in Geneva. One crisis at a time is enough!
                                                                    Yours ever,

Peter Carrington'
ENDS

---

1 No. 172.

No. 175

FCO to Sir L. Allinson, 20 November 1979, 4 p.m.[1]
Tel. No. 958 Flash, Confidential (Thatcher MSS (Churchill Archives Centre) THCR 3/1/4)[2]

MIPT: Rhodesia.[3]

1. Following is text of message from Prime Minister:

'Dear Kenneth

As you know, I had already addressed a message to you about the progress of the Rhodesia Constitutional Conference before news reached me about recent events. These I know have caused you much distress.

I can well understand the concern which you feel at the attacks which have taken place on your territory and the extremely difficult situation in which they have placed you and your people.

As I made clear to you when you were in London, it is my earnest desire to see that all such incidents come to an end and that normal relations can be restored between Rhodesia and Zambia as soon as possible.

Let me assure you, Kenneth, that we are doing all we can to see that this happens and that we have been urging both sides to show restraint. But the only way we can be sure of achieving our aim is to bring the war itself to an end. This is precisely what we are striving to do in this final phase of the Constitutional Conference. Peter Carrington and Iain [*sic*] Gilmour have been doing their utmost to impress on both the other delegations at Lancaster House the urgent need to make progress quickly.

One of the considerations which is uppermost in all our minds in this is the need to put an end to the loss of human life and the disruption of your economy which you are suffering as a result of the conflict in Rhodesia. To do this, we must get an agreement on a cease-fire here in London which will enable us to send our Governor out to Salisbury at once so that he can exert his authority over all the forces. Without a Governor we have no authority.

Having got agreement on the political basis for a settlement, it would be a tragedy if we now failed to get agreement on an end to the war, in the interests not only of the people of Rhodesia but of Zambia as well.

I do urge you to understand, Kenneth, that we are taking the situation very seriously indeed. At this vital moment, we must ensure that all the participants here concentrate on working without any further delay or interruption to reach agreement on a ceasefire at the earliest possible date. We must maintain the momentum of the talks at Lancaster House. We must get agreement within the next few days if the chance is not to slip from our grasp. I am sure that I can count on you for all possible help in this.

1 Lord Carrington was in Brussels on EEC related business. Repeated to Flash Lusaka, 21 November 1979, 2.46 p.m., and Information Immediate to UKREP Brussels (for PS to S of S), Washington, Dar es Salaam, Maputo, Deskby 20 November 4 p.m. to Gaborone; Priority to Luanda, UKMIS New York, Pretoria, Lagos, Mirimba, Salisbury.
2 No copy found in official files. Copy on the website of the Margaret Thatcher Foundation: https://www.margaretthatcher.org/document/119040.
3 Not printed.

If you think it would be helpful to have a word with me on the telephone to discuss this further, please do not hesitate to call me at once.

With warmest regards,

Margaret.'

No. 176

Lord Carrington to Sir L. Allinson (Lusaka), 20 November 1979, 7.30 p.m.[1]

Tel. No. 960 Confidential, Immediate (FCO 36/2442)

MIPT: Rhodesia Conference[2]

1. At a bilateral meeting this morning General Walls and other members of the Salisbury Delegation indicated that they could accept the main elements of our cease-fire proposals, but would wish to reserve judgement until we put forward detailed proposals. There were not prepared to negotiate on the basis of the Patriotic Front's proposals.

2. At a bilateral meeting this afternoon the Patriotic Front delegation led by Tongogara said that they were under instructions from Nkomo and Mugabe to say that they could only discuss the cease-fire in the presence of the Rhodesian delegation. They complained that the Rhodesians had not put forward their own proposals for a cease-fire and that this would have been the correct procedure. A long procedural argument ensued in the course of which we said that we could not oblige the Rhodesians to put forward proposals. What we were trying to do was to establish a basis on which it might be possible to reach agreement. We had offered since 17 November to hold discussions with the Patriotic Front to enable us to explain our proposals more fully to them and to discuss theirs.

3. The discussion then took a more constructive turn, with Tongogara admitting that in some important respects he saw merit in our proposals. It was clear that he was particularly attracted by the idea of a cease-fire commission, with representatives of the Commanders on both sides, under the Governor's Military Adviser, and that the primary responsibility for the enforcement of the cease-fire would rest with the Commanders on both sides. We were also able to explain that in our view there was a misconception in Patriotic Front thinking about the role of a peace-keeping or monitoring force. We explained that it could not be the role of such a force itself actually to enforce the cease-fire. This could involve it in conflict with either side (and this was not the role normally undertaken even by a 'peace-keeping' force). The cease-fire could only be maintained effectively by the forces on both sides. Our proposal for a monitoring force was designed to assist with this process. We also explained

---

1 And to Mirimba, Salisbury, Nairobi, Maputo, Gaborone, Dar es Salaam, Luanda, Lagos, Washington, Pretoria, Addis Ababa, Monrovia, Canberra, Ottawa, Wellington; Priority Peking, Moscow, Prague, Dakar, Kinshasa, Khartoum, Tokyo, EEC Posts, Kuwait, Kingston, Bridgetown, Dacca, New Delhi, Singapore, Georgetown, Freetown, Port Louis, Port of Spain, Lilongwe, Valletta, Banjul, Colombo, Accra, Kuala Lumpur, Nicosia, Oslo, Stockholm, Lisbon, Madrid, Athens, Mbabane, Abidjan; Information Immediate UKMIS New York, UKMIS Geneva; Information Saving Nassau, Maseru, Castries, Suva, Port Moresby, Honiara, Nuku'alofa, Victoria, Tarawa, UKDEL NATO, Sofia, Budapest, Bucharest, East Berlin, Belgrade, Cairo, Algiers, Tunis, Tripoli, Rabat, Tehran.

2 Not printed.

that we did not believe it possible to achieve agreement on the demarcation of areas under the control of the Patriotic Front and of the Rhodesian Security forces. Both sides claimed to control by far the greater part of the territory of Rhodesia. It would never be possible to reach agreement on the 'map' of the demarcation. Tongogara seemed reasonably receptive to these arguments and generally less doctrinaire than Mugabe. In conclusion he said that he had been telling his forces for fifteen years that they could only win power by fighting. He had to face the task of telling them otherwise. In order to be able to do so he had to be satisfied that the cease-fire would work. We said that General Walls had very similar pre-occupations.

No. 177

Transcript of a telephone conversation between Mrs Thatcher and President Kaunda, 22 November 1979
Unclassified (PREM 19/115)

Prime Minister: Is that Kenneth? This is Margaret.

President Kaunda: Good afternoon, Margaret.

PM: Oh, Kenneth, I'm so glad to have a chance to talk to you, because I think some very bad misunderstandings have arisen. Would you just like to say one or two things to me first?

President: Really, Margaret, things here, on my return from there, after I had gone through Rome and Baghdad, I found a very volatile situation here: the ways in which our bridges have been destroyed; continuous attacks on our people, resulting in murders and I just don't understand it at all. I have just come from London where after you received me, so well . . .[1] didn't want to find this position here at all. I called a press conference the day before yesterday at which I spoke very strongly. I was surprised of course by the silence of Western countries except for America which condemned the attacks on us, and I said at this press conference that Britain had the responsibility for this British colony—it's always been as far as I'm concerned—and then from there your British High Commissioner issued a very unfortunate statement indeed and this annoyed people here very much indeed.

PM: Well, I heard that and thought I would like to have one or two words with you. First, can I just say that I understand now that our British High Commission is all right and that the police and the army kept off the demonstration, and we're very grateful that they did and they acted to protect our people in the High Commission. Now secondly, Kenneth, what I'm very worried about is the misunderstanding that seems to have arisen about the powers we have at the moment. We don't have powers over Salisbury or General Walls until we can get a ceasefire actually signed and the Governor over there. Only then do we have the powers. Now Peter Carrington has been urging both sides to show complete restraint in particular during the cease-fire talks, and I am just as concerned as you are because I think that when you were here we were on the point of achieving success. Now let me tell you what is going to

---

1 All ellipses are in the original document.

happen now. We're going to have a full plenary session at 4 o'clock this afternoon. Peter Carrington having talked with both sides will be laying detailed proposals for a ceasefire for them to consider. The moment he lays his proposals he will ask both sides to come to an immediate agreement to prevent any further damage to Zambia. We shall ask for undertakings to come into effect simultaneously that no cross-border operations will be carried out by Rhodesia into Zambia and that no further movement of Patriotic Front personnel will take place from Zambia into Rhodesia. And we think it is vitally important that we secure those undertakings and will do all we can to persuade the parties to give them. Can I suggest one thing. We made those undertakings, we made the ceasefire agreement. It is vital to get it urgently because until we get that ceasefire agreement we are in a difficulty with no power over Rhodesia until we get a Governor in position. And that is what Peter was trying to say. We also are concerned, we have talked and tried to urge constraint and we will have another go this afternoon in the terms which I have indicated. But the vital thing, Kenneth, is to get that ceasefire agreement because the longer it takes now the more we are concerned that troubles of this kind—and we know how difficult they are and particularly for you—and that is why I have been worried that the talks are going on for such a long time. We'll do that at 4 o'clock this afternoon. Would that help?

President: Well I want you to know that really I am only speaking to you out of very personal respect and feelings for you.

PM: Well this is why I wanted to get on to you, because I thought if you and I talked about it it might help. I feel that only you can help to get us the ceasefire arrangements now and we do want them quickly if we are to get a Governor in position quickly and then deal with these matters. But in the meantime we will try to get undertakings from both sides, one, not to have any cross-border operations into Zambia and the Patriotic Front to agree that no further movement of their personnel will take place from Zambia into Rhodesia. And if we can get that, and the ceasefire agreement, then I believe we're on the verge of success.

President: Well I wish you the best of luck, Margaret, but honestly my time now is being spent on mobilising the small Zambian nation to self-defence and I cannot kid you that I will be paying any more attention to what is taking place in London. I just have no time at all for that now.

PM: I just hope that your people in London will urge the Patriotic Front to come to agreement on the ceasefire—and urgently. Because I feel, Kenneth, that it is urgent for your people as well for the whole future of Rhodesia. If we get a ceasefire agreement then we can act very quickly. Without it, it is difficult. You see, I can act within days of a ceasefire agreement, and we've got orders and Governors and everything else ready to come over. But we do need it and we need it quickly, and you need it, too, because it will . . . if we get the undertaking on the ceasefire then the things which have caused you such grievous trouble will, I believe, stop.

President: Look, Margaret . . . I don't think anybody has worked more for peace than I have done . . . I've done all these things. I responded to you . . . I came over . . . and I really must now organise my people for whatever happens . . . If we're going to be demolished because of the scale of power from the South—very well, but Margaret I keep saying to you, I'm talking to you only out of personal respect.

PM: I know that, I know that. But we very nearly got an agreement when you were here Kenneth and we just have to complete it now because if we do then the troubles that are causing you such grievous harm will, I believe, stop. We'll have a plenary at 4 o'clock; we'll ask both sides to come to an immediate agreement to prevent further damage to Zambia: one, to have no cross-border operations and the other to stop the movement of Patriotic Front personnel into Rhodesia and then go ahead and have the ceasefire quickly and I do beg of you to do anything you can to do that because I'm sure that's a quick way forward. Are you still there?

President: I'm listening, Margaret . . . I have to think as quickly as possible. I'm not sure it would be right for me to make promises which I can't fulfil. Really, nothing has disturbed me more these past few days. I don't know whether I would be effective in this shape or form in any of the things we would be trying to do together.

PM: I think we can still get through, Kenneth, if General Walls stops the attacks in return for Mr Nkomo stopping infiltration. Then we can go ahead with the ceasefire—and quickly. I know that you are having consultations in Dar es Salaam over the weekend and I hope everything will be done there to urge them to come to a ceasefire agreement quickly. Because we'll do our part here and we're constantly urging constraint because we're not going to put the whole of an agreement and a solution in jeopardy. We're just doing everything we can to stop the attacks and to have a constraint on both sides. So we'll do what we can, Kenneth, and I'm sure you'll do what you can because I think we are close to success and I think the worst is coming—the worst has come—just before success. Kenneth, you know I do personally wish you every success and I do thank you for what you did in coming over here and I just think we've got to hold on to the objective now to get the settlement, because that will be an end to your troubles and to Zimbabwe's.

President: Thank you for the messages, Margaret.

PM: If there are any further troubles, Kenneth, I will probably try to get on the telephone to you because I think you and I can perhaps try to deal with it more quickly than any other way. In the meantime, I know you'll look after all diplomatic people in Zambia.

President: Well I've made, not really an appeal, but an instruction to my countrymen of not acting anti-British at all . . . a lot of support from white subjects here . . . we have to protect the High Commission . . . nothing to do with ordinary British citizens here at all, nothing.

PM: Well, Kenneth. We'll do our best to stop both further attacks and infiltration and to get a ceasefire and I hope that if the other two come to Dar es Salaam they'll come back absolutely ready to take part in the ceasefire talks with a view to coming to a rapid conclusion.

President: Alright, Margaret. Thank you very much indeed.

PM: Thank you. My personal very best wishes, Kenneth.

President: Thank you Margaret. Thank you.

PM: Goodbye.

President: Goodbye now. God bless.

No. 178

Minute from Mr Renwick to Mr Walden, 23 November 1979
Confidential (FCO 36/2507)

Rhodesia: Consultations with the Americans

Mr Lanpher of the US Embassy called today to hand over the attached message for the Secretary of State from Mr Vance. I thanked Mr Lanpher for the action the Americans have taken on our request in support of our cease-fire proposals with all the front-line states before the meeting in Dar-es-Salaam. I also asked if the US Ambassador in Lusaka could make a particular effort—on lines already discussed with Mr Lanpher—with President Kaunda, if possible today.

R.W. RENWICK

ENCLOSURE IN NO. 178

Dear Peter,

I have received your message of November 20 and have instructed our Ambassadors in the front line states to impress on the governments the urgent need to complete the agreement quickly. They will be making this approach before the font line meeting in Dar es Salaam.

As you probably are already aware, the appropriate military authorities have already begun discussions on our helping to get heavy equipment for the monitoring force in Rhodesia. We will be in further touch with you on this issue.

You have my support in these final moments of the negotiations.

WITH BEST WISHES,
CY

No. 179

Lord Carrington to Sir A. Parsons (UKMIS New York), 23 November 1979, 8.43 p.m.[1]
Tel. No. 860, Immediate (FCO 36/2442)

Rhodesia: Statement by the British Government
Following is text of a Statement issued by No.10 Downing Street with the authority of the Prime Minister on 23 November. Copy addressees should bring it to the attention of the government to which they are accredited as quickly as possible. Dar es Salaam should ensure that copies reach those attending the Front Line States' Meeting as early as possible on 24 November.

Begins

The Lancaster House Conference has reached a critical point. I want everyone to be clear about the position of the British Government.

We are within an ace of success. The Conference has already agreed a constitution which, for the first time, guarantees genuine majority rule. It was agreed arrangements for a transitional period before independence. Only the cease-fire remains to be negotiated. All the parties have contributed towards these achievements. Everyone has made concessions. The United Kingdom does not wish that which has been achieved to be jeopardised by ill-judged actions or decisions: or by delaying the final phase of the Conference to the point where previous decisions are imperilled. Now is the time to bring the Conference to a successful close.

The British Government has put forward full proposals to bring a cease-fire into effect. These include a cease-fire Commission with military commanders from both sides: a monitoring force with Commonwealth participation: and disengagement of the opposing forces. If these proposals are accepted we envisage a cessation of hostilities within the next few days. This would bring immense benefits to the people of Rhodesia and of Zambia, Botswana and Mozambique, who have suffered so much in the course of the conflict. The British Government would help to bring about the return of the refugees.

Pending the implementation of a cease-fire, Lord Carrington has proposed that the Rhodesian authorities and the Patriotic Front leaders, with the cooperation of the Zambian authorities, should give undertakings about a cessation of all cross-border activities between Zambia and Rhodesia.

---

[1] Deskby to UKMIS New York 23 November 2130z.; and also sent to Dar es Salaam 24 November, Deskby 0700z; and to Immediate Mirimba, Salisbury, Nairobi, Maputo, Gaborone, Luanda, Lagos, Washington, Pretoria, Addis Ababa, Monrovia, Canberra, Ottawa, Wellington, Peking, Moscow, Prague, Dakar, Kinshasa, Khartoum, Tokyo, EEC Posts, Kuwait, Kingston, Bridgetown, Dacca, New Delhi, Singapore, Georgetown, Freetown, Port Louis, Port of Spain, Lilongwe, Valletta, Banjul, Colombo, Accra, Kuala Lumpur, Nicosia, Oslo, Stockholm, Lisbon, Madrid, Athens, Mbabane, Abidjan; Information saving Nassau, Maseru, Castries, Suva, Port Moresby, Honiara, Nukua'lofa, Victoria, Tarawa, UKDEL NATO, Sofia, Budapest, Bucharest, East Berlin, Belgrade, Cairo, Algiers, Tunis, Tripoli, Rabat, Tehran.

No. 180

Lord Carrington to Mr Brown (Lagos), 23 November 1979, 10.56 p.m.[1]
Tel. No. 886 Immediate, Confidential (FCO 36/2509)

Rhodesia: Nigerian Views

1. Alhaji Maitama Sule called on me this afternoon at his request accompanied by the Nigerian High Commissioner and Oba.

2. Sule pointed out that he had been sent as the President's personal emissary to make whatever contribution he could to the success of the Conference and would stay as long as necessary. The Nigerians were impressed by our achievements so far and were concerned that these should not be set at risk in the final stages.

3. Sule said that he had close contacts with the Patriotic Front and could understand their anxieties. In particular, with all the communications from Rhodesia blocked, except those to the south, the PF were afraid that their forces could be rounded up and dealt with. Hence the need for an effective third force to act as a deterrent. And an independent observer force would be essential to give a certificate of credibility to the elections.

4. Sule restated Nigeria's total commitment to African liberation which applied as strongly under the present government as under the FMG. This was not a matter of ideology but of Africanism. There was a danger of South African intervention in Rhodesia and consequently of wider involvement which Nigeria did not wish to see. The Nigerians had told the PF leaders that it was not in the general interest for them to allow the Conference to break up but their fears must be allayed by adequate security arrangements. Nigeria admired and respected Britain for her efforts so far. A successful outcome would help to strengthen bilateral ties and mutual commercial interests. But patience was needed at this stage. And it was essential that there should be agreement with both sides: Agreement with one side would not be acceptable to the international community.

5. I expressed thanks for Nigeria's help and interest so far. I described our concern about the situation in Zambia as a result of the recent Rhodesian raids and about the Front Line Meeting in Dar es Salaam. No one could believe that after 11 weeks of negotiations we could be so maladroit as to prejudice a successful outcome by conniving with the Rhodesians. And I asked Sule if the Nigerians would do anything they could to allay Kaunda's anxieties. As for the Dar Meeting we were afraid that the Zambian problem might sour the atmosphere, and the PF might return with unnegotiable demands. I asked that the Nigerians should urge upon the parties the need to maintain the momentum.

6. I explained, as Mr Luce had already done, our concept of the monitoring force and the necessity to see it in a realistic light. No arrangements for the ceasefire could be perfect: it would need dedication on both sides to see it work. We were putting forward proposals which we believed to be reasonable and we could not give a veto to either side.

---

1 Deskby to Lagos 24 November 0900z. And for information Priority to Lusaka, Dar es Salaam, Pretoria, Mirimba Salisbury, Washington, UKMIS New York.

No. 181

Minute from Mr Renwick to Mr Walden, 24 November 1979
Confidential (FCO 36/2480)

Rhodesia: Future Policy

1. At this point in the Conference, we need to pause to consider the courses of action open to us.

(*a*) *Maintaining the status quo*

If the Salisbury delegation withdraw in due course from the negotiations or fail to agree to arrangements we consider to be reasonable, it will be open to us to withhold a return to legality or the granting of legal independence and to continue to apply sanctions. We should not, however, be able to do so for very long under the existing administrative regulations. Following the lapse of the sanctions orders under Section 2, our present sanctions legislation has various inconsistencies. It will be argued strongly in Parliament that the Government should not continue to apply sanctions under the Export Import Act and the exchange control regulations without fresh legislative authority from Parliament to do so. Such authority could be provided under the Enabling Bill. The advantage of this course is that there would be no damage to our interests elsewhere in Africa or the Commonwealth. The disadvantages are that Bishop Muzorewa and his colleagues will argue that they have made all the concessions necessary to achieve recognition and the lifting of sanctions; that they were mis-led by the British Government; and that a return to legality, which they had expected, had been denied because of the non-participation of the Patriotic Front. Such a course could only be justified if the Rhodesians were clearly seen to be responsible for the break-down of the negotiations e.g. by launching further attacks on Zambian (as distinct from ZIPRA) targets. It would leave us in a position where we retained responsibility for Rhodesia (and continued to be held answerable by the Zambians and others for Rhodesia). The maintenance of sanctions and the withholding of recognition would be likely to be followed by South African intervention and/or gradual collapse of the situation inside the country leading to the more or less orderly evacuation of the white community. Since there are 130,000 British citizens or persons entitled to British citizenship, it would be very difficult for us to disclaim responsibility for assistance with the evacuation.

(*b*) *Proceeding directly to independence*

An alternative option would be to conclude at the end of the Conference that there is nothing more Britain can do to help solve the problem. The only action we can take is to recognise the reality of the situation, decide that Rhodesia must be accorded independence and that we can no longer preserve the fiction of British responsibility. We would then pass through Parliament as quickly as possible a Bill providing for independence. Sanctions would be lifted when independence was granted. The advantage of this course is that it would discharge our formal responsibility for Rhodesia and would minimise our involvement meanwhile. The very serious disadvantage is that we would get no international support. It would be argued very strongly in Parliament and internationally that we were granting independence without fulfilling the fifth principle or the Lusaka Communiqué; and that this was an abdication rather than a discharge of our responsibility. Since sanctions would be lifted only on the completion of the process, this would allow time for pre-emptive action to be organised against us in Africa, in the Security Council and the Commonwealth. We could find ourselves confronted with a generalised move by the Organisation of African Unity to break off diplomatic relations and to commit themselves to some form of economic retaliation. We would allow time for a series of moves to be made against us in the Security Council and would have to veto resolutions designed to affirm that we were not discharging our responsibility and that we could not lift sanctions without affirmative action by the Security Council.

(c) *The Return to Legality*

The alternative is to continue on our present course. This involves aiming to a comprehensive settlement in which the Patriotic Front as a whole or at any rate Nkomo might be brought in to participate; but being prepared, if we are forced to do so, to discharge our responsibility by the appointment of a Governor and the organisation of a rapid elections to be followed immediately by independence if the Patriotic Front will not agree to participate. If we have to proceed without the Patriotic Front we will not get much international support. But, depending on the timing, we may be able to get a fair measure of acquiescence—and to carry the Americans and some other governments with us. Furthermore, the only prospect of achieving a comprehensive settlement is to be prepared, if necessary, to begin to proceed without the Patriotic Front, but in such a way as to hold open the door for them to join in.

2. In terms of our tactics in the Conference in the next few days, our main objective must be to get the discussions back on to the substance of the matters before the Conference, i.e. our cease-fire proposals. We have American and EEC support for those proposals and quite a lot of Governments—and some members of the Patriotic Front—can see considerable attractions in them. They are the most practicable plan which can be produced; and they involve a very substantial British contribution.

3. The Salisbury delegation will accept proposals on 26 November. We have insisted that they must also state that they will be ready to discuss the arrangements for their implementation as soon as the Patriotic Front have accepted the proposals. The Rhodesians will maintain their offer to cease all cross-border operations if they receive any matching assurances from the Patriotic Front and the Zambians. Failing that they will attack no Zambian targets, though they will take action against ZIPRA forces moving towards or crossing into Rhodesia.

4. The Patriotic Front are likely to continue next week their tactics of refusing to discuss the substance of our proposals (whether or not they put forward counter-proposals of their own). They are finding it difficult to object to the main elements of our paper. Our objective must be to get the Patriotic Front to accept our proposals, subject to agreement on their implementation, by the end of the week. On his return from Dar-es-Salaam, we must work hard on Nkomo (and have already been trying to do so on Tongogara). But there will be no chance of bringing them to accept until they feel themselves to be under very strong pressure to do so. To apply that pressure we should be prepared to make the Order in Council concerning the Governor by the end of the week, leaving the Patriotic Front a day or two in which to reply. If that does not succeed, our next step could be to enact the Constitution before deciding the

point at which to send the Governor. This course offers the best chance of pushing the Patriotic Front towards a settlement.

5. If, despite these efforts, we are forced to proceed with the Salisbury parties alone it will be essential:

(a) to get the timing right and

(b) hold open the possibility of Patriotic Front participation.

Our main concern in that event will be for the security of the British community in Zambia (though we must also expect to face damage to our economic interests in Nigeria and a breach of diplomatic relations by *some* other African countries). In an effort to damp down Zambian reactions, we should make it clear that the Governor would insist on the immediate resumption of maize supplies to Zambia and would indeed offer a complete normalisation of relations.[1]

---

[1] In a minute of 26 November Mr Day thought that options (a) and (b) had little to commend them. Option (a) could create domestic political difficulties, even if it were possible to lay responsibility for the breakdown at the door of the Salisbury delegation. With option (b) there was a likelihood of complete international isolation, with the possible exception of South Africa. This was a situation to avoid at almost any cost. Like Mr Renwick, he favoured persisting with the present course of action as the only one likely to limit damage to national and international interests. He went on: 'Under Option (c) we have a good case to argue with the international community. We *have* achieved a respectable constitution; we *have* got agreement on the holding of elections under the authority of a British Governor. We *have* put forward proposals for a ceasefire which, though not perfect, are as good as anyone is likely to devise. We and other Commonwealth governments have committed ourselves to monitor the ceasefire. If the Patriotic Front insist on throwing all this away we can argue with some force that the fault is not ours or that of the internal parties and that we cannot reasonably hold up all further progress. What we must, however, ensure is that, in the next few days, we put ourselves in the best possible presentational light as far as our ceasefire proposals are concerned and that, as Mr Renwick says, we get the timing right if we have to go ahead with the internal parties alone.'

No. 182

Telephone conversation between Mrs Thatcher and Lord Carrington in the early evening of Sunday 25 November 1979
(PREM 19/115)

PM: Hullo.

FCS: Hullo Margaret.

PM: Peter. I just phoned to ask if you had any thoughts about the news from Dar es Salaam that they are not going to co-operate on the ceasefire and they are going to call your bluff, etc.[1]

FCS: Well I don't think we really know what happened. They didn't actually produce a communiqué.

PM: But Mugabe was on the news.

FCS: Tonight?

PM: Yes.

FCS: This evening?

PM: Yes. On the radio

---

[1] The Patriotic Front leaders had attended a meeting with Presidents of the Front Line States on 23-24 November.

FCS: We have heard nothing at the Foreign Office about that. What they will certainly do is not to answer tomorrow. But I don't think it necessarily follows that they won't go on talking. I think that they will say, you know, we haven't had the talks, and this that and the other. I hope Salisbury will say they accept the ceasefire tomorrow and then we shall try and play them along.

PM: Certainly. Though on the news tonight the BBC . . .[2] radio was one of four accounts that I have heard and it was very much that the Rhodesians say that Nkomo has been infiltrating people into us. But the Dar es Salaam people absolutely refuse to congregate in groups inside Rhodesia, because that would be unfair.

FCS: They won't congregate in groups?

PM: Yes.

FCS: Well in which case there can be no ceasefire.

PM: Well, and they are not going to co-operate and they are going to call your bluff, etc. The typical posturing stuff you would expect. In a way I was not displeased because it puts them back into the wrong. So it pleased me quite a lot from the viewpoint of public opinion it looks to me as if they have gone absolutely into the wrong.

FCS: Yes. I think that is rather good. You know they have done another raid.

PM: Oh no. On ZIPRA?

FCS: On ZIPRA, yes. And it is said to be a camp about 25 miles from Lusaka.

PM: Oh Lord it is right inside.

FCS: Well, you know one despairs of them doesn't one.

PM: Yes.

PM: Yes.

FCS: But somebody said they heard it on the news. Did it not appear on the six o'clock news?

PM: I didn't hear that on the six o'clock news, no.

FCS: Well may be it is a false report.

PM: They might have listened to television news you see.

FCS: No. This was earlier on at one o'clock.

PM: Oh. Well most certainly I don't think it was on the six o'clock.

FCS: Oh it might have passed off rather better than you might think. But so far as we can judge I have been in touch all day with all this, what's happened is that there has been no communiqué issued by the Front Line Presidents. But Mugabe gave a press conference in which he said he was going to call my bluff but . . .

PM: Yes well that must have been what we heard.

FCS: But nothing about concentrating or anything. That may have come later. In which case I agree with you. It puts them in the wrong.

PM: Yes. We were just talking Europe here. I can't see Peter that you are going to be able to come unless the thing breaks up before.

FCS: No, nor do I. It would come at this moment wouldn't it.

PM: I know. But if, they are coming back what, tonight or tomorrow morning?

FCS: They are coming back tonight.

PM: To arrive tomorrow morning?

---

2 All ellipses in original document.

FCS: Yes well they may turn up or they may not turn up in order to defy me because I asked them to give me an answer on Monday. But we shall be in a better position because if the Salisbury delegation agree to our ceasefire proposals, say that they won't hit ZIPRA, say they won't infiltrate, and also they will talk to them as soon as they have agreed. We are in a much better position.

PM: Much better. The blame is attached to the other side.

FCS: Well that's right and we are now getting the thing back on the ceasefire rather than on the Zambian thing. But I am afraid they have done themselves a lot of damage with all the people we want to support them. That is the problem. However we have just got to play this by ear really. I will give [you] a ring Margaret and find out ... I haven't been in touch with them for three or four hours.

PM: No. I am still at Chequers and will be here for another 2 1/2 hours.

FCS: Well if I find out anything else I will give you a ring.

PM: All right.

FCS: But

FCS: But I haven't heard that bit and I will see if they can confirm it.

PM: All right.

FCS: Thanks so much.

PM: Good bye.

***

FCS: Hullo Margaret.

PM: Yes Peter.

FCS: The report is inaccurate. What they said was that they were not going to have an ultimatum. They would go on negotiating in their own time. But our proposals did not give equality of status to the forces and that it if they were required to assemble then the Salisbury forces would have to assemble too.

PM: Oh. I see. Well that can't happen can it?

FCS: No. But it puts us of course in a more difficult position.

PM: In that case it would be far better if their forces got out, wouldn't it? But we can't ask that either.

FCS: But they won't do that. But they say because they hold more territory than the Salisbury forces.

PM: I See. So a ceasefire is going to be just about impossible to monitor.

FCS: It will be impossible to monitor because, I mean it is quite clear they won't assemble and you will have to use the other people to do it.

PM: To round them up?

FCS: Yes. But it will break down on that.

PM: Oh Lord.

FCS: I mean I would think that is what would happen, wouldn't you?

PM: I wonder if it is impossible for everyone to go back to barracks.

FCS: No because W[alls] won't. Because he said they won't assemble and there would be intimidation.

PM: He's right.

FCS: And he couldn't put the thing at risk.

PM: If they assembled you could use them for patrolling couldn't you? But you would have nowhere to go to . . .
FCS: But he won't accept that either.
PM: Oh well,
PM: Oh well, we'll have to think about it Peter.
FCS: Yes. But one thing is quite certain. After what he has done there is no paper.
PM: I entirely agree.
FCS: We will just have to think.
PM: Yes. Good bye.

No. 183

Minute from Mr Manning to Mr Walden, 26 November 1979
Confidential (FCO/2480)

Rhodesia: Future Policy

1. Mr Luce has seen Mr Renwick's minute of 24 November.[1] He considers that we have no alternative other than to proceed on our present course (Option (*c*)). Option (*b*) he considers is clearly not on, that way we would get the worst of all worlds: straight recognition of a Muzorewa government.

2. So far as Option (*a*) is concerned Mr Luce considers that in terms of parliamentary reality it would not be feasible to withhold recognition from or continue sanctions against a Muzorewa government even if it could be seen to have caused the breakdown of the talks. In any event blame for a breakdown is unlikely to be a clear-cut issue and no doubt both sides' propaganda machines will be able to convince their supporters that they are the injured party. For this reason Mr Luce does not think it would be reasonable to use the threat of non-recognition or continued sanctions to keep the Salisbury delegation at the conference. They could easily call our bluff. Rather he thinks that we should make it clear to the Salisbury delegation that their chances of *international* recognition will be slim if they walk out.

3. Mr Luce believes that we should make every effort to dissuade the Salisbury government from launching further attacks on Zambia. Given the helpful attitude of President Machel he thinks that it will be equally important to avoid further major assaults on Mozambique.

K.Q.F. Manning

1 No. 181.

No. 184

Lord Carrington to Sir L. Allinson (Lusaka), 26 November 1979, 8.20 p.m.[1]
Tel. No. 983 Confidential, Immediate (FCO 36/2442)

Rhodesia Conference

1. On their return from Dar es Salaam Mr Nkomo and Mr Mugabe asked to see me at noon today. They said that they were not in a position to reply to our cease-fire proposals and urged me not to press them for a 'yes or no' answer. They argued (pretty half-heartedly) that they could not discuss cease-fire proposals with us, but only with General Walls. They said that they had not had an opportunity to discuss our proposals and that if the Salisbury Delegation accepted them this would put them in a difficult position.

2. I said that we had been trying in vain to engage substantive discussions with the Patriotic Front ever since our original proposals were tabled on 16 November. I had repeatedly stressed the need to reach a quick decision on the cease-fire, otherwise there would be a danger of prejudicing the achievements of the Conference. We had held meetings at official level last week with the Patriotic Front but these had been profitless because of the Patriotic Front's insistence on procedural arguments. The Salisbury Delegation took the view that the Patriotic Front had refused to recognise their existence in the first two phases of the Conference. Mr Mugabe had repeatedly stated that he was prepared to negotiate only with the British Government. That was now the position of the Salisbury Delegation as well. They were not prepared for their military commanders to engage in negotiations without the involvement of the political leaders to whom they were responsible. I had, however, pressed them to agree that they would be prepared to discuss with us and the Patriotic Front the implementation of the cease-fire, with the involvement of their military commanders.

3. After a protracted argument, it was agreed that we would arrange full discussion of our proposals in a bilateral session tomorrow. I insisted repeatedly that the Patriotic Front must respond to the substance of our proposals and state what difficulties they saw in them. I also told the Patriotic Front that I could not cancel the Plenary session today. I had myself called the session and asked for a response to our proposals. I could not fail to hold a Plenary at whatever time one of the other delegations asked for it.

4. The Patriotic Front subsequently failed to attend the Plenary session this afternoon. Dr Mundawarara stated on behalf of the Salisbury Delegation that they could agree to our cease-fire proposals. He emphasised that this was a difficult decision, since it involved the placing of the Rhodesian security forces and the police under the authority of the Governor. He reiterated the offer to cease all cross-border military activity if the Patriotic Front would cease the infiltration of armed personnel

---

1 And to Immediate Mirimba, Salisbury, Nairobi, Maputo, Gaborone, Dar es Salaam, Luanda, Lagos, Washington, Pretoria, Addis Ababa, Monrovia, Canberra, Ottawa, Wellington, Priority Peking, Moscow, Prague, Dakar, Kinshasa, Khartoum, Tokyo, EEC Posts, Kuwait, Kingston, Bridgetown, Dacca, New Delhi, Singapore, Georgetown, Freetown, Port Louis, Port of Spain, Lilongwe, Valletta, Banjul, Colombo, Accra, Kuala Lumpur, Nicosia, Oslo, Stockholm, Lisbon, Madrid, Athens, Mbabane, Abidjan, UKMIS New York; Information Saving Nassau, Maseru, Castries, Suva, Port Moresby, Honiara, Nukua'lofa, Victoria, Tarawa, UKDEL NATO, Sofia, Budapest, Bucharest, East Berlin, Belgrade, Cairo, Algiers, Tunis, Tripoli, Rabat, Tehran.

into Rhodesia. He stated that the Patriotic Front had refused for seven weeks to acknowledge the existence of the Salisbury Delegation. They were now seeking direct negotiations with their military commanders. In Rhodesia the military commanders were responsible to the government. And direct negotiations would have to be conducted by the government. If the Patriotic Front were not prepared for such negotiations, they would have to negotiate with the British Government, as the Salisbury Delegation were doing. They had now been here for eleven weeks and were not interested in further general discussions. But they would be prepared to discuss the implementation of our proposals, with the involvement of their military commanders, if these were accepted by the Patriotic Front. The Lord Privy Seal thanked Dr Mundawarara for his positive response and explained that we would be having a bilateral meeting with the Patriotic Front tomorrow.

5. The present position therefore is that we have still had no substantive comments from the Patriotic Front on any aspect of our cease-fire proposals. Last week was wasted in procedural argument. We shall give the Patriotic Front tomorrow the fullest possible explanation of our proposals and will try to deal with their concerns about them. It will however be necessary to reach a point of decision on the proposals whether we can proceed to discuss their implementation later in the week.

No. 185

Minute from Mr Renwick to Mr Walden and Mr Day, 27 November 1979
Confidential (FCO 36/2442)

Rhodesia: Bilateral Meeting with the Patriotic Front: 27 November

1. Mr Barlow is preparing a brief for the meeting with the Patriotic Front this afternoon. The following thoughts are addressed purely to the questions of tactics and our objectives in the meeting.

Objectives

2. Our objectives must be:

(*a*) to bring the Patriotic Front towards acceptance of our cease-fire proposals (subject to their implementation—though without holding open any prospect of protracted negotiations on implementation); or, failing that

(*b*) to avoid wrong-footing ourselves and allowing the Patriotic Front to break off the negotiations on some issue on which they will get widespread support.

Tactics

3. Our tactics therefore should be to keep the discussion fairly general this afternoon and to seek to reassure the Patriotic Front on those points of legitimate concern to them (above all the security of their forces). We should emphasize that the Patriotic Front forces will not be required to lay down their arms; the Rhodesian forces will not be involved in the assembly process; they will be under the control of their commanders; the assembly places will be accompanied by monitoring groups (and will therefore be secure).

4. They will try to engage us in discussion of a large number of issues which we know to be secondary. These include the composition of the monitoring force (their

real concern is with its *size*); the South African dimension (open South African military intervention is much more likely if the war continues on in its present course and could not take place under a British Governor); the idea of 'zones' (which they know to be untenable) etc. Their real areas of concern are:

(*a*) the *size of the monitoring force*. We should resist any ideas of changing its composition. We should explain once again that a 'peace-keeping' force does not have an enforcement role. We should take note of their concern about the numbers (but without giving the impression that we can agree to a massive increase);

(*b*) the *integration of the forces*. We have stated repeatedly in earlier phases of the Conference that we do not believe the integration of the forces to be practicable in advance of the basic political choice to be made by the people of Rhodesia in elections. But we do agree that the object of the process must be reconciliation. We can see the need to give consideration during the interim period to the future role and careers of those at present in the forces on both sides. We hope that many of them will be prepared to return to civilian life and the British Government will be prepared to assist with this process;

(*c*) *the status and role of the Patriotic Front forces and of the Rhodesian forces*. It will be very important in the full bilateral session this afternoon to strike a balance between two conflicting and equally important considerations:

(i) we must not lead towards a situation in which the Governor does not have to make use of the Rhodesian forces without giving him a clear justification to do so. But it will be best to spell out that justification in *plenary* rather than in a bilateral session;

(ii) we must not leave it open to the Patriotic Front to claim that they are being required to assemble and accept the Governor's authority while the Rhodesian forces will be subject to no constraints.

5. We should bear in mind that this dilemma arises because the Patriotic Front's political and military objective is to assemble only a fraction of their forces and to leave the remainder in the field. The only way to deal with this problem, therefore, is to turn the argument back on the Patriotic Front. We should make it clear that the successful completion of the assembly process is crucial to the bringing into operation of an effective cease-fire. The Rhodesian forces will be required to dis-engage from the Patriotic Front forces while they assemble. Thereafter they will be required to comply with the directions of the Governor. (Their dispositions will depend on the dispositions of the Patriotic Front forces i.e. on the extent to which they assemble with their arms, accept the Governor's authority and are identified—as the Rhodesian forces will be.)

6. I am enclosing with this minute a suggested line to take on this point and on the way in which we deal with breaches of the cease-fire.[1] We have already included in our paper on the cease-fire (paragraph 13) the clear statement that 'in the event of a more general or sustained breaches of the cease-fire, the Governor will have to decide what action to take to deal with them with the forces which have accepted his authority'. We should *not* get driven much further down this road in the bilateral session today. If there is agreement on the cease-fire proposals—subject to their

---

1 Not printed.

implementation—we shall need to make the position clear in plenary session and that will be the moment to do so. We should not do more in the bilateral session than prepare the way for the kind of statement we will make in Conference.

R.W. RENWICK

No. 186

Record of conversation between Lord Carrington and Mr P.F. Botha, 28 November 1979, 3 p.m.
Confidential (FCO 36/2514)

Present:

The Rt. Hon. The Lord Carrington	Mr P.F. Botha
Mr J. Leahy	His Excellency Dr D. de Villiers
Mr G.G.H. Walden	Mr R. Killen

Lord Carrington thanked Mr Botha for his helpfulness in recent weeks. We had just overcome a difficult hiccough following the Rhodesian raids in Zambia. He quite understood that infiltration from Zambia to Rhodesia was at a high level. But politically the timing of the raids had made it harder for us to bring the Patriotic Front to the boil in the negotiations. If we had done so prematurely, the blame for a breakdown would have fallen on Salisbury. Now however we had succeeded in getting back to the ceasefire, and had just had a long bilateral meeting with the Patriotic Front. That afternoon he intended to give the PF the definitive UK position. This would attempt to reassure them on some points, but we would make it clear that we were looking for a swift response. He would see them before going to Dublin on 29 November, and again if necessary on his return, making it clear that there was no more negotiating fat on our position. We would then go ahead and appoint a Governor, make the Constitution, and begin putting through an Independence Bill. We would not however break the Conference, and make it clear that the PF were still free to join in if they wished. On Monday 3 December we would have to go ahead on that basis. The negotiations simply could not continue any longer, especially in view of the infiltration which was going on. The Salisbury parties were also fed up, though they themselves had lengthened the negotiations by one week. It was important that we should be in the best international position possible if there were a breakdown. He was grateful for South African forbearance.

2. *Mr Botha* said he was grateful for Lord Carrington's help over arranging this meeting. He had been worried about the press treatment of his visit, but the Ambassador had rectified this in 20 minutes. *Lord Carrington* said we had been concerned about charges of collusion, given the timing of Mr Botha's visit. *Mr Botha* said that he saw the difficulty. On Zambia, General Walls had told him that the Secretary of State had expressed understanding of the reasons for the Rhodesian attacks on Zambian bridges. It was important to realize how 'bloody terrible' the position on the ground was, where the guerrillas were crossing the border into

Rhodesia to murder and rape. In his view, Kaunda was finished (Mr Botha later alleged that Kapepwe[1] was recruiting Katangese, but seemed unsure of his facts). In Angola Dos Santos was also fighting for his life. South African monitoring of signals in Southern Angola showed that Government forces there, which number 13,000, including a Cuban element, had been cornered by Savimbi[2], and were refusing to obey their commanders until they were properly fed. Machel was also in trouble, and a new opposition movement (the MRN?[3]) was now active. Nyerere had also got into a mess in Uganda. The whole of Southern Africa was unstable, and South Africa face very difficult decisions. In Botswana, Russian activity was now very dangerous. The Russians had offered to identify British and American agents there in exchange for closer co-operation. Chief Jonathan was also like to be toppled within a month in Swaziland. He had asked Botha personally to improve his security, e.g. by providing him with better personal communications.

3. Against this background, delay at the Rhodesian Conference was unfortunate, though he recognized that this had largely been beyond Lord Carrington's control. He would be grateful if the Conference could be concluded as soon as possible. An ideal solution may not be possible. But a 'second-class solution' could bring about stability in time. A number of African countries would come to recognize Muzorewa: e.g. Senegal, Kenya, Swaziland, Botswana and Zaire. *Lord Carrington* said that this would only happen as a result of our going through the Lancaster House exercise. *Mr Botha* said he saw that, and agreed that the acceptance by the Patriotic Front of the Constitution had been an important achievement. But he was still afraid of a general flare-up in the region.

4. *Lord Carrington* said he was well aware of the problems, and again stressed that the Conference could not continue for much longer. But we would need as much international support as possible if we were to go ahead with a second-class solution. The Front Line States would continue to support the Patriotic Front in those circumstances, though with varying degrees of enthusiasm. We were also worried about British citizens in Zambia; Iran was a bad example. We would have economic difficulties with Nigeria. Nor could we expect much support from OAU members at the outset. However we would be able to demonstrate that we had spent 11 weeks trying to get a full settlement. Some Europeans were feebler than others (Mr Botha said that his list might be longer than Lord Carrington's) but we thought that others would come with us in the row over sanctions and the recognition of the Bishop. Even if we achieved the first-class solution, the ceasefire could be messy. The PF were unlikely to assemble their forces properly. If there were a breakdown of the ceasefire, we would also be accused of responsibility for it. But we still thought that we would be in a stronger position by attempting to achieve a ceasefire. Muzorewa had a good chance of getting a majority of seats, together with the Whites. (Mr Botha was clearly not familiar with the important provision in the draft Constitution whereby the Whites could only form a government with the largest political party. It was explained to him that Muzorewa would only need to gain a few seats more than his nearest rival to gain the support of the 20 White seats). Lord Carrington did not

---

1 Mr Simon Kapwepwe, Vice-President of Zambia, 1967-70.
2 Mr Jonas Malheiro Savimbi, founder of the National Union for Total Independence of Angola (UNITA).
3 Appears to be a reference to the Mozambican National Resistance party, formed in 1975.

think that Mugabe would win the elections, particularly in view of the activities of Mawema[4]. *Mr Botha* said he was not certain how important Mawema would be, but said that South Africa was helping him, and would help all anti-Marxist parties. He had just had a good talk with Sithole.

5. *Mr Botha* said that General Walls was nervous. His main fear was that some of our more junior officials (Walls had specifically exempted the Secretary of State and Mr Renwick) tended to give interpretations of our positions favourable to the Patriotic Front. Walls also feared that the Governor might interpret the provisions of any agreement in a sense favourable to the Patriotic Front. If there was no agreement he was afraid that the Governor might go out of his way to get the Patriotic Front in. *Lord Carrington* said that General Walls had clearly not understood the position. If the Patriotic Front did not answer our latest move, we would not break up the Conference. We would simply go ahead with the Governor, the Constitution and the Independence Bill, explaining that the Patriotic Front could come in within a period of x days, provided they accepted our ceasefire proposals. If they did not, the Government would fix the date of elections at the end of that period. *Mr Botha* said that it would be useful if Lord Carrington could explain this to General Walls, who felt that he had been left out of things recently. *Lord Carrington* said he would probably see the General on Saturday morning.

6. *Mr Botha* said that Ian Smith was already making overtures to Nkomo. *Lord Carrington* pointed out that he would only be able to make a coalition of the largest party. *Mr Botha* commented that many Rhodesians had no idea what was going on in London. In his view the situation still looked quite good, providing he could conclude the negotiations early. *Lord Carrington* said that he agreed with Mr Botha on time, but hoped no more bridges would be bombed. We had to understand President Kaunda's position to some extent. He had returned from London a hero, and had then been humiliated by the Rhodesian attack. *Mr Botha* said that Kaunda was emotional and histrionic. A number of members of the Zambian Government were in touch with the South Africans. Some of them favoured the Bishop, but Kaunda was personally committed to Nkomo, whom he wanted to see enthroned. The South Africans too had favoured Nkomo in 1974, but Smith had turned down Nkomo's terms. He thought that Nkomo would get no more than 20% of the vote. There was a danger of splitting all the parties, and of gangsterism. There were also problems in Malawi. As for Mozambique, he intended to stop helping Machel in Beira if the war in Rhodesia continued. If we could conclude the Conference soon, he knew from personal contact that there would be massive investment from the private sector for Muzorewa. The economic benefits would begin to flow in a matter of months. In a year, Lord Carrington would be seen as the man who had achieved a turnaround in the area. *Lord Carrington* said that we must achieve either a first or second class solution soon. In the latter case, we would appoint a different Governor and go for very quick elections. *Mr Botha* stressed that the South Africans wanted sanctions lifted very quickly.

7. *Lord Carrington* said that the Patriotic Front constantly alleged that the South Africans would invade Rhodesia if the Front won the elections. He had been taking

---

4 Mr Michael Andrew Mawema, Zimbabwe/Rhodesia nationalist leader.

the line that the South Africans would not interfere in an Administration run by a British Governor. *Mr Botha* said that this was an important issue which he wanted to get clear. The South Africans already had a presence in Rhodesia. He wanted to be frank. They had to help Muzorewa, otherwise there was no hope. The South Africans had to ensure the security of their trains passing through Rhodesia in remote areas. They also protected the Rhodesian end of the Beit bridge, which would otherwise be blown. *Lord Carrington* emphasised that he was not talking about South African equipment in Rhodesia, or about volunteers. But there must be no formed South African units which would attract the attention of observers and the press. If there were, this would put us in an impossible position. The South Africans must remember that we were talking about a ceasefire. If they had personnel in Rhodesia, they must be dressed in Rhodesian uniforms, and not come to notice in formations. He urged Mr Botha to discuss this with General Walls.

No. 187

Minute from Mr Lyne to Ms Spencer, 29 November 1979
Confidential (FCO 36/2613)

Rhodesia: Governor-Designate

Lord Soames rang me last night to say that he felt he was getting out of touch with Rhodesian developments. I briefed him on the position reached in the Conference, and you and Mr Day have kindly agreed to give him a fuller briefing at 4 p.m. this afternoon.

Specific points made by Lord Soames included in the following:

(*a*) He was very keen to have a meeting with General Walls and Acland at the earliest appropriate moment. We agreed that it would not make sense to hold such a meeting until we knew whether the Patriotic Front were accepting our cease-fire proposals. I assured Lord Soames that there would be time for such a meeting after the Patriotic Front's acceptance before General Walls left London. I have not committed us on the form which the meeting would take (e.g., it is possible that the Secretary of State would wish to be present).

(*b*) Lord Soames pressed again for the earliest possible announcement of his post. He asked if the announcement could be made before next Tuesday, when he is due to make a statement in the House of Lords on man-power cuts in the public service. If Lord Soames is to be Governor, he would like to hand over all matters connected with the man-power cuts, including negotiations with the trade unions, to his deputy, rather than to have to start dealing with the subject himself and then break off in the middle. I said that I would ask the Department to see whether it would be feasible to announce Lord Soames' appointment on Monday, if the Patriotic Front accepted our cease-fire proposals on Saturday; however, I thought there might be difficulties about this. It would be helpful if Lord Soames could be given further advice on the timing of the announcement at this afternoon's meeting.

(*c*) Lord Soames would like to receive more paper. He is already receiving Rhodesia policy distribution telegrams. We discussed certain other forms of paper which he might receive. I have sent him a copy of yesterday's conference statement by Lord Carrington. I have told his Private Secretary that you may bring further papers with you this afternoon.

(*d*) Lord Soames will be in London over the weekend. We should ring him as soon as we know the Patriotic Front's answer. He may then want to meet Lord Carrington and others to discuss the way forward.

R.M.J. LYNE

No. 188

Minute from Mr Walden to Mr Renwick, 29 November 1979
Confidential (FCO 36/2442)

Meeting between the Secretary of State and the Patriotic Front

At this morning's meeting with the Patriotic Front (at which the LPS, you and I were also present on our side), Nkomo began by acknowledging that Lord Carrington's statement yesterday was evidence that the British had moved on a number of points. Lord Carrington seemed to wish to reach agreement by movement on both sides, and this was a good thing. But it would be wrong to leave things undone (he mentioned the Rhodesian Air Force) and said that our proposals still needed to be 'knocked into shape'. The only way this could be done would be by sitting down with the Rhodesian side and getting down to details on maps.

Lord Carrington said that he knew that the Patriotic Front had difficulties, and we had tried to meet them. We could, for example, accept 1,000 monitors. He mentioned other concessions we had made. Assembly of the Patriotic Front forces was however crucial, as the start of a two-way traffic. He recognised that there was distrust on both sides, but reciprocal disengagement depended on the success of the assembly of the Patriotic Front forces. The Salisbury forces would be monitored from their bases. Nkomo said that he hoped that we were not talking about the Rhodesians' operational bases. Mugabe asked why the Rhodesians should not withdraw to barracks—that was the only possible meaning of movement on both sides. If the Rhodesian forces stayed in their operational areas, so would the Patriotic Front. Lord Carrington clearly had no notion about how the Patriotic Front forces were organised. Mr Nkomo said that all this needed to be discussed between them and the Salisbury people.

Lord Carrington said that as far as we were concerned, there was nothing more to discuss. Our wording had been carefully chosen. He hoped that the Patriotic Front could tell him tomorrow whether they could accept our proposals or not. In the meantime, we could give them any clarification they needed. We were now at the end of the road. Nkomo asked Lord Carrington not to talk about final discussions; the Patriotic Front were still a long way from the end of the road. Mugabe asked whether what we were saying was that the Rhodesians had refused to withdraw to their barracks. He was not going to stand by while his forces were pushed into 'slaughter points'. Mr Renwick explained that the Rhodesian forces, who would disengage to allow assembly, were hardly likely to slaughter the Patriotic Front forces before the eyes of the monitors. Mugabe argued that the Rhodesians were rebels, capable of anything, and that the monitors were inadequate. Nkomo said that we needed to establish where the Patriotic Front and Rhodesian operational bases were. If the Rhodesian forces stayed in theirs, so would the Patriotic Front.

Lord Carrington insisted that the Patriotic Front should tell him tomorrow night whether they accepted our proposals or not. Both Nkomo and Mugabe said that they would not reply tomorrow, but would re-pose their questions about assembly points and barracks.

G.G.H. WALDEN

No. 189

Minute from Mr Renwick to Mr Walden, 29 November 1979[1]
Confidential (FCO 36/2442)

Rhodesia: The Return to Legality

1. If the Patriotic Front accept our cease-fire proposals in the next few days, we have to devise a plan to deal with the otherwise serious danger of indefinitely protracted discussion of the arrangements for implementation. We should also consider taking advantage of the favourable circumstances which will then have been created to effect the return to legality in conditions in which we could aim to secure the acquiescence of much of the international community.

2. If the Patriotic Front accept the proposals, we should give them immediately the text of the independence Constitution. In doing so we should make it clear that this is not for negotiation. It was clearly established in the Conference that it would be for us to draft the Constitution. If their lawyers have any observations, these should be given to Mr Fifoot. The Constitution should be enacted by Order of the Council early next week. There would be serious hazards in any further delay, particularly in view of the proceedings now taking place in the Salisbury Parliament.

3. At the same time we should be prepared to make the Order in Council concerning the Governor. With the Patriotic Front participating in the discussions on implementation of the cease-fire, there would be very great advantage to sending an Acting Governor (Sir A. Duff) to Rhodesia as quickly as possible thereafter. This would bring about the return to legality and enable us to lift sanctions in conditions in which most western countries would be likely to consider this a reasonable step to take. There might be cries of foul from the Patriotic Front; but this would give them a very powerful incentive to agree quickly to the final package. There would cease, from their point of view, to be any advantage in further delay.

4. We could justify sending a Governor by the fact that the Patriotic Front had accepted the cease-fire proposals. In order to make the final arrangements for the implementation of the cease-fire, we need a presence in Salisbury. We cannot leave these to be settled by a Governor arriving on cease-fire day. In particular we also need to set in train the arrangements for the monitoring force.

1 Also sent to Mr Day.

5. We hope that the Patriotic Front would then agree quickly to the implementation of the cease-fire. If they did, Lord Soames might arrive in Salisbury on cease-fire day. If they did not, we should be well placed to proceed with the internal parties (or even, if absolutely necessary, to take the line that the return to legality had been effected in order to finalise the arrangements for the cease-fire, thereby leaving it open to us to withdraw the Governor and declare Rhodesia independent if it seemed hazardous to proceed with elections with the internal parties alone).

6. We must aim to introduce the independence Bill in the House of Commons next week. If a statement to that effect is not made, at the latest, on Thursday 6 December there will be serious parliamentary difficulties. We should not await the next parliamentary session to secure the passage of the independence Bill. If we were obliged to proceed with the internal parties alone, we might wish to complete the whole process before the next session. There will in any event be advantage in dealing with the legislative action concerning Rhodesia in a concentrated manner, rather than opening up a whole new round of legislative debate in the new session.

7. I *recommend*, therefore, that if the Patriotic Front accept the cease-fire proposals, we should make the Orders in Council concerning the Constitution and the Governor on Monday 3 or Tuesday 4 December. We should effect the return to legality by sending an Acting Governor to Salisbury as quickly as possible thereafter.

8. If the Patriotic Front do not accept our proposals, we should still be ready to set in train the legislative action set out above, in order to put final pressure on them to agree. But we should delay a decision about the date on which we should send a Governor.

R.W. RENWICK

No. 190

FCO to Mr Haydon (Dublin), 30 November 1979, 10.59 a.m.[1]
Tel. No. 259 Secret Flash DEDIP (FCO 36/2442)

Following for Lever from Lyne.

1. Renwick and Powell saw Nkomo early this morning.

Nkomo's objective seemed to be to see whether there were any further concessions to be extracted, and to frighten us that the Patriotic Front would not accept the cease-fire proposals.

2. Nkomo's main complaint was that you had adopted the wrong approach. Discussion had been going well. Had they been allowed to continue, there would be agreement by now. Instead you had again imposed an ultimatum. He recognised that your statement on 28 November contained positive and helpful elements. But there were other points which still needed to be discussed. He could not accept our proposals and your statement on a take-it-or-leave-it basis. If we could not agree, the fault would by yours because you refused to discuss.

---

1 For Lord Carrington who was in Ireland attending the European Council Summit meeting at Dublin Castle, taking place on 29-30 November 1979.

3. The only substantive point he raised was the composition of the Commonwealth Monitoring Force. There had to be other African countries in it. He could not accept it on the present basis.

4. Renwick and Powell said that there had been plenty of discussion and there could have been more still had the Patriotic Front not wasted a week arguing about procedure. Our proposals had been discussed and had theirs. Your statement on 28 November had been designed to take account of the concerns which the Patriotic Front had raised and help them. They were now being asked to accept the proposal as further clarified by your statement. The Conference could then go on to discuss implementation of the cease-fire. But without agreement of the proposals there would be nothing to implement. It would be a tragedy if Nkomo could not exert his authority and leadership to bring the Patriotic Front to the point of decision. There was very little time left for this. You would expect a decision this evening. As regards the monitoring force, it would be largely British under our direct auspices. The composition had been decided. What was important was the size, and here we had tried to meet Nkomo's concern.

5. The meeting ended with Nkomo still taking the line that he could not accept the proposals. Our assessment is that he does in fact intend to accept eventually (this is strongly supported by other evidence), but thinks that dragging out the process a little longer will in itself be a small triumph: and that by brinkmanship he may still gain a concession. We suspect that raising the composition of the monitoring force was a feint: we would expect him to make his last effort on disengagement and the disposition of the forces.

No. 191

Minute by Mr Day, 30 November 1979
Confidential (FCO 36/2442)

1. I agree with the recommendations in the first sentence of paragraph 7 and in paragraph 8.[1] I have reservations about the recommendation in the second sentence of paragraph 7 to bring about a return to legality and to lift sanctions whilst discussions on the ceasefire are continuing in Lancaster House.

2. I accept that we cannot start deploying the monitoring force to Rhodesia before a return to legality, and that there is a pressing need to set in train some of the monitoring arrangements. I also accept that a return to legality and the lifting of sanctions would act as a powerful incentive to the Patriotic Front to accept the detailed proposals for the implementation of the ceasefire.

3. However:

(*a*) the Secretary of State has made the following statements in the House of Lords:

(i) 'Sanctions will be lifted as soon as Rhodesia returns to legality with the appointment of a Governor and his arrival in Salisbury.' 7 Nov. Col. 830;

---

1 Of No. 189.

(ii) 'Sanctions will be taken off when the Governor takes over in Salisbury and he will take over when a ceasefire has been agreed. I would not say that all the shooting will have stopped but not until the ceasefire is agreed will he take over. Then at that point there is of course legality.' 7 Nov. Col. 834;

(iii) 'In the context that we are talking about [an agreement between all the parties at the Conference] it will obviously be necessary for a ceasefire and for the Governor to go as soon as it is arranged.' 7 Nov. Col. 835;

(iv) 'The Governor will go out to Salisbury as soon as a ceasefire is arranged.' 13 Nov. Col. 1102.

It is at least debatable whether these statements did not imply that there would be no return to legality until final agreement had been reached on a ceasefire;

(*b*) we may find some of our Western friends less disposed than Mr Renwick suggests to follow our lead on the basis of the appointment of an acting Governor at a time when discussions were still in progress in Lancaster House; there could also be implications for our position in the Security Council; and

(*c*) some countries who might otherwise give us the benefit of the doubt might think that we were guilty of sharp practice.

4. But what is the alternative? We could try, without the actual despatch of an acting Governor and all that flows from that, to bulldoze the Patriotic Front into early acceptance of the details of implementation. This may not work but it might be worth a try. The fact of making the Orders on the Constitution and the Governor would in itself be a form of pressure which might have some effect.

5. We do not have to take a final decision today on the sending of an acting Governor. The Order in Council can be worded in such a way that we can proceed or not as we wish. I suggest that we review this possibility when we are clearer about the Patriotic Front's intentions in respect of the ceasefire proposals.

D.M. DAY

No. 192

Minute by Sir I. Sinclair to Mr Walden,[1] 30 November 1979
Confidential (FCO 36/2442)

Rhodesia: The Return to Legality

1. I must confess to being concerned about certain aspects of the proposals made in Mr Renwick's submission of 29 November.[2]

2. I understand full well the danger that the Salisbury parties may run out if there is any further delay in making the necessary arrangements for the ceasefire. Nevertheless, I would suggest that the international repercussions of our acting in the manner proposed in paragraphs 3 and 5 of Mr Renwick's submission may well be serious. To send out an Acting Governor in advance of agreement on the implementation of the ceasefire could be represented as a piece of trickery on our part designed precisely to enable us to proceed with the internal parties alone. Any

---
1 Also sent to Mr Day.
2 No. 189.

'return to legality' predicated upon the arrival of an Acting Governor in advance of the agreement on the implementation of the ceasefire would inevitably be controversial, and it would be very difficult indeed to counter the criticism that the 'return to legality' was simply a ploy to enable us to proceed along the lines suggested in paragraph 5 of Mr Renwick's submission. Our argument on the lapsing of sanctions, already difficult enough, would be made considerably harder if it had to be based on a dubious 'return to legality' of this kind. I would think that Sir A. Parsons would have a very difficult time indeed in New York in answering the criticism that the despatch of the Acting Governor in the circumstances contemplated simply confirms a skilfully disguised determination on our part to proceed with the internal parties alone, and in mustering any support for our argument on sanctions.

3. If it is a question of seeking to bring further pressure to bear on the Patriotic Front to agree to reasonable arrangements for the implementation of a ceasefire, there would, in my view, be no objection to our proceeding immediately with the making of the Order in Council providing for the appointment of the Governor. This in itself would intensify the pressures on all parties to come to a final settlement, since it would then be open to us to indicate that we proposed to send out the Governor on such and such a date—thus in effect creating a deadline by which the arrangements for the implementation of the ceasefire must have been agreed.

4. As I understand the position, we will have hoped to achieve over the week-end a sufficient measure of agreement with all parties on the framework of the ceasefire; but there will still remain very difficult issues to be resolved in the context of the implementation of the ceasefire. If we have agreement with all parties on the general framework of a ceasefire, it will surely in any event be extremely difficult for us to proceed immediately to take controversial action of the nature contemplated.

IAN SINCLAIR

No. 193

Minute from Mr Walden to Mr Renwick, 30 November 1979
Confidential (FCO 36/2442)

Meeting between the Secretary of State and the Patriotic Front
Messrs Nkomo and Mugabe called again on the Secretary of State this evening, accompanied by Mr Chambati and Mr Kamba. The LPS, you and I were also present.

Mr Mugabe began by distributing and reading out a paper, which he described as the PF's reply to Lord Carrington. He said he would have preferred to do this at a full-scale bilateral meeting. Lord Carrington said that he found this reply most disappointing. It was not an answer, but an interpretative statement. The other side would also wish to make such statements if the PF did. In other respects, the paper was merely a reiteration of the PF's position. We had already taken account of the PF's problems, e.g. on monitoring where we were now thinking in terms of 1,200, thus trebling our initial figure. This was as far as we could go. As for the PF's concern about the Rhodesian Air Force, he could give a categorical undertaking that

Negotiations on the Cease-Fire and the Return to Legality

the airports would be adequately monitored. On the disposition of the forces, Lord Carrington then read out points (*a*)-(*h*) in your brief for the meeting.[1]

The Secretary of State stressed that there was no other way of reaching a ceasefire agreement, and no more negotiating fat on our position. It was for this reason that he had asked in good faith whether the Patriotic Front could accept our proposals or not. No more discussion was possible. Mr Mugabe said that there had been no discussion at all about disengagement on an equal basis. The PF were prepared to move to company basis if the Rhodesian forces were too. Mr Renwick said that we did not understand the proposals for a two-stage disengagement in the PF's document. Above all, the proposal in para 2(*d*) of that document (which suggests that movement into the second phase positions might be unnecessary) was not acceptable. Our own proposals were less complex. We were prepared to accept the monitoring of Rhodesian forces down to company level. Assembly was crucial. There could not be an adequate ceasefire with large numbers of PF forces across the country. The Rhodesians would fall back towards their bases as the PF assembled. Everyone would have to be satisfied, including the Governor, that the PF had assembled in sufficient numbers with their arms.

Mr Mugabe said that they accepted reciprocity, but our definition was not clear. Lord Carrington said that the details could be discussed in the talks and implementation. The point was that all the forces would be under the Governor, and would be monitored. Once they were separated there would be no more fighting. Mr Mugabe said that it was wrong to suppose that the PF forces could not be identified; they had provincial structures and commands. Mr Renwick said that if large numbers of the PF turned up, then the ceasefire would be successfully implemented. Mr Mugabe asked why the PF should be concentrated in fewer areas than the Rhodesian forces. The ZRSF[2] were not to be trusted. They were 'ferocious creatures'. In the final analysis, the PF would have to defend themselves since the Governor had no army and the monitors could only pray. Discussion of the problem would be much easier if the Rhodesians themselves were present.

Lord Carrington said that the main objective was to stop the war. He wanted to make it clear that there was nothing more he could say to the PF: they must decide whether or not they could accept our ceasefire paper, together with his statement at Lancaster House on 28 November which had been circulated as a conference document. Mr Mugabe said that the PF had given its answer in their paper; there must be an equality: if the Rhodesian forces withdrew to their battalion bases, the PF would too. Mr Nkomo became indignant, and asked what the PF were supposed to be accepting. Lord Carrington said that we could not accept the PF's interpretative paper. We had already rejected many of its arguments. He was not prepared to go through the whole business again. We were now at the end of the week, and he had a meeting with his senior colleagues on Monday. They knew that he had asked for a definitive answer. Decisions had to be taken on Monday about the next steps the Government would have to take. He would however be available to see the PF at 11 o'clock tomorrow morning if they wished.

1 Not printed.
2 Zimbabwe-Rhodesian Security Forces.

Mr Nkomo, in a noisy and heated intervention, said that Lord Carrington was making difficulties for himself; that the PF were not his students; and were not prepared to sing his song. Lord Carrington said that we had been discussing the ceasefire arrangements for over two weeks and had gone out of our way to allay the PF's fears. We had to have an answer. Mr Nkomo said that the PF were ready to agree on a ceasefire and want to go straight on to discuss the details. Lord Carrington said that the details could not be discussed until the PF had accepted our proposals.

G.G.H. WALDEN

No. 194

Extract from the minutes of a meeting of the Cabinet Defence and Oversea Policy Committee, 3 December 1979[1]
OD(79) 13th Meeting (CAB 148/183)

1. *Rhodesia*
Previous Reference OD(79) 12th Meeting.[2]
The Foreign and Commonwealth Secretary said that the Rhodesian Conference was now close to break-down because the Patriotic Front had not accepted the British proposals for a ceasefire. They had produced an entirely unacceptable paper in reply and it was proving very hard to carry matters forward by rational discussion. Their intentions were difficult to predict. It was possible that Mr Nkomo might be ready to come to an agreement without Mr Mugabe. Meanwhile the Salisbury delegation who had accepted the British proposals were reaching the end of their patience. To retain their co-operation, and to prevent the Patriotic Front appearing to have successfully ignored the deadline they had been given, he proposed, if the Committee agreed, to state publicly that the following action was being taken: an Order would be made at that evening's Privy Council meeting under which a Governor of Zimbabwe-Rhodesia could at the appropriate moment be appointed; both the Salisbury delegation and the Patriotic Front leaders would be given the full text of the new constitution which would be brought into force by Order in Council on 6 December; and preparations would go ahead for the passage through Parliament of an Independence Bill. Whatever happened, the Governor would almost certainly need to arrive in Rhodesia by early the following week. If a breakdown of the Conference proved unavoidable, Britain's position would be strengthened by the

---

1 Present were: The Rt Hon Margaret Thatcher MP, Prime Minister; The Rt Hon William Whitelaw MP; Secretary of State for the Home Department; The Rt Hon Lord Hailsham, Lord Chancellor; The Rt Hon Lord Carrington, Secretary of State for Foreign and Commonwealth Affairs; The Rt Hon Sir Geoffrey Howe QC MP, Chancellor of the Exchequer; The Rt Hon Francis Pym MP, Secretary of State for Defence; The Rt Hon Lord Soames, Lord President of the Council; The Rt Hon Sir Ian Gilmour MP, Lord Privy Seal; and The Rt Hon John Nott MP, Secretary of State for Trade.
The following were also present: The Rt Hon Sir Keith Joseph MP, Secretary of State for Industry; The Rt Hon John Biffen, Chief Secretary, Treasury; and The Rt Hon Sir Michael Havers, Attorney General (Items 1 and 2). Secretariat: Sir Robert Armstrong; Mr R.L. Wade-Gery; and Mr R.M. Hastie-Smith. The other items discussed were (2) Bingham Report and (3) Future United Kingdom Defence.
2 No. 146.

fact that international opinion was generally favourable to our ceasefire proposals, which the Patriotic Front leaders were being urged by their friends to accept. But there could still be very adverse effects on British interests.

The Prime Minister, summing up a short discussion, said that the Committee once again congratulated the Foreign and Commonwealth Secretary on the handling of the Conference and fully endorsed his proposals.

The Committee

1. Took note, with approval, of the Prime Minister's summing up of their discussion.

2. Invited the Foreign and Commonwealth Secretary to follow the course of action which he had proposed.

No. 195

Minute from Mr Lyne to Mr Renwick, 3 December 1979
Confidential (FCO 36/2442)

Call on Lord Carrington by the Salisbury Delegation,
Monday 3 December, 2.45 p.m.

Certain points from the meeting this afternoon between the Salisbury Delegation and Lord Carrington and the Lord Privy Seal (which officials continued after Ministers departed) should be recorded:

(*a*) Dr Mundawarara said that, if we could not name a date for the Governor's arrival in Salisbury, we would be allowing the Patriotic Front to exercise a veto. If it had not been for this 'PF veto', there would have been a Governor in Salisbury by now. He and others alleged that the British Government had let the Salisbury Delegation down. He said that we should allow the Patriotic Front four days after the Governor's arrival to join in. Dr Mundawarara said that the negotiation between the delegation and ourselves had been conducted up to the present on a basis of trust, but it was beginning to look as if the British had some particular reasons for delaying in sending the Governor.

(*b*) General Walls said that the Salisbury Administration had lost ground militarily, particularly during the last few days, by trying to be reasonable. (Air Vice-Marshal Hawkins said that the Government promised that the Salisbury Administration would not be disadvantaged: but they had now been disadvantaged, and every report received from Rhodesia stressed that Bishop Muzorewa's cause had suffered.) General Walls said that there was growing apprehension, based on comments in the press and elsewhere, that not only would the timetable slip further, but also that Britain's intentions towards Rhodesia were not irreversible. He asked if Lord Carrington could guarantee that his colleagues would definitely agree to send a Governor to Salisbury. Lord Carrington gave General Walls a categorical assurance that the Government would send a British Governor.

(*c*) Mr Allum said that earlier in the negotiations the British Government appeared to want to send a Governor to Salisbury with indecent haste and had pressed the Salisbury Government to dissolve their Parliament to make this possible. He asked why the Government could not now send a Governor to Salisbury within a few days.

(*d*) Professor Kamusikiri said that the British Government had lost the concept of time and were trying to get the Patriotic Front in at almost any price. He thought the British had misread the situation: the international community would not criticise the British Government for implementing a settlement if the Patriotic Front failed to agree after three months of negotiations. Air Vice-Marshal Hawkins interjected at this point (it was after Ministers had left) that the negotiations were beginning to 'look like a con'.

R.M.J. Lyne

No. 196

Lord Carrington to Sir L. Allinson (Lusaka), 3 December 1979, 6.40 p.m.[1]
Tel. No. 1034 Immediate, Confidential (FCO 36/2442)

My telno 1002: Rhodesia.[2]

1. I shall be giving a press conference this evening to explain that I have repeatedly asked for a response from the Patriotic Front to the cease-fire proposals we put forward after discussion on 22 November: which were accepted by the Salisbury Delegation on 26 November: and which have since been exhaustively discussed with the Patriotic Front. The text of my statement is in MIPT.[2] The full text of supplementaries will be sent in the Verbatim Series. I shall make clear that we are beginning to make the legislative provisions to bring a settlement into effect, but in such a way as to leave it open to the Patriotic Front to participate: and that our objective remains a comprehensive agreement in which all parties can participate.

2. The present position in the conference is that Nkomo is ready to accept our proposals and proceed to discuss their detailed implementation and Mugabe is not. All Posts except Maputo, Dar es Salaam and Addis Ababa may at their discretion make known to the Governments concerned that part of the Patriotic Front want to accept our proposals, but that other elements do not. We hope that the Patriotic Front will overcome their internal difficulties and be able to discuss the detailed implementation of the cease-fire tomorrow.

3. The Southern Rhodesia Constitution (Interim Provisions) Order, establishing the Office of Governor and vesting legislative and executive power in Rhodesia in the Governor, will be made this evening. You will be receiving the text in the Verbatim Series. At your discretion you may inform the governments to which you are accredited of the action we are taking. In doing so you should say that the only provision of the order which will be brought into operation immediately will

---

1 Deskby UKMIS New York 032300Z; Deskby Lusaka 040600Z; Deskby Mirimba, Salisbury, 040630Z; to Immediate Lusaka; and to Immediate Mirimba, Salisbury, Nairobi, Maputo, Gaborone, Dar es Salaam, Luanda, Lagos, Washington, Pretoria, Addis Ababa, Monrovia, Canberra, Ottawa, Wellington; Priority Peking, Moscow, Prague, Dakar, Kinshasa, Khartoum, Tokyo, EEC Posts, Kuwait, Kingston, Bridgetown, Dacca, New Delhi, Singapore, Georgetown, Freetown, Port Louis, Port of Spain, Lilongwe, Valletta, Banjul, Colombo, Accra, Kuala Lumpur, Nicosia, Oslo, Stockholm, Lisbon, Madrid, Athens, Mbabane, Abidjan; Information Immediate UKMIS New York; Information Saving Nassau, Maseru, Castries, Suva, Port Moresby, Honiara, Nukualofa, Victoria, Tarawa, UKDEL NATO, Sofia, Budapest, Bucharest, East Berlin, Belgrade, Cairo, Algiers, Tunis, Tripoli, Rabat, Tehran.
2 Not printed.

be that of creating the Office of Governor. Other provisions come into effect on a day to be appointed by the Secretary of State. As appropriate you should make the following points:

(*a*) The Conference has agreed that there should be a British Governor with full executive and legislative power. When the appropriate provisions of the Order are brought into operation, they will enable us to implement this Agreement. The Order creates the Office of Governor and establishes his powers and is thus an essential preparatory step to the appointment of the Governor.

(*b*) If you are asked whether we shall appoint a Governor without agreement being reached between all the Parties at the Conference, you should say that Agreement has already been reached on the Constitution and the Pre-Independence Arrangements[;] what remains to be settled are the details of implementing a cease-fire. The process of finalising the arrangements for the cease-fire will require a British Authority in Salisbury, the timing of sending the Governor will depend on progress in finalising the agreement.

4. We shall be giving both delegations the full text of the Constitution tomorrow morning (for guidance please see my telno 997).[2] This will be enacted by Order in Council later in the week, probably on Thursday 6 December.

No. 197

Letter from Mr Alexander (No. 10) to Mr Lyne, 4 December 1979
Confidential (PREM19/116)

Dear Roderic,

Call by Mr Ramphal

As you know, Mr Ramphal, the Commonwealth Secretary-General, called on the Prime Minister yesterday evening to discuss the present situation in the Lancaster House Conference. The Foreign and Commonwealth Secretary was present.

Mr Ramphal raised four issues.

The Conference

Mr Ramphal passed on to the Prime Minister a message from Mr Nkomo to the effect that Mr Nkomo recognised that 'the bus was on the move' and that he intended to be on it. Of the other members of the Patriotic Front, Mr Ramphal said that Mr Tongogara wanted a settlement and that Mr Mugabe probably did too although he was still 'in a dialectic'. The real difficultly lay with Mr Tekere who was still resisting agreement. However Mr Ramphal was confident that the Patriotic Front would come up to the mark, probably on the following day. He himself would be seeing both Mr Nkomo and Mr Mugabe later in the evening and would be telling them that the time for delay was past. Mr Sule, the Nigerian observer, would be doing the same. The Foreign and Commonwealth Secretary stressed that the Conference would have to be completed by the end of this week. He hoped that the Patriotic Front were clear about this and that they recognised that the discussions on implementation could only take a few days. Mr Ramphal thought there would be no difficulty about this. Mr Nkomo, at least, was desperate to get back to Rhodesia.

South African Involvement

Mr Ramphal said that the revelation that South African troops were present in Rhodesia had been very damaging. It had caused real concern within the Patriotic Front. They seemed to be alarmed lest the South Africans should remain in the country and subsequently get hold of planes and bomb them or take hostile action in some other form. Mr Ramphal said that he had told the Patriotic Front that they had no cause for alarm. A British Governor would not allow the South Africans to remain in the country. The Foreign and Commonwealth Secretary made it clear that he agreed with this. He had told Mr Pik Botha that, while he had no wish to be informed officially about whether or not there were South Africans in Rhodesia, any troops there should be removed as soon as possible. He was more worried about what would happen if the talks broke down. There was a real possibility that in those circumstances the South Africans would go into Rhodesia.

The Interim Period

Mr Ramphal said that the Patriotic Front were worried about the role of the Rhodesian Air Force, and in particular of their combat planes, during the interim period. Could the combat planes not be grounded? The Foreign and Commonwealth Secretary said that the Rhodesian Air Force planes would have to be used during the interim period for communications and monitoring purposes. It was absurd to suppose that the planes would be used to shoot up the Patriotic Front in their assembly areas. The Prime Minister pointed out that there would in any case be monitors in the assembly areas and that it was unlikely that anyone would take the risk of attacking them.

The Commonwealth Observers

Mr Ramphal said that he had not come to talk in detail about the Commonwealth observers but he had been in touch with the Canadian and Australian Governments and he thought they would agree to participate both in the national and in the collective Commonwealth effort to observe the elections. He thought that the views of a credible Commonwealth group would carry a great deal of weight with the world at large. The present mood of the Commonwealth was in any case helpful and constructive. The group would make it easier to control the views of potentially difficult countries like Nigeria. The Foreign and Commonwealth Secretary commented that the composition of the group proposed by the Secretary General seemed reasonable.

Mr Ramphal said as he left the meeting that Mr Nkomo had asked him to convey to the Prime Minister and the Foreign and Commonwealth Secretary his deep sense of appreciation of what they had done in trying to resolve the Rhodesia problem in recent months.

Yours ever,
MICHAEL ALEXANDER

No. 198

Lord Carrington to Sir L. Allinson (Lusaka), 5 December 1979, 9.16 p.m.[1]
Tel. No. 1012 Immediate, Confidential, (FCO 36/2443)

Rhodesia: Constitutional Conference

1. At a plenary meeting of the Conference today (5 December) the Patriotic Front expressed concern about the disposition of the forces, the grounding of the Rhodesian Air Force and the presence of South African forces in Rhodesia during a ceasefire. In reply I assured them again that:

(*a*) There will be no external involvement in Rhodesia under the British Governor. The position has been made clear to all the governments concerned (including South Africa); and

(*b*) The Rhodesian Air Force will be monitored effectively, and we have in mind a monitoring force adequate to the overall task in the vicinity of 1,200 men.

2. The PF then said that a number of details including the detail of the location and number of places for the disposition of the forces fell to be dealt with under the implementation of the ceasefire. They now felt that our proposals provided the basis for an agreement and for moving on quickly to settle the details of implementation.

3. My intention now is that conclusions should be reached on a formal ceasefire agreement (which I circulated [*sic*] to the Conference within the next two or three days) the main questions to be settled will be the date of the ceasefire and arrangements for assembly of the PF forces and deployment of the monitoring force.

4. Before the plenary meeting I had made the statement to Parliament[2] the text of which has been sent to you in VS [Verbatim Series] 111/79. Following the making of the Order in Council providing for the Appointment of Governor with full legislative and executive powers, the Independence Constitution will be enacted by Order in Council by the end of this week. The Government will introduce tomorrow the Zimbabwe Bill which will make the necessary provisions in UK law to enable Rhodesia to be brought to Independence on a date to be decided after elections have been held. A Governor will be sent to Salisbury in the next few days.

5. You should as necessary impress on the governments to which you are accredited that the purpose of all these steps, and in particular of the despatch of a Governor to Rhodesia, is to put the Government in a position to implement agreements reached at the Conference quickly. We cannot put elements of the Monitoring Force into Rhodesia until a British Governor has been installed. It is also only under the authority of a British Governor that we can take full responsibility for the arrangements to be made at the rendezvous points and assembly places for the Patriotic Front Forces. There will be serious dangers in any further delay.

1 And to Immediate Mirimba, Salisbury, Nairobi, Maputo, Gaborone, Dar es Salaam, Luanda, Lagos, Washington, Pretoria, Addis Ababa, Monrovia, Canberra, Ottawa, Wellington; Priority Peking, Moscow, Prague, Dakar, Kinshasa, Khartoum, Tokyo, EEC Posts, Kuwait, Kingston, Bridgetown, Dacca, New Delhi, Singapore, Georgetown, Freetown, Port Louis, Port of Spain, Lilongwe, Valletta, Banjul, Colombo, Accra, Kuala Lumpur, Nicosia, Oslo, Stockholm, Lisbon, Madrid, Athens, Mbabane, Abidjan; Information Immediate UKMIS New York; Information Saving Nassau, Maseru, Castries, Suva, Port Moresby, Honiara, Nukualofa, Victoria, Tarawa, UKDEL NATO, Sofia, Budapest, Bucharest, East Berlin, Belgrade, Cairo, Algiers, Tunis, Tripoli, Rabat, Tehran.
2 Parl. Debs., 5th ser., H. of C., 5 December 1979, vol. 403, col. 712.

No. 199

Extract from the conclusions of a meeting of the Cabinet, 6 December 1979[1]
CC(79) 24th Conclusions Secret (CAB 128/66)

3. Rhodesia

The Foreign and Commonwealth Secretary said that the Patriotic Front had now agreed to the proposed ceasefire arrangements. The Cabinet wholeheartedly congratulated him on the achievement of this further progress in the negotiations to bring first legality and then independence to Rhodesia. He warned, however, that there could still be serious difficulties over the implementation of the arrangements, on which negotiations were continuing. He would have preferred if possible to avoid appointing and sending out the Governor until they were complete. But momentum needed to be kept up, in order to ensure the irreversibility of the process and to sustain the Salisbury delegation's confidence. It would therefore be necessary to announce the Governor's appointment on 7 December and to make clear that he would arrive in Salisbury on the morning of 11 December. This would be a calculated risk. The Salisbury and Patriotic Front delegations might well put divergent interpretations on what had been agreed. Recrimination might then be unavoidable; and the ceasefire might break down because, as had been made clear to the Front's leaders, although there would be progressive disengagement in Rhodesia if the Patriotic Front forces assembled in accordance with the agreement, the Rhodesian security forces would have to be used by the Governor to keep the peace if the Front's forces failed to assemble adequately as the agreement required. That could lead to the British Governor, who would have been appointed as an appropriate person to preside over an agreed settlement, facing the very difficult context of the war continuing, for which a different appointment would have been more suitable. The recall of the Governor, leaving his Deputy in charge, might then have to be considered.

The Prime Minister, summing up a brief discussion said that the Cabinet endorsed the course of action proposed by the Foreign and Commonwealth Secretary, despite the real risks involved, and renew their warm congratulations on his achievement.

The Cabinet—

1. Took note, with approval, of the Prime Minister's summing up of their discussion.

---

[1] The following were present: The Rt Hon Margaret Thatcher MP, Prime Minister; The Rt Hon William Whitelaw MP, Secretary of State for the Home Department; The Rt Hon Lord Hailsham, Lord Chancellor; The Rt Hon Lord Carrington, Secretary of State for Foreign and Commonwealth Affairs; The Rt Hon Sir Geoffrey Howe QC MP, Chancellor of the Exchequer; The Rt Hon Sir Keith Joseph MP, Secretary of State for Industry; The Rt Hon Francis Pym MP, Secretary of State for Defence; The Rt Hon Lord Soames, Lord President of the Council; The Rt Hon James Prior MP, Secretary of State for Employment; The Rt Hon Sir Ian Gilmour MP, Lord Privy Seal; The Rt Hon Peter Walker MP, Minister of Agriculture, Fisheries and Food; The Rt Hon Michael Heseltine MP, Secretary of State for the Environment; The Rt Hon George Younger, MP, Secretary of State for Scotland; The Rt Hon Nicholas Edwards MP, Secretary of State for Wales; The Rt Hon Humphrey Atkins, Secretary of State for Northern Ireland; The Rt Hon Patrick Jenkin MP, Secretary of State for Social Services; The Rt Hon Sir Norman St John-Stevas MP, Chancellor of the Duchy of Lancaster; The Rt Hon John Nott MP, Secretary of State for Trade; The Rt Hon David Howell MP, Secretary of State for Energy; The Rt Hon Mark Carlisle QC MP, Secretary of State for Education and Science; The Rt Hon John Biffen MP, Chief Secretary, Treasury; The Rt Hon Angus Maude MP, Paymaster General. The following were also present: The Rt Hon Michael Jopling MP, Parliamentary Secretary, Treasury. Secretariat: Sir Robert Armstrong; Mr M.D.M. Franklin (Items 3 and 4) Mr R.L. Wade-Gery (Items 3 and 4) and four others.

No. 200

Record of a conversation between Mrs Thatcher and General Walls at 10 Downing Street, 6 December 1979, 12.30 p.m.
Secret (PREM 19/116)

Present:
Prime Minister   General Walls
Sir Antony Duff
Mr M.O'D.B. Alexander

After an exchange of courtesies, *General Walls* said that he expected the Patriotic Front would try to blame the Salisbury delegation for any difficulties which arose in the discussions of the implementation of the ceasefire. The *Prime Minister* said that in her view the Patriotic Front, in agreeing to the ceasefire, had crossed the Rubicon. It would be impossible for the Patriotic Front now to go back. For them to agree on the main issue and quarrel on detail would cast doubt on their good faith. She had been struck by the evident sense of relief all over the world at the agreement reached the previous day. Everyone considered that final agreement was now a fait accompli. The Prime Minister stressed that it was now the intention of the British Government to go 'all the way through to independence'.

General Walls said that he knew that the Prime Minister welcomed straight talking. He had a number of problems. The first was that under the British proposals he was divorced from political guidance. If he obeyed the British Governor, he could not consult Bishop Muzorewa who had agreed to stand aside during the interim. He had welcomed the 'under the counter' scheme for the Governor, the Prime Minister, and the present military Commanders to consult together during the interim. He envisaged this as a means of ensuring that their actions would be consistent with the policies of any incoming Government—always assuming that Government was a moderate one. Even so, two months was a long time for him to be without direct political guidance. Even one month would be a long time. He was very conscious of the responsibility which rested on his shoulders to ensure that the future of Rhodesia was protected. Many people had told him that he was being duped by the Prime Minister and the British Government. The Rhodesian people had put their faith in military Commanders, and in him, and he had to be certain that what he was doing was in the country's interest. He had to be sure therefore of his access to the Governor.

The Prime Minister said that it was her understanding that the Governor would be entitled to summon anyone to see him at any time. This included, of course, both Bishop Muzorewa and General Walls. It was no part of the British Government's intention to reduce the Governor's capability to keep law and order in Rhodesia. The Governor had to be in a position to create the right conditions for the elections. *Sir Antony Duff* said that he saw no difficulty in principle about access by General Walls to the Governor. Of course, some of the meetings would be informal.

General Walls said that what mattered was that there was no question of his being denied access to the Governor, and no question of his having to go through others to obtain that access. The *Prime Minister* confirmed that this was so. She said she would make it clear to Lord Soames both orally and in writing that he must have direct access to the Governor just as the Chiefs of Staff have direct access to her in this country. Moreover, General Walls should on occasion be present when the Governor was seeing Bishop Muzorewa.

As far as Rhodesia was concerned, the British Government had but one objective: to bring Rhodesia to independence. It was clear that the country's capability to maintain law and order, exercised through the Governor, had to be maintained.

General Walls said that he had taken the easiest of his problems first. He had often been told that previous Rhodesian leaders, like Sir Roy Welensky and Sir Edgar Whitehead[1], had been duped by Britain's methods of leading them on. He was concerned that a British Governor, under domestic and international pressure, might start wavering when it came to acting in the interests of Zimbabwe-Rhodesia. In reply to the Prime Minister's request for an example of what he had in mind, General Walls referred to the possibility of a build-up of guerrilla forces in one of the neighbouring countries. If such a build-up reached the point where the future of Zimbabwe-Rhodesia appeared to be threatened, General Walls said that he would hope that the Governor would agree that something had to be done. No doubt the Governor would hope to secure results by the exercise of diplomatic pressure. If he failed, he might be reluctant to envisage a cross-border operation while the military Commanders might want to take pre-emptive action. General Walls said that his critics were taking the line that once the Governor's authority had been accepted, the military Commanders would be prevented from taking such action.

The Prime Minister said she could not say how Lord Soames would react in these circumstances. She had given Rhodesia one of the ablest and strongest people in the British Government. He was not the sort of man who was likely to be intimidated or pressured. Everything would depend on the relationship between him and General Walls. There would have to be a determination on both sides to keep things straight. She could give no further undertakings. But she stressed the degree of her own commitment and the fact that she herself was unlikely to be intimidated. The Governments objective was to carry through the elections, and to bring Rhodesia to independence. They would not hesitate now.

Turning to the situation inside Rhodesia, which he said was the most difficult problem of all, *General Walls* said that he knew for a fact that the Patriotic Front did not intend to implement the ceasefire. They would continue to intimidate and threaten wherever they could. He believed that the British Government agreed that this was the case. He had to be in a position to assure people in Zimbabwe-Rhodesia that the armed forces would be able to counter intimidation. The British proposals allowed for a working arrangement whereby the present armed forces could provide protection and make possible the election of a responsible Government. The Governor must be ready to interpret these proposals in the same way as Lord Carrington had done in private conversations with General Walls. If the Governor were to waiver on this, and to try to reduce the ability of the armed forces to deal with the terrorists, General Walls would have forfeited the country's chance of

---

1 Prime Minister of Southern Rhodesia, 1958-1962.

survival. It was against this background that Lord Carrington had offered him a piece of paper. Perhaps Lord Carrington should not have offered the piece of paper, but its existence had enabled General Walls to reassure Bishop Muzorewa and the South African Government. The South African Government had been threatening to remove their men from Rhodesia which would, of course, be fatal to the country's chance of survival.

Lord Carrington had subsequently said that the piece of paper could not be given to General Walls and was now saying that there could be no piece of paper at all. He had also changed his position on the question of South African assistance to Rhodesia. Originally, he had said that he would encourage the South Africans to support Bishop Muzorewa's Government. Now he was saying that there must be no identifiable South African units in the country. If, as a result of Lord Carrington's new position on the question of a South African presence, the Governor were to give instructions for the withdrawal of the South Africans or to lay down conditions on their employment, then 'we'd be finished'. If it was no longer possible for him to have the piece of paper, General Walls said that he had to be 100% sure that the contents of the paper nonetheless represented the intentions of the British Government.

The Prime Minister said that the future of Zimbabwe-Rhodesia was at stake. So was the reputation of Lord Soames. So was her own reputation. Lord Soames had made a considerable gesture in agreeing to put his reputation at issue. She did not put her faith in pieces of paper. She put her faith in people. She shared with General Walls an immediate interest in the future of Zimbabwe-Rhodesia, since members of her own family lived there. She shared a larger interest in that she regarded the future of democracy in South Africa as being at stake. Her commitment was total. It was no part of her intention to reduce the capability of the only disciplined force in the country to maintain law and order there. General Walls and Lord Soames would, she was confident, be able to work out how to ensure that law and order, was kept. General Walls, she repeated, should be in no doubt about her commitment. She regarded Zimbabwe-Rhodesia as being in the front line of the defence of the Western way of life. It was on this commitment, rather than a piece of paper, that General Walls would have to put his faith. He could be assured of her continuing close interest in what was happening. Lord Soames and Sir Antony Duff, and through them General Walls, would be able to get in touch with her whenever they wished to do so.

General Walls said that he also did not put his faith in bits of paper. What the Prime Minister said was good enough for him. It was fine.

The discussion ended at 13:00 hours.

No. 201

Letter from Mr Lyne to Mr Alexander, 6 December 1979
Secret (FCO 36/2514)

Dear Michael,
   Rhodesia: Messages to the South African Government

As you know, we have had a number of exchanges this week with the South African Government over the role of their forces in Rhodesia following the arrival of a British Governor.

Mr Laurens van der Post has helped us to explain to the South Africans the reasons why we would not wish any identifiable units of the South African forces to remain in Rhodesia following the arrival of the British Governor. Mr van der Post called privately on Lord Carrington today. He said that the position over South African forces and equipment was now clearly understood in Pretoria. Mr van der Post strongly recommended that the Prime Minister and Lord Carrington should send private messages to Mr P.W. Botha and Mr Pik Botha as soon as possible, thanking the South Africans for their help and restraint. There was no need for the messages to deal with the details of military support for Rhodesia.

Mr van der Post said that such messages would have a very useful psychological effect, as the statements which we had been obliged to make in public about South African forces had left South African Ministers feeling that their positive efforts were going unrecognised. He was certain that the South Africans would be discreet about private messages from Mrs Thatcher and Lord Carrington.

Lord Carrington thinks this is a very helpful and sound suggestion, and recommends that the Prime Minister should send a short personal message of appreciation to Mr P.W. Botha as soon as possible. Such a message would help to balance the representations we have had to make about the need for the South Africans to remove identifiable military units from Rhodesia; and the public statements we have been obliged to make in response to Mr P.W. Botha's recent oblique reference to the presence of South African forces there. Although at times during the Lancaster House Conference the South Africans have had an unhelpful influence on its proceedings and on the Salisbury delegation, and continue to have doubts about whether we are pursuing the right course, in the past few weeks they have exercised considerable restraint and have taken a generally constructive line. We hope that sympathetic messages will encourage them to continue to do so. The South African Government are also said by Mr van der Post to have done all they can to contain and isolate Mr Ian Smith.

I enclose the texts of draft telegrams of instruction to HM Ambassador at Pretoria which, if the Prime Minister agreed, we would hope to despatch early tomorrow.

Yours ever,
R.M.J. Lyne

No. 202

Lord Carrington to Sir P. Moon (Dar es Salaam), 7 December 1979, 6.40 p.m.[1]
Tel. No. 411 Immediate, Confidential (FCO 36/2443)

Rhodesia

1. The Lord Privy Seal announced in Parliament today the appointment by Her Majesty the Queen of Lord Soames as Governor (Text in VS). Lord Soames will arrive in Salisbury next week on a date to be decided. The Salisbury Parliament will have to be dissolved before the Governor's arrival.

2. If you are asked about our intentions, you should say that agreement has been reached in the Conference on the Independence Constitution, the Pre-Independence arrangements and our cease-fire proposals. It is now necessary to finalise the details of implementation of the cease-fire. The Order in Council concerning the Governor enables us to give effect to a settlement and the appointment of Lord Soames, a senior Cabinet Minister, demonstrates the seriousness with which the Government is taking its intention to set Rhodesia on the road to Legal Independence. The date of Lord Soames' arrival in Salisbury will be decided early next week.

3. You may also point out that the presence of a British Authority is essential to enable us to bring a cease-fire into effect. Otherwise it will not be possible to bring the Rhodesian forces under our control or to make the practical arrangements to enable the Patriotic Front forces to assemble. Without a Governor in Salisbury we would also be unable to prevent cross-border military activity or to ensure the resumption of maize supplies to Zambia.

[1] And to Immediate Mirimba, Salisbury, Nairobi, Maputo, Gaborone, Luanda, Lagos, Pretoria, Addis Ababa, Monrovia; Priority to Dakar, Kinshasa, Khartoum, Tokyo, Bridgetown, New Delhi, Singapore, Georgetown, Freetown, Port Louis, Port of Spain, Lilongwe, Valletta, Banjul, Colombo, Accra, Kuala Lumpur, Nicosia, Oslo, Stockholm, Madrid, Athens, Mbabane, Abidjan; Information Saving to Nassau, Maseru, Castries, Suva, Port Moresby, Honiara, Nukualofa, Victoria, Tarawa, UKDEL NATO, Sofia, Budapest, Bucharest, East Berlin, Belgrade, Cairo, Algiers, Tunis, Tripoli, Rabat, Tehran.

No. 203

Minute from Mr Renwick to Mr Walden, 8 December 1979[1]
Confidential (FCO 36/2507)

The Secretary of State's meeting with Mr Vance: Rhodesia

1. Our recent exchanges with the Americans have revealed hesitations in Washington about the timing of the lifting of sanctions. The President, in deciding not to lift sanctions on 15 November, said that they would be lifted as soon as a British Governor arrived in Rhodesia and a process leading to fair elections had begun. As a result of recent consultations between the President and black Congressional leaders, Mr Vance wrote to Senator Helms that sanctions would be lifted 'within a

[1] Also sent to Sir A. Duff.

month' of the Governor's arrival in Rhodesia. In response to our representations about this, in which we impressed on the State Department the political dangers of getting out of step with each other on sanctions, the Americans asked if we could say 'something more concrete on the question of the electoral process'. We have pointed out that the ordinance establishing the Election Commissioner, and Election Council and assuming control of the Rhodesian election machinery will come into effect *immediately* on the Governor's arrival in Rhodesia (which really ought to satisfy the Americans on this point). But Mr Lake is now asking if we could announce the date for elections simultaneously with the date of the Governor's arrival. If this is really necessary to secure immediate US action in lifting sanctions, we should consider this (though the date would have to be changed to be brought forward if the Patriotic Front did not participate).

2. Against this background I *recommend* that the Secretary of State might take the line set out in the attached minute in his discussion with Mr Vance on 10 December. Sir A. Duff and I will have a preliminary discussion with Mr Lake.[2]

R.W. RENWICK

ENCLOSURE IN NO. 203

Rhodesia: Speaking Note

1. We are very close to a successful outcome of the Conference. But the Patriotic Front are engaged in another filibuster and show every intention of seeking to prolong the negotiations while they infiltrate as many more of their forces into Rhodesia as they can. The Americans will be aware of the movement of ZANLA forces from Tanzania and Mozambique; and the repeated attempts to infiltrate large ZIPRA units across the Rhodesia-Zambia border.

2. Against this background, unless agreement on a cease-fire is achieved in the next few days, it is unlikely to be achieved at all. If we do not get the Governor to Salisbury, the Rhodesians will launch further strikes into Zambia and Mozambique. There will also be a greater danger of increased South African involvement in Rhodesia.

3. The purpose of sending a Governor to Salisbury will be to assert our authority and limit these dangers. The Governor would immediately order the resumption of maize shipments to Zambia. A British authority in Salisbury is also essential in making the final arrangement for implementing the cease-fire. It is not possible to do this from a distance. We need control over the Rhodesian forces, police etc to ensure *inter alia* that adequate arrangements are made for the assembly of the Patriotic Front forces.

4. To anyone who has not been involved in the negotiations, it might appear that the solution is to agree the final details in the Conference; and arrange for the Governor to go once the final agreement has been signed. No-one who has negotiated with the Patriotic Front over the last 12 weeks will believe that this is feasible. They have a chronic inability to say either 'yes' or 'no'. On this occasion they are

2 In a minute of 8 December, Sir A. Duff agreed with the timing, except he thought that it would be very difficult to announce the date of the election on the Governor's arrival.

being asked to take the final plunge. It has only been possible to bring them to the point of decision on the three previous occasions by very strong pressures on them. It will not be possible to bring them to the point of decision without action by us. Unless and until the Patriotic Front are aware that the return to legality and the lifting of sanctions are actually underway, they will have no incentive to reach a final agreement on our proposals. They will be bound instead to continue to filibuster – because it is in their political and military interest to do so.

5. If, however, they are given a strong enough push, we believe that it should be possible to bring them into the settlement. This we intend to do by making a final presentation of our cease-fire proposals to the Conference tomorrow (Tuesday 11 December). In doing so, we will seek to meet the Patriotic Front's main concern of making it clear that if the Patriotic Front assemble their forces and cease all cross-border movement, the Rhodesian forces will not need to deploy from their company bases.

6. At the same time we will distribute a map indicating the Patriotic Front assembly places. These have been chosen in relation to their existing operational areas and in a manner which takes account of Tongogara's concern that they should not be 'encircled' by Rhodesian bases.

7. The return to legality will be effective with the arrival of the Governor in Salisbury and the acceptance of his authority on Wednesday 12 December. There can be no question of our continuing to apply sanctions against a British Governor: these will be lifted immediately, and we shall be looking to our friends and allies to follow suit. Sir A. Parsons will be instructed to address the attached letter to the President of the Security Council.

8. We have been very grateful for the action the President has taken at two previous moments of decision by sending messages to President Kaunda before his visit to London and to the front line Presidents before their meeting in Dar es Salaam. American support at this point could make a crucial difference to our success or failure in securing a comprehensive settlement. Despite Mugabe's negative tactics, the Zambian and Mozambique governments have a very strong interest in a successful outcome. We believe that there is a good chance of pushing the Patriotic Front into the settlement. This approach will only succeed, however, if our friends and in particular the Americans are prepared to give us strong support. We hope the Americans will be prepared to make immediately:

(*a*) a clear statement that the return to legality will be followed by immediate or very early US action to lift sanctions; and

(*b*) a public statement of strong support for our final cease-fire proposals.

9. This will exert real pressure on the Patriotic Front finally to agree to the settlement. But if doubt is created about the timing of the lifting of sanctions, US action could actually be self-defeating. If the Patriotic Front are left with the impression that they can afford to delay, they will be encouraged to hold out for different terms which will not be negotiable [while the United States would still end up lifting sanctions].[3]

[As necessary]

10. If this is crucial to the Americans' decision to lift sanctions, the Governor

---

3 Parentheses in the original.

probably could announce the date for elections immediately on his arrival in Salisbury. [But this could could actually render it rather more difficult for the Patriotic Front to participate.]

11. The cease-fire proposals are the best compromise that can be put forward. There is serious concern on the Patriotic Front side about the security of their forces, and we have moved to meet them on this. There is equally serious concern on the Rhodesian side that Patriotic Front will not assemble their forces (or more than a fraction of them) and that cross-border infiltration by Patriotic Front forces will continue.

12. The Prime Minister would find herself in a politically embarrassing situation in Washington if, by that time, there had not been a clear American decision about sanctions. We should not be able to endorse the continuance of sanctions even for a limited period against Rhodesia under a British Governor.

13. It is *not* possible to await the outcome of the Conference before sending a Governor. If we adopted that approach, the Conference would never come to the conclusion, and would be likely to collapse.

No. 204

Lord Carrington to Sir D. Tebbit (Canberra), 9 December 1979, 8.05 p.m.[1]
Tel. No. 609 Immediate, Secret (FCO 36/2443)

Rhodesia

1. We are very close to a successful outcome to the Conference. But Patriotic Front are engaged in another filibuster and show every intention of seeking to prolong the negotiations while they infiltrate more of their forces into Rhodesia. There has recently been a major movement of ZANLA (Mugabe) forces from Tanzania to Mozambique; and ZIPRA (Nkomo) are making repeated attempts to infiltrate large units across the Rhodesia-Zambia borders.

2. Against this background, unless agreement on a cease-fire is reached in the next few days it is unlikely to be achieved at all; and there will be a real risk of a further escalation of the conflict. The dangers of delay were high-lighted by the Rhodesian attacks on bridges in Zambia at the end of November and by the recent raids on ZIPRA targets in Zambia. If we do not get the Governor to Salisbury, the Rhodesians will launch further strikes into Zambia and Mozambique. There will also be a greater danger of increased South African involvement.

3. The purpose of sending a Governor to Salisbury will be to assert our authority and limit these dangers. The Governor will immediately order the resumption of maize shipments to Zambia. A British Authority in Salisbury is also essential for making official arrangements for implementing the cease-fire. It is not possible to

---

1 And to Immediate EEC Posts, Vienna, Ottawa, Madrid, Athens, Tokyo, Ankara, Oslo, Wellington, Lisbon, Berne; Information Immediate to Lusaka, Mirimba, Salisbury, Nairobi, Maputo, Gaborone, Dar es Salaam, Luanda, Lagos, Washington, Pretoria, Addis Ababa, Monrovia, Peking, Mosco, Prague, Dakar, Kinshasa, Khartoum, Tokyo, Kuwait, Kingston, Bridgetown, Dacca, New Delhi, Singapore, Georgetown, Freetown, Port Louis, Port of Spain, Lilongwe, Valletta, Banjul, Colombo, Accra, Kuala Lumpur, Nicosia, Stockholm, Mbabane, Abidjan, UKMIS New York, UKDEL NATO, Cairo, Algiers, Tunis, Tripoli, Rabat, Helsinki, Libreville, La Paz.

do this from a distance. We need control over the Rhodesian forces, police, etc., to ensure *inter alia* that adequate arrangements are made for the assembly of the Patriotic Front forces.

4. To those not involved in the negotiations it might appear possible to agree the final details in the Conference and arrange for the Governor to go once the final agreement has been signed. No-one who has negotiated with the Patriotic Front over the last twelve weeks will believe this to be feasible. Their negotiating tactics throughout the Conference have been based on a refusal to say either 'yes' or 'no'. On this occasion they are being asked to take the final decision. It has only been possible to bring them to the point of decision on the three previous occasions by very strong pressure. It will not be possible to do so on this occasion without action by us. Unless and until the Patriotic Front are aware that the return to legality and the lifting of sanctions are actually under way, they will have no incentive to reach final agreement on our proposals. They will be bound instead to continue to filibuster—because they believe that it is in their political and military interests to do so.

5. If, however, they are given a strong enough push, we believe that it should be possible to bring them into the settlement. This we intend to do by making a final presentation of our cease-fire proposals to the Conference on Tuesday 11 December. In doing so, we will seek to meet the Patriotic Front's main concern by making it clear that if the Patriotic Front assemble their forces and cease all cross-border movement, the Rhodesian forces will not need to deploy from their company bases. At the same time we will distribute a map indicating the Patriotic Front assembly places. These have been chosen in relation to their existing operational areas and in a manner which takes account of Tongogara's concern that they should not be 'encircled' by Rhodesian bases.

6. The return to legality will be effected with the arrival of the Governor in Salisbury and the acceptance of his authority on Wednesday 12 December. There can be no question of our continuing to apply sanctions against a British Governor: These will be lifted immediately, and we shall look to our friends and allies to follow suit. Sir A. Parsons will be instructed to address the letter in MIFT[2] to the President of the Security Council.

7. You will receive instructions to speak on these lines to the governments to which you are accredited, on the morning of Tuesday 11 December. Together with the final text of our presentation in the Conference. In doing so you should say:

(*a*) We are grateful for the support our friends and allies have given us in earlier critical phases of the Conference:

(*b*) We are aiming for a settlement involving the Patriotic Front, and believe there is a good chance of securing their final acceptance: but

(*c*) This will depend crucially on the extent of the support we get in this final, decisive stage of the Conference:

(*d*) We hope therefore that our friends and allies will give strong support to the action we are taking and to our cease-fire proposals:

(*e*) If we get solid international support, the pressures on the Patriotic Front to participate will be irresistible:

---

2 Not printed.

(*f*) Despite their tendency automatically to support Patriotic Front negotiating demands, the Front Line States are very concerned that a settlement should be reached this week:

(*g*) It will be very important that the interpretation of Sir A. Parsons' letter to the President of the Security Council should not be contested by other Western Members of the Council:

(*h*) We hope there will be no question of their continuing sanctions against Rhodesia under a British Governor:

(*i*) (As necessary). If our action is not supported, the Patriotic Front will be encouraged to hold out and make further demands which will be non-negotiable. There will then be a much greater danger of our friends having to make a choice between support for our position and (in effect) that of the Patriotic Front:

(*j*) The cease-fire proposals are designed to meet the concerns of both sides. The Patriotic Front are concerned about the security of their forces, and we have moved to meet them on this. There is equally serious concern on the Rhodesian side that the Patriotic Front will not assemble their forces (or more than a fraction of them) and that cross-border infiltration by Patriotic Front forces will continue:

(*k*) We should not be able to endorse the continuance of sanctions even for a limited period against Rhodesia under a British Governor:

(*l*) It is not possible to await the outcome of the Conference before sending a Governor, if we adopted that approach, the Conference would never come to a conclusion, and would be likely to collapse.

No. 205

Lord Carrington to Mr Papadopoulos (Maputo), 10 December 1979, 9.35 p.m.[1]

Tel. No. 173 Immediate, Confidential (FCO 36/2520)

MIPT Rhodesia[2]

Following is text of message (to be delivered if necessary in Baghdad).
Draft message from the Prime Minister to President Machel.
Dear President,

This morning, in the Rhodesia Conference, Peter Carrington made a final presentation of our detailed proposals for a ceasefire. As you know, we are proposing a ceasefire commission on which the military commanders of both sides will be represented and which will have the primary responsibility for supervising the ceasefire. The responsibility for ensuring the compliance of their forces with the ceasefire will rest with the commanders on both sides. We are proposing that the Patriotic Front forces should assemble at places in their operational areas, where their security, accommodation and other requirements can be provided for. They will assemble with their arms under the authority of their own commanders. The process of this

---

1 Deskby Maputo 11 December 07.30Z. It was also sent Immediate to Baghdad; and for Information Immediate to Washington, UKMIS New York.
2 Not printed.

engagement will be reciprocal. Provided that the assembly of Patriotic Front forces is complete and that there is a cessation of the movement of armed Patriotic Front personnel from neighbouring countries into Rhodesia, the process of disengagement will be complete, the forces will no longer be in contact, and the Rhodesian forces will not need to deploy from their company bases. We are also proposing a substantial monitoring force to assist with the observation and maintenance of the ceasefire. The force, which will include contingents from some other Commonwealth countries, is standing by and is ready to reach Rhodesia within the next few days.

We have already enacted the Independence Constitution on the basis of genuine majority rule: and there is agreement in the Conference that elections in which all parties can participate should be held under the authority of a British Governor with full executive and legislative powers.

The appointment as Governor of Rhodesia of Lord Soames, a very senior Cabinet Minister, demonstrates the importance which my Government attaches to the task of bringing the state of rebellion in Rhodesia to an end and enabling the country to be brought to legal independence. Lord Soames will be leaving London today to take up his appointment in Salisbury. When he arrives there tomorrow and his authority is accepted, the state of rebellion in Rhodesia will have been brought to an end. The Governor will set in hand immediately the arrangements for elections in which all parties can participate with an equal chance of success. He will also set in hand whatever action is necessary to normalise relations between Rhodesia, and Mozambique. Rhodesia will have returned to lawful Government as part of Her Majesty's dominions. A British authority in Salisbury is essential to the process of finalising the detailed arrangements for the ceasefire. It is indispensable that, for this purpose, we should have control over the Rhodesian armed forces, police etc. so that the logistic and other arrangements may be made for the ceasefire and for the security and accommodation and other agreed requirements of the Patriotic Front forces.

Britain has been urged for many years to assert its authority and carry out its responsibility to decolonise Rhodesia. This we are now doing. It is of course one of our essential objectives that all parties should participate in the settlement, provided they are prepared to put their political support to the test in free elections under our authority and commit themselves to campaign peacefully. I have no doubt that, with goodwill, final agreement on the details of the ceasefire can be reached in London in the next one or two days. We would wish to see the ceasefire come into effect immediately, thereby sparing the people of your country, as well as the people of Rhodesia any further suffering of the kind they have had to bear for the last fourteen years.

Your support has been of great importance in earlier phases of these negotiations. I hope that you will now exert your influence to persuade the Patriotic Front to accept the ceasefire proposals and to agree that they should be brought into effect immediately. We stand ready to assist with the process of bringing about the return of refugees to Rhodesia. We shall count on your cooperation in ensuring a cessation of cross-border military activity by the movement of Rhodesian forces into Mozambique or by the movement of Patriotic Front forces into Rhodesia. We are ready to establish military liaison arrangements for this purpose.

A settlement is now within our grasp. We are in a position to carry out our responsibilities and fully intend to do so. I hope that you will help to ensure that all parties participate in the elections.

With best wishes,

Margaret Thatcher

No. 206

Lord Carrington to Sir J. Thomson (New Delhi), 10 December 1979, 9.35 p.m.[1]

Tel. No. 833 Immediate, Confidential (FCO 36/2443)

Rhodesia:

1. Following a final presentation of our cease-fire proposals in the Conference on the morning of Tuesday 11 December, I shall be announcing in Parliament at 15:30 hrs GMT the Governor's departure for Salisbury. Lord Soames will arrive in Salisbury on 12 December. As soon as his authority has been accepted, Rhodesia will have returned to legality.

2. Please ensure that the message from the Prime Minister in MIFT[2] is delivered to President/Head of Government at 15.00 hrs GMT on 11 December. Nairobi should add the words 'as you know' before the penultimate sentence of the third paragraph, and the sentence 'I am most grateful for your help with this operation' at the end of this paragraph.

3. In delivering the message or in any discussion arising from it you should emphasise:

(*a*) The agreement at Lancaster House must be completed this week:

(*b*) In order to bring the final arrangements for a cease-fire into effect, it is indispensable to have a British Authority in Salisbury.

(*c*) My statement in the Conference is designed to meet the Patriotic Front's concerns about the security of their forces, the present disposition of the Rhodesian forces and the final disposition of the Rhodesian forces. On the latter point, if the Patriotic Front forces assemble with their arms and cease cross-border movement, the Rhodesian forces will not be deployed from their company bases.

4. In the light of these assurances, there can be no reason for the Patriotic Front not to complete the cease-fire agreement. It is our objective to bring the cease-fire into effect within the next few days. The monitoring force is standing by and can be deployed to Rhodesia within seven days: A settlement is within our grasp: but the chance of completing it depends on Front Line and Nigerian support.

5. For your own information we shall not be able to 'improve' on our final cease-fire proposals. In particular, any attempt to argue that, since the Patriotic Front are being required to assemble at fifteen places the Rhodesian forces should be limited to fifteen assembly places should be dealt with firmly.

---

1 Deskby to New Delhi on 11 November 0100Z; and to Immediate Dacca, Islamabad, Colombo, Singapore, Kuala Lumpur, Cairo, Khartoum, Rabat, Libreville, Kinshasa, Nairobi, Dakar, Accra, Georgetown, Freetown, Port Louis, Port of Spain, Lilongwe, Valletta, Banjul, Accra, Kingston, Lilongwe, Suva, Bridgetown; Information Immediate to Washington, UKMIS New York, Pretoria, Mirimba, Salisbury, Luanda, Ottawa, Wellington, Nassau, Nicosia, Dar es Salaam, Georgetown, Lusaka, Port Louis, Freetown, Port of Spain, Fort Moresby, Maseru, Mbabane.

2 Not printed.

No. 207

Minute from Mr Gomersall to Mr Renwick, 13 December 1979
Confidential (FCO 36/2443)

Rhodesia: Meeting with Mr Nkomo and Mr Mugabe

The Lord Privy Seal invited Mr Nkomo and Mr Mugabe to the office at 3.00pm today. Mr Chambati, Mr Mubaku, Mr Day and myself were present.

The *Lord Privy Seal* said that the Conference had progressed extraordinarily since September. There was now a great deal of agreement, but speed was necessary so that the Patriotic Front leaders could return to Salisbury to fight the election. *Mr Nkomo* agreed but regretted that the process had been rather rough. A number of issues were still not agreed. His lawyers had presented the British delegation with a note of points in the Constitution on which they were not satisfied. Some of these were serious. Despite what he understood to be an undertaking to remove references to the 'security forces' such references remained in the final Conference documents given to them.

Mr Mugabe said it was clear from our maps that our intention was to clear the Patriotic Front out of the centre of the country and place them on the periphery. If they agreed to that, others would move in to occupy their positions. What measures did we propose to contain or concentrate the auxiliaries who were also infiltrated among the people? They were happy with reciprocity so long as there was no imbalance. In further discussions of this question, the *Lord Privy Seal* clarified that the monitoring points indicated on our map were equivalent to a map of Rhodesian bases, though it did not say so. The assembly points had been selected in the light of our discussions with the Patriotic Front at official level, and of their expressed wish not to be encircled. *Mr Nkomo and Mr Mugabe* both denied that they had ever expressed such a wish. *The Lord Privy Seal* pointed out that although their forces would be assembled, their political wing would be free to move anywhere. *Mr Nkomo* said that they required both a practical and a psychological presence. Mr Nkomo argued that Rhodesian forces which had been displaced from the centre to the border areas would be able to move back inland as a result of the Patriotic Front assembly. However these points could be left to the officials who were meeting concurrently. *Mr Nkomo* complained that General Walls had not participated in these talks. There ensued some rehearsal about the old argument about bilaterals and the status of the Salisbury delegation. *Mr Mugabe* said that he thought that the Conference, far from alleviating suspicions between the delegations, had aggravated them. *The Lord Privy Seal* said he was sorry to hear this but thought Mr Mugabe had given as good as he got.

The Lord Privy Seal said that he hoped the Patriotic Front leaders understood that his honour and that of Lord Carrington were involved. There were deeply committed to making a settlement work and to proving that those who wished it to fail were wrong. He asked them to believe that the Government were totally committed to the success of this difficult task and had heavy obligations to both sides. *Mr Nkomo* said it was most useful to hear this. They too had come to the Conference committed to peace, and this explained their acceptance of the many things that the British delegation had imposed against their wishes. It was not their intention to break the ceasefire. It they did they would suffer the most. The *Lord Privy Seal* hoped that whatever the difficulties in the Conference it would be possible for the military commanders to meet and get to know each other soon on the Ceasefire Commission. This led to some discussion on the need for rules of procedure in the Commission. *Mr Nkomo* said that he and Mr Mugabe were of course the military commanders. *Mr Day* said it was up to the parties to nominate their own representatives on the Ceasefire Commission.

Finally, *Mr Nkomo* raised the question of security, not only of the political leaders but of the candidates in the elections. The *Lord Privy Seal* said that we made proposals in the Conference to cover the security of the leaders and he thought it was possible for the experts to agree arrangements for the rest. *Mr Nkomo* said that he would wish to give us his thoughts about this. The *Lord Privy Seal* said he hoped they would do so quickly. Lord Carrington was leaving with the Prime Minister for Washington on Sunday and it was important to get things tied up by then.

S.J. GOMERSALL

No. 208

Lord Carrington to Sir L. Allinson (Lusaka), 13 December 1979, 4.30 p.m.[1]
Tel. No. 1034 Immediate, Confidential (FCO 36/2443)

Rhodesia

1. In the Conference today Dr Mundawarara accepted the full cease-fire proposals on behalf of the Salisbury Delegation, subject to two provisions:

(*a*) He expressed concern that the Patriotic Front would not assemble all their forces inside the country. In that event the cease-fire would not be complete.

(*b*) Fully adequate arrangements must be made to prevent future cross-border movement by armed Patriotic Front personnel into Rhodesia.

2. The Lord Privy Seal thanked Dr Mundawarara for this statement and said that we agreed that for the cease-fire to be fully effective the assembly process must be complete and all cross-border movement must cease.

3. The statement was preceded by a procedural argument by Nkomo and Mugabe, who tried to prevent Dr Mundawarara making his statement on the grounds that the Salisbury Delegation no longer had any *locus standi*.[2] The Lord Privy Seal said that the Conference had begun with three delegations and would end with three delegations. The objective was to get the widest possible agreement. Bishop Muzorewa

1 And to Immediate Salisbury, Nairobi, Maputo, Gaborone, Dar es Salaam, Luanda, Lagos, Washington, Pretoria, Addis Ababa, Monrovia, Canberra, Ottawa, Wellington; Priority Peking, Moscow, Prague, Dakar, Kinshasa, Khartoum, Tokyo, EEC Posts, Kuwait, Kingston, Bridgetown, Dacca, New Delhi, Singapore, Georgetown, Freetown, Port Louis, Port of Spain, Lilongwe, Valletta, Banjul, Colombo, Accra, Kuala Lumpur, Nicosia, Oslo, Stockholm, Lisbon, Madrid, Athens, Mbabane, Abidjan; Information Immediate UKMIS New York; Information Saving Nassau, Maseru, Castries, Suva, Port Moresby, Honiara, Nukualofa, Victoria, Tarawa, UKDEL NATO, Sofia, Budapest, Bucharest, East Berlin, Belgrade, Cairo, Algiers, Tunis, Tripoli, Rabat, Tehran.
2 A legal term meaning the right of a party to appear and be heard before a court.

and his Delegation represented an important coalition of political parties, as did the Patriotic Front. In response to questions he said that General Walls was now under the authority of the Governor: so would General Tongogara be when the Patriotic Front accepted our cease-fire proposals. The Lord Privy Seal added that, as we understood it, the Patriotic Front had been fighting to achieve full majority rule, and against an illegal Government. The state of illegality had been ended: and majority rule had been achieved. The Patriotic Front were being offered the opportunity to participate in elections under our Authority. There could be no reason to go on fighting.

4. In separate discussions with the Patriotic Front military experts, they expressed satisfaction with the location of a number of Patriotic Front assembly places, but have been asking for more and different locations. The locations we have provided were designed to take account of the main Patriotic Front operational areas: the need for security for their forces: and the need also to achieve an effective dis-engagement from the Rhodesian forces. We shall not, therefore, be able to re-negotiate the location of the assembly places.

5. We have now circulated to both the other delegations in the Conference the text of the final documents. These include the Conference Report, the text of which will be telegraphed in the Verbatim Series: the Agreed Summary of the Constitution: The Agreed Pre-Independence Arrangements: the Cease-Fire Agreement (in accordance with the Agreed Cease-Fire Proposals): and the Schedule of Assembly Places for Patriotic Forces. It is stated in the Agreement that the disposition of the Rhodesian Forces will be as set out in my Statement of 11 December.

6. There is therefore no need for further substantive negotiation. The documents are now open for signature. The Salisbury Delegation have made clear that they are ready to sign them. We hope that the Patriotic Front can be brought to the point of decision in the next two days.

7. The New Zealand government lifted sanctions last night. The German and Swiss governments appear to be moving in that direction. We are hoping for an American announcement within the next two or three days.

No. 209

Brief by Rhodesia Department for Mrs Thatcher's visit to Washington (17-18 December), 13 December 1979
Confidential (FCO 36/2507)

Points to Make

1. We are concerned that the United States should take immediate action to lift sanctions against Rhodesia. The rebellion has been brought to an end. The Salisbury Parliament voted unanimously for a return to legality. The Governor's authority has been accepted.

2. It would cause serious difficulty if, in these circumstances, US sanctions were maintained against Rhodesia and a British Governor. Unless the United States have appeared to take action to lift sanctions quickly, there will be no further pressure applied to the Patriotic Front to accept our ceasefire proposals. In those circumstances,

American action may be self-defeating as it could actually encourage the Patriotic Front to stay out of an agreement. The leakage of Ambassador McHenry's recommendation against the lifting of sanctions has been very unfortunate.

3. There is a chance of bringing the Patriotic Front to accept; but not if they think they can hold out for better terms. We have been grateful for American support in earlier phases of the negotiations, including the messages from President Carter to the frontline Presidents; but this is the decisive phase. Delay will be prejudiced to the chances of securing a comprehensive agreement.

4. If the Patriotic Front participate in the settlement, the problem of maintaining the cease-fire will be formidable. There is a real danger that they will not assemble their forces and will not stop cross-border activity. Despite the risk, we are prepared to do our utmost to discharge our responsibility to bring Rhodesia to legal independence and to hold elections in which all parties which are prepared to do so peacefully can participate.

Background

5. The US government have given diplomatic support to our efforts to achieve a settlement. The President has addressed messages to the front line Presidents at various stages of the negotiations. The Americans are making transport aircraft available (subject to repayment by us) to airlift the remote monitoring force in Rhodesia. They have also made a statement in support of our ceasefire proposals, and indicating that no party can have a veto over a settlement.

6. Despite strong requests by us, the Americans have not yet begun any action to lift sanctions. We have pointed out that such action could have a decisive effect in pushing the Patriotic Front towards an agreement. The President is subject to conflict in domestic pressures. There is a majority in Congress for the lifting of sanctions. Mr Vance has strongly impressed on President Carter, the need to do so, and thereby to support our efforts to push the Patriotic Front into an agreement. But the President is concerned to retain the support of the black caucus in Congress; and therefore seems to be waiting for the Patriotic Front.

7. On the President's behalf, Mr Vance wrote to Senator Helms on 3 December that 'when the British Governor arrives in Salisbury to implement an agreed Lancaster House settlement and the electoral process begins the President will take action to lift sanctions. This will be done no later than one month after the Governor's arrival. If an agreed settlement is not reached at the conference, we will consult with the respective committee of the Senate and the house regarding the course of action which best serves the national interests.' The Secretary of State expressed his concern to Mr Vance about his formulation, which goes back to an earlier Presidential statement that sanctions would be lifted with the return to legality, and the beginning of a process leading to fair elections. The Prime Minister also spoke to Mr Vance.

8. In an attempt to help the Americans to argue that the electoral process has already begun, Lord Soames made a statement to that effect on his arrival in Salisbury. He promulgated on 12 December, ordinances establishing the authority of the Electoral Commissioner and making provision for the Election Council. He added: 'all parties which commit themselves to campaign peacefully will be able to do so freely. All parties which wish to participate in the elections should register

by 31 December. The British government is taking today the legislative action necessary to bring into force those parts of the independence constitution required for elections to be held.'

9. The State Department have issued a statement calling on the Patriotic Front to accept our cease-fire proposals; and that no party can exercise a veto. *The effect of this has been negated by the leakage of a memorandum from the US ambassador to the United Nations, Mr McHenry, recommending that the United States should not lift sanctions without positive action by the Security Council. This could cause the Patriotic Front to procrastinate; will cause additional difficulties for us in the Security Council; and will also cause some of the other allies to hesitate before lifting sanctions.*

10. The process of waiting for the Patriotic Front could cause considerable complications for the President in Congress. More seriously, it is unhelpful to the chances of pushing the Patriotic Front into an agreement. It is also liable to cause some of our other allies to delay taken action to lift sanctions.

No. 210

Record of a meeting between Lord Carrington and leaders of the Patriotic Front, 14 December 1979
Confidential (PREM 19/116)

Those Present:

Lord Carrington	Mr Joshua Nkomo
Sir Ian Gilmour	Mr Robert Mugabe
Mr G.G.H. Walden	Mr Chambati
Mr R.W. Renwick	

1. *Lord Carrington* said that since we were at the end of the Conference, it was time to look at what we had achieved. We now had genuine majority rule. The Patriotic Front had made concessions, e.g. over the 20 white seats; but the whites had too. During the transitional period, it would be a British Governor, and not the Bishop who would rule the country, in an attempt to get really fair elections. He had known Lord Soames all his life. He was a fair-minded man, with great personality and presence. He hoped that the position on the ceasefire, which he had outlined three days ago, was satisfactory. It had been a serious attempt to allay the PF's fears about reciprocal withdrawal. He recognised that the outcome was not ideal for the PF, for Salisbury, or for us. Nobody should forget that we too had our problems. We were responsible for making the agreement work. But it could not work if the PF and Salisbury did not help us.

2. He knew that there were also fears about personal security, and they understood these. It was our job to ensure personal security. And he would personally make this clear to the Governor. The PF leaders could also bring some of the people protecting them in London to Rhodesia if they wished. On the assembly areas, he

wished to make it clear that, if the PF forces assembled with their arms in numbers which posed difficulty in relation to the number and capacity of the assembly places allocated to PF forces, the Governor would have to make the necessary dispositions. We were now at the point of final agreement and we must all decide whether or not to accept. We should not allow the killing to go on. He had noted incidentally that the Salisbury people were still talking of 'terrorists'. Now that the Governor was there he would ensure that this stopped. With the Governor's presence, an irreversible process has begun. We were worried by the prospect of further delay. The PF must make a decision one way or the other. He was therefore calling a meeting at Lancaster House tomorrow morning. They had all had 14 difficult weeks of negotiation. But we had come along way. He had not expected to get so far when the negotiations had begun. There was only one final small jump to be taken. But there was a risk that, if it were not taken, everything could be lost. More people would then be killed.

3. The UK had shown great courage. The cowardly way out would have been to say on 3 May that there had already been elections, the five principles had been satisfied, and that Rhodesia could be given independence, even though the war might have continued and the South Africans might have been drawn in. The position he had taken up had not been very popular in his own party. We had shown our courage in accepting responsibility for what happened in the interim period. If it went badly, everyone would turn against us even our own friends.

4. *Mr Nkomo* asked whether we had already drawn up the list of election results? That seemed to be our manner of proceeding. *Mr Mugabe* said he hoped that Lord Carrington was aware of the PFs objections to our proposals on the disposition of the forces, and of the PFs own suggestions. Our positioning of the forces would not work, and was not acceptable. It would put the PF in an invidious position, in which the military balance would be tipped against them. The PF would have to defend itself in the last analysis, if the rebels attacked them again. Monitors would be no help; nor would the British, who were powerless. Why were the PF being moved from their operational areas to remote areas on the periphery of the country? They were being pushed away from the urban and industrial heartland of the country, leaving the field open to Rhodesian forces and Muzorewa's auxiliaries, who were already deployed amongst the people.

5. Mr Mugabe asked why we did not move Salisbury away from their operational areas. We had clearly agreed with Salisbury to concentrate the PF forces in 15 places. This was a non-starter. We clearly wanted to give maximum advantage to Muzorewa, and maximum disadvantage to the PF. *Lord Carrington* said that a ceasefire was to everyone's advantage. *Mr Nkomo* said that the PF completely accepted the principle of a ceasefire, and the idea of assembly. If the PF could not initial [the] agreement tomorrow, they would explain the reasons to the world. They simply would not be placed where we and the Rhodesians wanted to put them. They had been told that they themselves had asked to be on the periphery of the country. He wanted to make it clear that this was not so.

6. *Mr Renwick* explained that our military reconnaissance teams had been concerned to achieve an effective separation of the forces. In choosing the places in question, they had taken account of the PF's operational areas and their concern not to be encircled. We were talking about an election campaign, and not a military one.

The whole point was to enable the PF leaders to go to Salisbury and fight elections. *Mr Nkomo* said that the PF forces were being sent to forest areas and game reserves. *Lord Carrington* stressed that the PF's military commanders would be in Salisbury. *Mr Mugabe* said that the places we proposed suggested a surrender by the PF. Mr Mugabe asked why we did not say openly that we wanted the PF suppressed. *Lord Carrington* said that it would be misleading if he were to suggest that we could alter our proposals. *Mr Mugabe* said that this was because we had to fix things with Salisbury.

7. *Mr Renwick* said that both sides had difficulties. The Rhodesians were not keen on the PF being installed in Salisbury. Mr Mugabe said that we should monitor the PF in their bases, as with the Rhodesians. *Lord Carrington* said that the negotiations were over. There was nothing more to be said. We were at the end of the road. *Mr Mugabe* said that the PF were not at the end of their road. *Lord Carrington* said that the PF could do what they wished, but they must decide whether or not to initial the agreement tomorrow. There was no point in delay, and nothing more to be said.

8. *Mr Mugabe* said that he would never put his fighters in danger. Our Governor would be in charge of the Salisbury forces, and there would be war. *Lord Carrington* insisted that our proposals were fair. *Mr Renwick* said that the PF were not being asked to retreat, but to concentrate. In return they would get political advancement. *Mr Nkomo* said that he did not wish to be lectured about politics. *The Lord Privy Seal* stressed that the PF would be involved in a political campaign. *Lord Carrington* said he did not understand the PF's position, which seemed to assume that the hostilities would erupt before or after the elections.

9. *Mr Nkomo* appealed to Lord Carrington not to call a meeting tomorrow. *Lord Carrington* said that if the PF did not come, that would amount to a rejection of the agreement. They should note that our proposals were considered fair, in New York and elsewhere. The PF should think deeply before rejecting them. *The Lord Privy Seal* said that rejection would be a tragedy. *Mr Mugabe* said that Lord Carrington had proceeded unfairly throughout the conference, and particularly by sending a Governor to Salisbury before agreement was reached. *Lord Carrington* said he was deeply disappointed with the PF's reply, which could lead to tragic consequences.

No. 211

Letter from Mrs Thatcher to President Carter, 14 December 1979
Confidential (FCO 36/2507)

Dear Mr President,

I am sorry to have to raise Rhodesia with you when the very worrying situation in Iran is taking up so much of your time. I look forward to discussing both subjects with you on Monday. But there is one very important point on Rhodesia on which I hope we can make progress before then.

We have now to bring the Lancaster House Conference to a conclusion. The Patriotic Front are still trying to spin out the talking and avoid coming to a decision (and meanwhile are infiltrating more of their forces into Rhodesia). But we have completed the negotiations. We cannot hold up the implementation of a settlement much longer.

Our experiences at Lancaster House have shown that the Patriotic Front will not make up their minds unless and until they are brought up clearly against the need to do so.

Peter Carrington has therefore called a final session of the Conference for tomorrow. There is a fair chance that the Patriotic Front will initial the agreement then if it is made absolutely clear to them that they will get no support for staying out.

We have done everything we can to create the conditions for the Patriotic Front to participate in elections under the Governor's authority. We have presented detailed ceasefire proposals that Cy Vance was good enough to describe to Peter Carrington in Brussels as eminently fair. I am very concerned about the dangers of further delay in reaching agreement. This could result in a breakdown of the settlement as a whole.

The support of the United States, and the action you have taken with the parties and African governments have been a major factor in helping us to get this far. I hope that now you can help us to bring home to the Patriotic Front the need to agree to a ceasefire and participate in the elections. This might be done by a statement that the United States will not continue sanctions against Rhodesia under a British Governor. That would be the most effective approach, but in any case it would be very helpful if Kingman Brewster could speak in this sense directly to the Patriotic Front today. Action on these lines could help us to clinch the final agreement. I fear that if it is delayed, your decision would not have the same effect on the negotiations.

I hate troubling you at a time when you have such appalling troubles of your own. But I believe that action by you on the lines I have suggested would greatly increase the chances of a successful outcome. If you would like to discuss this I am available here all this evening.

With warm regards,
MARGARET THATCHER

No. 212

Lord Carrington to Sir L. Allinson (Lusaka), 15 December 1979, 3.35 p.m.[1]
Tel. No.1039 Immediate, Confidential (FCO 36/2443)

Rhodesia

1. A final Plenary Session of the Conference was held this morning. I made the statement in MIFT.[2] Mr Nkomo said that the Patriotic Front could accept the other aspects of the agreement but were still concerned about the number and location of the assembly places for their forces. Mr Mugabe, in a very different tune, said

---

[1] And to Immediate Salisbury, Cairo (Deskby151700Z), Nairobi, Maputo, Gaborone, Dar es Salaam, Luanda, Lagos, Washington, Pretoria, Addis Ababa, Monrovia, Canberra, Ottawa, Wellington; Priority Peking, Moscow, Prague, Dakar, Kinshasa, Khartoum, Tokyo, EEC Posts, Kuwait, Kingston, Bridgetown, Dacca, New Delhi, Singapore, Georgetown, Freetown, Port Louis, Port of Spain, Lilongwe, Valletta, Banjul, Colombo, Accra, Kuala Lumpur, Nicosia, Oslo, Stockholm, Lisbon, Madrid, Athens, Mbabane, Abidjan; Information Immediate UKMIS New York; Information Saving Nassau, Maseru, Castries, Suva, Port Moresby, Honiara, Nukualofa, Victoria, Tarawa, UKDEL NATO, Sofia, Budapest, Bucharest, East Berlin, Belgrade, Algiers, Tunis, Tripoli, Rabat, Tehran.

[2] No. 213.

that the Patriotic Front had not in fact agreed to the Independence Constitution, the pre-independence arrangements or the ceasefire proposals, unless military matters were decided to their satisfaction. He made various accusations against the British Delegation which I rejected.

2. The present position is, therefore, that Nkomo is still interested in a settlement, despite Mozambican pressures on him to settle, Mugabe, as is consistent with his behaviour throughout the Conference, is looking for a break. Underlying these problems is the fact that both the ZANLA and ZIPRA military commanders doubt their capacity to set their forces to assemble. The Rhodesians are extremely sceptical as to whether the Patriotic Front will assemble their forces with their arms in anything like the numbers involved, and whether they will stop cross-border movements. The Assembly places we have designated for the Patriotic Front Forces are in the heart of their operational areas. The Rhodesian Forces are heavily concentrated in the area between Salisbury/Gwelo/Bulawayo in which the Patriotic Front wish to install their forces. The Patriotic Front have never been able to achieve such a result by military means and Bishop Muzorewa's Government agreed to stand aside on the clear understanding that we would not agree to the siting of Patriotic Front military camps for political purposes.

3. In private discussions this morning I emphasised strongly to Nkomo and Mugabe that what we were talking about was an election campaign not a military campaign. The essential requirement therefore was to achieve an effective separation of the forces on both sides and this was fully provided for in our proposals. It was ridiculous to argue that Patriotic Front Forces were being asked to retreat when the Rhodesian Forces were also being required to concentrate, the Patriotic Front political and military leaders would be in Salisbury and the Patriotic Front would be campaigning throughout the country.

4. The political and psychological difficulty for the Salisbury Delegation of accepting this (as well as for Muzorewa in standing aside) was at least as great as any difficulties the Patriotic Front might face. In short, I did not see how it could be possible to justify the refusal to accept a cease-fire on these grounds. Mugabe made it clear that his objection to concentrating his forces was that they might have to start fighting again and would not be well placed to do so.

5. Nkomo said that he was anxious to have his forces in the 'political nerve centre' of the country. I said that he would have a complete political presence in that area. We could not site his forces in such a way as to enhance his political ambitions.

6. After the session, Dr Mundawarara initialled the Conference Report (text in VS) on behalf of Bishop Muzorewa and his Delegation and I did the same.

No. 213

Lord Carrington to Sir L. Allinson (Lusaka), 15 December 1979, 3.35 p.m.[1]
Tel. No.1040 Immediate, Unclassified (FCO 36/2443)

MIPT: Rhodesia[2]

1. I would like to open this session by reminding delegations of the achievements of this Conference. Agreement has been reached on an Independence Constitution providing for genuine majority rule and thereby removing the fundamental cause of the War. Bishop Muzorewa and his colleagues agreed to hand over authority to a British Governor who is now in Salisbury. The Governor's task is to organise elections in which all parties can participate freely. Agreement has also been reached on our cease-fire proposals. We have now set out their detailed implementation.

2. In order to meet various concerns expressed by the Patriotic Front and to explain our basic proposals, I made a statement on 23 November which was designed to help the Patriotic Front to agree to the cease-fire proposals: and I am very glad that this helped them to do so. In order to meet further concerns expressed by the Patriotic Front and to explain fully our detailed proposals I made a full statement on 11 December and circulated maps to the other delegates to the Conference. My statement of 11 December is incorporated in the final Conference documents.

3. The Patriotic Front have expressed concern about the number of assembly places allocated to them in relation to the size of their forces. Equally strongly felt anxieties have been expressed by the Salisbury Delegation as to whether there will be an effective assembly and a cessation of cross-border movement. I can assure the Patriotic Front, however, that if the Patriotic Front forces at present inside Rhodesia assemble with their arms and equipment in numbers [that] are greater than can be dealt with at the assembly places designated in the cease-fire agreement the Governor, will assess the need for additional sites in relation to the successful accomplishment of the assembly process by the Patriotic Front forces and in relation to the dispositions of their forces.

4. The Conference has now been in session for fourteen weeks. All the issues have been exhaustively discussed. With agreement on the Independence Constitution, a return to legality and free elections in which all the parties can participate there can be no reason for anyone to continue the war. The whole purpose of our proposals is to offer everyone an alternative to continuing the war. Of course we cannot oblige any party to accept that alternative: but we do not believe that others will readily understand a decision by any party to continue the war against a lawful authority established to enable elections to be held in which all parties can participate. It will

---

1 And to Immediate Mirimba, Salisbury, Nairobi, Maputo, Gaborone, Dar es Salaam, Luanda, Lagos, Washington, Pretoria, Addis Ababa, Monrovia, Canberra, Ottawa, Wellington; Priority Peking, Moscow, Prague, Dakar, Kinshasa, Khartoum, Tokyo, EEC Posts, Kuwait, Kingston, Bridgetown, Dacca, New Delhi, Singapore, Georgetown, Freetown, Port Louis, Port of Spain, Lilongwe, Valletta, Banjul, Colombo, Accra, Kuala Lumpur, Nicosia, Oslo, Stockholm, Lisbon, Madrid, Athens, Mbabane, Abidjan; Information Immediate UKMIS New York; Information Saving Nassau, Maseru, Castries, Suva, Port Moresby, Honiara, Nukualofa, Victoria, Tarawa, UKDEL NATO, Sofia, Budapest, Bucharest, East Berlin, Belgrade, Cairo (Deskby151700Z), Algiers, Tunis, Tripoli, Rabat, Tehran.
2 No. 212.

be a matter of very grave disappointment to us all if it is not possible to reach overall agreement at this Conference after all that we have achieved.

5. I hope that both delegations will be able to agree to the documents we circulated to the Conference on 13 December and to agree to initial them. Signature could then follow very quickly indeed. A cease-fire will then come into effect bringing peace to the people of Rhodesia and the neighbouring countries.

6. I cannot emphasise too strongly that it is my profound conviction that to deny the people of Rhodesia this opportunity to resolve their problems by peaceful means would be unforgivable. Immense benefits would flow from the signature of these agreements for them and for the people of the other countries who have suffered so much from the war. In other words a peaceful settlement is now within your grasp.

7. I cannot oblige anyone to take the decisions necessary to enable such a settlement to be put into effect. But I hope that everyone will reflect very seriously on the consequences and the responsibility for a failure to agree to a cease-fire, the essential purpose of which is to enable all the parties to campaign freely throughout the country in elections held under our authority.

No. 214

FCO to Lord Soames (Salisbury), 17 December 1979, 3.45 p.m.[1]
Tel. No 527 Flash, Confidential (FCO 36/2443)

Rhodesia

1. Both Nkomo and Mugabe now seem to have taken the decision in principle to accept the agreement. We do not know whether they are yet ready to take the final plunge but we shall be trying to get them to initial the Conference documents, with the addition of the Secretary of State's statement of 15 December and an assurance about one additional assembly place, later today.

2. It is clear that Mugabe has been under very strong pressure to accept from:
(*a*) Tongogara, who has been pressing for a settlement throughout
(*b*) Machel, who is fed up with the war.

---

1 Lord Carrington was in the US, accompanying Mrs Thatcher on her official visit. And for Information Flash to Washington (for Private Secretary to Secretary of State), UKMIS New York; Information Immediate to Lusaka, Lagos, Maputo, Gaborone, Pretoria, Dar es Salaam.

No. 215

FCO to Sir L. Allinson (Lusaka), 17 December 1979, 10.32 p.m.[1]
Tel. No. 1051 Immediate, Confidential (FCO 36/2443)

Rhodesia Constitutional Conference

1. The Patriotic Front agreed the final details on implementation of the cease-fire today (17 December), when Mr Nkomo and Mr Mugabe initialled the Conference Report and the Cease-Fire Agreement at a short ceremony at [the] FCO. Final signature is expected on 19 December.

2. This means that Phase One of the Cease-Fire will begin at midnight on 19 or 20 December. All movement by armed Patriotic Front forces in Rhodesia will cease at that time. Seven days later, Phase Two of the Cease-Fire will begin: all hostilities in Rhodesia will cease, contact between the forces will be avoided and the Cease-Fire Commission will be established. Assembly of the Patriotic Front forces should be complete seven days thereafter. Deployment of the Monitoring Force is beginning immediately.

3. With the agreement of the Salisbury Delegation we offered the Patriotic Front one further assembly place, at a position to be decided in the West Central area. This makes a total of sixteen assembly places instead of fifteen.

4. In my statement in the Conference on 15 December[2] I said that 'if the Patriotic Front forces at present inside of Rhodesia assembled with their arms and equipment in numbers greater than can be dealt with at the assembly places designated in the cease-fire agreement, the Governor will assess the need for additional sites in relation to the successful accomplishment of the assembly process by the Patriotic Front Forces'. There have already been attempts by the Patriotic Front to suggest that this means additional sites will be provided. If asked about this you should point out that the capacity provided for in the existing assembly places is 20,000 plus: and that it is an essential requirement of the cease-fire agreement that the Patriotic Front should move from the rendez-vous points to the assembly places and that the assembly process should be continuous. We are not therefore 'offering' additional sites to the Patriotic Front. Additional sites would only be considered if all the existing capacity was over-extended.

5. Nkomo has over the last few days been strongly in favour of a settlement on the lines now agreed. Mugabe has only been brought into the settlement by very strong pressure from President Machel and his commitment to it remains very doubtful. There will be serious problems ahead in making the cease-fire work and it remains to be seen how effective the Patriotic Front Commanders will be in assembling their

---

[1] Deskby to Lusaka on 18 December 0630Z; and to Immediate Salisbury, Nairobi, Maputo, Gaborone, Dar es Salaam, Luanda, Lagos, Washington, Pretoria, Addis Ababa, Monrovia, Canberra, Ottawa, Wellington, Khartoum; Priority Peking, Moscow, Prague, Dakar, Kinshasa, Tokyo, EEC Posts, Kuwait, Kingston, Bridgetown, Dacca, New Delhi, Singapore, Georgetown, Freetown, Port Louis, Port of Spain, Lilongwe, Valletta, Banjul, Colombo, Accra, Kuala Lumpur, Nicosia, Oslo, Stockholm, Lisbon, Madrid, Athens, Mbabane, Abidjan; Information Immediate UKMIS New York; Information Saving Nassau, Maseru, Castries, Suva, Port Moresby, Honiara, Nukualofa, Victoria, Tarawa, UKDEL NATO, Sofia, Budapest, Bucharest, East Berlin, Belgrade, Cairo, Algiers, Tunis, Tripoli, Rabat, Tehran.

[2] No. 213.

forces in accordance with the agreement: and whether cross-border movement by the Patriotic Front forces will cease. It is, however, encouraging that Tongogara has worked for a settlement throughout the negotiations.

No. 216

Record of a meeting between Mrs Thatcher and Dr Waldheim at the UN Secretariat Building, 18 December 1979, 11.45 a.m.[1]

Confidential (FCO 36/2551)

Present:

Prime Minister	Dr Kurt Waldheim
Secretary of State for Foreign and Commonwealth Affairs	Mr Brian Urquhart[2]
	Mr Rafi Ahmed[3]
Sir Michael Palliser	
Sir Anthony Parsons	
Mr. G.G.H. Walden	
Mr. M.A. Pattison	

Rhodesia

Dr Waldheim offered warm congratulations on the success of the Lancaster House Conference on Rhodesia. The United Nations had been delighted by the news, and he had cabled a message of congratulations to the Foreign and Commonwealth Secretary.

Lord Carrington said that there was still an outstanding difficulty. Bishop Muzorewa has now asked for clarification of news media reports of British concessions to the Patriotic Front. He believed this would prove to be last minute nerves. *Dr Waldheim* said that the United Nations had received the news of a ceasefire agreement with great enthusiasm. Rhodesia had been a difficult subject for the General Assembly, but the announcement at the President of the General Assembly's lunch of the initialing had been greeted by applause from even the most radical of representatives. The *Prime Minister* commented that this wholehearted support from all sides had been characteristic since the negotiation process had been set in hand at Lusaka. Everybody wanted success. The right moment had come. This did not mean that the problems were over. Battles were never finally won.

Dr Waldheim said that he hoped the achievement over Rhodesia would have an impact on the Namibian negotiations. The *Prime Minister* foresaw an impact on the whole of South Africa, and especially on the Front Line States. *Dr Waldheim* said that the Front Line States seemed to have been helpful. The *Prime Minister* said that they no longer wish to play host to the problems of Rhodesia. The success of

---

1 Sent by Mr Pattison (No. 10) to Mr Walden, 19 December 1979.
2 UN Under-Secretary for Political Affairs.
3 Chef de Cabinet, Executive Office of the UN Secretary-General.

The Lancaster House Conference and the Independence of Zimbabwe, 1979

the Conference was a blow for democracy in the heart of Africa, where democracy was not always in the ascendant. *Dr Waldheim* recalled a discussion with President Nyerere in Monrovia in the summer, where the President had assured him that he would press the Patriotic Front if the British were ready to set in hand the negotiating process. The *Prime Minister* commented that all the Commonwealth leaders have been very helpful at Lusaka. They had even been prepared to respond to her opening statement by re-drafting their own prepared speeches to pick up her theme. Work had then gone into a small group, once again proving that plenaries were always too big for worthwhile negotiations. Since then, a great deal of time had been spent on the negotiations. Ultimately, the strategy had proved effective. It was a tribute to the genius of the Foreign and Commonwealth Secretary and his staff. She recalled the decision to insist on negotiating an agreement on a constitution before allowing discussion of transitional arrangements. *Lord Carrington* commented that the agreement was still fragile, as that day's pronouncement from Bishop Muzorewa had demonstrated. All parties had been very nervous in the final days of discussion. The *Prime Minister* added that all the parties had concerns about their own security.

Dr Waldheim asked how the issue of bases had been solved at the final stage. *Lord Carrington* said that the Patriotic Front were all gathered on the Mozambique and Zambian borders. He had said that they should be assembled in those areas. The Patriotic Front claimed also to have significant concentrations of men in the centre of Rhodesia. The British Government were aware only of a few there, but had finally offered one additional base, in that area, with an understanding that the Governor would re-assess the situation if it proved that there were greater numbers of Patriotic Front forces in the central area. The Patriotic Front had declared 35,000 men, much more than the British Government's own information suggested. The United Kingdom estimated the Patriotic Front forces as in the region of 16,000 compared it with Bishop Muzorewa's Government forces of about 45,000. *Dr Waldheim* said that for presentational reasons the Patriotic Front may have wanted to claim a figure in that region.

No. 217

Extract from the conclusions of a meeting of the Cabinet, 20 December 1979[1]
CC(79) 26th Conclusions Secret (CAB 128/66)

2. The Foreign and Commonwealth Secretary said that, after last minute problems caused by Mr Mugabe's public attitude to the cease-fire arrangements and by the adverse reaction of Bishop Muzorewa, it was now agreed that the final documents of the Conference would be signed by all concerned (including the Lord Privy Seal as well as himself) at Lancaster House on 21 December. The main scene of action would now shift from London to Salisbury. Many problems still ahead, particularly as regards the operation of the cease-fire; although Mr Mugabe's military commander, Mr Tongogara, seemed disposed to make it work, Mr Mugabe's own attitude was less clear. But it was satisfactory that Britain had at last been able to lift all sanctions against Rhodesia without provoking the counter-action against British interests or the break-up of the Commonwealth.

The Cabinet—

1. Took note and congratulated the Foreign and Commonwealth Secretary and the Lord Privy Seal on the outstanding achievement in the face of so many difficulties.

---

1 The following were present: The Rt Hon Margaret Thatcher MP, Prime Minister; The Rt Hon William Whitelaw MP, Secretary of State for the Home Department; The Rt Hon Lord Hailsham, Lord Chancellor; The Rt Hon Lord Carrington, Secretary of State for Foreign and Commonwealth Affairs; The Rt Hon Sir Geoffrey Howe QC MP, Chancellor of the Exchequer; The Rt Hon Sir Keith Joseph MP, Secretary of State for Industry; The Rt Hon Francis Pym MP, Secretary of State for Defence; The Rt Hon James Prior MP, Secretary of State for Employment; The Rt Hon Sir Ian Gilmour MP, Lord Privy Seal; The Rt Hon Peter Walker MP, Minister of Agriculture, Fisheries and Food; The Rt Hon Michael Heseltine MP, Secretary of State for the Environment; The Rt Hon George Younger, MP, Secretary of State for Scotland; The Rt Hon Nicholas Edwards MP, Secretary of State for Wales; The Rt Hon Humphrey Atkins, Secretary of State for Northern Ireland; The Rt Hon Patrick Jenkin MP, Secretary of State for Social Services; The Rt Hon Sir Norman St John-Stevas MP, Chancellor of the Duchy of Lancaster; The Rt Hon John Nott MP, Secretary of State for Trade; The Rt Hon David Howell MP, Secretary of State for Energy; The Rt Hon Mark Carlisle QC MP, Secretary of State for Education and Science; The Rt Hon John Biffen MP, Chief Secretary, Treasury; The Rt Hon Angus Maude MP, Paymaster General. The following were also present: The Rt Hon Norman Fowler MP, Minister of Transport; The Rt Hon Michael Jopling MP, Parliamentary Secretary, Treasury; Mr Paul Channon, Minister of State, Civil Service Department (Items 4-6); Earl Ferrers, Minister of State, Ministry of Agriculture, Fisheries and Food (Item 1). Secretariat: Mr R.L. Wade-Gery (Items 2 and 3), Mr D.M. Elliott (Items 2 and 3) and five others.

The Lancaster House Conference and the Independence of Zimbabwe, 1979

No. 218

Lord Carrington to Lord Soames (Salisbury), 21 December 1979, 2.52 p.m.[1]
Tel. No. 594 Flash, Unclassified (FCO 36/2443)

1. The final Conference documents were signed at noon today at Lancaster House.

2. The Conference Report was signed by myself, the Lord Privy Seal, Bishop Muzorewa, Dr Mundawarara, Mr Nkomo and Mr Mugabe. The Cease-Fire Agreement was signed by the same members of the visiting delegations only.

3. The text of my concluding statement is being repeated to you in the Verbatim Series.

[1] And to Flash Canberra; Immediate Nairobi, Maputo, Gaborone, Lusaka, Wellington Dar es Salaam, Lagos, Washington, Pretoria (all Deskby 211630z), Luanda, Addis Ababa, Monrovia, Ottawa, UKMIS New York, Suva; Priority Peking, Moscow, Prague, Dakar, Kinshasa, Khartoum, Tokyo, EEC Posts, Kuwait, Kingston, Bridgetown, Dacca, New Delhi, Singapore, Georgetown, Freetown, Port Louis, Port of Spain, Lilongwe, Valletta, Banjul, Colombo, Accra, Kuala Lumpur, Nicosia, Oslo, Stockholm, Lisbon, Madrid, Athens, Mbabane, Abidjan; Information Immediate UKMIS New York; Information Saving Nassau, Maseru, Castries, Port Moresby, Honiara, Nukualofa, Victoria, Tarawa, UKDEL NATO, Sofia, Budapest, Bucharest, East Berlin, Belgrade, Cairo, Algiers, Tunis, Tripoli, Rabat, Tehran.

No. 219

Personal minute from Mrs Thatcher to Lord Carrington, 21 December 1979
No. M19/79T (FCO 36/2443)

The Rhodesia Conference

Today sees the successful conclusion of an extraordinary piece of diplomacy. The period ahead in Rhodesia is not going to be easy but the signature of the Agreement at the end of the Lancaster House Conference later this morning will nonetheless be a milestone of major significance.

The effort to secure an agreement between the various parties to the conflict in Rhodesia began not long after the present Government took office and has continued almost without pause ever since. It has been an exercise not only in negotiation, at Lusaka and Lancaster House, but also in international persuasion and has involved Embassies and High Commissions all over the world. It must have tested the resources of the Diplomatic Service to the full. Clearly the Service has been equal to the task.

You are well aware of my admiration for the way you and the Lord Privy Seal have conducted the negotiation as a whole and the Conference at Lancaster House in particular. But I should be grateful if you could arrange for my gratitude to be conveyed to everyone else who has played a part in the enterprise. They all have reason to be proud of what has been achieved.

MARGARET THATCHER

INDEX

Acland, John 312
Alexander, Michael 120, 147-50, 154, 282-83
Allinson, Sir Leonard xx, 13-14, 32-3, 106, 294
Angola 2, 31, 34, 43
Australia 32, 42, 245-46, 287, 324

Banda, Hastings Kamuzu 38, 43, 47
Barlow, P. J. 1
Botha, Pik xii, 285, 288-91, 324, 330; meeting with Thatcher 213-15; views on conference 106-8
Botha, P. W. 77-78, 201-2, 309-12, 330; views on conference 106-8
Botswana 2, 18, 31, 43, 286
Brewster, Kingsman 97, 98, 209-10, 273
Brown, Mervyn 115-18, 261-62
Byrd amendment 12

Cabinet, papers for 85-92; minutes of 92-4, 251-52
Cabinet Defence and Oversea Policy Committee (OD), minutes of 20-1, 75-6, 256, 258, 320-21, 326; papers for 14-18, 51-5, 68-74, 252-56
Callaghan, James ix, 259-61
Canada 10, 324
Carrington, Lord xv, xvi-xvii, xx, 30, 33-4, 155-56, 243-44, 291, 299, 320-23, 326, 331, 338; meeting with P. F. Botha, 309-12; meetings with Kaunda 267-68, 271-74, 281; meeting with Nkomo 247-48; meetings with Patriotic Front 157-58, 165, 179-81, 193-94, 206-08, 216-17, 220-21, 238-39, 241, 286-87, 293-94, 306-07, 313-14, 318-20; meetings with Muzowera/Salisbury delegation 60-5, 151-52, 159-61, 163, 220-21, 241, 284, 293-94, 321-22; meetings with Thatcher 36-7, 47-9, 147-50, 213-15, 251-52, 302-05, 323-24; messages to/meetings with Vance 22, 25-8, 204-05, 242-43; opening statement to conference 133-39; papers/minutes to Thatcher 112-15, 167-73, 200-02, 211-13, 252-56; views on conference xiii-xiv, 101, 130-31, 164
Carter, 'Jimmy' ix, 12-13, 22, 28, 43, 49, 98-9, 144
Cartledge, Bryan 36-7, 101
Carver, Field Marshal Lord Michael x, 104
Case-Javits amendment (see also US sanctions) 11, 22, 27-8

China 37
Chona, Mark 131-32, 143-44, 197
Commonwealth 17, 22, 42
Commonwealth Heads of Government Meeting (CHOGM), Lukasa (1979) xii, 10, 15, 20, 30, 33, 34, 37, 47, 73-4, 87-9
Commonwealth Monitoring Force 37, 204-5, 253, 274, 287, 316, 324;
Conservative Party 10, 13, 26
Cuba 27

Daily Telegraph 30
Day, Derek xiii, 34, 39-43, 55-6, 174-75, 249-50, 270-71, 281-82, 302, 316-17
de Villers, Dawie 154
Drinkwater, John 25-26
Doble, John 104-5, 108, 118-20
Duff, Sir Antony xi-xii, 11-12, 20, 23, 26-8, 29, 43, 47-8, 50-1, 57-8, 60-5, 106-8, 121, 131-32, 148-49, 152-53, 187, 189-91, 226-27, 326-29; views on Nkomo 109

European Economic Community (EEC) 26
Fenn, Nicholas xiv
Fifth Principle (see also Six Principles) 19, 20, 26
Fiji 287
Ford, Gerald ix
Fourie, Brand 107
France 4, 10, 110-11
Frontline States (FLS) xiv, xvi, 2, 10, 27-8, 29, 42, 43-7, 131, 204, 221-22, 239-40, 286-87, 298

Geneva Conference (1976) ix, xi, 126
Ghana 32
Gibbs, Sir Humphrey 234
Gilmour, Sir Ian xiv, xvi, 138, 158, 161, 241, 339-41; private meeting with Muzowera 226-27; private meeting with Nkomo 266-67
Giscard d'Estaing, Valéry 36
Group of Nine (G9) 3, 13, 32

Helms, Jesse 58-9, 146, 162, 331-32
Henderson, Sir Nicholas 275-79
Hughes, Cledwyn (Lord Hughes) 39
Hunt, Sir John xii, 9
Hurd, Douglas 216

355

India 42
Internal Settlement 6-7, 38-43
Ivory Coast 24, 32

Kaunda, Kenneth xii, xviii, 26, 30, 33-5, 36-7, 131, 164, 198-99, 242-44, 286, 292-93, 297, 310-11; meeting with Carrington 267-68, 271-74, 281; meetings with Thatcher 198-99, 271-72, 294-96
Kenya 19, 21, 24, 42
Khama, Sir Seretse 26, 33-34, 38, 47
Kissinger, Dr Henry ix, 12-13, 25

Labour Party 25, 259-61
Lake, Anthony 28, 218-19, 222-25, 332
Lancaster House xiv
Lancaster House Conference: citizenship 165, 176, 182-83, 191; constitutional reforms 38-43, 53-4, 91-2, 167-70, 176-79; defence reforms 178; land reforms/redistribution 119, 181-83; pre-election period/interim period 209-13, 263-64, 286-87; presidential system 158, 177; white minority representation in parliament 38, 53-4, 114, 165, 167, 177-78, 183-4
Leahy, John 285, 288-90
Lennox-Boyd, Alan (Lord Boyd) x, 9, 13, 14-16, 21, 25-26, 199
Liberia 32
Loewenstein, Allard 36
Lonrho (see also Tiny Rowland) 142-43
Lord Privy Seal (see Sir Ian Gilmour)
Luce, Sir Richard xiv, 25, 28, 29, 79-82, 142-43, 153, 166, 185, 221-22, 239-40, 285-86, 305
Lyne, Roderic xv, 129, 130-31, 200-2, 247-48, 264, 274-75, 312-13, 321-22, 330

Machel, Samora xiii, xvi, 26, 31, 33-4, 37, 187-88, 269-70, 305, 311, 336-38
Malawi 21, 43
Moore, Sir Philip 150-51
Moose, Richard 'Dick' 27, 144
Moyse, Jacqueline Arlette 37
Mozambique 2, 21, 30, 31, 43, 104-5, 305, 336-38
Mozambique Liberation Front (FRELIMO) 104-5, 121
Mugabe, Robert ix-xi, xvi, xxi-xxii, 7, 24, 26-7, 29, 31, 33-5, 36-7, 112-13, 121-22, 153, 290, 303, 310-11, 320, 322-23, 339-40; lunch with Henry Walston 268-70; meetings with Carrington (see also Patriotic Front) 180, 193-94, 206-8, 216-17, 306-7, 318-20; views on Nkomo 122, 269

Muldoon, Robert David 249
Muzorewa, Bishop Abel ix, xiii, xv-xvi, xviii, 2, 4, 8-9, 16, 20, 22, 23-4, 26-8, 29, 30, 38-43, 44-7, 51-3, 55-6, 106-8, 112-15, 123-24, 186-87, 288-91 300-1, 310-12, 327-29; 1979 election of 9, 11-12, 45; meetings with Carrington 60-5, 147-50, 151-52, 159-61, 163, 167-71, 211, 220-21, 239, 241, 247-48, 313-13, 321-22; meetings with Thatcher 60-5; private meeting with Gilmour 226-27
Namibia 10, 29, 289-90
Ndebele xxiii, 4, 123
Neto, Agostinho 31, 34
New Zealand 249, 287, 341
Nigeria 4, 15, 17, 21, 24-5, 27-8, 31, 42, 43, 115-18, 156-57, 261-62, 282-86, 299, 324
Nkomo, Joshua ix-x, xvi, 24, 26-7, 29, 31, 33-5, 36-7, 99-100, 106, 109, 112-13, 122-23, 153, 258-59, 279-80, 285, 288-91, 295-96, 300-2, 311, 315-16, 320, 322-23, 339-40; meetings with Carrington (see also Patriotic Front) 180, 193-94, 206-8, 216-17, 238-39, 241, 306-7, 313-14, 318-20; private meeting with Gilmour 266-67; views on conference 132; views on Mugabe 266-67
Non-Aligned Movement (NAM) 116
Nyerere, Julius xii, 26, 30, 33-4, 36, 45, 130, 141-42, 147-50, 164

Obasanjo, General Olusegun 33-34; views on conference 115-18
Organisation of African Unity (OAU) 32, 34, 42, 122
Ormsby-Gore, William David (Lord Harlech) xiii, 32-3, 33-4, 34-5, 36-7, 38-9, 47-9; Harlech Report 43-7
Owen, Dr David ix, x

Parsons, Sir Anthony 12-13, 83-4, 164, 261-65, 318
Patriotic Front (see also Zimbabwe African National Union, Zimbabwe African People's Union) xvi-xix, 2, 8-9, 10-11, 22, 23, 26, 29, 31, 33-34, 34-5, 38-9, 42-3, 112-14, 133, 140, 147-52, 167-71, 186-89, 230-31, 241, 300-2, 339-40; meetings with Carrington 157-158, 165, 191-94, 216-17, 220-21, 286-87, 306-7
Pearce Commission 45
Powell, Charles xvi, 279-80, 315-16, 320

Ramphal, Sir Shridath xii, xvi, xx, 76, 109, 323-24
Renwick, Robin xi, xvi, xvii, 11-12, 31-2, 38-9,

50-1, 57-8, 109-12, 121-25, 133, 185, 188-89, 221-22, 229-36, 237-38, 258-59, 279-80, 297, 300-2, 307-9, 314-20, 331-32; views on Carrington xi-xii
Rhodesia: election (April 1979) 9, 11-12, 45; Internal Settlement 6-7, 38-43
Rhodesian armed/security forces 107-8, 148-49, 187-88; incursions into Zambia 292, 294-96, 298, 300, 305, 309
Rowland, Tiny (see also Lonrho) 48, 142-3

Sanctions: on Rhodesia 3, 23, 278; UK sanctions (see also Southern Rhodesia Act) 6, 10, 13, 20, 26, 160-61, 218-19, 225, 230-31, 254-56, 300, 316-18; US sanctions 11, 22, 27-8, 162-63, 279, 331-34, 341-43
Salisbury Agreement (1978) 1
Senegal 24, 32
Shagari, Shehu 156-57, 261-62, 283-86
Sheinwald, Nigel xv
Shona xxiii, 4, 123
Sierra Leone 42
Sinclair, Sir Ian 65-8, 109-11, 170, 317-18
Sithole, Reverend Ndabaningi xiii, 36, 125, 161
Six Principles (see also Fifth Principle) 19, 20, 25, 41, 56
Smith, David xvi, 39, 124, 152, 155-56, 166
Smith, Ian x, ix, xiii, xv, 7, 9, 24, 26, 36, 39-40, 43, 45-6, 112, 124-25, 147, 150, 151-52, 154, 155, 160-61, 163, 170, 234, 311; return to Salisbury 186-87, 192, 194
Soames, Christopher (Lord Soames) xviii, xxi-xxii, 249-50, 281-82, 312-13, 315, 328-29, 331, 337, 338; governor of Rhodesia xxii, 185, 190-91, 212-13, 226, 249-50, 279-80, 300-02, 306, 308, 314-18, 321-23, 326, 331-34
Soames, Mary (Lady Soames) xxii
South Africa 2, 10, 24, 27, 77-8, 154, 194-97, 213-15, 285, 288-91, 330; military presence in Rhodesia 215, 270-71, 276, 308, 312, 324, 329
Southern Rhodesia Act, 1965 (see also sanctions) 6, 14-15, 66-8, 160
South West Africa People's Organisation (SWAPO) 10
Soviet Union see USSR
Spencer, Rosemary 166, 250, 282
Strategic Arms Limitation Talks (SALT) 36, 82
Sudan 32
Sule, Alhaji Maitama 299

Tanzania 2, 17, 21, 31, 43
Tekere, Edgar 83, 104-5, 108, 129; views on Thatcher 108

Thatcher, Margaret xi-xiii, 9-11, 20-1, 29-30, 33-5, 37, 58-9, 98-9, 130-31, 139-40, 211, 245-46, 251-52, 282-84, 292-93, 326-29, 336-38; Canberra Speech (1979) xii; meeting with Callaghan 259-61; meetings with Carrington 36-7, 47-9, 213-15, 302-5, 323-24; meetings with Salisbury delegation 60-5; meetings with Pik Botha 213-15; meetings with Kaunda 198-99, 271-72, 292-93, 294-96; statements to the Commons 87-8; views on conference 101, 120, 167-73
Tongogara, Josaiah xv, xx, 293-94, 323; death of xxiii

United Nations (UN) 12, 17, 42, 65-6, 164, 216, 265; peacekeeping force x, 218, 224, 238; Security Council 1, 21, 65, 109-12, 278; Security Council Resolution (30 April 1979) 10
USA 2, 11, 12-13, 22, 42, 50-1, 110-11, 143-46, 222-26, 236-38; US Congress 11, 144-46, 331-32
United African National Council (UANC) 26
Union of Soviet Socialist Republics (USSR) 17-18, 21, 27

Vance, Cyrus x, 15, 20-1, 22, 25-8, 29-30, 50-1, 187-88, 203-05, 275-79, 297, 331-32
van der Byl, P. K. 39, 234
van der Post, Colonel Laurens 154, 165-166, 194, 202, 330
Viscount airliner, downing of (1978) x, 153

Walden, George 11-12; 12-13, 165
Waldheim, Dr Kurt 164, 216
Wall, Stephen 33-34, 98
Walls, General Peter ix, xv, xix, 124, 149, 169, 259, 271, 276, 293-296, 304, 306, 309-12, 321-22, 327-29
Walston, Henry (Lord Walston) 268-70
West Germany (FRG) 10
Willson, John xv, 138
Winterton, Nicholas 139-40

Young, Andy 49

Zambia 2, 10, 17-19, 21, 31, 43, 287, 300-02, 305, 309-10; protests at British High Commission, Lusaka 294-96
Zimbabwe African National Liberation Army (ZANLA) x, 121, 149, 266, 332-34
Zimbabwe African National Union (ZANU) (see also Patriotic Front) ix, 7, 44, 82-3, 104-5, 108, 118-20, 121-22, 129-30, 133, 152-53, 185, 266

Zimbabwe African People's Union (ZAPU) (see also Patriotic Front) ix, 7, 44, 97-8, 122-23, 133, 152-53, 185; attack on delegation members 189-90

Zimbabwe People's Revolutionary Army (ZIPRA) x, xx, 122-23, 149, 300, 303-4, 332-34

Zimbabwe-Rhodesia, arrangements for new elections 220-21, 252-53; pensions/public service 184; Unilateral Declaration of Independence (UDI) ix

www.ingramcontent.com/pod-product-compliance
Lightning Source LLC
LaVergne TN
LVHW081518060526
838200LV00006B/211